Mastering VMware vSphere 6.7
Second Edition

Effectively deploy, manage, and monitor your virtual datacenter with VMware vSphere 6.7

Martin Gavanda
Andrea Mauro
Paolo Valsecchi
Karel Novak

D1571646

BIRMINGHAM - MUMBAI

Mastering VMware vSphere 6.7
Second Edition

Commissioning Editor: Vijin Boricha
Acquisition Editor: Devika Battike
Content Development Editor: Ronn Kurien
Technical Editor: Swathy Mohan
Copy Editor: Safis Editing
Language Support Editors: Storm Mann, Mary McGowan
Project Coordinator: Jagdish Prabhu
Proofreader: Safis Editing
Indexer: Rekha Nair
Graphics: Tom Scaria
Production Coordinator: Aparna Bhagat

First published: December 2017
Second edition: March 2019

Production reference: 1050319

Published by Packt Publishing Ltd.
Livery Place
35 Livery Street
Birmingham
B3 2PB, UK.

ISBN 978-1-78961-337-7

www.packtpub.com

Mapt is an online digital library that gives you full access to over 5,000 books and videos, as well as industry leading tools to help you plan your personal development and advance your career. For more information, please visit our website.

Why subscribe?

- Spend less time learning and more time coding with practical eBooks and Videos from over 4,000 industry professionals

- Improve your learning with Skill Plans built especially for you

- Get a free eBook or video every month

- Mapt is fully searchable

- Copy and paste, print, and bookmark content

Packt.com

Did you know that Packt offers eBook versions of every book published, with PDF and ePub files available? You can upgrade to the eBook version at www.packt.com and as a print book customer, you are entitled to a discount on the eBook copy. Get in touch with us at customercare@packtpub.com for more details.

At www.packt.com, you can also read a collection of free technical articles, sign up for a range of free newsletters, and receive exclusive discounts and offers on Packt books and eBooks.

Contributors

About the authors

Martin Gavanda has more than 10 years of experience, mainly for service providers offering IaaS solutions based on VMware vSphere products. He was responsible for the design and implementation of IaaS solution in CE region, he has also worked for one of the world's biggest service providers, supervising thousands of ESXi servers across the globe.

Currently, he is working as an independent cloud architect, focusing on large infrastructure projects and practicing as a VMware instructor. For the past year, he has led more than a dozen on-site VMware workshops. He has created several virtual classes focusing on the VMware vSphere platform, with thousands of students subscribed, and he runs his own blog about virtualization and the cloud.

I want to thank all my friends and family, who supported me during the writing of the book, and I want to thank all the people around me who support me in all the (crazy) things I do, with a special thanks to Martina Lupínková.

Andrea Mauro has more than 20 years of experience in IT, both in industry and the academic world. He works as a solutions architect and is responsible for infrastructure implementation, architecture design, upgrades, and migration processes. He is a virtualization and storage architect, specializing in VMware, Microsoft, Citrix, and Linux solutions. His first virtualized solution in production was built around ESX 2.x, several years ago. His professional certifications include not only several VMware certifications, but also other vendor-related certifications. He is also a VMware vExpert (2010-18), Nutanix NTC (2014-19), and Veeam Vanguard (2016-19), and he was a Microsoft MVP (2014-16).

I would like to thank my wife and my son for their patience (this book has taken a lot of my free time for three long months), my friends from VMUG.IT for their support, the co-authors Paolo and Karel for their support, without which this book would not have been possible (at least not with the proposed deadline), and Scott S. Lowe for his words and suggestions.

Paolo Valsecchi has worked in the IT industry for more than 20 years, and he currently works as a system engineer mainly focused on VMware vSphere, Microsoft technologies, and backup/DR solutions. His current role involves covering all tasks related to ensuring IT infrastructure availability and data integrity (including implementation, upgrades, and administration).

He holds the VMware VCP65-DCV and Veeam VMCE professional certifications, and he has been awarded the VMware vExpert title (2015-18) and the Veeam Vanguard title (2016-19).

A big thanks to Andrea and Karel for including me in this project, my family for their support and patience during this hard work, and all the people who supported me during this adventure.

Karel Novak has 18 years of experience in the IT world. He currently works as a senior virtual infrastructure engineer at Arrow ECS Czechia, and is responsible for implementation, design, and complete consultation when it comes to VMware and Veeam. As an instructor of advanced VMware and Veeam, he has delivered many courses. He specializes in VMware DCV, NSX, and, of course, Veeam. He has been using VMware for 12 years and Veeam from the first version. He is a VMware vExpert 2012-2018, VMware vExpert NSX 2016-2018, and a Veeam Vanguard 2015-2019. His highest certifications are VCI-Level 2, VCIX6-NV, VCIX6-DCV, VMCT-Mentor, and VMCA. He is also a VMware Certification Subject Matter Expert.

I must say thank you to Andrea and Paolo for this opportunity. Thank you to my amazing wife, who supports me in all my projects. Thank you to all those around me who support me in all the activities that I do.

About the reviewer

Mathias Meyenburg is managing director of vleet GmbH with more than 15 years of experience in the IT industry. Starting as a systems administrator, his career has progressed to operating and administering large-scale international data centers. He has constantly updated and expanded his know-how, and has acquired certifications such as CCNA, MCP, and VCP. vleet GmbH sought him out in 2016 as a solutions architect for the whole VMware SDDC stack, Horizon desktop virtualization, Horizon Cloud on Azure, and VMC on Amazon Web Services.

I would like to express my gratitude to my wife, Andrea, who had to carry the burden while I was occupied with this book and my career, and who lovingly looked after our kids while studying herself.

Packt is searching for authors like you

If you're interested in becoming an author for Packt, please visit authors.packtpub.com and apply today. We have worked with thousands of developers and tech professionals, just like you, to help them share their insight with the global tech community. You can make a general application, apply for a specific hot topic that we are recruiting an author for, or submit your own idea.

Table of Contents

Preface   1

Section 1: Getting Started

Chapter 1: Evolution to vSphere 6.7   9
  Introduction to VMware vSphere   9
    vSphere strategy – the foundation of your unified hybrid cloud   11
    Software-defined data center (SDDC)   12
    Virtualization versus containers   13
  VMware vSphere ecosystem   17
    Data centers and cloud computing   17
    Storage and availability   17
    Network and security   18
    End user computing   20
    Cloud management   20
    Cloud-native workloads   21
  Introduction to VMware Cloud on AWS   21
    Hardware specifications and sizing   22
    Physical location   23
    Pricing   23
    Interconnection with on-premises SDDC   24
    Connectivity to native AWS services   24
    Certifications   24
  What's new in VMware vSphere 6.7?   25
    Key features   26
      vSphere Client (HTML-5)   26
      Improved vCenter Server Appliance (vCSA) monitoring   27
      Improved vCenter backup management   28
      ESXi single-reboot upgrades   29
      ESXi Quick Boot   30
      Support for Remote Direct Memory Access (RDMA)   31
      vSphere persistent memory   32
      Virtual Trusted Platform Module (vTPM)   32
      TPM 2.0   33
      Microsoft virtualization-based security (VBS)   33
      Per-VM Enhanced vMotion Compatibility (EVC)   34
      Hybrid linked mode   35
      Instant Clone   36
    Configuration maximums   36
      Virtual machine hardware 14   37
      ESXi 6.7 hypervisors   38
      vCenter Server 6.7   39

VMware vSphere 6.7 Editions   39
   VMware vSphere Editions   40
   VMware vSphere Essentials Kits   44
   Remote Office Branch Office (ROBO) editions   44
Reasons for and against upgrading   45
  Why upgrade?   46
  Why shouldn't you upgrade?   47
   Upgrade paths   48
Summary   49
Questions   49
Further reading   51
Chapter 2: Designing and Planning a Virtualization Infrastructure   53
Planning a virtual infrastructure project   54
  Plan-Do-Check-Act (PDCA)   54
  Waterfall   55
  ITIL v3   56
  Improved waterfall   57
Physical hardware considerations   59
  Physical form factor considerations   59
   Standard rack servers   59
   Blade servers   62
   Hyper-converged servers   64
    Resource comparison   64
    Hyper-converged systems   65
  Storage design considerations   67
   Standard storage arrays   67
   Software-defined storage   67
  Network design considerations   68
   Three-tier architecture   69
    Access   69
    Distribution   70
    Core   70
   Leaf spine   70
Assess   71
  The design objective   72
  Requirements, constraints, assumptions, and risks   72
Design   73
  Conceptual design   74
  Logical design   75
  Physical design   77
   ESXi host   78
    Compute   79
    Storage   80
    Network connectivity   83
    Management   85
   vCenter Server   85
  How to provide good documentation   86

Best practices   86
Reference architecture   87
    VVD   88
Different scenarios   90
Enterprise   90
    Business requirements   90
    Possible constraints   91
    Main risks   91
    Some design decisions   91
Small and medium-sized business (SMB)   92
    Business requirements   93
    Possible constraints   93
    Main risks   94
    Some design decisions   94
ROBO   95
    Business requirements   96
    Possible constraints   96
    Main risks   97
    Examples of design decisions   97
Summary   99
Questions   99
Further reading   100

Chapter 3: Analysis and Assessment of Existing Environments   101
Analyzing a physical environment before virtualizing   103
Useful metrics from a physical environment   105
    Processor metrics   105
    Memory metrics   106
    Disk metrics   108
    Network metrics   108
Are all workloads good candidates to be virtualized?   109
Existing tools to analyze a physical environment   111
    VMware Capacity Planner (VCP)   112
    Virtual Storage Area Network (vSAN) sizing tools   112
    Dell Live Optics   113
    Microsoft Assessment and Planning (MAP) Toolkit   113
Assessing an existing virtual environment   114
Discovery and inventory   115
Health check   118
Benchmarks   118
    DVD Store   118
    Hyper-Converged Infrastructure Benchmark (HCIBench)   118
Existing tools for analyzing a virtual environment   119
    RVTools   121
    VOA   122
    VMware vSphere Health Check   123
Summary   124
Questions   124

Further reading   125
Chapter 4: Deployment Workflow and Component Installation   127
   vSphere components and workflow   128
   ESXi deployment plan   130
     Choosing the hardware platform   130
     Identification of the storage architecture   132
     Defining the network configuration   132
   ESXi installation   134
     Where should I install ESXi?   134
     Preparing for deployment   136
       Interactive installation   137
       Unattended installation   139
       Auto Deploy installation   143
     How Auto Deploy works   145
       Configuring DHCP   146
       Configuring TFTP   147
     Creating an image profile   148
     Creating deployment rules   149
     Auto Deploy modes   152
       Stateless installation   152
       Stateless caching installation   152
       Stateful installation   154
   vCenter Server components   154
     PSC   155
       Linked Mode   158
     vCenter Server   159
       Migration from vCenter for Windows to vCSA   160
     Where to install – physical or virtual?   161
   vCenter Server Appliance deployment   161
     Why deploy vCSA instead of the Windows version?   163
     Installing the vCSA PSC   164
     Installing the vCSA vCenter   166
     Installing the vCSA with Embedded Platform Service Controller   168
   vCSA HA   168
     vCenter HA configuration   169
   Summary   173
   Questions   174
   Further reading   175
Chapter 5: Configuring and Managing vSphere 6.7   177
   Using the VMware vSphere HTML5 client   178
   Configuring ESXi   178
     Management network configuration   179
       Enabling Secure Shell (SSH) access   180
       ESXi firewall   182
       Configuring the Network Time Protocol (NTP)   183

ESXi 6.7 partition layout 184
  Boot banks 187
  Scratch partition 187
Centralized log management 188
vRealize Log Insight 189
  Free syslog servers 190
  Syslog configuration 190
Backing up and restoring ESXi 190
Backing up and restoring ESXi using CLI 191
Backing up and restoring ESXi using PowerCLI 192
  Backing up using PowerCLI 192
  Restoring using PowerCLI 192
  Backing up all ESXi servers within a single vCenter server 192
Configuring vCSA 193
Basic setup using the vCenter Server Appliance Management
Interface (VAMI) 193
  Modifying the IP address and DNS 194
  Exporting a support bundle 194
  Configuring time synchronization 195
  Changing the vCSA password 195
Licensing 195
Roles and permissions 197
AD integration 200
  Configuring ESXi with AD authentication 202
  Installing the VMware Enhanced Authentication plugin 203
vCSA and PSC 204
  Repointing the vCSA to another external PSC 204
  Pointing the vCSA with an embedded PSC to an external PSC 205
  Resetting the SSO password 206
Exporting and importing the vCSA configuration 208
The vCSA backup procedure 208
vCSA restoration procedure 209
Managing data centers, clusters, and hosts 211
Creating a data center 212
Adding a host to the vCenter Server 213
  Disconnecting a host from vCenter Server 215
  Removing a host from vCenter Server 216
Creating a cluster 216
  Removing a host from a cluster 217
Managing hosts 218
  Using tags 219
  Tasks 220
    Scheduling tasks 220
  Managing host profiles 221
Automating tasks with scripts 224
Automating with PowerCLI 225
  PowerCLI script examples 228

vCenter REST API   229
Summary   231
Questions   231
Further reading   233

Chapter 6: Life Cycle Management, Patching, and Upgrading   235
Patching a vSphere 6.7 environment   236
Upgrade flow to vSphere 6.7   237
   Upgrading the workflow and procedure   237
     Step 1 – pre-migration   238
     Step 2 – migration   239
     Step 3 – validation   239
Upgrading vCSA 6.5 to vCSA 6.7   240
**Upgrading vCenter 6.5 for Windows to vCenter 6.7 for
Windows**   242
   PSC upgrade   243
   Upgrading vCenter Server   243
Migrating vCenter 6.5 for Windows to vCSA 6.7   244
   Migration procedure   245
Upgrading standalone ESXi servers   248
   ESXi compatibility checker   249
   Updating or patching ESXi hosts through the installation ISO   250
   Updating or patching ESXi hosts through the command line   251
   Rolling back to the previous version   253
VUM   254
   Configuring VUM   254
   Working with baselines   257
     Baseline groups   259
     Attaching or detaching baselines   260
   Scanning VMs and hosts   261
     Staging and remediating patches   262
   Upgrading hosts with VUM   264
   Upgrading VM hardware   266
   Upgrading VM Tools   267
Updating the vCSA   268
   Updating the vCSA through the command line   269
     Staging and remediating patches   269
   Updating the vCSA with VAMI   270
Summary   272
Questions   273
Further reading   274

Section 2: Managing Resources

Chapter 7: Managing Networking Resources   277
   Basic network overview   277

OSI model   278
Encapsulation and de-encapsulation   279
MAC tables and MAC learning process   280
Maximum Transmission Unit (MTU)   281
Virtual LAN (VLAN)   282
Transmission Control Protocol (TCP) versus User Datagram Protocol
(UDP)   283
IPv6   283
Virtual networking with switches   284
Standard virtual switch (vSwitch) overview   285
Distributed vSwitch overview   287
Comparing standard and distributed vSwitches   289
Managing standard virtual networking   290
Creating a new vSwtich   290
New vSwitch from ESXi host client   290
New vSwitch from vCenter Server   295
New vSwitch from ESXi CLI   296
Working with port groups   297
Creating a new port group from ESXi host client   298
Creating a new port group from vCenter Server   300
Creating a new port group from ESXi CLI   301
Working with VMkernel adapters   302
Creating a new VMkernel adapter from ESXi host client   302
Creating a new VMkernel adapter from vCenter Server   304
Working with physical NICs   305
TCP/IP stacks   307
Managing distributed virtual networking   310
Creating a distributed vSwitch   310
Attaching the ESXi host to the distributed vSwitch   312
Creating distributed port groups   316
Properties and configuration options of the distributed vSwitch   319
Topology   320
Link Aggregation Control Protocol (LACP)   321
Private VLAN (PVLAN)   323
NetFlow   324
Port mirroring   325
Health check   325
Ports, hosts, and VMs   326
Migrate VM networking   326
NIOC   327
Network resource pools   328
Direct allocation on VM   330
Advanced network functions   331
Single Root I/O Virtualization (SR-IOV)   331
Enabling SR-IOV   332
Configuring VM for SR-IOV   333
Traffic filtering and marking   333

Summary 335
Questions 335
Further reading 337

Chapter 8: Managing Storage Resources 339
  Storage basics 340
    Storage arrays 341
      Storage performance 342
        The RAID level 343
        Deduplication 343
        Replication 344
        Physical storage device types 344
      SSDs and AFAs 345
      Asymmetric Logical Unit Access (ALUA) arrays 346
  VMware vSphere storage types 346
    Storage types at the ESXi logical level 348
    Storage types at the ESXi physical level 349
    Storage types at VM logical levels 350
    Storage types at the VM physical level 352
      Persistent memory (PMem) 353
  VMware vSphere storage configuration 355
    FC storage 355
      FCoE storage 357
    iSCSI storage 358
    NFS storage 361
  SIOC and storage DRS 362
    SIOC 362
      Reservations, limits, and shares 363
        Reservations 363
        Limits 363
        Shares 364
      RLS calculations 364
      SIOC versions 365
    Storage DRS 368
      Datastore clusters 370
      Anti-affinity rules 370
  Advanced storage features 371
    Virtual Machine File System (VMFS) 6 371
    Automatic space reclaim 372
    Instant clones versus linked clones 373
    Storage DRS versus storage tiering 374
    RDM 375
    Permanent Device Loss (PDL) and All-Paths-Down (APD) 375
    Flash Read Cache 377
  Storage integration 378
    VMware vSphere SPBM 378
    Pluggable Storage Architecture (PSA) 379

Multipathing | 380
VMware vStorage API for Array Integration (VAAI) | 381
VMware vSphere APIs for I/O Filtering (VAIO) | 382
VASA | 382
VVols | 382
Introducing VMware vSAN | 384
Planning and designing | 385
Device considerations | 386
vSAN configuration | 386
Health monitoring | 389
vSAN policies | 390
Creating VM on vSAN | 390
Summary | 391
Questions | 392
Further reading | 394

Chapter 9: VM Deployment and Management | 395
The components of a virtual machine | 396
Virtual hardware | 396
vCPUs | 397
Memory | 397
Network adapter | 398
Virtual disks | 399
Storage controller | 401
File structure | 403
Changing the default file position | 405
Virtual machine tools | 405
OVT | 407
Deploying VMs | 408
Creating a new VM | 409
Hardware version | 411
Setting the default hardware version | 412
Installing the OS | 413
Installing Virtual Machine Tools | 414
Cloning a VM | 415
Deploying a VM from a template | 416
VM customization Specifications | 418
Content library | 421
Creating a content library | 422
Local content library | 422
Subscribed content library | 423
Working with the content library | 426
Uploading ISO images | 427
Uploading templates and OVF files | 428
Deploying VMs from the content library | 429
ISO files from the content library | 430
Managing VMs | 431

Adding or registering an existing VM 431
Removing or deleting a VM 433
Managing the power state of a VM 434
Managing VM snapshots 435
Creating a snapshot 436
Reverting to a snapshot 438
Committing changes 438
Snapshot consolidation 438
Importing and exporting VMs 439
Deploying Open Virtual Format (OVF) and Open Virtual Appliance
(OVA) templates 439
Exporting a virtual machine and an Open Virtual Format (OVF) 442
Converting VMs 443
P2V conversion 443
V2V conversion 445
Summary 445
Questions 446
Further reading 447

Chapter 10: VM Resource Management 449
Virtual machine resource management 450
Reservations, limits, and shares 450
Shares 451
Reservations 452
Limits 452
CPU resources 452
Memory resources 454
VM swapping 456
ESXi host memory states 457
TPS 461
Ballooning 463
Compression 464
Host swapping 465
Virtual machine migration 465
Compute vMotion 466
Storage vMotion 470
vMotion without shared storage 472
DRS 473
Virtual network-aware DRS 477
Managing DRS rules 477
VM-VM affinity rule 478
VM-Host affinity rule 479
DRS recommendations 481
DRS utilization 482
Managing power resources 482
Resource pools and vApps 484
Resource pool configuration 484

Expandable resource pool 488
Resource allocation monitoring and calculations 490
Managing resource pools 491
vApps 492
Network and storage resources 495
Summary 495
Questions 496
Further reading 497

Section 3: Advanced Topics

Chapter 11: Availability and Disaster Recovery 501
VMware vSphere HA 502
vSphere HA configuration 502
vSphere HA heartbeats 504
vSphere HA network heartbeats 504
vSphere HA storage heartbeats 505
vSphere HA protection mechanism 507
Virtual Machine Component Protection (VMCP) 507
Proactive HA 509
Admission control 510
VM restart and monitoring 512
VMware vSphere FT 513
FT configuration 516
Working with FT-enabled VM 518
FT performance implications 518
Virtual machine clustering 520
Clustering features available in VMware vSphere 521
RDM device and multi-writer flag 523
Virtual machine backup 525
Transport modes 526
Backup solutions for VMware vSphere 526
Veeam Backup and Replication 527
NAKIVO Backup and Replication 527
Altaro VM Backup 528
Vembu VMBackup 529
Deduplication appliances 529
Hyper-scale solutions 529
Cohesity 530
Rubrik 530
VMware vSphere Replication 530
vSphere Replication installation 531
Working with vSphere Replication 532
Configuring vSphere Replication 533
Disaster recovery and disaster avoidance 534
DR of a virtual data center 536
DR versus disaster avoidance 537

DR versus stretched clusters   538
VMware solutions   539
VM Replication   540
Stretched cluster   541
SRM   542
Summary   544
Questions   544
Further reading   546

Chapter 12: Securing and Protecting Your Environment   547
Security and hardening concepts in vSphere   547
Hardening vSphere   548
Authentication and identity   549
SSO configuration   549
Password management   550
Role-Based Access Control (RBAC)   552
Active directory integration   554
MFA   554
Smart cards   555
RSA SecurID   557
vCenter Server, ESXi, and VM hardening   557
ESXi hardening   558
Lockdown mode   559
Networking   560
Transparent Page Sharing (TPS)   560
VIB acceptance level   561
Host encryption mode   561
ESXi Secure Boot   562
vCenter hardening   563
VM hardening   563
VM Secure Boot   564
Other security aspects   565
Log management   566
Monitoring protocols   566
Certification management   567
Encryption options of the vSphere   569
Protecting the data at rest   570
VM encryption   571
Protecting data in motion   575
Encrypted vMotion   575
Summary   577
Questions   577
Further reading   579

Chapter 13: Analyzing and Optimizing Your Environment   581
Monitoring a virtual environment   581
vSphere monitoring   582

vCenter Server statistics levels   582
Performance monitoring with vCenter Server   583
ESXi health   587
Working with alarms   588
CLI monitoring   590
ESXTOP   591
PowerCLI   592
VM optimization   594
Using the default VM templates   594
Using only the necessary virtual hardware   594
Choosing the correct virtual network adapter   595
VMware tools   595
Paravirtual SCSI (PVSCSI) storage controller   595
Don't use snapshots in production   595
Don't oversize your VMs   596
VMware OS Optimization Tool (OSOT)   596
Log management   597
vRealize Log Insight   598
vRealize Operations   600
vRealize Operations installation   600
vRealize Operations analytics   603
vRealize Operations integrations   605
Other monitoring tools   606
Veeam ONE   607
Opvizor   609
Summary   610
Questions   611
Further reading   612

Chapter 14: Troubleshooting Your Environment   613
What is troubleshooting?   613
Troubleshooting a virtual environment   615
CLI tools   615
esxcli commands   615
esxcfg-*   618
Ruby vSphere console   619
vim-cmd   620
vcsa-cli   622
PowerCLI   623
Logs   623
ESXi host logs   624
Troubleshooting vSphere components   627
Troubleshooting the vCenter Server   627
Troubleshooting the ESXi host   629
Troubleshooting cluster HA or DRS   630
Troubleshooting a virtual network   630

Troubleshooting storage   632
Troubleshooting VMs   632
Summary   634
Questions   634
Further reading   635

Section 4: Building Your Lab Environment

Chapter 15: Building Your Own VMware vSphere Lab   639
The importance of lifelong learning   640
Why build a lab?   640
VMware Hands-On Lab (HOL)   640
VMware forums   641
Blogs   642
Choosing the right platform   642
Standard rack servers   643
Desktop PC   644
Small, dedicated PCs   645
Cloud-based solutions   645
A dedicated server in a data center   646
Software components and licensing   646
VMware licensing   647
VMware EVALExperience   647
Windows licensing   649
Other software components   649
Storage   649
Networking   649
Architecture and logical design   650
The architecture of the lab   651
The Master ESXi hypervisor   652
iSCSI storage   652
Virtual router   652
Management station   652
AD   652
IP address plan   653
Management network   653
vMotion network   653
iSCSI network   654
Production network   654
A detailed implementation guide   655
Master ESXi server configuration   655
Network configuration   656
Virtual switches   656
Port groups   657
Virtual machines   658
Virtual router   659
Virtual router configuration   660

Firewalls and access to the virtual router 661
DNS configuration 663
License configuration 664
VLAN configuration 665
Windows infrastructure 666
DC01.learnvmware.local 666
DC02.learnvmware.local 670
Mgmt.learnvmware.local 671
iscsi.learnvmware.local 673
Storage design 673
iSCSI target configuration 674
DNS configuration 676
Centralized management 678
iSCSI target configuration 679
ESXi servers 682
Network configuration 684
vSwitches 684
Port groups 685
VMkernel ports 687
Network verification 687
Storage configuration 688
The vCenter Server 692
vSphere configuration 696
Summary 698
Assessment 699
Other Books You May Enjoy 711
Index 715

Preface

VMware vSphere provides a powerful, flexible, and secure foundation for next-generation applications to help you achieve an effective digital transformation efficiently.

Mastering VMware vSphere 6.7, Second Edition, begins by covering an overview of all the products, solutions, and features of the vSphere 6.7 suite, comparing 6.7 with previous releases. You'll learn how to design and plan a virtualization infrastructure to drive performance analysis and then proceed with workflows and the installation of components. Along with new network trends that will help you in optimally designing the vSphere environment, you will also learn the best practices involved in configuring and managing virtual machines in a vSphere infrastructure. With vSphere 6.7, you'll make use of more powerful capabilities for patching, upgrading, and managing the configuration of the virtual environment and focus on specific availability and resiliency solutions in vSphere. The concluding chapters of the book will provide information on how to save your configuration, data, and workload from your virtual infrastructure and teach you different approaches on how to build your own VMware vSphere lab to help you run even the most demanding workloads.

By the end of the book, you'll have learned about VMware vSphere 6.7, right from design to deployment and management.

Who this book is for

If you are an administrator, infrastructure engineer, IT architect, or an IT consultant and analyst who has some basic knowledge of VMware vSphere and now wants to master it, then this book is for you.

What this book covers

`Chapter 1`, *Evolution to vSphere 6.7*, provides a general overview of all the products, solutions, and features of the vSphere 6.7 suite, comparing 6.7 with previous releases. This chapter will explain why you should choose (and why you should not choose, in some cases) vSphere 6.7 over previous versions or other products. Also, it will briefly describe the different editions and licenses of vSphere.

Chapter 2, *Designing and Planning a Virtualization Infrastructure,* describes how to plan a virtualization project and build proper infrastructure by providing an approach both for planning and design.

Chapter 3, *Analysis and Assessment of Existing Environments,* explains how to analyze and assess an existing physical or virtual environment in order to gain data that's useful for planning your migration, upgrade, or improvement. Different tools and approaches are described as a way of reaching this goal.

Chapter 4, *Deployment Workflow and Component Installation,* starts by explaining the components of vSphere and the roles and services they provide. We will walk through the main aspects to consider in terms of the preparation of a deployment plan for your environment, analyzing the criteria for hardware platform selection, storage, and network requirements.

Chapter 5, *Configuring and Managing vSphere 6.7,* describes the different ways to manage a vSphere 6.7 infrastructure, including the new HTML5 clients, and also contains an introduction to the scripting and automation tools. ESXi, vCenter, VMware cluster-related configuration, and management topics are covered in this chapter.

Chapter 6, *Life Cycle Management, Patching, and Upgrading,* looks at how, with vSphere 6.7, administrators will find significantly more powerful capabilities for patching, upgrading, and managing the configuration of the virtual environment using the Update Manager and Host Profile features. We also cover the upgrade path and considerations to make regarding upgrading or migrating your virtual environment.

Chapter 7, *Managing Networking Resources,* is dedicated to virtual networking, both with standard and distributed virtual switches, and covers the design, management, and optimization of a virtual network in a vSphere environment.

Chapter 8, *Managing Storage Resources,* details the storage aspect of a virtual infrastructure, starting from local block-based storage and extending into shared block storage with Fibre Channel (FC), FC over Ethernet (FCoE), internet Small Computer System Interface (iSCSI) protocols, and NFS-based NAS storage.

Chapter 9, *VM Deployment and Management,* introduces the practices and procedures involved in deploying, configuring, and managing Virtual Machines (VMs) in a vSphere infrastructure. Different types of VM provisioning are considered, including use of templates, the content library, and OVF.

Chapter 10, *VM Resource Management*, provides a comprehensive view of vSphere resources management, including reservations, limits, and shares, and how to balance and optimize them in your environment. Finally, we will discuss different migration techniques for moving your workload across different environments.

Chapter 11, *Availability and Disaster Recovery*, focuses on specific availability (and resiliency) solutions in vSphere, including the new vSphere High Availability (HA) features, proactive HA, vSphere Fault Tolerance (FT), and other solutions, such as guest clustering.

Chapter 12, *Securing and Protecting Your Environment*, looks at how security has become a critical part of any implementation, including virtual environments. In addition to the security and hardening aspects of vSphere, the new 6.7 version brings other important related features (though some were introduced with version 6.5), such as VM encryption, encrypted vMotion, secure boot support for VMs, and secure boot plus cryptographic hypervisor assurance for ESXi.

Chapter 13, *Analyzing and Optimizing Your Environment*, covers the native tools used to monitor your environment for performance analysis or for possible issues in order to improve the virtual environment and workloads. This chapter focuses on monitoring different critical resources, such as computing, storage, and networking resources, across ESXi hosts, resource pools, and clusters. Other tools, such as vRealize Operations and third-party tools, will also be described briefly .

Chapter 14, *Troubleshooting Your Environment*, covers the native tools used to troubleshoot performance issues and other issues in a vSphere environment. Also, the chapter provides some examples and methods for troubleshooting approaches.

Chapter 15, *Building Your Own VMware vSphere Lab*, goes into the basics of why you should build your own lab environment, looking at what the benefits of running such a lab are in comparison with using VMware Hands-On Labs (HOLs). Different approaches to how labs can be designed will be covered.

To get the most out of this book

This book assumes a basic level of VMware vSphere and virtualization knowledge, which you will need in order to understand all the concepts.

This book requires the following minimum software components: VMware vSphere 6.7, and VMware vCenter Server 6.7. There is also other optional software.

The best way to practice without the need for software licenses or hardware components is to try VMware HOLs (`https://labs.hol.vmware.com/`), which cover different products and technologies. The first ones that you should use, if you are new to the features of vSphere 6.7, are listed here:

- HOL-1911-01-SDC – What's New in VMware vSphere 6.7
- HOL-1911-91-SDC – vSphere 6.7 Lightning Lab
- HOL-1904-02-CHG – vSphere 6.7 – Challenge Lab

If you would prefer your own lab, there are several suggestions for what type of hardware to use, whether a single big server with nested ESXi hypervisors, or a cloud service such as Ravello (which can also host nested ESXi hosts). There are also suggestions on how to deploy all software components. One interesting way of doing so is using AutoLab (`http://www.labguides.com/autolab/`), or you can see the blogs of Alan Renouf and William Lam, where you can find some powerful scripts for building an entire vSphere 6.5 environment (also with vSAN and NSX!).

Download the color images

We also provide a PDF file that has color images of the screenshots/diagrams used in this book. You can download it here: `https://www.packtpub.com/sites/default/files/downloads/9781789613377_ColorImages.pdf`.

Conventions used

There are a number of text conventions used throughout this book.

`CodeInText`: Indicates code words in text, database table names, folder names, filenames, file extensions, pathnames, dummy URLs, user input, and Twitter handles. Here is an example: "At the `runweasel` command line, type `ks=usb:/ks.cfg`."

A block of code is set as follows:

```
vmaccepteula
rootpw mypassword
install --firstdisk —overwritevmfs
keyboard English
network --bootproto=dhcp --device=vmnic0
reboot
```

When we wish to draw your attention to a particular part of a code block, the relevant lines or items are set in bold:

```
esxcli system syslog config set —loghost tcp://SYSLOG_IP:514
esxcli system syslog reload
```

Any command-line input or output is written as follows:

```
cd /usr/lib/vmware-sso/
openssl x509 —inform PEM —in xyzCompanySmartCardSigningCA.cer >>
/usr/lib/vmware-sso/vmware-sts/conf/clienttrustCA.pem
```

Bold: Indicates a new term, an important word, or words that you see onscreen. For example, words in menus or dialog boxes appear in the text like this. Here is an example: "Under **Settings**, switch to **General** and click the **Edit...** button."

Warnings or important notes appear like this.

Tips and tricks appear like this.

Get in touch

Feedback from our readers is always welcome.

General feedback: If you have questions about any aspect of this book, mention the book title in the subject of your message and email us at customercare@packtpub.com.

Errata: Although we have taken every care to ensure the accuracy of our content, mistakes do happen. If you have found a mistake in this book, we would be grateful if you would report this to us. Please visit www.packt.com/submit-errata, selecting your book, clicking on the Errata Submission Form link, and entering the details.

Piracy: If you come across any illegal copies of our works in any form on the Internet, we would be grateful if you would provide us with the location address or website name. Please contact us at copyright@packt.com with a link to the material.

If you are interested in becoming an author: If there is a topic that you have expertise in and you are interested in either writing or contributing to a book, please visit `authors.packtpub.com`.

Reviews

Please leave a review. Once you have read and used this book, why not leave a review on the site that you purchased it from? Potential readers can then see and use your unbiased opinion to make purchase decisions, we at Packt can understand what you think about our products, and our authors can see your feedback on their book. Thank you!

For more information about Packt, please visit `packt.com`.

Section 1: Getting Started

This part introduces the new features of vSphere 6.7 and the vSphere ecosystem. We will cover the different logical and physical considerations of your vSphere projects, and we will show you how to assess your existing environment. Different types of project management techniques for IT-related projects will be described as well. At the end of this section you will see how to deploy your first vSphere infrastructure, and we will cover essential management skills. We will also cover different update approaches so your infrastructure is always up to date.

This section includes the following chapters:

- Chapter 1, *Evolution to vSphere 6.7*
- Chapter 2, *Designing and Planning a Virtualization Infrastructure*
- Chapter 3, *Analysis and Assessment of Existing Environments*
- Chapter 4, *Deployment Workflow and Component Installation*
- Chapter 5, *Configuring and Managing vSphere 6.7*
- Chapter 6, *Life Cycle Management, Patching, and Upgrading*

Evolution to vSphere 6.7 1

VMware vSphere 6.7 is the latest version of the most used enterprise virtualization platform. A good understanding of this product and its features is crucial for a successful implementation of the vSphere infrastructure.

In this chapter, we will provide you with a better understanding of the VMware product portfolio, the VMware vision, and the evolution of the product. We will also learn what is new in vSphere 6.7 and introduce the different solutions, features, and editions of vSphere. Furthermore, we will provide tips for choosing the right editions and version of vSphere and choosing when (and when not) to upgrade to vSphere 6.7.

This chapter will cover the following topics:

- Introduction to VMware vSphere
- VMware vSphere ecosystem
- Introduction to VMware Cloud on AWS
- What's new in VMware vSphere 6.7
- Reasons for and against upgrading

Introduction to VMware vSphere

With more than 500,000 customers globally, VMware remains a proven leader not only in virtualization but also in all technologies related to digital transformation. This year marks 20 years since the creation of VMware by Diane Greene, Mendel Rosenblum, Scott Devine, Ellen Wang, and Edouard Bugnion in 1998.

VMware has always focused on virtualization and its flagship product—VMware vSphere—proves that this was the right choice. The first version of ESXi hypervisor was released in 2001 and the first version of vCenter was then released two years later in 2003.

The VMware vSphere suite includes ESXi (the evolution of ESX Server) for the virtualization layer and the vCenter Server for the management layer.

Compute virtualization is only the first step here; to move to a real cloud computing infrastructure, you will not only need to compute resource abstraction (provided by virtualization) but also operation automation and agility (both of these are only partially obtainable through virtualization). Finally, this approach should not only be applied to the compute virtualization but also to the other resources, such as storage, networking, and security.

Today, VMware products can be used to fulfill this vision. There are three infrastructure pillars that VMware virtualizes:

- Compute resources—VMware vSphere
- Storage resources—VMware vSAN
- Network resources—VMware NSX

Together, these products build a unified platform for delivering any service with unmatched performance.

In this book, we are focusing primarily on VMware vSphere, but we will also touch on vSAN and NSX. However, this won't be covered in too much detail, as we will mainly look at compute virtualization using VMware vSphere.

> *"VMware is helping our customers and partners to achieve unlimited possibilities, while a shift to the digital is accelerating a technology supply to invent new products, deliver new services and find new ways to work and grow a business. Our solutions enable a business to build precisely what is needed in the way it is needed for today and tomorrow."*

> *– Pat Gelsinger, VMware CEO*

The digital transformation journey has four IT priorities that VMware focuses on:

- **Modernizing data centers**: Software-defined data center architecture to modernize existing data centers painlessly and automation to run enterprise and cloud-native workloads.
- **Integrating public clouds**: Provides extra agility and cross-cloud architecture. Cloud freedom brings a choice, and you can easily extend your on-premises infrastructure to include any vSphere-based-public cloud.

- **Empowering the digital workspace**: Introduces an exceptional mobile experience by providing users with a secure and digital workspace. VMware delivers virtualized applications and offers the ability to manage apps, access, and endpoints securely.
- **Transforming security**: This transformative approach to security delivers secure infrastructure, networks and applications, data, and access from end to end, securing on-premises data centers through a cloud connected to the endpoint and device.

vSphere strategy – the foundation of your unified hybrid cloud

"The Software-Defined datacenter is VMware technology architecture for building a data center where all infrastructure is virtualized, and control of the data center is fully automated with software."

– June Yang, VMware Sr. Director for vSphere

Based on this strategy, there are three key pillars that VMware follows:

- **Continuous innovation and integration of vSphere core components**: A software-defined data center is more scalable, provides better performance, and is secure as well as easier to manage and operate.
- **Unified hybrid cloud capabilities**: Customers want the choice to run applications on both the private and public cloud. The idea here is to provide the agility and flexibility that is required by a business while enabling the right level of performance, continuity, and security that IT is responsible for delivering.
- **Any application**: vSphere is the best platform to run any application from traditional enterprise applications to cloud-native workloads. VMware is very successful when running traditional applications, and now the goal is to extend this to cloud-native workloads as well.

Software-defined data center (SDDC)

In 2012, former VMware CTO Steve Herrod explained this vision with the new concept of the SDDC, where all infrastructure elements (computing, networking, storage, and security) are virtualized and delivered as a service using a cloud computing model:

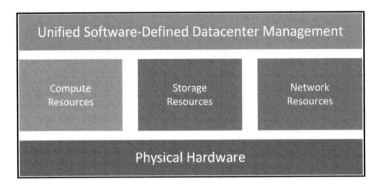

Virtualization is no longer the final destination of the digital transformation journey; it has become the starting point, an essential requirement, and a foundation for digital businesses. VMware has addressed these needs by extending both its product portfolio and its vision.

Together, VMware vSphere, NSX, and vSAN are unified building blocks which form an SDDC. As we will explain later, this approach incorporates nicely with hyper-converged infrastructure, a physical server that contains not only computer resources but also local storage devices for building software-defined storage. Hyper-converged servers are physical infrastructure blocks for SDDCs.

As an extension to this approach, the **Cloud Foundation** product can be leveraged. VMware Cloud Foundation is an integrated software platform that automates the deployment and life cycle management of a complete SDDC on a standardized hyper-converged architecture. This can be deployed on-premises on a broad range of supported hardware, or consumed as a service in the public cloud (VMware Cloud on AWS or VMware Cloud Providers).

The following represents a high-level overview of the VMware Cloud Foundation product:

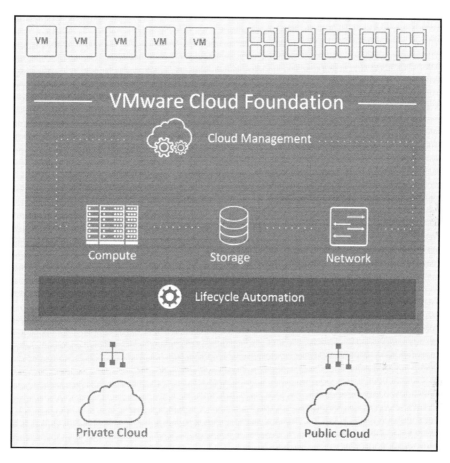

For more information about VMware Cloud Foundation, feel free to visit the official product brief at `https://www.vmware.com/content/dam/digitalmarketing/vmware/en/pdf/datasheet/products/vmware-cloud-foundation-datasheet.pdf`.

Virtualization versus containers

Containers and VMs have similar resource isolation and resource allocation benefits, but function differently, because containers do not include the operating system part (or at least not the kernel part of it). Containers are also more lightweight, so they are potentially more portable and efficient.

With containers you do not need an underlying operating system for each container but individual Containers are run on the shared **Host Operating System** through **Docker Engine**:

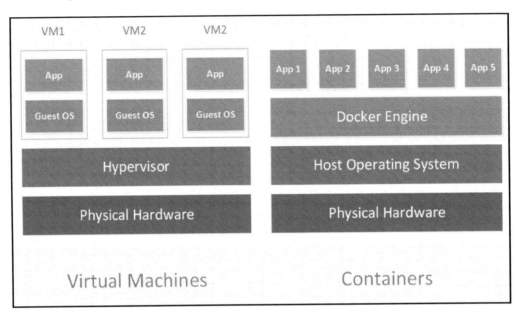

Both virtual machine and container approaches have their pros and cons, so there is no winner. Different workloads may require different infrastructure platforms to meet the IT and business requirements or objectives.

In the vSphere 6.5 release, VMware introduced **vSphere Integrated Containers** (**VIC**), a platform to bring containers into an existing vSphere environment simply and easily. With VIC, it is possible to deliver an enterprise container infrastructure that provides not only agility for developers (by using the containers) but also full control for vSphere operations teams, where containers can now be managed with the same concepts and skills as standard VMs, without requiring any changes in processes or tools.

VIC are structured into the following components:

- **VIC engine**: Docker remote is an API-compatible engine which is deeply integrated into vSphere (6.0, 6.5, 6.7) for instantiating container images that run as VMs, with support for distributing images to remote offices/branch offices.

- **Container management portal**: This portal is designed to allow apps teams to manage the container repositories, images, hosts, and running container instances. It provides **Role-Based Access Control (RBAC)** with support for **Lightweight Directory Access Protocol/Active Directory (LDAP/AD)**.
- **Container Registry**: This securely stores container images with built-in RBAC and image replication. The container registry provides vulnerability scanning, content trust with security policies, and also supports third-party registries:

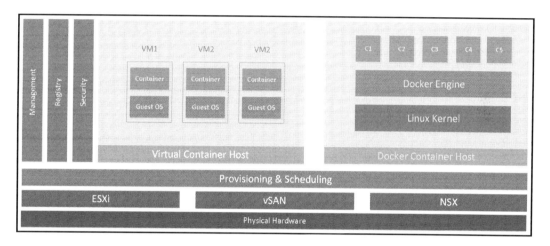

Using VIC, vSphere administrators can provide a full Docker-compatible interface to their developers, using the existing vSphere infrastructure with native capabilities and features, including VMware NSX for security and VMware vSAN for storage. The new version 1.2 (released in September 2017) adds a native Docker container host from a unified management portal.

A second product that focuses on containers is the **Pivotal Container Service (PKS)**. In contrast to VIC, PKS focuses on multi-cloud deployments where you can natively run your containerized applications using a Kubernetes engine. Kubernetes is an orchestration platform for running Docker containers, but compared to Docker Swarm, it provides more functionality.

With PKS, you can efficiently manage one homogeneous environment, providing the same compute, network, or storage capabilities for your containerized workloads in multi-cloud environments.

PKS is structured into the following different components:

- **PKS Control Plane**: This is a critical component of the PKS infrastructure that is responsible for self-service access, life cycle and on-demand deployment of the Kubernetes clusters. Using APIs, the requests are sent to BOSH, which is responsible for the automation itself.
- **Kubernetes**: Kubernetes is an open source, portable, extensible orchestration framework for managing containerized workloads and services. Applications are run within Kubernetes clusters, providing optimized resource access and maintaining a consistent application state within clusters.
- **BOSH**: This is an open source tool for maintaining large-scale distributed deployments. Using BOSH, you can deploy applications to many Infrastructure as a Service solutions from supported partners to on-premises infrastructure. BOSH allows interconnection with OpenStack, VMware vSphere, AWS, Microsoft Azure, or **Google Cloud Platform (GCP)**.
- **VMware NSX-T**: This is a network virtualization tool from VMware that can be deployed not only within VMware vSphere but also within other hypervisors. NSX provides sophisticated network functions from layer 2 up to layer 7. This includes micro-segmentation, load balancing, or transparent L2 bridging, for example.
- **Project Harbor**: This is an open source tool that acts as a centralized cloud registry for your application images as well as providing RBAC to your users using LDAP or AD integration.

Here is an overview of the components of PKS:

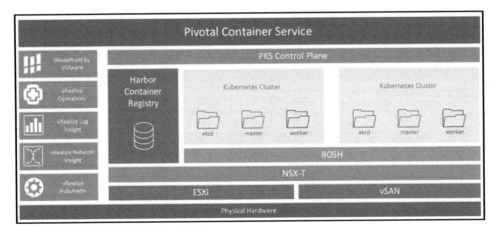

VMware vSphere ecosystem

As well as the well-known vSphere product line, VMware has plenty of products available today. Let's have a look at the different segments that VMware currently covers.

Data centers and cloud computing

VMware vSphere is a flagship in VMware's portfolio. However, there has been a rise in popularity of other products, as enterprise companies already broadly adopted VMware vSphere as a virtualization platform.

VMware vSphere has been around for more than 15 years now (the first version of a vCenter server with vMotion was released in 2003), yet with every new release, there are significant improvements.

Gartner named VMware as a leader in x86 virtualization Gartner's **Magic Quadrant (MQ)** many times, proving that this technology was broadly adopted by enterprise companies as well as honoring VMware's clear vision of the product itself.

There is not much more to say here except that VMware vSphere was, is, and will always be one of the most commonly deployed and trusted platforms for data center and cloud computing.

Storage and availability

Storage and availability products focus on the improved reliability of your storage subsystem and the overall uptime of your data center, utilizing business recovery and disaster recovery avoidance technologies.

In storage and availability, you can find two major products:

- **VMware vSAN**: This is an implementation of hyper-converged, software-defined storage. With this approach, you can utilize your local storage in your ESXi servers and form a uniform storage resource that is used as your shared storage. Together with VMware, vSphere, and VMware NSX-V, vSAN forms an SDDC:

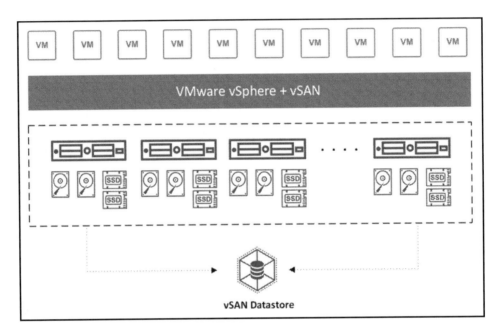

- **VMware Site Recovery Manager (SRM)**: This is an orchestrator to simplify the site disaster recovery plan in a single-click procedure, with the capability to test it in safe mode and to handle not only the failover procedures (planned or unplanned), but also failbacks.

Network and security

NSX—a product developed based on technology acquired from Nicira, enables the creation of entire networks in software. NSX is integrated with the distributed vSwitch and thus runs directly on the ESXi hypervisor. Using this approach you can easily abstracted the network functions from the underlying physical hardware.

Any network component that is supported by NSX can be provisioned in minutes, without touching the application or the physical environment:

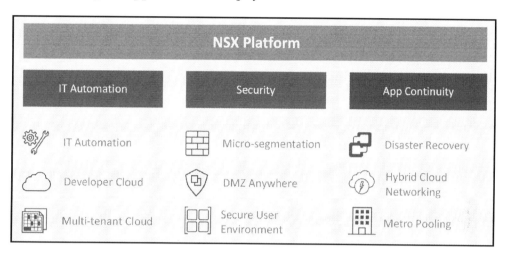

There are two versions of NSX today:

- **NSX for vSphere (NSX-V)**: This is tightly integrated with vSphere components requiring both ESXi (used both as a data plane and also for hosting some NFV and VMs used as a control plane) and vCenter. (The NSX manager is paired with this, and the management interface is just an extension of the vSphere Web Client.)
- **NSX Transformers (NSX-T)**: This is a multi-hypervisor aware SDN stack brought to the likes of vSphere, KVM, OpenStack, Kubernetes, and Docker. NSX-T is designed to address emerging application architectures that have heterogeneous endpoints and technology stacks. One of the primary use cases for NSX-T is providing a network infrastructure for containers. In today's virtualization, we can see that more and more applications are running in environments outside of virtual machines.
- **NSX Cloud**: This is an NSX implementation that focuses on public clouds. Using NSX Cloud you can manage both your private datacenter and public cloud as a single network and security entity.
- **AppDefense**: Datacenter endpoint security product. AppDefense is focusing on understanding the application logic and behavior rather then hard limits or rules.

End user computing

This product line closely follows VMware's vision of *any application on any device*. You can find several products here, but the most important are **Workspace ONE** and **Horizon 7**:

- **Workspace ONE:** Centralized solution that allows users to access any application on any device no matter where the application is running. With Workspace One you can also unify the access to all company-wide applications utilizing Single-Sign On functions.
- **Horizon 7:** Solution that is focusing on delivery of virtualized remote desktops and applications to the users through a centralized platform.

Cloud management

Today, the biggest struggle in maintaining a unified cloud is centralized management and automation. Although the majority of VMware vSphere day-to-day tasks can be accomplished by vCenter Server itself, for those who are seeking a more advanced management platform, the vRealize product line can be leveraged:

- **vRealize Operations**: Delivers continuous performance optimization at a minimal cost, driven by business and operational intent, efficient capacity management and planning, and intelligent remediation. It automates and simplifies IT operations management and provides unified visibility from applications to infrastructure across physical, virtual, and cloud environments.
- **vRealize Automation**: Cloud automation platform that accelerates the delivery of IT services through automation and pre-defined policies, providing a high level of agility and flexibility for developers, while maintaining frictionless governance and control for IT teams.
- **vRealize Network Insight (vRNI)**: Helps you to build an optimized, highly available and secure network infrastructure across multi-cloud environments. It accelerates micro-segmentation deployment, minimizes business risk during application migration, and enables customers to manage and scale NSX deployments confidently.

Cloud-native workloads

Container technologies have been used for many years. However, with modern tooling that provides orchestration, scheduling, and massive scalability, containers have gained new interest from enterprises. Combined with DevOps practices, containers are leveraged as part of **Continuous Integration/Continuous Deployment (CI/CD)** to deliver applications faster, much like web-scale companies. Although application developers are starting to adopt containers and DevOps, taking applications to production often entails a broader set of conditions that involve IT administrators.

Containers do not require virtualization at all because they can run on bare metal. Moreover, you can use different solutions for managing and deploying them.

There are different methods for providing a **Containers-as-a-Service (CaaS)** solution with different approaches:

- **Using VIC**: This is useful if you have containers that you need to put into production and still use your existing production VM monitoring systems to monitor individual containers
- **Using PKS**: This is used for multi-cloud workloads
- **Using vRealize Automation:** This is used to deploy VMs (with Photon OS or CoreOS) that can host multiple containers

VIC is a comprehensive container solution built on VMware's industry-leading virtualization platform, vSphere, which enables customers to run both modern and traditional workloads in production on their existing SDDC infrastructure today with enterprise-grade networking, storage, security, performance, and visibility.

VMware PKS is a Kubernetes-based container solution that integrates advanced networking functions allowing rapid deployment and operations of Kubernetes clusters on both private and public clouds.

Introduction to VMware Cloud on AWS

VMware Cloud on AWS is the only hybrid cloud solution that allows VMware vSphere customers to modernize, protect, and scale mission-critical applications leveraging AWS, the world's leading public cloud. With the inclusion of VMware **Hybrid Cloud Extension (HCX)** in the base offering, VMware has made it extremely easy to migrate applications at scale to VMware Cloud on AWS.

VMware Cloud on AWS provides the performance, availability, and scale required to support the most resource-intensive applications, including Oracle databases, middleware, applications, and Microsoft SQL Server. Running VMware vSphere, vSAN, and NSX on Amazon's EC2 dedicated, elastic, bare-metal infrastructure delivers the predictable, high-performance infrastructure required for these workloads:

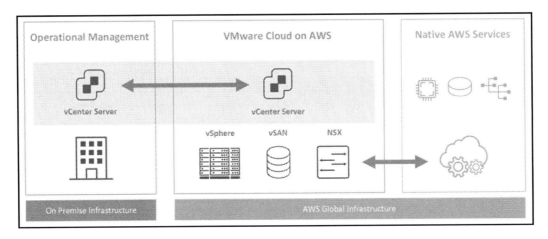

Hardware specifications and sizing

The VMware Cloud on AWS's minimum standard configuration contains three hosts. Each host is an Amazon EC2 `i3.metal` instance. These hosts have dual 2.3 GHz CPUs (custom-built Intel Xeon processor E5-2686 v4 CPU) with 18 cores per socket (36 cores total), 512 GiB RAM, and 14.3 TB raw NVMe storage (3.6 TB cache plus 10.7 TB raw capacity tier).

The minimum size of the cluster is three ESXi hosts, and you can scale up with increments of one unit up to a total supported cluster size, which is 32 ESXi hosts.

For service sizing based on your assumed workloads, you can look at *VMware Cloud on AWS Sizer and TCO calculator* at `https://vmcsizer.vmware.com/home`.

Physical location

With VMware Cloud on AWS, you can choose where your SDDC will be deployed. Most of the AWS regions are available for VMware Cloud, such as the following:

- AWS US West
- AWS US East
- AWS GovCloud (US)
- AWS Europe
- AWS Asia Pacific

Pricing

The overall price of the service is based on a number of ESXi hosts per hour.

VMware Cloud on AWS costs $8.3681/hour per host. The minimum size of the infrastructure is three ESXi hosts.

With a minimum cluster size of three, ESXi hosts give you 108 physical CPU cores at 2.3 GHz, 1,536 GB of memory and 42.9 TB of NVMe Storage for roughly $600 per day. This may sound a bit expensive, but you receive everything as a service without any additional management or licensing costs at all. In addition, with a 1-year subscription, you get a 30% discount and with a 3-year subscription, you get a generous 50% discount.

VMware Cloud on AWS is not only physical hardware—you get a complex service consisting of the following features:

- vSphere, vSAN, and NSX
- Multi-cluster, multi-AZ
- High availability, SLA
- Term commitment discounts
- Hybrid loyalty discounts up to 25%
- $8.3681/hour for each additional host after the first four hosts

You can check current prices as well as an advanced calculator at the following page at `https://cloud.vmware.com/vmc-aws/pricing`.

Interconnection with on-premises SDDC

You can run all your workloads on VMware Cloud on AWS without having a single server on-premises, but you will likely have existing infrastructure in place. One of the most exciting capabilities of VMware Cloud on AWS is native interconnection with your existing VMware vSphere infrastructure. Using **Hybrid Linked Mode (HLM)**, you can access both your on-premises and cloud-based infrastructure from a single, unified vCenter management portal. Here, you can freely migrate your workloads between those two environments without any disturbance to your services, all thanks to vMotion technology.

Connectivity to native AWS services

VMware Cloud on AWS is directly interconnected with your customers AWS **Virtual Private Cloud (VPC)** using the **Elastic Network Interface (ENI)**. Thanks to this interconnection, customers can use all essential AWS services directly from virtual machines running within VMware Cloud on AWS. There is no limit regarding AWS services so you can access anything from a broad set of available AWS services such as EC2 instances, Amazon S3 object storage, or **Elastic Load Balancing (ELB)**, using either a public API endpoint or even a private connection.

Certifications

VMware Cloud on AWS has been independently verified to comply with ISO 27001, ISO 27017, ISO 27018, SOC 1, SOC 2, SOC 3, and HIPAA. VMware Cloud on AWS also complies with the **General Data Protection Regulation (GDPR)**.

 For more information about VMware Cloud on AWS, feel free to go to `https://cloud.vmware.com/vmc-aws/resources`.

What's new in VMware vSphere 6.7?

In every VMware vSphere edition, there are a lot of new features available, and version 6.7 is no different. VMware vSphere 6.7 was released on April 17 2018, and by the end of 2018 there should be an upcoming U1 release.

 Detailed VMware vSphere 6.7 release notes can be found at `https:/ /docs.vmware.com/en/VMware-vSphere/6.7/rn/vsphere-esxi-vcenter-server-67-release-notes.html`.

At a high level, the new version focuses on the following four main areas of innovation:

- **Simplified and efficient management at scale**: There are several improvements in scaling and managing large deployments.
- **Comprehensive built-in security**: You should be able to run your workloads anywhere while still offering unmatched security features to your virtual machines.
- **Universal app platform**: Following the VMware vision, vSphere 6.7 could be a single platform to support any application on any cloud, as discussed previously.
- **Seamless hybrid cloud experience**: This is all about integration with cloud environments, especially, with VMware Cloud on AWS.

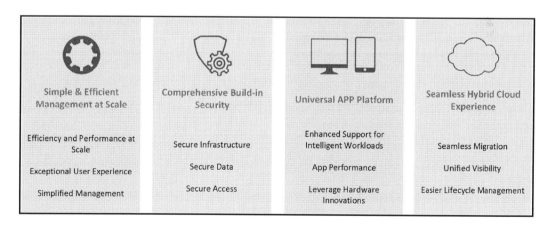

Key features

Let's dive a little bit deeper. At a technical level, the different improvements are as follows:

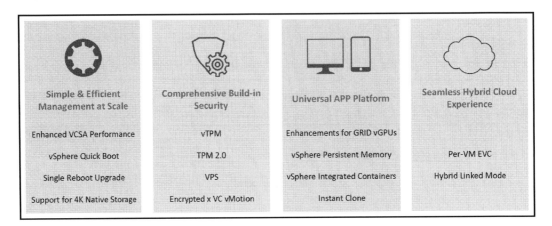

Simple & Efficient Management at Scale	Comprehensive Build-in Security	Universal APP Platform	Seamless Hybrid Cloud Experience
Enhanced VCSA Performance	vTPM	Enhancements for GRID vGPUs	
vSphere Quick Boot	TPM 2.0	vSphere Persistent Memory	Per-VM EVC
Single Reboot Upgrade	VPS	vSphere Integrated Containers	Hybrid Linked Mode
Support for 4K Native Storage	Encrypted x VC vMotion	Instant Clone	

vSphere Client (HTML-5)

There is not much to say about the new HTML-5 client. Everyone has been waiting for this, and at this stage, more than 95% of the features are fully integrated into the new HTML-5 client.

 In the upcoming release of VMware vSphere 6.7U1, everything will be available in the HTML-5 client as stated at `https://blogs.vmware.com/vsphere/2018/08/under-the-hood-vsphere-6-7-update-1.html`.

The HTML-5 interface is much faster than the old Flex client, and from my perspective, it is more intuitive than the old client:

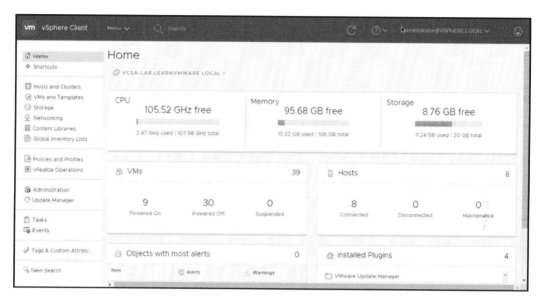

Improved vCenter Server Appliance (vCSA) monitoring

The management of the vCSA has been redesigned (you can access it through a web browser through `https://IP` or FQDN of `VCSA:5480`) and there are a whole bunch of improvements.

The overall health of all services is visible in the VAMI interface, and you can restart individual services directly from the UI as well as seeing when a particular disk is running out of space:

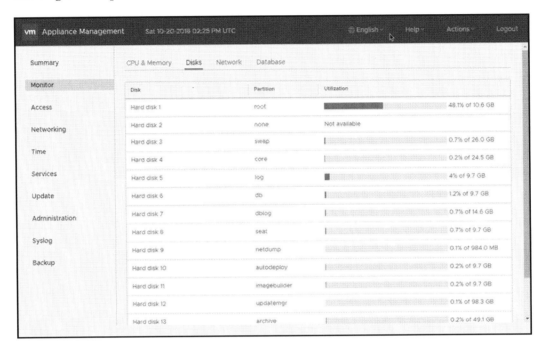

Improved vCenter backup management

Until version 6.7, you had the option to create a manual backup only, but everybody was missing an option to define the backup schedule as well. Of course, it was possible to do that through the CLI and with a bit of scripting, but that was not convenient. However, this is no longer the case. In VMware vSphere 6.7, you can easily define a backup schedule directly from vCSA management interface:

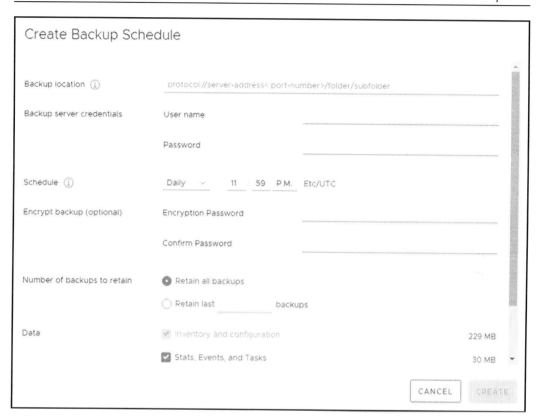

ESXi single-reboot upgrades

A lot of improvements were made regarding an upgrade procedure between major vSphere versions. In the past, there were two reboots. However, since vSphere 6.7, only one reboot has been required during the upgrade. That does not seem like a big thing, but when working with complex infrastructures, this can save a lot of time. Also, please note that when upgrading from VMware vSphere 6.5 to 6.7, you will experience this feature as well.

ESXi Quick Boot

To keep things simple, Quick Boot is a way of restarting ESXi without going through the physical hardware reboot process. This is the first implementation of this feature, so only a limited subset of physical hardware is supported. So, *how does it work?* A second ESXi image is created and updated and, when rebooting new ESXi, the image is booted directly instead of doing a full reboot. Again, the purpose here is to save time.

Currently, the following hardware platforms are supported:

- HPE ProLiant DL360 Gen10 Server
- HPE ProLiant DL360 Gen9 Server
- HPE ProLiant DL380 Gen10 Server
- HPE ProLiant DL380 Gen9 Server
- Dell R640
- Dell R630
- Dell R740
- Dell R740xd
- Dell R730
- Dell R730xd

 To check whether or not your system is compatible with Quick Boot, run this command on the ESXi host from the shell: `/usr/lib/vmware/loadesx/bin/loadESXCheckCompat.py`. You can also have a look at the knowledge base at `https://kb.vmware.com/s/article/52477`.

Support for Remote Direct Memory Access (RDMA)

vSphere 6.7 introduces new protocol support for **RDMA over Converged Ethernet (RoCE)** (pronounced *rocky*) v2, a new software **Fiber Channel over Ethernet (FCoE)** adapter, and **iSCSI Extension for RDMA (iSER)**. This feature is particularly useful for applications that require extremely low latency and high bandwidth. Please note that when RDMA is used, most of the ESXi network stack is bypassed, and when used in pass-through mode, this also means that vMotion is not available, so this will be useful specifically for scale-out applications with their high-availability mechanisms:

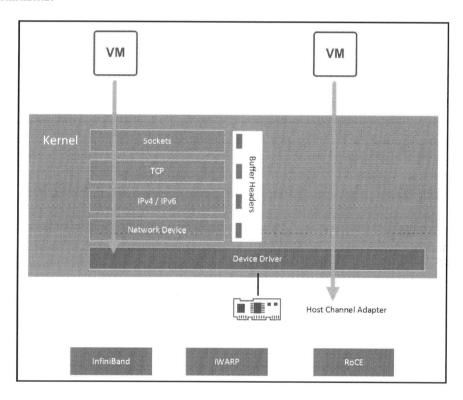

vSphere persistent memory

Persistent memory is a new storage class used for extremely demanding workloads. Persistent memory, also called **non-violated DIMM (NVDIMM)**, provides much higher performance compared to SSDs at lower costs than DRAM. Furthermore, latency is minimal—around 1 microsecond compared to low milliseconds with SSDs. To use vSphere persistent memory, you must use the latest hardware version, 14. The virtual machines can be configured with one NVDIMM controller and a maximum of 64 NVDIMM devices:

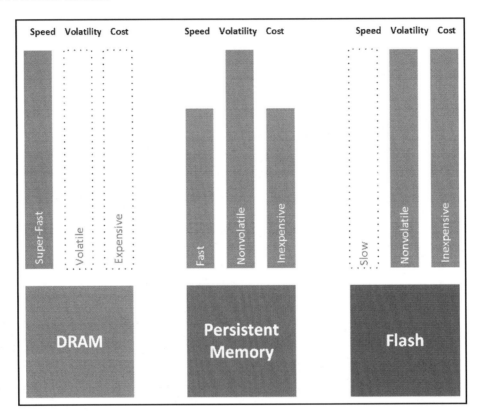

Virtual Trusted Platform Module (vTPM)

In physical systems, TPM is a chip that securely stores secrets which are used to authenticate the physical platform (PC, server). The secrets can be passwords, private keys, or certificates. The use of TPM is particularly useful for securing a system and ensuring that the data held in it is safe in case of theft, for example.

A vTPM is similar to a physical TPM device, except the cryptographic operations are performed in the vSphere layer. Instead of storing the secrets in a hardware component, they are stored in the .nvram file which is encrypted using VM encryption. vTPM is not dependent on the physical TPM at all so you can leverage this feature even if you do not have a physical TPM device.

TPM 2.0

Since vSphere 5.x, there has been support for TPM 1.2. In vSphere 6.7, VMware introduced support for TPM 2.0. Please note that TPM 2.0 and TPM 1.2 are two entirely different implementations and there is no backward compatibility with these.

 If you are running 6.5 on a server with TPM 2.0, you will not see the TPM 2.0 device because there's no support in 6.5 for TPM 2.0. New features in 6.7 do not use the TPM 1.2 device.

The TPM module is used to store the fingerprint of the ESXi image securely. If there is any manipulation of the image, or if it is not correctly signed, the digitally signed fingerprint will not match.

By enabling TPM, you can then ensure that ESXi has booted using only digitally signed code.

Microsoft virtualization-based security (VBS)

Microsoft VBS is a Windows 10 and Windows Server 2016 security feature that enhances security by creating an isolated region of memory called a memory enclave, using the hypervisor capabilities of Windows. This is used to protect critical systems or security assets such as authenticated user credentials with a credential guard.

To leverage VBS in a VM, the virtual machine must be presented with the same hardware as a bare-metal server. The only difference is that the hardware is virtualized. The following requirements must be met:

- Virtual hardware version 14
- Nested virtualization enabled
- Secure boot enabled
- EFI firmware

Here is an overview of Microsoft virtualization-based security:

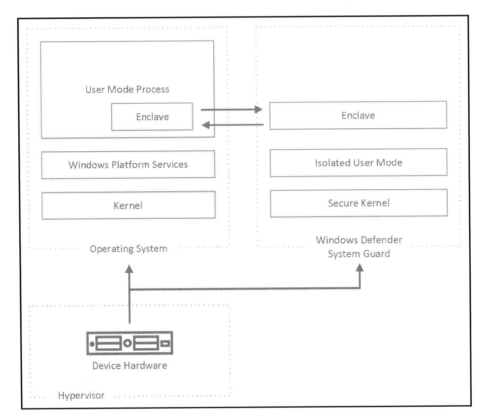

Per-VM Enhanced vMotion Compatibility (EVC)

EVC is a cluster-level feature which makes it possible to vMotion virtual machines across different generations of a CPU within the cluster by masking CPU features based on your baseline. vSphere 6.7 has taken EVC to the next level. In VMware vSphere 6.7, you can even configure EVC on a per-VM basis so every single virtual machine can have its own EVC configured. The idea here is to be able to freely move your VMs across different environments, particularly to VMware Cloud on AWS:

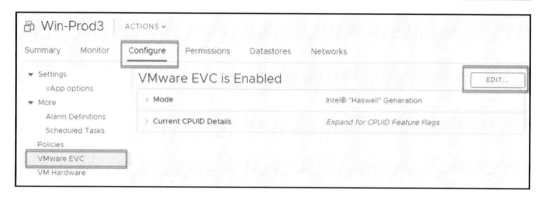

Hybrid linked mode

This feature allows you to link your on-premises vCenter **Single Sign-On (SSO)** domain with a vCenter Server located in VMware Cloud on AWS.

The idea here is to be able to access both on-premises and cloud environments from the single vCenter web client as well as to be able to vMotion your workloads between those two environments. You will also have the option to share tags and categories across vCenter Servers as well as finally sharing unified users and groups management:

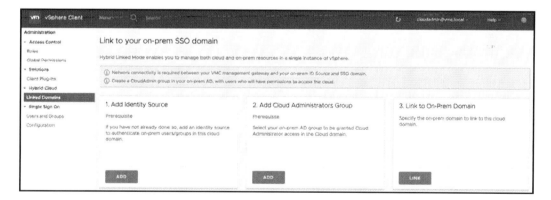

Instant Clone

One of the new features in vSphere 6.7 is **Instant Clone**. This is not exactly a new feature, however. In the past, the technology was referred to as a **VMFork**; since vSphere 6.7, it has been fully integrated into vSphere itself as the Instant Clone feature. So, *what is it?* Imagine a situation in which you need to instantly create and customize (new IP addresses, DNS names, and so on) dozens or even hundreds of VMs from a source VM, and you need to customize them as well.

The way that it works internally is similar to snapshot technology, in which the new changes are written to a delta disk, so all the VMs have a similar base disk at the beginning of their life cycle, but individual changes in those VMs are not affecting each other. You can now add memory as well, so you have new VMs running from the same point in time as the source VM. This feature might be particularly useful in CI/CD workflows where you need to test your application on a large number of nodes:

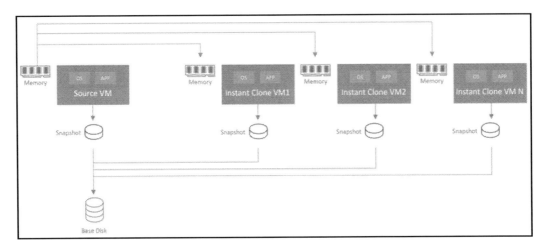

Configuration maximums

In every version of VMware vSphere, there is an increase in configuration maximums. VMware released a new website on which you can compare different versions with each other. Please note that only versions 6.0 and newer are supported here since version 5.5 is no longer officially supported (general support ended September 19, 2018).

You can check different VMware vSphere configuration maximums for different versions at `https://configmax.vmware.com/repcomp/compare`.

Let us explore the most interesting configuration maximums and the comparison between VMware vSphere 6.7 and previous versions.

Virtual machine hardware 14

Every new version of VMware vSphere brings a new version of the virtual machine virtual hardware. Currently, the most recent version of VM virtual hardware is 14. Some features, like NVDIMM devices, a virtual TPM, or a Microsoft VBS are available only with the newest virtual hardware version.

A complete feature list and corresponding configuration maximums can be found in hardware features, available with virtual machine **Compatibility** settings.

The following table summarizes some of the maximum numbers for each VM virtual hardware in the different version of vSphere:

Feature	ESXi 6.7 and later	ESXi 6.5 and later	ESXi 6.0 and later
Hardware version	14	13	11
Maximum memory (GB)	6,128	6,128	4,080
Maximum number of logical processors	128	128	128
Maximum number of cores (virtual CPUs) per socket	128	128	128
NVMe Controllers	4	4	N/A
Maximum video memory (MB)	128	128	128
Maximum graphics memory (GB)	2	2	2
PCI passthrough	16	16	16
Serial ports	32	32	32
Virtual RDMA	Y	Y	N/A
NVDIMM controller	1	N/A	N/A
NVDIMM device	Y	N/A	N/A
Virtual I/O MMU	Y	N/A	N/A
Virtual TPM	Y	N/A	N/A
Microsoft VBS	Y	N/A	N/A

A few other changes exist in version 14:

- The maximum number of virtual disks per **Paravirtual SCSI (PVSCSI)** adapter raised to 64 for a total maximum of 256 disks per VM (60 before)
- Support for per-VM EVC

As usual, it is always recommended to upgrade to the newest version of VM virtual hardware, but as always, this is not required. There are some reasons not to upgrade, for example, backward ESXi compatibility. It is not recommended to run a mixed environment without having all hosts or clusters on the same version. However, if you want to use any of the new features mentioned here (such as persistent memory or Microsoft VBS) you will have no choice but to upgrade.

Upgrading the VM virtual hardware does require a reboot of the virtual machine, so take this into consideration and plan such a task during the maintenance window.

ESXi 6.7 hypervisors

In vSphere 6.7, the ESXi host limits increased only slightly compared to version 6.5, and new hardware and new devices are now supported. New 50 GbE and 100 GbE network interface cards were also made available in version 6.7.

The following table summarizes the configuration maximums for an ESXi host:

Feature	ESXi 6.7	ESXi 6.5	ESXi 6.0
Logical CPUs per host	768	576	480
Virtual CPUs per host	4,096	4,096	4,096
Virtual CPUs per core	32	32	32
RAM per host	16 TB	12 TB	12 TB
Virtual machines per host	1,024	1,024	1,024
LUNS per host	1,024	512	256
Non-volatile memory per host	1 TB	N/A	N/A

vCenter Server 6.7

There is no change in configuration maximums for the vCenter Server compared to version 6.5. Please keep in mind that vCSA should be your default choice when installing a new vCenter Server and VMware vSphere 6.7 is the last supported version for vCenter Server on Windows. Furthermore, only vCSA will be available:

vCenter Server maximums	vCenter Server 6.7	vCenter Server 6.0	vCenter Server 6.0
vMotion operations per datastore	128	128	128
Storage vMotion operations per host	2	2	2
Storage vMotion operations per datastore	8	8	8
Non-vMotion provisioning operations per host	8	8	8
Hosts per vCenter server	2,000	2,000	2,000
Total number of libraries per VC	1,000	1,000	20
Powered-on virtual machines per vCenter server	25,000	25,000	10,000
Total items per library	1,000	1,000	20
Registered virtual machines per vCenter server	35,000	35,000	15,000
Linked vCenter servers	15	15	10
Total content library items per VC (across all libraries)	2,000	2,000	200
Hosts in linked vCenter servers	5,000	5,000	4 000
Powered-on virtual machines in linked vCenter servers	50,000	50,000	30,000
Registered virtual machines in linked vCenter servers	70,000	70,000	50,000

VMware vSphere 6.7 Editions

Different license levels are available from VMware, covering everything from small business to remote office and branch office, all the way up to a standard enterprise license. In each license type, there are usually multiple options available, each covering a different subset of VMware vSphere functionality.

VMware vSphere Editions

VMware vSphere Editions are the key licensing options available. These focus on standard enterprise companies, and the license is assigned to each physical CPU installed. Please note that you always need to buy a license for the vCenter server itself as well.

There are two vCenter Server licenses available:

Product feature	vCenter foundation	vCenter standard
Host manageable	Max four ESXi hosts	Unlimited ESXi hosts
vCenter **High Availability (HA)**	Not available	Only for the vCSA
vCenter backup and restore	Not available	Only for the vCSA
Linked mode	Not available	Yes

vCenter Foundation is a vCenter server that has a limited functionality (although it provides all cluster services, such as VMware HA an **Distributed Resource Scheduling (DRS)**) as well as the maximum number of supported hosts. vCenter Standard has no limitations at all.

Once you have your vCenter Server, then you need to assign a proper license to your ESXi host, and again, multiple options are available.

In VMware vSphere 6.7 U1 (which was announced during the writing of this book but has not been released yet), the new edition will be available as VMware vSphere Platinum.

VMware vSphere Platinum edition has the same capabilities as Enterprise Plus but with one big advantage—**AppDefense**.

 If you are interested in more information about AppDefense, feel free to have a look at `https://www.vmware.com/products/appdefense.html`.

Let's focus on features you can find in different vSphere editions:

- **Business Continuity and Security**: Features focusing on improved availability, enhanced uptime, and advanced security features are as follows:

Product features	VMware vSphere Standard	VMware vSphere Enterprise Plus	VMware vSphere with operations management	VMware vSphere Platinum
vMotion	Cross-vSwitch/Cross-vCenter/Long Distance/Cross-Cloud	Cross-vSwitch/Cross-vCenter/Long Distance/Cross-Cloud	Cross-vSwitch/Cross-vCenter/Long Distance/ Cross-Cloud	Cross-vSwitch/Cross-vCenter/Long Distance/ Cross-Cloud
vSphere HA	Y	Y	Y	Y
Storage vMotion	Y	Y	Y	Y
Fault Tolerance	2-vCPU	8-vCPU	8-vCPU	8-vCPU
vShield Endpoint	Y	Y	Y	Y
vSphere Replication	Y	Y	Y	Y
Support for 4K Native Storage	Y	Y	Y	Y
vSphere Quick Boot	Y	Y	Y	Y
vSphere Single Reboot	Y	Y	Y	Y
vCenter High Availability	vCenter Server Standard	vCenter Server Standard	vCenter Server Standard	vCenter Server Standard
vCenter Backup and Restore	vCenter Server Standard	vCenter Server Standard	vCenter Server Standard	vCenter Server Standard
vCenter Server Appliance Migration Tool	vCenter Server Standard	vCenter Server Standard	vCenter Server Standard	vCenter Server Standard
vCenter Server Appliance Converge Tool	vCenter Server Standard	vCenter Server Standard	vCenter Server Standard	vCenter Server Standard
TPM 2.0 Support and Virtual TPM	Y	Y	Y	Y
FIPS 140-2 Compliance & TLS 1.2 Support as Default	Y	Y	Y	Y

Product features	VMware vSphere Standard	VMware vSphere Enterprise Plus	VMware vSphere with operations management	VMware vSphere Platinum
Cross vCenter Encrypted vMotion	Y	Y	Y	Y
Virtual Machine Encryption		Y	Y	Y
Automated Discovery of Application Assets, Intent, and Communication				Y
Contextual Intelligence of Application State				Y
Orchestrated or Automated Responses to Security Threats				Y
Integration with Third-Party Security Operations Tools				Y

- **Resource prioritization and enhanced application performance:** Features aimed for improved performance, workload optimization, and application control:

Product features	vSphere Standard	vSphere Enterprise Plus	vSphere with operations management	vSphere Platinum
Virtual Volumes	Y	Y	Y	Y
Storage Policy-Based Management	Y	Y	Y	Y
Distributed Resource Scheduler (DRS)		Y	Y	Y
Distributed Power Management (DPM)		Y	Y	Y
Storage DRS		Y	Y	Y
Storage I/O Control		Y	Y	Y

Product features	vSphere Standard	vSphere Enterprise Plus	vSphere with operations management	vSphere Platinum
Network I/O Control		Y	Y	Y
Single Root I/O Virtualization (SR-IOV) support		Y	Y	Y
vSphere Persistent Memory		Y	Y	Y
NVIDIA GRID vGPU		Y	Y	Y
Proactive HA		Y	Y	Y
Predictive DRS			Y	

- **Automated administration and provisioning:** Features enabling streamlined operations and automation of the environment:

Product features	vSphere Standard	vSphere Enterprise Plus	vSphere with operations management	vSphere Platinum
Content Library	Y	Y	Y	Y
vCenter Server Appliance Enhanced Linked Mode with Embedded Platform Services Controller	vCenter Server Standard	vCenter Server Standard	vCenter Server Standard	vCenter Server Standard
Storage APIs for Array Integration, Multipathing	Y	Y	Y	Y
Distributed Switch		Y	Y	Y
Host Profiles and Auto Deploy		Y	Y	Y

VMware vSphere Essentials Kits

VMware vSphere Essentials Kits are for small businesses and combine virtualization for up to three physical servers with centralized management using VMware vCenter Server® for Essentials. vCenter Server for Essentials has a similar capability to vCenter Foundation, but the limit is only three ESXi hosts. Also, Essentials Kits are bundled in a single SKU which contains ESXi licenses as well as the vCenter Server license. There are two different Essentials Kits available:

	vSphere Essentials Kit	**vSphere Essentials Plus Kit**
Overview	Server virtualization and consolidation with centralized management	Server virtualization and consolidation plus business continuity
vCenter Server	vCenter Server for Essentials	vCenter Server for Essentials
License entitlement	Three servers with up to two processors each	Three servers with up to two processors each
Features	ESXi	ESXi, vMotion, high availability, vShield endpoint, vSphere replication

Remote Office Branch Office (ROBO) editions

VMware vSphere ROBO is designed for IT infrastructure located in remote, distributed sites. This delivers improved service levels, standardization, availability, and compliance.

The idea of ROBO edition is that you have one vCenter Server in your HQ and then different ROBO sites that you centrally manage. You can, of course, deploy vCenter Server Foundation as a local management platform in each ROBO site as well.

You can run up to 25 VMs in a single ROBO site, but you can't assign multiple license packs in the single site. However, you can distribute the single license among multiple sites (ROBO site 1 contains 5 VMs, ROBO site 2 contains 10 VMs, and ROBO site 3 contains 10 VMs):

	vSphere ROBO Standard	**vSphere ROBO Advanced**
Overview	Remote site server virtualization platform with business continuity and backup features	Remote site server virtualization offering business continuity and backup with advanced features such as standardization of host configurations
Centralized management	vCenter Server for Essentials	vCenter Server for Essentials
License entitlement	Pack of 25 virtual machines	Pack of 25 virtual machines
vCenter Server (sold separately)	vCenter Server Standard	vCenter Server Standard
Features	ESXi, vMotion, Storage vMotion, High Availability, Fault Tolerance (2-vCPU), vShield Endpoint, vSphere Replication, Hot-add, Content Library	ESXi, vMotion, Storage vMotion, High Availability, Fault Tolerance (4-vCPU), vShield Endpoint, vSphere Replication, Hot-add, Content Library, Host Profiles, Auto Deploy, Distributed Switch

Reasons for and against upgrading

VMware vSphere 6.7 does not represent a major release of vSphere compared to 6.5, but some exciting features might encourage you to think about going for the update. This is especially the case if you are interested in a hybrid cloud solution and interconnection with AWS; vSphere 6.7 is a clear way to go. Furthermore, the features described here are only available in the newest version of VMware vSphere. If you need to use some of those features, then make the update. There are almost no difference in configuration maximums, so scalability is probably not the most significant issue there.

Finally, don't forget to check that your physical hardware is supported by vSphere 6.7. This is necessary as there were some changes, especially with several CPU models that are no longer supported. Don't forget to consider all third-party code, including drivers, services, kernel modules, all vCenter plugins, or integration with external software such as backup products.

You can check all your components with the hardware compatibility List to see if they are fully supported in VMware vSphere 6.7 at https://www.vmware.com/resources/compatibility/search.php.

You can also try one of the newest **VMware flings**: ESXi compatibility checker. This is a Python script that can validate VMware hardware compatibility and resolve ESXi issues.

You can download the ESXi compatibility checker Python script for free from VMware labs at https://labs.vmware.com/flings/esxi-compatibility-checker.

Why upgrade?

There can be several reasons to upgrade vSphere to the latest version:

- **To extend the support and the life cycle of the product**: VMware vSphere 5.5 is no longer supported (since September 2018) and VMware vSphere 6.0 is only supported until March 2020.
- **HTML-5 web client**: Brings a big improvement for day-to-day administration of the environment.
- **To have a new product**: vSphere 6.7 provides new features but new hardware (and other new software) may require or benefit from this version.
- **New infrastructure functions**: This may include Instant Clone or the vTPM.

- **Storage benefits**: If you require a super-fast storage subsystem, persistent memory is a big deal.
- **Cloud integration**: VMware Cloud on AWS offers a genuinely cloud-based environment with the same capabilities as your on-premises vSphere environment.

Why shouldn't you upgrade?

There can be a few reasons to avoid upgrading vSphere 6.7:

- You may have a software or hardware part that does not support this version.
- *Does the new version support existing servers?* vSphere 6.7 drops the support for some old hardware and software. vSphere 6.7 no longer supports the following processors:
    - AMD Opteron 13xx Series, 23xx Series, 24xx Series, 41xx Series, 61xx Series, 83xx Series, and 84xx Series
    - Intel Core i7-620LE Processor
    - Intel i3/i5 Clarkdale
    - Intel Xeon 31xx Series, 33xx Series, 34xx Series, 34xx Series, 35xx Series, 36xx Series, 52xx Series, 54xx Series, 55xx Series, 56xx Series, 65xx Series, 74xx Series, and 75xx Series
- *Do you really need the new functions?* If you are involved in a digital transformation, you will probably need the new platform (AWS for vSphere or vSphere for integrated container management require the new version). However, for SMBs, most of the new functions are not usable or useful yet.
- *Can you really use the new functions?* Most of the new features are only for the Enterprise Plus edition (see the next paragraph for more details about the different editions).
- *Is the new version mature and stable enough?* Some customers prefer to wait several months for the upgrade to make sure that there are no significant bugs in the code.

Upgrade paths

vSphere 5.5 does not have a direct upgrade path to vSphere 6.7. If you are currently running vSphere 5.5, you must first upgrade to either vSphere 6.0 or vSphere 6.5 before upgrading to vSphere 6.7.

 There is no supported upgrade path from vSphere 6.5 Update 2 to vSphere 6.7, as described at `https://kb.vmware.com/s/article/53704`. However you can upgrade to vSphere 6.7U1

If you have a complex vSphere environment, you should update all components in the correct order, otherwise you might face troubles with the infrastructure. The correct update sequence for VMware vSphere 6.7 and related products is as follows:

- **vRealize Automation (vRA)**
- **vRealize Orchestrator (vRB)**
- **vRealize Business for Cloud (vRBC)**
- **vRealize Operations (vROps)**
- vRealize Operations Manager Endpoint Operations Agent
- **vRealize Log Insight (vRLI)**
- vRealize Log Insight Agent
- VMware **vSphere Storage APIs for Data Protection (vADP)**-based backup solution
- NSX for vSphere (NSX-v)
- **Platform Services Controller (PSC)** External
- vCenter Server
- **vSphere Update Manager (VUM)**
- **vSphere Replication (VR)**
- **Site Recovery Manager (SRM)**
- ESXi
- vSAN
- Virtual hardware
- VMware tools

 You can find detailed steps for upgrading multiple vSphere components at `https://kb.vmware.com/s/article/53710`.

Summary

This chapter has covered a general overview of modern data center concepts as well as all key products and solutions from VMware.

In this chapter, we also covered VMware Cloud on AWS, a new option for utilizing VMware vSphere infrastructure as a service, its benefits, and guidance for migration from on-premises infrastructure.

We have also looked at new features of the vSphere 6.7 suite, comparing its evolution with the previous releases, and we have covered the differences between the most commonly used VMware vSphere editions currently available.

Finally, in this chapter, we have explained why you should or should not choose to upgrade to vSphere 6.7, and we have also briefly touched on upgrade paths from previous versions.

In the next chapter, we will focus on how to plan a virtualization project in order to build a proper infrastructure solution and reliable data center.

Questions

1. What are three essential products for fulfilling the SDDC concept?

   a) VMware vSphere
   b) VMware Cloud on AWS
   c) VMware Site Recovery Manager
   d) VMware vSAN
   e) VMware Cloud Foundation
   f) VMware NSX

2. Based on the following use case, which licensing option will be the most effective?

The customer has an existing central data center with VMware vSphere Enterprise Plus licenses. Additionally, the customer wants to deploy two secondary sites in a branch location, each serving only a small amount of virtual machines. The customer also needs to use vSphere Distributed vSwitch in branch locations:

   a) VMware vSphere Enterprise Plus edition
   b) VMware vSphere Essentials edition
   c) VMware vSphere ROBO edition
   d) VMware vSphere Standard edition

3. What are the benefits of using VMware Cloud on AWS?

   a) Full integration with on-premises infrastructure
   b) Deep integration of VMware vSphere, vSAN, and NSX
   c) Pay-as-you-go payment model based on the number of ESXi hypervisors
   d) Fully managed environment
   e) Zero investment costs
   f) Dedicated hardware

4. Can you manage cloud-native workloads (containers) using VMware vSphere?

   a) Yes
   b) No

5. Regarding configuration maximums of the vCenter server, are there any differences between vCenter Server for Windows and vCenter Server Appliance?

   a) Yes
   b) No

6. What features are available in VMware vSphere Enterprise Plus licenses that are not available in VMware vSphere Standard edition?

    a) VMware High Availability
    b) VMware Distributed vSwitch
    c) VMware Distributed Resource Scheduler
    d) VMware Fault Tolerance
    e) VMware vMotion
    f) Network I/O Control

7. What is the primary constraint when planning the upgrade of the ESXi hypervisor?

    a) Hardware support
    b) License costs
    c) Upgrade complexity

Further reading

For more information, feel free to check the following resources:

- **Building VMware Software-Defined Data Centers**: In this book, Valentin Hamburger explores the unified software-defined data center concept using all three essential products from VMware—vSphere, vSAN, and NSX. `https://www.packtpub.com/virtualization-and-cloud/building-vmware-software-defined-data-centers`.

- **VMware cross-cloud architecture**: If you are looking for unified hybrid cloud solutions, this book is the answer. `https://www.packtpub.com/virtualization-and-cloud/vmware-cross-cloud-architecture/`.

- **VMware product pages**: You can have a look at the official VMware product pages for additional white-papers, technical documentation, and datasheets of each product you are interested in.
  - `https://www.vmware.com/products.html`
  - `https://labs.hol.vmware.com/HOL/catalogs/catalog/681`

2
Designing and Planning a Virtualization Infrastructure

This chapter describes how to plan a virtualization project and build proper infrastructure by providing an approach both for the planning and the design. We'll start with how to map business requirements to technical requirements, and then how to move from conceptual design to logical and physical design.

To support those different phase methodologies, documents such as best practices, reference architectures, and guidelines will be suggested.

In this chapter, we will learn about the following:

- Planning a virtual infrastructure project
- Physical hardware considerations
- Assess
- Design
- Approaching different scenarios—SMB, ROBO enterprise

Planning a virtual infrastructure project

A virtualization project is like any other business-related project and should follow the same set of methodologies and processes for successful project delivery. There are different methodologies that are commonly used, but they usually contain the same building blocks:

1. **Assess:** This phase covers all the pieces of information needed for successful design, from the project objectives, business requirements, service level objectives, and agreements, possible risks, or constraints. It is essential to understand and capture all those inputs as they will define the resulting design and architecture.
2. **Design:** During this phase, the design is created based on the information gathered in the previous step and must cover all the requirements defined by the organization's goals, requirements, or constraints.
3. **Deploy:** In this phase, the production environment is deployed according to design documents.
4. **Verify:** Lastly, in this phase, after the production environment is configured, you conduct various tests to check whether your design objectives, requirements, or **service level agreement** (SLA) match with the design specifications. This phase can have multiple iterations if additional changes are required to resolve possible conflicts with the design objective.

Plan-Do-Check-Act (PDCA)

This method is a general framework for every project. Based on PDCA, generally, you can deliver anything from business projects such as cost savings or restructuralization, all the way to infrastructure projects such as data center relocation or even virtualization projects.

PDCA has four main phases, but the fundamental concept is that PDCA runs in cycles, meaning that, after each iteration of one cycle, the next one begins until the project is done. In each additional run, you optimize or narrow the expected outcomes from the process:

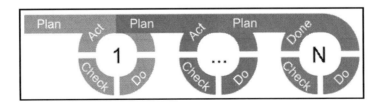

The four main phases are explained as follows:

- **Plan**: This is the first phase of PDCA. During the planning phase, you establish the objectives and processes necessary to deliver all of the business requirements. In this phase, you will also produce a design for the solution.
- **Do**: This is the implementation phase, according to the previous plan. Small changes are usually implemented or tested and data is gathered to see how effective the change is.
- **Check**: During the check phase, the data and results gathered from the do phase are evaluated. Data is compared to the expected outcomes to validate the design and improve or correct it if needed.
- **Act**: In this phase, with the results of previous phases, the final implementation can be executed. If needed, the cycle can be reiterated, generally before the end of the lifetime of the assets, or periodically to revalidate or improve the infrastructure.

There are many flavors of the PDCA, such as **Plan-Do-Study-Act (PDSA)**, **Observe-Plan-Do-Check-Act (OPDCA)**, **Standardize-Do-Check-Act (SDCA)** , or **Define-Measure-Analyze-Improve-Control (DMAIC)**. However, from my perspective, there are even better methods that you can use, especially related to infrastructure projects. Let's explore several of the methods you can use to drive your infrastructure projects.

Waterfall

Let have a look at the standard waterfall model. Sometimes it is also referred to as a linear-sequential life cycle model. It is a straightforward and easy to use model, since each phase must be successfully completed before you can proceed to the next phase:

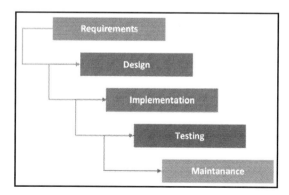

The five sequential phases in the waterfall model are as follows:

1. **Requirement gathering and analysis**: Requirements are captured in this phase as well as business justification for the project. All variables and inputs are documented.
2. **System design**: Based on the requirements specified in the first phase system, the design is prepared. Based on the system design, all hardware and software requirements are documented, and the system architecture is prepared.
3. **Implementation**: The project is implemented using your system design.
4. **Integration and testing**: System implementation is tested according to the expected behavior defined in system design. The entire system is tested for any faults and failures.
5. **Deployment of system**: Once the functional and non-functional testing is done, the service is deployed in the customer environment or approved for production.
6. **Maintenance**: Day-2 operations of the environment are covered by maintenance. The environment is monitored, changes are implemented to further improve the solution, and support and management is provided.

Over the years, the waterfall model evolves to better address continually changing the environment, but I tend to stick with a standard waterfall model with several improvements.

This model is based on the fact that, before you move to the next phase, you check that the outcome of the next phase corresponds with the requirements defined in the previous and, if not, you reassess either your business requirements or the infrastructure.

In the end, the maintenance process itself is reworked and extended based on the **Information Technology Infrastructure Library (ITIL)**.

ITIL v3

The **IT Infrastructure Library (ITIL)** framework consists of five books (sometimes referred as a stages) that are part of every IT service. Each stage contains several core processes or functions that are aligned with IT organization structure. Usually, companies adopt some of these processes, that are suitable for their teams but it is not required to implement the whole set of processes from all stages. Therefore, ITIL is quite flexible regarding adoption.

The following is a diagram of the ITIL service life cycle stages:

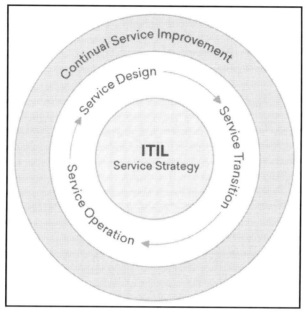

Core ITIL Processes:

- **Service Strategy**
- **Service Design**
- **Service Transition**
- **Service Operation**
- **Continual Service Improvement**

Improved waterfall

As described previously, the standard waterfall has its limitations, and for infrastructure projects, I tend to use this improved waterfall model.

Some of the stages from the classical waterfall are also mapped to the design process, as used in **VMware Certified Design Expert 6 – Data Center Virtualization (VCDX6-DCV)** at https://www.vmware.com/education-services/certification/vcdx6-dcv.html.

VCDX contains three phases of design, as shown in the following diagram:

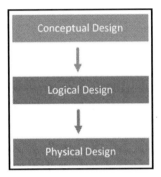

- Discover the inputs (conceptual model)
- Develop the solution (logical design)
- Design the architecture (physical design)

From my perspective, the improved waterfall approach gives you better control because of constant verification: the outcomes from each phase are compared to the requirements in each phase. In addition, it is more detailed, following the VDCX-DCV structure. You can easily use this project management framework even for the service operation as it includes core components of the service operation process defined in ITILv3:

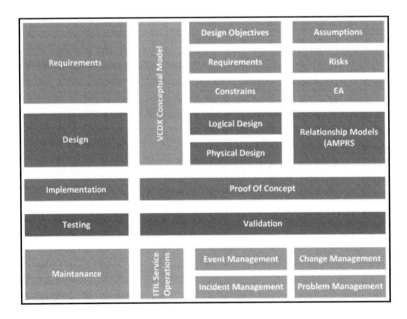

Please keep in mind that an infrastructure project can't be successfully delivered without cooperation between multiple stakeholders. You'll need to have customer involvement during all phases, of course, with various types of people during the different phases. For the assess and design phases, stakeholders should be involved to provide appropriate input into the design process. For the deploy and validate phases, you need the customer's operators and administrators (in all the technologies involved in the project) to understand the new technology and operational changes that will be needed.

Physical hardware considerations

Before we jump to planning the project design, we're going walk through several hardware platforms that you can use with your designs later on.

It is essential to understand the pros and cons of different hardware solutions, as well as some basic hardware component considerations. We will cover those components in more depth in upcoming chapters, but for now a basic knowledge will do.

Physical form factor considerations

Today, there are many form factors you can use for your virtualization projects, from standard rack servers, to blade servers or hyper-converged solutions. All of the platforms are standard x86 servers, with similar capabilities concerning CPU, memory, or storage resources with their own pros and cons from technical, design, and business perspectives.

Standard rack servers

Standard rack servers are the mainstream you would find in every datacenter and every company.

They have been around for decades, and you've probably seen them before:

Standard rack servers can vary in size (regarding rack units, also known as **U-size)** which usually defines the maximum number of storage disks you can install into the server.

The key characteristics of a standard server are that each physical unit equals the individual server. All the I/O modules are installed directly to the server; in addition, each server has its own power supply, although usually you will see two independent power supplies for redundancy.

Today's mainstream are dual-socket servers that can be equipped with two CPU packages, although single-socket servers or quad-socket servers are also available.

In the next two charts, you can find the typical server sizing is based on the VMware customer improvement experience program.

CPU socket and CPU core distribution:

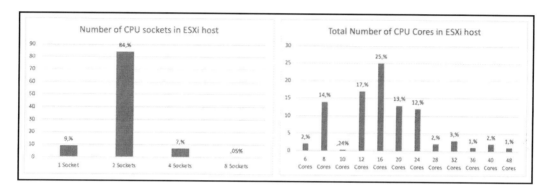

And, here's the installed memory size distribution:

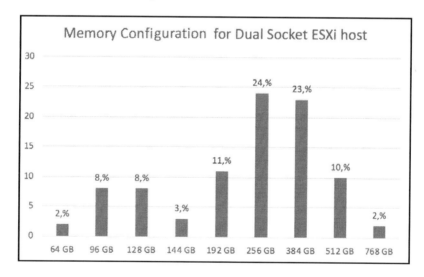

Standard servers are independent, meaning that you can install them into a 19 rack anywhere. There is no need for any special wiring or interconnection between systems, and you can even start the server on the floor of the data center. Standard servers are also cheaper compared to blade systems.

You can easily switch the vendors because there is no dependency at all, meaning with standard rack servers you can be more agile and flexible.

On the other hand, management of large-scale installation of standard servers can be quite challenging. There is no central management at all, so every server acts as an individual unit, meaning a large operational overhead. Also, imagine a situation when you have a full rack of servers, and you need to make some physical adjustments. Sometimes, it is quite difficult to maneuver around the server due to the extensive cabling. Lastly, not all components are located from the front. I/O modules are usually at the back while disk devices are located in the front.

Standard rack servers also generate much additional heat and pull a lot of power compared to blade systems. Although they're getting better, rack systems need a lot of cooling and high volumes of airflow to keep their components at a proper working temperature.

Blade servers

A blade server is a special form-factor, where all unnecessary hardware is removed from the server and placed in the blade chassis which is a mandatory piece of equipment. Blade servers are mounted into the blade chassis (sometimes called enclosure) and those chassis hold the shared equipment like power supplies, fans, network adapters or shared management.

The idea is to keep the data center footprint at a minimum. In the standard 42U rack, you can install up to 42 standard rack servers, but in the case of blade servers, it can even be hundreds, depending on the physical design of the blade server and chassis. In more traditional chassis designs—HPE blades, for example—you can install up to 4 blade chassis in the 42U rack and each chassis can be equipped with 16 servers giving a total number of 64 dual-socket servers, which is roughly a 33% denser deployment compared to standard rack servers:

Another significant advantage of blade servers is centralized management through the blade chassis. You can manage and configure the whole system from a single interface covering all your blade servers in the chassis, and usually (depending on your blade system vendor) you can even link multiple chassis into a single management domain.

Similarly, because some components have been removed, the overall power consumption is lower compared to traditional servers. In blade systems, you have only a few highly efficient power supplies for the whole chassis instead of many power supplies in each standard rack server.

Also, the interconnection is done differently. As there are now I/O modules on the blade servers themselves, everything is, again, done on the chassis level. You can install several interconnection modules to the chassis, and then the blade servers are internally attached to those interconnection modules. You can imagine this interconnection as a switch (for a network interconnection module), and such a switch has several ports; some of the ports are accessible, through which you can connect your chassis with the physical network, and some ports are internal, which are connected to the blade servers, but internally through the backplane itself, rather than using cables.

There are many interconnection modules available—from standard network modules, to fiber-channel modules, or even high-speed modules such as **InfiniBand** (**IB**). The most significant disadvantage of blade systems is their proprietary technology. You can mix and match blade servers from different vendors in a chassis. In the beginning, you select your vendor—HPE, Dell, IBM, or any other and that's it, you will always need to use this vendor.

The second disadvantage is the internal storage of blade servers. There is just no space for a large number of disk devices. The maximum is usually two, meaning you would need to have some centralized storage array for all your data.

Hyper-converged servers

I would like to talk about hyper-converged servers a little bit deeper than about standard and blade servers. These servers are the best combination of the form factors we've been through, giving you the best of both worlds. In addition, they are perfect for the **software-defined-data center** (**SDDC**) concept, as we discussed in the previous chapter. So, let's dive a bit deeper into the hyper-converged servers.

The key concept used in hyper-converged servers is that each unit provides all three core resources—**computing**, **storage**, and **network**.

Although you might argue that you can achieve the same with standard servers, you are only partially right.

Hyperconverged servers have evolved since standard rack servers, although they still fit into standard cabinets. There are many vendor-specific designs, but they share the same concept—multiple systems in a single, physical unit.

From the front view, it looks like a standard 2U rack server; however, when you look to the rear side, you will see four fully independent systems.

Independent in this context means that each unit is a standalone server with its CPU, memory, disk, network controller, and I/O cards. The only shared resource within the physical unit are the power supplies.

Resource comparison

Let's have a look at a comparison of standard servers. We are assuming the same configuration for every system:

- Two-socket servers, Intel Xeon 2680 v4 (14 cores)
- 512 GB RAM
- 1.6 TB NVMe SSD (maximum installable amount)
- 42U cabinet size, 2U dedicated for networking hardware

With our standard servers, we will utilize one cabinet for standard servers, and a second cabinet will be used for standard storage arrays (assuming storage nodes with 2U size and 24 SFF disks per node).

For hyper-converged servers, we will utilize a 4-node HCI configuration in a single 2U chassis (total storage capacity is 24 SFF disks for 4 nodes).

Infrastructure type	Standard servers	Hyper-converged
Number of compute servers	40	0
Number of standard storage arrays	20	0
Number of hyper-converged servers	0	40
Number of hyper-converged nodes	0	160
Total CPU capacity (physical CPU cores)	1 120 CPU cores	2 240 CPU cores
Total memory capacity (installed memory size)	20 480 GB	40 960 GB
Total storage capacity (raw capacity)	768 TB	1 536 TB

As you can see, with hyper-converged servers you can achieve twice as many compute resources and 50% more storage resources compared to standard servers in the same footprint.

Hyper-converged servers are usually deployed in SDDC solutions where all of the core components (compute, storage, and network) are managed by software to provide simplicity and flexibility when compared with legacy solutions.

Hyper-converged systems

With VMware, there are several options when talking about hyper-converged infrastructure, but they always include three major components—VMware vSphere, VMware vSAN, and VMware NSX.

- **vSAN ReadyNode**: vSAN ReadyNode is a standard x86 server, available from all the leading server vendors, that have been pre-configured, tested, and certified for VMware **Hyper-Converged Infrastructure (HCI)** software. Each ReadyNode is optimally configured for vSAN with the required amount of CPU, memory, network, I/O controllers, and storage (SSDs, HDDs, or flash devices).

 For more information about vSAN ReadyNodes, feel free to check the official website at `http://vsanreadynode.vmware.com/RN/RN`.

- **Integrated solutions**: Some vendors can deliver a complete SDDC as a turnkey solution. Everything is preconfigured and tested, and all you need to do is plug in the cables. This way, not only is the hardware preconfigured, but the software is as well. You do not need to spend time with the configuration of NSX or vSAN. This approach can save a lot of time and cut down on administration, and so is ideal either in case of limited time or lack of advanced skills.

  One example of such a product is Dell EMC VxRack. Based on your requirements, the whole solution is designed by Dell EMC technical specialists and contains everything including racks, physical network switches, servers, all software components, and centralized management.

- **Building your own system**: Building your own system is probably the most challenging approach, but gives you the greatest flexibility. You can decide how to combine and configure resources based on your specific requirements. Although you must still ensure hardware and software compatibility, you get to select the server, network, storage, and other components. This lets you put together a system that best suits your business needs. You can configure your server independently, such as by adding memory, swapping out disks, upgrading CPUs, all the while still scaling out by adding complete nodes.

  This granular scalability is thanks to the ability to use commodity hardware, rather than being locked into the types of custom-engineered systems that many vendors sell. With commodity hardware, you can build a hyper-converged platform with less investment, replace and scale up components when necessary, and reuse the parts for other purposes when the time comes to decommission them.

There are also other players in the HCI market that are not using VMware as a central control plane for SDDCs, like **Nutanix** or **SimpliVity** (currently owned by HPE), and instead are using their modified hypervisor and software-defined storage and network products.

 For more information regarding HCI, feel free to have a look at the well-known *Gartner Magic Quadrant* where you can learn about the strengths and weaknesses of different vendors in the HCI market: `http://learn.vmware.com/44045_REG`.

Storage design considerations

Once you have figured out what server platform you would like to choose, you need to have a look at different storage approaches and benefits. At this level, we will not cover in-depth technical details about the actual implementation or benefits of different storage protocols, as that all will be covered in later chapters. Instead, we'll focus on the bigger picture. For now, there are two main roads to follow.

Standard storage arrays

Better the devil you know than the devil you don't. We all know them and probably use them. Many storage professionals tend to stick with standard storage arrays because of their maturity. They have been around for decades, evolving and improving. Standard storage arrays vary from small size storage, which look like a standard server, all the way up to storage systems spanning multiple racks and storing petabytes of data.

You can find various systems, but usually, when talking about virtualization projects, you are interested in dual controller systems for better availability and multiple disk chassis connected to the controllers hosting all your disk devices.

Many storage vendors offer advanced functionality, such as storage tiering, all-flash solutions, or replication between storage systems for business continuity and disaster recovery when the whole site is unavailable.

On the other hand, standard storage arrays are a significant vendor lock-in. Once you choose your storage system, there is no way out except moving to an entirely new solution. You can't expand current storage arrays with different disks or chassis from other vendors, and usually, you are forced to buy an expensive disk from your storage vendor (although they are usually the same—just different proprietary firmware compared to stock magnetic disks or solid-state disks). Additionally, the license costs might skyrocket if you are using some advanced storage features.

Software-defined storage

Software-defined storage is the opposite to the standard storage arrays. You can use any hardware, as all the intelligence is done in the software layer, precisely the same way as compute virtualization works.

Eric Burgener, research director for storage, IDC., said the following:

> *"For IT organizations undergoing digital transformation, SDS provides a good match for the capabilities needed—flexible IT agility; easier, more intuitive administration driven by the characteristics of autonomous storage management; and lower capital costs due to the use of commodity and off-the-shelf hardware. As these features appear more on buyers' lists of purchase criteria, enterprise storage revenue will continue to shift toward SDS."*

You might argue that, because you are using commodity hardware, you can easily replace this layer without compromising your investment in the hardware itself. Benefits of software-defined storage usually fit into three main categories—reduced vendor lock-in, scalability, and flexibility:

- You can use non-proprietary, commodity components that allow systems to be built by you. The software-defined storage solution can consume standard hard drives, SSDs, and work within a typical server chassis.
- You can change hardware platforms at will, without complex and risky data migrations, as the data lives in the software layer and is abstract from the hardware.
- You can change software storage vendors, as most provide a standard storage service and no *borders*.
- You can start small, but as you grow, you can scale the solution without any interruptions, downtime, or migrations of the workloads that run on the storage platform.
- You can manage the solution as one distributed storage array from a single management plane, or even through APIs or CLI.

Network design considerations

Lastly, you should think about your network design. We will cover detail guidance in the following chapters, but for now let's have a look at two different network architectures.

Three-tier architecture

Until recent years, three-tier architecture was the mainstream. Three-tier architecture was designed mainly for north-south types of traffic (traffic from the data center):

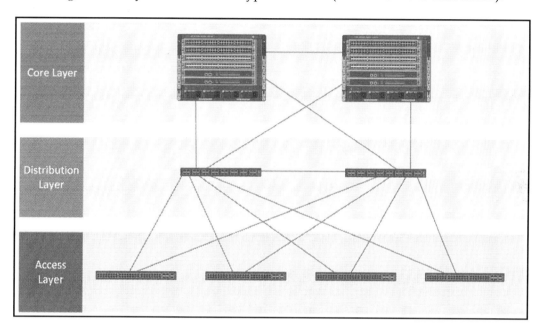

As the name suggests, this architecture consists of three main layers:

- Access
- Distribution
- Core

Access

The Access Layer is the one closest to the devices. The primary purpose of this layer is to connect users and servers to the network itself.

At this layer, you can usually find simple fixed form-factor L2 switches because advanced functions are provided by the upper layers.

Distribution

The Distribution Layer bridges the access layer to the core layer. In most deployments, default gateways for all the VLANs reside at the Distribution Layer.

At this layer L2/L3 switches are commonly used to provide basic L3 functions. Stackable switches or Multi-Chassis Link Aggregation technologies are commonly used at the Distribution layer to provide a scalable layer for the access switches.

Core

In the three-tier architecture, the Core Layer is the center of the network. The core interconnects all distribution layers and sometimes it is referred as the backbone.

At this layer you can usually find the most powerful and advanced switches. Compared to the Access and sometimes the Distribution layer, such switches have multiple redundant components and sometimes even modular form factor. All advanced L3 functions, such as BGB routing, are provided by the Core layer.

Leaf spine

Leaf-spine architecture is one of the mostly deployed topologies that is quickly replacing traditional solutions. Compared to traditional three-tier topology, multiple connections between core switches (spine switches) and access switches (leaf switches) exists to support high-performance and low-latency networks. The role of the leaf is to provide connectivity to the endpoints in the network, including compute servers and storage devices or any other networking endpoints—physical or virtual, while the role of the spine is to provide interconnectivity between the leaves:

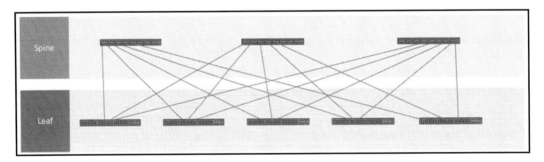

The requirements applying to the leaf-spine topology include the following:

- Each leaf connects to all spines in the network
- The spines are not interconnected with each other
- The leaves are not interconnected with each other

A leaf-spine network is comprised of two layers of networking equipment. The backbone of the network is the Spine Layer, while secondary activity occurs on the Leaf Layer. Every router (a device used to link different networks together) on the Spine Layer connects to every switch (or point of connection between devices on a network) on the Leaf Layer. With this network design, every leaf switch on the network is the same distance away.

Compared to the traditional three-tier architecture, the leaf-spine architecture design reduces latency and provides predictable performance. All leaves are connected to all spines, and unplanned downtime of the spine switch will reduce your overall throughput of the network (*N-1*).

Assess

While this stage is referred to as *requirements* in the waterfall model, I prefer to refer to it as *assess*, because in this phase, you are gathering all the required inputs that will form your infrastructure design.

In this phase, it's really important to identify and interact with the key stakeholders, and to collect all the requirements in order to deliver a design that meets all customer and business needs. Sometimes, the importance of this phase is underestimated, or it is simply not performed at all, perhaps because of time or budget constraints. This can be a huge risk for the project itself.

Also, remember that if you are providing a professional service (as a consultant or as a solution partner), you should prepare for this phase with pre-engagement planning and a kick-off in order to be prepared for the engagement. Furthermore, if the project is handled internally inside the organization, a successful engagement requires the right participants, defining the different roles, and good sponsors.

Tasks in the assessment phase include the following:

- Identifying all the business needs and design objectives
- Reviewing the current state of the existing environment (if there is one)
- Mapping design objectives to requirements and constraints
- Making some assumptions for the missing input
- Performing risk management on all those pieces of information

The design objective

The design objective is a crucial part of every project. *What are you trying to achieve and why? What are the business goals of this project?* The design objective is usually not related to the technology itself, but it is based on business requirements.

Here are some examples of business requirements:

- We need to decrease the operation costs of our environment
- We need to increase the availability of our environment to support business-critical applications
- We need to consolidate our data center footprint to reduce costs.

Requirements, constraints, assumptions, and risks

Requirements describe, in business or technical terms, the necessary properties, qualities, and characteristics of the desired solution. The customer should provide all requirements, but a good interview with the right people is needed to gain all the requirements that form the basis for the design. It's possible that different requirements may conflict with each other, or that they may change through discussion and negotiation. Requirements can be divided into two main categories:

- Functional requirements
- Non-functional requirements

Functional requirements (FRs) describe *WHAT* functionality a system should deliver, while **non-functional requirements (NFRs)** describe *HOW* a system should behave.

Constraints are not necessarily issues or limitations; they can also be related to business processes, a business decision, a business policy, or a technical limitation. In most cases, they are mandatory requirements. Some common constraints include the usage of existing hardware (or using a specific vendor for all the hardware) and regulatory requirements. Budget restrictions and timelines could be classified as constraints (for example, if there is a mandatory milestone in the timeline) or requirements, depending on the case.

Assumptions could also be expectations about the implementation, but usually, they are related to what cannot be confirmed during the assessment or design phases. Of course, at some point, assumptions must be validated; otherwise, the respective design areas will be at risk (and you must analyze their impact through risk management).

Risks must be documented and rated based on the severity of the risk and the type of impact, and must be addressed with a mitigation plan or recommendation. There could be risks that can't be mitigated, or the mitigation cost will overweight the potential risks. In this case, the risk must still be documented but, based on your risk analysis, you might decide to do nothing about such risks.

Design

The design process is well covered in the **VMware vSphere Design Workshop** course.

The VMware vSphere Design Workshop course includes the following modules:

- Design process overview
- VMware vSphere storage design
- VMware vSphere network design
- Compute resources design
- Virtual machine design
- VMware vSphere virtual data center design
- Management and monitoring design

 vSphere Design Workshop is a three-day, instructor-led class at
`https://mylearn.vmware.com/mgrReg/courses.cfm?ui=www_edua=`
`oneid_subject=79170`.

VCDX certification also provides some useful information; the entire path of VCDX-DCV certification provides a complete VCDX methodology. This methodology focuses on how to identify business needs and how to map them to design and implement decisions.

 You can find more information about becoming VCDX at `https://www.vmware.com/education-services/certification/vcdx-application-defense.html`.

Furthermore, if you are not VCDX certified, you can learn about this type of approach from the VCDX Boot Camp, the VCDX Blueprint, or the books and posts written by other VCDX users.

Following the VCDX methodology or a similar one, you can have an in-depth look at how a large number of variables can affect the design of a virtual infrastructure. Some effects may define some creativities or risks, but also, any assumptions that are unknown or that you are unsure of should be considered risks. This is because, depending on their probability and how critical such requirements are, they could cause your project to fail.

Conceptual design

The conceptual design provides a high level of conceptual diagrams for the solution, using the data collected from the current state analysis of the existing environment (if existing), the application requirements, and the business needs and goals. All the data collected during the assessment is arranged into different categories:

- **Requirements**: This provides the business requirements that the designed solution must meet.
- **Constraints**: These are the conditions that provide boundaries to the design.
- **Assumptions**: These list the conditions that are believed to be true but are not confirmed. All assumptions should be validated before deployment.
- **Risks**: These are factors that might have an adverse effect on the design.

All business requirements, assumptions, and constraints must be used to support design and implementation decisions suited for mission-critical applications, also considering how risk can affect design decisions and how it can be mitigated.

Non-functional requirements map to the design qualities—availability, manageability, performance, recoverability, and security:

- **Availability**: Everything related to the system uptime and prevents the failures. For example, preventing **single point of failure (SPOF)**.
- **Manageability**: All requirements that are related to how a system must be managed are covered by Manageability; for example, centralized management for infrastructure and storage.
- **Performance**: Performance NFRs cover the desired performance of the system or how quickly the system should respond. Number of **input/output operations per second (IOPS)** or **response times for end users** can be used here.
- **Recoverability**: Recoverability requirements dictate how fast the system must be back online after the failure. **RPO** and **RTO** requirements are typical recoverability NFRs.
- **Security**: Everything that is related to the system protection and how it is secured. **Single Sign-On (SSO)** and **role-based access control (RBAC)** are typical examples of security NFRs. These describe *HOW* a user should log in to the system and how they can use it.

So, in short, a conceptual design describes the owner's view and why the system is being built in the first place.

Logical design

Logical design is something that architects sometimes struggle with because of its abstraction. This is particularly the case for architects who have been working with specific technology for a long time because they tend to build the design using the specific technologies they know (from a hardware or software perspective).

In general, a logical design should be an abstract, vendor-agnostic design with functional specifications of what you want to build. It should not contain any references to specific technologies or vendors because you might use conceptual designs together with logical design as a part of **request for information/request for proposal (RFI/RFP)** when selecting your vendor for such a solution.

If you skip logical design or build it based on a specific vendor, you lock yourself into one particular vendor and miss the opportunity to catch your exact functional requirements. This leads to vendor preselection, and might not bring the desired value to the customer. (This occurs if the solution is more complicated than necessary, or the costs are not balanced.)

A logical design must include the logical design overview, before covering every infrastructure component you will be deploying:

- Compute design
- Network design
- Storage design
- Backup and recovery design
- Disaster recovery design
- Security design
- Cloud automation design
- **Virtual Desktop Infrastructure** (**VDI**) design

Examples of bad logical design decisions include the following:

- Four or more ESXi hosts required per HA/DRS cluster
- vSphere HA used for protection against host failures and VM failures
- The ESXi cluster based on HP DL360 G10 hosts needing to be installed across multiple racks

The preceding can be rewritten as great logical design decisions:

- A minimum of four hypervisors deployed in compute cluster.
- A native workload protection mechanism within the hypervisor with the necessary functionality to restart virtual machines if the hypervisor or virtual machine is unresponsive.
- Hypervisor hosts must be deployed in separate cabinets. Form-factor of the server must fits to the standard datacenter cabinet.

Here is an example of a logical design:

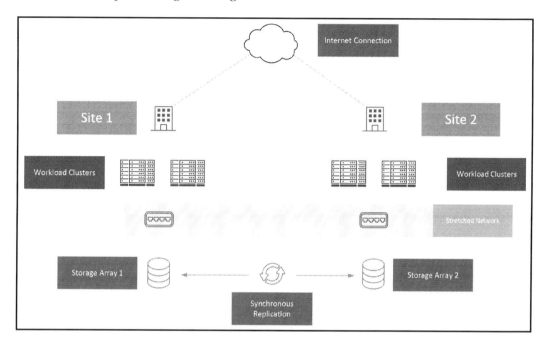

Physical design

The physical design details the logic design, where each major infrastructure component is already present, at a high level (with the right design decisions and motivations).

Hardware sizing, for both the capacity and the performance aspects, could be assisted by the initial assessment of existing infrastructure, as will be described in Chapter 3, *Analysis and Assessment of Existing Environments.*

In a Physical design, you start to build your exact solution. However, in comparison to logical design, at this stage you go much, and you are referring to specific technologies and components. The same approach as with logical design is used—first, there is a physical design overview, and then each significant component has its physical design section:

- Compute design
- Network design
- Storage design

- Backup and recovery design
- Disaster recovery design
- Security design
- Cloud automation design
- VDI design

The following is an example of the physical design of the ESXi hypervisor:

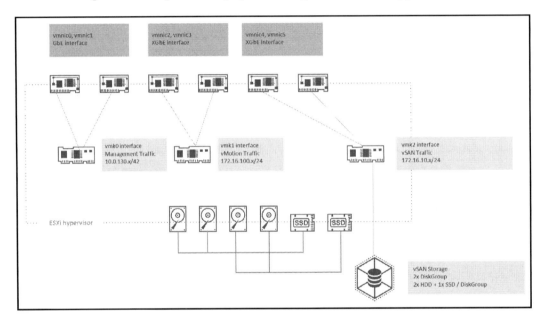

In the upcoming chapters, we will look at specific hardware and software components in more detail.

ESXi host

For ESXi hosts, there are several considerations concerning sizing and configuration. Based on your business requirements and assumed workloads, you should look at several categories regarding your server.

Compute

By compute, we mean CPU and memory considerations. For the hosts, you can use different types of approaches for cluster design:

- **Scale-out**: More hosts in a single cluster, each mid-sized
- **Scale-up**: Fewer hosts in a single cluster, each usually with many resources

Common processors now have many cores inside, and considering that VMware ESXi licensing is generally per socket (except in some specific cases), you may prefer a few processors with many cores. The bi-processor configuration is more common for the virtualization hosts. However, also remember other licenses, such as the new license model for Windows Server 2016, where the number of cores is also counted.

With new AMD EPYC processors, some architects have started to think about AMD as well when talking about processors in virtualization servers, but Intel is a safe choice. With a wide range of Intel Xeon Scalable family processors, you can cover all imaginable workloads from Bronze processors such as Intel Xeon Bronze 3106 (8 cores) to Intel Xeon Platinum 8180 (28 cores).

Frank Denneman and Niels Hagoort published a great book called *VMware vSphere 6.5 Host Resources Deep Dive*, and based on the extensive research through the **Customer Experience Improvement Program** (CEIP), most companies are using ESXi hypervisors installed with two physical CPUs.

The second part of the compute configuration aims to determine the amount of memory installed in the server.

You will usually deploy servers ranging from 128 GB of memory up to around 512 GB of memory. It is essential to understand your workloads and the correlation between CPU and memory requirements. Although you can equip your servers with up to 3 TB of memory (HP DL 380 G10 with 64 GB LRDIMM modules), you might not have enough CPU power to spin as many VMs that would require that amount of memory.

You should be aware of one additional detail here—**non-uniform memory access (NUMA)**.

Modern dual-socket servers can be equipped with one or two processors and, based on the setup, corresponding memory modules are used. This means that, if you have a dual socket motherboard and you install only one CPU, you can't use modules that belong to the second CPU.

However, *what happens if you have both CPUs installed? Can the first CPU touch memory that is connected to the second CPU?* It can, but there are several consequences of doing such thing.

The following is an example of virtual machine resources mapped to physical resources:

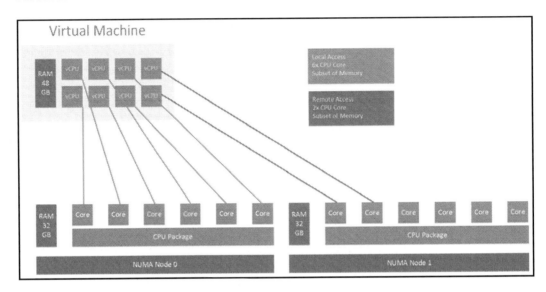

Each CPU has its local memory connected directly to the CPU. This memory is called **local memory**.

If the CPU wants to access memory that belongs to the second CPU, it must use some interconnecting link between CPUs. In such a case, we are talking about remote memory.

What are the consequences? The main consequence is latency of such an operation. If the first CPU needs to touch the memory belonging to the second CPU for whatever reason, it will be much slower compared to local memory access. This is why the NUMA approach has been developed.

VMware ESXi fully understands underlying physical NUMA architecture, so what happens by default is that with a dual socket server with dual CPUs installed, ESXi will see two NUMA nodes—**node0** and **node1**. As you create VMs, the ESXi server will try to keep them on the single NUMA node, so there is no impact regarding performance.

Storage

There are two main reasons why you need to design your storage subsystem carefully: the ESXi installation disk and storage from your virtual machines will be run:

- **ESXi installation disk:** In this situation, we are primarily talking about a reliable storage subsystem for the ESXi server itself. If the disk where your ESXi kernel resides fails, the whole ESXi server will be unavailable. For such resiliency, ESXi server is usually installed on a RAID1 volume where two individual identical disks form one logical disk that operating systems see. If one disk fails, nothing happens, and the system is still available through the second disk. If you want to configure a RAID1 array, you need RAID adapter in your server. For RAID1 arrays, even the basic RAID adapters (sometimes located on the motherboard) can be used. There is no need for advanced functions such as cashing, battery backup, and so on in this scenario. Some vendors also support installation on the SD cards.

  It is also possible to use a SATADOM device instead of disks. A SATADOM device looks like a small flash drive that is plugged directly to the motherboard through onboard SATA ports. In such a case, you can usually configure RAID1 with such devices, so your system depends on a single device. This approach creates a single point of failure but, based on your design, it might be an acceptable risk, especially if you are working with a large number of ESXi servers (if you lose 1 of 100 ESXi servers due to such a hardware failure, overall this is 1% of compute power loss). On the other hand, if you are working with four ESXi servers and you lose one, this is a 25% power loss. In such a case, I would not recommend using SATADOM devices:

- **Shared storage for virtual machines:** All ESXi hosts must have access to the storage subsystem, so you can't directly use local disks. First, you need to create some logical shared storage using software-defined storage software (such as VMware vSAN, EMC ScaleIO, or HPE StoreVirtual).

Different software solutions might have different requirements for storage subsystems—especially requirements about how the RAID adapters should be configured and how the individual disks should be accessed, so please, carefully read those requirements.

Regarding storage devices, we are talking about magnetic disks (HDDs), **solid-state drives** (**SSDs**), and NVMe devices. Those devices are connected either to SATA or SAS RAID adapters (each type provides different latency and maximum bandwidth) or directly to PCIe bus (NVMe devices):

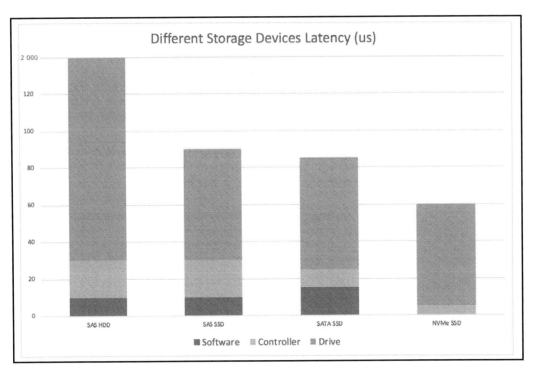

Based on your estimated workloads, you need to scale the storage in terms of total capacity. (Be aware that there might be a big difference between **RAW** capacity and **USABLE** capacity; RAW capacity is the sum of all your devices while USABLE capacity is RAW capacity minus any overhead based on your storage protection level.)

Network connectivity

A general recommendation is to use 10 GbE network interface cards for your ESXi server connectivity. There might be some specific use-cases where only 1 GbE NICs will be sufficient, but you should prefer 10 GbE NIC.

Again, the number of NICs would be determined based on your network design and assumed workloads. I usually prefer to separate the management network from the production network, meaning that two 1 GbE NICs are used for management purposes only, and two 10 GbE NICs are used for everything else. Of course, those pairs of NICs are always connected to two, individual, independent switches to eliminate any single point of failure in your design:

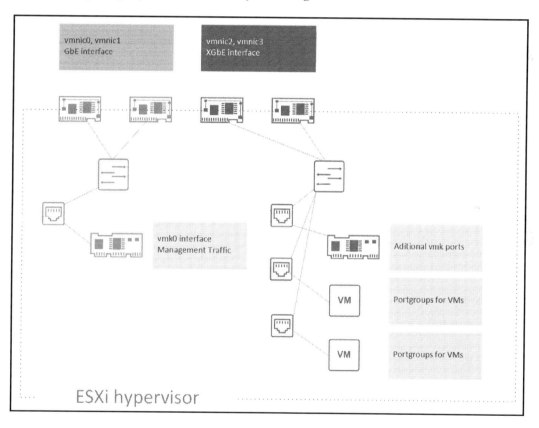

There are specific use cases in which you may require more than 10 Gbps as a port speed. In such a case, I would strongly recommend looking at 100 GbE network switches and skipping 40 GbE switches and NICs. There ware big discussion if 40 GbE is a next 10 GbE or if it is 100 GbE. Many architects and system engineers prefer to skip 40 GbE implementations at all and start to deploy infrastructures based on 100 GbE switching solutions.

With 100 GbE switches, you get more significant flexibility compared to 40 GbE switches. 100 GbE is internally formed by four 25 GbE lines, while 40 GbE is four times 10 GbE. What this means is that, from a single 100 GbE port on your physical network switch, you can create four 25 GbE ports connecting your ESXi servers using breakout cables:

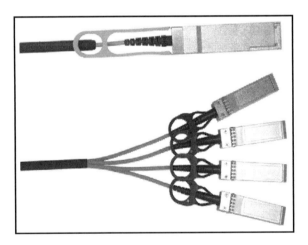

Today, 100 GbE switches are usually configured with 32 physical QSFP28 ports so you can connect up to 120 25 GbE ports to such a switch (leaving two 100 GbE ports as an uplink, or even more depending on your desired over-subscription). Once you decide to upgrade your servers, you reconfigure your switch, and from the single QSFP28 port, you create two 50 GbE ports for your server.

We will discuss the network architecture more deeply in upcoming chapters, as well as looking at advanced configurations.

Management

Always look for servers with some dedicated onboard management that allows you to connect the server over IP protocol, even if the server is unresponsive. This is handy for initial installation as well as for ongoing support. Different vendors name this remote functionality differently—iLO (HPE), iDRAC (DELL), or IPMI (Supermicro).

All hardware must be classified as VMware vSphere-certified, or it must match the VMware **Hardware Compatibility List** (**HCL**) between the hardware components, the firmware version, the drivers, and the proper VMware vSphere version.

vCenter Server

In the past, there were many considerations when deploying the vCenter Server. This is not the case today. **vCenter Server Appliance** (**vCSA**) is the recommended way of deploying a new vCenter Server. You can deploy vCenter Server on Windows, and version 6.7 is the last version that supports such a configuration. With newer versions, this deployment type will be unavailable, so I strongly suggest using vCSA, even today.

In the past, there were differences regarding configuration maximums and scaling vCSA but since version 6.5 the limits are identical compared to vCenter Server on Windows. As a benefit, you get an integrated database as well, so you do not need to take care of the database layer anymore.

Based on your deployment type, vCSA installer will suggest the corresponding hardware configuration, so you do not need to do any calculations here:

Deployment size	vCPUs	Memory (GB)	Storage (GB)	Hosts (upto)	VMs (upto)
Tiny	2	10	300	10	100
Small	4	16	340	100	1,000
Medium	8	24	525	400	4,000
Large	16	32	740	1,000	10,000
X-Large	24	48	1,180	2,000	35,000

You need to decide if you will install **Platform Service Controller** (**PSC**) on a dedicated machine or not, but we will cover this in `Chapter 4`, *Deployment Workflow and Component Installation*.

There is no need to use dedicated PSC unless you need to configure linked-mode. There are no performance benefits of doing so at all and, with VMware vSphere 6.7U1, you an also use enhanced linked-mode, in which case you do not need to deploy external PSC at all.

How to provide good documentation

All design steps have some deliveries, usually in the form of a document representing the specific design and explaining the different choices. Also, consider that simplicity could be the key to a successful project; the more complicated a project is, the more complicated its documentation will be. As well as this, the more risks you have in the deployment and implementation phase, the more complex supporting and troubleshooting it will be, and the more effort management will need to be devoted to. Of course, scripting and automation could help in the deployment and management of complex infrastructure, and proper monitoring tools could help to prevent issues, and documentation is also a valuable asset for troubleshooting. If you still try to keep things simple and clear, you can have some advantages.

For big projects, you need something more. Usually, the documentation is used as a building block approach with different pods (or blocks) based on reference architecture, designed from use cases or best practices.

Supporting documentation should include the following documents:

- Implementation plan
- Configuration guide
- Test plan
- Standard operating procedures

Best practices

A best practice is a method, technique, or approach that is generally accepted because it produces better or more reliable, repeatable results. You can consider this as a standard way of doing some things. However, it's not a law that must be universally followed. Using best practices requires you to know the background of the best practice, and how it applies to your specific situation and design.

Anyway, best practices remain a useful pattern for the design of virtual infrastructures in a proper way; it is also valuable for validating the design itself, and provides compliance with possible future support feedback or requests.

You can find several best practices for VMware in different documents, such as the following:

- **Performance Best Practices for VMware vSphere 6.7**: https://www. vmware.com/content/dam/digitalmarketing/vmware/en/pdf/techpaper/ performance/vsphere-esxi-vcenter-server-67-performance-best- practices.pdf
- **VMware vCenter Server 6.5 High Availability Performance and Best Practices** (no updated version available for vSphere 6.7): https://www. vmware.com/content/dam/digitalmarketing/vmware/en/pdf/techpaper/ vcha65-perf.pdf
- **VMware vSphere Availability 6.7**: https://docs.vmware.com/en/VMware- vSphere/6.7/vsphere-esxi-vcenter-server-67-availability-guide.pdf
- **Best practices for upgrading to vCenter Server 6.7**: https://kb.vmware. com/s/article/54008

Remember that there are also vendor-specific best practices, such as for storage or networking (but also for servers). When VMware has a general suggestion (such as, in storage, the multipath choice), the specific vendor will usually have more detailed information for the configuration part. For this reason, try to apply the more specific recommendations based on best-practices, but always check that there aren't any conflicts between different recommendations.

Reference architecture

Typically, a reference architecture is a business-ready design with configurations for some common virtualization cases such as virtual desktops or small businesses. It could be, based on use cases, preconfigured, easy-to-order bundled solutions designed to aid in the ordering, deployment, and maintenance of a virtual infrastructure.

You can find several documents from both VMware, usually on specific products, verticals, or use cases, and other vendors where there could also be pre-packaged solutions.

For SDDC design, one of the more complete sources of documents and blueprints is **VMware Validated Design** (VVD).

VVD

The VVD is a pre-built end-to-end SDDC cloud infrastructure designed to perform in a predictive way, to scale, and to be reliable and resilient. More importantly, it is already pre-validated, all by matching VMware's best practices and leveraging the real-world expertise of VMware solution architects. This design is intended to be a building block for virtual infrastructure design, valuable for large deployment, and with a reduced timeframe for the implementation of the project (and also the design phase):

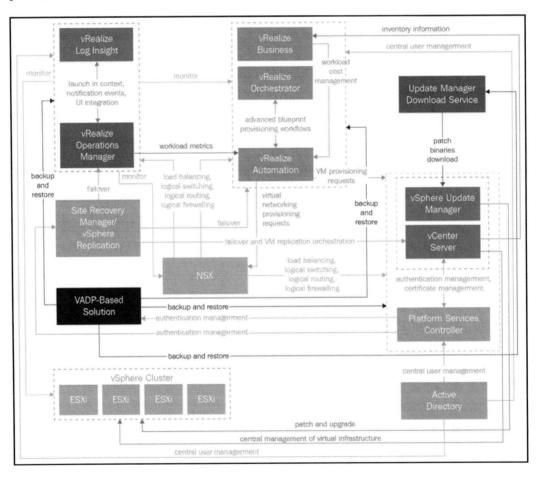

Unlike specific reference architectures, which are usually focused on an individual product or purpose, the VVD gives a global overview of the full stack, with different products using a holistic approach to the design. Also, even if you don't plan to use the product in this kind of design (for example, the storage part based on vSAN), the design itself could be very valuable and good support for your project.

> The VVD documentation page provides all these documents, at `https://www.vmware.com/go/vvd` or `https://www.vmware.com/support/pubs/vmware-validated-design-pubs.html`.

The VVD is based on a set of different VMware products with specific versions, which are included in the VMware CEIP. CEIP is an optional program that provides VMware with information on which customers use products and features, and it's used to improve VMware products and features. If you don't have specific regimentation or security constraints (or concerns), you can join this program by selecting this option during product installation.

VVD is a complete multi-site and cross-cloud design, but it also supports some specific use cases. In both cases, it is optimized for integration, expansion, and Day-2 operations, as well as specific maintenance tasks like upgrades and updates.

The latest version of VDD is **VMware Validated Designs 4.3** (17 July 2018), and already includes the following:

- VMware Validated Design for SDDC
- VMware Validated Designs for Management and Workload Consolidation
- VMware Validated Design Use Cases Documentation
- VMware Validated Design for Micro-Segmentation
- VMware Validated Design for IT Automating IT

VMware Validated Design 4.3 is currently based on the following versions:

- vSphere 6.5 U2
- vSAN 6.6.1 U2
- NSX 6.4.1
- vRealize Log Insight 4.6
- vRealize Operations 6.7
- vRealize Business 7.4
- vRealize Automation 7.4

Different scenarios

There are different types of typical scenarios where most use cases can fit, but much can also depend on the type of workload and business requirements.

We will consider and discuss, at a high level, just three different cases—Enterprise, SMB, and ROBO. For other, more specific examples, such as for VDI, there are several reference architectures, and also some specific VVDs.

Enterprise

Large companies are usually qualified, by their size, as enterprise or corporate. Their business needs are usually very strictly defined and almost all workloads can be business-critical, including infrastructure workloads such as the vCenter Server.

The number of workloads is usually high; that probably means more workload clusters and more attention paid to performance and scaling aspects in order to adapt the infrastructure to business growth. Hybrid cloud could also be used to provide more flexibility, capacity, scaling, and so on. Furthermore, the managed data might be considered significant (hundreds of TBs or PBs are becoming quite common).

These kinds of organizations have grown to the point where they need dedicated, full-time IT staff with specific expertise to manage specific applications or parts of the entire infrastructure; these individuals, such as the storage administrator, Windows administrator, database administrator, and so on, may work on specific technology silos, but for the infrastructure part, it is becoming more common to have cross-technology capabilities, or at least to build a shared team of people with different competencies.

Business requirements

Applications, services, and workloads are all typically (or mostly) business-critical, and the infrastructure part could need a very high level of availability. For example, in a vRealize Automation private cloud, or in a VDI environment, the lack of a vCenter Server will stop the provisioning of new services or new virtual desktops, with a potentially massive impact on the business.

Possible constraints

For an enterprise, the main constraints could be related to regulations and compliance requirements, or specific laws or internal standards. However, there can be a lot of other constraints related to infrastructure or product choices, resource assignments, naming conventions, or limited capabilities in negotiating the different requirements. Also, if budget is not a constraint, but the project size is too big, or the requirements are too strict and require costly solutions, that could become a constraint.

Main risks

The main risk could be having limited visibility on a project. If you don't have time to interview all the different stakeholders, that means that you don't have all the requirements (and constraints) and you may make too many assumptions based on uncertain information.

A lousy timeline during project implementation could be another risk; maybe you spend too much time during the PoC, or define a design so sophisticated that the time to implement the entire solution does not match the required time to market.

Some design decisions

Enterprise scenarios usually require a high availability level, greater than 99.99% for most workloads. Using just vSphere HA features is not enough, not for all workloads. For workloads that require a level better than 99.99%, you have to consider vSphere FT or guest clustering (building a clustered solution across VMs). Alternatively, design your application to provide a better resiliency and a high availability level.

Performance and scaling are also crucial, and the design needs a proper initial assessment and has to consider future growth. Real-time monitoring is needed to verify the right service level, from both the availability and the performance point of view. To help in the design phase, the VVD documents provide a great example as well as good and validated reference architecture for most of the projects. Trying to customize too much to adapt to specific requirements, or to deviate from the blueprints could make the design too complex and costly regarding money or time.

In this type of project, there could also be the engagement of VMware Professional Services, at least to support the design or validate the solution.

Typically, for an enterprise, both the ESXi Enterprise Plus and vCenter Standard editions are used, but there are also specific bundles, such as the vCloud suite, that include more of VMware's products. For large environments, there are specific licenses such as the **Enterprise License Agreement (ELA)**.

Note that there is one particular design option for enterprise environments—a multi-tenant environment, typical for service or cloud providers, but also needed in some big enterprises where different organizations need the flexibility of cloud computing, as well as the ability to manage their resources in a self-provisioning way.

VMware has two different products—vCloud Director for Service Providers or vRealize Automation for enterprises. For cloud service providers, there is a specific license model called **VMware Cloud Provider Program**.

Small and medium-sized business (SMB)

An SMB is a company with a small number of employees, maybe with only a part-time individual managing its data center. In comparison to an enterprise, it does not have the same budget capabilities, but still has similar business needs and requirements.
The number of employees can vary, but for example, Gartner defines a company as an SMB if the number of employees is less than 100 (for small) or less than 999 (for medium). There are also some criteria based on annual revenue, with less than $50 million (for small) or less than $1 billion (for medium).

The size parameters may also differ depending on the country. For example, in Italy, a small company has less than 50 employees and less than €10 million in revenue, whereas a medium company has less than 250 employees and less than €50 million. There is also the mid-market size called **small and medium-sized enterprise (SME)**. This sized organization has some full-time employees dedicated to managing its data centers. However, these individuals have generalist IT skills and have to manage two or more IT-related tasks (backups, databases, network, servers, support, and so on) without a specialized role.

There are also **Small Office/Home Office (SOHO)**, which are usually too small for a real virtual environment or could be more effective using some public cloud solution. Historically, SMB companies have relaxed requirements, due to the limited budget (compared to enterprise), but the digital transformation also affects this type of reality, in some cases more than with the enterprises. The main consequence is that SMBs can now have similar (in some cases, the same) requirements to the enterprises (like a high level of availability), but still without the same type of budget and other specific types of constraints.

Small Office/Home Office (SOHO) sites can remain more flexible in comparison to enterprises regarding timing, the type of constraints, the ability to talk directly with the C-level of the company, and, of course, the numbers. This is because the number of SMBs is usually much greater than the number of enterprises.

Business requirements

Requirements could be a little more relaxed compared to the enterprise scenario, but you still have to design your project with availability, reliability, performance, scalability, security, and manageability in mind.

The lack of specialized technical people makes the manageability aspect potentially much more crucial; the solution must be as simple as possible to manage, with high-level tools (like the GUI) in the hands of just a few people who have limited skills in vSphere environments.

Possible constraints

For SMBs, the budget is usually the main constraint, and you have to plan your solution carefully to consider the entire costs (including licenses) to fit in the budget. It's also possible that there is a budget spread across different years; in this case, you have to build a modular design where more parts can be added in the future to improve it (for example, the disaster recovery solution).

There can be some constraints on the devices, hardware, and software that can be used. For example, hold services must be recycled to optimize the investments.

Main risks

There can be several other risks with regards to the locations designed for the data center, where racks may not be present at all, or may not be designed for the chosen type of servers, or the uninterruptible power supply may be outdated or may not have enough power for the entire environment. Existing switches may lack in redundancy or performance (perhaps they have just 1 Gbps ports). Environmental conditions must also be verified in order to validate that cooling and HVAC systems are sized well.

Some design decisions

Even if the public cloud is an option for SMB cases, most of them are still building their on-premises infrastructures. In SMB scenarios, a reasonable availability level could be between 99% and 99.9%, but some workloads may require a higher level of availability (or others that are not critical at all). The vSphere HA features could be enough for most cases.

Performance isn't usually a problem due to the computing capacity of a typical server today. A single host can potentially handle all the workloads, but of course, it represents a single point of failure. For this reason, two or more (commonly three) hosts are the typical configuration. The sizing of those hosts is not usually critical, and reducing the cost could also be interesting, considering single-socket configurations.

For the licenses aspect, VMware has a specific bundle called Essential Plus Kit with limited features but an affordable price that can cover an infrastructure with up to three hosts. Other vendors have similar bundles to simplify the adoption in this scenario, or perhaps a subscription model. In this case, the design is quite simple, because you have to build a two- or three-node cluster and think about the resiliency and the recoverability aspects. The three node limits could be enough for SMBs unless we also want to include a disaster recovery part (but you can use other licenses on the second site).

For the storage part, you can use some hyper-converged solution (although, for vSAN, three hosts are just the minimum). Alternatively, we can use external storage, maybe with a direct SAS connection to avoid the need for fabric.

An exciting design option has been introduced with VMware vSphere 6.5 Update 1. Now you can manage up to four hosts with vCenter Server Foundation (not only three nodes, as in the past).

What are the possible implications of this? With four nodes, you can do exciting things that you can now plan in your design:

- **vSAN cluster**: Technically, three nodes are the minimum, but I don't like to build a vSAN cluster with only three nodes. I prefer to have four in order to plan a better resiliency.
- **vSAN two-node cluster**: For some cases just a two nodes cluster and the witness appliance on a third node can provide desired availability. This is something that can now be considered.
- **Production and DR cluster managed by the same vCenter**: This is also possible with three nodes, but it is limited to 2+1. In this case, you have more flexibility.
- **Scale out instead of scale in**: In some cases it is better to run several smaller hosts but, in the others, fewer hosts with more resource capacity is the better choice.

Instead, for small environments or budgets, some other minimal solutions can be considered if you reduce the availability and recoverability requirements. For example, just two nodes with the Essential license (that is the cheapest one, but it does not provide any cluster functionality) can provide desired capacity and availability, one active, and one in manual standby (for each workload) with a VM-based replication solution to have a minimum level of recoverability. (Several third-party backup solutions provide VM replication across hosts.)

For an SMB scenario, there could be a risk in using licenses based per VM or instance, considering that the estimated number could increase in the future (VM spread). However, if the growth could be estimated carefully, it could make sense to consider licensing based per VM or space. Note, that for VMware vSphere, the Essential Plus (or in some minor cases, the Essential) bundles remain the most popular, and they license three bi-processor hosts.

ROBO

A ROBO is an office located on a different site or in a geographically remote area from other offices of the same company or holding. Usually, there is a headquarters that acts as the main office. Several organizations have one (or more) central office, as well as remote offices in different cities, countries, or continents. Those organizations may have, in each remote office, some local IT infrastructure and assets, usually for data locality, but also to provide local services.

Considering the size of a remote office, it's similar to a small company, because there are usually just a few servers running a few workloads to support local needs. Therefore, they could be very similar to the SMB scenario described previously.

However, in reality, if you look at the entire infrastructure, it's more similar to an enterprise scenario, with significant numbers (entirely), full enterprise needs, and some specific challenges.

Business requirements

Each remote site should have at least some level of high availability as at the central site, but other business requirements might be important as well. Let's have a look at several example requirements:

- **Central management**: The solution should be easy to manage and monitor. Local IT staff might not have enough experience, so centralized management is usually required.
- **Availability and compliance**: Although limited resources are available within site, the solution should provide a sufficient level of high-availability as well, as the solution should comply to regulatory requirements.
- **Data protection**: The data running in the local site should be protected using an affordable backup and recovery solution.
- **Standardization and repeatability**: Since the solution might be deployed to other sites, deployment standards should exist to easily reproduce the design to other sites.
- **Service-oriented infrastructure**: You should focus on Service and the Business Objectives rather than the technology itself.
- **Scalable solution**: The solution must be able to scale-up along with the growth of the site.

Possible constraints

The budget could be the one main constraint; more are the remote offices, and much is the total cost. Also, it could be complicated to find the right building block that matches the requirements and the budget constraint.

However, there could also be some limitations in local IT facilities; space could be minimal, available electrical power could be capped, and UPS capacity limited. Also, the lack of local IT support and people must be considered for both the deployment and the maintenance of the remote infrastructure.

Main risks

In a ROBO scenario several risks might be involved, such as, the following:

- Remote sites usually have limited equipment and, in particular, the datacenter footprint can't be a huge constraint, or the rack cabinets might not be deep enough to host modern servers.
- UPS systems might not be present or they do not provide sufficient power to the infrastructure. Physical switches might not have enough ports, or the port-speed is limited (for example only 1 Gbps but not 10 Gbps).
- Business Continuity and Disaster Recovery plans might lack the desired complexity. RTO and RPO for backups might not be as low as required and the physical security could have considerable limits.
- Network connection to the WAN network might be limited due to the physical location of the site or lack of service providers who might be able to offer adequate connectivity. Bandwidth and latency should be checked and verified.

Examples of design decisions

You can potentially centralize everything in the main office environment or in the public cloud. The desktop could also be centralized using VDI or a RemoteApp. From a management point of view, this solution is easy because all is centralized and managing and monitoring will be more comfortable.

However, there can be some risks—network connectivity becomes much more critical, not only from the bandwidth point of view (where you need enough bandwidth for each service and each user) but also because latency and reliability can impact the business continuity requirements and user experiences in the worst way. If the risk is too high, local workloads are needed at the remote offices.

In ROBO scenarios, a reasonable availability level could be between 99% and 99.9%, but some workloads may require the higher level of availability. The vSphere HA features could be enough for most cases.

Performance isn't usually a problem due to the computing capacity of a typical server today. A single host can potentially handle all the workloads, but of course, it also represents a single point of failure. For this reason, the two node cluster configuration is the most typical for this scenario. The sizing of those hosts is not usually critical, and if the cost is the biggest constraint, you should consider single socket configurations.

Storage is more tricky due the budget constraints as well as the possible space constraints; you still need storage with reasonable reliability and shared capabilities in order to use a VMware cluster, but a proper external storage could be costly and provide more complexity in the infrastructure (external switches, more components, and so on). Fortunately, there are some specific hyper-converged solutions for ROBO scenarios, both from VMware (vSAN for ROBO configuration, with a specific license based per VM) and other vendors (for example, StorMagic, and StarWind).

In ROBO scenarios, it is usually vital to minimize the license cost of each office in order to keep the entire project in the estimated budget. Cost per VM or space could be attractive, considering their low number.

The VMware vSphere ESXi licenses that are most interesting for remote offices are the ROBO SKU that are sold per VM (25 VMs SKU). The ROBO license is independent of the number of hosts, sockets, or cores, but please note that each VM counts as a license, including management VMs (such as VSA or other VAs).

Windows Server remains licensed per socket (and starting with Windows Server 2016, they also limit the total number of cores). With just a couple of VMs, Windows Standard edition could be considered to limit costs.

Storage licenses depend on the type of storage. This can be included in the cost of the storage itself, but for software-based storage such as vSAN or other VSA-based storage, it can be licensed in different ways: per capacity (for instance, several VSA solutions), per socket (for instance, vSAN), or per VM (for instance, vSAN for ROBO).

For VMware vSAN, the ROBO SKU could be attractive for a small number of VMs in each remote office, compared to the other license options.

Summary

This chapter has explained how to approach a virtualization project using reference architectures and best practices. This has covered everything from the analysis of requirements, constraints, and risks to the different types of design (conceptual, logical, and physical). We explored network and storage aspects, as well as different vCenter Server and ESXi design and planning aspects.

Three different scenarios have been used as examples of some design decisions—SMB, Enterprise, and ROBO.

In the next chapter, we will discuss the other phases, such as the initial assessment for an existing environment and rightsizing of the virtual environment. This is important for the correct planning and design of the infrastructure.

Questions

1. What are the main logical steps in every project?

   a) Plan
   b) Assess
   c) Configure
   d) Do
   e) Maintain
   f) Check
   g) Act

2. What are the key benefits of blade servers?

   a) Individual server blade management
   b) Better power utilization compared to standard servers
   c) Higher density
   d) I/O cards are installed in individual blade servers
   e) Centralized management through blade chassis

3. Which network architecture is usually deployed with hyper-converged servers?

   a) Three-tier architecture
   b) Leaf-spine architecture

4. Which three main design blocks should be covered in the design phase?

     a) Disaster recovery design
     b) Conceptual design
     c) Network design
     d) Logical design
     e) Physical design
     f) vSphere design

5. AMPRS stands for which of the following?

     a) Automation, Management, Performance, Recoverability, and Scalability
     b) Availability, Management, Performance, Redundancy, and Scalability
     c) Availability, Maintenance, Persistency, Recoverability, and Security
     d) Availability, Management, Performance, Recoverability, and Security
     e) Automation, Management, Persistency, Recoverability, and Security

Further reading

Read the following articles for more information:

- **vSphere High Performance Cookbook - Second Edition:** https://www.packtpub.com/virtualization-and-cloud/vsphere-high-performance-cookbook-second-edition.
- **VMware vSphere Design Essentials:** https://www.packtpub.com/virtualization-and-cloud/vmware-vsphere-design-essentials.
- **Complexity simplified:** Here you can also find a comprehensive guide towards VMware VCDX certification with real-world examples and guidance. https://vcdx133.com/

Analysis and Assessment of Existing Environments

3

It is crucial to find a simple and effective way to analyze an existing environment; this task could become an essential aspect of your system that must be appropriately planned and executed.

These are some situations in which you may need to analyze an existing environment:

- **Before planning a virtualization project**: Before starting on your virtualization journey, it is essential to understand your current IT infrastructure and how the virtualization process will impact it; this is not only to clarify whether virtualization is possible but also to match or better transform existing procedures in the new environment.
- **Before a migration:** It doesn't matter whether we are talking about an entire platform migration, a migration from one hypervisor to another, or merely a migration across vSphere (maybe different versions, in the case of a hardware refresh, or sometimes also across the same version); performing this task without right-sizing and planning the target could be really business-critical.
- **Before an upgrade:** In the case of an in-place upgrade, usually the system is already sized. However, some minor considerations may be taken into account, such as different overheads—for example, for virtual appliances or ESXi itself. Note that upgrades require more attention and considerations, and we will cover those aspects in Chapter 6, *Life Cycle Management, Patching, and Upgrading*. Also, an upgrade that is not in-place falls into the migration category.
- **On a running system:** Finding a baseline for your environment or a simple document may be an essential task if it wasn't already covered during the deployment of the infrastructure. Also, it may be useful to prepare for other tasks.

- **Before an audit process:** Compliance, security, and regimentation are typical cases where you need an in-depth and targeted analysis of your environment but there can also be other cases, such as a simple verification that the environment matches the business needs, or specific aspects such as performance.

Different types of analysis can be performed to achieve different goals, depending on the applicable scenario:

- **Discover and inventory:** This is useful for capturing your assets, to build your documents, or check the inventory. Usually, you need some detailed information from your hardware, such as firmware releases or merely the exact names and models for a device or I/O card.
- **Solution readiness:** Normally, this is related to a new virtualization project where you need to verify the effective possibility of virtualizing your workloads. However, it could also be useful in any upgrade process, or in every migration, such as from a different type of hypervisor.
- **Health check or sanity check or configuration audit:** Doing a health assessment of your environment is critical in several situations, such as any migration or upgrade process. However, it could also be beneficial to perform it periodically to discover wasted resources, misalignment with the documentation or with best practices from VMware or other vendors, and possible optimization or changes.
- **Risks and compliance assessment or audit:** This is useful when your focus is on the security or compliance aspects. Licensing validation could also fit in this case.
- **Capacity planning:** This is usually used to find out whether capacity meets the business requirements.
- **Optimization assessment:** Based on your current workloads, you can ensure proper sizing of your virtual environment. Sometimes, you can discover that current resource sizing is not optimal (either oversized or undersized) and, based on such analysis, you can adjust the resources for your virtual machines to get best possible performance.

There are also other types of analysis that could be related to the rest of the infrastructure, such as storage or network parts, that sometimes must be performed in more depth and need to be specific to the vendor, products, and solutions used. Some other analysis could be needed for other layers, such as the application layer, the database level, the network and storage level, the application architecture, and so on.

In this chapter, we will cover the following topics:

- Analyzing a physical environment before virtualizing it, and important performance metrics
- How to assess an existing virtual environment

Analyzing a physical environment before virtualizing

Virtualization is typically used to provide workload consolidation, but this means, without the right resource management, just blending everything; this could become a risk, like putting all your eggs in one basket without taking any precautions. Besides, all shared components of your infrastructure will most likely be affected in some way by this significant change (for example, storage or the network). Moreover, standard procedures such as monitoring, backups, patching, and administration will also be affected.

Before you start with the virtualization of the existing physical environment, you should carefully assess all components of the existing infrastructure. With servers, you should focus on the utilization and any potential performance bottlenecks, but you should also assess the other components of the infrastructure such as physical switches, storage devices or the datacenter itself.

Of course, ensure you have a healthy environment before attempting to virtualize it, to avoid incorrect measures, such as workloads with existing performance or application issues, to avoid the risk of just moving those issues to the virtual environment. Depending on the data that you collect, your conceptual and logical design (as described in the previous chapter) may remain the same, but the physical design should take account of real and objective data to ensure a successful project. The existing environment could be physical, as was typical in the past, or mixed with some physical and virtual workloads, or already fully virtualized.

Most virtualization projects will involve migrating your current physical servers to virtual machines using a **physical-to-virtual (P2V)** conversion, or, even better, using an application/service migration to a new virtual environment. Therefore, it is vital that you thoroughly understand your current environment before attempting to move it to a virtual environment. By doing this, you can ensure that you purchase properly-sized server hardware for the hosts and define the correct storage, both for capacity and performance. For this purpose, you will need to collect some critical metrics, as discussed in the next section.

However, it's not always the technical aspects; you need to consider the licensing impact, not only for the virtual environment (for example, more hosts, more VMware licenses), but also for applications and services and operating systems where you may need new or different licenses.

Also, it's essential to identify whether the old physical hardware could be reused for virtualization—for example, for disaster recovery, or for other purposes (such as physical domain controller servers or backup server roles). In this case, you have to consider both the technical possibilities (for example, *does the server have enough resources?*) and the practical and organizational possibilities. (Is the server still supported and *how much does it consume and cost during operation compared to a new server?*)

For P2V conversions, you can use VMware Converter, which allows such P2V or V2V conversions. VMware Converter is a free tool from VMware:

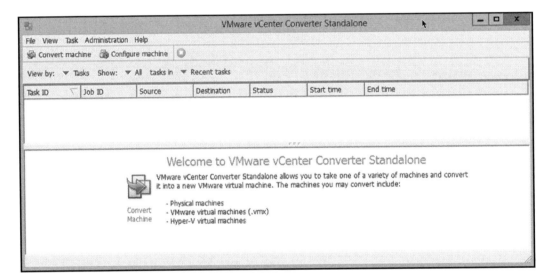

 For more information about VMware Converter, feel free to visit https://www.vmware.com/products/converter.html.

Useful metrics from a physical environment

There are four key resources you should focus on—processor, memory, disk, and network, as those resources define the core resource components of every virtualization project. It is important to gather those metrics from the physical environment and you should capture such data for a longer time—a minimum of a week, but preferably even longer to discover any specific usage patterns over the time or peaks.

As a best-practice you should capture the performance data during a representative time period such as during business hours or during the running of business-critical applications (if they are not run constantly).

Only if you have the representative data, will you be able to correctly right-size you environment and cover any peaks and spikes in the resource usage.

Processor metrics

Statistically, most servers have low overall CPU usage (< 25%), which is the main reason why server virtualization is so effective and used for server consolidation. However, you also have to consider the peaks, which could be near 100% in some cases and, depending on how frequent they are, how long-lasting, and how they are correlated, could become critical for sizing the virtual infrastructure.

The CPU is usually overcommitted and, depending on the workload, a 4:1 ratio between virtual and physical resource could be a reasonable target if you don't have CPU-intensive (or CPU-bound) workloads.

The Dell white paper, *Demystifying CPU Ready (% RDY) as a Performance Metric*, establishes the following `vCPU:pCPU` guidelines:

- 1:1 to 3:1 is no problem
- 3:1 to 5:1 may begin to cause performance degradation
- 6:1 or higher will often cause a problem

You can use this general rule for the assessment, but it always depends on your specific workloads how the vCPU-to-pCPU ratio will affect your infrastructure.

Note that the ratio should be calculated on the physical (real) cores, not the logical processors that VMware ESXi sees, because hyper-threading could increase this number. It could also be essential to define how the workload could be scaled with more cores or sockets and how it could depend on the architecture (not all applications perform the same on different types of processor family) or merely the speed of the processor (some old applications require GHz instead of cores).

For the CPU, the following table suggests the main metrics to be considered:

Metric	Description	Notes
% processor time (average and peaks)	Percentage of elapsed time that the processor spends to execute a non-idle thread.	Based on this performance counter you can correctly right-size the CPU resources for the new VM.
Processor queue length (average and peaks)	Number of threads in the processor queue but not currently able to use the processor resource.	If other process is running, you can't assign the processor to other tasks. This performance counter might indicate that you need more vCPUs for your VM

Finally, remember to compare apples with apples; a different processor may perform differently, and an application may perform differently by simply changing the type of processors.

 To compare processor power, you can use a variety of CPU Benchmarks, but I tend to use SPEC located at `https://www.spec.org/cgi-bin/osgresults?conf=cpu2017`.

Memory metrics

RAM could be overcommitted (assigning VMs more memory than the host physical RAM) on an ESXi host, and this was one of the historical advantages of VMware products. However, just because you can, it does not necessarily mean that you should.

Now, in most cases, it is not recommended anymore because it will degrade the performance of your environment (for example, memory ballooning or swapping also have an impact on storage). So, the right memory sizing could be crucial, not only for the workload but also for high-availability aspects. (We will discuss this more in Chapter 11, *Availability and Disaster Recovery*.)

If you are assessing an existing virtual environment, you can have a look at the difference between **consumed memory** and **active memory**:

- Consumed memory means the total amount of memory that the virtual server has accessed

- Active memory means the total size of memory that the virtual server is accessing in the physical memory of the ESXi server

 You can find more information about memory counters here: `https://www.vmware.com/support/developer/converter-sdk/conv51_apireference/memory_counters.html`.

Note also, that there are more and more workloads that are becoming more memory-bound—consider, for example, all in-memory databases. In those cases, you should design the hosts carefully and maybe consider a specific cluster for those workloads (depending on the numbers and the recommended practices from the software vendor).

For memory, the following table suggests some possible metrics:

Metric	Description	Notes
Available free memory (average and least)	Amount of physical memory available for allocation to a process or system. It is equal to the sum of memory assigned to the standby (cached), free, and zero page lists.	This performance counter might help you to correctly right-size the amount of memory for the VM. If the server does not use assigned memory, there is no need to configure such an amount for the VM. On the other hand, if the value is close to zero, it might be useful to add more memory for the VM.
Pages swapped/sec (average and peaks)	Pages/sec is the rate at which pages are read from or written to disk to resolve hard page faults. This counter is a primary indicator of the kinds of faults that cause system-wide delays.	You should avoid swapping at all. If you discover that the server is using swap extensively, you should assign more memory to the virtual machine.

Disk metrics

The disk can be the first bottleneck for your virtual environments; for this reason, it's essential to understand how much is used and how it is used, both for the capacity (but this could be quite easy) and for the expected performance. Using a simple **input/output operation per second** (**IOPS**) approach could work in several cases but does not appropriately qualify the type of I/O and cannot always help in storage sizing and design. Storage will be discussed in detail in Chapter 8, *Managing Storage Resources*.

For the disk, the following table lists some of the common metrics:

Metric	Description	Notes
% disk time	Percentage of elapsed time that the selected disk drive was busy servicing read or write requests.	Usually you can discover I/O bottlenecks using this performance counter.
Disk latency (average and peaks)	Observed latency of disks. Warning zone of latency is typically around 10-20 ms.	Increased latency usually corresponds with disks or other storage overutilization.
Disk bytes/sec	Represent the rate of the bytes per second that are transferred to or from the disk during write or read operations.	You can use this performance counter to right-size the required throughput of your storage area network and storage array.

Network metrics

The network is usually the latest bottleneck for your virtual machines, except in the case of VMs with massive network traffic or when networks are shared between VM traffic and other types of traffic (such as IP storage, but also vMotion or **Fault Tolerance** (**FT**) traffic).

Depending on the **Network Interface Card** (**NIC**) types, you may have two different but common situations for the VM traffic—dedicated NIC ports (typically for 1 Gbps ports where you may have several available ports) or shared ports (typically for 10 or more Gbps ports, where the number of ports is usually limited). Networking will be discussed in depth in Chapter 7, *Managing Networking Resources*.

For the network, throughput is usually the common metric used for sizing, as described in the following table:

Metric	Description	Why it's important
Bytes total/sec	Bytes total/sec is the rate at which bytes are sent and received over each network adapter	You can use this performance counter to right-size the required throughput of your local area network and physical switches.

Are all workloads good candidates to be virtualized?

Starting with vSphere 5, almost all servers and workloads can be virtualized, considering the large number of resources that you can provide to a monster VM.

However, there are some cases where you may keep a workload physical instead of migrating it to the virtual environment, as described in the following table:

Boundary condition	Why virtualize?	Why keep it physical?
High-resource utilization servers	When virtualizing these types of server, you may be able to have only one or two VMs on a host server, but you can take advantage of some of the features that virtualization offers such as snapshots, vMotion, HA, disaster recovery, and data protection, that are more difficult and costly to implement in a physical environment.	Very highly-utilized servers might not bet he ideal candidates for virtualization since the virtual machine will not benefit from resource sharing within the virtual infrastructure. It might also compromise the overall performance of the infrastructure, since the server will try to access as many resources as possible.

Boundary condition	Why virtualize?	Why keep it physical?
Vendor licensing models	Thankfully, most vendors today have specific license rules for virtual environments, and in some cases are also virtualization-friendly. (For example, with a Windows Server data center, you can run unlimited instances on a properly licensed host.)	Some applications, such as Oracle, do not have virtualization-friendly licensing, and require you to license their software based on the number of physical CPUs in the host server and not the number of virtual CPUs assigned to the VM that is running the application. Several applications require that you license all physical CPUs where the virtual machine could run, not the number of vCPUs assigned to the virtual machines. That might be the big constraint in terms of the costs. For example, Oracle is well-known for its virtualization-non-friendly licensing model.
Licensing restriction or limitation	There are some possible ways to accommodate these types of licensing scheme on virtual servers, such as USB redirection or specific network appliances (or Digi AnywhereUSB).	Certain applications use stricter licensing controls, such as hardware dongles (parallel/serial port/USB device keys), MAC address, or hardware serial controls.
Hardware that cannot be virtualized	Some applications might require specific hardware to run. With PCI passthrough or Serial-Over-IP technologies of ESXi server, you can benefit from virtualization, even for such specific applications.	Some servers might have non-standard hardware such as a fax and modem.
Application support	Very few vendors do not support virtualization, but in those cases, you may consider keeping some physical server to reproduce the issue on them, and still have the right support.	Some vendors will not provide support for their application if it is running on a virtual server.

Boundary condition	Why virtualize?	Why keep it physical?
Avoid too many eggs in the same basket	You can still consider different clusters (for example, a management cluster) or use proper QoS solutions.	Shared infrastructure could mean shared problems (for example, storage performance).
Dependency or risk prevention	You can still consider different clusters (for example, a management cluster) or a different site.	Sometimes you have a circular dependency that can be a risk in the case of a major failure. Dependencies are also needed to understand how to power-off or power-on the entire infrastructure.

Existing tools to analyze a physical environment

For a physical environment, you need to collect all the data from the different operating systems, and then analyze and aggregate them all to right-size your ESXi hosts.

Different tools could be used, but you can use standard tools provided by the different operating system, for example, **Performance Monitor** in a Windows system and `top`, `vmstat`, `sar`, and other command-line tools, in a Linux system. However, using those tools is time-consuming even in a relatively small data center, because acquiring meaningful and useful inventory information requires manual aggregation of the results, and the approach is impractical in medium-to-large data centers.

VMware provides different tools or services to provide support during the initial assessment of a physical environment, with the purpose of right-sizing the new virtual environment.

VMware Capacity Planner (VCP)

VCP is a powerful tool that automatically collects all relevant performance metrics on each Windows server in your environment and prepares a report that you can use to determine your hardware requirements for your virtual environment. It can identify trends in your environment and make recommendations for physically grouping servers on virtual hosts. It uses built-in Microsoft performance counters and does not require that an agent is installed on each server that will be analyzed (it uses the **Windows Management Instrumentation (WMI)** and the Remote Registry service). Using VCP is the best method for collecting data from your servers and reporting on it because it was developed specifically for infrastructure assessment and data analysis and will provide consolidation estimates, recommendations, and capacity assessments.

This tool is limited to VMware **Professional Services Organization (PSO)** or authorized partners.

 For more information, refer to the service page at `https://www.vmware.com/products/capacity-planner.html`.

Virtual Storage Area Network (vSAN) sizing tools

This tool can be used for sizing the underlying **hyper-converged infrastructure (HCI)** based on your assumed virtual workloads. Different tools can be used, for example **vSAN ReadyNode™ Sizer** (`https://vsansizer.vmware.com/login?src=%2Fhome`).

However, there are also other tools from different vendors; third-party workload-sizing tools can also be a valid option, but the prices and capabilities of these tools vary.

Dell Live Optics

This tool can be used for free for a variety of assessments of your physical or virtual environments. All you need is to install the agent on the target server (Windows, Linux, and macOS are supported) which collects all your required data. You can run even long-term monitoring to get the actual utilization of your system (usually 24 hours or more). The collector runs remotely and uploads all data to the cloud dashboard, gathering core metrics such as disk I/O, throughput, free and used capacity, and memory utilization, as you can see in the following screenshot:

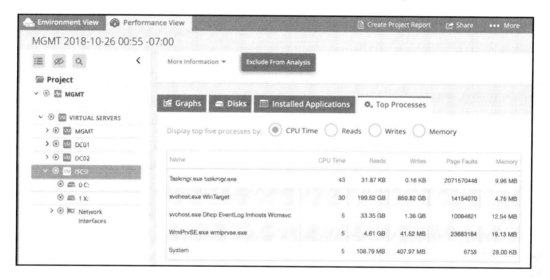

Feel free to have a look at the product page at `https://app.liveoptics.com/register?ref=stpchatlink`.

Microsoft Assessment and Planning (MAP) Toolkit

Although it might seem it's only for Microsoft-based environments, this tool allows you to connect to both Windows and Linux servers (physical or virtual) and collect both inventory and performance data from the system.

With MAP Toolkit you do not need to install any monitoring agent to the guest operating system and it provides support for multiple products (not only from Microsoft).

The report functionality is quite extensive, providing you with comprehensive sets of hardware and software information:

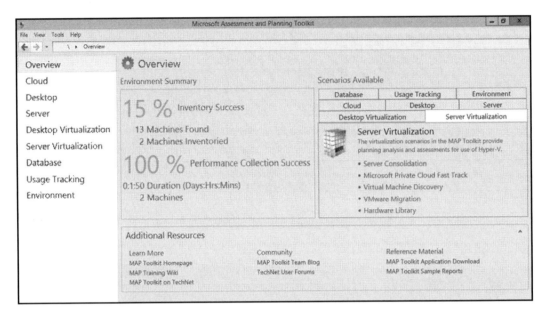

The output is not provided as a graphic report, unlike Live Optics, but as a complex CSV file you can then process as you need.

The following is an example of a MAP performance report:

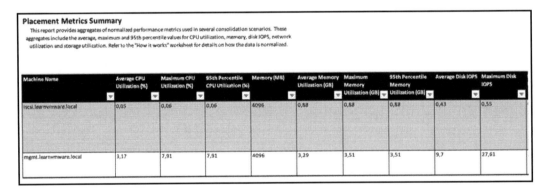

You can download MAP from the following website: https://www.microsoft.com/en-us/download/details.aspx?id=7826.

Assessing an existing virtual environment

For virtualized workloads, the data is already there and can be used for the design (we will discuss later how to get and use it); maybe a greater complexity can be found with other hypervisors, where host-related metrics could not be easily comparable with a vSphere environment. However, data collected at the virtual machine level might be good enough and quite useful.

Monitoring could be handled in the same way as with the physical environment, with the same tools and the same metrics, but it's easy to gain more information directly from your vCenter Server without having to deal with every single guest operating system. Monitoring and collecting (performance) data from a virtual environment will be discussed in depth in Chapter 13, *Analyzing and Optimizing Your Environment.*

However, it's not all about metrics; you may also need to perform a health check or a full inventory of your environment.

If you are planning a new virtual infrastructure, you can use the following assumptions to size the environment. Please note that the virtual machine configuration may vary a lot but, based on the global statistics, a typical virtual machine has the following configuration and storage behavior:

Compute	2 vCPU
Memory	8 GB RAM
Disk size	100 GB HDD
Disk IO	50-150 IOPS
Disk latency	15 ms latency
Disk I/O size	8K IO size
Disk read versus write	80% read IO
Random versus sequential	80% random IO

Discovery and inventory

Building an inventory of your infrastructure is also very easy with standard vSphere clients because you have a list of all your VMs or ESXi hosts with several columns. (You can easily customize it with the information you want, and you can order or search your data.)

Note that you can export several pieces of information, such as the hosts or a VM list, using the vSphere Web Client and the export function in the **VMs** or **Hosts** tab:

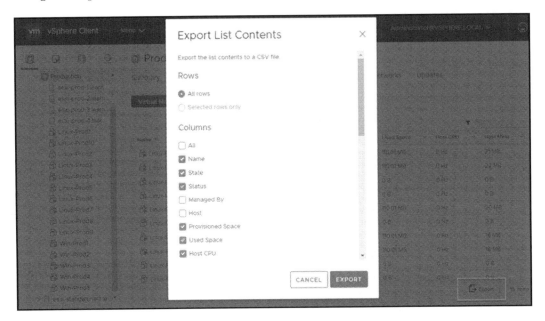

However, if you need more detailed data, such as the firmware version of your I/O cards or the space used inside the **Virtual Machine Disk (VMDK)**, this may need more effort or specific tools.

You can also write PowerCLI scripts to get all required information in a single CSV or output the results to the console:

```
Name             : vcsa-lab.learnvmware.local
NumCpu           : 2
MemoryGB         : 10
PowerState       : PoweredOn
SCSI controller  : {@{Type=VirtualLsiLogic}, @{Type=VirtualLsiLogic}}
NICs             : @{Type=Vmxnet3}

Name             : SGL-INT-1
NumCpu           : 1
MemoryGB         : 2
PowerState       : PoweredOn
SCSI controller  : @{Type=ParaVirtual}
NICs             : @{Type=Vmxnet3}

Name             : SGL-INT-2
NumCpu           : 1
MemoryGB         : 2
PowerState       : PoweredOn
SCSI controller  : @{Type=ParaVirtual}
NICs             : @{Type=Vmxnet3}
```

One interesting case where you need a good inventory, is during the upgrade procedure, where you first need to verify the **hardware compatibility list (HCL)**, with details on all hardware and their firmware and driver versions. Besides, you have to check all the software versions to ensure interoperability and guarantee the right upgrade paths. If the second task is quite easy to achieve, the first could be a little more complicated.

Sometimes, you can use VMware GUI or CLI functions; otherwise, you may need other tools, such as specific vendor-related tools. Remember also that several servers have a specific out-of-band card (called **iDRAC** on Dell PowerEdge, **Integrated Lights-Out (iLO)** on HPE ProLiant, and so on) that can also provide many details about hardware configurations.

For the host's hardware details, there are some ways to obtain more information, as follows:

Asset	How to obtain this information from VMware
Service tag	This information is stored in the motherboard's BIOS and usually can be read in the configuration/processor area
BIOS	Can be read in the configuration/processor area using the GUI
I/O cards	Some information is available from the GUI, but details on the model and the chipset are possible with specific commands, described in **KB 1027206: Determining Network/Storage firmware and driver version in ESXi 4.x and later** at `https://kb.vmware.com/kb/1027206`, or by using vendor-specific management plugins for vCenter
Storage details	Vendor-specific management plugins for vCenter

Using proper documentation to inventory your assets could be useful for their lifecycle management. For this purpose, you can use traditional documents or spreadsheets, which may be shared in some way, or specific collaborative tools such as SharePoint, Wiki, or custom web applications.

Health check

Doing a health check or health assessment of your current environment is critical, especially before some tasks, such as migrations or upgrades. However, it can also be used during the entire life cycle of your environment—for example, to discover wasted resources, possible issues, and mismatches with best practices, tools, and so on. Depending on how often your environment changes, you may need to perform this kind of task more frequently.

From a budget perspective, most companies do an in-depth health check on their environment every six or twelve months, but this may vary in each case. From a management point of view, a continuous health check would be best, but of course, in this case, you need to automate it as much as possible and use the right tools. Several tools could also be used to perform other analyses, not only the health check.

Benchmarks

Benchmarks are a great way to compare performance results between different environments, either physical or virtual. Based on this comparison, you can get a better understanding of your environments, especially if you are performing a migration from a physical to a virtual environment.

DVD Store

DVD Store is a database performance benchmark. You need to install the supported database first. (Currently the MS SQL, Oracle, MySQL, and PostgreSQL databases are supported.) DVD Store benchmark will assess your database performance by running multiple SQL queries resulting in overall transactions per second performance of the system. Feel free to download DVD Store at `https://github.com/dvdstore/ds3`.

Hyper-Converged Infrastructure Benchmark (HCIBench)

HCIBench is an extension to the commonly used **Vdbench** open-source benchmark tool with a focus on Hyper-Converged Infrastructure testing and automation.

The idea of the tool is to provide a simplified solution to test the customer's **proof-of-concept (PoC)** using a fully automated approach where you do not need to deploy multiple VMs manually, as the tool will do everything for you.

HCIBench can be used to assess any HCI-based infrastructure, although the primary focus is on VMware vSAN.

HCIBench is available as a Fling from VMware labs at `https://labs.vmware.com/flings/hcibench`.

Existing tools for analyzing a virtual environment

Some VMware tools can help by providing reports on your current environment. Most of these tools come with a 60-day evaluation period, which is enough time to get the information needed, and they are listed as follows:

- **VMware vSphere Health Check**: VMware or professional partner services provide this and it's based on a virtual appliance (or also a standalone package) that can connect to your VMware infrastructure and analyze it, with a great report generator. At this point, it's only available for VMware employees or selected partners. For more information refer to `https://www.vmware.com/content/dam/digitalmarketing/vmware/en/pdf/products/vsphere/consserv-vmware-vsphere-health-check-datasheet.pdf`

- **vSphere Optimization Assessment (VOA)**: Using this tool you can access the overall reports for your multi-cloud environments from the single console. The primary focus is on the optimization, right-sizing, capacity and costs. For more information refer to `https://www.vmware.com/assessment/voa`.

- **VMware vRealize Operations**: The primary purpose of this tool is monitoring, in a proactive way, a virtual (and in some parts, also physical) infrastructure. However, it can also provide some useful insights for capacity and resource planning, and also for resource optimization and resource reclaiming. For more information refer to `https://www.vmware.com/products/vrealize-operations.html`.

- **Hybrid Cloud Assessment:** Ideal for companies interested in multi-cloud operations, how to move workloads, optimization, and cost analysis. For more information see `https://www.vmware.com/hybrid-cloud-assessment.html`
- **Virtual Network Assessment (VNA):** The VMware tool called **vRealize Network Insight (vRNI)** is used to extract the data flow across your physical and virtual infrastructure. VNA provides a comprehensive set of reports of traffic flows between your VMs, applications, VLANs or VXLANs.
- **vSAN Assessment:** Collect data about your existing vSphere storage environment in just one week and get the technical and business recommendations you need for a vSAN design.
- **Virtual Desktop Infrastructure (VDI) assessment**: This is a specific assessment for a VDI environment that identifies the best candidates both for users and desktops, if they can be moved into a virtual desktop environment, and the order in which those groups and desktops should be virtualized for a successful VDI project.

Then, there are tools from other vendors, or also community scripts, or your personal set of scripts. Note that, VMware does not officially support community tools as they can also vary or change (many scripts are quite old). However, scripting could be the best way to check some specific details, for example, to check whether the number of paths for each shared storage device is what you expect.

The following is a partial list of some of these tools:

- **RVTools:** Probably the most powerful and straightforward (you have to connect to your vCenter or hosts) tool with which to inventory your environment. It also provides some health check capabilities; for more information, see `http://www.robware.net/rvtools/`.
- **VMware {code} vCheck vSphere:** A community script, useful both for inventories and health checks; for more information, see `https://code.vmware.com/samples/823/-vcheck-vsphere`.
- **VisualESXtop**: A GUI frontend to the standard ESXtop command for performance metrics of individual ESXi servers—available from the VMware labs page at `https://labs.vmware.com/flings/visualesxtop`.

Some cloud-based monitoring tools with assessment and/or health check functions are as follows:

- **Runecast**: https://www.runecast.biz/
- **Opvizor**: http://www.opvizor.com/
- **CloudPhysics**: https://www.cloudphysics.com/

Most of them can also verify how best practices are used and applied. The best way to learn more is to try them or ask for a demo:

- **Veeam ONE**: This provides advanced monitoring, reporting, and capacity planning capabilities designed to help you protect your virtual and backup environments. It also provides some useful reports for the assessment of a virtual environment; for more details, see https://www.veeam.com/one-vmware-hyper-v-monitoring-reporting.html.
- **Turbonomic virtual monitor**: This is a free product that provides virtualization monitoring and reporting in an unlimited fashion across vSphere, Hyper-V, XenServer, and Red Hat virtualization, not only for network monitoring but also to provide insights into risk and efficiency information and potential improvements across the environment. For more information, see https://turbonomic.com/downloads/virtual-health-monitor/.

The most exciting and useful tools are RVTools and some assessment tools from VMware. (VMware vSphere Health Check is probably the most interesting but unfortunately it cannot be directly used by customers or end users.) Note that there are also situations, such as application dependency mapping, where other tools could be useful—for example, the vRealize Infrastructure Navigator.

RVTools

RVTools is a Windows .NET 4.0 application that uses the **VMware Infrastructure Software Development Kit (VI SDK)** to display information about your virtual environments. It's a free application that can run on a server or a Windows client machine and it can read information from all versions of the VMware vSphere platform, from virtual infrastructure 3.x through vSphere 6.7 versions.

Using RVtools you can extract the different lists that contains information about your virtual infrastructure like VMs, datastores, HBAs, ESXi host, networking and much more:

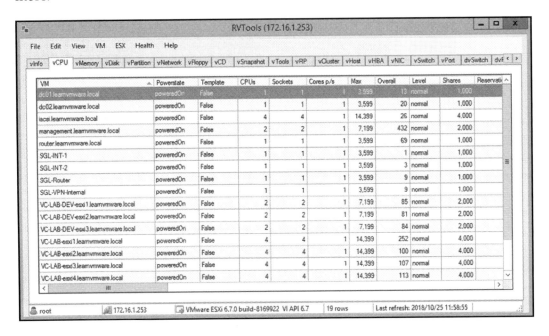

The main pros of RVTools are that it is free, requires minimal installation, and supports all versions of vSphere. More importantly, it's able to export all that data in Excel or CSV formats.

VOA

VOA can improve the performance, efficiency and availability by addressing the health, performance, and capacity management of the IT infrastructure and applications in your virtualized data center, as well as across heterogeneous and hybrid cloud environments.

This tool can provide a different series of analytic reports that assess the configuration, performance, and capacity of your vSphere environment:

- **Configuration health**: Get a comprehensive report on vSphere configuration errors and security hardening suggestions. See a sample configuration health report at `https://www.vmware.com/content/dam/ digitalmarketing/vmware/high-touch-eval/pdf/vmw-voa-phase-1- configuration-reporting-en.pdf?exp=b`.
- **Performance assessment:** It is useful to understand performance issues affecting your virtual environment and find possible bottlenecks. See a sample performance bottlenecks report at `https://www.vmware.com/ content/dam/digitalmarketing/vmware/high-touch-eval/pdf/vmw-voa- phase-2-performance-reporting-en.pdf?exp=b`.
- **Capacity assessment**: This builds a customized capacity optimization report based on current usage and trends, which is useful for reclaiming underutilized resources or identifying over-provisioned VMs. See a sample capacity utilization report at `https://www.vmware.com/content/dam/ digitalmarketing/vmware/high-touch-eval/pdf/vmw-voa-phase-3- capacity-reporting-en.pdf?exp=b`.

VMware vSphere Health Check

VMware vSphere Health Check is a tool that is only available for VMware's partners (or VMware PSOs), but it can collect some data from a virtual environment, analyze the configuration, and provide a Word document with a lot of usable structural information in the following areas:

- Major findings and recommendations
- Organizational
- Operational
- Technical
- Health check assessment and recommendations
- Compute
- Network
- Storage
- Data center
- VM
- Security
- vSAN

The technical recommendations section is the most interesting because it tries to check the existing configuration according to VMware best practices and classify all non-compliance at different priority levels. Then, there is an inventory part, as with RVTools, but with the advantage that it's more structured for a readable document, instead of just being contained in some sheets in a spreadsheet.

Summary

This chapter explained how to perform an analysis and assessment of an existing physical or virtual environment and to gain all the data you need to plan your migration, upgrade your environment, or improve it. Different tools and approaches were described as a way to reach the goal. Specific application-level tools were not considered, but must be part of a complete analysis.

The key takeaway lessons from this chapter are how to analyze a physical or virtual infrastructure, how to collect data from an existing environment to drive planning or performance analysis, and how and when to perform a health check of your environment.

With the next chapter, we are now able to start using the vSphere product, starting from the deployment of its components.

Questions

1. Which of the following conditions may be a constraint on virtualization of the system?

    a) More than two 10 GbE NICs
    b) An application requires an HW USB key connected to the system
    c) Application vendor limitations
    d) High-performance system with a lot of compute resources
    e) Proprietary hardware used within the system

2. Name at least two available tools that you can use to assess your virtual or physical infrastructure.

3. Microsoft Assessment and Planning Toolkit is intended to be used in Microsoft environments only.

    a) True
    b) False

4. Please describe all of the products, tools, or services offered by VMware:

    a) VMware vSphere Health Check
    b) VMware vRealize Operations
    c) vSAN Assessment
    d) vSphere Optimization Assessment

5. Different benchmarking tools can be used to assess the health of the vSphere environment.

    a) True
    b) False

Further reading

Managing Virtual Infrastructure with Veeam ONE: `https://www.packtpub.com/virtualization-and-cloud/managing-virtual-infrastructure-with-veeam-one`.

4
Deployment Workflow and Component Installation

VMware vSphere 6.7 is a sophisticated product with several components to install and set up. Understanding the correct sequence of tasks required to install and configure vSphere is the key to a successful deployment. The chapter starts by explaining the components of vSphere with the roles and services they provide. We will walk through the main aspects to consider for the preparation of a deployment plan for your environment, analyzing the criteria for hardware platform selection, storage, and network requirements.

The host deployment plan will then describe the different ways to install ESXi, including Auto Deploy, and other solutions for deploying the host. We'll also detail the deployment of **Platform Services Controller (PSC)** and **vCenter Server Appliance (vCSA)**.

In this chapter, we will cover the following topics:

- vSphere components and workflow
- ESXi deployment plan
- ESXi installation
- vCenter Server components
- vCenter Server Appliance deployment
- vCSA **High Availability (HA)**

vSphere components and workflow

To provide services to the infrastructure, vSphere relies on two core components: the hypervisor, which is the virtualization layer for the complete environment, and vCenter Server, which centralizes the management of the ESXi hosts and allows administrators to automate and secure the virtual infrastructure. To complete the vSphere deployment, it is essential to know the interaction between ESXi and vCenter. Let's examine these two components to figure out their role:

- The **ESXi hypervisor** is the platform on which VMs and virtual appliances run. Its primary function is to provide the resources to workloads regarding CPU and RAM, but it can also provide storage resources through vSAN. To manage the ESXi resources, ensuring performance and reliability, an additional component is necessary—vCenter Server.
- **vCenter Server** is a central management platform that manages ESXi hosts connected in a network and allows you to pool and manage the resources of multiple hosts. VMware vCenter Server can be installed in a virtual or physical machine with Windows Server, or deployed as a vCSA. The installation of vCSA can be launched from Windows, macOS, and Linux OS. Any host you plan on connecting to vCenter Server 6.7 must be running version 6.0 or above.

The **vCenter Server Appliance (vCSA)** is a preconfigured Linux-based (with VMware Photon OS) virtual machine that provides all the services required to run vCenter Server and its components. As compared to previous versions, vCSA 6.7 has the capability of providing all services as the Windows-based vCenter Server. **vSphere Update Manager (VUM)** is also completely integrated, and you no longer need to install a separate Windows server to host it. In a vSphere environment, vCenter Server is not an essential requirement to deploy the ESXi hosts, and VMs can run without it. However, advanced features available in vSphere can't be used without vCenter Server. You won't be able to provide services such as **vMotion, Distributed Resource Scheduler (DRS), HA, FT**, and **Update Manager**, to mention a few.

The services required to run vCenter Server and vCenter components are now bundled in the VMware PSC, a component introduced in version 6.0 of vSphere that provides common infrastructure services for VMware products.

For a correct installation sequence, the PSC (which will be discussed later) must always be installed before deploying the vCenter Server. Depending on the vSphere design, the PSC can be installed embedded in the vCenter Server or installed externally in the vCenter Server.

A correct VMware vSphere 6.7 deployment requires a specific installation sequence to avoid problems due to missing components or services and can be summarized as follows:

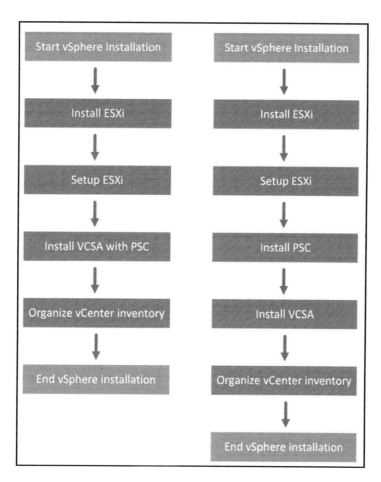

With a good design and following the correct workflow, the deployment procedure of vSphere 6.7 is straightforward and shouldn't raise problems. Let's have a look at the following points:

- **ESXi installation**: In this step, you have to verify whether the chosen hardware platform is included in the HCL, and determine what installation method to use and which destination to use to boot the hypervisor.
- **ESXi setup**: This step involves the initial configuration of the ESXi server, especially its management network.

- **vCenter Server and PSC deployment**: You should identify what deployment model best fits in your environment for vCenter Server and the PSC. The vCenter Server can be deployed with an embedded or an external PSC depending on the design (multiple vCenter Server instances, for example). vCenter Server and the PSC can be installed on a Windows machine (physical or virtual) or a vCSA.
- **Connect to vCenter Server**: Use the integrated vSphere Web Client to complete the configuration of the vCenter Server.

When the required steps are clear, let's start the vSphere deployment by examining the first core component of the infrastructure—the ESXi hypervisor.

ESXi deployment plan

A successful vSphere deployment requires an appropriate plan to avoid problems of incompatibility, performance, and instability with the commitment of remaining within the available budget.

Three main areas should be considered when planning a vSphere deployment:

- Choosing the hardware platform
- Identification of the storage architecture and protocols (NFS, iSCSI, FC, or FCoE)
- Network configuration (number of NICs, FC adapters, 1 GbE, or 10 GbE NICs)

Choosing the hardware platform

An important decision to take when planning an ESXi deployment is the choice of the hardware platform of the server. ESXi doesn't support all the hardware available on the market (storage controllers, NICs, and so on) and has some restrictions that can prevent the successful installation of the hypervisor.

Only tested and supported hardware ensures that your ESXi can be installed without any problem and can operate as expected. Before purchasing the hardware for your server, it is strongly recommended you verify whether ESXi supports the chosen hardware platform.

To check for hardware compatibility, you can refer to the VMware Compatibility Guide available at `https://www.vmware.com/resources/compatibility/`. The list of tested hardware is large, and you can find the supported hardware from the leading manufacturers, such as HP, Dell, IBM, and Cisco.

When new hardware is released and certified for compatibility, the list of supported vendors is updated accordingly.

Choosing the right server for your installation is not an easy task, especially if your environment grows quickly and the business requirements change frequently. Capability, scalability, availability, and support are the elements of the server you need to evaluate carefully to be sure the final choice fits in the available budget without affecting the global design.

In some scenarios, it is better to have more, smaller servers in a cluster to provide the required resources than a few big servers.

There are several considerations you need to think about:

- Fewer servers with more resources are usually cheaper compared to the same amount of resources distributed among more smaller servers (you always need to buy a chassis, a motherboard, and power supplies for every server).
- With more smaller servers you can have multiple fault domains. For example, if you have 10 ESXi hypervisors in four racks, when one rack (fault domain) becomes inaccessible, you still have other fault domains compared to 15 powerful servers in a single rack.
- When your ESXi server becomes unavailable, you lose part of the computing power. If you have 10 large servers, you will lose 10% of the total capacity if you encounter downtime. If you have 50 smaller servers, you will lose only 2%.
- With more servers, you will need adequate network infrastructure concerning the physical 1/10/40/100 GbE ports.

The challenge is to find a server that provides the number of resources that meets the requirements but at the same time supports enough expansion (scalability) if the demand for resources grows.

Another factor you should consider is the expected performance of the server. The default hardware BIOS settings of the chosen hardware do not always ensure the best performance. To optimize performance, you should check some of the following in your server's BIOS settings:

- Hyperthreading should be enabled for processors that support it.
- Enable turbo boost if your processors support it.
- In NUMA-capable systems, disabling node interleaving (leaving NUMA enabled) will give you the best performance.
- Hardware-assisted virtualization features, such as VT-x, AMD-V, EPT, and RVI, should be enabled.
- Consider whether you should disable any devices you won't be using from the BIOS (Serial/Parallel ports, unused PCIe cards, and so on).
- For power management, you can choose to enable max performance or leave the control in ESXi with OS Controlled mode.

Identification of the storage architecture

Choosing a suitable storage solution is another piece of the deployment plan. You should consider what protocols will be used and their direct dependencies. For instance, a **Fibre Channel (FC)** storage device requires FC adapters to be installed on the server. vSphere supports software and hardware initiators (also known as **host bus adapters (HBAs)** or **converged network adapters (CNA)**) that add flexibility to your storage architecture design.

An ESXi host may use multiple storage protocols in the same installation to support the design requirements. It is not unusual to see different ESXi installations with FC and NFS storage devices connected at the same host and, in some scenarios, also with the addition of an iSCSI storage. Storage will be discussed in detail in Chapter 8, *Managing Storage Resources*.

Defining the network configuration

For a successful deployment plan, you should consider the impact on your environment and how the deployment will integrate with the existing network infrastructure. This is another crucial point to keep in mind, because it is strictly related to the hardware chosen for the server and the storage protocols used. Networking will be discussed in depth in Chapter 7, *Managing Networking Resources*.

ESXi generates network traffic that must be controlled and sized to properly manage advanced features such as vMotion, FT, and VM traffic without congesting the network. The question is, *how many NICs should I use?*

The number of NICs supported by the server can profoundly influence the network design and, consequently, the overall host performance. If the server has only four slots available to accommodate the adapters and FC storage is used, the server needs to be equipped with at least two FC adapters to provide FT, taking precious slots intended for additional NICs.

Depending on the design of your ESXi server, general guidelines you might consider when defining the number of NICs to use are the following:

- **ESXi management network**: One NIC is required; two would be better for redundancy.
- **vMotion**: At least one NIC and, due to the amount of data involved during a vMotion process, a **Gigabit Ethernet (GbE)** must be used. More NICs can provide more bandwidth, with the right configuration.
- **vSphere FT**: It requires at least 1 GbE NIC but, depending on how many vCPU and FT-enabled VMs are configured, a 10 GbE NIC could be a better choice. A second NIC is recommended for redundancy.
- **Storage**: Except for FC, which uses different adapters, NFS or iSCSI storage protocols need at least a 1 GbE or, better, 10 GbE. Also, for this configuration, more NICs are recommended for redundancy and performance.
- **VM traffic**: To better distribute and balance the load, two or more GbE NICs are recommended.

A general recommendation is to have always two NICs available for specific traffic, although multiple traffic types can be combined into the single NIC. By using two (or more) NICs you can eliminate the possible network outage regarding switch failure, cable to cut or similar situation.

I tend to use 2x GbE NICs for management and 2x 10 GbE NICs for everything else and to separate traffic using Network I/O Control (we will discuss Network I/O Control in `Chapter 7`, *Managing Networking Resources*) or at least using VLANs if the license does not allow use NIOC.

When you have defined the server and the number of NICs you need for your design, the ESXi installation plan raises a new question—how should I install ESXi?

ESXi installation

Once you have defined the hardware platform and the storage and network setup, you are ready to deploy the ESXi host. The installation is pretty simple and takes only a few minutes.

The latest release of vSphere made an essential enhancement regarding security, introducing a new feature for the hypervisor—Secure Boot. Secure Boot is a solution that ensures that only the trusted EFI firmware loads code before the OS boots. The trust is given by the UEFI firmware that validates the digitally signed ESXi kernel against a digital certificate stored in the UEFI firmware.

Once you have defined the design of the virtual infrastructure, you should evaluate which installation option is suitable for your environment. vSphere 6.7 offers three options to deploy ESXi:

- **Interactive**: Manually providing answers to installation options
- **Unattended**: Using installation scripts
- **Automated**: Using the vSphere Auto Deploy feature

The deployment method to adopt depends on the size of your environment and on the number of hosts to install. Interactive installation is definitively the most straightforward procedure you can use but requires more time if you have several hosts to deploy. Automated installation is more complicated to implement but for large environments is always the preferred choice.

There are, of course, additional steps to follow for unattended or automated installation, but in the end, it will save you a lot of time.

Once you have defined how to install ESXi, you should ask yourself the following question: *where should I install ESXi?* Let's examine the available options you may consider.

Where should I install ESXi?

Before installing ESXi, you need to decide where to store the ESXi files. A local disk, SD card, SAN (LUN), FC, or USB device are all possible destinations you can use for ESXi, but what solution is the best and what you should use is very hard to say. The choice to make depends on your infrastructure design and network configuration, and the installed devices in your target machine.

You can use a remote device available through your SAN (for hardware-based HBAs such as fiber channel, fiber channel over Ethernet, or iSCSI) but you can use this method with software-based initiators for iSCSI and FCoE. An extra configuration is required to set up LUNs and zoning . Anyhow, the use of SAN LUN creates a dependency on an external storage array that, in the case of failure, makes the ESXi unusable, but your storage array and SAN need to be highly available anyway.

From my perspective, using a SAN device for booting is always preferable if your hardware infrastructure allows it since you do not need additional local disks installed in your server.

Using local disks as the destination for the ESXi files is a solution that, until a few years ago, was popular in most ESXi installations because it is a cost-effective solution and doesn't require any extra configuration. If the local hard disk is your choice, I strongly recommend configuring **RAID 1** to provide fault tolerance. There is no need to invest in SSDs as booting devices, because there is no benefit from using them at all. The smallest available disk from your vendor will do the job.

A valid alternative to HDDs is the use of SD cards which offer better performance and, compared to years ago, are more significant and more cost-effective. To use SD cards, the target server needs to be equipped with **Secure Digital** (**SD**) bays, but if your server has only one bay available, it won't be able to provide fault tolerance. Luckily, certain hardware manufacturers, such as Dell and HP, provide servers equipped with double bays for SD cards you can mirror, like you would an HDD, and fit perfectly in this installation method.

The downside of using SD cards is the requirement of some additional configuration. The scratch partition of ESXi (which will be covered in `Chapter 5`, *Configuring and Managing vSphere 6.7)* needs to be placed in persistent storage (VMFS or NFS volumes attached to the server) to store `vm-support` output, which you need when you create a support bundle.

The USB stick is another possible option you can use for ESXi installation. It is the most economical destination device, but for production servers, I don't recommend its use since you don't have any redundancy in case of failure.

As with SD cards, for USB sticks, no log files will be stored locally (a scratch partition needs to be configured). Although a 1 GB USB or SD device suffices for a minimal installation, it is recommended you use a 4 GB or larger device.

Did you notice that fault tolerance is a recurrent caveat for devices? Is there any reason for that? Yes, of course. Let's talk briefly about the importance of having fault-tolerant components. *What happens if you use just one device for your ESXi installation and suddenly the device fails?* The ESXi stops working, stops providing its resources, and in a situation of inadequate infrastructure design, the network services may be no longer available to users. For this reason, a good design for ESXi should consider the use of two devices configured in mirror RAID 1 to provide fault tolerance and performance.

Preparing for deployment

When the destination for your ESXi has been chosen, you should decide what method to use for the ESXi deployment. Before proceeding with the installation, you can download the installation files at `https://my.vmware.com/web/vmware/downloads/`. The installation files are typically provided in ISO format to be quickly burned to a physical CD/DVD or mounted to a server.

The installation using a physical CD/DVD can be considered old-fashioned and time-consuming, but to install the ESXi, you have also the option of using an USB flash drive, through the network using the **Preboot Execution Environment** (**PXE**), or mounting the ISO installation file (virtual CD) if your server is equipped with the remote management tool (iLO, iDRAC, IPMI, or similar). Perhaps the USB key is the fastest solution to use if your server doesn't have any integrated remote management tool since you need to create a bootable USB key. Tools such as **UNetbootin** or **Rufus** can do that using the ISO file without burning any CDs.

Some manufacturers, such as HP, Dell, and Super Micro, provide servers with an integrated remote management tool that allows the use of the virtual CD feature, which remains an excellent way to install your ESXi without the need to burn the ISO (you can sit at your desk without getting cold inside the data center):

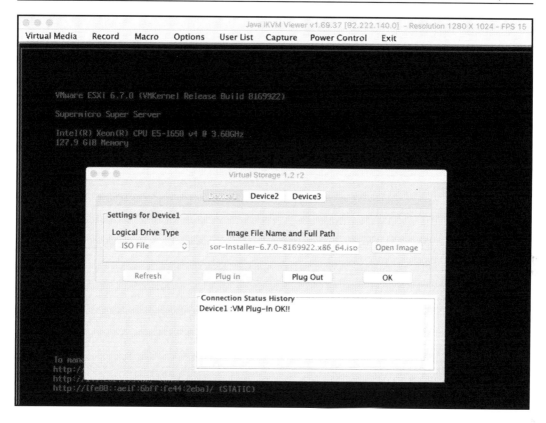

Let's examine the three possible installation options.

Interactive installation

Interactive installation is straightforward, because the procedure makes use of a comfortable and intuitive interface that guides the user during the entire process. The installer is booted from a CD/ DVD, from a bootable USB device, or by PXE booting the installer from a location on the network. The interactive installation method best applies to small environments where the number of ESXi hosts to install is limited. You can install ESXi in a few minutes directly launching the installer from the installation media, and no scripts or dedicated network configurations are required to complete the procedure. If you need to install a few ESXi hosts, this is definitively the fastest and most straightforward option.

Depending on the ESXi installer media used (CD/DVD, USB flash drive, or PXE), remember to set the BIOS server accordingly to configure the correct boot sequence. Perform the following steps to proceed with an interactive installation:

1. Insert the installation medium (CD/DVD, USB flash drive) and power on the server. When the server boots, the installer will display the Boot Menu window.

2. Select the ESXi installer and press *Enter*. The system loads the ESXi installer and displays the welcome screen. Press *Enter* to continue.

3. Accept the **End User License Agreement (EULA)** by pressing *F11* and continue with the installation.

4. The next screen displays the available devices on which to install the ESXi, divided into local devices and remote devices (see the following screenshot). Select the desired destination and press *Enter*. Since the disk order shown in the list is determined by the BIOS, make sure the selected device is operative. To get the details of any previous ESXi installation and what VMFS datastore is detected, press *F1*.

5. In the disk selection window, SATA disks, SD cards, SATADOM, and USB flash drives are listed as local devices, while SAN LUNs and SAS devices are listed as remote:

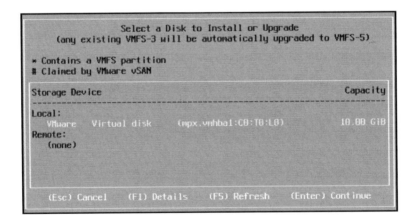

6. If the selected device contains a previous ESXi installation or a VMFS datastore, you have three clear choices to select:

- **Upgrade ESXi, preserve VMFS datastore**
- **Install ESXi, preserve VMFS datastore**
- **Install ESXi, overwrite VMFS datastore**

7. The keyboard layout selection is the next screen. Select your language then press *Enter*.

8. Enter the root password twice and press *Enter*. For security reasons, keep the password in a safe place.

9. At the confirm install screen, press *F11* to proceed with the installation. The procedure only takes a few minutes and begins re-partitioning the disk and installing the host in the selected device.

10. After the installer completes, remove the installation CD/DVD or USB flash drive, and press *Enter* to reboot the host.

11. Once the host has rebooted, the procedure is complete. For new installations, or if an existing VMFS datastore is overwritten, VFAT scratch and VMFS partitions are created on the host disk (only if the destination device is not an SD card or USB stick).

By default, the ESXi is configured to obtain an IP address from a DHCP server used for its management. If your network doesn't have any DHCP server installed, the ESXi won't be able to obtain an IP address, and you will need to configure it manually. The configuration of a static IP address and the post-installation configuration of the ESXi will be discussed in `Chapter 5`, *Configuring and Managing vSphere 6.7*.

Unattended installation

While interactive installation is straightforward, you need to repeat the same steps for each server to install. If the number of hosts to install increases dramatically, the interactive installation method may not be the most suitable choice. The installation process can be automated using a script to provide an efficient way to deploy multiple hosts.

ESXi supports the use of an installation script to automate the installation process and can be useful if you want to have a consistent configuration for all hosts. Using an installation script, you can quickly deploy multiple instances of ESXi, creating unattended installation routines. These scripts can be saved on a USB flash drive or in a network location accessible through NFS, HTTP, HTTPS, or FTP.

The following table indicates some common boot options for unattended ESXi installation. For a complete list of supported boot options, refer to the *vSphere Installation and Setup Guide* available on the VMware website at `https://docs.vmware.com/en/VMware-vSphere/6.7/com.vmware.esxi.upgrade.doc/GUID-61A14EBB-5CF3-43EE-87EF-DB8EC6D83698.html`:

Boot option	Description
`BOOTIF=hwtype-MAC address`	Similar to the `netdevice` option, except in the PXELINUX format as described in the IPAPPEND option under SYSLINUX at `syslinux.zytor.com`.
`gateway=ip address`	Sets the default gateway to be used for downloading the installation script and installation media.
`ip=ip address`	Used to set a static IP address to be used for downloading the installation script and the installation media.
`ks=cdrom:/path`	Specifies that the path of the installation script, which resides on the CD in the CD-ROM drive. The path of the script must be written in uppercase characters (for example, `ks=cdrom:/KS_CUST.CFG`).
`ks=file://path`	Performs a scripted installation with the script at `path`.
`ks=protocol://serverpath`	Specifies that the script is located on the network at the given URL. Supported protocol can be HTTP, HTTPS, FTP, or NFS (for example, `ks=nfs://host/porturl-path`).
`ks=usb`	Indicates that the installation script is located in an attached USB drive. `ks.cfg` must be in the root directory of the drive. Only FAT16 and FAT32 are supported. If multiple USB flash drives are attached, the system searches until the `ks.cfg` file is found.
`ks=usb:/path`	Specifies the path of the installation script that resides on the USB (for example, `ks=usb:/ks.cfg`).
`ksdevice=device`	Tries to use a network adapter device when looking for an installation script and installation media. If the script has to be retrieved over the network, the first discovered plugged-in NIC is used if one is not specified.

`nameserver=ip address`	Specifies a domain name server to be used for downloading the installation script and installation media.
`netdevice=device`	Tries to use a network adapter device when looking for an installation script and installation media. The device can be specified as `vmnicXX` name. If the script has to be retrieved over the network, the first discovered plugged-in NIC is used if not specified.
`netmask=subnet mask`	Specifies the subnet mask for the network interface that downloads the installation script and the installation medium.
`vlanid=vlanid`	Used to specify the VLAN for the network card.

Common boot options for unattended ESXi installation

The installation script is a text file often named `ks.cfg` that contains supported commands useful to provide the required installation options to the ESXi installer. In the installation medium, VMware includes a default installation script that can be used as a reference to perform an unattended ESXi installation to the first detected disk. You can use this script if it is suitable for your ESXi installation.

The default sample script is as follows:

```
#
# Sample scripted installation file
#
# Accept the VMware End User License Agreement
vmaccepteula
# Set the root password for the DCUI and Tech Support Mode
rootpw mypassword
# Install on the first local disk available on machine
install --firstdisk --overwritevmfs
# Set the network to DHCP on the first network adapter
network --bootproto=dhcp --device=vmnic0
# A sample post-install script
%post --interpreter=python --ignorefailure=true
import time
stampFile = open('/finished.stamp', mode='w')
stampFile.write( time.asctime() )
```

To create a custom installation script or modify the default script, you should use the supported commands available.

A complete list of supported commands to use with installation scripts can be found in the **vSphere Installation and Setup Guide**: https://docs.vmware.com/en/VMware-vSphere/6.7/vsphere-esxi-67-installation-setup-guide.pdf.

To configure an unattended installation booting from a USB stick, perform the following steps:

1. Navigate to the installation media and edit the boot.cfg file. Replace kernelopt=runweasel with kernelopt=runweasel ks=usb:/ks.cfg. This allows the system to automatically use the script located on the USB drive. Make sure you use an editor that can handle UNIX encoding.

2. Create a ks.cfg file in the root directory of the USB device that the installer will use for the unattended installation. Edit the file and create the script. You can use the following simple script as an example:

```
vmaccepteula
rootpw mypassword
install --firstdisk —overwritevmfs
keyboard English
network --bootproto=dhcp --device=vmnic0
reboot
```

3. Save and close the file. Plug in the USB stick and power on the server.

4. To manually run the installer script when the ESXi installer window appears, press *Shift + O* to edit boot options. At the runweasel command line, type ks=usb:/ks.cfg. To specify the path to an installation script, you may also use the ks=http://ip_address/kickstart/ks.cfg command, where the IP address refers to the machine where the script resides.

5. The system will boot from the USB stick and do an unattended installation.

The main benefit of using unattended installations for ESXi is not only that it speeds up the installation process, but it also ensures a consistent configuration of all ESXi hosts.

There are certain caveats when using unattended installation such as an IP configuration. Generally, you do not want to use a dynamically assigned IP address, but instead use a statically configured address. To do that without any additional modifications, you would need to have individual config files for each ESXi server you want to configure and select them during the boot process: `ks=http://ip_address/kickstarts/ks_ESXi-36.cfg`.

You can automate the whole procedure using some scripts.

The first requirement is to have MAC address mapping to the individual ESXi servers since the DHCP server knows the mapping between MAC address and the IP address.

Once your ESXi servers connect to the web server where the script resides over IP, you will know which ESXi server it is thanks to this mapping. Now, based on this information, you can dynamically create the correct `kickstart` file with appropriate IP address for the management interface or other variables individual for each ESXi server, such as DNS settings.

You can, of course, use the more convenient method, Auto Deploy, which will do all the work for you, but this feature is only available in Enterprise editions of vSphere.

Auto Deploy installation

Auto Deploy installation is a way to PXE-boot your ESXi hosts from a central Auto Deploy server. This method is based on the use of master images with some set of rules to deploy ESXi with the desired specifications. Auto Deploy can also be used with the vSphere Host Profile feature (this will be detailed in Chapter 5, *Configuring and Managing vSphere 6.7*) to customize all ESXi hosts, ensuring a consistent configuration within the infrastructure. In a large environment, setting up the vSphere Auto Deploy feature to handle ESXi installations is the most efficient and suitable method to use.

Auto Deploy relies on several components, and the configuration required is more complicated. A vCenter Server must be already present in the vSphere infrastructure to provide the Auto Deploy feature. You also need a DHCP server and a **Trivial File Transfer Protocol (TFTP)**.

The Auto Deploy feature in VMware vSphere 6.7 introduces a new graphical user interface for managing ESXi images and deployment rules that reduces complexity and helps users during the configuration. PowerCLI is still available and has been enhanced with a new script bundle that allows administrators to add a post-deployment script once all the configurations have been applied to a stateless ESXi host.

The Auto Deploy feature is installed with the vCSA but by default is disabled. To use this functionality, you need to enable the service:

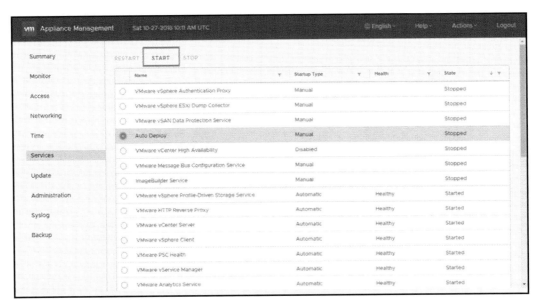

 Please note that from the web management of the vCSA you can only start the service, but you can set it to automatic startup.

To start the services and set the automatic startup, you need to use vSphere Web Client (not the HTML5 client):

1. Log in to the vSphere Web Client as administrator.
2. Go to **Administration** | **System Configuration** | **Services**.
3. Right-click on **ImageBuilder** and **AutoDeploy Service** and select **Edit Startup Type**. Choose **Automatic** and click **OK**.

4. Select **ImageBuilder** and **AutoDeploy Service** and choose **Start**.
5. Log out of the vSphere Web Client and log in once again. The Auto Deploy icon should now be visible.

Before digging into the installation procedure, let's see how vSphere Auto Deploy works and the configuration of the required components (DHCP, TFTP).

How Auto Deploy works

To take advantage of this deployment method, it is essential to understand how Auto Deploy works and what steps and services are involved during the ESXi deployment process. Different components interact with vSphere Auto Deploy when a fresh host boots:

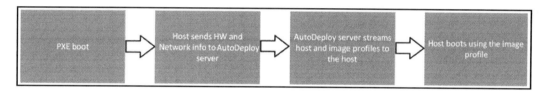

The ESXi booting process through the Auto Deploy feature involves the following steps:

1. When the server first boots, the host starts a PXE boot sequence. The DHCP server provides an IP address giving instructions to the host on how to contact the TFTP server (DHCP configuration will be discussed later).
2. When the host establishes the connection with the TFTP server, it downloads the iPXE file (executable boot loader), named `undionly.kpxe.vmw-hardwired` for legacy BIOS or `snponly64.efi.vmw-hardwired` for UEFI BIOS, and a configuration file.
3. During the iPXE execution, the host makes an HTTP boot request to the vSphere Auto Deploy server (this info is stored in the iPXE configuration file) to get hardware and network information.
4. The vSphere Auto Deploy server streams the required components as the image profile to the hosts based on the defined rules.
5. Host boots using the image profile assigned by the deploy rule. If a host profile has been assigned as well, it is applied to the host.
6. The host is added to the same vCenter with which Auto Deploy is registered. If any rule does not specify the inventory location, the host is added to the first data center displayed in the vSphere Web Client UI.

Configuring DHCP

To support vSphere Auto Deploy, the DHCP server has to be configured accordingly. First, we have to define basic settings to configure a DHCP scope including the default gateway. If you want to assign a specific IP address to the host to be better identified, you can use DHCP reservation to accomplish this.

When the necessary settings are ready, you need to specify two additional options:

- **Option 66**: In this option, you should specify the **Boot Server Host Name** to be used by the system.
- **Option 67**: The **Bootfile Name** must be specified. The filename `undionly.kpxe.vmw-hardwired` can be found in the Auto Deploy configuration tab in the **BIOS DHCP File Name** field.

If VLANs are used in your vSphere Auto Deploy environment, make sure you set up end-to-end networking correctly because, during the host PXE booting, the firmware driver has to tag the frames with proper VLAN IDs. Changes must be set manually in the UEFI/BIOS interface. If you are running a Windows-based environment, the easiest way is to install a DHCP server role.

Once the DHCP server role is installed, you need to configure desired options.

At the least, you need to configure your new DHCP scope (IP Address Range for DHCP clients) and Option 66 and Option 67.

If the vCenter Server is not on the same L2 network, you also need to configure Option 003 – Default Gateway for your DHCP client, and preferably DNS servers using Option 006:

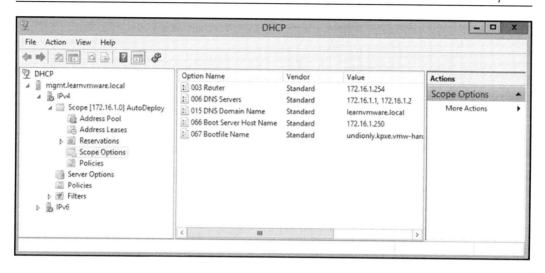

Configuring TFTP

vCenter Server does not include TFTP server, so you need to install third-party TFTP server as well and store the boot files from your vCenter Server.

To access those files, navigate to the **Configure** tab of your vCenter Server, select **Auto Deploy**, and **Download TFTP Boot Zip**:

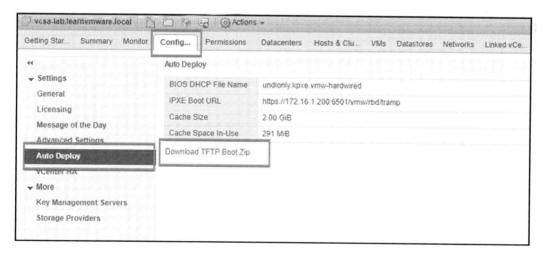

As the TFTP server, you can use some free tools such as **Pumpkin TFTP** server available at `http://kin.klever.net/pumpkin/binaries`, **SolarWind TFTP Server** available at `http://www.solarwinds.com/free-tools/free-tftp-server`, or **Tftpd32** available at `http://tftpd32.jounin.net/`.

When you boot a new server, it gets the IP address from the DHCP and connects to the TFTP server through Option 66 and Option 67 specified during the DHCP configuration. Your new host will be available in the **Discovered Hosts** tab of **Auto Deploy configuration**, you will be able to see the host with an assigned IP address, or it will be automatically added to the inventory based on your deployment rule.

Creating an image profile

Image profiles are a set of **vSphere Installation Bundles** (VIBs), a collection of files packaged into a single archive to facilitate distribution and used to boot the ESXi hosts. Image profiles are built and made available in public depots by VMware and VMware partners. You can create custom image profiles, usually by cloning an existing image profile and then adding the required software packages VIBs to the image created.

To create an image profile, you should add at least one software depot, but you can add multiple software depots. A software depot can be a structure of folders and files stored on an HTTP server (online depot) or, more commonly, in the form of a ZIP file (offline depot). The software depot contains the image profiles and software packages VIBs that are used to run ESXi.

You can either use the official VMware depot which contains all VMware ESXi images or you can create your own **Software Depots** and upload your existing **Image Profile:**

> If you want to use the official VMware online depot, all you need is to create a new online depot using the following URL: `https://hostupdate.vmware.com/software/VUM/PRODUCTION/main/vmw-depot-index.xml`.

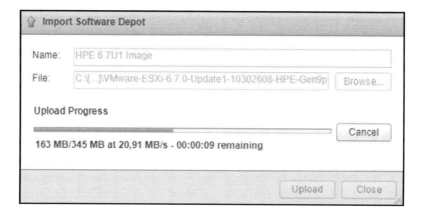

For custom image profiles such as the official profiles from hardware vendors you can follow this steps:

1. Go to the **Auto Deploy** configuration page then select the **Software Depots** tab
2. Click on the green arrow to import a software depot
3. Type a name in the **Name** field and select the file to use an image then click **Upload**

Once the depot is successfully added, you can browse all available image profiles associated with the depot.

An image profile doesn't contain any configuration (virtual switch, security settings, and so on) and you should use the vSphere Host Profile feature to store the desired ESXi configuration in vCenter Server providing the parameters to the host to provision. If syslog is not configured in the host profile, logs are lost every time the host is rebooted since they are stored in memory.

Creating deployment rules

Deployment rules are used to link the image profiles to hosts and VIBs defined in a specific image profile. To make an image profile available to hosts, VIBs are copied to the Auto Deploy server to be accessible from hosts.

To start provisioning hosts through Auto Deploy, you should define a deployment rule to apply. To create a new deployment rule, proceed with these steps:

1. Select the **Deploy Rules** tab and click on the **New Deploy Rule** icon. Enter a name in the Name field and specify to which hosts the rule should apply. If you want to apply the rule only to specific hosts, select one or more patterns that the hosts should match. In the example, we want to install the host with the IP address 172.16.1.253, previously listed in the **Discovered Hosts** tab. Then click **Next.**

2. Select the image to assign to the host then click **Next.**

3. Select the host profile to apply. If you don't have any host profiles available, flag the **Do not include a host profile** option and click **Next.**

4. Specify the location, cluster, or folder where the host should be added and click **Next.** I tend to use a dedicated empty cluster called Deployment or similar, so my new ESXi host is added to a dedicated cluster first before everything is tested.

5. Click **Finish** to create the rule. By default, the rule is disabled and must be activated using the **Activate/Deactivate rules...** button as well as specifying the deploy rule order. To modify an existing rule, the rule must be first deactivated from the **Activate/Deactivate rules...** button to allow editing:

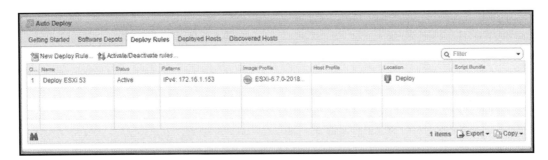

6. Restart the host.

The boot process of the ESXi provisioned with vSphere Auto Deploy is different from the interactive or unattended installation methods:

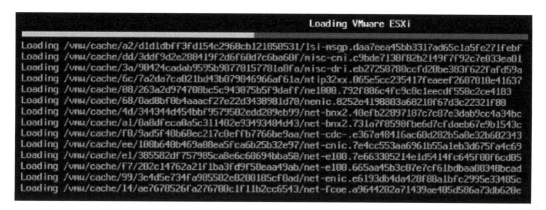

Once the server is up and running, you will see it in the vCenter Server inventory in the location you have specified by the deployment rule:

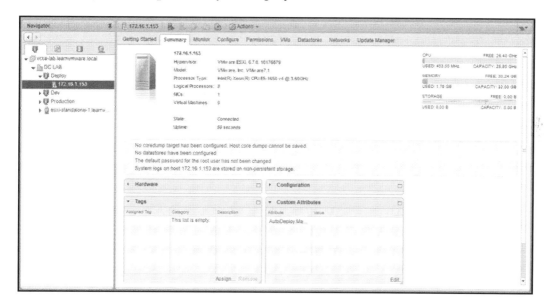

As you can see, there are several notifications associated with our new host. This is because we did not include a host profile in the deployment rule that specifies how the host should be configured.

Auto Deploy modes

Having completed the Auto Deploy installation procedure, let's walk through the different modes you can use to configure vSphere Auto Deploy. There are three possible installation types you can use:

- **Stateless**: The ESXi image is not technically installed, but it is loaded directly into the host's memory as it boots.
- **Stateless caching**: The image is cached on the local disk, remote disk, or USB. If the Auto Deploy server is not available, the host boots from the local cache.
- **Stateful**: The image is cached on the local disk, remote disk, or USB. As compared to stateless caching, the boot order is inverted; the host boots first from local disk then from the network.

Let's have a look at the different procedures to configure Auto Deploy installations.

Stateless installation

Stateless installation follows the procedure previously seen where the host receives the configured image profile when it boots. This installation method requires an available image profile and a deployment rule that applies to the target host.

When you make a change to the Host Profile that is associated with the ESXi server in the Auto Deploy rule, the change will be applied to the host during the boot.

In this case, the Auto Deploy infrastructure must always be available. Otherwise, the ESXi server won't boot.

Stateless caching installation

During the ESXi deployment through Auto Deploy, the image is cached on local disk, remote disk, or USB drive. vSphere Auto Deploy always provisions the host, but if the server becomes unavailable due to bottlenecks (for example, hundreds of hosts that attempt to access the Auto Deploy server simultaneously), the host boots from the cache and attempts to reach the Auto Deploy server to complete the configuration.

The stateless caching solution is primarily intended to prevent situations where the deployment process may fail due to server congestion, a typical scenario that occurs in large environments.

To enable stateless caching mode, follow these steps:

1. From vCenter Server, navigate to **Home | Host Profiles**.
2. Edit an existing host profile attached to hosts to provision or create a new one.
3. Under **Advanced Configuration Settings**, select **System Image Cache Configuration**.
4. From the drop-down menu, select **Enable stateless caching on the host** and click **Finish** to save the configuration. You can specify a comma-separated list of disks to use (by default, the first available will be used) using the syntax shown in Table 4.1 to configure an unattended installation:

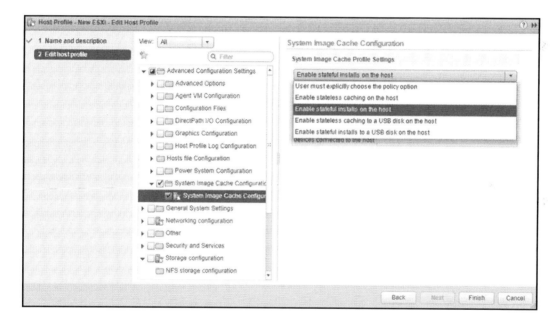

    The host profile configuration must be modified to enable stateless caching.

5. Configure the boot order from the BIOS of your server to boot from the network first then from the local disk. Reboot the host to get a fresh image.
6. After a successful boot, the Auto Deploy image loaded in memory is saved to the local disk.
7. When you reboot the host and Auto Deploy is not available, the host boots from the cached image on local disk.

Stateful installation

The stateful installation method is almost the same as the stateless caching mode, with the exception that the boot order in the host's BIOS is inverted. Stateful installation is a method to perform a network installation because, after the first successful boot, Auto Deploy is no longer needed.

To enable stateful mode, follow these steps:

1. From vCenter Server, navigate to **Home | Host Profiles**. Edit an existing host profile attached to hosts to provision or create a new one.
2. Under **Advanced Configuration Settings**, select **System Image Cache Configuration**.
3. From the drop-down menu, select **Enable stateful installs on the host** and click **Finish** to save the configuration. You can specify a comma-separated list of disks to use (by default, the first available will be used).
4. Configure the boot order from the BIOS of your server to boot from the local disk first then from the network. Reboot the host to get a fresh image. During the boot process, settings stored in the host profile are applied to the host.
5. When the host boots, it will enter maintenance mode. At this stage, the settings passed with the host profile configured with Auto Deploy must be applied to the host. The host remediation action must be performed to complete the deployment process.

We will discuss host profiles in more detail in upcoming chapters, so do not worry.

vCenter Server components

vCenter Server is a service that centralizes the management of the ESXi hosts and the VM that run on the hypervisor. This vSphere core component not only interacts with ESXi hypervisors, but also integrates with other VMware products—vRealize Automation, Site Recovery Manager, and vSphere Update Manager, to give you some examples.

vCenter Server is not limited to act as a central management tool. The advanced features such as a **sign-on server (SSO)**, centralized authentication, vMotion, DRS, HA, and FT are all services that come into play only when vCenter Server is present in the infrastructure. With vCenter Server, you can manage resources, ESXi hosts, VM, templates, logs and stats, alarms and events, and so on. Besides, vCenter Server provides all the functionalities needed to distribute and manage the network services, ensuring the availability of resources and data protection. vSphere management will be discussed in detail in Chapter 5, *Configuring and Managing vSphere 6.7*:

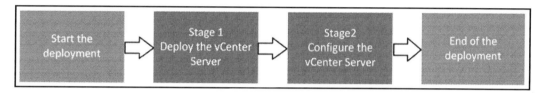

Starting from vSphere 6.0, the vCenter installation includes the deployment of two components:

- Platform Service Controller
- vCenter Server

PSC

Introduced in vSphere 6.0, the PSC is a component used to provide common infrastructure services for VMware products.

The PSC is an essential component in the design that provides services not only for vCenter Server and vSphere but the VMware product suite in general. SSO, for example, can also be shared with other VMware products to provide centralized user authentication (for example, vRealize Orchestrator, and vRealize Automation).

Depending on your environment and the infrastructure design, vCenter Server and the PSC can be deployed in two different ways—embedded or external:

- **Embedded**: Preferred deployment for single-sites where you do not need to interconnect different vCenter Servers to the SSO domain. vCenter Server can be deployed with an embedded PSC to simplify the management and, because both components are not connected over the network, outages due to connectivity and name resolution issues between vCenter Server and PSC are avoided. If the vCenter Server used is the Windows-based version, you can also save some Windows licenses. If you install vCenter Server with an embedded PSC, you can reconfigure the setup and switch to vCenter Server with an external PSC later on.
- **External**: Installing the vCenter Server with an external PSC is a solution suitable for large environments with the benefit that shared services in the PSC instances consume fewer resources. This setup increases the management complexity and, in the event of connectivity issues between the vCenter Server and PSC, could cause some outages.

Which method to use strictly depends on the requirements regarding availability for your vCenter Server. You can have a PSC that serves multiple sites or a highly available PSC in a single cluster.

VMware recommends six high-level PSC topologies:

- vCenter Server with embedded PSC
- vCenter Server with external PSC
- PSC in replicated configuration
- PSC in HA configuration
- vCenter Server deployment across sites
- vCenter Server deployment across sites with a load balancer

 For more information about moving from a deprecated to a supported vCenter server deployment topology before upgrade or migration, you can visit `https://docs.vmware.com/en/VMware-vSphere/6.7/com.vmware.vcenter.upgrade.doc/GUID-080CA000-4BD0-40F8-8324-DABB3A136390.html`.

Some topologies have changed from version 5.5 and are now deprecated. The choice of the right topology depends on different aspects, such as features (do you need enhanced linked mode between multiple vCenters?), availability, scalability, physical topology, and so on.

Although a mixed environment is supported, it is recommended that you use the same platform (only appliances or only Windows-based installations) for both vCenter Server and PSC to ensure easy manageability and maintenance.

There are three core services provided by the PSC essential for the vSphere functionality— SSO, VMware License Service, and certificate management:

- **SSO:** This is a prerequisite to installing vCenter Server (it cannot be installed without SSO). This service solves the problem of authentication in an environment with multiple ESXi hosts. Using a secure token mechanism, vSphere components can communicate with each other without requiring a separated authentication for each component. For each administrator who needs access to a specific server, without having a vCenter Server in your environment, you need to create a separate user account and grant access permissions for each ESXi. If the number of ESXi hosts grows, the number of accounts to manage also grows. Joining the ESXi to AD to centralize the authentication can be an option (Active Directory integration will be covered in `Chapter 5`, *Configuring and Managing vSphere 6.7*), but adds another dependency in the infrastructure—the **Domain Controller (DC)**. The SSO authentication service is easier to manage and more secure for the authentication against VMware products.

- **VMware License Service:** This centralizes the management of all the information related to the license of the vSphere environment and VMware products that support PSC. This capability allows licensing information between vCenter Servers not configured in the Linked Mode group installed in geographically different locations to replicate every 30 seconds (by default). vCenter Servers in a Linked Mode group will be examined in detail in `Chapter 5`, *Configuring and Managing vSphere 6.7*.

- **Certificate Management:** This is required to communicate securely with each other and, with ESXi hosts, vCenter Server services make use of SSL. The **VMware Certificate Authority (VMCA)** provisions ESXi hosts and services with a certificate signed by VMCA by default.

Other services provided by PSC are as follows:

- VMware Appliance Management Service (only in appliance-based PSC)
- VMware Component Manager
- VMware Identity Management Service
- VMware HTTP Reverse Proxy
- VMware Service Control Agent
- VMware Security Token Service
- VMware Common Logging Service
- VMware Syslog Health Service
- VMware Authentication Framework
- VMware Directory Service

Additional details and configuration of PSC will be discussed in `Chapter 5`, *Configuring and Managing vSphere 6.7*.

Linked Mode

Linked Mode is a feature where you can link multiple vCenter Servers to the same PSC, allowing you to manage multiple vCenter Servers from the single vSphere client.

With this, you can join multiple vCenter Server systems using vCenter Linked Mode, and this will enable them to share information with each other. You can also view and manage the inventories of other vCenter Server systems when a server is connected to it using Linked Mode:

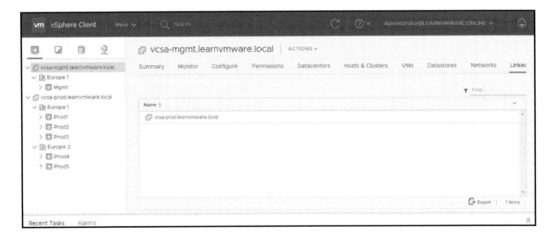

In the past, there were some limitations regarding Linked Mode and vCSA. Those limits no longer apply, and you can even link multiple vCSA appliances with embedded PSC. This mode is called Embedded Linked Mode.

vCenter Embedded Linked Mode is supported starting with vSphere 6.5 Update 2 and suitable for most deployments:

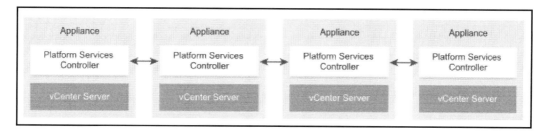

According to the vSphere-vCenter installation guide, `https://docs.vmware.com/en/VMware-vSphere/6.7/vsphere-vcenter-server-67-installation-guide.pdf`, the other features of vCenter Embedded Linked Mode include the following:

- No external PSC. This provides a more simplified domain architecture than an external deployment along with the enhanced linked mode.
- Provides a simplified HA process, removing the need for load balancers.
- Up to 15 vCenter Server Appliances can be linked together using vCenter Embedded Linked Mode and displayed in a single inventory view.

vCenter Server

VMware vSphere 6.7 is the last version that will support vCenter for Windows deployment. From the next version, vCSA will be the only option to run vCenter Server.

If you want to install vCenter for Windows with version 6.7 it is still fully supported deployment, but keep in mind that with the next upgrade, you will have to migrate vCenter for Windows to the vCSA.

vCenter Server provides the following services:

- **Web Client**: The vSphere Web Client lets you connect to vCenter Server instances by using a web browser so that you can manage your vSphere infrastructure.
- **Inventory Service**: This stores vCenter server inventory data and server application data. It also allows you to search the inventory objects across linked vCenter server instances.
- **Profile driven storage**: This is a component in VMware vSphere that allows users to intelligently provision applications, mapping VMs to storage levels according to pre-defined service levels, storage availability, performance requirements, or cost.
- **Auto Deploy**: This feature allows you to deploy and provision hundreds of physical servers and automatically install the ESXi hypervisor. Optionally, you can specify host profiles to apply to the hosts and a vCenter Server location (folder or cluster) for each host.
- **Syslog Collector**: ESXi system logs can be redirected to a vCenter server over the network, rather than storing them on a local disk. Using Syslog Collector, you can centralize the log management of all your ESXi servers.
- **Network Dump Collector**: This is the vCenter Server support tool. ESXi can be configured to save the VMkernel memory to a network server, rather than saving it to a disk when the system encounters a critical failure. Such memory dumps over the network will be collected by the vSphere ESXi Dump Collector.

Since version 6.5, vCenter Server Appliance is a preferred deployment type, and vCenter Server for Windows is still fully supported in vSphere 6.7 as well. If you want to follow VMware best practices, you should switch to vCSA.

Migration from vCenter for Windows to vCSA

If you are thinking about moving from vCenter for Windows to vCSA, you can use the migration wizard that is fully integrated into the vCSA installation.

During the migration, new vCSA appliance and PSC will be provisioned with a temporary IP address.

Once the temporary appliance (or appliances if you have a dedicated platform service controller) is up and running, the migration wizard will connect to the source vCenter for Windows (and PSC) and migrate the configuration and all performance data to the new vCSA.

In the end, the migration wizard will disconnect the source vCenter Server from the network (if you run the vCenter server in a virtualized environment) and change the temporary IP address of the new vCSA appliance to the production IP address of the previous vCenter server.

Where to install – physical or virtual?

One recurrent question about vCenter Server installation is whether it should be installed on a physical server or a VM. Technically, vCenter Server can be installed on both destinations, but I prefer deploying on a VM. Why?

If you have the vCenter Server installed on a VM and the ESXi that hosts the vCenter Server fails, HA will restart the VM on another node, ensuring service availability. If a physical server with vCenter Server installed fails, you lose not only the vCenter Server but all the services it provides. The best option would be having a management cluster with vCenter running on it (this perhaps makes more sense for large environments), but it would be an expensive solution the business could not afford/approve.

Another option could be placing the vCenter Server in the running cluster of your vSphere environment, a common approach for small environments. In large environments, if you need to shut down the infrastructure or perform some maintenance, it could be useful to know precisely which ESXi is hosting the vCenter Server without wasting time on research between hosts.

VMware recommends deploying vCenter Server on a VM, suggesting the use of the vCSA. vCSA is replacing the Windows-based vCenter Server which will be deprecated quite soon.

vCenter Server Appliance deployment

vCSA is prepackaged and preinstalled Photon Linux-based VM that provides vCenter and PSC services. As compared with old versions, vCSA now offers the same capabilities provided by the Windows-based version plus some exclusive services, such as native HA, native backup and restore, a migration tool, and improved appliance management.

With vSphere 6.7 you can run the vCSA GUI and CLI installers on Microsoft Windows 2012 x64 bit, Microsoft Windows 2012 R2 x64 bit, Microsoft Windows 2016 x64 bit, and macOS Sierra. The new capabilities make the appliance complete and ready to take over the Windows-based version.

The following is a short description of features available in vSphere 6.7:

- **Native HA**: This feature, available for vCSA only, is a solution to provide HA to your vCenter. You could have the active vCSA in one data center and the passive vCSA located in a DR or secondary data center. It removes the dependency on expensive third-party database clustering solutions of RDMs.
- **VUM**: This is now embedded into vCSA. You no longer need a separate Windows VM and an additional license.
- **HTML5 interface:** You no longer need to use the old Flex client. In vCenter 6.7, almost 95% of features are fully integrated into the new HTML5 client. VMware promises that all features will be available in vCenter 6.7U1, which should be available in Q4 2018.
- **Native backup and restore:** The process has been simplified with a new native file-based solution. It restores the vCenter Server configuration to a new appliance and streams backups to external storage using HTTP, FTP, or SCP protocols (vCSA only).

The installation procedure has been simplified, and now vCSA, and PSC installation is a two-stage process:

- **Stage 1:** Deploying OVF
- **Stage 2:** Configuration

This is a significant enhancement and provides not only better validation checks, but also you can take a snapshot between stages for rollback. Besides, you can create a template for additional deployments.

Introduced with vSphere 6.0 Update 1, the Appliance Management client (accessible at the address `https://<VCSA_IP>:5480`) simplified the configuration and upgrade process. Now you can patch or upgrade the appliance through ISO-or URL-based patching, simplifying the process and allowing you to save precious time.

vCSA updates can be applied directly from the VAMI using an intuitive GUI:

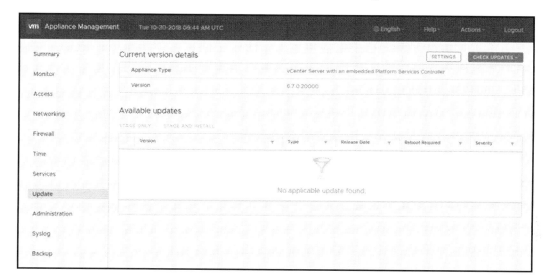

Please note that the update of vCSA is available only between minor versions, for example, from 6.7.0.10000 to 6.7.0.20000, not between major versions.

There are many more features of the management interface of vCSA, such as backup configuration, services overview, and storage consumption.

Why deploy vCSA instead of the Windows version?

There are several reasons why you should deploy vCSA:

- Being a packaged and installed vCenter, the deployment is quick, and you only need to supply a few details.
- The embedded PostgreSQL database supports up to 2,000 hosts and 35,000 VMs, so there is no difference in configuration maximums between vCenter for Windows and vCSA.
- No need for extra Microsoft Windows licenses. Since VUM is now embedded, there is no need for a separate Windows box.

- Having now identical features, it's only a matter of time before VMware drops the vCenter Windows version permanently.
- vCSA 6.7 runs on Photon Linux OS and generally is a more secure OS compared to Windows.
- Less hardware to use since vCSA can be deployed only as a VM. This allows you to reduce costs.

After having analyzed the reasons for making vCSA the preferred choice for your vCenter Server and the benefits it brings, let's walk through the installation process.

Installing the vCSA PSC

As the vCSA installer with a new look, independent of a browser, now also support macOS, Linux, and Windows, you can use the system you are more familiar with. Before proceeding with the installation, make sure you enter the new host in the DNS to both forward and reverse resolve. Perform the following steps:

1. Mount the ISO and run the installer.
2. When the main screen appears, there are four actions you can do—**Install**, **Upgrade**, **Migrate**, and **Restore**. Click on **Install**.
3. Click **Next** to begin stage 1. When prompted, accept the EULA and click **Next**.
4. As seen previously, the deployment type to use depends on the size of your environment. For this example, we are going to install vCenter Server with an external PSC. Select the option and click **Next**.
5. vCenter Server can be deployed with an external PSC by selecting the correct option in the installation wizard.
6. Specify the ESXi or vCenter target settings and the host credentials. Click **Next**.
7. Click **Yes** to accept the self-signed SSL certificate.
8. Enter the PSC name and the root password then click **Next**.
9. Next, you need to specify storage options. Here, you have the option to enable thin-provisioned disks, but this is not recommended for production environments. Click **Next**:

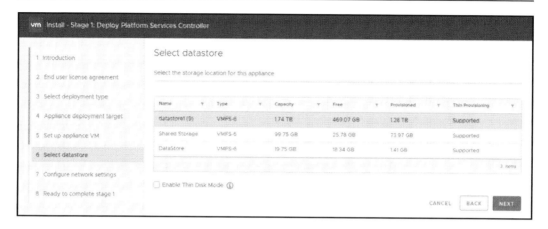

10. Configure the networking the vCSA appliance should use. Make sure the DNS for the IP used can both forward and reverse resolve to avoid errors. Click **Next**.

11. In the **Summary** window, click **Finish** to deploy the PSC.

12. When the deployment completes, click **Continue**. Stage 1 is now complete.

At this point, you can take a snapshot before proceeding with stage 2.

The installation continues with stage 2, performing the configuration of NTP and SSO services:

1. From the main screen, click **Next** to begin.

2. Time synchronization is the first option to configure to avoid communication issues with hosts. Here, you can also enable or disable SSH. Click **Next**.

3. Configure SSO, specifying a domain name, password, and site name. Click **Next**.

4. Feel free to join the **Customer Experience Improvement Program (CEIP)**. Make your choice and click **Next**.

5. In the Summary window, click **Finish**. This will complete stage 2 and the installation of the PSC

When the installation process is complete, the PSC is fully working and can be accessed via the browser.

Installing the vCSA vCenter

To install the vCSA vCenter, you should run the installer once again, repeating a similar procedure to that which was used to deploy the PSC component:

1. During the vCenter Server deployment procedure, at step 3 click **vCenter Server (Requires External Platform Services Controller)** under the **External Platform Services Controller** option and then click **Next**:

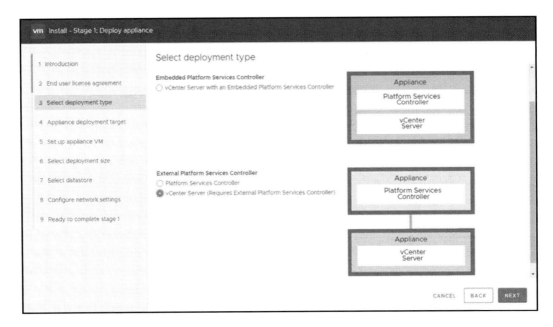

2. After specifying the storage options, in step 8 during stage 1 of the PSC deployment, you should specify the deployment size for the vCenter based on your environment. Make your choice then click **Next**.
3. Continue the installation procedure by following the remaining steps until you complete stage 1.
4. When the stage 2 installation process begins, click **Next**.

5. Specify NTP servers in the NTP servers (comma-separated list) field and set the SSH access option as Enabled. Click **Next** to continue the configuration.

6. In the SSO configuration page, specify the PSC appliance to connect, enter the SSO domain and SSO password, then click **Next**. You can create a new, or join an existing, SSO domain.

7. In summary, click **Finish** to complete the vCenter Server installation

In vSphere 6.7, the only way to log in to vCenter is through the two integrated web clients:

- **Flash-based web client**: `https://<VCSA_IP>/vsphere-client`
- **HTML5 web client**: `https://< VCSA _IP>/ui`

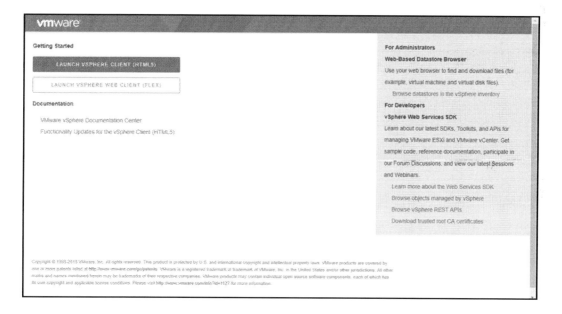

Installing the vCSA with Embedded Platform Service Controller

If you do not need to run separated Platform Service Controllers, the installation procedure is the same except in step 3 of the installation wizard. At this point, select **vCenter Server with an Embedded Platform Services Controller** as the deployment type:

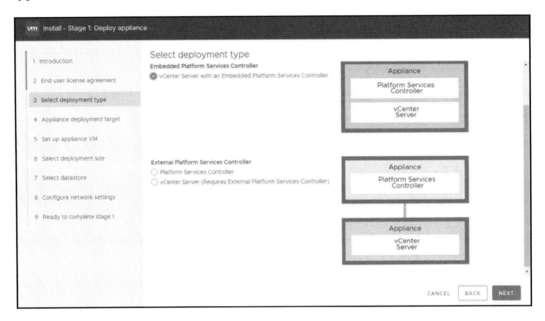

In stage 2 of the installation, instead of pointing your vCenter Server to the Platform Service Controller, you will have an option to create new SSO domain – a similar one as with PSC stage 2 configuration.

If you do not need to run separated PSCs (for example, because of the mixture of vCSA and vCenter Server for Windows), there is no need to run a dedicated PSC.

vCSA HA

In the past, you could only rely on vSphere HA which would automatically restart your vCSA in case of the hardware failure, but this might lead in the corrupted system state as with any other OS.

If you aren't familiar with vCenter HA, it is a feature introduced in vSphere 6.5 and available only for the vCSA. When you enable vCenter HA, secondary passive vCSA is deployed along with the witness appliance.

vCenter HA provides short RTO (about five minutes) for recovery of the vCenter Server. When the hardware where the active node is running fails, the passive vCenter Server will take over, shortening the total downtime of the vCenter Server. vCenter HA is a part of the vCenter Server Standard license, so no additional licensing is required.

vCenter HA is only available in the vCSA, and you can't deploy this configuration with vCenter for Windows.

vCenter HA configuration

The configuration of vCenter HA is pretty simple, and it's done from the vCenter server web client. At this stage, you can't use the new HTML5 interface, and the configuration is done through the older FLEX client:

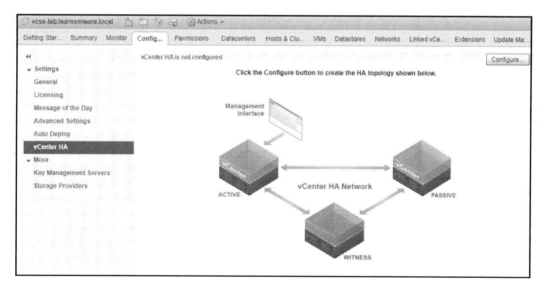

There are two deployment modes—basic and advanced.

With basic deployment, you need to run vCSA on the same environment that vCSA is managing. If you have a dedicated management cluster where your vCSA is installed, you need to perform advanced configuration since, during the vCenter HA setup, the source vCSA will be cloned, and this won't be possible if the vCSA is not located within the same environment, of course:

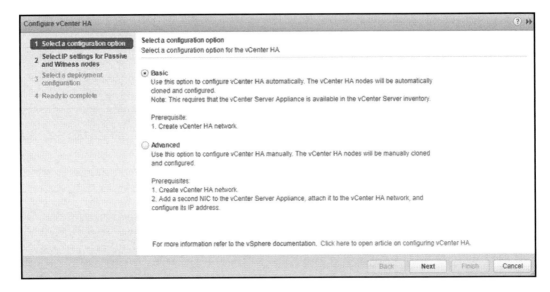

Once you have decided what deployment type you will need, you need to set up the HA network. The HA network is used for internal communication between two vCSA servers and the witness appliance.

As the last step, you need to configure settings for the peer vCSA and the witness appliance. On which datastore the appliances will be stored, portgroup association or cluster on which the VMs will be run:

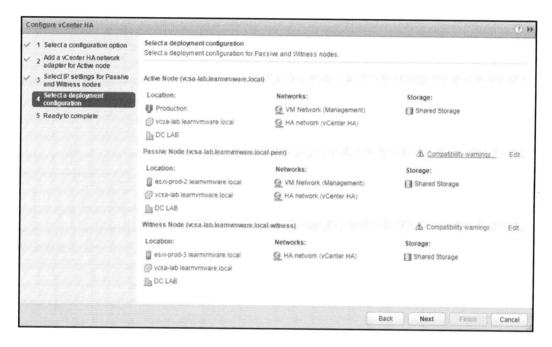

In this case, the configuration wizard complains about using the same datastore as the production VMs, which is not the best practice. You should always use dedicated datastores for your management and the production workloads. Once you hit **Finish**, you can check your running tasks to see at what stage the deployment is.

Once the deployment is finished, you will see the current state of the cluster, which is the active node, and the state of the passive node and witness appliances:

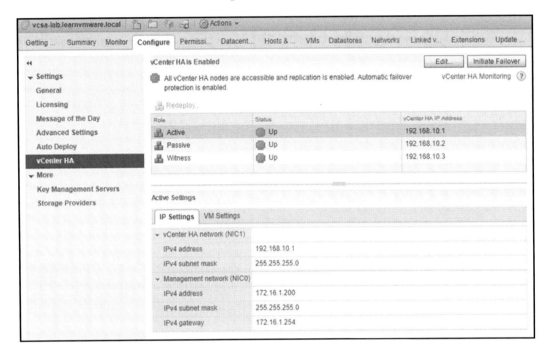

In the case of hardware failure, the passive appliance becomes active, and you will still be able to manage your environment even if the originating vCSA appliance is no longer available:

Please note that the failover process takes several minutes. If you try to access the web client of the vCSA during the failover, you will see that the failover is in progress.

Summary

For the successful deployment of VMware vSphere 6.7, understanding all the steps involved not only ensures the correct sizing of the hardware components but helps to avoid potential misconfigurations.

This chapter walked through the core components of vSphere 6.7, explaining the roles and services provided. The ESXi host is responsible for providing resources to workloads, while the vCenter Server is used to manage hosts and resource availability. To ensure a successful deployment, a deployment plan must be drawn up to define the correct hardware platform to use, storage architecture and protocols, and network configuration.

We explained in detail the different installation methods available to users for vSphere components to finalize the deployment. There are three ways to install ESXi hosts depending on the environment size—interactive installation, unattended using installation scripts, and automated which uses the vSphere Auto Deploy feature to install ESXi through PXE. The Auto Deploy feature is the most suitable method for the deployment of a large number of ESXi hosts, automating the process and ensuring configuration consistency within the whole environment.

The chapter also covered the vCenter Server components and how to install them correctly. vCSA 6.7 requires the deployment of two components—the PSC (used to manage SSO, License Service, and certificate management) and the vCenter Server. The vCenter Server can be installed with an embedded PSC or with an external PSC. As stated by VMware, the vCSA replaces the deprecated Windows-based vCenter Server.

You have also learned about vCSA HA, which provides enhanced availability for your management plane in the case of hardware failure.

Now that all the different vSphere components have been deployed, in the next chapter, we will discuss how to configure the entire virtual infrastructure.

Questions

1. What are the two core components of VMware vSphere deployment?
2. Can you directly update VMware vSphere 6.5 U2 to VMware vSphere 6.7?

   a) Yes
   b) No

3. What is VMware HCL?

   a) Hardware Configuration Layout
   b) Hardware Compatibility List
   c) Hyperconverged Classification List
   d) Hyperconverged Compatibility List
   e) Hardware Capacity List

4. Name three ESXi installation options.
5. What is a remote device in terms of ESXi installation?

6. Can you upgrade your ESXi installation using installation image?

    a) Yes
    b) No

7. TFTP server is bundled in vSphere AutoDeploy server:

    a) True
    b) False

8. What is PSC?

    a) Platform Solution Controller
    b) Persistent Storage Center
    c) Platform Service Controller
    d) Performance Service Center

9. Name at least three benefits of using vCSA over vCenter for Windows.
10. vCenter HA is available in all versions of vCenter Server:

    a) True
    b) False

Further reading

- **VMware Vsphere 6.5 Host Resources Deep Dive:** https://www.amazon.com/Vmware-Vsphere-Host-Resources-Deep/dp/1540873064/.

- **vSphere High Performance Cookbook - Second Edition:** https://www.packtpub.com/virtualization-and-cloud/vsphere-high-performance-cookbook-second-edition.

5
Configuring and Managing vSphere 6.7

This chapter will cover the configurations required by ESXi and vCenter Server to provide services and resources to a **virtual machine** (**VM**). We will look at how to set up the hypervisor properly, how to assign the correct IP address, and how to configure a time-synced network to get a working infrastructure.

This chapter will also walk through the configuration of the main parameters and features of **vCenter Server Appliance** (**vCSA**), such as **single sign-on** (**SSO**), **Active Directory** (**AD**), roles, permissions, and more. We'll explore how to manage data centers, clusters, and hosts efficiently using the new vSphere Client (HTML5 client). We will also focus on backing up the configuration of the ESXi hypervisor and vCSA.

The use of PowerCLI and the vSphere REST API are other important topics that will be covered in this chapter, because time-consuming tasks can be automated and executed in seconds using scripts, therefore reducing the workload for IT staff.

In this chapter, we will cover the following topics:

- Using the VMware vSphere HTML5 client
- Configuring ESXi
- Backing up and restoring ESXi
- Configuring vCSA
- Exporting and importing vCSA configuration
- Managing data centers, clusters, and hosts
- Automating tasks with scripts

Using the VMware vSphere HTML5 client

The HTML5 client was introduced in VMware vSphere 6.5 and it evolved significantly between that and VMware vSphere 6.7. vSphere 6.7 U1 was released on October 27, 2018, and, according to the enhancement list, the HTML5 interface now supports all the functions available in the FLEX client.

The new client, called vSphere Client (in this book, we will call it the HTML5 client to clarify the type of client), comes from the vSphere HTML5 Web Client Flings project (`https://labs.vmware.com/flings/vsphere-html5-web-client`). This client is still available if you want to add this functionality to a vSphere 6.0 infrastructure. With the release of vSphere 6.7, the reach of the HTML5 client development increased, covering 95% of the workflow.

The new client is entirely built on HTML5. It requires no plugins and is lighter and much faster than the flash-based client. The vSphere **Client Integration Plugin** (**CIP**) has been deprecated, and it no longer works for connecting vSphere 6.7 components. Both the flash and HTML5 clients are automatically installed as part of the vCenter deployment process. The HTML5 client can be accessed through `https://<VCSA_IP>/u`.

To log in to the ESXi host, version 6.7 provides a new built-in HTML5 client, which is available at `https://<VESXi_IP>/ui`. The HTML5 client started as the Flings project (`https://labs.vmware.com/flings/esxi-embedded-host-client`) and was later integrated into ESXi 6.0 U2, becoming the only client in version 6.7.

Configuring ESXi

When the installation of the ESXi host is complete, there is some configuration you need to do to connect the hypervisor with the network infrastructure. There are also other suggested configurations that you should perform after a clean installation of the ESXi hypervisor.

In this section, we'll walk through the main settings that you should configure.

Management network configuration

By default, ESXi is configured to receive the IP address for the management console through the **Dynamic Host Configuration Protocol (DHCP)**. If no DHCP server is present in your network, the hypervisor doesn't obtain an IP, and you won't be able to connect.

Assigning a dynamic IP address to ESXi is not a recommended configuration because management and services are linked to specific IP addresses assigned to the server. If the IP changes (after rebooting the host or for an expired lease), some services may not work as expected. If the server has multiple physical **network interface controllers (NICs)** installed and the DHCP assigns an IP address to an NIC linked to a wrong vSwitch, you may experience connectivity issues that will impede the connection to the management console, and you may not be able to manage the host.

Configuring a static IP address to the ESXi management console is the recommended configuration to adopt. The ESXi management console can be configured by accessing the **Direct Console User Interface (DCUI)** directly, or through the iLO, iDrac, IPMI, or similar (if your server has an integrated remote management console). Proceed with the following steps:

1. Access the ESXi console and press *F2* to access the **Customize System/View Logs** option.
2. When requested, enter the root password set during the installation process.
3. Select **Configure Management Network** from the **System Customization** menu and press *Enter*.
4. Select **Network Adapters** from the **Configure Management Network** menu and press *Enter*.
5. Using the spacebar, select the NIC to use for the ESXi management and press *Enter*. Press *D* to see details related to the selected NIC (for example, the attached vSwitch).
6. Now, select **IPv4 Configuration** and press *Enter* to assign a static IP address.

7. Use the spacebar to select the **Set static IPv4 address and network configuration** option, then configure the **IPv4 Address**, the **Subnet Mask**, and the **Default Gateway**. Press *Enter* to save the configuration, as demonstrated in the following screenshot:

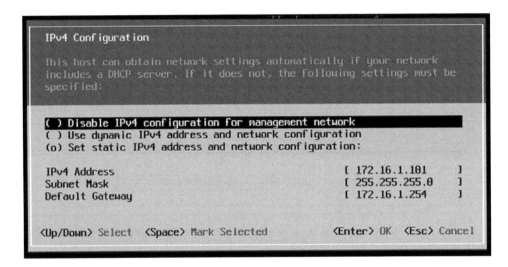

8. Select **DNS Configuration** to specify the **primary and alternate DNS servers** and the **hostname**. Press *Enter* to confirm the settings.
9. Select **Custom DNS Suffixes** to specify the suffix to use (lab.local, for instance). Press *Enter* to confirm.
10. Press *Esc* to exit the **Configure Management Network** console. Press *Y* to apply the changes when prompted.

As a best practice, you should always configure the DNS name of the system and use the **fully qualified domain name** (**FQDN**) when adding a host to vCenter Server.

Enabling Secure Shell (SSH) access

You may need to access the hypervisor through SSH for troubleshooting, or to perform some actions using **command-line interface** (**CLI**) commands. To access the ESXi host through SSH, you must enable the SSH protocol first, because it is disabled by default. For security reasons, it is suggested that you keep the SSH protocol disabled if it is not used. A warning message advises you that the SSH protocol is enabled, as shown in the following screenshot:

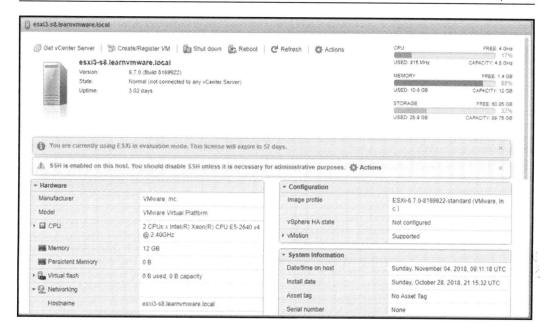

To enable SSH from the web console, log in to ESXi, and right-click the host. Select **Services | Enable Secure Shell (SSH)**.

To enable SSH from the DCUI, perform the following steps:

1. From **System Customization**, select the **Troubleshooting** option and press *Enter*.
2. Select **Enable SSH** and press *Enter* to change. SSH is now enabled.
3. The same procedure must be performed if you want to enable the ESXi Shell.
4. Press *Esc* to exit.

Based on VMware best practices and security hardening (which will be discussed in `Chapter 12`, *Securing and Protecting Your Environment*), I prefer to keep SSH running all the time. If there is an issue that needs to be troubleshot, I prefer to connect directly to the system without additional configuration steps.

If you don't like the warning notification that is displayed when the SSH service is enabled, you can alter the behavior with advanced configuration parameters. To configure the advanced parameters, perform the following steps:

1. From **Navigator**, select **Manage**, then from the **System** tab, select the **Advanced settings** option
2. Find the `User.Vars.SuppressShellWarning` variable
3. Edit the value of the property and change it to `1`

ESXi firewall

If you would like to harden the access to any ESXi service, you can also use the integrated firewall option of the ESXi hypervisor, so that only a limited number of IP addresses or IP ranges can access the service, as demonstrated in the following screenshot:

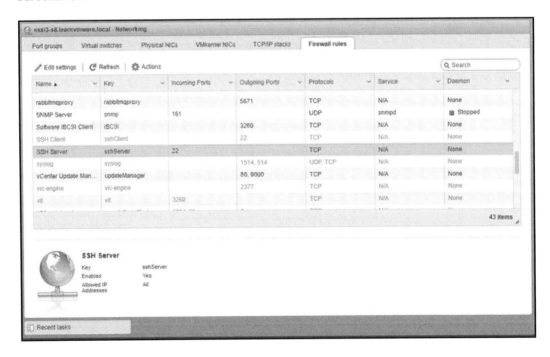

To reconfigure the ESXi firewall, perform the following steps:

1. Select **Networking** in **Navigator** and switch to **Firewall Rules**
2. Select the service you want to protect by a firewall

3. Click **Edit settings**
4. Configure the desired IP addresses or IP ranges

Note that you need to perform this configuration on every ESXi hypervisor. Also, keep in mind that misconfiguration can lead to several network-related consequences, as different VMware products may need to connect to the ESXi server as well.

 More information about the required TCP and UDP ports can be found at the following link: `https://kb.vmware.com/s/article/1012382`.

Configuring the Network Time Protocol (NTP)

Time synchronization in your network should always be configured, but sometimes users underestimate its importance because they believe that having the network time-synced is not that important. It is, however, critical. If the ESXi hosts are not in sync, you might face some communication issues between vSphere components that could cause a service outage. If you use AD in your network, for example, the **Domain Controllers** (**DCs**) and clients must be time-synced to avoid authentication problems. If the time between the DCs and clients differs by more than five minutes, Kerberos tickets will fail, and you will not be able to log in. By default, machines joined to a domain will contact the DC that holds the **Primary Domain Controller** (PDC) emulator role to synchronize the time.

If your network is not time-synced, you may experience authentication issues between **vCenter Server** and the **Platform Services Controller** (**PSC**). When vSphere components are not time-synced, the login procedure may fail due to communication issues between the PSC and vCenter.

VMs use VMware Tools (which will be discussed in `Chapter 8`, *Managing Storage Resources*) to synchronize the time with the host. Although a VM can be time-synced with the ESXi host using VMware Tools (VMs automatically synchronize the time when specific events occur, such as VM vMotion, snapshot creation, or guest OS reboots), it is recommended to synchronize the guest OS time with the NTP source instead.

To keep the time synchronized, ESXi supports the NTP, which you can configure through the vSphere Client. As a time source for your network, you should use a reliable external source, such as the `pool.ntp.org` project (a big virtual cluster of time servers providing a reliable, easy-to-use NTP service) or an internal source, such as a DC synchronized with an external time source.

Let's take a look at how to configure an NTP in your ESXi by performing the following steps:

1. Open the vSphere Client by typing the address, `https://<ESXi_IP>/ui` into your favorite browser, and log in to the host.
2. In the **Navigator**, select **Manage**. Go to the **System** tab and select **Time & date**.
3. Click **Edit settings** to open the time configuration window.
4. Select **Use Network Time Protocol (enable NTP client)** to specify the NTP parameters.
5. Select **Start and stop with port usage** (the recommended option) in the NTP service startup policy drop-down menu. In the NTP servers field, enter the NTP server to use. Specify the `pool.ntp.org` NTP servers to point the host to an external source directly, or enter the AD DC that holds the PDC emulator role configured to synchronize the time to an external source, to ensure the correct time.
6. Click **Save** to save the configuration.
7. Click **Action** and select **NTP service | Start** to start the service.

The time of the ESXi host is now synchronized with a reliable NTP server.

 VMware recommends that you use NTP instead of VMware Tools time synchronization, as NTP provides more precise timekeeping on VMs. For resiliency, you should always use two independent time source servers.

ESXi 6.7 partition layout

Regardless of the installation method you have chosen for your host, once the ESXi has been installed on the destination device, a specific partition layout is created on the disk. It is not possible to modify the partition layout during the installation process, and all the partitions are created automatically.

To identify the partition layout created by the installer in vSphere 6.5, you should use the `partedUtil` command, because the `fdisk` command was compatible with previous releases only. With the introduction of the **GUID Partition Table (GPT)** partition from ESXi 5.x, the `fdisk` command has been deprecated because it doesn't work anymore. To display the partition table, you need to access the ESXi console and run some specific commands.

Proceed as follows to display the partition table information:

1. SSH the ESXi and run the `ls /dev/disks -lh` command to identify the name of the system disk (usually, it is the only disk with more than one partition). As you can see in the following screenshot, the `mpx.vmhba0:C0:T0:L0` device has multiple partitions:

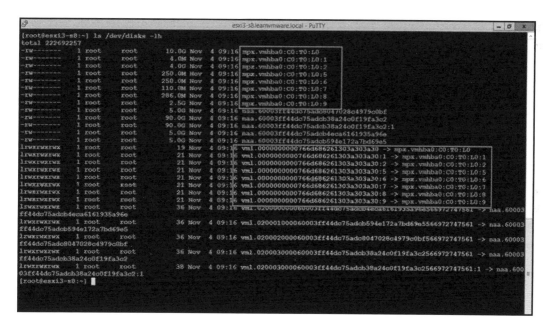

2. Once you have identified the system disk, you can use
   the `partedUtil` command with the `getptbl` option to see the partition
   size, as shown in the following screenshot:

```
esxi3-s8.learnvmware.local - PuTTY

[root@esxi3-s8:~] partedUtil getptbl /dev/disks/vml.0000000000766d686261303a303a30
gpt
1305 255 63 20971520
1 64 8191 C12A7328F81F11D2BA4B00A0C93EC93B systemPartition 128
5 8224 520191 EBD0A0A2B9E5443387C068B6B72699C7 linuxNative 0
6 520224 1032191 EBD0A0A2B9E5443387C068B6B72699C7 linuxNative 0
7 1032224 1257471 9D27538040AD11DBBF97000C2911D1B8 vmkDiagnostic 0
8 1257504 1843199 EBD0A0A2B9E5443387C068B6B72699C7 linuxNative 0
9 1843200 7086079 9D27538040AD11DBBF97000C2911D1B8 vmkDiagnostic 0
2 7086080 15472639 EBD0A0A2B9E5443387C068B6B72699C7 linuxNative 0
[root@esxi3-s8:~]
```

You can also check the partition layout from the ESXi web client, as follows:

1. Select **Storage** from **Navigator** and switch to the **Devices** tab
2. Click on the device that was used for the installation

Looking at the preceding screenshots, the ESXi 6.7 host partition layout created by the
ESXi installer can be composed of up to eight partitions. Partitions 2 and 3 may not be
visible if the host is installed on SD cards or USB flash drives. Here are details
regarding the partitions:

- **1 (systemPartition 4 MB)**: The partition needed for booting.
- **5 (linuxNative 250 MB—/bootbank)**: The core hypervisor VMkernel.
- **6 (linuxNative 250 MB—/altbootbank)**: This partition is initially empty
  because no previous version of ESXi is available.
- **7 (vmkDiagnostic 110 MB)**: This partition is used to write the host dump
  file if ESXi crashes.
- **8 (linuxNative 286 MB—/store)**: This partition contains the VMware Tools
  ISO file for the supported OS.
- **9 (vmkDiagnostic 2.5 GB)**: This is the second diagnostic partition.
- **2 (linuxNative 4.5 GB—/scratch)**: This partition is created to store the VM-
  support output needed for VMware support. It is not created on SD cards
  or USB flash drives.
- **3 (VMFS datastore)**: The available and unallocated space of the disk is
  formatted as VMFS5 or VMFS, depending on the ESXi version. This
  partition is not created on SD cards or USB flash drives.

Boot banks

Looking at the preceding partition list, you may notice that partitions 5 and 6 are named **primary boot bank** and **alternate boot bank**. These partitions are a failsafe. The ESXi system has two independent banks of memory, each of which stores a full system image. When a fresh ESXi installation is performed, partition 6 is empty.

During the system upgrade, the new version is loaded into the inactive bank of memory and the updated bank is set to be used when the ESXi reboots. If the boot process fails for any reason, the system automatically boots from the previously used bank of memory. You can also manually choose which image to use for that boot at boot time.

Scratch partition

In the partition layout, we saw that a scratch partition is created during the ESXi installation procedure. A scratch partition is a 4 GB VFAT partition used for storing temporary data, including logs, diagnostic information, and system swaps. Although a scratch partition is not required, VMware recommends that ESXi has a persistent scratch location available. If a scratch partition is not configured, /scratch is located on the **ramdisk** linked to /tmp/scratch.

Leaving the scratch partition on the ramdisk will affect the performance and the memory optimization, so it is recommended to create the partition in a suitable destination. If ESXi is installed on a destination, such as an SD card or a USB stick, the scratch partition is not created. As a result, an annoying warning message will be displayed in the UI, which advises you to set persistent storage for logs.

To configure the scratch partition, it is necessary to have a VMFS or NFS volume attached to the server to host the log files, but of course, you would have that anyway, for your VM to live on.

Perform the steps as follows:

1. Access ESXi using the **vSphere Client** and click the **Manage** item.
2. Go to the **System** tab and select **Advanced settings** to access the advanced settings.

3. In the search field, type `scratch`, then press **Enter** to find the parameter key needed to modify the partition location. The `scratchConfig.CurrentScratchLocation` key contains the current location of the scratch partition. Edit the `ScratchConfig.ConfiguredScratchLocation` key and enter a unique directory path for this host, such as `/vmfs/volumes/DatastoreUUID/DatastoreFolder`.

4. Reboot the host for the changes to take effect.

Messages from the VMkernel and other system components are useful to identify the status of the host. Potential issues are written to the log by the ESXi's syslog service, `vmsyslogd`.

To modify or configure the log location, you should perform the following steps:

1. Open the vSphere Client and select **Manage**.
2. Go to the **System** tab and click **Advanced settings** under **System**.
3. Search for the `Syslog.global.logDir` key that specifies where the logs are stored. The `/scratch` directory can be located on mounted NFS or VMFS volumes using the `[datastorename] path_to_file` syntax, where the path is relative to the root of the volume backing the datastore.
4. Click **OK** to save the configuration. Changes to the syslog options take effect immediately.

Centralized log management

As a best practice, you should consider using a centralized system for all logs in your infrastructure to cover all elements, instead of only using VMware vSphere to correlate events.

For example, let's say that at 17:01:03, your ESXi hypervisor loses half of the active paths to the storage array. If you have a centralized log management system in place, you can easily search the logs, and you might find that at the same time, your data center switched to the UPS system because of a power failure, but one of the switches went down (the power supply in the switch was not connected to the UPS system).

There are several products you can use for this kind of task. Some are free, and others aren't.

vRealize Log Insight

vRealize Log Insight is a product offered by VMware that has many capabilities on a single syslog server.

It has powerful add-ons that help you better understand your vSphere environment and it allows you to easily drill down through your whole environment.

vRealize Log Insight comes as an OVA appliance that you can quickly deploy to your vSphere environment. Using its powerful HTML5 interface, you can access all the logs from the entire infrastructure, as demonstrated in the following screenshot:

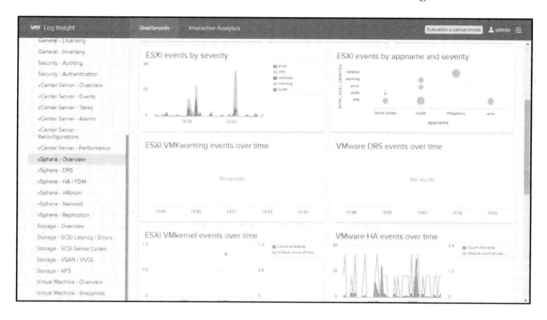

In the past, Log Insight was a free product that was available automatically with your vCenter server license. Recently, however, there were changes in the licensing. vRealize Log Insight 4.6 is the last available version that you can use for free.

VMware is announcing the **End of Availability (EoA)** of vRealize Log Insight for vCenter Server starting with the next release and all future releases of Log Insight. The current version of Log Insight, version 4.6.x, is the last release that will support the Log Insight for vCenter Server capability. The next release will not accept vCenter Server license keys for activation. For more information, please visit the following link: `https://blogs.vmware.com/vsphere/2018/07/ vrealize-log-insight-for-vcenter-server-end-of- availability.html`.

Free syslog servers

There are many free syslog servers that you can easily install to your Windows or Linux environment to provide centralized log management capabilities, including the following:

- **Splunk Light**: `https://www.splunk.com/en_us/download/splunk-light. html`
- **Kiwi syslog server**: `https://www.solarwinds.com/free-tools/kiwi- free-syslog-server`
- **PRTG**: `https://www.paessler.com/free_syslog_server`

Syslog configuration

To configure the syslog server, you should perform the following configuration tasks on each ESXi hypervisor:

1. From **Navigator**, select **Manage | System | Advanced settings**
2. Search for the `Syslog.global.loghost` configuration value
3. Click **Edit Settings** and provide the **IP address or FQDN** of your syslog server

Backing up and restoring ESXi

ESXi hypervisor is the same as any other server or network device, so you need to take into account the **configuration backup**. While the installation only takes a couple of minutes, the backup contains configuration files concerning virtual switches and their configuration, shared storage (datastore configurations), multi-paths, local users and groups, and also licensing information.

This is why you should perform regular backups of your ESXi infrastructure. If something goes wrong, you can install a new ESXi hypervisor and restore the configuration to get the desired state within the blink of an eye.

Backing up and restoring ESXi using CLI

If your infrastructure is not that big, you can perform individual backups of the ESXi servers using CLI. This might not be a good approach for larger infrastructures, for which you might prefer to automate the whole task.

To perform an individual backup using CLI, perform the following steps:

1. Connect to the ESXi server using SSH
2. Run the following command: `vim-cmd hostsvc/firmware/sync_config` And `vim-cmd hostsvc/firmware/backup_config`
3. As an output, you will receive a URL, from which you can download the backup file

To restore an individual ESXi server, perform the following steps:

1. Upload the backup file to the ESXi hypervisor (either using the SCP protocol with WinSCP, for example, or by directly uploading the file to the datastore).
2. Connect to the ESXi server over SSH.
3. Enter **Maintenance Mode** using `vim-cmd hostsvc/maintenance_mode_enter`.
4. The backup file should be located in the `/tmp/` folder. To copy the file to the location, you can use the `cp` command: `cp /vmfs/volumes/datastore1/RESTORE/configBundle-esxi-prod-4.learnvmware.local.tgz /tmp/configBundle.tgz`.
5. Restore the configuration using `vim-cmd hostsvc/firmware/restore_config /tmp/configBundle.tgz`.
6. ESXi will automatically reboot so be prepared for this.

Backing up and restoring ESXi using PowerCLI

Sometimes, you might want to either automate the backup tasks, schedule them to run periodically, or perform them on dozens of ESXi hypervisors. Using a simple CLI approach is not the most effective way to do this, but you can use PowerCLI, an automation tool, to perform these kind of operations. We will discuss PowerCLI itself later in this chapter, so at this stage, let's take a look at how to use it.

Backing up using PowerCLI

To perform a backup of the ESXi server, perform the following steps:

1. Launch PowerCLI
2. Connect to the ESXi server using the `Connect-VIserver` command
3. Issue the `GetVMhostFirmware` command to receive the backup file

Restoring using PowerCLI

If you need to restore the ESXi server, perform the following steps:

1. Launch PowerCLI
2. Connect to the destination ESXi server using `Connect-VIserver`
3. Place the host in maintenance mode using `Set-VMhost ESXi-name -State Maintenance`
4. Restore the configuration through `Set-VMhostFirmware`

It might look as though something went wrong, and the restore operation did not happen, but this is not the case. Again, immediately after issuing this command, the host initializes the reboot cycle, so PowerCLI loses its connection to the ESXi server.

Backing up all ESXi servers within a single vCenter server

Let's have a look at a simple script that will backup all of your ESXi servers that are connected to a single vCenter Server.

The most simple version of the script will include the following commands:

```
connect-viserver -server VCSA_FQDN -user administrator@vsphere.local -
password PassW0rd

$esxi_all = get-vmhost

foreach ($esxi in $esxi_all){
 Get-VMHostFirmware -vmhost $esxi -BackupConfiguration -
DestinationPath c:\esxibackups
 }
```

Now, if you check your backup folder, you will see the backups from all ESXi servers.

You can easily tweak the script to save the files in dedicated folders for each ESXi server, and store several versions of the configuration based on your preferences and backup schedule.

Configuring vCSA

When the deployment of the vCSA is complete, as part of the installation, the vSphere Web Client and the new HTML5 client are available to access the appliance. Both clients rely on the Tomcat web service to access the appliance, and no third-party software is required. As explained in Chapter 4, *Deployment Workflow and Component Installation*, in vSphere 6.5, login to the appliance can be done using both flash-based and HTML5-based web clients.

In your favorite browser, type the following addresses:

- **Flash-based client (vSphere Web Client)**:
  `https://<VCSA_IP>/vsphere-client`
- **HTML5 client (vSphere Client)**: `https://< VCSA _IP>/ui`

Basic setup using the vCenter Server Appliance Management Interface (VAMI)

Let's walk through the basic configuration that you should do on your vCenter Server instance to ensure the correct functionality. The configuration of the vCSA can be easily managed using the VAMI, which allows you to export logs, configure NTP, enable/disable SSH, and more. The same configuration can also be made using the vSphere Client.

Modifying the IP address and DNS

Although you configure the IP address and DNS during the deployment process, you can further modify the parameters through the VAMI. The steps to do this are as follows:

1. To modify the IP address and DNS, log in as root to the VAMI and select **Networking**.
2. Access the **Manage** tab and click the **Edit button** in the **Hostname**, **Name Servers**, and **Gateways** area and modify the network parameters.
3. Click **OK** to apply the new settings.

Exporting a support bundle

For diagnosing and troubleshooting purposes, you can export a support bundle that contains the log files of the running vCenter Server instance. The bundle can be submitted to VMware support for assistance or analyzed locally on your machine.

To export the log files, proceed as follows:

1. Log in as root to the VAMI
2. Click on the **Actions** and select a **Create Support Bundle** button to save the bundle in the `.tgz` format somewhere in your local machine, as demonstrated in the following screenshot:

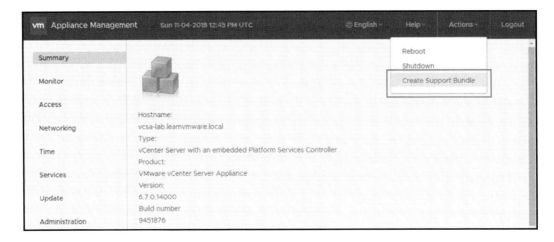

Configuring time synchronization

We have already discussed the importance of having the network time synchronized. If vCenter Server is connected to an external PSC and the time is not synchronized, you may experience authentication issues. To avoid this problem, make sure you configure the same time synchronization source.

To configure time synchronization, follow these steps:

1. From the VAMI, go to the **Time** tab to configure the time zone and time synchronization.
2. In the **Time zone** area, click the **Edit** button to configure the correct time zone.
3. In the **Time Synchronization** area, click the **Edit** button and set the **Mode** field as NTP, then specify the **NTP source servers**.
4. Click **OK** to save the setup.

Changing the vCSA password

Changing the vCSA root password on a regular basis is a good way to enforce security.

The steps for changing the vCSA password are as follows:

1. From the VAMI, go to the **Administration** tab to change the password
2. Under the **Password** area, click **Change** and type the current password and enter a new one twice
3. Click **Submit** to save the changes

Licensing

VMware vSphere 6.7 is available as a 60-day, fully working trial, to give administrators the opportunity to test the product's functionalities and the services provided. When the evaluation license expires, you need to insert a valid license composed of a 25-character alphanumeric string to re-enable the functionalities in ESXi and vCenter Server in order to avoid a service outage.

The available services are strictly related to the applied license. VMware vSphere ESXi is licensed per processor, and this means that you need a valid license key for each physical CPU installed in the physical server. The license key can be used on different servers since it doesn't contain any server-related information and it's not tied to a specific hardware. You don't have any restrictions concerning physical cores or physical RAM, and the number of VMs you can run is unlimited if the proper license is applied.

VMware vSphere 6.7 comes in the following three editions:

- **vSphere Standard Edition**: This is the entry-level solution that allows for basic server consolidation.
- **vSphere Enterprise Plus Edition**: This edition offers all the features of vSphere and ensures application availability and business continuity.
- **vSphere with Operations Management Enterprise Plus Edition**: This edition offers all the features of vSphere.

Besides this, there are two Essential editions provided as full kits developed for small environments that need to save costs, where you can have up to three hosts with a maximum of two physical CPUs each (each kit includes six processor licenses and one vCenter Server Essential license):

- **Essential**: This provides basic functionality only and doesn't protect the running VM if one ESXi fails.
- **Essential Plus**: This offers services, such as vMotion or vSphere HA, to ensure business continuity and data protection.

You can refer to `Chapter 1`, *Evolution to vSphere 6.7*, for additional information about licensing.

To centralize the management of ESXi hosts and VMs and enable the available services, you need one instance of a vCenter Server. vCenter Server comes in the three following editions:

- **vCenter Server Essentials**: This is used for management of vSphere Essential kits and is integrated with the bundle.
- **vCenter Server Foundation**: This license is bundled with several vSphere bundles, especially with ROBO licenses. This vCenter server can manage a maximum of four ESXi hypervisors.
- **vCenter Server Standard**: This allows you to take advantage of all of the features available in vSphere, such as vSphere vMotion, vSphere HA, vSphere DRS, and so on.

Using vCSA is the simplest method to apply and manage the license across the infrastructure. Bear in mind that licensing is a service provided by the PSC.

 If you configure the vCenter Server HA feature, you don't need to license a separate vCenter Server Standard instance for the Passive or Witness node.

To enter a new vCenter Server license, proceed with the following steps. First, you need to install the license itself. Installing the license does not mean that you assign it:

1. From the vSphere **Web Client**, go to the **Administration** and select **Licenses** under the **Licensing** option. Click on the **Add New License** button to insert a new license key.
2. Fill in the license key you want to add to the inventory. It might be vCenter Server license, an ESXi license, or any other VMware product.
3. Once the license is installed, you can browse all your available licensed products in the **Assets** tab.
4. To assign a license to a windows server, go to the **Configure** tab of your vCenter Server.
5. Under **Settings**, click **Licensing**.
6. Click **Assign License** and select the license you want to assign to this vCenter Server.

Depending on the license you have chosen, in the **Overview** tab, you will see which license is currently assigned, the license expiry date (some of the licenses may be valid only for a limited time), and which features are included in the license.

Roles and permissions

Permissions specify the privileges (the tasks a user can perform) an authenticated user or group has on a specific vCenter Server object and can be assigned at different levels of a hierarchy. For example, you can assign permissions to a cluster object or a data center object. The best practice is to assign only the required permissions, to increase the security and to have a more explicit permissions structure. The use of folders to group objects based on specific permissions makes the vSphere administration simpler.

There are also global permissions that are applied to a global root object to grant the user or group privileges for all objects in all hierarchies. Use global permissions carefully, because you assign permissions to all objects in the inventory.

Roles are a set of permissions you can assign to users to perform specific tasks on inventory objects. There are some default roles predefined on vCenter Server, such as **Administrator, Read-only**, and **No access**, which cannot be modified. Other roles, such as network administrator, are defined as sample roles. You can create new roles or clone and modify existing roles. It is advisable to clone an existing profile instead of creating a new one to avoid potential security issues.

From vSphere 6.5, there is a new role called no cryptography administrator. This role contains the same set of permissions as the administrator role, but the user assigned with this role is not able to perform any encryption or decryption tasks. The idea is that sometimes you need to ensure that the VMs stay encrypted at all costs, but at the same time your vSphere administrators must be able to perform any configurations necessary. For this reason, no cryptography administrator role was introduced.

You can manage the vCSA roles from the **Administration** menu. Follow these steps to create or modify a new role:

1. To create a new role, select the role you want to start from and click on the clone role action icon.
2. Specify a role name, add a description (optional), then click **OK**.
3. Select the just-created role and click the edit icon to edit the role action.
4. Enable all the actions the new role should be able to perform, then click **Next**.
5. You can modify the role name and the description of the role if necessary. Click **Finish** to save the role configuration. You can navigate the **DESCRIPTION**, **USAGE**, and **PRIVILEGES** tabs to get an overview of the granted permissions and to which objects the created role has been assigned, as shown in the following screenshot:

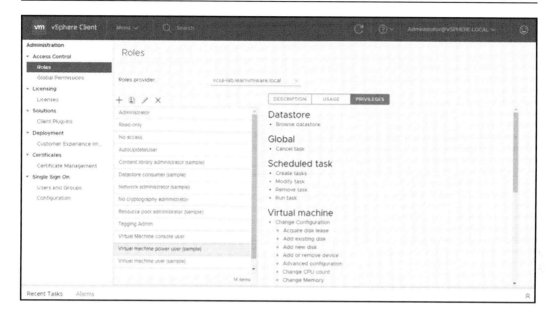

Once a role has been defined, you need to assign the role to an authenticated user or group. Where possible, it's recommended to assign permissions to groups instead of users for better and more efficient management.

To assign a role to a user or a group, proceed with the following steps:

1. From the vSphere Client, select the object you want to assign permissions to and click on the **Permissions** tab.
2. Click the add icon button to access the wizard.
3. Specify the domain to use from the **User/Group** drop-down menu, then search for or type the user or group name you want to use. The user or group can be a member of localos, SSO domain, AD, or other identity sources.
4. From the **Role** drop-down menu, select the role you want to assign to the selected user or group. It is recommended to enable the **Propagate to children** option to also apply the role to child objects. This will not only propagate the permission to the current child, but to the newly created children as well.
5. Click **OK** to save the settings.

6. **Defined In** refers to which objects in the hierarchy the permission is configured on. Let's assume that we have created a permission somewhere within the hierarchy. If you click on any object that is a child of that object, you will see the level on which the permission was configured.

AD integration

The vCenter Server can be integrated with an external identity source, so you do not need to configure individual user accounts or groups on the vCenter Server level, but instead use a centralized database.

There are three possible integrations, as follows:

- **Active Directory** through **Integrated Authentication**
- **Active Directory** through **LDAP**
- **LDAP server**

As you can see, you can use either Active Directory as a central user and groups database or any LDAP-enabled identity source. In most environments, you will find that Active Directory through the Integrated Authentication mode is used more than the traditional LDAP approach since the configuration is much simpler. If you want to configure the Integrated Authentication mode, you must join the PSC instance or the vCSA to the AD domain. This allows the AD users to log in to vCenter Server using the Windows session authentication **Security Support Provider Interface** (**SSPI**).

The procedure to join vCenter Server to an AD domain depends on how the vCSA and the PSC have been deployed:

- If you deployed the **vCSA with an embedded PSC**, you need to join the vCSA to the AD domain
- If you deployed the **vCSA with an external PSC**, you need to join the PSC to the AD domain

 The use of a **Read-Only Domain Controller** (**RODC**) in an AD domain to join a PSC or a VCSA with an embedded PSC is not supported. Only a writable DC must be used to join the AD domain.

To join a vCSA with an embedded PSC to the AD, follow these steps:

1. Select **Administration**, **Single Sign-On**, and **Configuration**.
2. Click on the **Active Directory** tab and click **Join AD**.
3. Enter the domain to join in the **Domain** field and, optionally, the organizational unit. Specify the AD username in the UPN format (`username@domain.com`) with the privileges to join the PSC and the password. Click **OK** to confirm.
4. When the process completes, the joined domain is listed in the **Domain** field, and a new **Leave** button is displayed.
5. You need to reboot the node to enable the changes. Since this option is not available from the vSphere Client, switch to the VAMI management of the vCSA and, from **Actions**, click **Reboot**.
6. When the node has been rebooted, navigate to **Configuration | Identity Sources** to add the AD domain. Click to open the **ADD IDENTITY SOURCE** wizard, as demonstrated in the following screenshot:

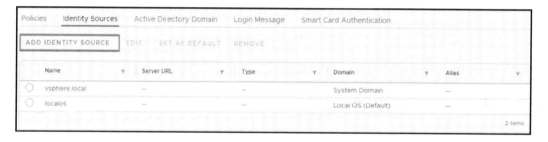

7. Select the **Active Directory (Integrated Windows Authentication)** option and enter the joined FQDN domain name if it's not displayed automatically.
8. Select the **Use machine account** option to use the local machine account as **Service Principal Name** (**SPN**). If you expect to rename the machine, don't use this option, because it will break the authentication process. Click **OK** to confirm the specified AD domain as the new identity source.
9. In the **Identity Sources** tab, the joined AD domain is now displayed. You can assign permissions to users or group members of the AD domain.

You can select the added **AD domain** and click on the **Set as Default Domain** icon to make the new identity source the default domain.

Once the integration is done, you can assign the permissions for Active Directory Users or Groups. All you need to do is select the Active Directory domain instead of the default single sign-on domain.

Configuring ESXi with AD authentication

An ESXi host can also be joined to an AD domain to allow users and groups to manage the hypervisor. When the host is added to AD, the domain group **ESX Admins** is granted full administrative access to the host, as follows:

1. Log in to the host through a web console by entering the address `https://<ESXi_IP>/ui` in your favorite browser, then select the **Manage** menu.

2. Go to the **Security & users** tab and select the **Authentication** sub-menu. Click on the **Join domain** field to join the host to the domain, as shown in the following screenshot:

3. Enter the domain name and the credentials of an AD user with sufficient permissions to join computers to the domain. Click on the **Join Domain** button.

You might also change the default group that is granted an administrator role within ESXi by changing the advanced default configuration setting `Config.HostAgent.plugins.hostsvc.esxAdminsGroup`.

Once you have created the **ESX Admins** Active Directory group and assigned an Active Directory user to it, you can try to **log in** to the ESXi server using AD credentials, as shown in the following screenshot:

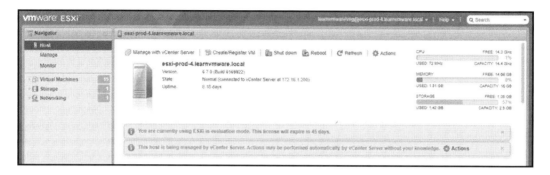

Of course, you can also assign individual Active Directory users or groups specific permissions on the ESXi itself. There is one caveat, however, which is that the web UI of the ESXi server is not able to browse the Active Directory itself, so you need to manually enter the username or the group name using `domain\user_or_group` as the user account.

Installing the VMware Enhanced Authentication plugin

To allow users to log in using **Integrated Windows Authentication**, you need to install the **VMware Enhanced Authentication** plugin. This plugin replaces the **Client Integration Plugin** (**CIP**) from vSphere 6.0.

In addition to Integrated Windows Authentication, the VMware Enhanced Authentication plugin also provides Windows-based smart card functionality. If you have the old CIP from a previous vSphere version installed on your machine, both plugins can coexist, and there are no conflicts.

The installation of the plugin is simple and straightforward:

1. Using your favorite browser, open the vSphere Client by typing the address of your vCenter Server, `https://<VCSA_IP>/ui`.
2. Click the **Download Enhanced Authentication** plugin option at the bottom of the page.
3. Save the plugin on your machine and run the installer.
4. When the installation has completed, refresh your browser. A **Launch Application** window may pop up in this step, asking for permission to run the **Enhanced Authentication** plugin.

If the VMware **Enhanced Authentication** plugin is installed from an Internet Explorer browser, you need to disable **Protected Mode** and enable pop-up windows.

vCSA and PSC

As seen previously, from vSphere 6.0, vCenter is composed of the PSC and vCenter Server components. The PSC is a multi-master model component that provides licensing, authentication, and certificate services. If the PSC fails, these services stop working and consequently, the entire infrastructure will no longer work.

During the design of your virtual infrastructure, you should consider the option of installing and configuring two PSCs at the site to ensure availability. You may need to connect vCenter Server to another external PSC or to point the vCSA with an embedded PSC to an external PSC.

Let's see how to configure vCenter Server to point to different PSCs.

Repointing the vCSA to another external PSC

If the external PSC fails, or if you want to distribute the load of an external PSC, you can configure the vCenter Server instance to point to a different PSC in the same domain and site.

The steps are as follows:

1. SSH the vCenter Server instance using the root credentials and enable the shell.
2. To repoint vCenter Server, run the following command:

   ```
   cmsso-util repoint --repoint-psc psc_fqdn
   ```

   Here, `psc_fqdn` is the FQDN (the value is case-sensitive) or the static IP address of the external PSC.

3. Using the vSphere Client, log in to the vCenter Server instance to verify that the instance is running and that you can manage it. The vCenter Server instance is now registered with the new PSC.

For more information visit the official VMware **Knowledge Base** (**KB**): https://kb.vmware.com/s/article/2113917.

Pointing the vCSA with an embedded PSC to an external PSC

If the vCenter Server instance has been deployed with an **embedded PSC** and you want additional vCenter Server instances in your SSO domain, you can modify the vCenter Server instance configuration to point to an external PSC. This configuration is a **one-way process** only, and it's not possible to switch back to the previous configuration with an embedded PSC.

Before proceeding, take snapshots of both the vCenter Server with the embedded PSC and the external PSC, so that you can go back if anything goes wrong during configuration.

To point the vCSA with an embedded PSC to an external PSC, you should perform the following steps:

1. SSH the vCenter Server with the embedded PSC using the root credentials and enable the shell.
2. Verify that all services are running in the PSC using the following command:

```
service-control --status --all
```

The services that must be running are as follows:

- VMware License Service
- VMware Identity Management Service
- VMware Security Token Service
- VMware Certificate Service
- VMware Directory Service

3. To reconfigure the vCenter Server, use the following command:

```
cmsso-util reconfigure --repoint-psc psc_fqdn --username
username --domain-name domain --passwd password
```

4. Using the vSphere Client, log in to the vCenter Server instance to verify that the instance is running, and that you can manage it. If the procedure has completed successfully, the vCenter Server with the embedded PSC is now demoted and redirected to the external PSC.

Resetting the SSO password

There are some situations in which you need to reset the SSO password to recover access to the PSC due to a forgotten password.

Follow this procedure to reset the SSO password:

1. SSH the PSC or vCenter Server with the embedded PSC appliance as a root user and enable the shell with the `shell.set --enabled true` command, then type `shell`. Press *Enter*.
2. Run the `/usr/lib/vmware-vmdir/bin/vdcadmintool` command to load the console and manage the password reset.
3. Select **option 3**. Reset the account password and, when prompted, enter the account UPN (such as `administrator@vsphere.local`), as shown in the following screenshot:

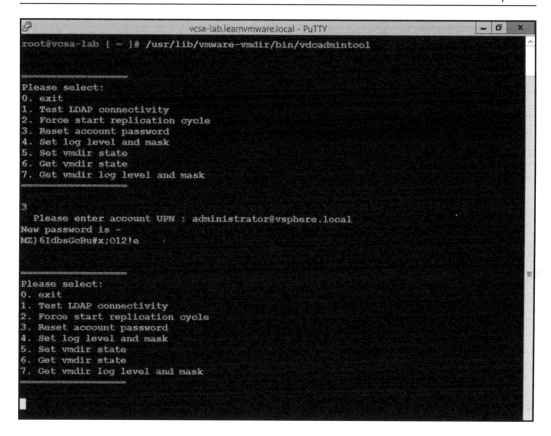

4. A new password is generated. Use this password to log in to the system with the user for which you want to reset the password (for example, `administrator@vsphere.local`).

5. Once you are successfully logged in to the vSphere Client using the password generated by the system, click **Users and Groups** under the **Single Sign-On** menu, and then select the **Users** tab.

6. Select the account used to log in and click the edit icon to set a **new password**. Enter the new password twice and click **OK** to confirm the change.

Exporting and importing the vCSA configuration

As we have already described, backing up your infrastructure should be a routine task. This should also be the case for the vCSA. In the past, it was possible to configure a one-time backup of the vCSA using the VAMI, but for periodical backups, you have to create a custom shell script. This is not required anymore; with VMware vSphere 6.7, you can even configure a backup schedule through the VAMI.

The vCSA backup procedure

To configure a backup of the vCSA, follow these steps:

1. Connect to the vCSA VAMI
2. Select **Backup** from the left-hand menu
3. Click **Configure** to configure a backup schedule
4. You have the option to configure several parameters of the backup schedule, as follows:
    - **Backup location**: Points to the `ftp/scp/nfs` location that will be used for backups
    - **Backup server credentials**: The login used to access the backup server
    - **Schedule**: Indicates when the backup should be performed
    - **Encryption**: You might choose to encrypt the backup if the data is stored in a non-secure location
    - **Number of backups**: How many backups should be retained
    - **Data**: Which tables should be saved in the backup
5. Once the backup is configured, it will start to perform the backups based on your schedule, as demonstrated in the following screenshot:

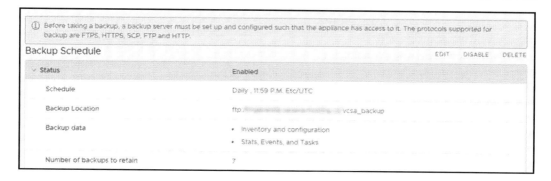

In the **Activity** window, you will see all backups that were performed and some additional information about them. From here, you have the option to take a manual backup outside of the configured backup schedule.

You can also explore the backup server location. Depending on the backup server configuration, you might use, for example WinSCP, to browse the backup server (for SCP or FTP backup-type locations).

As you can see, at this time, I have only one backup on the backup server. We can see that it was a manual backup (as indicated by the M_ in the name) with the timestamp when the backup was taken.

vCSA restoration procedure

To restore your vCSA from a backup, you need the installation image of the vCenter Server containing the same vCSA version that you are about to restore. The restoration process installs a fresh new vCSA server and then performs a restoration from the backup location. It does not repair the existing vCSA, as follows:

1. Based on your operating system, launch the installation wizard.
2. From the main menu, select **Restore**.
3. The wizard follows the same steps as the installation itself. In the third step, you need to specify the backup location. You do not need to provide the full path to the backup. A first-level backup folder will do the trick.
4. Once you click **Next**, the backup browser will appear. Select the folder containing the backup you want to restore.

5. Once you have selected the backup folder, you can confirm the selection in the backup review.

6. The next steps are the same as for the clean installation. Select the deployment target, configure the VM name and the root password, and select the deployment size, and the datastore where the vCSA will be deployed.

7. You do not need to configure the network settings since the information from the backup file will automatically populate them.

8. In the last step, you may review all the settings and, once ready, click **Finish**.

Once the first stage of the installation is complete, you can continue with the second stage. For this stage, you need to provide a password. If you have selected **Encrypted Backup**, everything else is already preconfigured.

If the original vCSA is still available, shut it down as the wizard suggest to avoid any network conflicts, as shown in the following screenshot:

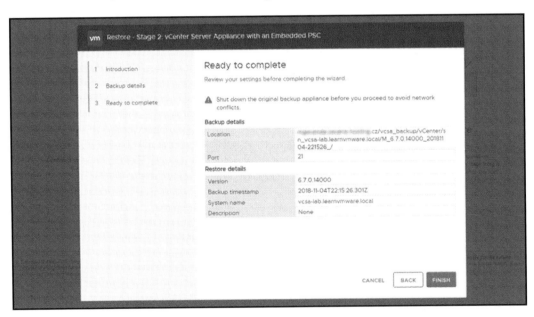

Once the restoration is done, you will be able to access your original vCSA at the configured FQDN with all the hosts in the inventory and all the performance metrics until the time that the backup is available.

Please note that if you have vCSA HA configured, it won't be configured after the restoration and you will need to deploy passive and witness vCSA again using the vCSA HA configuration wizard.

Managing data centers, clusters, and hosts

vCenter Server is a core component of the infrastructure that allows a centralized administration of hosts and VMs for your environment. To ensure the maximum efficiency of the infrastructure, you need to consider how to administer VMs and their resource demands.

For an optimal organization of the inventory, you need to create some virtual objects in the vCenter Server to define a logical structure. The organization of the inventory requires the following tasks to be performed:

1. Create data center(s)
2. Create cluster(s)
3. Add hosts to the cluster
4. Build a logical infrastructure using folders
5. Set up networking (vSS and vDS)
6. Configure the storage system (the datastore and the datastore cluster)
7. Create clusters (resource consolidation, vSphere HA, and vSphere DRS)
8. Create a resource pool (flexible management of resources)

In vCenter Server, there are four main views available to manage the inventory:

- **Hosts and clusters**: Clusters, hosts, resource pools, and VMs. From this view, you can manage the resource allocations of VMs and their locations.
- **VMs and templates**: Folders, VMs, and templates. This view can be used to group VMs in a logical structure (by role, location, department, and so on) using folders. You can also manage the templates from which you can deploy new VMs.

- **Storage**: Datastore and datastore cluster. From this view, you have an overview of installed datastores in your virtual infrastructure, regardless of the data center membership. You can configure and manage all device configurations, including the datastore clusters.
- **Networking**: **vSphere standard switch (vSwitch)** and **vSphere distributed switch (vDS)**. The setup of services, such as vMotion, vSphere FT, vSAN, and so on are managed from this view.

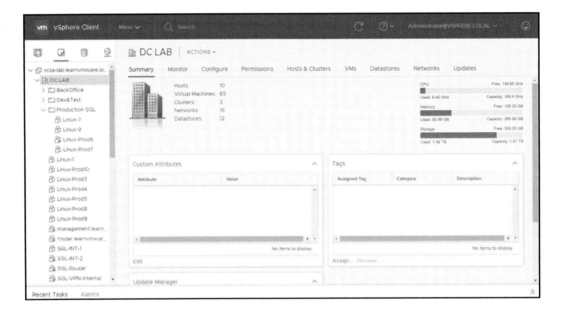

Creating a data center

The vCenter Server is composed of a data center object that acts as a core container for all other objects. To add hosts and VMs to the vCenter Server, at least one data center object must be created.

You can configure more than one data center per vCenter Server since multiple data center objects within a single instance are supported. Data center objects are shared among the four views, allowing for a better organization of the view based on the corporate policies, therefore simplifying management.

A data center object usually represents either a physical location in your infrastructure, such as the name of the physical data center, a physical location in the data center, or even an individual data center room.

To create the data center object, proceed with the following steps:

1. From the vSphere Client, right-click on the connected vCenter Server and select the **New Datacenter** option.
2. Enter a name in the **Name** field and click **OK** to create the data center object. Once the data center has been created, you can add the hosts to the inventory, as demonstrated in the following screenshot:

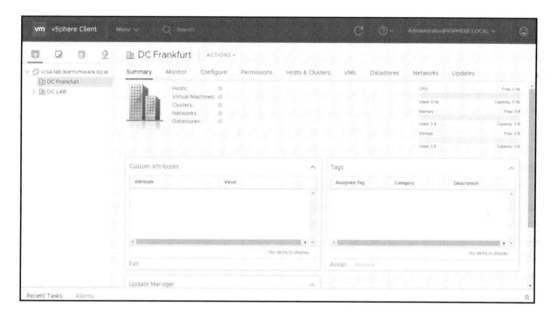

Adding a host to the vCenter Server

Since the vSphere environment strongly relies on DNS, before configuring the vCenter Server, make sure that the name resolution is working correctly in your network.

Verify that the vCenter Server can resolve ESXi hostnames added to the inventory and that the added ESXi hosts can resolve the vCenter Server hostnames used to manage them. Ensure that all the hypervisors added to vCenter can resolve the hostnames of other ESXi hosts.

To add ESXi hosts to vCenter Server, follow these steps:

1. From the vSphere Client, log in to the vCenter Server.
2. In the **Hosts and Clusters** view, right-click on the configured data center object and select the **Add Host** option.
3. Enter the **ESXi hostname or IP address** and click **Next**. In this step, it is suggested to use **FQDN** instead of the IP address.
4. Enter the root credentials and click **Next**. When prompted, click **Yes** to trust the host and to accept the host's certificate.
5. On the host summary page, click **Next** to continue. On this page, information related to the added host is displayed.
6. Select an **available license** to assign to the host. A 60-day evaluation license can be assigned if no license keys have been entered previously. Click **Next**. If you haven't purchased a vSphere Enterprise Plus license, using the 60-day evaluation license, you have all the vSphere features available to complete the configuration of the environment, taking advantage of some automation and functionalities included in the Enterprise Plus license only. For example, you could take advantage of the Storage DRS feature to optimize the performance and resources across different storage devices in your vSphere environment.
7. Configure **Lockdown** mode. By default, Lockdown mode is set as **Disabled**. Select **Normal** to manage the host through the local console or the vCenter Server, or **Strict** to allow access to the host only through the vCenter Server, stopping the DCUI service. You might use Lockdown mode for hardening access to your ESXi servers. Select the option you want to use and click **Next**.
8. Specify the location to which you want to move existing VMs running in the selected host and click **Next**.
9. Review your settings and click **Finish** to add the host to the vCenter Server. Repeat the same procedure to add all other required hosts to this vCenter Server instance.

You can add a host to the data center object itself. In this case, the ESXi hypervisor will be considered as a standalone host, or you can add the ESXi host directly to the cluster as a member of the cluster. You can quickly move your ESXi hypervisors between different clusters or data centers; it's not a fixed configuration.

When you enter the root password to add the host to the vCenter, the password is used to establish a connection with the host and to install the vCenter agent. The process sets different credentials that maintain the communication and authentication between ESXi and vCenter, even if ESXi's root password is changed.

Disconnecting a host from vCenter Server

Once ESXi is connected to vCenter Server, you can always disconnect or remove the host later on. It's important to understand that disconnecting the host from vCenter Server is different to removing the host. Disconnecting a managed host from vCenter Server doesn't remove ESXi from the vCenter Inventory as well as the VM registered in the host. When the managed host is disconnected, vCenter Server suspends monitoring and management activities for that host. If you disconnect a host and then connect it again, all the performance metrics will be kept.

It's a different story if you remove the host from the vCenter Server. Removing a managed host from the vCenter Server means the host and its VM are removed from the vCenter Inventory. If you remove a host from the inventory and then add it again, it will be considered a new object and no historical performance metrics will be available.

To disconnect a managed host from the vCenter Server, proceed with the following steps:

1. From the vSphere Client, log in to the vCenter Server that manages the host to disconnect.
2. Right-click the managed host, select the **Connection** | **Disconnect** option and click **OK** to confirm. Once the host is disconnected from the vCenter Server, in the inventory view, the ESXi and all the VMs associated are marked as disconnected.

To reconnect the host, you operate from the vCenter Server, as follows:

1. Right-click on the disconnected host and select the **Connection** | **Connect** option, then click **OK** to confirm.
2. Click **Next** in the **Name** and **Location** tab, then enter the root credentials of the host to reconnect. Click **Next**.
3. In the host summary, click **Next**, then specify where to locate the VM in the **VM Location** tab. Click **Next** to continue.

4. Click **Finish** to reconnect the host. When the procedure has completed, the disconnect label is removed from the host and its VM. The host is available to the vSphere environment again.

Removing a host from vCenter Server

Removing a host from vCenter Server stops all the vCenter Server monitoring and managing activities. You should remove the managed host while still connected to remove the vCenter agent as well.

To remove a managed host, follow this procedure:

1. From the vSphere Client, log in to the vCenter Server that manages the host to remove.
2. Power off all running VMs, right-click on the host, and select **Maintenance Mode | Enter Maintenance Mode**. Click **Yes** to confirm.
3. Right-click on the host once again and select the **All vCenter Actions | Remove from Inventory** option. Click **Yes** to confirm the removal. The host and its VM are removed from the vCenter Inventory; the license assigned to the host is removed from the vCenter list and retained by the host.

When the host has been removed, the vCenter Server is no longer able to manage the host. To access the VM, you need to access the host directly.

Creating a cluster

A vSphere cluster is a configuration that manages the added hosts pooling the available resources. Once the cluster has been created, you can move the hosts to the cluster. When the hosts are added to the cluster, the cluster manages the available resources and allows you to enable the vSphere HA, vSphere DRS, and vSphere FT features that are only available with clusters. These features will be covered in Chapter 11, *Availability and Disaster Recovery* .

To create a cluster, proceed as follows:

1. From the vSphere Client, log in to the vCenter Server.
2. In the **Hosts and Clusters** view, right-click on the configured data center object and select the **New Cluster** option.

3. Enter the name of the cluster and select the features you want to enable. Click **OK** to create the cluster. To better understand the available features displayed in the wizard, the HA feature provides business continuity, while DRS is used to balance the workload across the hosts.

Enhanced vMotion Compatibility (EVC) is a feature that allows VMs to vMotion across hosts with different processors in the same cluster. The caveat is that all processors must be from the same vendor (Intel or AMD) since a mixed cluster is not supported. Pay attention when you install a new ESXi server in the same cluster.

To add hosts to the created cluster, the easiest way is to drag and drop the ESXi hosts into the cluster. Alternatively, you can right-click on the hosts, select the **Move To** option, select the target cluster, then click **OK**. You can also use scripts to automate the process of adding hosts to the cluster. If you are prompted about resource pool management, leave the default option and click **Yes**.

Removing a host from a cluster

When you remove a managed host from a cluster, the cluster loses the resources provided by the removed host, reducing the total capacity. All historical data remains in the vCenter Server database. Before removing a host from a cluster, make sure that the cluster has enough resources to provide to the workloads to avoid performance issues or service disruption.

If the vSphere DRS feature is not enabled in the cluster, make sure to migrate all running VMs to a new host using vMotion before putting the host in **Maintenance Mode**. If not migrated, powered off, or suspended, VMs will remain associated with the removed host:

Follow these steps:

1. From the vSphere Client, right-click on the host you want to remove from a cluster.
2. Right-click the host to remove and select the **Maintenance Mode | Enter Maintenance Mode** option, then click **OK** to proceed. If DRS is enabled, powered-off (you need to enable the option), and running VMs are migrated to other hosts in the cluster.
3. When the host enters **Maintenance Mode**, the host icon changes. Right-click on the host and select the **Move To...** option.
4. Select the destination (data center, folder, or a different cluster) of where you want to move the host to and click **OK**.

5. When the host has moved off the cluster, right-click on the host and select **Maintenance Mode** | **Exit Maintenance Mode**.

 If you want to move a host in a cluster from one vCenter Server to another, you can disconnect the host and move it without putting the host in **Maintenance Mode**.

Managing hosts

vCenter Server is a core component of VMware vSphere that centralizes host administration, offering some powerful features that simplify the management process. vCenter Server provides a single pane of glass for your environment and allows access to the installed hosts and their configurations.

To access the ESXi management area, select a host from the vSphere Client. If you navigate from the available tabs, you can access the different configuration areas to set up the host matching the business requirements.

Let's have a look at the main areas:

- **Summary**: This displays information related to the ESXi, such as the resources in use, the tags, the global configuration, and more.
- **Monitor**: From this tab, you can track issues and alarms related to configuration problems and check the host's performance information, tasks, and events related to the selected host and the hardware health, to keep the status of the hardware components under control.
- **Configure**: From this tab, you can modify the host configuration. Storage configuration (such as storage adapters, and storage devices), network settings (such as vSwitches, VMkernel adapters, and TCP/IP), system components (such as host profile, firewall, security profile, and more), and hardware changes can be done in this section.
- **Permissions**: This tab is used to add permissions that specify users and roles.
- **VMs**: This shows the list of VMs and VM templates registered in the selected host. Double-click on an object to access its configuration area.
- **Datastores**: This displays the list of attached storage, showing details such as status, type, storage capacity, and free space.

- **Networks**: This displays a list of virtual switches and distributed virtual switches configured in the selected host.
- **Updates**: This displays a list of attached baselines from the **Update Manager** and the object compliance with the baselines.

Using tags

A tag is a label that you can apply to vCenter Server objects (such as datastores, VMs, and hosts) to simplify searches, allowing for a better sorting process. When a tag is created, it must be assigned to a category that groups related tags. A category also specifies whether you can assign one or multiple tags to an object. The creation and management of tags and categories are done through an intuitive configuration area, which can be reached by going to the menu, and then **Tags & Custom Attributes**, as follows:

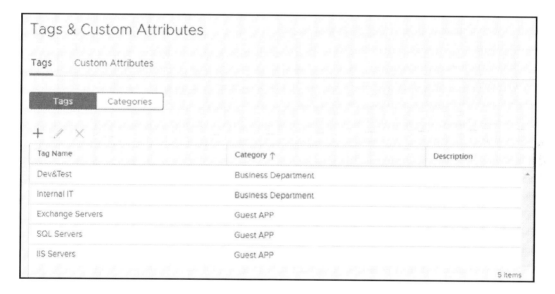

For instance, you can use tags to classify your application type or the business department that is responsible for a VM.

To assign a tag, right-click on an object in the vCenter Inventory and select **Tags & Custom Attributes | Assign Tag**.

Some software backup solutions make use of tags to group VMs with the same backup policy (for example, RTO), making the administration process more straightforward.

Tasks

Tasks are activities performed by the system that occur on an object of the vCenter Inventory (to power on or power off a VM, for example) and can be executed in real-time or be scheduled.

The task list can be viewed in the vSphere Client by selecting the **Tasks** option from the menu. The list displays all tasks that occurred to a specific object, detailing information, such as the target, status, initiator, and more. By default, tasks listed for a single object also include tasks executed on the child objects. The list can be filtered by typing the keywords in the search field on the right.

Scheduling tasks

Tasks can be scheduled to run at specific times or recurring intervals. A task cannot be scheduled to run on multiple objects. The available tasks you can schedule from the vSphere Web Client are the following:

- Add hosts and check the compliance of a profile
- Change the power state, clone, create, deploy, migrate, make a snapshot, or edit the resources of VMs
- Change the cluster power settings
- Scan for updates
- Remediate the object

Tasks not included in the list can be scheduled using the vSphere API. To schedule a task, proceed as follows:

1. From the vSphere Web Client, select the object on which you want to schedule a task and select **Monitor** | **Tasks & Events**. Click **Scheduled Tasks** to create a new schedule.
2. From the **Schedule**, in the **New Scheduled Task** drop-down menu, select the task to schedule (available tasks depend on the selected object).

3. Configure task-related options and the scheduling settings. Enter an email address to be notified when the task is complete and click **OK** to save the task schedule, as demonstrated in the following screenshot:

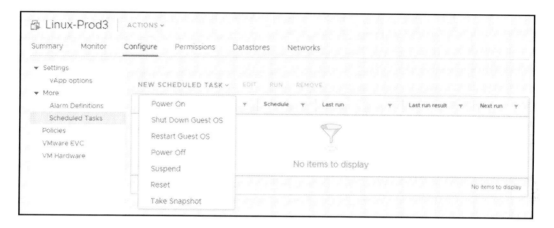

Managing host profiles

Host profiles are a feature of vSphere that allow you to include the ESXi configuration in a profile (template) to ensure that all hosts installed across the infrastructure have the same configuration and are compliant with the setup policy you have in your organization.

Generally, after completing the deployment of an ESXi host, there are several settings you should configure to ensure the host's services match your infrastructure:

- **Network configuration**: Creating VMkernels and VM port groups, assigning IPs to VMkernels, setting up NIC-teaming, and mor
- **Storage configuration**: Configuring software iSCSI adapters, port bindings, and CHAP.
- **Time synchronization**: Configuring and enabling the NTP service
- **Enable services:** Enabling services such as SSH and shell
- **Firewall**: Opening specific ports that are required by some services

If you have just a few hosts to install, you can quickly and easily use the interactive ESXi installation method and once, completed, manually set up the required host's parameters. If the environment to build is large and you have 100-1,000 hosts to set up, manually performing the configuration for each hypervisor is a tedious and time-consuming task, and human error can occur at any moment: incorrect IP addresses assigned, wrong NIC to a VMkernel port group mapping, and so on.

Using host profiles mean we can avoid these kind of configuration errors. You profile a host by creating a template containing the configuration extracted from a reference host, and then you apply this template to any host of the infrastructure to ensure consistency. Once created, the host profile can be edited to change, enable, or disable properties. If a host profile is applied to a cluster, all the member hosts are affected, ensuring a consistent configuration.

Host profiles can also be used together with the *Auto Deploy* feature (*Auto Deploy* was covered in `Chapter 4`, *Deployment Workflow and Component Installation*) to automate the provisioning process fully.

The overall process can be summarized as follows:

1. Set up and configure the reference host. Because the configuration will be saved to the host profile, make sure the ESXi setup is correct and verified.
2. Create the master host profile, extracting the configuration from the reference host.
3. Attach the created host profile to a host or cluster to apply the standard configuration.
4. Check the compliance of processed hosts to the host profile to ensure they all have the same configuration.
5. Remediate the host to apply the settings. The ESXi host attached to the selected host profile modifies its configuration only at this stage.

To create a host profile, perform the following steps:

1. From the vSphere Web Client, right-click on the hypervisor used as a reference host and select **Host Profiles** | **Extract Host Profile**.
2. Enter a profile name and a description. The description is useful to identify the scope of the profile but is optional. Click **Next** when done.
3. Click **Finish** to start the host profile creation. When the process has completed, the created profiles can be found in the **Home** | **Policies & Profiles** | **Host Profiles** area of the vSphere Web Client.

To apply settings saved in the profile to a host or cluster, you need to attach the created host profile. To attach the host profile, proceed as follows:

1. From the vSphere Web Client, right-click on the host to process and select the **Host Profiles** | **Attach Host Profile** option.
2. Select the host profile to attach and click **OK**. At this stage, you can customize the host (for example, configure the IP address and DNS server) or enable the **Skip Host Customization** option to avoid host customization during the process.

Once a host profile is attached to a host, the configuration is not automatically applied, but you must perform a compliance check first to compare the current host configuration with the configuration stored in the profile.

To run the compliance check, follow these steps:

1. Right-click on the host to check and select **Host Profiles** | **Check Host Profile Compliance**. If the checked host is found to be non-compliant, a warning message is displayed in the **Summary** tab, as demonstrated in the following screenshot:

2. If you click on **Details**, you will see which configurations are done differently compared to the host profile. In this case, the ESXi server, `esxi-prod-2`, does not have the syslog server configured (advanced configuration option `Syslog.global.logHost`).

3. You can remediate the host to match the Host Profile (the configuration from the host profile will be applied to the host) using the **Remediate** button.

Host profiles can be modified to change some settings by editing the desired profile. To modify a host profile, proceed as follows:

1. From the vSphere Web Client, go to **Home | Profiles & Policies | Host Profiles**

2. Select the profile you want to modify from the list and click on the **Edit Host Profile**

Automating tasks with scripts

The administration of the vSphere environment often requires you to perform repetitive tasks that can be time-consuming, involving the same activities to be done for each component of the infrastructure. Examples of these kinds of activities include migrating VMs or deploying new VMs from a template.

The chance to automate some tasks will allow you to optimize your time, improving efficiency and ensuring consistency. Manually modifying the configuration of thousands VMs, for example, will require a lot of time, with the risk of missing some steps or making some errors. Automation can perform the same tasks in seconds with no errors and ensure consistency within the network, reducing the workload of IT staff.

VMware offers some tools to automate tasks, such as PowerCLI, vCLI, **vRealize Orchestrator (vRO)**, and the vSphere Web Services SDK. **vSphere Management Assistant (vMA)** has been deprecated, and version 6.5 is the final release.

Perhaps the most popular tool for system administrators is PowerCLI, but of course, the optimal solution is only what is suitable for your environment and needs.

Automating with PowerCLI

The most common automation tool provided by vSphere is PowerCLI, a command-line and scripting tool built on Windows PowerShell that provides cmdlets used for managing and automating vSphere and other VMware products.

Today, two versions of PowerShell and PowerCLI exist:

- **PowerCLI 6.5**: This version is based on the standard **Windows PowerShell**
- **PowerCLI 10.0**: This version is based on **PowerShell Core**, which is a multi-platform implementation of PowerShell

PowerShell Core can be installed on Windows, Linux, and macOS and it is the recommended version of PowerShell to use. Microsoft is going to deprecate old Windows PowerShell, so you should switch to PowerCLI 10 if you have not done so already. As mentioned, PowerShell Core can be installed even on macOS. You can use PowerCLI directly from your macOS, and you do not need to use Windows to jump hosts anymore!

The following screenshot shows PowerCLI running directly on macOS X:

```
● ● ●                           ⌂ gavis — pwsh — 101×31
PS /Users/gavis> get-vm


Name                   PowerState Num CPUs MemoryGB
----                   ---------- -------- --------
router.learnvmwar...   PoweredOn  1        0.500
management.learnv...   PoweredOn  2        4.000
dc01.learnvmware....   PoweredOn  1        2.000
vcsa.learnvmware....   PoweredOn  2        10.000
SGL-Router             PoweredOn  1        0.125
SGL-VPN-Internal       PoweredOn  1        0.125
dc02.learnvmware....   PoweredOn  1        2.000
VC-LAB-esxi2.lear...   PoweredOn  4        16.000
VC-LAB-esxi3.lear...   PoweredOn  4        16.000
VC-LAB-esxi4.lear...   PoweredOn  4        16.000
VC-LAB-DEV-esxi1....   PoweredOn  2        10.000
VC-LAB-DEV-esxi2....   PoweredOn  2        10.000
VC-LAB-DEV-esxi3....   PoweredOn  2        10.000
VC-LAB-esxi1.lear...   PoweredOn  4        16.000
VC-LAB-Standalone...   PoweredOn  8        12.000
SGL-INT-1              PoweredOff 1        2.000
SGL-INT-2              PoweredOn  1        2.000
vESXI1                 PoweredOn  8        32.000
iscsi.learnvmware...   PoweredOn  4        4.000
psc-prod.learnvmw...   PoweredOn  2        4.000
vcsa-prod.learnvm...   PoweredOn  2        10.000
vcsa-mgmt.learnvm...   PoweredOn  2        10.000
vcsa-lab.learnvmw...   PoweredOn  2        10.000


PS /Users/gavis> ▊
```

If you have not install PowerShell Core yet, check the official manual of PowerShell Core at the following link: `https://docs.microsoft.com/en-us/powershell/` `scripting/setup/installing-powershell?view=powershell-6`.

Once the PowerShell Core is installed, you can easily install PowerCLI directly from the PowerShell Core.

The installation process of PowerCLI 10 has been simplified and requires us to run a command from the PowerShell console.
To install PowerCLI, follow this procedure:

1. Open the PowerShell console and run the following command:

```
Install-Module -Name VMware.PowerCLI
```

2. To see the installed modules, run the following command:

```
Get-Module vmware* -listavailable
```

3. Before you start to use PowerCLI, don't forget to change the default behavior of PowerShell Core if you are using self-signed certificates. By default, they are not trusted:

```
Set-PowerCLIConfiguration -InvalidCertificateAction Ignore
```

To try PowerCLI, open the PowerShell Core console where the VMware PowerCLI module has been installed. From the console, connect the vCenter Server instance to query, then run the following command (enter the login credentials when prompted):

```
Connect-VIserver -server VCSA_fqdn
```

To get a list of VMs running in the selected vCenter Server instance, enter the following command:

```
Get-vm
```

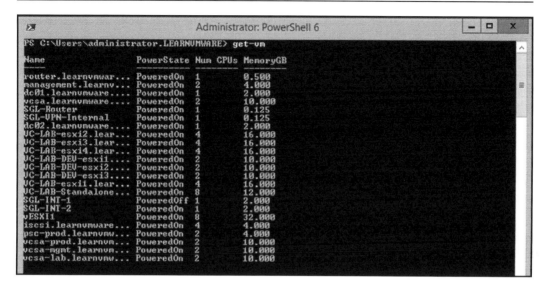

Remembering all PowerCLI commands and the correct syntax is not easy for most people, and the documentation is not always available to help. A useful cmdlet is available in PowerShell that provides information about a specific command is Get-help. To find the correct syntax to use with a specific cmdlet, Get-help helps you to find the information you need. For example, to find which parameters can be used with the Get-VM cmdlet to retrieve the list of running VMs, you can enter the following:

```
Get-help Get-VM
```

You get a brief explanation of the command, the syntax to use, and the description. If you append -example at the end of the command, the system also displays examples of how to use the command. You can pipeline multiple PowerShell cmdlets to build a script in a single line of code.

Sometimes, the Get-* command will retrieve only the necessary information about the object, such as PowerState, number of CPUs, and memory size, but there may be more properties of the object.

To get the full list, you can append `Select-Object` `*` on the command, as follows:

```
Get-vm -name Linux-Prod1 | Select-Object *
```

The output of the command is displayed in the following screenshot:

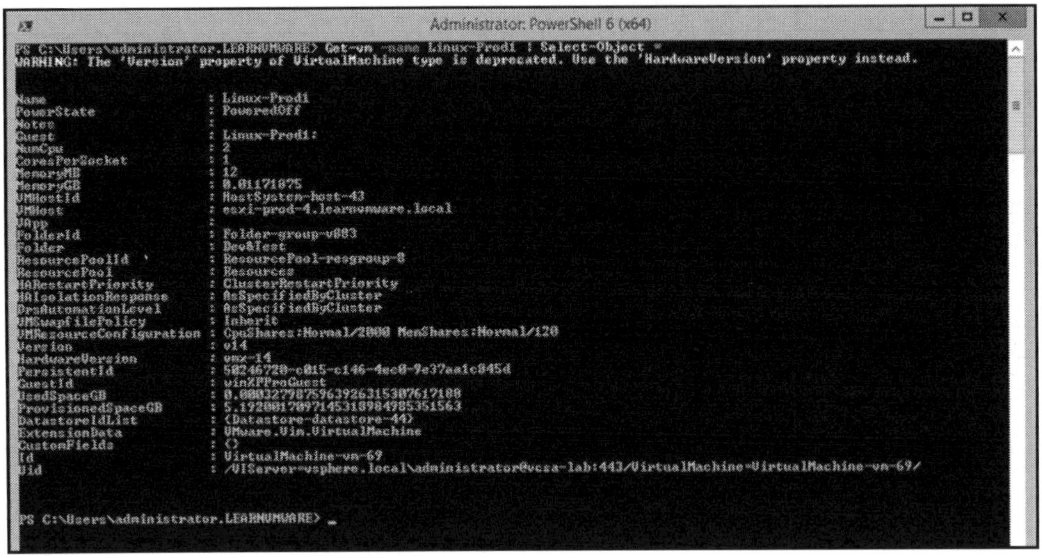

PowerCLI script examples

Here are some of the examples of PowerCLI scripts that are used to perform some tasks in the vSphere environment, as follows:

- **To move VMs to another host**, use the following script:

```
get-vmhost -name esxi-prod-3.learnvmware.local | get-vm |
Move-VM -Destination (Get-VMHost-name esxi-
prod-1.learnvmware.local)
```

- **To move a single VM to a different host**, use the following script:

```
Move-VM -VM VM_name -Destination esxi-prod-1.learnvmware.local
```

- **To get information about the VMs**, previously, we used the `Get-VM` command to retrieve a list of running VMs in the vCenter Server instance. You also have the option of exporting the list of VMs in a `.csv` file, including some properties you want to specify:

```
Get-VM | Select-Object Name,NumCPU,MemoryMB,PowerState,Host |
Export-CSV VMinfo.csv -NoTypeInformation
```

- **To find out on which host a specific VM runs**, use the following script:

```
Get-VMHost -VM (Get-VM -Name VMname)
```

- **Configuring NTP**: We have already discussed the importance of having the hosts time-synced to avoid authentication issues. The following cmdlet configures the NTP server for the specific host, as well as setting the service to automatically start with the host:

```
Add-VmHostNtpServer -VMHost $vmhost -NtpServer
172.16.1.1,172.16.1.2
Get-VmHostService -VMHost $vmhost | Where-Object {$_.key -eq
"ntpd"} | Start-VMHostService
Get-VmHostService -VMHost $vmhost | Where-Object {$_.key -eq
"ntpd"} | Set-VMHostService -policy "on"
```

As you can see, with PowerCLI you can automate everything, and I would strongly suggest getting used to PowerCLI, because it is a powerful tool that can save you a lot of time, especially with repetitive tasks.

vCenter REST API

A new feature introduced in vSphere 6.5 is a REST API, which is a more modern, more straightforward-to-use, and more developer-friendly vSphere API. Compared to the capabilities provided by the vSphere API, at the time of writing, not all functions are supported by the REST API. However, compared to vSphere 6.5, the range of supported functions has been extended significantly.

Embedded in the vCSA, there is an API Explorer that allows you to access the documentation of the new REST APIs.

Access your vCSA at the address `https://<VCSA_IP>/apiexplorer` to reach the API Explorer and click on the **Select API** drop-down menu to select the available endpoints, as shown in the following screenshot:

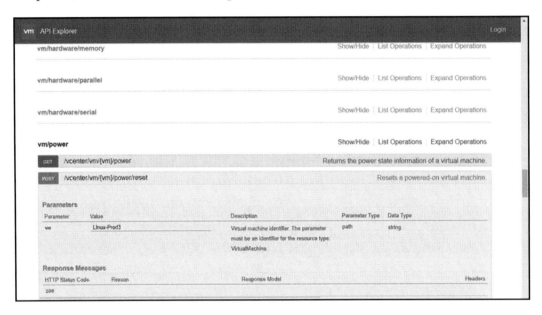

To get the complete documentation on a specific API (description, required fields, request body, and more), click the **Show/Hide** option to expand the available sections. For example, to reset a running VM, I can use the following URL:

```
https://vcsa-lab.learnvmware.local/rest/vcenter/vm/Linux-Prod3/power/r
eset
```

The whole command for CURL is as follows:

```
curl -X POST --header 'Content-Type: application/json' --header
'Accept: application/json' --header 'vmware-api-session-id:
7d884f11981fbd6e7b383ca737277834'
'https://vcsa-lab.learnvmware.local/rest/vcenter/vm/Linux-Prod3/power/
reset'
```

Summary

A correct configuration of the vSphere components ensures business continuity and improves performance. We have already discussed the ESXi installation procedures, where settings, such as the NTP and the IP address, should be configured to avoid authentication issues and accessibility problems.

We also explained the scratch partition used for storing temporary data, including logs, and diagnostic information. By configuring the vCSA accordingly, roles and permissions can be assigned to users or groups to manage the infrastructure on different levels, and the integration with AD provides domain users with the capability to manage vSphere based on assigned roles.

You have learned how to perform backups of both essential vSphere components—ESXi hypervizors and vCenter Server, and how to restore from such backup-in-case of failure.

The management of vSphere objects was another topic covered in this chapter, describing the virtual objects to be created in the vCenter Server to define a logical structure and to better organize the inventory – data centers, clusters, and resource pools. To simplify the host configuration, the vSphere host profile feature ensures that all hosts have the same configuration settings.

This chapter ended by showing you how to speed up and avoid repetitive tasks, using the PowerShell and REST API tools to automate some tasks using scripts or command-line commands.

In the next chapter, will look closely at the specific configurations related to the network infrastructure.

Questions

1. Which protocols can be used to manage the ESXi hypervisor?

       a) HTTP
       b) RDP
       c) HTTPS
       d) Telnet
       e) SSH
       f) VNC

2. Why should you configure the NTP client on the ESXi server?
3. There are three partitions created by default on the ESXi server during installation:

   a) True
   b) False

4. Describe why you should perform periodic backups of ESXi server and vCSA.
5. The IP address and the DNS settings of vCSA can't be changed after the installation:

   a) True
   b) False

6. What is the difference between vCenter Essentials, vCenter Foundation, and vCenter Standard?
7. You can integrate vCenter Server to the remote identity source. What are the valid sources for your users and groups?

   a) Active Directory, Open LDAP, LocalOS, and Local Domain
   b) Open LDAP, Local Domain, and LocalOS
   c) Active Directory, Lotus Notes, Open LDAP, and Local Domain
   d) Active Directory, Novell Netware, and Open LDAP

8. Which components can be integrated with Active Directory?

   a) ESXi server and vCSA
   b) vCSA only
   c) ESXi only

9. Can you point your vCenter Server to a different PSC?
10. The maximum number of vSphere clusters is 64:

    a) True
    b) False

11. Name at least two solutions you can use to automate your vSphere environment.

Further reading

- **VMware vCenter Cookbook**: `https://www.packtpub.com/virtualization-and-cloud/vmware-vcenter-cookbook`
- **Learning PowerCLI – Second Edition**: `https://www.amazon.com/Learning-PowerCLI-Robert-van-Nieuwendijk-ebook/dp/B01D8HIII2/`

6
Life Cycle Management, Patching, and Upgrading

vSphere 6.7 simplifies and enhances the capabilities for patching and upgrading ESXi hosts and the **vCenter Server Appliance** (**vCSA**). In addition, vSphere 6.7 introduces many new features and improvements, such as the vCSA with the integrated **vSphere Update Manager** (**VUM**), vCenter HA, and more. Thanks to those features, migration to the latest release is highly recommended.

The VUM service is now fully integrated into the vCSA and no longer requires an additional external Windows server. The embedded VUM can also benefit from the vCenter HA feature for redundancy. VUM is enabled by default, and only a minor configuration is required so that you have a system that's ready to handle patches and upgrade tasks. You will also learn how to patch ESXi hosts using the command line in situation where you do not have vCenter Server.

vSphere 6.7 includes a migration tool that allows administrators to easily and quickly migrate from vCenter for Windows to VCSA.

In this chapter, we will cover the following topics:

- Patching a vSphere 6.7 environment
- Upgrading workflow and procedures
- Upgrading the vCSA
- vCenter 6.5 for Windows to vCenter 6.7 for Windows.
- vCenter 6.5 for Windows to vCSA 6.7 migration
- Upgrading standalone ESXi servers
- VUM
- Updating the vCSA

Patching a vSphere 6.7 environment

Keeping ESXi hosts and vCenter Servers up-to-date is not only an essential best practice, but it's strongly recommended to ensure the correct functionality of the virtual platform and protection from bugs. Several methods are available for patching ESXi hosts via the use of VUM (this will be discussed later in this chapter) to update all hosts automatically. Alternatively, if no vCenter Servers are present in the network, the command line of the ESXi server can be used as well. Also, the vCSA can be patched in different ways, all of which will be analyzed later on.

There are two different upgrade types:

- **Minor updates**: From one build to a higher one, but still within the same major version. For example, from ESXi 6.5 U1 (build 5969303) to ESXi 6.5 U2 GA (build 8294253).
- **Major updates**: From one major version to a higher major version. For example, from ESXi 6.5 U2 GA (build 8294253) to ESXi 6.7 GA (build 8169922).

 You can check versions and corresponding builds at `https://kb.vmware.com/s/article/2143832`.

If you are performing a minor update of your ESXi servers, it is not necessary to upgrade your vCenter Server. If you are performing a major update, vCSA must be updated before you update your ESXi servers, otherwise it will not be able to manage the newer hosts.

 Feel free to check out the **VMware Product Interoperability Matrices** at `https://www.vmware.com/resources/compatibility/sim/interop_matrix.php` to get a better understanding of compatibility requirements between different products.

Upgrade flow to vSphere 6.7

The latest version of the VMware virtual platform, vSphere 6.7, comes with exciting new features and improved capabilities that bring tremendous benefits for the network regarding improved functionality, management, security, and more that were not available in previous versions.

The entire upgrade process needs to follow a specific sequence and flow; first, all PSCs, then all vCenter Servers, then all ESXi hosts. However, if you have more VMware products, the entire sequence could be much more complicated.

 For more information, see **KB 53710: Update sequence for vSphere 6.7 and its compatible VMware products** at `https://kb.vmware.com/s/article/53710`.

Upgrading the workflow and procedure

For a successful migration to the new version, the overall procedure must be carefully planned with a precise and well-executed workflow to avoid potential issues, such as service disruption or compatibility issues with running components. The migration procedure plan can be split into three main steps, as shown in the following diagram:

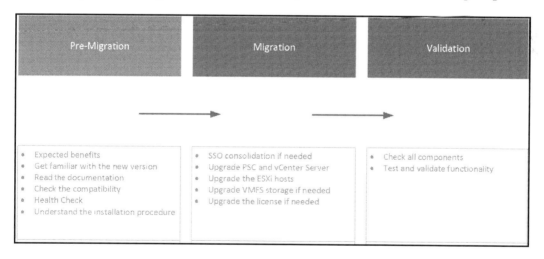

Let's look at these steps in more detail.

Step 1 – pre-migration

The pre-migration step includes a plan of the tasks that should be done before starting the actual migration. An analysis of the expected benefits of the new features should be done to determine the added value to your business and justify the investment to management. Try to obtain as much documentation as you can, such as guides, release notes, and tips of the new release, to limit possible problems with the upgrade. Explaining how the new release and new features should be implemented and configured is also an essential point for a successful migration.

Make sure that running programs in the current vSphere environment are also supported in the release you are going to install. If other VMware products are used in your network, validate the compatibility of each product by using the **VMware Product Interoperability Matrices** that are available on the VMware website at the following URL: `https://www.vmware.com/resources/compatibility/sim/interop_matrix.php`.

 Ensure that the backup solution in use supports the new version to ensure the protection of your workload. In the event of incompatibility, take all the necessary actions (upgrades, replacement) to ensure full support before migrating.

Performing a health assessment for your current vSphere environment is useful for detecting objects that are no longer needed but are still consuming resources. They also help fix misconfigurations to avoid issues during migration and network cleanup.
There are several tools available on the market that allow you to perform a healthcheck on the vSphere environment. In addition to solutions that require a license, some free tools can also be used to health check your virtual platform.

The following are some examples of commercial and free products that you can use to health check your environment:

- **Licensed**: VMware vRealize Operations Manager, **vSphere Optimization Assessment** (**VOA**), Runecast Analyzer, or Opvizor Health Analyzer
- **Free**: Turbonomic Virtual Health Monitor, Veeam ONE Free Edition, or RVTools

Step 2 – migration

Plan all the involved steps accordingly, evaluating the impact of new features and the improvements that can be applied to the current environment. An upgrade order of the virtual components should be established to avoid potential problems. For example, the vSphere platform requires first upgrading the vCenter Server and then the ESXi hosts to avoid communication issues within vSphere components.

Since VMware has deprecated the Windows-based version of vCenter Server, it's worth migrating directly to the Linux-based vCSA. This takes advantage of the new features that were introduced in version 6.5, such as embedded VUM, **vCenter High Availability** (**VCHA**), and built-in file-based backup restore, which is available in the vCSA only. If you have vCenter Servers with external **Platform Services Controllers** (**PSCs**), get both components on the same version to take advantage of new features.

You can perform an upgrade of vCSA 6.5 to 6.7 using the following tools:

- **Graphical interface**: Using this, you can insert the new vCSA ISO image into your management station as well as by using guided installation
- **CLI interface**: On the vCSA ISO file, you can also find the CLI that allows you to upgrade vCSA in unattended mode

When PSCs and vCenter Servers have been upgraded, you can start migrating ESXi hosts. ESXi 5.5 is not supported in version 6.7 at all, so you must upgrade those ESXi hosts before managing them through vCenter 6.7. ESXi 6.0 or 6.5 can be managed by vCenter 6.7, although new features won't be available for such hosts.

For large environments, you could schedule the upgrade in different maintenance windows by upgrading the vSphere environment in stages. You can start by upgrading all PSCs, followed by the vCenter Servers, and then the ESXi hosts. Planning the upgrade process in different steps reduces the maintenance of the environment in three shorter time frames, thus limiting downtime. To avoid issues, upgrade each vCenter **Single Sign-On** (**SSO**) or PSC one at a time.

Step 3 – validation

Ensure that the upgrade has been completed successfully and that all components work as expected. Verify the full functionality of the vSphere infrastructure and integration with third-party products (such as backup software) according to plan. Once the validation has succeeded, the migration procedure is complete.

Upgrading vCSA 6.5 to vCSA 6.7

VMware made a significant effort to simplify the migration process to vSphere 6.7. They did this by introducing direct upgrades from the installation media of vCenter Server Appliance from an existing vCSA and PSC Appliance 6.5 or a Windows-based vCenter Server to the new version. The tool supports vCenter Servers running version 6.0 and higher.

The upgrade process comprises two stages:

1. vCSA deployment
2. Making a copy of the configuration from the vCenter Server source

The automated upgrade process requires the **Distributed Resource Scheduler (DRS)** feature in the cluster, in which the source vCenter Server is installed but not set to fully automated mode.

The upgrade procedure is straightforward and guided through a simple and clear UI in which you must specify source and target network parameters in the upgrade wizard when requested.

Before you start with the update, don't forget to create a backup of an existing vCSA appliance from the **vCenter Server Appliance Management Interface (VAMI)**, as discussed in the previous, `Chapter 5`, *Configuring and Managing vSphere 6.7*.

You can't upgrade to the new major version directly from the VAMI interface of vCSA. Those upgrades are between minor versions. As you can see, on my vCSA 6.5, I only have the option to upgrade to a newer build of vCSA 6.5, not 6.7:

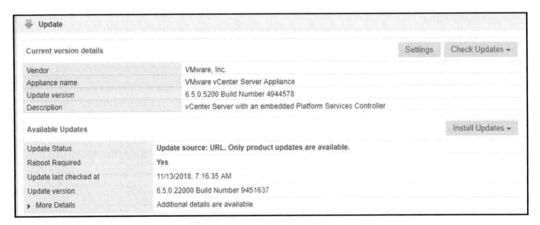

The upgrade itself is not an in-place upgrade. The original vCSA won't be touched. Instead, a new vCSA will be deployed, and the data will be migrated.

To perform an upgrade of vCSA 6.5 to 6.7 with an embedded PSC, the following steps are required:

1. Mount the ISO installation media of vCSA to your management station.
2. Launch the GUI installer located at `CDROM:\vcsa-ui-installer\win32\installer.exe`.
3. Select the **Upgrade** option.
4. The **Upgrade** wizard looks similar to the installation one, and only a few steps are different. After you accept the end user agreement, you need to connect to the existing vCSA and fill in the required password for vCSA itself and the ESXi host that is being managed by the current vCSA.
5. In the next steps, you need to provide a destination ESXi host or vCenter Server where the new vCSA will be deployed. You also need to provide the new vCSA VM name and root password.
6. After you have selected the deployment size based on your inventory size and datastore, which will be used to host new vCSAs, you need to specify networking of the new vCSA. Keep in mind that you need to assign a different IP address to the new vCSA that will be used during migration. Once the migration is done, the IP will be changed to the original one.
7. Once stage 1 is complete, stage 2 configuration (the actual migration) will start.
8. Stage 2 is slightly different from the new vCSA installation. First, the pre-check is performed, and you will see the output of the pre-check in the wizard.
9. Once you resolve the warnings from the pre-check, you can select what data you need to migrate to the new vCSA. This decision will significantly affect the overall duration of the migration.
10. Once all the information is gathered, you can double-check everything before you start with the actual upgrade.
11. In the last step, you need to confirm that the original vCSA will be shut down during the process. Once the data is migrated, the old vCSA will be powered off, and a new one will get an original IP address.
12. Once the whole procedure has finished, you can see different messages based on your vSphere infrastructure and its configuration.
13. After the process has completed, you can log in to the VAMI interface of the vCSA (at the original IP address or FQDN), and you should see that the new version is running.

Now, if you log in to the vSphere client (HTML5 or Flex), you will see that the new VM has been deployed that hosts vCSA 6.7, but you will also see that the old VM is still available but powered off, as shown in the following screenshot:

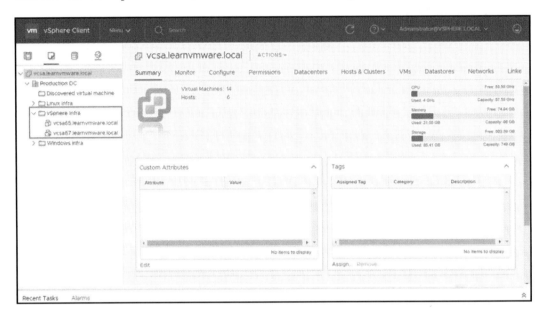

The migration process doesn't delete the old vCenter Server and its configuration, but copies data to the new vCSA and then powers the source vCenter off. This allows you to quickly restore the old vCenter Server if the upgrade process fails.

Upgrading vCenter 6.5 for Windows to vCenter 6.7 for Windows

vCenter for Windows is a fully supported deployment type in VMware vSphere 6.7, but keep in mind that this is the last version that supports vCenter for Windows. In the next release, vCSA will be the only supported deployment.

The upgrade consists of two steps:

1. Upgrade PSC (the embedded version is not used)
2. Upgrade vCenter Server

PSC upgrade

Before you upgrade vCenter for Windows to vCSA, the PSC must be migrated to the corresponding vSphere version, which in our case is vSphere 6.7.

If you are migrating vCenter for Windows with an embedded PSC, you can skip this step. You can follow these steps to upgrade your PSC:

1. Perform a backup of the Windows Server that hosts the PSC.
2. Mount the installation image of vCenter Server for Windows to the external PSC and start the installation wizard of vCenter Server.
3. The installation will realize that it has been launched on a system that contains a previous version of the vSphere component and the upgrade wizard will be launched.
4. Accept the license agreement and provide an SSO user account.
5. You can change the default ports that PSC will be bound to as well as the installation directories.
6. At the summary windows, you must check that the Windows server was backed up. If not, the installation will not be permitted.
7. Only after the upgrade is completed can you continue with the next steps.

Upgrading vCenter Server

The upgrade of vCenter Server for Windows consists of the same steps as the PSC upgrade:

1. Perform a backup of the Windows Server that hosts the vCenter Server as well as the SQL database (if external is used).
2. Mount the vCenter Server for Windows 6.7 installation image.
3. Start the installation of the vCenter Server for Windows.
4. The installation will discover that the previous version of vCenter is running and the upgrade will be performed instead.
5. Follow the installation wizard, provide the SSO administrative password, and customize the installation directories if necessary.
6. In the summary of the upgrade, you need to explicitly confirm that the backup was taken. Otherwise, the **Upgrade** option will be grayed out.

After you log in to the vCenter Server, you will see that the configuration is intact (for example, custom virtual machine folders) and that you are running vCenter 6.7:

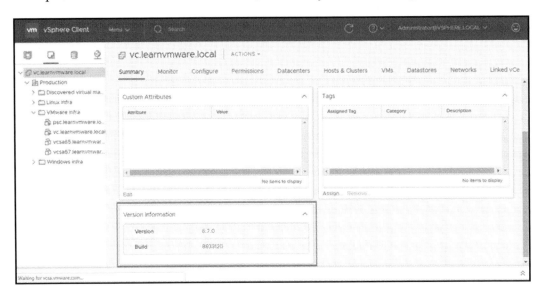

Migrating vCenter 6.5 for Windows to vCSA 6.7

Historically, many infrastructures were based on vCenter for Windows, especially those that were not deployed after vSphere 6.5 was announced. Before vSphere 6.5 was introduced, the vCSA was an appliance with a limited set of features and many companies preferred to use a full-feature vCenter Server running on Windows.

From vSphere 6.5, vCSA is the preferred vCenter deployment option, and vSphere 6.7 is the last release that supports vCenter for Windows. Customers are encouraged to perform the migration from vCenter for Windows to vCSA.

VMware introduced the vCenter for Windows to vCSA migration wizard in vSphere 6.5 as an integrated part of the vCSA installation.

Migration procedure

The migration from the vCenter Server for Windows to vCSA has several steps, depending on your vSphere deployment:

- With an external PSC, migrate to the dedicated vCSA machine that will be used as an external PSC. Migration from an external PSC to an embedded one is not supported.
- Migrate vCenter for Windows 6.5 to vCSA 6.7. If you have installed a dedicated vCenter server and PSC, the result will be two appliances, one running vCenter Server and the second one running the PSC. With the embedded Windows deployment type, the result will be a single vCSA appliance holding both the vCenter and PSC roles:

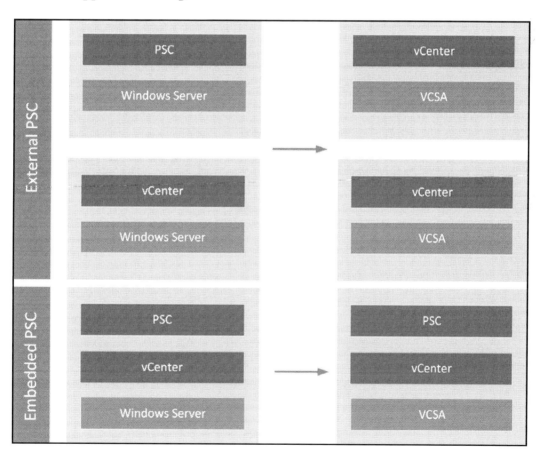

Migrate in this context means migrate and upgrade in a single step. Check the following documentation for additional information about vCenter for Windows to vCSA migration: `https://docs.vmware.com/en/VMware-vSphere/6.7/com.vmware.vcenter.upgrade.doc/GUID-9A117817-B78D-4BBE-A957-982C734F7C5F.html`.

The migration itself is a straightforward process, as all you need to do is launch the migration wizard.

The migration wizard supports all kinds of vCenter for Windows deployments:

- vCenter for Windows with embedded PostgreSQL database and embedded PSC
- vCenter for Windows with embedded PostgreSQL database and external embedded PSC
- vCenter for Windows with an external database and embedded PSC
- vCenter for Windows with an external database and external embedded PSC

If you have an external PSC, perform the migration of the PSC first, then continue with vCenter Server. If you have vCenter Server with an embedded PSC, only migrate the vCenter Server.

To migrate vCenter for Windows with an internal PostgreSQL database and an embedded PSC to vCSA with an embedded PSC, follow this procedure:

1. From the source Windows vCenter Server, launch the migration assistant from the installation ISO image of the vCSA 6.7. The migration assistant is located at `CDDRIVE:\migration-assistant\VMware-Migration-Assistant.exe`:

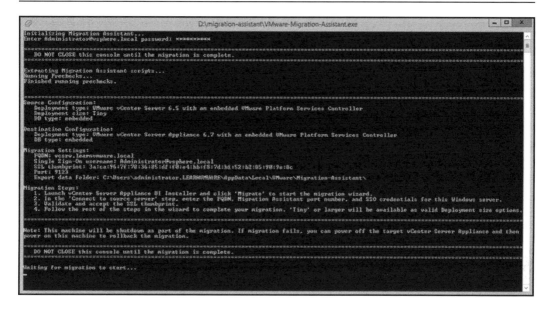

2. Plug in the vCSA installation image to your management station and select **Migrate**.

3. After you have agreed with the license terms, you need to connect to the source—vCenter Server for Windows.

4. The **Appliance deployment target** step can be an ESXi server or a vCenter Server, as you already know. The next steps are the same as for a new vCSA installation. Here, you need to provide the VM name of the new vCenter Server, root password, deployment size, and datastore.

5. In the **Configure network settings** step, you need to provide a temporary IP address that will be used during the migration process. Once the migration has finished, the new vCSA will be reconfigured with the old IP address that's currently configured in the vCenter for Windows.

6. In the last step, you can check everything and if the configuration is correct, start with the deployment.

Once stage 1 is complete (initial VCSA deployment), you can continue with the actual migration:

1. Based on your vSphere environment, you might see different warnings and notices once the stage 2 migration wizard connects to the source vCenter for Windows.
2. If your vCenter Server for Windows is a member of an **Active Directory (AD)**, you will be prompted for AD credentials so that you can join the new vCSA to the AD.
3. You have an option to select which data will be migrated to the new vCSA appliance.
4. Next, you can join the **Customer Experience Improvement Program (CEIP)**, and in the final step, you have to confirm that the backup of the source vCenter for Windows was done.
5. During the migration, the source vCenter Server for Windows will be powered off.
6. Now, the actual migration will be performed based on your configuration settings.
7. If the migration was successful, you should see a screen with the results of the operation.

Once the migration has finished, you can log into the web interface of the new vCSA appliance (running on your original IP address) and verify that the configuration was moved, as well as that the version installed matches the targeted version.

At this stage, vCenter 6.7 should be running in your environment (either upgraded from the previous vCSA version, migrated from vCenter for Windows, or running as a Windows service in the case of vCenter for Windows). It is now time to upgrade your ESXi hypervisors.

Upgrading standalone ESXi servers

Once you have successfully upgraded your vCenter server to version 6.7, you can start with the ESXi servers.

It is crucial to check that your hardware is supported in the targeted version of VMware vSphere by using the **Hardware Compatibility List (HCL)**. Over time, some older hardware platforms will no longer be supported in the new vSphere releases.

The **ESXi Compatibility Checker** Python tool can be used to verify such compliance for you in an automated way.

ESXi compatibility checker

The ESXi compatibility checker tool which is available as a Fling from VMware labs at `https://labs.vmware.com/flings/esxi-compatibility-checker`, can save you from taking the time of going through the HCL manually. To use this tool, you have to install Python on your management station, as described in the **Requirements** tab of the tool in the preceding link.

 Flings are small projects that are being developed by VMware employees in their spare time. Why Flings? A Fling is a short-term thing, not a serious relationship but a fun one.

Once the tool has been successfully installed, you can quickly launch it, which will connect you to the ESXi server when you use the following command:

```
Compchecker.py -s IP or FQDN of ESXi -u root
```

The output of the preceding code is as follows:

```
C:\compchecker>compchecker.py -s esxi-prod-5.learnvmware.local -u root
    The authenticity of host 'esxi-prod-5.learnvmware.local' can't be established.
    RSA key fingerprint is 29:0E:3F:44:76:13:01:58:FB:87:30:08:B8:9E:57:4F:ED:7F:7F:4B.
    Are you sure you want to continue connecting (yes/no)? yes
    Warning: Permanently added 'esxi-prod-5.learnvmware.local' (RSA) to the list of known hosts.

    Enter password for host "esxi-prod-5.learnvmware.local" and user "root":

> Connecting host esxi-prod-5.learnvmware.local

> collecting host information...
    Please wait, this may take few minutes depending on the number of ESXi hosts...
    [WARNING] The compatible status may not be fully accurate, please validate it with the official VMware
Compatibility Guide

    [1]   esxi-prod-5.learnvmware.local: VMware ESXi 6.5.0 build-4564106

HostAgent esxi-prod-5.learnvmware.local> _
```

Once you have connected to the ESXi server, you can check what versions are available for upgrade based on the currently installed version:

- `host 1`: Selects the host (you might connect to the vCenter Server as well, and so multiple ESXi servers will be available. In the case of the standalone host, only one host, `host 1`, is available).
- `comp s`: Verifies the compatibility of the server hardware.
- `up`: Displays all versions that are available for upgrade.

Once you have decided which version you would like to upgrade to, you can verify the compatibility of the physical hardware using the following command:

```
upto 6.7.0 -s
```

The following screenshot shows the output of the preceding command:

```
HostAgent esxi-prod-5.learnvmware.local> upto 6.7.0 -s

  [OK] The specified release (VMware vSphere Hypervisor (ESXi) 6.7.0) is upgradable from this 6.5.0

  Hostesxi-prod-5.learnvmware.local: May Not Be Compatible

  [SERVER: Warnings] Server 'VMware Virtual Platform may not be compatible for ESX 6.7.0
  [IO: Warnings]  Some IO devices may not be compatible for ESX 6.7.0

  Compatibility issues:
    - IO Device 'vmxnet3 Virtual Ethernet Controller' (PCIID:15ad:07b0:0000:0000) is certified
      but current driver (nvmxnet3) is not supported
      More information: http://www.vmware.com/resources/compatibility/detail.php?deviceCategory=io&produ
ctid=45617

HostAgent esxi-prod-5.learnvmware.local> _
```

As you can see, in this case, the server might be upgraded to ESXi 6.7, but the current driver version of **VMXNET Generation 3 (VMXNET3)** is not supported.

Once you have confirmed that your hardware is compatible with the targeted version of VMware vSphere, you can decide how to perform the upgrade:

- **Using ISO installation media**: The ESXi server boots directly to the installation of the ESXi server and you can perform the upgrade from there
- **Using CLI:** Through SSH, you can connect to the running ESXi server and perform the upgrade from the running hypervisor

Updating or patching ESXi hosts through the installation ISO

You can boot into the installation image of ESXi server and perform the upgrade from here:

1. Insert the installation ISO image of the ESXi hypervisor to the physical CD-ROM (or the virtual one by using IPMI, iLO, or iDRAC, as discussed in `Chapter 2`, *Designing and Planning a Virtualization Infrastructure*).
2. Reboot the server and boot from the virtual CD-ROM.
3. The installation wizard is exactly the same one that appeared for installing the new ESXi servers on the physical hardware.

4. During installation, you can select where you can select a disk. When installing the ESXi servers, you will see an asterisk mark (*) that indicates that the previous version is already installed on the disk.

5. If you select a disk, you will have following options:
    - **Upgrade and preserve VMFS datastore**: Configuration will be preserved as well as the local datastore.
    - **Install and preserve VMFS datastore:** Configuration will be set to default, but the datastore will be preserved.
    - **Install and overwrite VMFS datastore**: Configuration will be set to default, and the datastore will be re-written. Be careful with the last option. If you have any existing virtual machines on such a datastore, they will be lost.

6. If you do not have any existing datastores on the disk, only the **Upgrade** or **Install** options will be available.

Once the installation or upgrade is done, reboot the server and verify the installed version in DCUI.

Updating or patching ESXi hosts through the command line

Patches and updates for ESXi are combined in a bundle provided by VMware in the .zip format that includes some **vSphere Installation Bundle** (**VIB**) ESXi software packages containing fixes and updates.

To proceed with the update, you need to obtain the latest available patches from the VMware website at https://my.vmware.com/group/vmware/patch. Patches and upgrades are cumulative, and the patch bundle is provided, which includes all past security and critical updates.

Once the patch bundle has been downloaded, proceed with the following steps:

1. From vSphere Client, log in to the ESXi host to upload the downloaded bundle to a local datastore that's reachable by the host. In the navigator area, select **Storage** and then select **Datastores** on the right-hand side.

2. From the available datastores, select the location on which you want to upload the patch and click **Datastore browser**.

3. Create a new folder or select an existing folder, and then click the **Upload** button to upload the patch. Click **Close** when the upload has completed.

Alternatively, you can use a tool such as WinSCP to copy the patch bundle directly to a local datastore on the ESXi host. This may be an option if ESXi hosts to be patched into the network don't have access to the same shared storage.

4. SSH the host using a tool such as PuTTY and log in to the host by entering the root credentials. If the SSH shell is not enabled, from vSphere Client, right-click the **Host** item and select **Services | Enable Secure Shell (SSH)** or enable the SSH service directly from the DCUI, as discussed in Chapter 5, *Configuring and Managing vSphere 6.7*.

5. Before patching the host, it can be useful to identify the currently installed build version by running the following command:

```
esxcli system version get
```

The following screenshot shows the output of the preceding command:

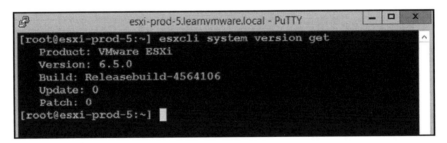

6. Before applying the patch, the host must be put in maintenance mode to migrate the running VM off the host and preventing new VMs to be placed in the hypervisor. To enter the host in maintenance mode, run the following command from the command line:

```
esxcli system maintenanceMode set --enable true
```

7. Make sure that the ESXi is in maintenance mode, and then proceed with the update procedure by running the following command:

```
esxcli software vib update -d
/vmfs/volumes/datastore/folder/patch_bundle.zip
```

8. When the patch has been applied successfully, you may need to reboot the host. Run the following command to do this:

```
reboot
```

9. When the ESXi host has been rebooted, exit the host from maintenance mode with the following command:

```
esxcli system maintenanceMode set --enable false
```

10. Check the host version after the update to confirm that the update was successful by running the following command:

```
esxcli system version get
```

Rolling back to the previous version

If something went wrong, thanks to the two independent boot banks, you have the option to roll back to the previous version.

To perform the rollback, follow these steps:

1. Reboot your ESXi server.
2. When the hypervisor progress bar starts loading, press *Shift* + *R*. You will see the following warning:

```
                    VMware Hypervisor Recovery
Installed hypervisors:

   HYPERVISOR1: 6.7.0-8169922 (Default)
   HYPERVISOR2: 6.5.0-0.0.4564106

CURRENT DEFAULT HYPERVISOR WILL BE REPLACED PERMANENTLY.
DO YOU REALLY WANT TO ROLL BACK?
```

3. Press *Y* to roll back the build.
4. Press *Enter* to boot.

 For more information, visit the official **KB1033604 – Reverting to a previous version of ESXi** at `https://kb.vmware.com/s/article/1033604`.

VUM

The VUM service is a tool that allows you to efficiently manage patches and updates for VM, hosts, and vApps that are installed in the virtual environment. In comparison to previous versions, VUM no longer requires the installation of an additional external Windows server. This is because, since vSphere 6.5, the Update Manager server and client components have become part of the vCSA.

VUM is installed during the vCSA installation, and it's enabled by default. VUM uses a PostgreSQL database that is bundled with the appliance to store its data. Although both vCenter Server and VUM share the same PostgreSQL database, they use a different database instance.

 In vSphere 6.7, a Windows-based Update Manager 6.7 instance cannot be connected to vCSA 6.7 during the installation procedure because it will fail with an error.

If Update Manager doesn't have access to the internet, you can install the optional **Update Manager Download Service (UMDS)** module to download virtual appliance upgrades, patch binaries, patch metadata, and notifications. UMDS must be installed on a machine with internet access and, in version 6.7, it's available for both Windows and Linux-based OSes.

Although VUM is integrated into the vCSA, the UI of the VUM is not yet fully supported in the HTML5 client. To use all of the features of VUM, you need to use an old FLEX Client. In VMware vSphere 6.7U1, it is fully integrated.

Configuring VUM

Default settings configured during the vCSA installation can be modified from the Update Manager administration area, and these changes are only applied to the Update Manager instance that's specified. If you have multiple Update Manager instances in your SSO domain, changes are not propagated to other instances in the group. To specify the Update Manager instance to work with, you have to select the name of the vCenter Server on which the Update Manager instance is registered.

To configure VUM from the vSphere Web Client, select **Home** | **Update Manager** and specify the vCenter Server instance to edit. In the **Manage** tab, you can specify the following VUM configuration settings:

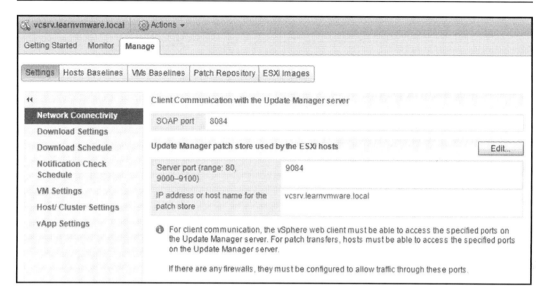

You can see the following tabs in the configuration settings:

- **Network Connectivity**: From this tab, you can only change the IP address or the hostname for the patch store.
- **Download Settings**: Edit this area to specify the patch type to download and additional custom URLs to specify third-party patch repositories. By enabling the **Use a shared repository** option, you can specify the URL of the UMDS instance that's used to centralize the downloads. If a proxy is used to access the internet, edit the **Proxy Settings** area to specify the correct parameters. Patches in ZIP format can also be imported into the repository by using the **Import Patches** button.

 Since the service strongly relies on DNS resolution, use an IP address whenever possible to avoid any potential DNS resolution problems. If you use a DNS name, make sure that the specified DNS name can be resolved by vCenter Server and from all ESXi hosts managed by Update Manager.

- **Download Schedule**: In this area, you specify the frequency of patch downloads with the option of sending a notification email (SMTP settings must be configured in vCenter Server by accessing **Configure | General area**).

- **Notification Check Schedule**: This is used to specify the frequency that's used by Update Manager to check the VMware repository for notifications about patch recalls, new fixes, and alerts.
- **VM Settings**: You can specify whether a snapshot of the VM should be taken before applying the patch. In case the remediation fails, you can quickly roll back to the snapshot taken before the remediation. Since snapshots affect VM performance, it's strongly recommended that a snapshot retention policy is defined to delete the created snapshots, saving precious storage space.
- **Host/Cluster Settings**: This area allows you to control the operations that are required during remediation. To apply the updates, the target host must be put in maintenance mode, and the running VM must be migrated to other hosts of the cluster to ensure availability. The operation can be automated if vSphere vMotion is configured and DRS is enabled in the cluster. You can also specify that you wish to install patches on PXE booted hosts, but updates are lost after the host reboots if the patch is not included in the host image as well.

The configuration of these settings may vary, depending on the setup of your infrastructure. However, as a general guideline, you can configure host and cluster settings as follows:

- **Disable any removable media devices**: Removable devices may prevent the host from entering in maintenance mode
- **Disable admission control**: It is suggested that this parameter is disabled to make additional resources available to the cluster, especially if you have a few hosts
- **Disable FT**: This is required if you have only two hosts

> When a new ESXi patch is available, ensure that you update the image that's used for PXE booted hosts as soon as possible to have the patch applied persistently.

- **vApp setting**: Enabled by default, this allows you to specify the use of the smart reboot feature to reboot the virtual appliances, thus maintaining the correct startup dependencies.

Working with baselines

To upgrade objects in your vSphere environment, you can use predefined hosts and VM baselines that are created during the installation of the vCSA. Baselines are used during the scan of the VM to determine the compliance level of scanned objects (**hosts, VM**, and **virtual appliances**).

While host baselines can be customized, you cannot create custom VM or VA baselines.

 In vSphere 6.5 Update 1, VUM was integrated into vSAN, providing an automated update process to ensure a vSAN cluster is up-to-date with the best available release to keep your hardware in a supported state.

VUM provides some predefined baselines that can only be attached or detached to the inventory objects, without the ability to edit or delete them:

- **Hosts baselines**: This provides critical host patches and non-critical host patches options
- **VMs/VAs baselines**: This provides a VMware Tools Upgrade to Match Host, a VM Hardware Upgrade to Match Host, and VA Upgrade to Latest

To create a new host baseline, proceed as follows:

1. From vSphere Web Client, select **Home | Update Manager** and select the vCenter Server instance on which Update Manager is registered.
2. Select **Manage | Hosts Baselines** and click **New Baseline**.
3. Enter a name in the **Name** field and description in the **Description** field for the new baseline and specify the baseline type area from the three available options. Click **Next**.
4. Specify the type of baseline patch you want to use and click **Next**. You have two baseline types to choose from:
   - **Static baseline**: The baseline doesn't change, even if new patches are added to the repository. You can create a static baseline to ensure that a specific patch is applied to all the hosts of your environment.
   - **Dynamic baseline**: This is useful to keep systems current as patches change over time. Dynamic baselines specify a set of patches that meet the criteria specified during the configuration, thus adding or removing some specific patches.

5. If a dynamic baseline type has been specified, you have to define the criteria to determine what patches to include in the baseline. For example, to create a host baseline specifically for critical bug fixes, you can select the parameters that meet your needs in the **New Baseline** wizard. You can also specify a release date range to restrict patches that will be included in the baseline:

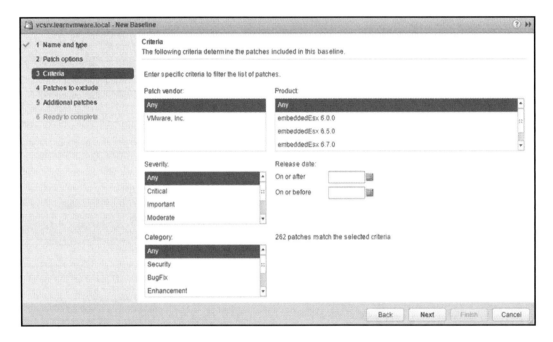

6. Select patches to exclude from the baseline and click **Next**.
7. Specify additional patches, if any, to include in the baseline and click **Next**.

8. When the parameters have been defined, click **Finish** in the **Summary** window to create the new baseline.

To verify which hypervisor is not compliant with the parameters that were configured in the created baseline, the new baseline must be attached to the ESXi hosts executing the **scan** procedure (host scans will be discussed later in this chapter in the *Scanning VMs and hosts* section).

Baseline groups

In addition to baselines, you can define baseline groups that are used to put together different existing baselines to meet specific needs for your environment. For example, baseline groups can be used if you want to update ESXi hosts in your environment, ensuring that a specific patch is applied during remediation. You can create a baseline group by combining a dynamic baseline for patches and a static baseline with the specific patch you want to apply. To install the latest updates and host extensions to ESXi hosts, using a baseline group allows you to combine different baseline types, performing the task in a single step and simplifying the overall procedure.

To create a new baseline group, from vSphere Web Client, select **Home** | **Update Manager** and click the **Manage** tab. You need to follow these steps:

1. Select **Hosts Baselines** and click the new baseline group button. Enter a name and description and then click **Next.**
2. Specify the upgrades to apply, if any, and then click **Next.**
3. Select the patch baseline to use and click **Next.**
4. Select the extension to apply to the hosts and then click **Next.**
5. In the **Summary** window, click **Finish** to create the new baseline group:

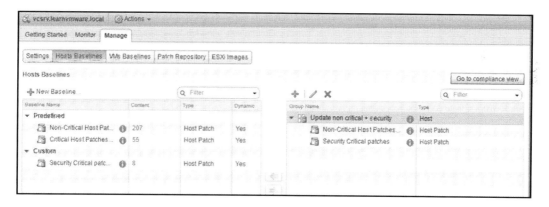

To edit or delete a baseline, right-click the baseline to process and select the **EDIT** or **DELETE** baseline option accordingly.

Attaching or detaching baselines

Once a baseline or a baseline group has been created, you must attach it to a host or VM to scan and determine whether the object is compliant. By attaching a baseline at a higher level in vCenter Server, it will also be applied to child objects. You can attach different baselines at different levels if you need to apply specific baselines to specific objects.

To attach or detach baselines or baseline groups to hosts or VMs, proceed with the following steps:

1. Using vSphere Web Client, from the inventory, select to view the object level on which you want to attach the baseline or baseline group and select the **Update Manager** tab.
2. Click the **Attach Baseline...** button to select the baselines to use from the list and then click **OK.**
3. To detach a baseline, right-click the baseline or baseline group to remove it and click the **Detach Baseline...** button:

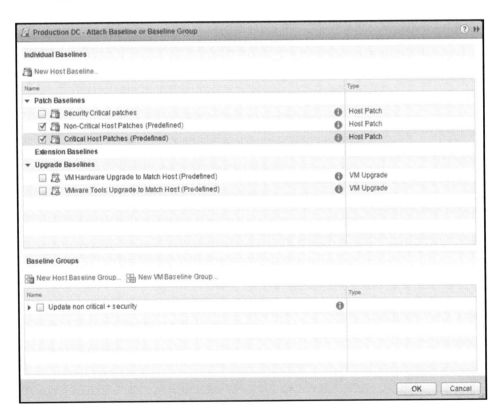

Use the **Hosts and Clusters** view to attach baselines to ESXi hosts, and the **VMs and Templates** view to attach baselines to VMs.

Scanning VMs and hosts

The scanning process allows for the identification of hosts, VMs, or virtual appliances that are not compliant with the attached baselines and baseline groups.

Object scans can be initiated manually or scheduled. To perform a manual scan, select the vCenter Server, data center, cluster, or the host object and then select the **Update Manager** tab:

1. To scan hosts, click the **Scan for Updates...** button to open the dialog box. Select **Patches** and **Extensions** and **Upgrades** as types of updates to scan for, and then click **OK**.

2. To scan VMs and vApps, the procedure to follow is similar to what is performed for hosts. Click the **Scan for Updates...** button and select any of the three available options – **Virtual appliance upgrades**, **VMware Tools upgrades**, and **VM Hardware upgrades**. Click OK to proceed with the scan.

The **Compliance Status** column indicates whether the scanned objects are **Compliant** or **Non-Compliant** against the attached baselines and baseline groups. If the value reported is **Non-Compliant**, you need to perform the remediation of missing patches or updates:

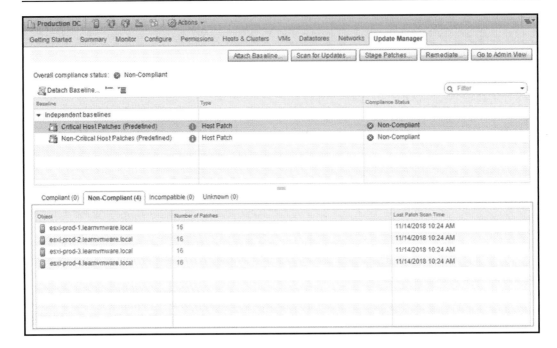

Staging and remediating patches

If the scanned hosts are marked as non-compliant, you need to remediate them to apply missing patches or updates. You have the option to stage or remediate patches and updates.

Let's see the differences between the two processes:

- **Staging**: Patches are copied from Update Manager to the ESXi hosts across the network. This allows you to reduce the remediation time. Staging host patches is not a required step, and it is not necessary to put hosts in maintenance mode while patches are staged. If you have hosts connected to Update Manager over slow WAN, staging patches can reduce the ESXi outage that's required for remediation.
  To proceed with staging from vSphere Web Client, click the **Stage Patches...** button in the **Update Manager** tab and follow these steps:
  1. Select the baselines to attach and click **Next.**
  2. Specify the hosts on which you want to stage patches and then click **Next.**

3. Select the patches and extensions to be staged in the selected hosts and click **Next.**

4. Review the settings selection and then click **Finish** to begin the staging process.

- **Remediating**: The remediation process applies patches and upgrades to the objects that are non-compliant with the attached baseline. To remediate hosts from vSphere Web Client, click the **Remediate...** button in the **Update Manager** tab and follow these steps:

    1. Select the baseline to apply to the hosts and click **Next.**

    2. Select the hosts to remediate and click **Next.**

    3. Select the patches and extensions to apply to selected hosts and click **Next.**

    4. In the **Advanced options** step, you can schedule the remediation task by specifying the name of the task, description of the task, and remediation time. You can also choose to ignore warnings for unsupported hardware devices that may stop the remediation procedure. When you are done with this, click **Next.**

    5. In the **Host remediation options**, be sure to leave the VM power state as set to **Do Not Change VM Power State** to avoid VM downtime, allowing the system to vMotion the VMs to other hosts. Also, tick the **Disable any removable media devices connected to the virtual machines on the host** option. After doing this, click **Next.**

    6. Specify the **Cluster remediation options** to apply to the selected cluster during remediation. Disable DPM, FT (if you have only two hosts in the cluster), and HA admission control (if you have a few hosts in the cluster), and click **Next.**

 By default, the remediation process runs sequentially for host members of a cluster. You can enable the remediation in parallel by ticking the appropriate option in the **Cluster remediation options** step.

    7. After reviewing the settings selection, click **Finish** to begin the remediation procedure for the selected hosts. When the remediation process is complete, ESXi hosts will be patched/upgraded and ready to host a VM.

If you do not have a DRS license (for vSphere Standard or Essentials), the host won't switch to the maintenance mode automatically because DRS will not be able to migrate the VMs from the hosts. You have to perform the vMotion of running VMs manually. The same applies if you have your cluster DRS configuration set to **Partially automated**. If the DRS is set to automatic, migration will be invoked by the system user, just like any vMotion that is invoked by DRS.

Once the remediation process finishes, the scan will be invoked automatically, and you should see that all ESXi hosts are compatible with the attached baselines.

Upgrading hosts with VUM

VUM allows you to upgrade an ESXi host from a previously supported version to the current version.

The first step is the creation of the baseline so that you can attach the hosts to upgrade:

1. From vSphere Web Client, select **Home** | **Update Manager** and select the vCenter Server instance you wish to configure. Select the **Manage** tab.
2. Navigate to **ESXi Images** and click the **Import ESXi Image** button to import the image file that's used to upgrade the ESXi hosts.
3. From the wizard, click on the **BROWSE** button and select the ISO file to use for the upgrade, and then click **Next** to upload the image into VUM.
4. When the upload has been completed, a review of the ESXi image information is displayed. Click **Close** to exit the import wizard. The uploaded image listed in the **ESXi Images** tab will be used to create the baseline.
5. Go to the **Hosts Baselines** tab and click the **New Baseline** button. In the wizard, enter the name of the new baseline and, optionally, add a description. This is useful for identifying the baseline scope. Under **Baseline Type**, select **Host Upgrade** and then click **Next**.
6. Select the ESXi image to use for the upgrade and then click **Next**.

7. A review of the settings selection is displayed. Click **Finish** to create the baseline and exit the wizard:

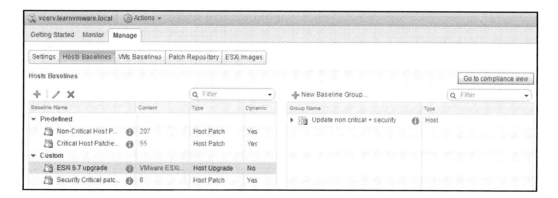

8. Click the **Go to compliance view** button to attach the new baseline to the hosts to upgrade.
9. In the **Update Manager** tab, click the **Attach Baseline...** button to specify the baseline to attach to the object level (cluster) that contains the ESXi hosts you need to upgrade to the new version and click **OK**.
10. Click the **Scan for Updates...** button to verify the host's compliance against the attached baseline. In the **Confirm Scan** wizard, specify **Upgrades** as the scan for the option and then click **OK**.
11. Click the **Remediate** button and select the created baseline to apply to the ESXi hosts. Click **Next** to continue.

Before starting the remediation process of the hosts, back up the current ESXi configuration to quickly restore the hypervisor in case something goes wrong with the upgrade.

12. Select the target ESXi hosts to remediate and then click **Next**.
13. Accept the EULA and click **Next** to continue the upgrade procedure.
14. Follow the remediation steps, as we discussed previously.

As a result of the remediation procedure, the processed ESXi hosts will now be compliant against the applied baseline.

You can verify the installed version in the **Summary** tab of the ESXi server.

If you are upgrading host members of a cluster, it is suggested to upgrade one host at a time to prevent cluster failure in the event of problems during the remediation process.

Upgrading VM hardware

Another useful feature of VUM is the option to automate and schedule the upgrade of VM hardware version. A VM with an outdated hardware version cannot take advantage of new features that are introduced in the latest VMware vSphere releases. VUM allows admins to easily identify VMs that don't have a current hardware version and upgrade them automatically.

VUM comes with a predefined VM hardware baseline that you can't change or delete, but you should use to upgrade the VM hardware to the current version (vSphere 6.7 introduces hardware version 14).

 Hardware upgrades can be performed only while the VM is powered off. If you plan a hardware upgrade of your VM, you should consider that this process will cause downtime.

The hardware upgrade steps are similar to what we have discussed already:

1. From vSphere Web Client, go to the **VMs and Templates** inventory view and select the object level (data center, for example) on which you want to attach the baseline.
2. Select the **Update Manager** tab and click the **Attach Baseline...** button. Select the **VM Hardware Upgrade to Match Host** option and click **OK**.
3. Click the **Scan for Updates** button to check the VM's compliance against the attached baseline. In the **Scan for Updates** wizard, specify **VM Hardware upgrades** as the scan option to allow VUM to detect outdated VM hardware. Then, click **OK**.
4. Now, click **Remediate** to configure the task and upgrade the hardware version for outdated VMs.
5. The remediation procedure requires the selection of the baseline to attach and the selection of the objects to remediate.

6. The remediation task can be scheduled to be executed in the correct maintenance window where the downtime is due to the upgrade having a minor impact on the production environment. By defining a task name and a task description, you can remediate the VM on power cycle, or you can specify three different schedules depending on the state of the VM: powered on, powered off, or suspended. By default, all three options are configured to run the action immediately, so you should pay attention before confirming the remediation execution. Click **Next** to continue.

7. Specify the remediation **Rollback options** step to revert the VM to the state before the remediation if something goes wrong during the upgrade process. It's recommended to configure snapshot retention so that you can delete the snapshot after a specified time. This will help you avoid performance issues. Click **Next** to go to the final step.

8. Review your settings selection and click **Finish** to execute or schedule the remediated task.

Upgrading VM Tools

VUM can also be used to automate the VMware Tools upgrade process for the VM in the inventory. During the powering on or the restart of a VM, Update Manager can be configured to check the VMware Tools version that's installed in the VM and perform the upgrade to the newest version that's supported by the host that is running the VM. The upgrade of VMware Tools can be scheduled to avoid VM downtime during working hours.

The procedure is the same as what's used to upgrade the hardware version of a VM:

1. From vSphere Web Client, go to the **VMs and Templates** inventory to attach the requested baseline.

2. Once the **VM Tools Upgrade to Match Host** baseline has been attached
   (through the **Attach baseline...** button), click **Scan for Updates...**, selecting
   VM Tools upgrades as the option to check the VM's compliance against the
   attached baseline. After doing this, click **OK:**

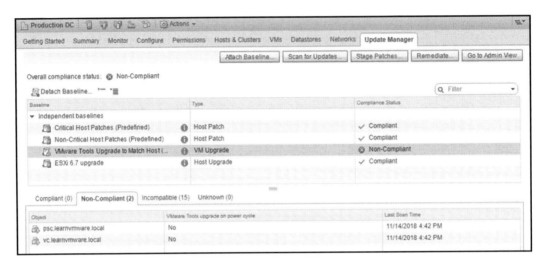

 If the virtual machines do not have VMware Tools installed, they
will be listed in incompatible objects.

3. To remediate a non-compliant VM, click the **Remediate** button to upgrade
   the VM Tools for an outdated VM.
4. Now follow the steps we used previously to upgrade the hardware version
   to complete the remediation procedure.
5. Once the upgrade has been performed, you will see that the previously
   non-compliant objects are now in a compliant state.

Updating the vCSA

You should check for minor updates of the vCSA to keep it up-to-date. For minor
upgrades on the same major version, you do not need to use a vCSA installation ISO
image – the upgrade can be performed from the VAMI interface of the vCSA or CLI.

Updating the vCSA through the command line

Since vSphere 6.5, upgrading the vCSA has also been simplified. There are two ways to patch the vCSA—through VAMI, which was introduced in vSphere 6, or by using the command line. From the VMware website, download the latest vCenter Server update that's provided in ISO format and save it anywhere on your computer. The ISO image containing the patches must be uploaded to shared storage that's accessible from the vCSA that's present in the network. The ISO image can also be attached to the CD/DVD drive of the vCSA.

 Before proceeding with the update, take a snapshot of the vCSA to quickly revert to a working state in case something goes wrong during the patching process.

Staging and remediating patches

Patches from the ISO file that were previously downloaded from the VMware website can be staged to the vCSA for updates. This can be done by attaching the ISO image to the CD/DVD drive of the vCSA or by specifying a datastore ISO file.

Staging patches is a useful procedure for speeding up the remediation process because patches are already available locally on the vCSA and the downtime during remediation is reduced.

Mount the ISO image patch to the vCSA VM and SSH the vCSA using a tool such as PuTTY. Enter the root credentials to log in to the vCSA and proceed with the upgrade procedure of the vCSA.

To check the current vCSA version from the CLI, you can use the following command:

```
vpxd -v
```

The following screenshot shows the output of the preceding command:

```
Command> shell
Shell access is granted to root
root@vcsrv [ ~ ]# vpxd -v
VMware VirtualCenter 6.7.0 build-8833179
root@vcsrv [ ~ ]#
```

To stage packages to the vCSA, run the following command:

```
software-packages stage --url
```

Staged patches information can be checked with the following command:

```
software-packages list --staged
```

If a mistake is made during the patch staging procedure, you can always unstage the staged patches by running the following command:

```
software-packages unstage
```

To install staged patches, run the following command from the command line:

```
software-packages install --staged
```

Staging patches is not a requirement and updates can be installed directly from an attached ISO image. To install patches directly from the ISO image, run the following command:

```
software-packages install --iso
```

The patch installation process requires a few minutes to complete, and a reboot may be necessary.

After the reboot, check the installed version again with the vpxd -v command:

```
Command> shell
Shell access is granted to root
root@vcsrv [ ~ ]# vpxd -v
VMware VirtualCenter 6.7.0 build-10244857
root@vcsrv [ ~ ]#
```

Updating the vCSA with VAMI

To make the overall procedure simpler, the vCSA can also be updated using the UI through the VAMI. To access the VAMI, type https://<VCSA_IP>:5480 into your favorite browser and enter the root credentials.

Perform the following steps to install the available updates from the repository or the ISO image:

1. Access the **Update** tab and select the **Check Updates | Check Repository** option to check the available updates from the default VMware repository:

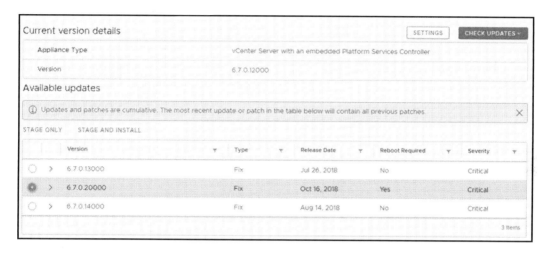

2. If the ISO image has been mounted to the vCSA VM, from the **Update** tab, select the **Check Updates | Check CDROM** option to install the available updates directly from the ISO image.
3. If a new update has been detected, the **Available updates** area displays the information related to the available update, but the current release doesn't provide a list of patches that will be installed in the system. Click **Install updates** to proceed with the update installation.
4. The installation requires a few minutes to complete, and a reboot of the vCSA may be required to complete the update process. Click **OK** to proceed with the upgrade.

If a vCSA in your network is configured with an external PSC, patches or updates must be applied to the PSC and its replicating partners first, and then, if installed, in the vCenter SSO domain.

If a proxy is enabled in the network configuration of your vCSA, you might experience a generic download failed error (both PSC and vCenter Server are affected) when you try checking for updates online through VAMI.

To quickly fix this issue, perform the following steps:

- **From the vCSA UI**, enable the **Proxy Settings** in the **Networking** area.
- From CLI, SSH the vCSA, edit the `/etc/sysconfig/proxy` file, and manually enter a valid HTTP proxy address in the `HTTPS_PROXY` line, as in this example:

```
HTTPS_PROXY="https://proxy.domain.com:3128/"
```

Once the appliance has been upgraded, you should see the correct version installed in the **Summary** window in the VAMI interface.

Summary

To keep the infrastructure healthy, ESXi hosts and vCenter Servers must be patched on a regular basis.

We covered all three ways of getting vCenter 6.7: upgrading the vCSA, upgrading the vCenter for Windows, and migrating from vCenter for Windows to vCSA.

You have learned that ESXi hosts can be patched and updated using the command line if a vCenter Server is not available in the network using different methods and the automated method using VMware Update Manager was covered as well. Update Manager can be also used to upgrade VMware Tools, hardware version of the VM and Virtual Appliances.

The vCSA itself can be patched and updated using the command line by staging and remediating the mounted ISO image patch file or through the VAMI that provides a visual UI.

The next chapter will focus on virtual ,machines. We will cover the different virtual hardware can be used and describe the difference between emulated and paravirtualized devices and all virtual machine options. Templates and snapshots will be discussed, as well as their benefits.

Questions

1. What are the supported vSphere 6.7 Upgrade or migrate paths?

    a) vCenter Server for Windows with embedded PSC to vCSA with External PSC
    b) vCSA 6.5 with embedded PSC to vCSA 6.7 with embedded PSC
    c) vCenter Server for Windows with embedded PSC and external database to vCSA with Embedded PSC and external database
    d) vCenter Server for Windows with external PSC to vCSA with External PSC
    e) vCSA 6.5 with external PSC to vCSA 6.7 with external PSC
    f) vCenter for Windows 6.5 with embedded PSC and embedded database to vCenter 6.7 for Windows with embedded PSC and embedded database

2. vCSA should be deployed as a best practice compared to vCenter for Windows:

    a) True
    b) False

3. ESXi hypervisor can be upgraded using which of the following methods?

    a) vSphere Update Manager
    b) The `vi-cfg` tool
    c) The `esxcli` tool
    d) ISO installation media
    e) The `esxi-update` tool

4. Update Manager can be used for the automation of vSphere upgrades:

    a) True
    b) False

5. What default baselines are available in Update Manager?
6. It is not necessary to perform a backup of vCSA when upgrading through VAMI, and the backup is done automatically:

    a) True
    b) False

7. Please describe the purpose of the migration assistant during the migration from vCenter for Windows to vCSA.

8. If you perform an upgrade of vCSA, it is considered an in-place upgrade:

   a) True
   b) False

Further reading

During the launch of VMware vSphere 6.7, VMware introduced several posts regarding the upgrade procedure, the upgrade of the different parts of the vSphere, and much more. Feel free to check the whole series:

- **Preparing to Upgrade:** `https://blogs.vmware.com/vsphere/2018/07/vsphere-upgrade-series-part-1-preparing-to-upgrade.html`
- **Upgrading vCenter Server:** `https://blogs.vmware.com/vsphere/2018/07/vsphere-upgrade-series-part-2-upgrading-vcenter-server.html`
- **Upgrading vSphere Hosts:** `https://blogs.vmware.com/vsphere/2018/07/vsphere-upgrade-series-part-3-upgrading-vsphere-hosts.html`
- **VMware tools and VM Compatibility:** `https://blogs.vmware.com/vsphere/2018/09/vsphere-upgrade-series-part-4-upgrading-vmware-tools-and-vm-compatibility.html`
- **Upgrading VMFS Storage:** `https://blogs.vmware.com/vsphere/2018/09/vsphere-upgrade-series-part-5-upgrading-vmfs-storage.html`
- **Upgrading vSphere Networking:** `https://blogs.vmware.com/vsphere/2018/09/vsphere-upgrade-series-part-6-upgrading-vsphere-networking.html`
- **Migrating to the vCenter Server Appliance**. You can have a look at a different walkthrough for any upgrade scenario that's available in VMware vSphere 6.7 here: `https://blogs.vmware.com/vsphere/2018/10/vcenter-server-windows-migrations.html`

2
Section 2: Managing Resources

This section focuses on the virtual machines and infrastructure that's required to support them. We will start with the network configuration, and we will cover all the essential techniques that allow you to access the network in the most effective way. Then, storage components will be introduced, including the logical design of different types of storage and advanced storage features such as Storage DRS and Storage I/O Control. Lastly, we will cover virtual machines, how to work them, and how to assign resources to them in the most efficient way.

The following chapters are included in this section:

- Chapter 7, *Managing Networking Resources*
- Chapter 8, *Managing Storage Resources*
- Chapter 9, *VM Deployment and Management*
- Chapter 10, *VM Resource Management*

Managing Networking Resources

7

bIn this chapter, we will be discussing networking from the basics to advanced network functions. Networking is an essential part of the VMware infrastructure, and we should have a deep understanding of the configuration options as well as the overall concepts.

In this chapter, we will cover the following topics:

- Basic network overview
- Virtual networking with switches
- Managing standard virtual networking
- Managing distributed virtual networking
- **Network I/O Control** (**NIOC**)
- Advanced network functions

Basic network overview

Without a basic understanding of different network technologies, it might be quite complicated to understand the nuances in virtual networking correctly, so before we dive into virtual networking, let's have a look at some necessary technologies, acronyms, and features that will give you a better understanding of the whole networking concept.

We will start with the basics, and then we will cover selected features and technologies that you will get in touch concerning virtual networking in VMware vSphere.

OSI model

The OSI model is a conceptual model that is used to describe how data flows in a network from one device to another. There are seven layers, from the lowest (physical media) all the way up to the application layer as shown in the following diagram:

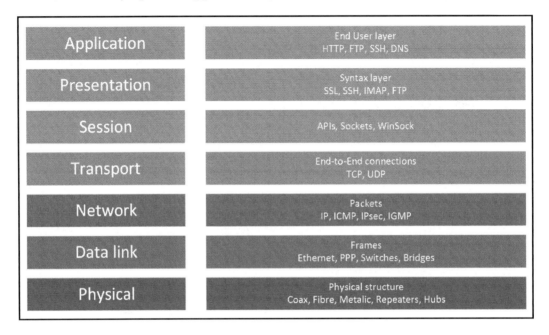

As an example, let's have a look at the HTTP communication between client and server.

In the beginning, a user wants to access some web page from a web browser.

We will skip the DNS communication that precedes the HTTP communication to keep it simple. We will also skip the three upper layers (Application, Presentation and Session layer). *What happens?* The browser will issue an HTTP request to URL `http:/` `/www.learnvmware.online`. This request contains application-specific data, such as which object we want to receive from which session from the browser. This application data is then encapsulated by the transport layer. In the case of HTTP, the data is divided into several TCP fragments. Each TCP fragment contains information about the source and destination TCP ports. Those fragments are then sent to the underlaying layer—Network Layer and information about the source and destination IP address are added to the packet.

Next, this packet is sent to the data link, which will add source and destination MAC addresses, and lastly the frame is sent to the physical link as a stream of ones and zeros.

Once those bits are received on the receiving side, the process is done backward. First, the bits are translated to the Ethernet frames, from there to the IP packets, then to the TCP segments, and finally received by the application—the HTTP server.

For details, see `https://learningnetwork.cisco.com/docs/DOC-30382`.

Encapsulation and de-encapsulation

Information that is transmitted over the network must undergo a process of conversion at the sending and receiving ends of the communication. The conversion process is encapsulation and de-encapsulation. You can imagine this as an onion and its layers. Sometimes you need to encapsulate one packet or frame (depending on which OSI layer the encapsulation takes place).

For instance, in software-defined networking, VXLANs are used. In this case, the original packet is encapsulated by VXLAN headers and travelers across the network, and on the receiving side, the VXLAN packet is de-encapsulated to the original packet:

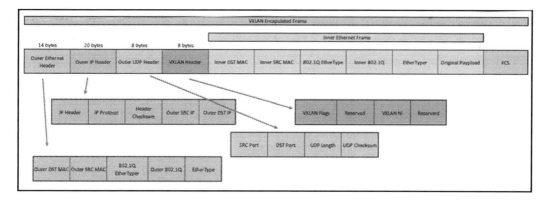

For details about VXLAN, refer to `https://blogs.vmware.com/vsphere/2013/04/vxlan-series-different-components-part-1.html`, or you can have a look at generic encapsulation techniques at `http://www.firewall.cx/networking-topics/the-osi-model/179-osi-data-encapsulation.html`.

MAC tables and MAC learning process

Physical switches use MAC tables to perform frame forwarding. Physical switches learn and build the MAC table. The switch reads the **Ethernet headers** and learns the MAC address of the device and makes an entry in its MAC table.

By populating MAC tables, the switches learn on which physical port the corresponding client MAC address is located. This is the example output from the Juniper physical switch:

```
admin@sw-dc-1> show ethernet-switching table
 Ethernet-switching table: 245 entries, 230 learned, 0 persistent
entries
 VLAN MAC address Type Age Interfaces
 lan * Flood - All-members
 lan 00:07:4d:6a:64:3d Learn 3:00 ge-1/0/15.0
 lan 00:0c:29:20:4c:bf Learn 0 ge-0/0/1.0
 lan 00:0c:29:53:1b:64 Learn 0 ge-0/0/1.0
 lan 00:10:db:ff:10:00 Learn 0 ae0.0
 lan 00:15:70:d9:00:8f Learn 0 ge-0/0/18.0
 lan 00:15:70:d9:94:11 Learn 0 ge-1/0/16.0
```

Address Resolution Protocol (ARP) can discover a MAC address that corresponds to a known IP address, in order to permit the building of the layer 2 packets. From ESXi, you can see the ARP packets with this command:

```
[root@esxi-prod-1:~] tcpdump-uw arp
tcpdump-uw: verbose output suppressed, use -v or -vv for full protocol
decode
listening on vmk0, link-type EN10MB (Ethernet), capture size 262144
bytes
16:46:09.101046 ARP, Request who-has 172.16.1.2 tell 172.16.1.1,
length 46
16:46:09.118221 ARP, Request who-has 172.16.1.254 tell 172.16.1.1,
length 46
16:46:11.694890 ARP, Request who-has esxi-prod-1.learnvmware.local
(00:50:56:a7:b4:2d (oui Unknown)) tell 172.16.1.250, length 46
16:46:11.703010 ARP, Reply esxi-prod-1.learnvmware.local is-at
00:50:56:a7:b4:2d (oui Unknown), length 28
```

On ESXi, there is a local ARP table for all the VMkernel interfaces, and you can print it with the `esxcli network ip neighbor list` command:

```
[root@esxi-prod-1:~] esxcli network ip neighbor list
 Neighbor Mac Address Vmknic Expiry State Type
 ------------ ------------------ ------ -------- ----- -------
 172.16.1.250 00:0c:29:60:69:d4 vmk0 1180 sec Unknown
```

```
172.16.1.85 00:0c:29:3d:df:9a vmk0 662 sec Unknown
172.16.1.1 00:0c:29:e0:d6:2d vmk0 1197 sec Unknown
172.16.1.2 00:0c:29:a5:68:75 vmk0 1187 sec Unknown
```

You will see all IP addresses, corresponding MAC addresses and VMkernel adapters on which such an entry is visible.

Maximum Transmission Unit (MTU)

According to the original IEEE 802.3 specifications, a valid Ethernet frame size is from 64 to 1,518 bytes. A standard Ethernet header is 18 bytes in length in total so the payload (or content) of the frame ranges from 46 to 1,500 bytes.

However, since the original Ethernet specification was defined, different IEEE standards have been developed that support additional, expanded frame types, listed here as follows:

- **VLAN tagging (802.1Q)**: This is with an additional four bytes in the Ethernet header.
- **Provider Bridge (PB) 802.1ad**: This is with an additional eight bytes to the original frame to support service and customer tagging.
- **FCoE frames**: These have an MTU of 2,500 bytes.
- **Multiprotocol Label Switching (MPLS)**: This increases the maximum Ethernet frame size to *1,518 bytes + (n * 4 bytes)*, where *n* is the number of stacked labels.
- **VXLAN**: This adds another 50 bytes.
- **Jumbo frames**: These are Ethernet frames with more than 1,500 bytes of payload, typically around 9,000 bytes. They are mostly used for IP-based storage traffic.

Which is the recommended MTU? If you plan to use jumbo frames for iSCSI or NFS traffic, there is a specific **KB 1007654: iSCSI and Jumbo Frames configuration on VMware ESXi/ESX** at https://kb.vmware.com/s/article/1007654. For VXLAN traffic, the recommended MTU is 1,600.

Generally, as a best practice, you should use jumbo frames (MTU 9,000) for iSCSI or NFS traffic. If you do not use jumbo frames, the overhead from *chopping* the large packets to the smaller frames can affect the performance of your IP storage.

Keep in mind that all network devices within the path must be configured for the jumbo frames. Otherwise, the packets will be divided into the smaller ones on the way.

MTU unit details can be found at `https://tools.ietf.org/html/rfc791`, `https://tools.ietf.org/html/rfc1191` and `https://en.wikipedia.org/wiki/Maximum_transmission_unit`.

Virtual LAN (VLAN)

VLAN is a broadcast domain so that you can be segmenting Ethernet broadcast domains with VLANs. Network ports might be configured with one (access or untagged mode) or multiple VLANs (trunk or tagged mode).

802.1Q trunking modifies Ethernet frames to add a numeric tag. Using this tag can forward frames to different VLANs. Native VLAN is the untagged VLAN on an 802.1Q trunked switch port. VMware vSphere supports **external VLAN tagging** (only at a physical switch level), **virtual switch VLAN tagging**, and **VM VLAN tagging**. In the following diagram, you can see which Ethernet fields are part of the Ethernet frame:

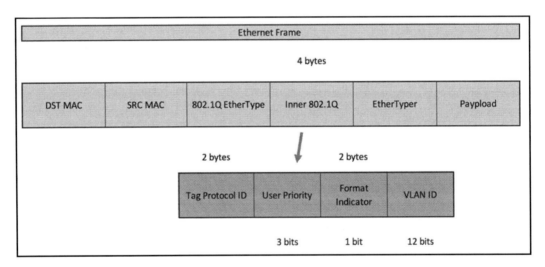

With VLANs, we can logically isolate different types of traffic even using the same shared physical media. For more information, refer to `https://tools.ietf.org/html/rfc3069`.

Transmission Control Protocol (TCP) versus User Datagram Protocol (UDP)

TCP is connection-oriented; once a connection is established, data can be sent bidirectionally, and TCP provides guaranteed delivery packets. UDP is a simpler, connectionless protocol that provides a network without the overhead of a reliability mechanism.

With TCP, the communication is reliable; if the packets are not received, they will be retransmitted. UDP, on the other side, is more like fire-and-forget.

Some vSphere-related services are based on TCP or UDP, depending on the type of service.

For more information about UDP, see `https://tools.ietf.org/html/rfc768`.
For more information about TCP, see `https://tools.ietf.org/html/rfc793`.

IPv6

Starting with vSphere 4.1, there is support for both IPv4 and IPv6, although IPv6 support was initially disabled by default. With vSphere 5.1, IPv6 has become enabled by default for VMkernel traffic.

For guest OSes, both on Linux and Windows systems, it becomes challenging to disable it, and Microsoft does not recommend disabling IPv6. We do not recommend that you disable IPv6 or its components, or some Windows components may not function correctly.

You can find more details on IPv6 at `https://www.ietf.org/rfc/rfc2460.txt`.

Virtual networking with switches

Before we jump to the details about vSwitches, we have to understand which critical components of vSphere networking are available. We will dive deeper in to the individual components and the configuration options later on, but for now, let's have a brief look at them:

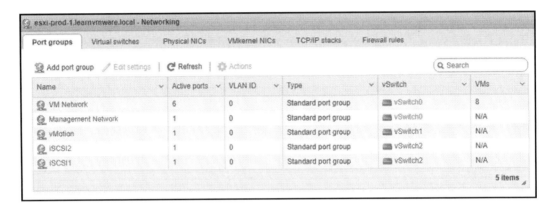

These are the components as seen in the preceding screenshot:

- **Port groups**: This is a logical container that is used to interconnect your VMs. On the port group, you can define to which VLAN a port group belongs, and by default the port group will inherit the configuration from the virtual switch, but you can override such settings if you need to.
- **Virtual switches**: In the VMware world, we have two types of virtual switches, which are classified as **vNetwork Standard Switch (vSS)** and **vNetwork Distributed Switch (vDS)**. The vSS is configured on every ESXi host, meaning independently on each ESXi host in your environment. The vDS is managed from a vCenter Server at the datacenter level.
  The virtual switch is a software construct running in the VMkernel. The virtual switch provides two connectivity types between physical network interface cards to the VM (VM port group) and the hypervisor services (VMkernel ports).
- **Physical NICs**: These are the physical network interface cards available in the ESXi server. These physical NICs are connected to the physical network infrastructure, and on the other side they are the uplinks for your standard or distributed vSwitches.

- **VMkernel NICs**: If the ESXi server needs to communicate over the network, it uses the VMkernel NIC. VMkernel NICs are IP-enabled interfaces of the ESXi server, and you can create multiple VMkernel NICs for different IP services of the ESXi server (vMotion, **Fault Tolerance** (**FT**), management traffic, and others).
- **TCP/IP stacks**: We can compare these to virtual routing instances in physical networking. By default, you can have only a single default gateway, thus you need to use static routes if you have a complex layer 3 network topology. By using different TCP/IP stacks, you can simplify such configurations.
- **Firewall rules:** As we have already discussed, you can configure the built-in firewall of the ESXi server there. For instance, you can limit the connections to the management interface of the ESXi server even without configuring a physical firewall or **access control lists** (**ACLs**) on the physical router.

Standard virtual switch (vSwitch) overview

Let's have a look at the standard vSwitch defined in the ESXi server. As we have said, the vSwitch is used to interconnect your VMs and VMkernel ports with the physical uplink network interface cards:

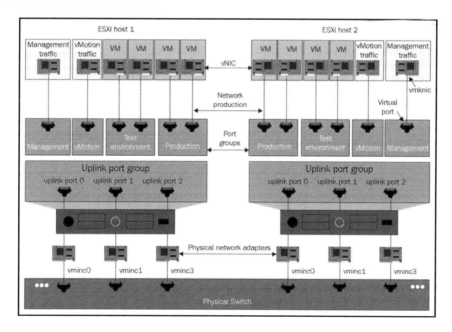

Each vSwitch configuration can be viewed in the vSphere Client.

To access the vSwitch configuration, follow these steps:

1. Click **Networking** in the navigator
2. Then select the **Virtual Switches** tab
3. Select the vSwitch you are interested in:

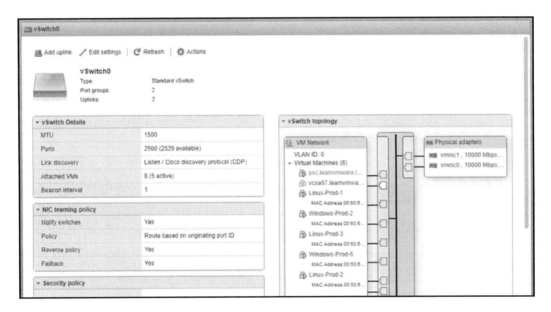

The same can be achieved from the CLI:

1. Connect to the ESXi server using SSH.
2. Issue the `esxcli network vswitch standard list` command:

```
[root@esxi-prod-1:~] esxcli network vswitch standard list
vSwitch0
Name: vSwitch0
Class: cswitch
Num Ports: 2560
Used Ports: 12
Configured Ports: 128
MTU: 1500
CDP Status: listen
Beacon Enabled: false
Beacon Interval: 1
Beacon Threshold: 3
Beacon Required By:
```

```
Uplinks: vmnic1, vmnic0
Portgroups: VM Network, Management Network
```

Distributed vSwitch overview

The following diagram shows what your typical vDS should look like. The entire configuration is performed on the vCenter servers, where you define what the vSwitch looks like, and then this template is pushed to the ESXi servers:

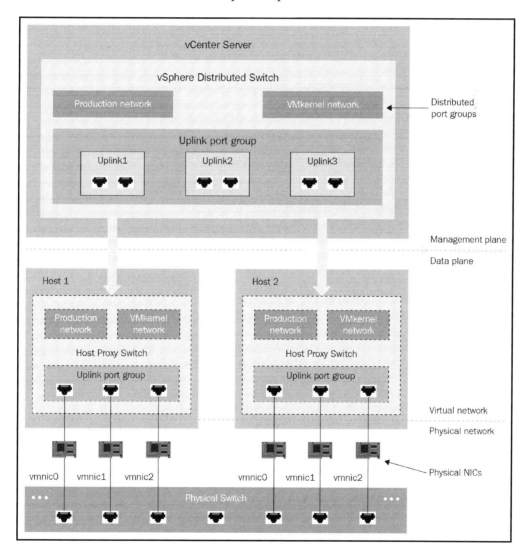

To configure a distributed vSwitch, launch the vSphere client of the vCenter server and switch to the networking view:

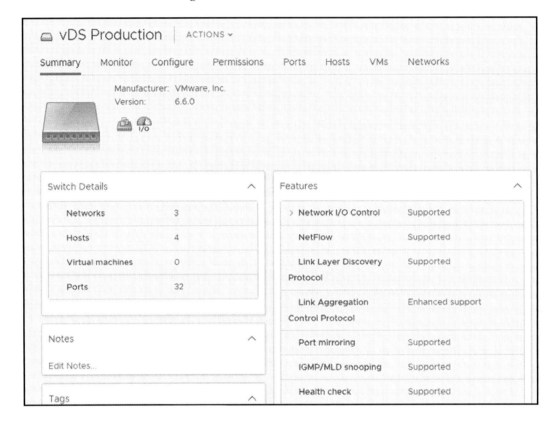

Once the vSwitch is configured on the vCenter level and the ESXi hosts are connected to the vDS, you can use the CLI on the ESXi server to see the configuration of the vSwitch:

```
[root@esxi-prod-1:~] esxcli network vswitch dvs vmware list
vDS Production
Name: vDS Production
VDS ID: 50 0e c6 0a 05 ec f9 76-ea 0e 00 7f 74 6b ab a0
Class: cswitch
Num Ports: 2560
Used Ports: 5
Configured Ports: 512
MTU: 1500
CDP Status: listen
Beacon Timeout: -1
Uplinks: vmnic6, vmnic7
VMware Branded: false
```

Comparing standard and distributed vSwitches

Although we have said that distributed vSwitches are centrally managed from the vCenter server, there are many more features that are available only with a distributed vSwitch:

Feature	Standard vSwitch	Distributed vSwitch
L2 forwarding	Yes	Yes
VLAN support	Yes	Yes
NIC teaming	Yes	Yes
Outbound traffic shaping	Yes	Yes
Inbound traffic shaping	No	Yes
Centralized management	No	Yes
PVLAN support	No	Yes
Netflow export support	No	Yes
Port mirroring	No	Yes
Multicast support	No	Yes
Traffic filtering	No	Yes
Network IO control	No	Yes

As you can see, the configuration options of a distributed vSwitch are much more extensive than the standard vSwitch, but keep in mind that the distributed vSwitch is only available in the Enterprise Plus edition of VMware vSphere.

Managing standard virtual networking

Let's start with the standard vSwitch. In this part, we will describe how to add, edit, and configure vSS using the GUI and the CLI. Then we will cover port groups, VMkernel NICs, TCP IP stacks, and physical network interface cards.

Creating a new vSwtich

As a first step, we need to create virtual switches before we can connect our VMs to the network.

After the installation, **vSwitch0** is created automatically because it is used for the management network.

New vSwitch from ESXi host client

To create a standard vSwitch, follow these steps:

1. Connect to the ESXi server using the host client
2. Select **Networking** from the navigator
3. Switch to the **Virtual Switches** tab
4. Click **Add standard virtual switch** and a new window will open, as shown in the following screenshot:

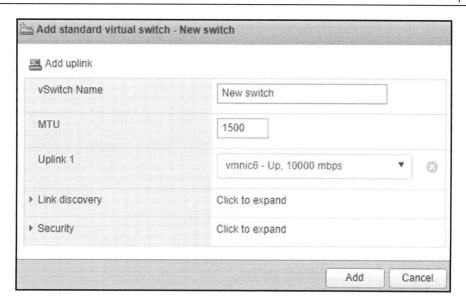

Let's have a look at the fields in the preceding screenshot:

- **vSwitch Name**: Each virtual switch has a name. Please keep in mind that the name can not be changed after creation.
- **MTU**: As we have discussed, if you want to use jumbo frames, all devices within the network must be able to handle those, including the vSwitch.
- **Uplink 1**: Usually, each virtual switch has a physical NIC assigned as an uplink. By default, the first unassigned physical NIC will be chosen as **Uplink1** of the new vSwitch. You can assign multiple physical NICs as an uplink using the **Add uplink** button, and as a best practice you should do so to eliminate any single point of failure within your network.
- **Link discovery**: Standard vSwitches support **Cisco Discovery Protocol (CDP)**, so you can use your standard network management tools to discover network devices. You can choose which mode will be used:
  - **Listen (default)**: The vSwitch will accept CDP frames from the network, and based on these it will show you, for example, to which physical switch the uplink port is connected.

- **Advertise**: The vSwitch will advertise itself to the physical network, so on the physical switch you will see which physical ports are connected to which virtual switch on which ESXi server.
- **Both**: The ESXi server will listen and advertise.
- **None**: CDP will not be used at all.

- Security: You can choose how the vSwitch will be configured regarding specific security features:
    - **Promiscuous mode**:
        - **Reject**: This is the default option. The guest OS does not receive frames for another VM.
        - **Accept**: All frames that pass the virtual switch are forwarded to all VMs connected to the virtual switch (or port group).This can be useful to detect and monitor traffic or when you want to use traffic sniffer analyzers.

    - **MAC address changes**:
        - **Reject**: The guest OS changes the MAC address of the adapter to a value different from the address in the .vmx configuration file. The switch will block the port.
        - **Accept**: This is the default option. The guest OS can change the MAC address of the network adapter, and the adapter receives frames at its new address.

    - **Forged transmits**:
        - **Reject**: The switch drops any outbound frame with a source MAC address that is different from the one in the .vmx configuration file.
        - **Accept**: The switch does not perform filtering and permits all outbound frames.

Once the standard vSwitch is created, you can access its configuration and view the topology. In the following screenshot, you can see the topology of a standard vSwitch:

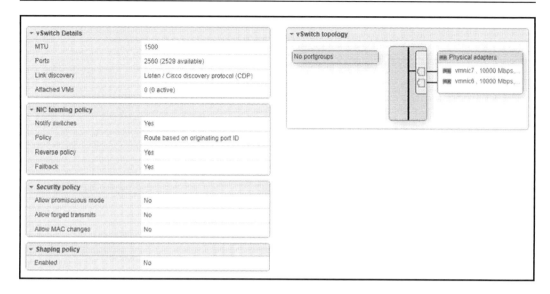

Once the vSwitch is created, we have more configuration options compared to the new virtual switch wizard. We can change the settings we configured during creation, but we also have two new configuration options:

- **NIC teaming**
- **Traffic shaping**

In **NIC teaming,** we can specify how the traffic will be balanced between multiple physical NICs, as well how the failure detection is configured:

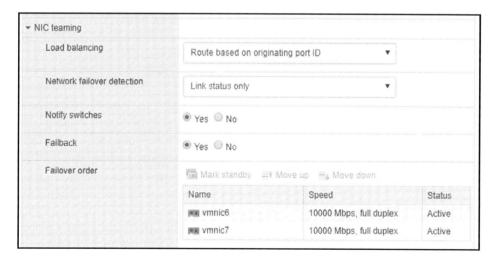

- **Load balancing**: This option determines how network traffic is distributed between the network adapters in a NIC team, according to one of these algorithms:
  - **Route based on originating virtual port (default)**: The virtual switch selects uplinks based on the VM port IDs on the vSS or vDS. This method is without extra configuration on the physical switch and has low overhead.
  - **Route based on source MAC hash**: The virtual switch selects an uplink for a VM based on the VMs MAC address. To calculate an uplink for a VM, the virtual switch uses the VM MAC address and the number of uplinks in the NIC team. This method is a support for all physical switches and has low overhead.
  - **Route based on IP hash**: The virtual switch select uplinks for VMs based on the source and destination IP address of each packet. The IP-based method requires 802.3ad link aggregation support or EtherChannel.
  - **Use explicit failover order**: There's no actual load balancing with this policy. The virtual switch always uses the first uplink that is in the active adapter list. If not possible, one of the other active adapters will be used instead of the standby adapter.
- **Network failure detection**: This option is how you understand that one link is not usable. You can specify two methods for failover detection:
  - **Link status only**: This is the default option. Only link failures are detected. For example unplugged cables or problem on the physical switch.
  - **Beacon probing**: When you want to use this detection mode, you must have at least three NICs in the team for beacon probing. *How does it work?* It sends out and listens for Ethernet broadcast frames that physical NICs send to detect a link failure in all physical NICs in a team. ESXi hosts send beacon packets every second.
- **Notify switches**: This option is a single option (by default it's enabled) used to speed up the change of the network topology at the physical switch level. When the physical port used for the VM traffic must be re routed to a different physical port (for example, due to link failure), then the virtual switch sends notifications over the network to update the lookup tables on the physical switch. The same happens during vSphere vMotion migration. The protocol used is **Reverse Address Resolution Protocol (RARP)**.

- **Failback**: This option is another single option (again, by default it's enabled) that determines how a physical adapter is returned to active duty after recovering from a failure. By default, the adapter returns to active duty immediately.
- **Failover order**: This option specifies how the different uplinks (the physical NICs) are used:
  - **Active adapters**: These continue to use the uplink when it is up as active.
  - **Standby adapters**: If there are no active adapters that are up, then the next uplink from the standby adapter list will be used.
  - **Unused adapters**: Never use this uplink.
- **Traffic shaping**: This can be used to allow only specific bandwidth to traverse over the virtual switch. With only the standard virtual switch on outbound network traffic can be shaped. When you need bidirectional control, you must use vDS inbound and outbound traffic. This option is disabled by default.
  The following configuration options are available:
  - **Average bandwidth (kbit/s)**: Establish the number of bits per second to allow across a port, averaged over time. This number is the allowed average load.
  - **Peak bandwidth (kbit/s)**: The maximum number of kilobits per second to allow across a port when it is sending a burst of traffic. This number is more than the bandwidth that is used by a port whenever the port is using its burst bonus.
  - **Burst size (KB)**: The maximum number of kilobytes to allow in a burst. This is useful if you want a permit whenever bandwidth peaks (a larger amount than the average bandwidth) for a limited time. Note that the burst is not expressed in time, but size.

New vSwitch from vCenter Server

If your ESXi host is already connected to the vCenter Server, you can easily create a new vSwitch from there:

1. Connect to the vCenter server using HTML5 or FLEX client
2. Switch to the **Host and Clusters** view
3. Select the ESXi server you want to configure

4. Switch to the **Configure** tab and select **Virtual switches** under **Networking**:

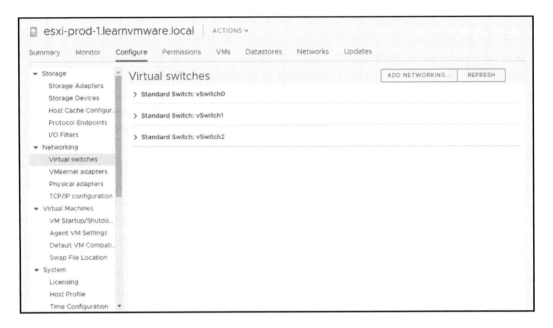

5. Click **ADD NETWORKING...** and select **Physical Network Adapter**.
6. Assign the physical network adapters

Once the virtual switch is created, you can edit its configuration by clicking on the Edit button.

New vSwitch from ESXi CLI

If you need to, for example, during the initial configuration of the environment using automation tools, you can create a standard vSwitch from the CLI of the ESXi server:

1. Connect to the ESXi server using SSH
2. Create a new vSwitch using `esxcli`:

```
esxcli network vswitch standard add --vswitch-name=vSwitch3
```

3. Set the MTU and CDP settings:

```
esxcli network vswitch standard set --cdp-status=listen --
vswitch-name=vSwitch3

esxcli network vswitch standard set --mtu=9000 --vswitch-
name=vSwitch3
```

4. Assign an uplink port:

```
esxcli network vswitch standard uplink add --uplink-
name=vmnic6 --vswitch-name=vSwitch3

esxcli network vswitch standard uplink add --uplink-
name=vmnic7 --vswitch-name=vSwitch3
```

5. Configure the load balancing policy:

```
esxcli network vswitch standard policy failover set
-vswitch-name=vSwitch3
```

6. Configure a security policy:

```
esxcli network vswitch standard policy security set
-vswitch-name=vSwitch3
```

7. Configure a shaping policy:

```
esxcli network vswitch standard policy shaping set
-vswitch-name=vSwitch3
```

Working with port groups

Port groups are used to connect our VMs and VMkernel ports to the virtual switches.

By default, two port groups are created during the installation:

- **VM network**: This port group does not contain any VMs but can be used for new VMs that are connected to the default **vSwitch0** created during the installation.
- **Management network**: This port group is used for our first VMkernel NIC—**vmk0**—which is used for management of ESXi.

As we have said, VMs and VMkernel NICs are not connected directly to the vSwitch, but instead, they use port groups, a logical container that has the desired network configuration.

Usually, you will create a port group for every VLAN that you intend to use in the VMware vSphere.

Creating a new port group from ESXi host client

To create a new port group, select **Networking** in the navigator and switch to the **Port group** tab:

1. Click **Add port group**. Fill in the name of the port group. Keep in mind that the name cannot be changed once the port group has been created.
2. Specify **VLAN ID**. If the uplink ports are not trunk ports, keep the value as **0;** otherwise, select to which VLAN the VMs should be connected.
3. Select a virtual switch to which the new port group will be connected. This can't be changed once the port group is created.
4. You have an option to override the security settings on the port group. By default, the settings inherited from the virtual switch will be applied:

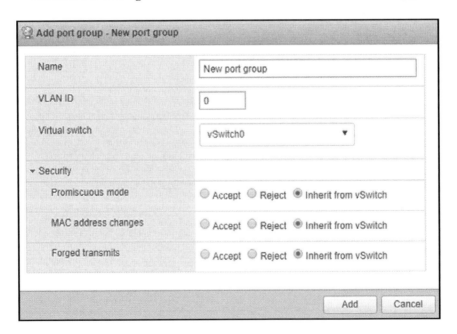

Once the port group is created, you can have a look at the details just by clicking on the port group you are interested in.

On the left side, you can see the topology view—which VMkernel NICs or VMs are connected to the port group, to which virtual switch the port group is connected, and finally which uplink physical NICs are used by such a virtual switch. On the right side, there is the configuration of the port group itself.

If you need to change the settings, click the **Edit settings** button:

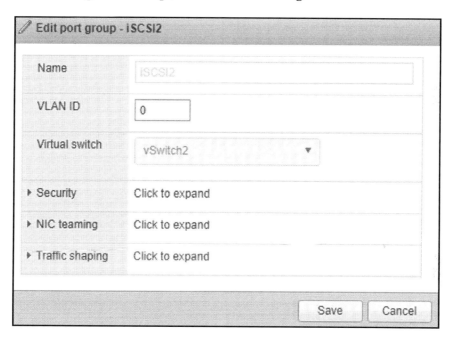

Following the virtual switch configuration, once the port group is created, you can define the NIC teaming and traffic shaping as well.

By default, the configuration is inherited from the virtual switch, but you can override it based on your needs. In my example, a VMkernel port connected to the **iSCSI2** port group will not be using both physical network interface cards as the vSwitch does, but only one will be set to active:

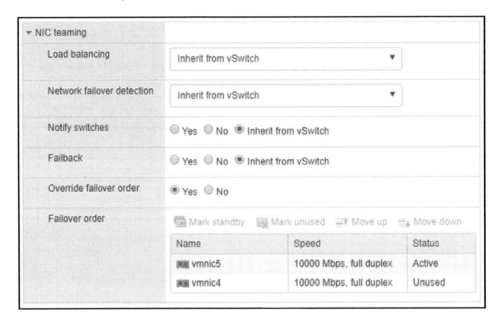

Creating a new port group from vCenter Server

If you instead prefer to use vCenter Server when working with port groups, you can, but keep in mind that, even though you are working on the vCenter Server, port groups connected to standard virtual switches must be configured on every single ESXi hypervisor.

To create a new port group, perform the following operation:

1. Switch to the **Hosts and Clusters** view and select the ESXi server you want to configure
2. Switch to the **Configure** tab
3. Under **Networking**, select **Virtual Switches**
4. Click **Add Networking** and select **Virtual Machine Port Group for a Standard Switch**, as shown in the following screenshot:

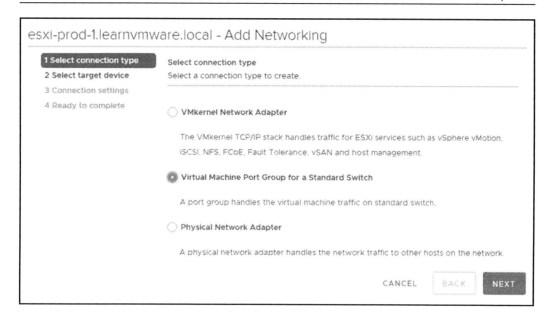

5. Select an existing virtual switch, or you can create a new one directly in the wizard
6. Specify the port group name and VLAN ID

Creating a new port group from ESXi CLI

Of course, you can create port groups from the CLI of the ESXi hypervisor using the `esxcli` command:

1. Connect to the ESXi server using SSH
2. Issue the `esxcli network vswitch standard port group add` command:

   ```
   esxcli network vswitch standard portgroup add --portgroup-
   name=PGname --vswitch-name=vSwitch1
   ```

3. To specify the VLAN ID of the port group, you can use the `set` command:

   ```
   esxcli network vswitch standard portgroup set -p PGname --
   vlan-id 1234
   ```

4. Finally, override the configuration of security, teaming, and shaping the policy of the virtual switch:

```
esxcli network vswitch standard port group policy set
```

Working with VMkernel adapters

The VMkernel port (or the VMkernel adapter or interface) is used for VMkernel services when we need to connect to the physical network. VMkernel adapters are used (and needed) for IP-based storage (such as NFS or iSCSI), for vSAN, for vMotion traffic, for vSphere FT logs, for management interfaces, for vSphere Replication, and for NSX-VTEP or VSAN.

The following services are supported on VMkernel NICs:

- Management traffic
- vMotion traffic
- Provisioning traffic
- IP storage traffic and discovery
- Fault tolerance traffic
- vSphere Replication traffic
- vSphere Replication NFC traffic
- vSAN traffic

Again, VMkernel adapters can be configured from ESXi host client, vCenter Server, or the CLI.

Please note that a port group can either be used for VMs or VMkernel ports, not both simultaneously. You can, of course, create two port groups with the same VLAN ID for this reason.

Creating a new VMkernel adapter from ESXi host client

The procedure is almost the same as with port groups or virtual switches. In the ESXi host client, switch to **Networking** in the navigator and then select VMkernel adapters:

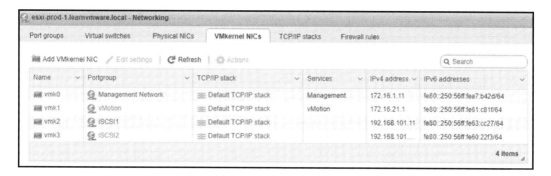

To create a new VMkernel adapter, you can follow this procedure:

1. Click on **Add VMkernel NIC**.
2. You can create a port group to which the VMkernel NIC will be assigned directly from the wizard, or you can select an existing port group.
3. If the VMkernel NIC is used for traffic such as iSCSI or NFS, set the MTU value to 9,000 (jumbo frames).
4. In the IP version, you can select which IP version will be supported on the interface. You cannot create an IPv6-only interface; the options are IPv4 only or IPv4 and IPv6.
5. Next, based on your selection, you need to specify the IP address. It is strongly suggested to use a static IP address and not a DHCP client option.
6. In the TCP/IP stack, you can select to which stack the VMkernel interface will be connected.
7. Lastly, you can select which services will be available on this interface.

 Please note that not all options are available in the ESXi host client. Services such as vSAN can be configured only from the vCenter Server.

Once the VMkernel adapters are created, you can have a look at the detail configuration, or you can easily adjust the settings:

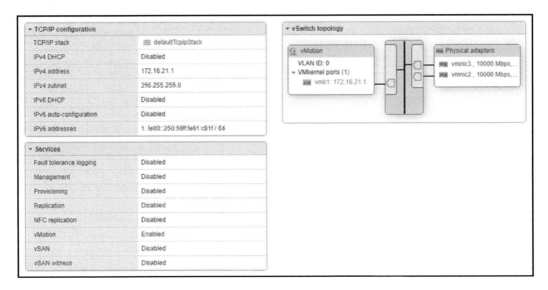

Creating a new VMkernel adapter from vCenter Server

It is possible to create a new VMkernel NIC directly from the vCenter Server. As you already know, VMkernel NICs are IP interfaces of the ESXi server, thus you need to perform this configuration on every single ESXi hypervisor:

1. Switch to the **Hosts and Clusters** view
2. Select one of the ESXi servers
3. Switch to the **Configuration** tab
4. Under **Networking**, select **VMkernel adapters**, as shown in the following screenshot:

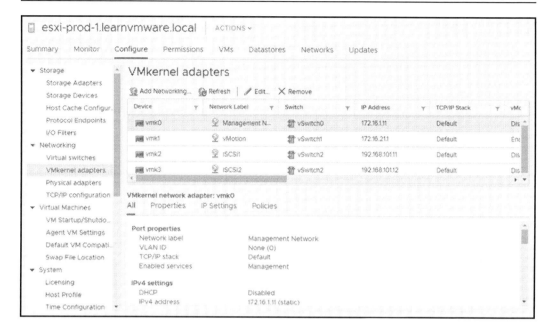

5. Click **Add Networking...**
6. Select the VMkernel network adapter
7. Configure the IP address, MTU, and associated services as already described

Working with physical NICs

Physical adapters (also called pNICs) are usually used as the virtual switches' uplinks. There is not much you can configure here. The view is just a representation of the physical network cards your ESXi server has, which driver is used with particular physical network interface card, and the MAC address of the physical interface itself.

In the ESXi host client, you can find this view under the **Physical NICs** tab:

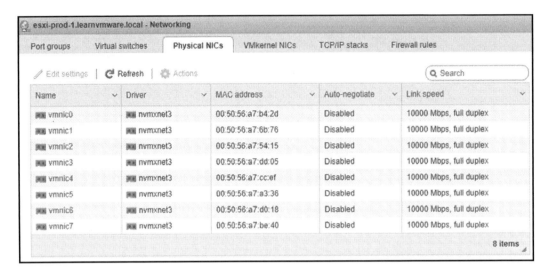

In the vCenter Server, you would find the same view. Just navigate to the **Configure** tab of the ESXi hypervisor, and under **Networking** select **Physical adapters**.

You can get the same information by using `esxcli` from the ESXi hypervisor:

```
[root@esxi-prod-1:~] esxcli network nic list
 Name PCI Device Driver Admin Status Link Status Speed Duplex MAC
Address MTU Description
 ------ ------------- -------- ------------- ------------ ----- ------- --
 --------------- ---- ------------------------------------------------
 vmnic0 0000:0b:00.0 nvmxnet3 Up Up 10000 Full 00:50:56:a7:b4:2d 1500
VMware Inc. vmxnet3 Virtual Ethernet Controller
 vmnic1 0000:13:00.0 nvmxnet3 Up Up 10000 Full 00:50:56:a7:6b:76 1500
VMware Inc. vmxnet3 Virtual Ethernet Controller
 vmnic2 0000:1b:00.0 nvmxnet3 Up Up 10000 Full 00:50:56:a7:54:15 9000
VMware Inc. vmxnet3 Virtual Ethernet Controller
 vmnic3 0000:04:00.0 nvmxnet3 Up Up 10000 Full 00:50:56:a7:dd:05 9000
VMware Inc. vmxnet3 Virtual Ethernet Controller
```

TCP/IP stacks

Before vSphere 6.0, the TCP/IP configuration was mainly managed by a single network stack. But now we can have multiple and different TCP/IP stacks (also called **netstacks**) for different VMkernel interfaces.

These are the built-in TCP/IP stacks available in vSphere:

- **Default TCP/IP stack**: General-purpose stack that can be used for any VMkernel service.
- **vMotion TCP/IP stack**: Stack optimized for vMotion. The goal is to fully isolated vMotion traffic. Once used, the vMotion traffic will be removed from the default TCP/IP stack.
- **Provisioning TCP/IP stack**: Dedicated stack that is used to isolate several VM operations as migrations, cloning, or traffic generated by snapshots.

By using a separate TCP/IP stack, you can handle different network traffic according to the topology of the network and as required for your organization:

- **Route the traffic by using a default gateway**: The gateway must be different from the gateway assigned to the default stack on the host
- **Assign a separate set of buffers and sockets**: Certain traffic types might consume enormous numbers of connections
- **Avoid routing table conflicts**: These might appear when many features are using a common TCP/IP stack
- **Isolate traffic**: To improve security

Currently, there is no option to create a new TCP/IP stack from the UI (either the ESXi host client or vCenter Server). To create the custom TCP/IP stack, follow these steps:

1. Connect the ESXi server over SSH
2. Use `esxcli` to create a new stack:

```
esxcli network ip netstack add -N Custom-Stack
```

Once the stack is created, you can configure it from the UI.

Please note that the routing table will be empty unless you create a new VMkernel interface and assign it to the new TCP/IP stack. When creating a new VMkernel adapter, don't forget to check the override default gateway option to specify a different default gateway for this interface, as seen in the following screenshot:

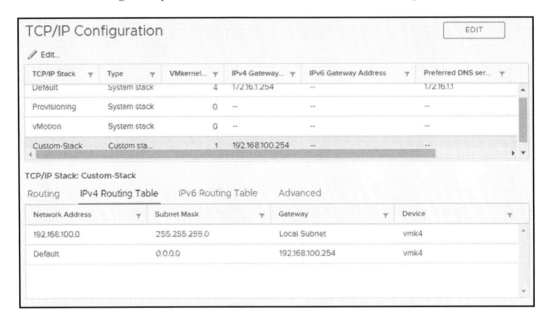

You have to be very careful when you need to ping or list routes. You must specify each time which TCP/IP stack you want to use. For example, when we want to ping on the VMkernel port that is on another host in the TCP/IP stack named `Custom-Stack`, you must specify the TCP/IP stack you would like to use.

When you need to check the correct connection between the two ESXi hosts, you can use `vmkping`, but specify which VMkernel interface you want to use and specify the TCP/IP stack you want to use:

```
vmkping ++netstack=Custom-Stack 192.168.10.200 -I vmk4
 PING 192.168.10.200 (192.168.10.200): 56 data bytes
 64 bytes from 192.168.10.200: icmp_seq=0 ttl=64 time=0.232 ms
 64 bytes from 192.168.10.200: icmp_seq=1 ttl=64 time=0.210 ms
 64 bytes from 192.168.10.200: icmp_seq=2 ttl=64 time=0.218 ms
```

One typical use case of the TCP/IP stack is to provide a different default gateway address for a specific VMkernel interface (for example, to use vMotion across datacenters).

Another use case is to provide a specific routing path without the need to specify a static routing table; that is a tricky task on ESXi, as described in **KB 2001426: Configuring static routes for VMkernel ports on an ESXi host** at `https://kb. vmware.com/kb/2001426`.

To provide a different default gateway for each stack, you can use both the GUI and the CLI:

* The first option used is the GUI:

* The second option is using the CLI with the `esxcli` command:

```
esxcli network ip interface ipv4 set –i vmknic –t static
–g gateway –I IP address –N mask
```

Managing distributed virtual networking

In the previous section, we covered standard virtual networking, but as already explained some of the functionality is only available in the distributed vSwitch only:

- **Inbound traffic shaping**: Ability to limit not only the egress traffic but also the ingress direction
- **Centralized management:** Instead of creating multiple standard vSwitches on every ESXi server, only one instance is configured centrally
- **PVLAN support**: Possibility to use PVLANs in your environment
- **NetFlow**: Ability to export NetFlow data to the central NetFlow collector
- **Port mirroring**: Different types of traffic mirroring
- **Multicast support**: Standard vSwitch is not able to intelligently work with multicast
- **Traffic filtering:** Network ACLs on the virtual switch itself
- **NIOC**: Smart control over the network bandwidth on shared physical media

Before we can start playing with the configuration, we need to create the distributed vSwitch first.

Creating a distributed vSwitch

To create a new distributed vSwitch using the vSphere Client, follow these steps:

1. Switch to the **Networking** inventory view. This specific inventory view is the logical container of the vDS definition and configuration.
2. Right-click on the data center and from the contextual menu, choose the **Distributed Switch** menu and then the **New Distributed Switch** option, and fill in the name of the distributed virtual switch:

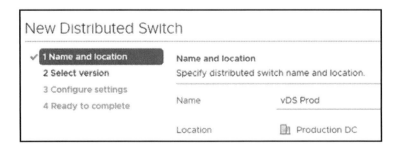

3. In the next part, we must specify the version of vDS. This step is crucial because each different version has different features and enhancements, but of course, the newest versions are not compatible with the previous version of ESXi and vSphere. To learn more about the features and capabilities of the different versions of vDS, you can click on the small blue icon in the vSphere Client.

4. The next step is to configure the settings as follows:
   - **Number of uplinks**: You can specify the maximum number of allowed physical connections to the distributed switch per host. It does not mean that each ESXi server must be connected to the vDS by the exact amount of physical uplinks.
   - **Network I/O Control**: You can prioritize the access to network resources for workloads.
   - **Default port group**: If the first distributed port group is created.
   - **Port group name**: The name for the default port group.

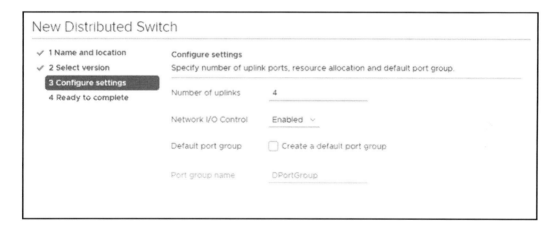

Now we have successfully created the vSwitch, but before we can start using it, we need to connect our ESXi servers to the distributed vSwitch.

Attaching the ESXi host to the distributed vSwitch

The procedure is quite straightforward:

1. Right-click on the distributed vSwitch and select **Add and Manage hosts.**

2. Select which hosts will be connected to the distributed vSwitch. ESXi hosts can be connected to multiple distributed switches:

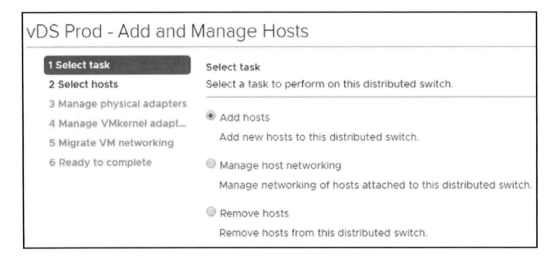

3. In **Manage physical adapters**, you need to assign which physical network interface cards of the ESXi host will be connected to the distributed vSwitch.

4. You have two options here:
   - Manual assignment of all pNICs of all ESXi servers
   - Template mode

With the manual assignment, you need to select every single pNIC you would like to connect to the ESXi server. To do so, select pNIC and click assign:

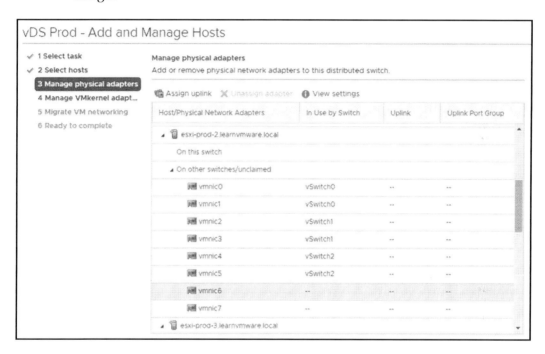

Depending on your configuration of the vDS and the number of configured uplinks, you will have the possibility to select to which logical uplink the pNIC will be assigned.

Once the assignment is done, you will see how the pNICs will be assigned:

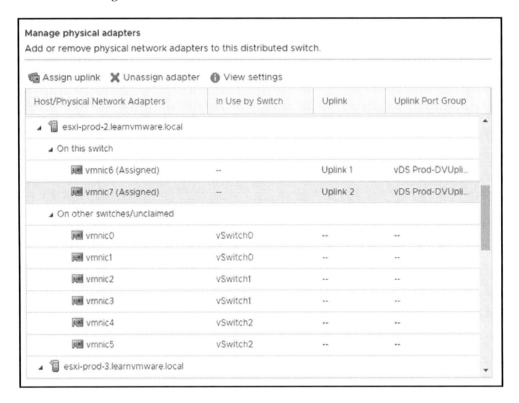

With template mode, you can speed up the operation a bit, but keep in mind that you need the same environment (concerning the number of pNICs in each server you are connecting with the same configuration on the physical switches).

In template mode, you can check **Apply this uplink assignment to the rest of the hosts**, as shown in the following screenshot:

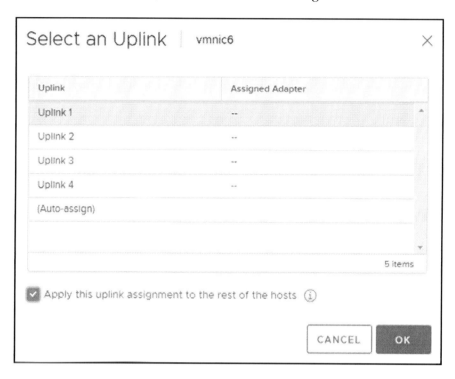

In this case, every single pNIC **vmnic6** will be assigned as an **Uplink1** for all ESXi hypervisors.

5. Next, you can automatically migrate your VMkernel networking from the standard virtual switch to the new distributed one. At this stage no distributed port groups were created so we can skip this option.
6. In the last step, you have an option to migrate the VM networking.

Once the host is connected to the distributed vSwitch, you will see it in the **Overview** tab of the distributed vSwitch:

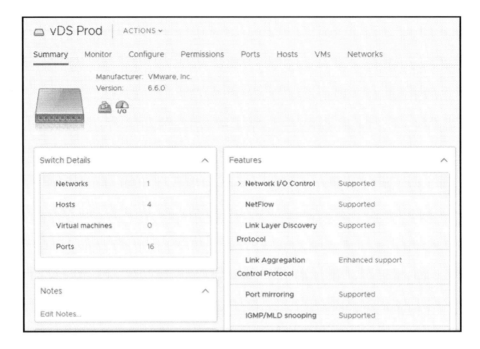

Creating distributed port groups

While working with distributed vSwitches, new port groups can be easily created from the vSphere UI:

1. In the **Networking** view, right-click on your **Distributed vSwitch**, and select **Distributed Port Group** and **New Distributed Port Group...**
2. Provide the name of the new port group:

3. In the configuration step, you have several options:
   - **Port binding**: We have the following two options under port binding:
     - **Static binding**: When you connect a VM to a port group configured with static binding, a port is immediately assigned and reserved for it, guaranteeing connectivity at all times. The port is disconnected only when the VM is removed from the port group. You can only connect a VM to a static-binding port group through vCenter Server.
     - **Ephemeral binding**: In a port group configured with ephemeral binding, a port is created and assigned to a VM by the host when the VM is powered on, and its NIC is connected. When the VM powers off or the NIC of the VM is disconnected, the port is deleted.
   - **Port allocation**: We have the following two options under **Port allocation**:
     - **Elastic**: The number of ports available on the distributed vSwitch will automatically increase and decrease as needed.
     - **Fixed**: Exact number of ports.
   - **Number of ports**: Only usable with fixed port allocation. Keep in mind that each vNIC or VMkernel port connected to the port group will consume one port.
   - **Network resource pool**: This can be later on used with **Network I/O Control** (**NIOC**) to guarantee or limit the overall bandwidth of the port group.
   - **VLAN type**: This will specify if the VLAN tagging will be performed on the port group.
   - **Customize default policies configuration**: This will give you an option to change the default policies from the distributed vSwitch.

4. In the **Security** settings, you can adjust the security settings of the port group as with a standard vSwitch.

5. **Traffic shaping** enables you to specify the maximum ingress and egress bandwidth of the port group.

6. In **Teaming and failover**, you can override the default teaming and failover policy of the virtual distributed switch:

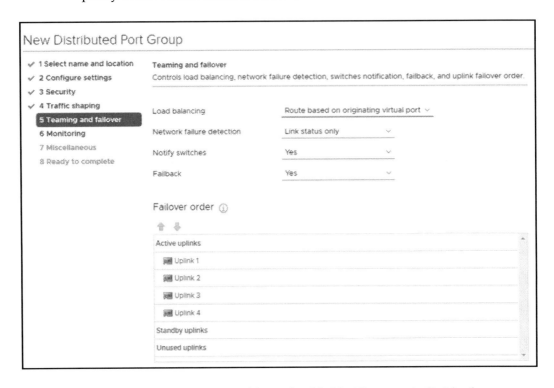

7. In **Monitoring**, you can enable or disable NetFlow per individual port group.
8. Also, you have the option to block all ports so the VMs connected to the port group will not have network access.

Once the port group is created, you will see it under your virtual distributed switch:

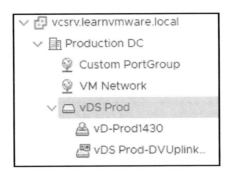

Properties and configuration options of the distributed vSwitch

Like every vSphere object, a distributed vSwitch has its configuration and properties. Simply select the newly created distributed vSwitch, then choose the **Configure** tab and the **Properties** menu to see all the settings of your vDS:

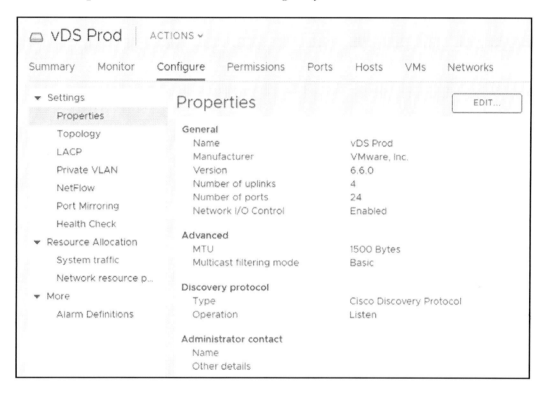

You can change the settings by clicking on **EDIT...** in the right corner. Distributed switched settings are grouped in a general section (for the common settings) and in an advanced section (for the advanced settings):

- **General**: You can change the name of the vDS, change the number of uplinks (and their names), enable or disable NIOC, or add a description to your vDS.

- **Advanced**: Advanced settings include the possibility to change the MTU, multicast filtering mode, discovery protocol, and add an administrator contact. Under **Multicast filtering mode**, you can set the filtering mode as follows:
  - **Basic filtering:** In basic multicast filtering mode, a vSS or vDS forwards multicast traffic for VMs according to the destination MAC address of the multicast group.
  - **Multicast snooping:** In the multicast snooping mode, a vDS provides IGMP and MLD snooping according to RFC 4541. For more details, refer to `https://tools.ietf.org/html/rfc4541`.
- **Discovery protocol**: There are two different supported protocols. First is the **Cisco Discovery Protocol** (**CDP**), which is proprietary from Cisco, but also supported by some other switches. The second is a vendor-neutral standard called **Link Layer Discovery Protocol** (**LLDP**). Note that vSS only supports CDP. You can choose the discovery protocol, and if it is enabled you can also choose in which directory it can be used (advertise, to announce at the physical switch, or listen, to receive information from the physical switch).

Topology

The next part of the vDS configuration and settings is the **Topology** section, where there is a view of your vDS and port groups:

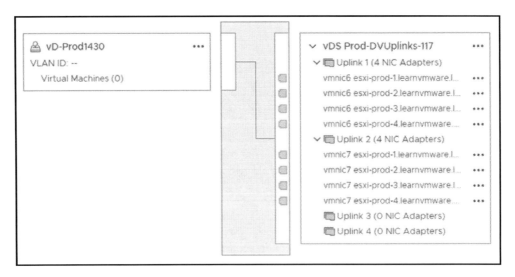

You will see the list of all ESXi hosts and their pNICs connected to the uplink ports on the right side and on the left, all your distributed port groups and the VMs connected to them.

This view can be handy to check the network connections and find possible problems, such as links that are down or blocked ports.

Link Aggregation Control Protocol (LACP)

The LACP protocol is fully supported with vDS (note that it's not available for vSS). You can connect the ESXi host to physical switches by using dynamic link aggregation. LACP must be prepared correctly for the physical part of the networking. You create a **Link Aggregation Group** (**LAG**), and every LAG group has two or more ports.

If you want to use LACP, you need to create a LAG first:

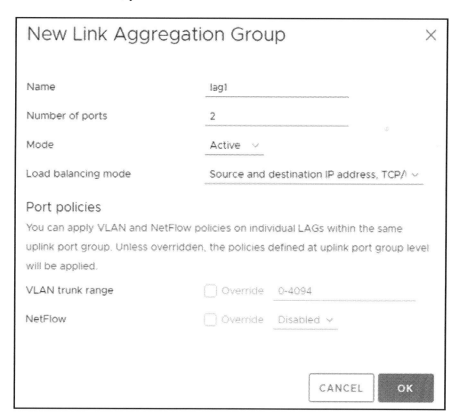

Mode settings depend on your physical switch configuration:

- **Active**: All LAG ports are in an active negotiating mode. The LAG ports initiate negotiations with the LACP port channel on the physical switch by sending LACP packets.
- **Passive**: The LAG ports are in passive negotiating mode. They respond to LACP packets they receive but do not initiate LACP negotiation.
- **Load balancing mode**: This must match the configuration on the physical switch. Once the LAG is created, you will see it on the list:

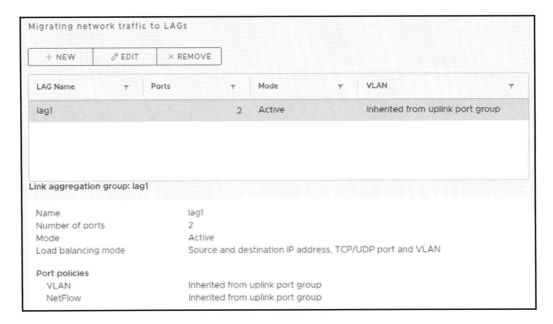

Once the LAG is created, you can assign the physical NICs to the LAG instead of uplink ports.

To do so, select **Add and Manage Hosts...** as a contextual option of the distributed vSwitch and select **Manage host networking**. The wizard is the same as when we ware creating a new virtual distributed switch, but at this time we have an option to select LAG as an uplink.

Once both pNICs ware assigned, you will see them in a summary window:

As you can see, our pNICs **vmnic6** and **vmni7** are now assigned to **lag1-0** and **lag1-1** instead of **Uplink1** and **Uplink2**.

Private VLAN (PVLAN)

Private VLANs are used to solve limitations and segmentation broadcast domains.

There are three private VLANs:

- **Promiscuous**: Private VLAN communicates with primary VLAN
- **Isolated**: They communicate only with promiscuous VLANs

- **Community**: Communication with promiscuous VLANs and with ports in the same secondary VLAN:

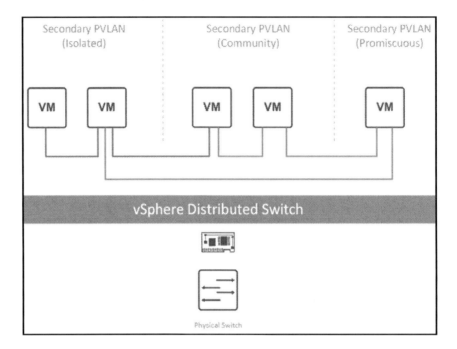

To configure the PVLAN, click the edit button and create your PVLAN design.

NetFlow

To monitor vDS and analyze its network traffic, you can use NetFlow. For example, **vRealize Network Insight** (**vRNI**) acts as a NetFlow collector, but there are also other possible products and solutions.

By using NetFlow, you can quickly get visibility into the traffic. In NetFlow, no actual data is stored, only the identification of the individual flows (source/destination IP, TCP/UDP ports, duration, timestamp, and so on).

If you want to test the functionality, you can use **NfSen**, an open source project that serves as a NetFlow collector with an HTTP-based GUI where you can search for traffic patterns, individual flows, or overall statistics.

For more information, check out the project at http://nfsen.sourceforge.net.

Port mirroring

Port mirroring sends a copy of packets from one switch port to another switch port. This feature is usefully especially during troubleshooting when you need to see the exact copy of the data traveling the network. Other use cases are out-of-band intrusion detection and prevention systems that need to see the data.

To monitor such a data flow, you can use **Wireshark** (`https://www.wireshark.org`) or `tcpdump` installed on a VM that will be used as a destination for such mirroring.

The most common scenarios are as follows:

- Distributed port mirroring (SPAN)
- Remote mirroring source and remote mirroring destination (RSPAN)
- Encapsulated remote mirroring (L3) source (ERSPAN)

Health check

This technology is used to monitor changes in vDS and helps with the troubleshooting process. You can check the MTU, teaming policy, and VLAN trunk. You would very quickly get information about misconfiguration between the ESXi host and a physical switch.

The following checks are performed:

- **VLAN**: Checks whether the vSphere distributed switch VLAN settings match the trunk port configuration on the adjacent physical switch ports
- **MTU**: Checks whether the physical access switch port MTU settings per VLAN matches the vSphere distributed switch MTU settings
- **Network adapter teaming**: Checks whether the physical access switch ports EtherChannel settings match the distributed switch port group IP hash teaming policy settings

Once the health check is enabled, you can switch to the **Monitor** tab of the virtual distributed switch and select health to access the health check information.

Ports, hosts, and VMs

The other tabs relevant for network configuration are the port, host, VM, and network tabs, and are discussed as follows:

- **Ports**: Using this tab, it is possible to view all ports connected to the vDS and find useful information on all ports. For example, it is possible to check the state of the port and other configuration-related pieces of information:

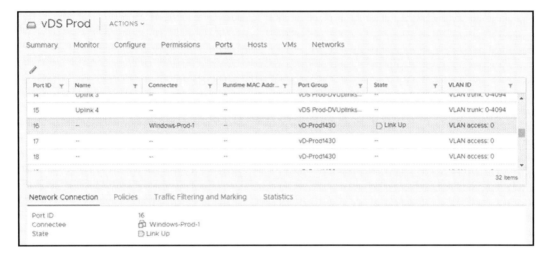

- **Hosts**: This provides some details, such as which hosts are connected to the vDS.
- **VMs**: In this view, you can see all VMs connected to the vDS.

Migrate VM networking

Once you have created all your distributed port groups, and the virtual distributed switch is configured, you can move existing VMs to them.

One option is to manually reassign the adapter from the standard port group to the distributed port group for every single VM you would like to migrate:

1. Edit the settings of the VM
2. Select the virtual NIC
3. Click on **Browse** in the port group assignment

4. Select the targeted distributed port group
5. Confirm the configuration

This procedure might work for a limited number of VMs, but if you have a lot of VMs where you need to move to the distributed port group, it might not be the most effective procedure. Fortunately, you can migrate the VMs using a simple wizard that will do the trick for you:

1. Switch to the **Networking** view, select your source port group, and select **Migrate VMs to Another Network....**
2. A new wizard will appear and based on your selection, the source network will be already filled in. All you need is to specify the destination port group.
3. In the next step, you have the option to migrate either all VMs attached to the source port group, or you can select individual VMs.

Once you confirm the operation, every single VM that was selected for migration will be reconfigured to the new port group. You can use the same wizard even for migration between distributed port groups.

NIOC

A function called NIOC provides the entire network's resource allocation and management. When you are using NIOC v3, you can manage the network resources, such as shares, reservations, and limits, in a similar way to resource pools for computing. NIOC is a vDS-only feature that allows the VMware administrator to prioritize different types of network traffic.

Network traffic can be managed using the same resource concepts used for CPU and memory (for example, in resource pools):

- **Limit**: The maximum bandwidth that a system traffic type can consume on a single physical network adapter.
- **Shares**: From 1 to 100 reflects the relative priority of system traffic type against the other system traffic types that are active on the same physical network adapter. Shares are applied only when the congestion occurs.
- **Reservation**: The minimum bandwidth that must be guaranteed on a single physical network adapter. If an object does not use the bandwidth with a reservation, it might be used by another object.

The total reserved system traffic types can be configured up to 75% of the total bandwidth of a single physical network interface card (if you are using a 10 Gbps uplink, the maximum reservation that is allowed is 7.5 Gbps).

If we enable NIOC, the reservation can be configured for the different types of network traffic. See the following example:

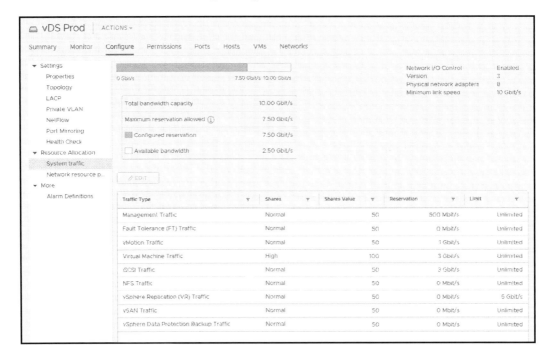

In VM traffic, we assign a 3 Gbps reservation for VM traffic that is used in admission control. When you power on a VM, the admission control verifies that the bandwidth is effectively available.

Network resource pools

You can create a network resource pool that will be assigned to the port groups. In the network resource pool, you can configure the reservation for the bandwidth guaranteeing that the VMs connected to the port group with the network resource pool will always have a certain amount of bandwidth available at all times:

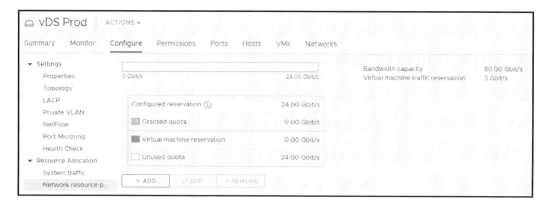

In the previous screenshot, you have a summary page with the following information:

- **Granted quota**: This is taken from network resource pools
- **Virtual machine reservation**: This is taken from the configuration VM that is not connected to the distributed port group with the network resource pool assigned
- **Unused quota**: Free reservation capacity that can be used for additional resource pools or vNIC reservations

To create a network resource pool, perform the following configuration steps:

1. You must define the reservation for VM traffic first
2. Switch to network resource pools under the configuration of the vDS
3. Click **Add** to create a new network resource pool
4. Specify the name and the reserved bandwidth

Once the network resource pools have been created, you will see all of them with the corresponding bandwidth reservations.

You might be wondering why we have configured a reservation of 24 Gbps even though we have configured a 3 Gbps reservation for VM traffic.

The calculation is simple—we have four ESXi hypervisors, each with two 10 GbE NICs. On each pNIC, we have reserved 3 Gbps for VM traffic, so in total it's 6 Gbps per host multiplied by the number of hosts.

Once the network resource pool is configured, you can attach it to the distributed port group. Go to **Edit settings...** of the port group and select the corresponding network resource pool in the **General** tab.

Direct allocation on VM

If you need to, you can configure the network bandwidth allocation directly on an individual VM:

1. Edit the settings of the VM
2. Expand the properties of a vNIC
3. Specify the **Limit**, **Shares**, or **Reservation** for each vNIC
4. Commit the change by clicking on **OK**:

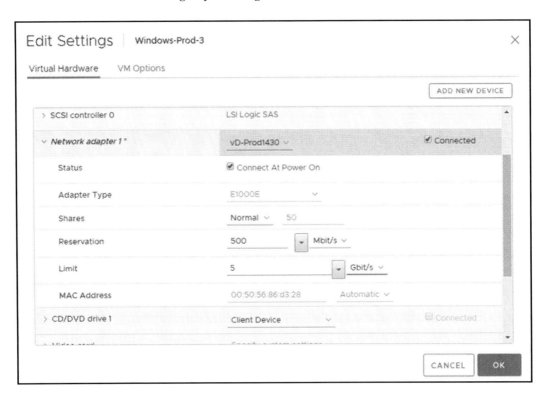

Advanced network functions

We have walked through the configuration of standard and distributed networking, and we have learned how to connect VMs to the port groups to get network connectivity. We have also explained the difference between core network components, but there are a few more advanced features that you might want to use in your environment.

Single Root I/O Virtualization (SR-IOV)

SR-IOV is a specification that allows a single **Peripheral Component Interconnect express** (**PCIe**) physical device under a single root port to appear as multiple separate physical devices to the hypervisor or the guest operating system.

SR-IOV uses **physical functions** (**PFs**) and **virtual functions** (**VFs**) to manage global functions for the SR-IOV devices. PFs are full PCIe functions that are capable of configuring and managing the SR-IOV functionality. It is possible to configure or control PCIe devices using PFs, and the PF has full ability to move data in and out of the device. VFs are lightweight PCIe functions that support data flow but have a restricted set of configuration resources.

The vSphere SR-IOV functionality is based on the interaction between VFs and PFs. Once the SR-IOV is enabled and the VM is configured with VF instead of the traditional vNIC, the VM adapters directly tap into the PF function of the physical network interface card through the VF.

On an ESXi host without SR-IOV, the vSwitch sends external network traffic through its ports on the host from or to the physical adapter for the relevant port group.

The vSwitch also applies the networking policies on managed packets:

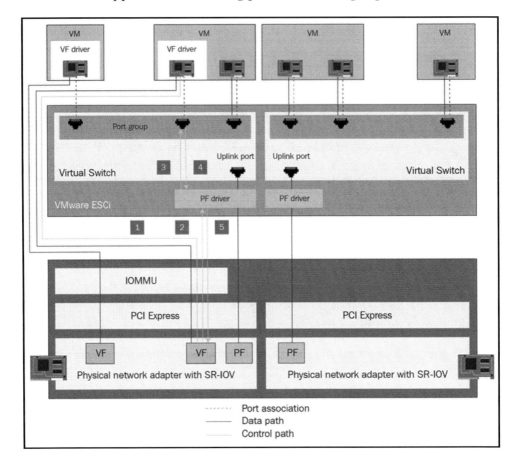

Enabling SR-IOV

SR-IOV is a feature of the physical network interface card, and you can enable SR-IOV only on physical NICs that support it. You can check the **Hardware Compatibility List** (**HCL**) to see if the selected network interface card supports SR-IOV.

If the physical network interface card supports SR-IOV, you can easily enable SR-IOV:

1. From the list of available physical network adapters, select the adapter on which you want to enable SR-IOV
2. Edit the settings of the physical adapter
3. Define the number of maximum supported virtual functions (how many VMs might be connected to the adapter)
4. Reboot the host

Configuring VM for SR-IOV

Once the SR-IOV has been enabled on the physical NIC, you can configure VMs with an SR-IOV-enabled NIC:

1. Power off the VM.
2. Edit the settings of the VM.
3. From the **New device** drop-down menu, select the new network card.
4. Expand the **New Virtual Network** section, and connect the VM to a port group. The virtual NIC does not use this port group for data traffic. The port group is used for the networking properties like VLAN tagging.
5. From the **Adapter Type** drop-down menu, select **SR-IOV passthrough**.
6. From the **Physical function** menu, select the physical adapter to connect the pass through VM adapter.
7. It is possible to configure the MTU of packets from the guest operating system, using the **Guest OS MTU Change** option.
8. Expand the **Memory** section, select **Reserve all guest memory (All locked)**, and click **OK**. The VM must have all memory reserved so that the passthrough device can access the memory by using **direct memory access (DMA)**.
9. Power on the VM.

Traffic filtering and marking

With a distributed switch, by using the traffic filtering and marking policy, you can protect the virtual network from unwanted traffic and security attacks or apply a **Quality of Service (QoS)** tag to a specific type of traffic.

The traffic filtering and marking policy represents an ordered set of network traffic rules for security and QoS tagging of the data flow through the ports of a distributed switch. In general, a rule consists of a qualifier for traffic, and of an action for restricting or prioritizing the matching traffic.

The vSphere distributed switch applies rules to traffic at different places in the data stream. The distributed switch applies traffic filter rules to the data path between the VM network adapter and distributed port, or between the uplink port and physical network adapter for rules on uplinks:

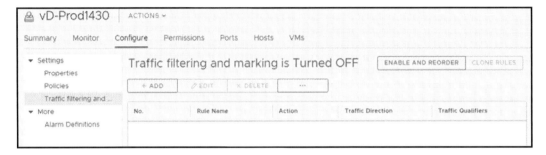

To configure filtering and marking follow this procedure:

1. On the selected port group, switch to the **Configure** tab and the **Traffic Filtering and Marking** section.
2. Add rules that you want to apply.
3. **Action**: Allow, drop (for filtering) and tag (for marking). If you select **Tag**, then you can assign required DSCP or CoS tag.
4. **Traffic Direction**: Ingress, egress, or both.
5. **Traffic Qualifiers**: These allow you to mark or filter only specific traffic. You have a broad set of options including the simple source/destination MAC addresses, but you can go all the way up to the TCP/IP layer and specify specific TCP ports that should be allowed, blocked, or marked.

Once the rules are created, enable the traffic filtering by clicking on the **ENABLE AND REORDER** button.

Summary

This chapter described networking concepts and specific network configuration and features of vSphere 6.7. Virtual networking concepts are covered, both with standard and distributed virtual switches and its broad set of configuration features.

We have learned how to attach our VMs to the network and how the traffic flows from the VM, through the port group, virtual switch, and physical network cards of the ESXi hypervisor.

We have also covered advanced network functions. We have looked at how to provide fast and reliable network connection to the VMs using SR-IOV, how to guarantee or limit the throughput of different services, VMs, and network resource pools using NIOC, and we have learned how to filter and mark specific traffic flows using the traffic filtering and marking feature of the virtual distributed switch.

The next chapter will focus on another essential component of the infrastructure—storage.

Questions

1. The OSI model consists of five layers:

   a) True
   b) False

2. What is the purpose of using VLANs?
3. Using a lower MTU value, you can increase the network's performance.

   a) True
   b) False

4. Name at least four features that are available in a vSphere distributed switch and are not part of vSphere standard switch.
5. Name four key components of vSphere networking.

6. What are the three security policies we can configure?

   a) Copy mode
   b) Promiscuous mode
   c) MAC address changes
   d) IP address changes
   e) Forged transmits
   f) Ethernet security

7. You can override the NIC teaming policy on the individual port group:

   a) True
   b) False

8. Under the failover order option, to which physical NICs can we assign the different configuration?

   a) Active adapters
   b) Failback adapters
   c) Standby adapters
   d) Dedicated adapters
   e) Unused adapters

9. VLAN ID is defined on the vSwitch.

   a) True
   b) False

10. A distributed vSwitch can be configured from the ESXi hypervisor.

    a) True
    b) False

11. Distributed vSwitches support two protocols used for network discovery. Which two?

12. What items can health check on the Distributed vSwitch check?

    a) MTU configuration
    b) VLAN configuration
    c) iSCSI offload availability
    d) VXLAN settings
    e) NIC teaming
    f) Port speed

13. Network I/O Control can only be used to guarantee specific bandwidth for VMs.

    a) True
    b) False

14. What are the benefits of using SR-IOV technology?

Further reading

Read the following articles for more information:

- **vSphere Networking**: `https://docs.vmware.com/en/VMware-vSphere/6.7/vsphere-esxi-vcenter-server-67-networking-guide.pdf`
- **VMware NSX Cookbook**: `https://www.packtpub.com/virtualization-and-cloud/vmware-nsx-cookbook`.
- **CCNA Routing and Switching 200-125 Certification Guide**: CCNA Routing and Switching 200-125 Certification Guide covers topics included in the latest CCNA exam, along with review and practice questions. `https://www.packtpub.com/networking-and-servers/ccna-routing-and-switching-200-125-certification-guide`.

Managing Storage Resources

8

Storage is usually the most critical part of a virtual infrastructure, due to the need to provide enough performance and capacity for the entire cluster and all the workloads inside it. To provide features such as vSphere **High Availability (HA)**, vSphere **Distributed Resource Scheduler (DRS)**, and other cluster-related capabilities, you need common shared storage for all the ESXi hosts on the cluster. You might also want to have more storage per cluster, or use the same storage for other clusters as well.

This chapter details storage aspects of a virtual infrastructure, starting from local block-based storage and extending into shared block storage with **Fibre Channel(FC)**, **Fibre Channel over Ethernet (FCoE)**, **Internet Small Computer System Interface (iSCSI)** protocols, and NFS-based NAS storage.

In this chapter, we will learn about the following topics:

- Storage basics
- VMware vSphere storage types
- VMware vSphere storage configuration
- **Storage I/O Control (SIOC)** and Storage DRS
- Advanced storage features
- Storage integration
- Introduction to VMware vSAN

Storage basics

There are different types of storage, with different protocols, architectures, scaling capabilities, and purposes. In a virtual environment, you will need a resilient and reliable storage solution that meets your required performance and that can scale for the future. This is only possible using enterprise storage products, with some exceptions for the ROBO and SMB scenarios, as discussed in `Chapter 2`, *Designing and Planning a Virtualization Infrastructure*.

Enterprise-class storage can be classified in different ways:

- **Direct-Attached Storage (DAS)**
- **Network Attached Storage (NAS)**
- **Storage Area Network (SAN)**
- **Object-based storage/cloud storage**

For VMware vSphere, the first three storage classes are the most relevant as they are the only solutions that can be used for running VMs. Object-based storage, however, could be used by other solutions (such as backup products), and maybe also by vSphere in the future. The main differences between these different types of storage are the types of services the provide, the different ways in which they can be used, their performance, and how they can scale.

Several storage solutions are based on the DAS storage type but provide shared storage for an ESXi server. Using SAS switching, you can connect multiple SAS HBA adapters to an SAS storage device, but compared to SAN or NAS solutions these storage arrays have limits regarding scaling, and hence are fine for smaller projects but not large-scale virtualization projects.

All enterprise storage can be classified according to its architecture. There are many different enterprise storage architectures. The two most commonly used solutions are as follows:

- **Scale-in or scale-up**: This is where the storage grows in capacity (and initially also in performance) by adding new disk shelves.
- **Scale-out:** This is where more arrays are managed as a single logical storage performance and the capacity can scale by adding new arrays.

From a performance perspective, storage arrays or storage types are commonly classified into the following tiers:

- **Tier 0**: Very high-performance storage, such as the **All-Flash Array** (**AFA**). Tier 0 storage is getting more and more popular as the prices of Enterprise-class SSDs are dropping. It provides unmatched I/O performance.
- **Tier 1 or primary storage**: This is usually the main storage and corresponds to the VMware side in different datastores.
- **Tier 2 or secondary storage**: This is storage not (usually) used from VMware production environments. It stores online archives, backups, cold data, and so on.
- **Tier 3**: This can be long-term and offline archival storage repositories, such as tapes, or copies of backups on public cloud storage.

Storage arrays

The storage market has slightly changed in recent years, moving from appliance solutions (mainly based on hardware features) to software-defined solutions. More importantly, flash technologies have changed the components of storage arrays, and now almost all solutions include flash devices inside each product, with two primary types of array:

- **AFAs**: This is where only flash memories are used, maybe with different types of flash device
- **Hybrid array:** This is where both flash and HDD are used

Moving to a software-defined approach and the use of flash technologies has made it possible to implement a lot of new storage functions, such as tiering, compression, and deduplication. Also, storage architectures have evolved, especially scale-out architectures, with new models (hyper-scaling or HCI) in which each node is not only a storage array but also a computing node. We will describe **Hyper-Converged Infrastructure** (**HCI**) in more detail later on in this chapter.

Concerning the protocols used for frontend interfaces (this does not apply to HCI, but only to external shared storage), the main types of protocol supported in VMware vSphere and their typical use cases are as follows:

Protocol type	Type of service	Interface speed	Typical usage
SAS	Block	6 or 12 Gbps	Shared storage with limited host scaling
FC	Block	8, 16, 32 Gbps	Shared storage, typically for enterprises
FCoE	Block	10, 25, 40, 50, 100 Gbps	Shared storage, typically for enterprises and mid-sized businesses
iSCSI	Block	1, 10, 25, 40, 50, 100 Gbps	Shared storage
NFS	File	1, 10, 25, 40, 50, 100 Gbps	Shared storage

Storage performance

When we talk about storage performance, we are mainly talking about the amount of read and write I/O per second that the storage can serve. There are many factors that affect the overall I/O performance of the store, such as the physical disks or SSDs that are used by the storage, the maturity of the storage controller, the physical media, and the protocols used, or the IO size. Usually, the most important components are as follows:

- The **Redundant Array of Independent Disks (RAID)** level of the logical volume presented to the ESXi servers
- The device type that is used to form a logical volume

The RAID level

The idea of the RAID level is to use multiple physical devices that form a logical volume. There are two main reasons for working with logical volumes instead of single devices:

- **Redundancy**: The goal is to have multiple devices (HDDs or SSDs) in a single logical volume. Based on the RAID level, we can tolerate one or more failures without affecting the availability of the logical volume.
- **Performance**: Some RAID levels have better performance characteristics than other types, but usually the trade-off is capacity. Higher performance means less capacity and vice versa.

The most commonly used RAID levels are as follows:

- **RAID 0**: This is also called **striping**. Both disks are used simultaneously, giving you twice the performance (for reading operations). The overall capacity also equals the sum of both disks. However, keep in mind that with RAID 0 there is no redundancy at all.
- **RAID 1**: This is a simple **mirror**. The data is written to two disks simultaneously. If one disk fails, the other will take over. With Raid 1, you have 50% of the overall capacity and no performance benefits.
- **RAID 5**: This is also called **erasure-coding**. You have multiple disks, and one disk (or better, the total capacity that is equal to one disk) is used for control checksums. If one of the disks fails, the data can still be reconstructed from the control checksum.
- **RAID 10**: This is striping and mirroring together. It is ideal for production workloads as it has the best performance of all standard RAID levels (not counting RAID 0 because of the lack of redundancy), but only 50% of the overall capacity is usable.

Deduplication

This technology can be found in more expensive (or highertier) hardware- or software-based storage arrays. As the name suggests, the idea is that we do not need to store data that is already written to the storage; only data that is different is stored.

Deduplication usually works in blocks. Each block (containing the actual data) has its *hash calculated*. If the hash already exists, then the data is not written but is instead pointed to the location of the data that is already stored.

There are two types of deduplication:

- **In-line**: Data is deduplicated as it is being written to other storage. This commonly involves a cache. The data is written to the persistent cache, the hash is calculated and compared to the stored blocks, and then the data is written to the storage itself (if it is not already stored).
- **Off-line**: The data is written to the storage *as-is*, and at a defined interval, the deduplication process is invoked to deduplicate the data.

Replication

Replication is usually part of the software stack of mid-range or high-range storage arrays. It allows you to replicate the data between two (or sometimes even more) physical storage arrays transparently. Replication is usually used for disaster recovery scenarios where you want to protect your infrastructure from complete site downtime.

There are two types of replication:

- **Synchronous**: When the ESXi server issues an SCSI command to the underlying storage, the data is first written to the primary storage, before being written to the secondary storage. Only once the secondary storage acknowledges that the data has been written is the acknowledgement sent to the VM. For synchronous replication, you need a high-performance storage area network because any delay caused by the interconnection between two storages will affect the overall latency of the VM. When the primary array fails, you do not lose any data because it is on both arrays simultaneously.
- **Asynchronous**: When the SCSI command is received, it is written to the primary storage, and an acknowledgement is immediately sent to the VM. Then, after a pre-defined replication interval, the data is synced to the secondary storage. If the primary storage fails, you will lose the data that has not yet been replicated to the secondary array.

Physical storage device types

So far we have been talking about the performance of the storage infrastructure. The main factor that affects the overall performance is the device type that we use within the storage array.

Before we move on to looking at the actual device types, we need to understand the different physical ports on the devices:

- **SATA**: These devices have a single port. They cannot be connected to both service processors simultaneously.
- **SAS**: The device has two ports and can be connected to two service processors simultaneously. SAS devices are usually faster.

SSDs and AFAs

There are different types of SSD available today. These range from customer-oriented devices using the **Multi-Level Cell (MLC)** technology through to **Enterprise Multi-Level Cells (eMLCs)** and enterprise **Single-Level Cell (SLC)** chips. The critical difference is the durability of the chips and the device itself. You should never use customer SSDs in your infrastructure because they are not intended to run continuous workloads at all.

The endurance of SSDs is often defined as the amount of **Drive Writes Per Day (DWPD)**. The DWPD number will show you how often you can rewrite the whole SSD every single day within the warranty of the SSD. If you continuously go over this number, the chip cells will not be able to handle the load, and errors start to appear until the whole device is completely unusable.

Today, manufacturers have introduced several SSD types based on their designated use:

- **Write intensive SSDs**: These devices are usually equipped with SLC chips and they have a high DWDP, usually around 10, meaning that you can rewrite them ten times every single day. Write-intensive SSDs are commonly used as a caching tier, so the data is always written to these devices and altered during the destaging process to lower performing devices. The capacity is usually up to 1 TB (±800 GB).
- **Read-intensive SSDs**: The DWDP of these devices is much lower than write-intensive SSDs, usually under 1, meaning that you should not rewrite the whole capacity within a single day. They have a much higher capacity than write-intensive SSDs (3.84 TB for SATA3 devices), and they are also cheaper. They do not use SLC chips but eMLC chips instead. The primary use case for this kind of device is the capacity tier.

- **Mixed-use SSDs:** This is a compromise between WI and RI devices. They have a higher DWDP then RI SSDs but a lower DWDP than WI devices (usually between 2 and 5). Their capacity and price are also in between RI and WI devices. They are often used as a single, all-purpose device. If you do not want to create multiple storage tiers, mixed-use SSDs are the way to go.

Asymmetric Logical Unit Access (ALUA) arrays

It is essential to understand that not all storage arrays are the same, even if they look the same. Here, we are talking about ALUA arrays. Although they have two independent controllers, the interior design is different compared to higher-tier storage. In ALUA arrays, only one service processor (the controller) *owns* the device (the logical volume). This means that if an I/O request is received by the service processor that owns the device, there is no impact on the performance. On the other hand, if the service processor that does not own the device receives the I/O request, the I/O is first internally forwarded to the service processor that owns the device, and then the actual I/O is processed.

VMware vSphere storage types

VMware vSphere supports different types of storage architecture, both internally (in this case the controller is crucial; it must be in the HCL) or externally with shared SAS DAS, SAN FC, SAN iSCSI, SAN FCoE, or NFS NAS (in this case, the HCL is fundamental for external storage, the fabric elements, and the host adapters). Different storage types and their properties are displayed in the following table:

Technology	Protocols	Transfer	Interface
FC	FC/SCSI	Block access	FC HBA
FCoE	FCoE/SCSI	Block access	Converged network adapter (hardware FCoE) NIC with FCoE support (software FCoE)
iSCSI	IP/SCSI	Block access	iSCSI HBA-or iSCSI-enabled NIC (hardware iSCSI) Network adapter (software iSCSI)
NAS	IP/NFS	File access	Network adapter

Different storage types have different vSphere characteristics:

Storage type	Boot ESXi	Run VMs	vMotion	Datastore	RDM	VM clustering (guest OS)	VMware HA and DRS	Storage APIs – data protection
Local Storage	Yes	Yes	No	VMFS	No	Yes	No	Yes
Fibre Channel and FCoE	Yes*	Yes	Yes	VMFS	Yes	Yes	Yes	Yes
iSCSI	Yes*	Yes	Yes	VMFS	Yes	Yes	Yes	Yes
NAS over NFS	No	Yes	Yes	NFS3 and NFS 4.1	No	No	Yes	Yes

 Please note that you can only boot from FCoE or iSCSI if you are using a hardware adapter, not a software-based equivalent.

One of the most critical metrics in the storage world is the latency of the storage. Latency in this case refers to how long it takes until the underlying storage receives the SCSI command. Many factors affect the overall latency, one of which is the different types of protocol. The following diagram shows the flow of the SCSI command from the guest OS down to the physical network:

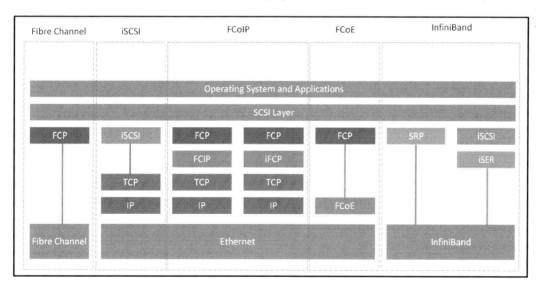

The more steps between the SCSI layer and the physical layer, the larger the latency will be, because every additional step takes some time.

Storage types at the ESXi logical level

At a high level, VMware vSphere will access each storage using datastores—a logical paradigm for abstracting all storage types, such as how a common operating system uses letters or mount points to access a filesystem.

VMware vSphere 6.x has the following four main types of datastore:

- **VMware FileSystem (VMFS) datastores**: All block-based storage must be first formatted with VMFS to transform a block service to a file and folder oriented services.
- **Network FileSystem (NFS) datastores**: This is for NAS storage.
- **VVol**: This is introduced in vSphere 6.0 and is a new paradigm for accessing SAN and NAS storage in a uniform way and by better integrating and consuming storage array capabilities.
- **vSAN datastore**: If you are using a vSAN solution, all your local storage devices could be polled together in a single shared vSAN datastore.

New datastores could be provisioned from the new HTML5 client, starting from a **data center**, a **cluster**, or a **host**; just right-click on the object, choose **Storage**, and then **New datastore**.

For local disks, if you have configured the right RAID level from the controller (remember that ESXi does not provide software RAID features), you can just *format* the logical disks with a VMFS datastore.

But before external storage, before adding a new datastore, you must first configure the ESXi host, the fabric (if present), and the storage itself. This depends on the storage type and vendor and will be discussed later. You cannot directly add a vSAN datastore; the vSAN configuration is quite different, but the final result will be a vSAN datastore with its own format.

Of course, on the same host you can have multiple datastores, also with different types:

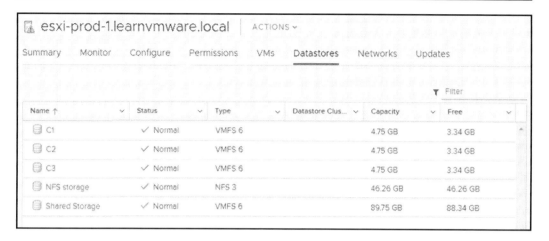

On the datastore level, there isn't any difference between DAS or SAN; they are just block-based storage types and both become VMFS datastores. The functional difference is that a SAN disk could be shared across multiple hosts, not local DAS disks (but there are also shared SAS storages that are formally classified as DAS storage).

Storage types at the ESXi physical level

Excluding vSAN, which has a specific configuration, at the physical level there are three main types of storage:

- **Block-based storage accessed by a hardware adapter**: This includes DAS storage or SAN FC storage.
- **Block-based storage accessed by a software adapter**: This is like SAN iSCSI storage when the software initiator is used. In this case, you first need to configure the network connectivity properly. After that, it becomes very similar to the first case.
- **NFS storage**: This is where you first have to configure the IP network connectivity to your storage and then connect the NFS datastore.

For the physical storage adapters, VMware ESXi supports several types of protocols and technologies (refer to the hardware compatibility list to check the supported level):

- **Fibre Channel Host Bus Adapter (FC HBA)**: This is the standard way to implement FC-based storage using a dedicated full fabric.
- **iSCSI HBA**: These are specialized PCIe cards that implement the entire iSCSI stack completely in the hardware, reducing the load on the host CPU.
- **CNA adapters for FCoE or iSCSI**: These are mostly 10 Gbps (or higher) Ethernet adapters providing hardware (or hardware-assisted) FCoE or iSCSI functionality on converged (or dedicated) networks.
- **RDMA over Converged Ethernet (RoCE)**: This is a network protocol that allows **remote direct memory access** (**RDMA**) over an Ethernet network. Starting with vSphere 6.5, RoCE certified adapters can be used for converged networks.
- **InfiniBand HCA**: Mellanox Technologies InfiniBand HCA device drivers are available directly from Mellanox Technologies. Mostly used for the network instead of the storage, they can be interesting in converged networks, and also in vSAN implementation.

Storage types at VM logical levels

There are different types of virtual disks depending on the provisioning method—pre-allocated or dynamic. The types of virtual disks have mainly stayed the same since vSphere 4.0:

- **Eager zeroed thick Virtual Machine Disk (VMDK)**: An eager zeroed thick disk has all the space allocated and wiped clean of any previous content on the physical media at creation time. Such disks may take a long time to create compared to other disk formats. The entire disk space is reserved and unavailable for use by other VMs.
- **Thick or lazy zeroed thick VMDK**: A thick disk has all space allocated at creation time. This space may contain stale data on the physical media. Before writing to a new block, a zero has to be written, increasing the **input/output operation per second (IOPS)** on new blocks compared to eager disks. The entire disk space is reserved and unavailable for use by other VMs.
- **Thin VMDK**: The space required for the thin-provisioned virtual disk is allocated and zeroed on demand as space is used. Unused space is available for use by other VMs.

You can choose a disk provisioning type during virtual disk creation, but you can change the type using a cold VM migration across two data stores, or by using Storage vMotion (if you have at least the ESXi Standard edition). Note that you can also change the type of each disk by choosing **Configure per disk** in the HTML5 client, as shown in the following screenshot:

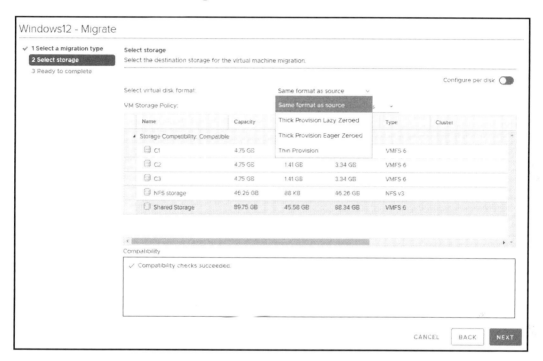

There are also **Raw Device Mapping (RDM)** disks where a disk at the ESXi level is mapped 1:1 to a VM (such as a passthrough mode), with two different types of compatibility (virtual or physical mode). Unless you are building guest clusters (clusters across VMs on different hosts), there is no need to use this type of disk.

There is no significant difference in performance for sequential I/O between the different types of virtual disks. For random I/O, thin VMDKs have the worst performance and higher latency (for the lazy thick virtual disk format, it depends on whether you have to write a new block).

Storage types at the VM physical level

To access a block device, such as a virtual disk's VMDK, a virtual CD/DVD-ROM, or other SCSI devices, each VM uses storage controllers; at least one is added by default when you create a VM.

There are different types of controller available for a VM running on ESXi. These are described as follows:

- **BusLogic**: This was one of the first emulated SCSI virtual controllers available in VMware ESX. It's now a legacy controller used mainly for legacy operating systems. It does not support VMDKs larger than 2 TB.
- **LSI logic parallel**: This was formally known as LSI Logic and was the other SCSI virtual controller available formerly in VMware ESX. It is used for operating systems such as Windows Server 2003.
- **LSI logic SAS**: This was introduced in vSphere 4.0 and is the evolution of the parallel driver. It works as an SAS virtual controller and is used in Windows Server 2008 or newer.
- **VMware paravirtual (or PVSCSI)**: This was introduced in vSphere 4.0. It's a SCSI virtual controller designed to support very high throughput with minimal processing cost, working not in emulation mode, but in paravirtual mode (it requires VMware Tools to be recognized).
- **NVMe**: Virtual NVMe devices have reduced guest I/O processing overheads (over 50% compared to AHCI SATA SCSI device), which allows more VMs per host or more transactions per minute. Each VM supports four NVMe controllers and up to 15 devices per controller.

Others virtual controllers are also possible in a VM, such as AHCI SATA (introduced in vSphere 5.5), IDE, and also USB controllers, but usually for specific cases (for example, SATA or IDE are usually used for virtual DVD drives).

Persistent memory (PMem)

Introduced in VMware vSphere, 6.7 ESXi supports next-generation persistent memory devices, also known as **Non-Volatile Memory** (**NVM**) devices. These devices combine performance and speed of memory with the persistence of traditional storage. They can retain stored data through reboots or power source failures.

Virtual machines that require high bandwidth, low latency, and persistence can benefit from this technology. Examples include VMs with acceleration databases and analytics workload.

Let's have a look at the core building blocks of PMem technology:

- **PMem datastore:** After you add persistent memory to your ESXi host, the host detects the hardware, and then formats and mounts it as a local PMem datastore. ESXi uses VMFS-L as a file system format. Only one local PMem datastore per host is supported. The PMem datastore is used to store virtual NVDIMM devices and traditional virtual disks on a VM. The VM home directory with the vmx and vmware.log files cannot be placed on the PMem datastore.

- **Direct-access mode:** In this mode, a PMem region can be presented to a VM as a virtual **non-volatile dual in-line memory module** (**NVDIMM**) module. The VM uses the NVDIMM module as a standard byte-addressable memory that can persist across power cycles. You can add one or several NVDIMM modules when provisioning the VM.
  The VMs must be hardware version ESXi 6.7 or later and have a PMem-aware guest OS. The NVDIMM device is compatible with the latest guest OSes that support persistent memory, for example, Windows 2016. Each NVDIMM device is automatically stored on the PMem datastore.

- **Virtual disk mode:** This mode is available to any traditional VM and supports any hardware version, including all legacy versions. VMs are not required to be PMem-aware. When you use this mode, you create a regular SCSI virtual disk and attach a PMem VM storage policy to the disk. The policy automatically places the disk on the PMem datastore.

- **PMem storage policy:** To place the virtual disk on the PMem datastore, you must apply the host-local PMem default storage policy to the disk. The policy is not editable. The policy can be applied only to virtual disks. Because the VM home directory does not reside on the PMem datastore, make sure to place it on any standard datastore.

  After you assign the PMem storage policy to the virtual disk, you cannot change the policy through the VM **Edit Settings...** dialog box. To change the policy, migrate or clone the VM. If a PMem device is installed in your ESXi hypervisor, you will see the available size under the **Configure** tab, hardware section and memory:

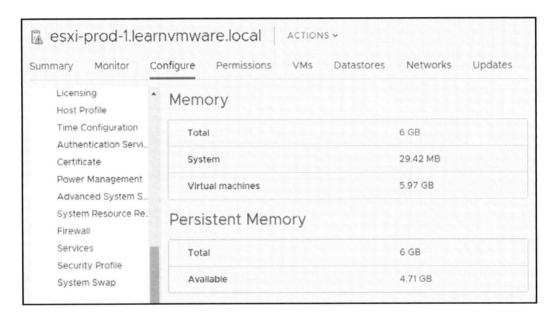

The local PMem datastore is automatically created for PMem devices, although it is not visible in the vCenter Server. You must use the ESXi host client to access the datastore:

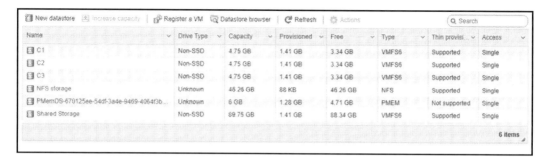

You can find more information about PMem in the following technical paper:
`https://www.vmware.com/content/dam/digitalmarketing/vmware/en/pdf/`
`techpaper/performance/pmem-vsphere67-perf.pdf.`

VMware vSphere storage configuration

For shared storage, the ESXi configuration varies a lot depending both on the storage type and the protocols used. There is a specific guide from VMware, but what's more important is to follow specific storage vendor guides, including possible reference architectures or configuration suggestions.

FC storage

FC is an entire high-speed network stack used to implement storage area networks. Starting with vSphere 6.0U2, ESXi supports 32 Gbps FC for all the supported HBA.

When using ESXi with FC SAN, follow the recommendations and best practices of both VMware and the storage vendor to avoid possible issues. Note that storage vendor specifications could be more restrictive than VMware's; for example, the HCL could be smallest or restricted on specific firmware/driver versions. In those cases, it's essential to use the vendor specifications.

On the ESXi side, you have to only plug in the supported FC HBA (with the correct firmware and drivers) and cable them properly, usually following a full fabric topology, as shown at the following diagram:

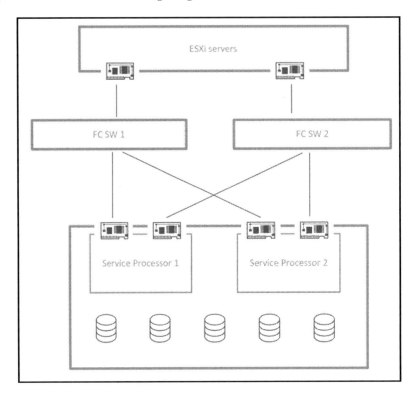

VMware may support point-to-point topologies (such as a DAS storage, for a small environment), but first you have to verify if the storage vendor supports it. After that, you only have to configure the fabric with the correct zoning at the port level or better at the **World Wide Name** (**WWN**) level (again, refer to what your storage vendor requires or recommends); and finally, the storage with the correct **LUN masking** to present the logical disks to the hosts. At this point, there isn't any difference, at the ESXi level, between local or remote storage: you need to format the logical disk from one host and then re-scan the datastore from all the others. That's all!

Most storage requires that each ESXi host is registered with the array, to map the hosts correctly to the arrays and also to authorize the connections (FC does not provide strict authentication capabilities). ESXi usually performs automatic host registration by sending the host's name and IP address to the array, but if you prefer to perform manual registration, you can disable the ESXi auto-registration feature by changing the advanced settings, `Disk.EnableNaviReg`, to 0.

> For troubleshooting or monitoring FC connectivity, you can use the `resxtop` or `esxtop` command-line utilities. For more information see **KB 1003680: Troubleshooting fibre channel storage connectivity** (`https://kb.vmware.com/kb/1003680`).

FC usually does not require specific tuning at the host level, except maybe the HBA settings or the queue depth for the driver (refer to storage vendor best practices).

Since the FC device is configured before the OS is booted, you can quickly boot from the SAN using FC adapters. There is no difference when it comes to VMware vSphere configuration; all you need to do is to provide an additional, usually small, disk that will be used as a destination device in the installation procedure. This is especially handy when working with blade servers because you do not need to buy local disks just for the installation of the ESXi hypervisor.

FCoE storage

FCoE encapsulates FC frames over Ethernet networks, using 10 Gbps (or higher) Ethernet networks at layers 1 and 2. However, the rest remain FC protocols stacks (note that FC is a complete network stack, so no IP, UDP, or TCP protocols are used), and you still need specific FC skills (for example, for fabric zoning), plus specific new skills for converged networks (such as datacenter bridging protocols).

For CNA cards, you can use **network partition (NPAR)** and enable hardware-assisted FCoE at the ESXi level with the right driver. You will see a new VMware storage adapter called **vmhba** acting like a traditional FC HBA. The rest of the configuration is all at the fabric and storage levels as described before.

In vSphere 5.0, VMware introduced a new software FCoE adapter, useful for NIC with a partial FCoE offload. In this case, you also need to configure the virtual switch part to bind a VMkernel port to a virtual switch connected to this NIC. FCoE traffic does not go through the virtual switch, but to manage DCB and other control traffic, you need this network configuration to forward Ethernet frames to the **dcbd** service the is run in the user space.

iSCSI storage

The iSCSI is a different way to implement SAN storage; instead of using a dedicated network stack FC, iSCSI relies on the standard TCP/IP stack. Like FC protocols, there are two different leading roles—the initiator (at host side) and the target (at storage side). Also, of course, the fabric, that is a traditional Ethernet network (maybe with new protocols, such as **datacenter bridging (DCB)**).

ESXi can be one of the following iSCSI initiator types:

- **Software iSCSI adapter**: Use one or more VMkernel network interfaces and the virtual switches to manage the entire iSCSI traffic. With the software iSCSI adapter, you can use iSCSI technology without purchasing specialized hardware.
- **Dependent hardware iSCSI adapter**: VMware manages iSCSI management and configuration, and it may also be the part of the network that must be implemented at the virtual switch level. Ethernet NIC with iSCSI offload capabilities falls into this category. At the ESXi level, those NICs are presented with two different components—a hardware iSCSI adapter and a corresponding standard networking NIC.
- **Independent hardware iSCSI adapter or iSCSI HBA**: This is like the FC HBA. All of the network stack is implemented in hardware inside the adapter. On the ESXi side, you will see one or more vmhba, like with all other block storage adapters. Network configuration must be performed at the card level, using BIOS management, or specific tools (there are also plugins for vCenter to manage the configuration inside vSphere).

The main difference between one mode and another lies in how the network is configured; for independent hardware iSCSI adapters, you configure at the adapter firmware level; for a software initiator, you have to build a proper virtual network configuration. Performance can change slightly across those modes, but in most cases could remain similar; not so with the host **CPU load**, which usually decreases when moving from software to **HBA mode**.

Some iSCSI storage arrays work with a network topology exactly like the FC fabric, two different switches with isolated networks. That means two different logical networks and two different IP classes. This is a solution that does not require any inter-switch connection and provides better resilience (switches are fully independent and isolated from each other). For example, the iSCSI version of Dell-EMC VNX or Compellent storage works in this way. If you are using a software initiator, you need at least two different VMkernel interfaces, one on each logical network.

However, there is also another possibility, a single flat network on both layer 2 and layer 3. That means that the physical switches (to provide resilience and redundancy you want at least two) must be in the same broadcast domain and must be (directly or indirectly) interconnected. For example, Dell-EMC EqualLogic needs this kind of network configuration. Using stacking, a virtual chassis, or similar functions to build a single logical switch could be an option, mainly to simplify management. However, plan it carefully to ensure the right network resilience (for example, some stacked switches need to reboot all the switches during a firmware upgrade). Also, in this kind of network topology, using a software initiator, more VMkernels may be needed, but in this case, you have to bind all of them to the iSCSI adapter:

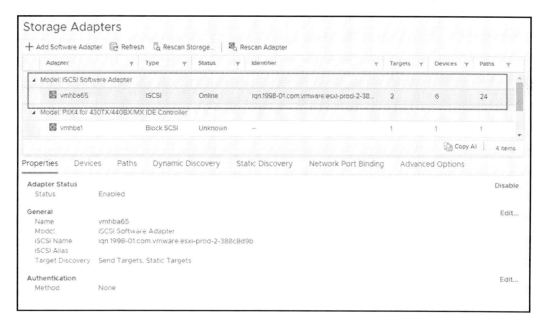

There isn't a specific service type for the VMkernel interface to tag it for iSCSI network traffic; the choice of the proper interface is made depending on your routing table. For this reason, be sure to use dedicated network ranges for iSCSI only when you have more interfaces on the same network. You need iSCSI NIC binding. Otherwise, only one interface will be used.

As compared to FC storage, there are several different possible tweaks and optimizations for iSCSI, but check what your storage vendor recommends:

- **Jumbo frames (9000 bytes for Ethernet frames)**: iSCSI traffic can usually benefit from jumbo frames, but is only enabled end-to-end across initiator and target; that means at the VMkernel and virtual switch level (configuration is possible under MTU settings), at the physical switch level (for all the ports used by iSCSI), and at the storage level.
- **DCB**: If you use converged networks and your storage supports them, DCB can provide **Quality of Service (QoS)** for storage traffic. It's usually configured on the ESXi side on CNA adapters.
- **iSCSI initiator advanced setting delayed ACK**: Some storage vendors suggest disabling this.
- **iSCSI initiator advanced setting login timeout**: The default value is quite low; some storage vendors suggest increasing it (for example, to 60 seconds).
- **TSO and LRO of the physical NICs**: Sometimes you have to change these settings using **KB 2055140: Understanding TCP Segmentation Offload (TSO) and Large Receive Offload (LRO) in a VMware environment** (https://kb.vmware.com/kb/2055140).
- **TCO of the physical NICs**: Sometimes you have to change this setting using **KB 2052904: Understanding TCP Checksum Offloading (TCO) in a VMware Environment** (https://kb.vmware.com/kb/2052904).

Note that iSCSI can provide initiator (and also target) authentication in different ways:

- **IP based**: With some storage arrays you can add a list of authorized IPs (or networks).
- **iSCSI Qualified Name (IQN)**: Each initiator and target has at least one IQN that can be used for authorizing specific hosts. Note that the default ESXi software initiator identifier is based on the hostname (when you activate the software iSCSI adapter) followed by a random string such as `iqn.1998-01.com.vmware:esx01-789fac05`, but you can change it (this requires a host reboot), or add an alias to use a different string.
- **Challenge Handshake Authentication Protocol (CHAP)**: This is a real authentication using a shared password, and can also be mutual, so not only does the storage authenticate the host, but the host can also authenticate the storage.

NFS storage

The only types of **network-attached storage** (**NAS**) supported by ESXi are those with NFS protocols, NFS 3, or NFS 4.1 (starting with vSphere 6.0), both over TCP (by default NFS is on the UDP transport protocol). Like software iSCSI, an ESXi host needs a proper VMkernel and virtual network configuration to access a remote NFS server.

Note that there isn't a specific type of VMkernel interface for NFS traffic; depending on your routing table, the right interface is chosen correctly.

To add a new NFS datastore, proceed with the following steps:

1. Choose to add new data store
2. Select the NFS type
3. Choose the right protocol—NFS 3 or NFS 4.1, based on your storage array configuration
4. Provide storage information, that is, at least a folder on the share (usually the full path) and the name or IP of the storage, as follows:

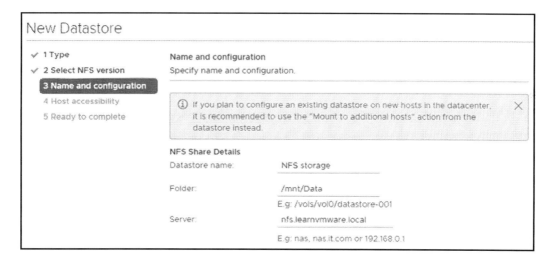

NFS 3 uses one single TCP connection between client and server. For this reason, ESXi does not support multiple paths, and the only solution is to work with more IPs at the storage side and use link aggregation. NFS 4.1 provides multipathing for servers that support session trunking. When trunking is available, you can use multiple IP addresses to access a single NFS volume. Client ID trunking is not supported. Storage vendors usually detail the required configuration to provide better scalability, the best resilience, and also if some specific tuning could be requested.

Virtual disks created on NFS datastores are thinly provisioned by default. To have thick-provisioned VMDK as well, you must have VAAI-compatible storage that supports the Reserve Space operation. VAAI will be discussed later.

SIOC and storage DRS

SIOC and Storage DRS are techniques that either prevent contention or provide fair access to the storage resources when the contention occurs.

Storage contention is one of the worst situations you, as a VMware vSphere administrator, could be in. In such a situation, the overall performance of the environment is affected, your VMs suffer high latency when accessing storage, and applications become very slow.

SIOC

With SIOC, which is enabled at the datastore-level, you can prioritize storage resource consumption of VMs during contention. Since storage is shared between all VMs, when a particular VM starts to issue a heavy I/O load, it might compromise the overall storage capacity, resulting in poor performance for all VMs.

SIOC provides several capabilities that can be used to ensure that your critical VMs will not be affected during storage contention.

In a situation when the configured latency or I/O threshold is reached, the datastore is considered congested, and the storage resources are servers based on configured shares. By default, all VMs have the same shares configured on all virtual disks; however, you can assign the shares as **High**, **Normal**, or **Low**.

When you enable storage I/O control, ESXi hypervisors start to monitor every SIOC-enabled datastore, and device latency together with the number of I/O operations per second are stored in `.iormstats.sf` file.

Each ESXi server can access the `.iormstats.sf` file, which is created for each datastore and writes its own observations of latency and I/O, thus enabling all hosts to read the file and observe the datastore-wide latency and overall I/Os.

Reservations, limits, and shares

Once the SIOC is enabled, you can start to play with the RLS settings of the virtual disks. Let's have a look at the following scenario.

A storage array can handle 10,000 IOPS and the following VMs are deployed with specific reservations, limits, and shares:

Virtual machine	Reservation	Limit	Shares
VM1	2,000 IOPS	5,000 IOPS	4,000
VM2	1,000 IOPS	5,000 IOPS	2,000
VM3	500 IOPS	5,000 IOPS	1,000
V4	2,000 IOPS	5,000 IOPS	2,000

We have four VMs, each of which has different reservations, limits, and shares assigned, and they want to access single storage concurrently. All VMs wants to perform as many IOPS as possible. *What will be the active IO assignment?* Let's have a look at the Reservations, Limits and Shares calculations.

Reservations

Reservation is the number of resources that will always be available to the VM (or virtual disk respectively in this case). If the reserved resources are not used, the remaining number of resources will be used to satisfy the needs of other VMs, but once a machine with a reservation wants to access those resources, it will even if others are using them as well.

Limits

This is a hard cap on resources. The VM (or virtual disk) will not consume more than the resources configured by a limit.

Shares

Shares come into play only when congestion occurs. VMs want to access more resources than the storage can provide. In this situation, each VM will get a fair number of resources calculated using shares.

RLS calculations

Based on our example, the I/O resource distribution will be as follows:

Virtual machine	No contention	Contention situation
VM1	Max 5,000 IOPS	4,000 IOPS
VM2	Max 5,000 IOPS	2,000 IOPS
VM3	Max 5,000 IOPS	1,000 IOPS
VM4	Max 5,000 IOPS	3,000 IOPS

During no contention state, the maximum IOPS will be determined by a defined limit. In contention situations, first reservations are applied. The sum of all reservations is 5,500 IOPS and, based on our storage performance, we have 4,500 IOPS available to be assigned by shares.

The total sum of all shares is 9,000. Thus a single share equals 0.5 IOPS:

Virtual machine	Shares	Effective IOPS
VM1	4,000	2,000 IOPS
VM2	2,000	1,000 IOPS
VM3	1,000	500 IOPS
V4	2,000	1,000 IOPS

SIOC versions

With vSphere 6.7 there are two different SIOC versions:

- **SIOC V1**: It is disabled by default. It needs to be enabled on a per datastore level, and it is only utilized when a specific level of latency has been reached. By default, the latency threshold for a datastore is set to 30 ms, as mentioned earlier. If SIOC is triggered, disk shares (aggregated from all VMDKs using the datastore) are used to assign I/O queue slots on a per-host basis to that datastore. In other words, SIOC limits the number of I/Os that a host can issue. The more VMs/VMDKs that run on a particular host, the higher the number of shares, and thus the higher the number of I/Os that particular host can issue. The throttling is done by modifying the device queue depth of the various hosts sharing the datastore. When the period of contention passes, and latency returns to normal values, the device queue depths are allowed to return to their default values on each host.
- **SIOC V2**: This can now be managed using **Storage Policy Based Management (SPBM)** policies. Since vSphere 6.5, VM storage policies have had a new option called **common rules**, used for configuring data services provided by hosts, such as SIOC and encryption.

SIOC V1 and SIOC V2 can co-exist on vSphere 6.7.

To build a new SIOC storage policy and enable SIOC:

1. Switch to the **Datastores** view in the vSphere client

2. Right-click on the storage and select **Configure Storage IO control**:

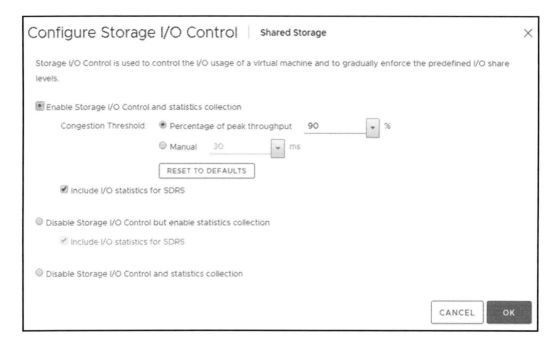

If you want to use SIOC v2, follow these steps:

1. Switch to **Policies and Profiles** using the menu.
2. Select **VM Storage Policy.**
3. Select **Create VM Storage Policy.**
4. Then you need to define the name of the policy.
5. In the next step, select the policy structure. In this case, we are working with host-based rules:

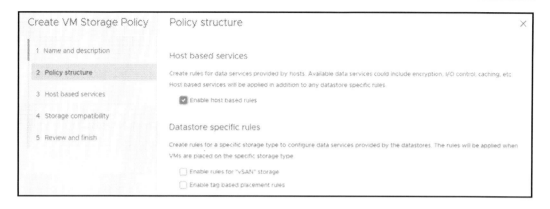

6. Under **Host based services**, switch to the **Storage IO Control** tab, and either use the standard storage component from the drop-down menu, or define your own RLS settings for the policy.

7. In the next section, you will see which datastores you might use this policy on.

8. Lastly, review the settings and finish the wizard.

Once the policy is defined, you can attach the policy to the virtual disk:

1. Switch to the VMs and templates

2. Select your VM and click **Edit settings...**

3. Select the virtual disk to which you want to assign the policy:

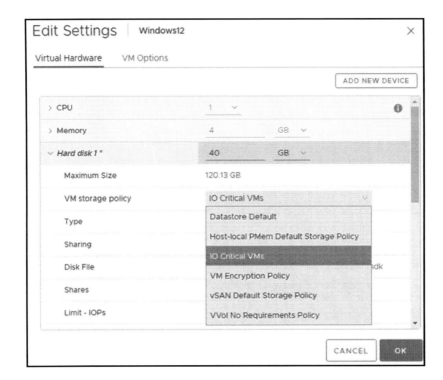

So that's it! Now your virtual disk will have RLS settings configured from the policy instead of manual settings.

Storage DRS

Storage Distributed Resource Scheduler (**SDRS**) was introduced in vSphere 5.0 to efficiently manage a pool of datastores as a single logical datastore (a datastore cluster). VM optimization and distribution were based on two metrics—**space** and **I/O**.

SDRS fully supports VMFS and NFS datastores. However, it does not allow the addition of NFS datastores and VMFS datastores into the same datastore cluster. Starting with vSphere 6.0, SDRS is now aware of the storage capabilities available through VASA 2.0 and can use storage policies (see later in this chapter). It will only move or place VMs on a datastore within the datastore cluster that can satisfy a specific VM's storage policies.

When you enable Storage DRS, the following functions will be available:

- **Space load balancing:** All datastores will be utilized evenly in terms of free space
- **I/O load balancing:** All datastores will be utilized evenly in terms of overall I/O load
- **Initial placement:** New VMs will be placed on the least utilized datastore

To enable Storage DRS on a datastore cluster, follow these steps:

1. Browse to the **Datastores** view and select **Datastore Clusters** in the vSphere Client
2. Click the **Configure** tab and click **Services**
3. Select **Storage DRS** and click edit
4. Select **Turn ON vSphere Storage DRS** and click **OK**, as shown in the following screenshot:

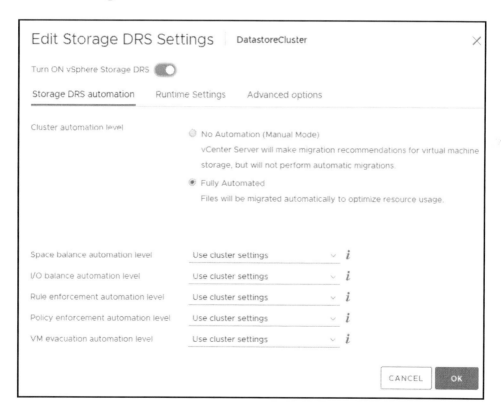

5. Select either manual mode or fully automated mode
6. In **Runtime Settings**, enable I/O metrics for SDRS recommendations and configure the desired parameters
7. In **Advanced options**, you can select default VM affinity policy, the I/O imbalanced threshold, and how often the SDRS will run

Datastore clusters

A datastore cluster is a set of datastores that you manage as a single logical entity in which to store your VMs. **Storage DRS** can be enabled only in a datastore cluster, not an individual datastore.

Datastore clusters are not only useful for simplified storage management. You can also use datastore maintenance mode for individual datastores. When there is some operation that might affect the availability for the datastore, you can efficiently evacuate all VMs residing on the datastore using datastore maintenance mode.

Anti-affinity rules

You can use anti-affinity rules with VM disks, allowing you to specify on which datastore the virtual disks should be stored. By default, all virtual disks are stored on the same datastore, but in some cases it is better to keep the virtual disks on different datastores.

There are two types of anti-affinity rule:

- **VM anti-affinity rules**: You can specify which VMs will never be stored on the same datastore
- **VMDK anti-affinity rules**: You can specify what disks on the single VM will never be kept on the same datastore:

Advanced storage features

vSphere version 6.7 brings a lot of improvements to storage levels, and some new features in different areas, from VMs to datastores, to low-level storage; we will discuss in the next paragraphs.

Virtual Machine File System (VMFS) 6

VMFS 6 introduces two new internal block size concepts for file creation—**Large File Block (LFB)** with a size of 512 MB and **Small File Block (SFB)** with a size of 1 MB—and these are used to back up files on the VMFS 6 volume. Note that the VMFS block size remains 1 MB. **Small File Blocks (SFBs)** are used to back thin disks. **Eager Zeroed Thick (EZT)** or **Lazy Zeroed Thick (LZT)** disks are backed by LFBs as much as possible; SFBs are used for the portion of the disk that does not fit into an LFB. For more information, see `http://cormachogan.com/2017/08/16/vmfs-6-large-small-file-blocks/`.

Datastore format upgrades from VMFS-5 (or previous versions) to VMFS-6 are not supported, but ESXi 6.7 can still work with VMFS-5 datastores. Since there is no direct in-place upgrade, you have to build new a datastore and migrate VMs across from the old datastores. VMFS-3 datastores are no longer supported in vSPhere 6.7

In VMFS 6, most datastore management tasks remain the same as VMFS 5, such as increasing the capacity of a datastore, designating a datastore, managing the pointer block cache, and checking metadata consistency with **vSphere On-disk Metadata Analyzer (VOMA)** (for more information, see the storage guide available at `https://storagehub.vmware.com/`).

Automatic space reclaim

VAAI UNMAP was introduced in vSphere 5.0 to reclaim free space when a VM had to be moved or deleted from a datastore that is thin provisioned at the storage level. vSphere 6.0 introduced some improvements to UNMAP that facilitated the reclaiming of stranded space from within a guest OS.

However, in this case, the reclaim operation was performed manually, as described in **KB 2057513: Using the esxcli storage vmfs unmap command to reclaim VMFS deleted blocks on thin-provisioned LUNs** at `https://kb.vmware.com/kb/2057513`. In vSphere 6.5 and with the new VMFS6, there is now an automated UNMAP mechanism for reclaiming dead or stranded space on datastores. Now UNMAP runs continuously in the background if enabled at the datastore level.

There are currently two settings available—**none** and **fixed**. The previously available **Low** method is no longer supported.

With vSphere 6.7 a new method, **fixed**, is available, which allows you to configure an automatic UNMAP rate between 100 MBps and 2,000 MBps, configurable both in the UI and CLI:

```
esxcli storage vmfs reclaim config set
```

In vSphere 6.0, there was limited in-guest UNMAP (note that TRIM is the ATA equivalent of SCSI UNMAP) support for reclaiming in-guest dead space natively. This was limited to Windows 2012 R2 initially, primarily because of the vSCSI version. Linux distributions check the SCSI version, and unless it is version 5 or higher, do not send UNMAPs. With SPC-4 support, as introduced in vSphere 6.5, Linux guest OSes will now also be able to issue UNMAPs.

One way to monitor automatic UNMAP operations is to use `esxtop`. Run this command and type `u` (switch to disk device), then `f` for define custom field, then set **VAAI statistics** to **0.** The `DELETE` column is related to **UNMAP operations**. Space reclaim remains manual for VMFS 5 datastores if you disable it at the datastore level, or if you disable it at the host level.

Instant clones versus linked clones

Starting with VMware Horizon 7, it's possible to choose two different ways to deliver virtual desktop pools in a space-optimized way: using **VMware Composer** and **Linked Clones** technology, or using the **VMware Instant Clones** technology introduced in vSphere 6.0.

Both technologies share a virtual disk of a parent VM between multiple VMs and therefore consume less storage than full clone VMs. It's like differential disks in other virtualization solutions. However, instant clones (also called just-in-time VM delivery or VM Fork) are significantly faster than linked clones.

An overview of instant clones and an example workflow is shown in the following diagram:

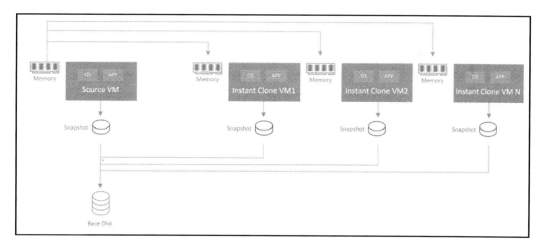

Transparent page sharing is automatically enabled because clones can also share the memory of a parent VM, making them not only space-efficient on the storage side, but also the memory side. Unfortunately, there isn't a direct way to create them from management interfaces, but only from other products. Instant clones can be used in **VMware Horizon Enterprise** and from **vSphere Integrated Containers** or using **PowerCLI** as described by William Lam at `https://www.virtuallyghetto.com/2018/04/new-instant-clone-architecture-in-vsphere-6-7-part-1.html`.

Storage DRS versus storage tiering

Storage Distributed Resource Scheduler (SDRS) was introduced in vSphere 5.0 to efficiently manage a pool of datastores as a single logical datastore (a datastore cluster). VM optimization and distribution were based on two metrics—**space** and **I/O**.

SDRS fully supports **VMFS** and **NFS** datastores. However, it does not allow adding NFS datastores and VMFS datastores into the same datastore cluster. Starting with vSphere 6.0, SDRS is now aware of the storage capabilities available through VASA 2.0 and can use storage policies (see later in this chapter). It will only move or place VMs on a datastore within the datastore cluster that can satisfy specific VM's storage policies, based on several features, including the following:

- **Deduplication**: SDRS will be aware of deduplication domains, and when datastores belong to the same domain, moving a VM will have little to no effect on capacity.
- **Storage tier**: SDRS will not move VMs while the storage auto-tier is promoting or demoting blocks to a lower or higher tier.
- **Thin provisioning**: SDRS can recognize if more thin-provisioned datastores have a common backing pool to avoid migrating VMs.
- **Storage replica (SR)**: SDRS will recognize replica VMs and avoid resource constraints between storage vMotion and replication.

Always refer to the storage vendor's guides to verify if SDRS is supported and with which settings (usually auto-tiering storage is incompatible with SDRS I/O balance).

Also note that **SDRS cannot replace the tiering** mechanism implemented in some storage (especially hybrid storage); just because a single VMDK can only stay in one single datastore and not split across multiple datastores, there is no way for SDRS to move hot blocks to a fast datastore and cold blocks to a slow datastore.

Datastore cluster and SDRS management remain the same as in vSphere 5, with similar considerations, such as keeping disks with the same capabilities in the same datastore cluster. However, with vSphere 6.0 you can now mix datastores with different capabilities in the same datastore cluster, using the right storage policies at the VM level.

RDM

RDM is a mapping technique that provides **direct access** to a LUN on a SAN storage system for a VM.

Virtual machines can directly access the storage device using RDM, and the RDM mapping file contains metadata which controls the disk access to the physical device. RDM gives you some of the advantages of direct access to a physical device while keeping some advantages of a virtual disk in VMFS. As a result, it merges VMFS manageability with raw device access.

There are two types of RDM compatibility mode:

- **Virtual compatibility mode** allows an RDM to act exactly like a virtual disk file, including the use of snapshots
- **Physical compatibility mode** allows direct access to the SCSI device for applications that need lower-level control

RDM is usually used when clustering on the guest OS is performed, especially when clustering virtual and physical machines into a single cluster.

Permanent Device Loss (PDL) and All-Paths-Down (APD)

Starting with vSphere 6.0, in vSphere HA configurations, there is a new storage-related feature, **VM Component Protection** (**VMCP**), that protects VMs from possible storage issues.

VMCP can manage two different types of condition:

- **PDL**: This occurs when the storage array issues an SCSI sense code indicating that the device is unavailable (for example, a failed LUN)
- **APD**: Usually, related to an underlying storage/networking issue, which is different from a PDL because the host doesn't have enough information to determine if the device loss is temporary or permanent

A typical response could be to restart the VM in the case of a PDL, because this condition may indicate that the storage device does not expect the device to return any time soon. However, you can configure PDL with different responses:

- **Disabled**: No action will be taken to the affected VMs
- **Issue events**: No action will be taken against the affected VMs; however, the administrator will be notified when a PDL event has occurred
- **Power off and restart VMs**: All affected VMs will be terminated on the host, and vSphere HA will attempt to restart the VM on hosts that still have connectivity to the storage device

An APD condition is more of an unknown situation; when an APD occurs, a timer starts. After 140 seconds, the APD is declared, and the device is marked as APD time out. There are different types of responses for APD:

- **Disabled**: Same as before, no action will be taken against the affected VMs
- **Issue events**: Same as before, no action will be taken against the affected VMs. However, the administrator will be notified when a PDL event has occurred
- **Power off and restart VMs (conservative)**: vSphere HA will not attempt to restart the affected VMs unless it has determined there is another host that can restart the VMs
- **Power off and restart VMs (aggressive)**: vSphere HA will terminate the affected VMs even if it cannot determine that another host can restart the VMs

Note that there is also a response recovery option to retry before APD times out.

All settings are also available with the vSphere Client (HTML5), as shown in the following screenshot:

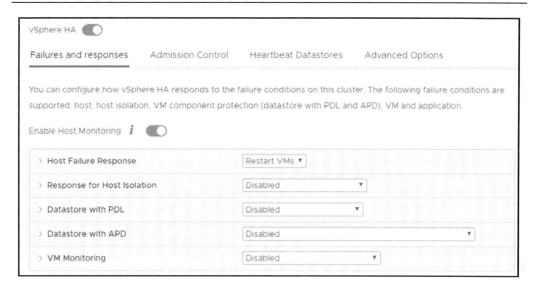

For more information, see the following:

- **Permanent Device Loss (PDL) and All-Paths-Down (APD) in vSphere 5.x and 6.x** at `https://kb.vmware.com/kb/2004684`
- **Lost or degraded connectivity to the storage device** at `https://kb.vmware.com/kb/1009553`

Flash Read Cache

Flash Read Cache, also known as **vFlash**, is a feature introduced in vSphere 5.5 and available in the Enterprise Plus edition that can improve VM storage performance by using host local flash devices as a cache. The **performance boost** depends on your workload type and working set size. Only read-intensive workloads, with working sets that fit into the cache size, can benefit from the Flash Read Cache feature. vSphere Flash Read Cache offers legacy support for the swap-to-SSD feature introduced in vSphere 5.0; it was previously way to use a local SSD to host VM-related swap files.

You can reserve a Flash Read Cache for any individual virtual disk that is created only when a VM is powered on; it is discarded when a VM is suspended or powered off. When you migrate a VM, you can migrate the cache (default option); otherwise, if you do not migrate the cache, the cache is rewarmed on the destination host. Flash Read Cache does not support RDMs in terms of physical compatibility. Virtual compatibility RDMs are supported with Flash Read Cache as vSphere HA and DRS, but not FT.

Storage integration

VMware vSphere has several different types of storage integration solutions and technologies; some started with version 4.1 (such as VAAI), others more recently (such as VVol), directed towards building a fully **software-defined storage** (SDS) stack.

VMware vSphere SPBM

SPBM is an extension of VM Storage Policies and the foundation of the SDS control vision from VMware. SPBM enables vSphere administrators to simplify storage provisioning and management, by assigning to each VM the required storage features and capabilities. VM will be automatically provisioned on the right datastore that respects these requirements.

SPBM interprets different storage requirements and dynamically composes different storage services, such as by placing the VM on the right storage tier, allocating capacity, providing snapshots, replication, and so on. To understand storage features and capabilities, **vStorage APIs for Storage Awareness** (VASA) could be used, but it's not formally mandatory.

Since vSphere 6.5, storage policies are used widely, also for **VSAN, VVols, SIOC v2, VM encryption** (see `Chapter 12`, *Securing and Protecting Your Environment*).

Please consider the following points:

- Policies are stored and managed by the vCenter server but can be applied to VMs in one or more clusters.
- Each vCenter in Enhanced Linked Mode has its own set of policies.
- A maximum of 1,024 policies can exist per vCenter server.
- The storage policy name can consist of up to 80 characters. The storage policy name is not the correct identifier because, like for VM names, a unique identifier is used instead.
- Storage policy can define one or many rules regarding performance, availability, space efficiency, and so on.
- Storage policies are not additive. Only one policy (that contains one or more policy rules) can be applied per object.
- A storage policy can be applied to a group of VMs, a single VM, or even a single VMDK within a VM.

To learn more, see this blog post—**Understanding Storage Policy-Based Management** at `https://blogs.vmware.com/virtualblocks/2017/01/16/understanding-storage-policy-based-management/`.

Pluggable Storage Architecture (PSA)

The PSA framework (introduced in vSphere 4.0) is a collection of **VMkernel APIs** that allow partners to insert specific functions into the ESXi storage layer.

These third-party plugins fall into one of three categories:

- **Third-party native multipathing plugin (NMP)**: Provides new multipath rules to VMware NMP
- **Third-party storage array type plugin (SATP)**: Used to recognize some storage capabilities, not recognized by VMware SATPs
- **Third-party path selection plugin (PSP):** Similar to the previous one, but usually used to identify the default multipath rule for new storage

The following diagram summarizes the PSA architecture:

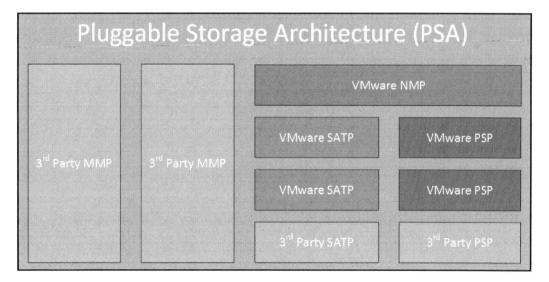

Multipathing

Multipathing is a technique that lets you efficiently and reliably use more than one physical path to transfer data between the host and an external storage array.

VMware supports different types of storage architectures as follows:

- **Active-active storage system:** All controllers (or all ports) are active; that means all the paths are active unless a path fails. In this storage, it is possible to access a LUN simultaneously through all the storage paths that are available without significant performance degradation.
- **Active-passive storage system:** Usually one controller is active (on a specific LUN) and the second is passive (but could be active on another LUN). If access through the active storage port fails, one of the passive storage processors can be activated by the servers accessing it.
- **Asymmetrical storage system:** Supports **Asymmetric Logical Unit Access (ALUA)**, where all ports could be active, but with different levels of access per port. With ALUA, hosts can determine the states of target ports and prioritize paths; some active paths are primary, and others are secondary.
- **Virtual port storage system:** Supports access to storage services through a single virtual port. Virtual port storage systems are active-active storage devices, but hide their multiple connections through a single port; for example, with iSCSI, it is possible to work with a single virtual IP instead of each IP of each port, or for FC it is possible to build a virtual WWN (if the switches support NPIV). These storage systems handle port failovers and connection balancing transparently (transparent failover).

Depending on the storage type, you need specific multipath criteria. VMware ESXi has three main types of path selection policy (provided by NMP) described as follows:

- **Fixed**: The host uses the designated preferred path if it has been configured. Otherwise, it selects the first working path discovered at system boot time. This is the default policy for most active-active storage, and there is also `Fixed_AP` which extends fixed functionality to active/passive and ALUA storage.

- **Most Recently Used (MRU)**: The most recent path is selected as active and only this path is used. When the path is marked unavailable, the host will select another available path as active. This is the default multipath policy for most active-passive storage.
- **Round Robin (RR)**: The host uses all available paths. The I/O is served through all active paths in the batches. The first set of I/O commands is sent over first path, the second set of I/O commands over the second, and so on. This policy can be used with both active-active and active-passive storage arrays to balance the I/O over multiple paths.

 If the path selection for your storage is not recognized correctly or you want to change the default, you must use PSA-related commands for NMP and SATP. Refer to your storage vendor documentation and best practices for VMware vSphere.

VMware vStorage API for Array Integration (VAAI)

VAAI are a set of features introduced in vSphere 4.1 that provide hardware acceleration and offload functionality for some types of operation. Initially designed only for block-based storage, with vSphere 5.0 this has also been extended to NFS datastores.

In vSphere 6.x VAAI isn't changed, but now it's available for the Standard edition. VAAI is enabled by default, and you can control it with the following ESXi advanced settings:

Advanced parameter	Description
HardwareAcceleratedLocking	ATS that is used during creation of files on the VMFS volume
HardwareAcceleratedMove	Clone Blocks/Full Copy/XCOPY, used to copy data
HardwareAcceleratedInit	Zero blocks/write same, used to zero-out disk regions

For more information, see **KB 1021976: Frequently Asked Questions for vStorage APIs for Array Integration** (https://kb.vmware.com/kb/1021976).

VMware vSphere APIs for I/O Filtering (VAIO)

VAIO, introduced in vSphere 6.0 U1, permits the addition of seamless new third-party software-based data services; the technology's partners can now put their solution directly into the I/O stream of a VM through a filter that intercepts data before it goes to the disk. It enables the secure filtering of a VM's I/O safely in the kernel, with a well-defined framework and according to storage policies. VAIO is totally storage-agnostic and works with VVOLs, vSAN, and legacy storage.

VAIO could be integrated both in traditional and software-defined storage.

Caching and replication are the initial use cases (for replication, the next version 10 of Veeam Backup and Replication will use VAIO for the new **Continuous Data Protection (CDP)** feature), but potentially can also work for anti-virus, data inspections, and other services.

VASA

APIs for storage awareness are a set of APIs (introduced in vSphere 5.0) that will enable vCenter to see the capabilities of the datastores at storage side, making it much easier to select the appropriate datastore for VM placement. Storage capabilities, such as the RAID level, thin or thick provisioned, replication state, and much more, can now be made visible within vCenter, without the need for a specific plugin. You need a VASA provider (usually a web service) that exposes all of those capabilities.

VASA minimizes the need to manually manage information on the capabilities of each LUN, usually performed by documentation or naming conventions, and simply guarantees the right **Service Level Agreement (SLA)** to VMs.
With vSphere 6.0, a new VASA (2.0) has been introduced to manage VVols.

VVols

Introduced in vSphere 6.0, VVols are a new integration and management framework that abstracts and virtualizes SAN/NAS storage with a software-defined storage approach, based on SPBM.

The VVols architecture has five major components, which are described as follows:

- **VVol object**: It can be config-VVol (metadata), data-VVol (VMDKs), mem-VVol (snapshots), swap-VVol (swap files), or other-VVol (vendor solution specific).
- **Protocol Endpoint (PE)**: Although storage systems manage all aspects of VVols, ESXi hosts have no direct access to virtual volumes on the storage side. Instead, ESXi hosts use a logical I/O proxy, called the PE, to communicate with VVols and virtual disk files that virtual volumes encapsulate. ESXi uses PE to establish a data path on demand from VMs to their respective VVols.
- **Storage Container (SC)**: Unlike traditional LUN-and NFS-based vSphere storage, the VVols functionality does not require preconfigured volumes on a storage side. Instead, VVols uses an SC, which is a pool of raw storage capacity or an aggregation of storage capabilities, that a storage system can provide to VVols.
- **VASA provider (2.0)**: A VVols storage provider, also called a VASA provider, is a software component that acts as a storage awareness service for vSphere. The provider mediates out-of-band communication between the vCenter Server and ESXi hosts on one hand and a storage system on the other.
- **Array**: This implements VVols features; note that not all storage vendors implement VVols in the same way, so it depends on the maturity of their solution.

For more information, see **KB 2113013**: **Understanding Virtual Volumes (VVols) in VMware vSphere 6.0** (https://kb.vmware.com/kb/2113013).

vCenter and the VASA provider are critical for VVols, and the lack of them can affect some operations, such as powering a VM (a swap object must be created), or adding new virtual disks. For more information see this blog post at https://cormachogan.com/2015/12/04/losing-vasa-vcenter-in-vvols/.

Today, the bind operation happens out-of-band using the control path through the VASA provider, and the goal for the future is to bring it in-band to the data path through the PE instead. Still, some features, such as NFS v4.1 support and in-band binding, are not yet present (and will probably be implemented in the next major release).

There are a lot of papers and documentation on how VVols could be useful in a vSphere environment; for example, IDC research VVols provide powerful application-aware management for vSphere environments. However, there is not much data on real adoptions in production; that seems to still be limited. Also, it is a technology that depends too much on storage vendors implementations (VMware provides just the framework).

Introducing VMware vSAN

Hyper-converged infrastructure (HCI) are specific solutions that combine computing and storage (and sometimes also networking) capabilities from more hosts to achieve a shared pool of resources. A vSphere cluster already does this for the computing part. Some storage products extend this to the storage part, making more external storage unnecessary and making the HCI market an important trend; it is not only growing fast, with more attention from the big storage vendors, but it is also changing fast.

We have already discussed HCI hardware in Chapter 2, *Designing and Planning a Virtualization Infrastructure*, so let's focus on VMware vSAN, the software-defined storage from VMware.

Note that there are also some specific HCI solutions for ROBO scenarios, or small clusters (usually HCI starts from at least three nodes), for example, from **StarWind** or **StorMagic**.

VMware vSAN is formally a new product from VMware, but the code is already included in all vSphere versions starting from v5.5U1. It's so tightly bound with vSphere that the vSAN version depends on the vSphere versions, just because the only way to upgrade vSAN is by upgrading your vSphere version.

Like other HCI solutions, it provides shared storage with standard features from a pool of local disks. The first big difference is that each host must have at least one flash disk (SSD or also NVMe), plus other disks (HDD or other flash drives); vSAN configuration can be hybrid or AFA and can work with a caching tier (the faster option) or a capacity tier (the other option). An overview of vSAN deployment is shown as follows:

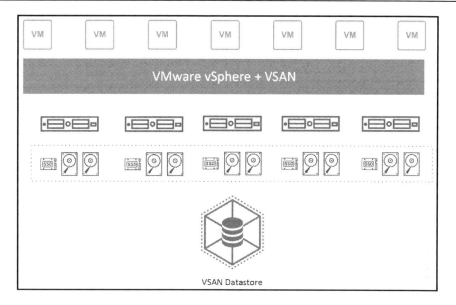

VSAN Datastore

There are many features, such as compression, deduplication, and erasure coding, but most of them can only be used in AFA configuration. vSAN also supports the stretched cluster both for the hybrid and AFA configuration. One specific case of a stretched cluster is the two-node configuration useful for ROBO scenarios.

For more information about vSAN licensing and a feature comparison, feel free to check the official guide at `https://www.vmware.com/content/dam/ digitalmarketing/vmware/en/pdf/products/vsan/vmware-vsan-66-licensing- guide.pdf`.

Planning and designing

Planning and design are quite essential to define your architecture, the expected performance, the capacity, and how your infrastructure can scale. The HCL of vSAN is a subset of all the HCL of vSphere, just because the choice of the disks and the storage controller is very critical.

If you are planning to use an All-Flash configuration, also consider using dedicated pairs of 10 GbE network cards for isolating vSAN traffic and provide adequate bandwidth for vSAN traffic.

The Leaf–Spine network topology is also commonly used for a high-performance network fabric that is needed for larger-scale vSAN deployments.

Device considerations

vSAN has two operating modes :

- **Hybrid deployment**: A mixture of fast caching devices (SSDs) and magnetic devices for capacity. In hybrid deployments, you can't use features such as erasure coding (RAID 5/6) or deduplication and compression.
- **All-flash**: In this case, high-performance SSD is used as a caching device (usually NVMe), and standard SSDs are used for a capacity tier. All-flash configuration provides unmatched I/O performance.

You always need one caching device and several capacity devices for each disk group you configure. A maximum of five disk groups can be configured, each containing a maximum of seven capacity devices.

vSAN configuration

vSAN is tightly integrated into VMware vSphere; thus, enabling vSAN is easy compared to other SDS solutions. All you need to do is to enable the vSAN service on the cluster:

Please note that you need to have the VMkernel adapter configured with the vSAN service first. Also, HA cannot be enabled on the cluster level when vSAN cluster is being configured.

To create a new vSAN cluster, follow these steps:

1. Click the **Configure** button under **vSAN | Services.**
2. You have to select what type of vSAN cluster is being configured.
3. Next you need to specify advanced services that you want to enable on the vSAN cluster.
4. Now you have to claim devices that will be contributing to the vSAN cluster:

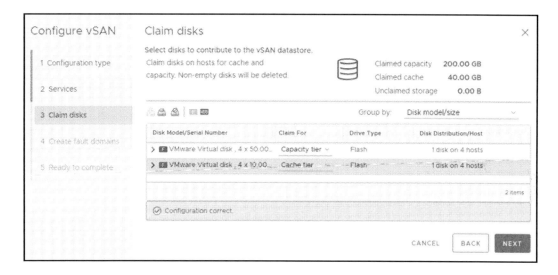

5. In the next step, you may configure fault domains. Fault domains are an isolated part of the vSAN cluster, meaning that by using several fault domains you can prevent unavailable data when part of the cluster becomes unavailable (for example, one datacenter cabinet is considered as a one-fault domain) and vSAN will ensure that replicas of the objects will not be stored within a single fault domain. For mirroring (RAID 1), you need at least three fault domains.

6. Lastly, review the settings and confirm the vSAN creation.

Once the vSAN datastore is created, you will see it as a standard datastore:

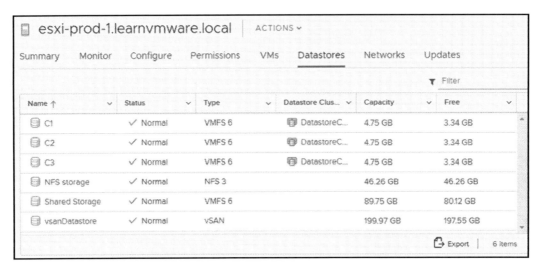

Health monitoring

Monitoring your vSAN health is crucial. There are multiple built-in checks that vSAN performs, and any discrepancy might result in either poor performance of the vSAN cluster to even data corruption. The following screenshot displays a vSAN health overview:

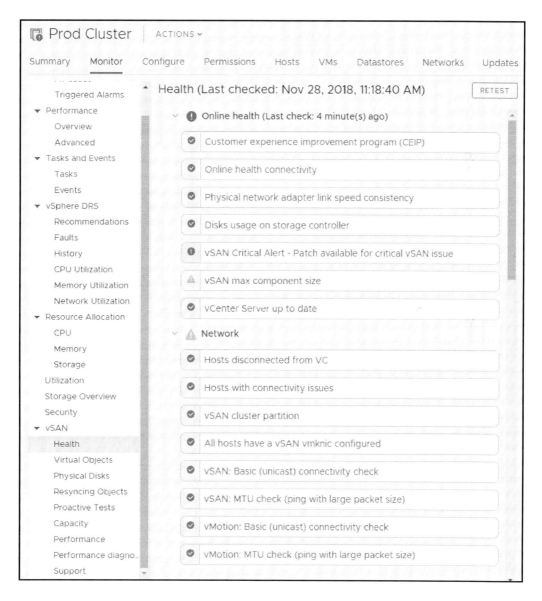

vSAN policies

When you want to deploy VM on the vSAN datastore, you need to attach the VM to the correct storage policy. There is a default vSAN storage policy, but I would suggest defining different storage policies based on your availability requirements:

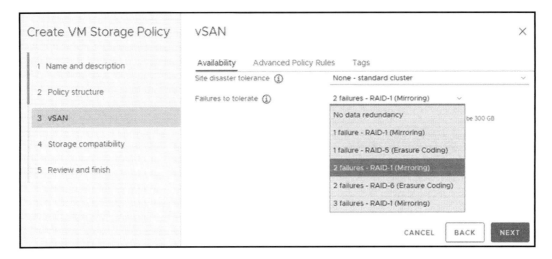

Creating VM on vSAN

Once the storage policies have been defined, you can create a new VM on the vSAN datastore.

In the **Select storage** option, choose the correct storage policy, and you will see what storage is compatible with your policy:

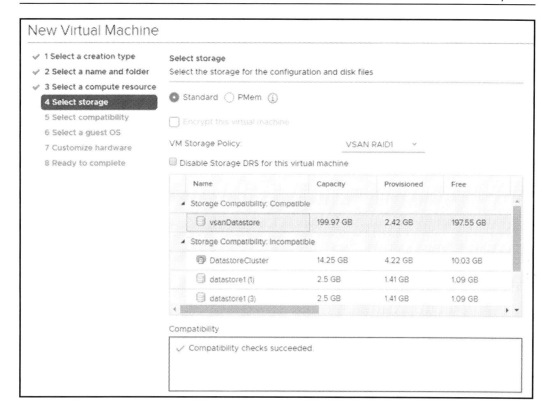

It is beyond the scope of this chapter to go more deeply into vSAN, but we have demonstrated how the logic within vSAN works and how to create a simple vSAN datastore. There are many more configuration options and design choices you need to make for successful vSAN deployment so do not use this guide as a *production-ready* walk-through.

Summary

This chapter was dedicated to the storage part of a virtual infrastructure, starting from local block-based storage and extending into shared block storage with the FC, FCoE, and iSCSI protocols, and NFS-based NAS storage.

For each of them, we considered the different optimization techniques, integration, and storage features provided by vSphere. Other types of storage architectures were also considered, especially HCI solutions. To learn more, a great source of information on storage aspects is the VMware StorageHub at `https://storagehub.vmware.com/`.

In this chapter, we introduced the main storage concepts and features, and described how to manage local, block, and NAS storage and how to configure vSphere to use them.

Also, we explained how to integrate vSphere with storage using VAAI, VASA, VVols, storage profiles, vCenter plugins, and so on.

In the final part, there was a short introduction to vSAN and its initial configuration.

In previous chapters, we described how networking and storage are configured in VMware vSphere, and in the next chapter we will explore VMs in depth.

Questions

1. Please describe the difference between All-Flash Arrays and Hybrid Arrays.
2. In VMware vSphere, we can use different protocols to connect our storage. Name some of them (environments are generally based on five storage protocols).
3. Redundant Array of Independent Disks, also known as RAID, is used to create logical volumes from independent disks. RAID 10 provides more space than RAID 5, but RAID 5 provides better performance than RAID 10:

    a) True
    b) False

4. What is the difference between RAW capacity and USABLE capacity?
5. Can you boot ESXi hypervisors from a NFS datastore?

    a) Yes
    b) No

6. What are the hardware components of the Fibre Chanel infrastructure?

   a) Host Bus Adapters
   b) Network Interface Cards
   c) Local cashing device
   d) Ethernet Switches
   e) SAN Switches
   f) SAN WWN replicator
   g) DAS SSDs

7. What is the difference between block-based storage accessed by a hardware adapter and block-based storage accessed by a software adapter?

8. Thick or lazy zeroed thick VMDK has all its space allocated and wiped clean of any previous content on the physical media at creation time.

   a) True
   b) False

9. What can storage controllers be used in the VM?

   a) LSI Logic Parallel
   b) BusLogic Logic SAS
   c) VMware Paravirtual (or PVSCSI)
   d) NVMe Controller
   e)Persistent Memory Controller

10. Please describe the difference between a software iSCSI adapter, a dependent hardware iSCSI adapter, and an independent hardware iSCSI adapter (iSCSI HBA)?

11. NFS 3 and NFS 4.1 provide support for multipath:

    a) True
    b) False

12. Using Storage I/O Control, you can define RLS. What does the RLS stand for?

    a) Resources, Limits, and Shares
    b) Reservations, Logging, and Security
    c) Reservations, Limits, and Shares
    d) Reserved, Local, and Storage
    e) Reservations, Logic, and Shares

13. **VM Component Protection (VMCP)** manages two storage-related conditions. What are they?

14. VMware vSAN can be configured only from vSAN Configuration Appliance:

    a) True
    b) False

15. How many caching and capacity devices can be managed by a single ESXi server using vSAN?

Further reading

- **vSphere Storage** : `https://docs.vmware.com/en/VMware-vSphere/6.7/vsphere-esxi-vcenter-server-67-storage-guide.pdf`.
- **VMware Storage Hub**: Different storage and availability technical documents are avaliable through this single site. For more information, refer to `https://storagehub.vmware.com/`.
- **Best practices for running VMware vSphere on iSCSI**: `https://storagehub.vmware.com/export_to_pdf/best-practices-for-running-vmware-vsphere-on-iscsi`.

9
VM Deployment and Management

Once the setup of the vSphere environment has been completed, the final step involved in firing up your virtual infrastructure is deploying the virtual machines. When the hosts and vCenter Server are in place, they provide physical resources to the VMs that physically reside on the storage device shared within the environment.

This chapter will look closely at the structure of VMs and their configuration to better understand how they work and which options we should configure in order to obtain the best performance. The use of templates is a key point in the management of VMs since it simplifies the management of the environment, allowing VMs to be created easily and deployed quickly. Compared to physical machines, VMs deployed from a template don't need to be installed from scratch, which saves you time.

We will also look at the content library, which allows us to centrally store all our ISO images and templates. We can easily replicate its content over the network to vCenter servers in different sites.

We will cover how to work with virtual machines and which operations can be performed on VMs, such as snapshots. We will also have a look at different physical-to-virtual and virtual-to-virtual conversions.
In this chapter, we will cover the following topics:

- The components of a virtual machine
- Deploying VMs
- The content library
- Managing VMs

- The content library and its features
- Importing and exporting VMs
- Converting VMs

The components of a virtual machine

A VM behaves in the same way as a physical computer, but it's a software computer that runs an OS and applications supported by the host's provided resources. A VM supports all the same functionalities and devices as a physical machine, but it's easier to manage and more secure.

Typically, a VM can be configured to run on ESXi hosts, data centers, clusters, or resource pools, and includes three main components:

- Virtual and hardware resources
- Virtual machine tools
- Guest operating system

Virtual hardware

When you create a VM, the ESXi host presents the hardware as a specific set of resources to the VM. The hardware type provided by the configuration wizard is selected by VMware to ensure the highest level of compatibility with the supported OS.

Every VM has a CPU, memory, and disk resources. Virtual devices in the VM perform the same functions as the hardware on a physical computer. You can configure most of the virtual devices present in the VM, but certain virtual hardware cannot be modified or removed, such as the VMCI device.

When you create a VM, specific virtual hardware is presented to the VM. Sometimes you need to adjust the default hardware to meet the requirements of the guestOS or the applications that will be installed inside the VM. To access the virtual hardware configuration, right-click on the VM and select the **Settings** option.

Let's walk through the main components you need to configure in a VM.

vCPUs

One or more virtual processors can be defined in the VM, but the amount cannot exceed the number of logical processors (sockets x cores x 2 if hyperthreading is enabled) present in the host. The number of vCPU sockets specified in the configuration determines the number of cores available. One VM could have virtual sockets and virtual cores. By default, for each vCPU, a single socket with a single core is assigned as virtual hardware. You can change the default behavior and assign multiple CPU cores per single socket. You might need to do this for licensing reasons, for applications running inside the guest OS (for example, the latest SQL Express can work with more cores, but not with more sockets).

If you have more than eight vCPUs, **virtual NUMA (vNUMA)** is enabled, and ESXi distributes the VMs in more NUMA nodes if it is not possible to fit them in just 1.

> For more information about NUMA and vNUMA, visit `https://blogs.vmware.com/performance/2017/03/virtual-machine-vcpu-and-vnuma-rightsizing-rules-of-thumb.html`.

If you are running a vSphere Enterprise Plus license, you can also enable Hot Plug for CPU. This option will enable you to add more vCPUs even if the virtual machine is running. You are usually not allowed to change the number of vCPUs while the virtual machine is powered on.

Hot Plug for CPU can be easily enabled by selecting the **Enable CPU Hot Add** checkbox:

The maximum number of supported vCPUs per VM is 128.

Memory

A default amount of RAM is configured based on the selected guest OS. The specified RAM is the memory the OS will present to its system; it's also the maximum amount of RAM the VM can claim from the physical memory installed on the host.

Assigning memory to the virtual machine does not automatically mean that the amount of memory will no longer be available on the ESXi hypervisor level. If the virtual machine is not accessing the memory (see the active memory used performance metric), memory over-commitment techniques can be used to spin more virtual machines.

Note that if you are using over-commitment techniques for memory, you should carefully monitor the active memory used, so it does not exceed the total available amount of memory on the ESXi hypervisor. Otherwise, swapping might occur, affecting the performance of the virtual machines.

Memory optimization techniques are mostly the same as they were in previous versions of VMware vSphere, but with one significant difference. From vSphere 6.0, in **Transparent Page Sharing** (**TPS**), page sharing is enabled by default within VMs (intra-VM sharing), but is enabled between VMs (inter-VM sharing) only when those VMs have the same salt value. This change was made to ensure the highest security between VMs.

 For more information, see **KB 2080735: Security considerations and disallowing inter-Virtual Machine Transparent Page Sharing** at `https://kb.vmware.com/kb/2080735`.

In vSphere 6.7, a VM supports a maximum of 6,128 GB of RAM (with the latest virtual hardware versions).

Network adapter

During the VM configuration, you must select the adapter type and the network it will connect to. Depending on the VM compatibility and the guest OS, the supported NIC types are the following:

- **E1000E**: This is the default adapter for Windows 8 and Windows Server 2012. It emulates the Intel 82574 Gigabit Ethernet NIC.
- **E1000**: This driver is available in most newer guest OSes and emulates the Intel 82545EM Gigabit Ethernet NIC.
- **Flexible**: This identifies itself as a Vlance adapter, an emulated version of the AMD 79C970 PCnet32 LANCE NIC. Most 32-bit guest OSes have the driver for this NIC type. When installing Virtual Machine Tools, the adapter changes to the higher-performance VMXNET adapter.

- **VMXNET**: This is optimized for VM performance. To provide the driver, it requires Virtual Machine Tools to be installed.
- **VMXNET 2 (Enhanced)**: Based on the VMXNET adapter, this provides high-performance features, such as jumbo frames and hardware offloads. A limited set of guest OSes support it.
- **VMXNET 3**: This offers all the features available in VMXNET 2 and it's a paravirtualized NIC designed for performance. Multiqueue support (known as RSS in Windows), IPv6 offloads, and MSI/MSI-X interrupt delivery are some of the additional features offered by this adapter. It requires VM hardware version 7 or later, and a limited set of guest OSes support it.

By default, the MAC address is automatically generated from the vCenter Server MAC address pool, but you can set a manual MAC address if you need to.

> You can't change the adapter type once the adapter is created. The option to set the adapter type is only available when creating a new network adapter.

Virtual disks

A virtual disk stores the actual VM data and the VM can be configured to use a new disk, attach an existing disk, or map a SAN LUN. A LUN to a VMFS map is referred to as a **Raw Device Mapping** (**RDM**) that points to the raw LUN. In this case, the .vmdk file (.vmdk files will be discussed later in the file structure) doesn't store data, as the data is stored in the LUN, but it contains the mapping to the LUN disk information.

Virtual disks can be moved across different data stores connected to the host on which the VM runs. When a new disk is created, it can be provisioned in three different formats, depending on the requirements:

- **Thick provision lazy zeroed**: This is the default format; space on the datastore is allocated when the VM is created, and data on the physical device is not erased.
- **Thick provision eager zeroed**: This is the format used to support specific configurations, such as vSphere FT or some SQL installations; it allocates space on the datastore when the disk is created. Compared to the lazy zeroed format, data on the physical device is zeroed out at creation time. The thick provision eager zeroed format takes longer to be provisioned.

- **Thin provision**: This is used to save space; it's the fastest method to create a new disk. This format doesn't allocate all the requested disk space upon creation. At first, it only uses the space required by the initial operations of the disk, growing in size until the maximum configured size is reached.

The following screenshot shows the different **Disk Provisioning** types:

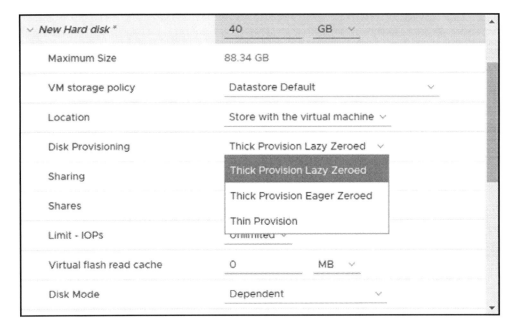

Each virtual disk has a disk mode, as follows:

- **Dependent**: Dependent disks are included in snapshots. Snapshots will be discussed in the *Managing VMs* section.
- **Independent-Persistent**: Independent disks act the same as dependent disks, but the writes are committed to the disk immediately and the disks are not affected by the snapshots. Even if you create a snapshot, the data will be directly written to the disk.
- **Independent-Nonpersistent**: Any writes made to non-persistent disks are discarded when you power off or reset the virtual machine.

Virtual disks can only be connected to a single SCSI controller. You can connect an existing virtual disk to a different SCSI controller. For example, once the VM tools are installed, you can assign a new PVSCSI controller, as shown in the following screenshot:

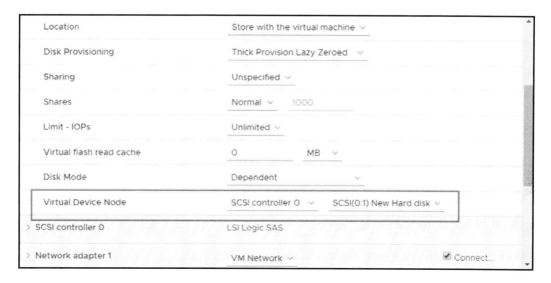

Storage controller

Added by default during VM creation, the storage controller is used to access virtual disks, CD/DVD devices, and SCSI devices. Storage controllers are presented to VMs as different types of storage controllers, such as BusLogic Parallel, LSI Logic Parallel, LSI Logic SAS, VMware Paravirtual SCSI, AHCI, SATA, and NVMe, as described in Chapter 8, *Managing Storage Resources*.

Generally, the default controller optimized for best performance is assigned to the VM based on the guest OS selection, the device type, and VM compatibility. A maximum of four SATA, four SCSI, and four NVMe controllers are supported for each VM. If, during the creation of the VM, the Windows Server 2008 or 2012 guest OS is selected, for example, the LSI Logic SAS controller is assigned by the system.

The following list contains the options that are available today (visit `https://blogs.vmware.com/vsphere/2014/02/vscsi-controller-choose-performance.html` for more information):

- **BusLogic**: This was one of the first emulated vSCSI controllers available in the VMware platform.
- **LSI Logic Parallel (formerly known as just LSI Logic)**: This was another emulated vSCSI controller available initially in the VMware platform.
- **LSI Logic SAS**: This is an evolution of the parallel driver to support a new future-facing standard.
- **VMware Paravirtual (also known as PVSCSI)**: This has been designed to support a very high throughput with minimal processing costs. The vSCSI controller is virtualization-aware and is, therefore, the most efficient driver.

When a VM is created, two storage controllers are assigned by default:

- **SATA**: This controller is assigned to access CD/DVD devices and supports up to 30 devices. If you have multiple disks, to distribute the load and improve performance, you can add up to four controllers per VM. An AHCI SATA controller is supported for VMs with ESXi 5.5 and later compatibility. A SATA controller is supported by most guest OSes and is assigned by default to CD/DVD devices.
- **SCSI**: Depending on the guest OS, many VMs have this controller configured by default. A single controller supports up to 15 devices. If you have multiple disks, to distribute the load and improve performance, you can add up to four controllers per VM. In the new SCSI controller, you can enable SCSI bus sharing to allow the virtual disk to be shared by the VM, for example, for building a guest cluster. There are three options available:
    - **None**: The virtual disk cannot be shared
    - **Physical**: The virtual disk can be shared by a VM on the same host
    - **Virtual**: The virtual disk can be shared by a VM on any host

File structure

A VM is composed of several files that typically reside on a datastore in the VMs folder. The VM settings are managed through vSphere Client, but you can also use the command line using PowerCLI, vCLI, or the vSphere Web Services SDK. The core files that compose a VM are as follows:

- .vmx: This is a plaintext file that stores the configuration of the VM. The file contains information related to the hardware that resides in the VM, such as the processor number, the amount of RAM, the disks, the MAC address, the virtual hardware version, the number of NICs connected, the virtual disk location, and other configurations of the virtual machine, as shown in the following example:

```
config.version = "8"
virtualHW.version = "14"
nvram = "Windows12.nvram"
pciBridge0.present = "TRUE"
svga.present = "TRUE"
floppy0.present = "FALSE"
svga.vramSize = "8388608"
memSize = "4096"
powerType.powerOff = "default"
powerType.suspend = "default"
powerType.reset = "default"
...
```

  The .vmx file contains a list of keys and related values that identify the components configured in the selected VM. To determine, for example, the configured RAM or the installed OS in the VM, you need to scroll down the list and identify the keys, memSize, and guest OS, which indicate the requested information. The .vmx file is only the configuration file of the VM and doesn't store any data from the guest OS. The virtual hard disk file with a .vmdk extension is responsible for storing the actual data of the VM.

- .vmdk: Identifies the virtual hard disk of the VM that holds the data of the guest OS instance. A VM can have one or more .vmdk files depending on the disks configured in the .vmx file. For instance, if you configure disks **C:** and **D:** in a VM running Windows OS, you will have two .vmdk files, one for each configured drive.

If you browse the datastore where the VM resides, you can see only a single
.vmdk file (if the VM is configured with a single drive). Technically, the
virtual hard disk is composed of two files with the same extension: a VMDK
descriptor and a flat.VMDK file. Let's take a look at the roles of these files.
The .vmdk file is the descriptor file, a plaintext file that contains the
configuration information and pointers to the flat file. Generally, the .vmdk
descriptor file is a small file. -flat.vmdk is generally a large binary file that
contains the actual data of the VM. Its size is defined in the .vmx
configuration file. The .vmdk file can start from a few GB in size and can
grow up to 62 TB (the maximum size supported in vSphere 6.7). To see
both the .vmdk and -flat.vmdk files, you need to access the command
line, navigate to the datastores folder where the VM resides, and run the ls
-lah command, as shown in the following screenshot:

```
esxi-prod-1.learnvmware.local - PuTTY                          _ □ X

[root@esxi-prod-1:/vmfs/volumes/5bfd67c0-72feebdf-aa85-000c299f4b65/Windows12] ls -lah
total 3328
drwxr-xr-x    1 root     root       72.0K Dec  1 11:28 .
drwxr-xr-t    1 root     root       72.0K Nov 28 08:45 ..
-rw-------    1 root     root        4.0K Nov 28 08:51 Windows12-01d62f107daab0ae.vmfd
-rw-r--r--    1 root     root         236 Nov 27 15:52 Windows12-5587bfce.hlog
-rw-------    1 root     root       40.0G Nov 27 15:52 Windows12-flat.vmdk
-rw-------    1 root     root        8.5K Nov 28 08:52 Windows12.nvram
-rw-------    1 root     root         552 Nov 28 08:51 Windows12.vmdk
-rw-r--r--    1 root     root           0 Nov 27 15:52 Windows12.vmsd
-rwxr-xr-x    1 root     root        2.8K Dec  1 11:28 Windows12.vmx
-rw-r--r--    1 root     root      185.2K Nov 27 16:34 vmware-1.log
-rw-r--r--    1 root     root      199.1K Dec  1 11:04 vmware.log
[root@esxi-prod-1:/vmfs/volumes/5bfd67c0-72feebdf-aa85-000c299f4b65/Windows12] █
```

- .nvram: This is a binary file that cannot be edited and contains the VM
  BIOS or EFI configuration. If you delete this file, it will be automatically
  recreated when the VM is powered on.
- .log: This is saved in the same directory as the VM configuration files and
  contains the logs of the VM activities. It can be used for troubleshooting if
  you encounter a problem. A new .log file is created every time the virtual
  machine experiences a power cycle.
- .vswp: For each powered-on VM, two files are used as swap files in case of
  RAM contentions. The biggest is usually the size of the vRAM of the VM
  minus the vRAM reservation.

Snapshot-related files will be described in the *Managing VMs* section.

Changing the default file position

By default, all VM-related files are in a single folder with the original VM name (or the VM name after a VM storage migration). You can place the different files in different datastores based on your needs. The following files are part of the virtual machine:

- **VMDK files**: Having virtual disks in different datastores allows you to choose the proper type of disks with the proper performance and service level. You can choose a new location when you add a new virtual disk or choose different locations for each VMDK when you apply a storage migration.

- **Swap file**: Migrating VM swap (`.vswp`) files to a different datastore is possible and described in **KB 2003956: Migrating virtual machine swap (.vswp) files from one datastore to another** (`https://kb.vmware.com/kb/2003956`). You can also use an SSD datastore for this purpose, but usually, the need for a different position occurs when storage array replication is used, and you need to avoid swap file replication.

- **Log files**: By default, ESXi/ESX hosts store VMs specific logging in the same directory as the VM configuration files. VM logs can be reconfigured to archive at different intervals, with different names, in different volumes, or when the log reaches a specific size. For more information, see **KB 1007805: Locating virtual machine log files on an ESXi/ESX host** (`https://kb.vmware.com/kb/1007805`).

- **Snapshot files**: All files with snapshots are created in the VM working directory, which, by default, is the same directory as that of the VM. The working directory can be changed with **KB 1002929: Creating snapshots in a different location than default virtual machine directory for VMware ESXi and VMware ESX** (`https://kb.vmware.com/kb/1002929`).

Virtual machine tools

Virtual machine tools is a set of utilities installed on the guest OS that improves the overall performance and provides better control of the VM, making administration easier. Virtual machine tools is not installed by default.

Although a guest OS can run without virtual machine tools, the management of power controls and other features is not available unless you install virtual machine tools. Shutdown or restart options, for example, are not available without virtual machine tools. An improved graphics interface, better mouse control, and the ability to copy and paste files are some of the main benefits you will notice after installation.

There are three types of virtual machine tools that you can install:

- ISOs (containing installers)
- **Operating System Specific Packages (OSPs)**
- **open-vm-tools (OVT)**

You can find more information at `https://docs.vmware.com/en/VMware-Tools/10.2.0/com.vmware.vsphere.vmwaretools.doc/GUID-5D9177F3-A098-42F7-B87F-551F61BA434E.html`.

The following list includes some of the features of virtual machine tools:

- Integration with the vSphere suite as a DNS and IP propagation
- Improved network adapter performance (VMXNET driver)
- Improved storage controller performance (PVSCSI driver)
- Smooth mouse experience
- Copying, pasting, and dragging and dropping files
- Improved video resolution
- Improved sound
- The ability to take quiesced snapshots of the guest OS

The **IP Addresses** and **DNS Name** propagated to the vCenter client is shown in the following screenshot:

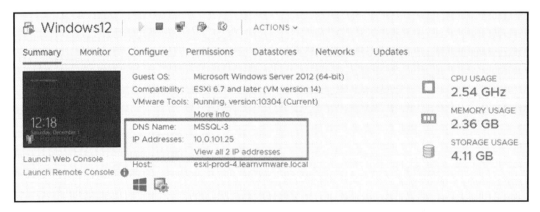

Virtual machine tools include the following components:

- **VMware device drivers**: This gives you drivers for virtual hardware, including network adapters. Drivers provide smooth mouse operations and improved sound, graphics, and performance.
- **VMware user process**: This gives you the ability to copy and paste text between the VMware Remote console and the host operating system.
- **VMware services**: This handles communication between the guest and host operating system.

 For more information on **Virtual Machine Tools**, see the blog post at `https://blogs.vmware.com/vsphere/2017/11/every-vsphere-admin-must-know-vmware-tools.html`.

A recommended practice is to upgrade to the latest Virtual Machine Tools version included in your ESXi. VMware vSphere 6.7 includes Virtual Machine Tools version 10.2.0.

OVT

OVT is an open source implementation of Virtual Machine Tools specific for Linux that allows you to bundle the tools into the guest OS, avoiding the management of the Virtual Machine Tools life cycle. OVT is delivered with RPM packages or with `yum` or `apt`. To install OVT in a VM, perform the following steps.

1. Access the system console and run the following command:

```
yum install open-VM-tools
```

The preferred option is to use the ISO image installation type for Virtual Machine Tools. With Open VM tools, you cannot use the vSphere Update Manager to upgrade the version of the VM tools.

2. To check which version of VM tools is installed quickly, click on **More info** under VMware Tools in the virtual machine overview:

Deploying VMs

The creation of VMs in vSphere 6.7 is a core task, and different methods are available for deployment. The most suitable deployment method to use depends on the goal of the VM, the configuration, and the type of infrastructure the VM will run on.

You can create a VM using the following methods:

- **Creating a VM from scratch**: This is used if you need a VM with a specific configuration, OS, or application, and it's not already present in your environment.
- **Using templates**: If a VM has the requirements you need and is deployed frequently, the use of a template (a master copy of a VM) is a good option to consider. This option requires a minor setup stage after the deployment and allows you to save time. Templates also allow you to further customize the system using guest OS customization templates for supported guest operating systems.
- **Cloning**: If similar VMs are deployed in your environment, the cloning option requires less time than creating and configuring a VM from scratch.

To identify which method is suitable for your environment, let's have a closer look at these options to understand the differences between them.

Creating a new VM

You create a new VM when you need a VM with a specific configuration and a specific OS, and it is not already installed on your virtual infrastructure. When the VM is created from scratch, you can define the virtual hardware to use (CPU, RAM, or a hard disk). The default disk assigned to the VM can be removed and you can add new one, either selected from an existing disk or a new RDM device.

To create a new VM, follow this procedure:

1. From the vSphere Client, access the vCenter Server and right-click a valid parent object from the inventory (it can be a datacenter, cluster, resource pool, or host), then select the **New Virtual Machine** option.
2. From the **New Virtual Machine** wizard, select the **Create a new virtual machine** option to proceed with a new installation:

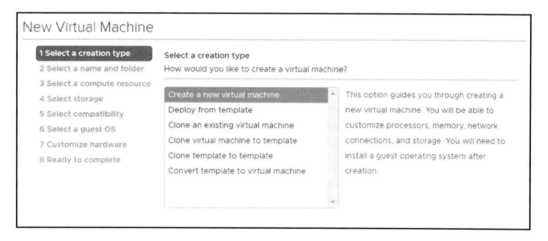

3. Enter a VM name, specify the location for the VM, then click **Next**. If you place the VM into a cluster with DRS disabled or set in manual mode, you need to specify the host on which to create the VM.

4. Select a computer resource (cluster, host, or resource pool) the VM will access to take the resources and click **Next**. In this step, a compatibility check is performed against the selected location to avoid compatibility issues. If the checks succeed, you can proceed with the next step.

5. Select the datastore or datastore cluster to store the configuration and the virtual hard disk files that meet the VM requirements (performance, size). Make sure you have enough space for VM creation and the operations related to the VM operations (for example, snapshots). If you are using storage policy, only compatible datastores will be listed based on the selected storage policy. Click **Next**:

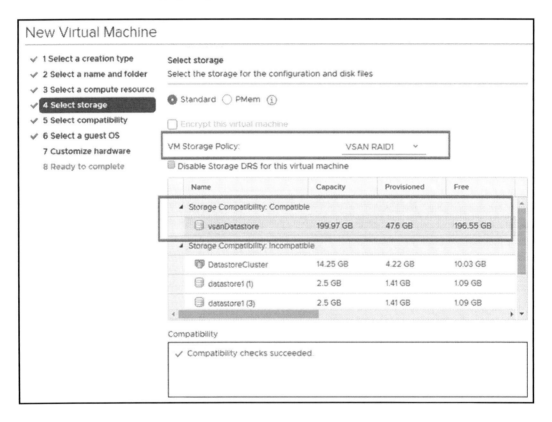

6. Select the VM compatibility. From the compatible with drop-down menu, specify the version of ESXi the machine can run on. This setting determines the virtual hardware (hardware versions are covered in the following section) available to the VM, such as the available virtual PCI slots, the maximum number of CPUs, and the maximum RAM configuration.

7. Select the OS family (Windows, Linux, or other) and the version of the guest OS the VM will run. The OS selection determines the supported devices and the vCPU number available for the VM.

8. On the **Customize hardware** screen, you have the option to customize the virtual hardware presented to the VM. You can adjust the number of vCPUs to use, specify the amount of RAM, add a new NIC, add a new virtual disk, or remove a device that is not needed (such as a floppy drive), and so on. The VM compatibility settings determine what virtual hardware is available and the configuration maximums. Click **Next** when done.

9. Review the VM settings and click **Finish** to create the VM. Keep in mind that you are creating just the configuration of the virtual machine and no OS has yet been installed. Once created, the VM will appear in the vCenter Server inventory.

Hardware version

The hardware version defines the virtual hardware available to the VM that corresponds to the physical hardware available on the host. vSphere 6.7 introduces hardware version 14 and supports VMs created with previous hardware versions. Each hardware version supports at least five major or minor vSphere releases. By default, the compatibility of the VM is given by the host version on which the VM is created, or by the inventory object on which the default VM compatibility is set.

You might be wondering which hardware version to use. This depends on which version of ESXi your environment uses. If you have multiple hosts with different versions, you should choose the correct hardware version to match the lowest version host used in the infrastructure. However, a lower version will have reduced functionality, and a VMware product won't support a VM with a higher hardware version that is configured with a lower version. If your environment runs vSphere 6.7, you should configure the running VM with the highest hardware version available to take advantage of the latest features.

Different VM versions can be created, edited, and run on a host if the host supports that version. Actions on a host are limited, or the VM might not have access to the host if the VM's configured hardware version is higher than the version supported by the host.

The VM hardware versions can be summarized as follows:

ESXi/ESX version	Version 14	Version 13	Version 11	Version 10	Version 9
ESXi 6.7	Create, edit, run	Create, edit, run	Create, edit, run	Create, edit, run	Create, edit, run
ESXi 6.5	Not supported	Create, edit, run	Create, edit, run	Create, edit, run	Create, edit, run
ESXi 6.0	Not supported	Not supported	Create, edit, run	Create, edit, run	Create, edit, run
ESXi 5.5	Not supported	Not supported	Not supported	Create, edit, run	Create, edit, run

The chosen version determines not only the hardware available to the VM but also the supported OS. During the deployment of the VM, the OS supported depends on the hardware version configured.

To run Windows Server 2016, you need at least virtual hardware version 10. Otherwise, the Windows Server 2012 guest OS option won't be available.

Setting the default hardware version

By default, the VM compatibility is configured to use the datacenter settings and the host version. In vCenter Server, you can define a default hardware version for VM creation on a host, cluster, or datacenter.

To configure the default hardware version, perform these steps:

1. From the vSphere Client, log in to the vCenter Server, right-click on the object to configure, and select **Edit Default VM Compatibility**.
2. In the **Compatible with** option, using the drop-down menu, select the hardware version to use and click **OK** to confirm. When a VM is created in this cluster, the default compatibility setting is used.

Installing the OS

Once the VM has been created, you need to install the OS as you would for a physical machine. There are two methods available to install the OS on a VM:

- **Using PXE**: You don't need any installation media for this installation type, but the guest OS you install must support PXE installation, and PXE infrastructure must be in place. The VMware vSphere suite does not include the PXE infrastructure, except for the Auto Deploy feature.
- **From media**: You install the guest OS from a CD/DVD media or an ISO image.

Using an ISO image is generally the fastest method to install a VM OS. Let's do so:

1. Download the ISO image file, then upload the guest OS media to install on a VMFS or NFS datastore that is accessible by the host. Alternatively, you can also use a content library (this will be discussed later in this chapter) to store the ISO image file.
2. From the vSphere Client, right-click on the virtual machine to install and select **Edit Settings**. Access the **Virtual Hardware** tab and expand **CD/DVD drive 1**.
3. From the **CD/DVD drive 1** drop-down menu, select the installation method you want to use from the available options:
    - **Client Device**: The CD-ROM of your machine will be accessed to install the guest O
    - **Host Device**: The CD-ROM of ESXi will be accessed to install the guest OS
    - **Datastore ISO File**: The ISO image file of the guest OS is selected from the datastore to which you previously uploaded the file
    - **Content Library ISO File**: Select the ISO image to mount from the content library (the creation of a content library is discussed in the *Content library* section)
4. Do not forget to check **Connect At Power On** under **Status**. Otherwise, the virtual machine will be equipped by the CD ROM with the associated ISO file (or the client or host device), but, from the perspective of the VM, the media will be ejected. Select the method to use and click OK to confirm.
5. Right-click on the VM to install and select **Power | Power On**. Make sure you have set the correct boot order. By default, the virtual machine will try to boot from the disk first. If the operating system is not installed, the second option to use is a CDROM boot followed by a PXE network boot.

Follow the installation options of the guest OS to complete the installation.

Installing Virtual Machine Tools

Although a VM can run without Virtual Machine Tools, VMware highly recommends installing the latest version to enable advanced features (graphic, networking, mouse, storage, and so on). If no VM tools are installed, you will see the following notification in the **Summary** tab:

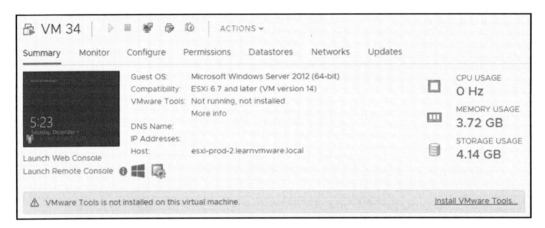

The installation of Virtual Machine Tools can be performed in three ways:

- **Using vSphere Client**: You can install or upgrade Virtual Machine Tools on a single VM at a time.
- **Using VUM**: If more VMs need to install or upgrade Virtual Machine Tools, you can automate the process using VUM (VUM will be covered in Chapter 6, *Life Cycle Management, Patching, and Upgrading*).
- **Using other tools**: You can also use tools such as a Linux repository or a standalone version of Virtual Machine Tools, which is downloadable from the Driver and Utilities tab at my.vmware.com.

To install the Virtual Machine Tools, follow these steps:

1. From the vSphere Client, right-click the running VM to process and select **Guest OS | Install Virtual Machine Tools** to mount the disk image in the virtual CD/DVD of the VM
2. Access the guest OS and proceed with the installation

The installation takes a few seconds and may require a reboot of the VM. A quick way to perform the installation is by clicking the Install Virtual Machine Tools link from the warning message in the **Summary** tab of the VM.

Virtual Machine Tools is included in the ESXi distribution and the bundled tools' ISO image files are located in the `/locker/packages/` directory. If you want a central repository in a shared datastore, take a look at **VMware KB 2129825: Installing and upgrading the latest version of Virtual Machine Tools on existing hosts** (`https://kb.vmware.com/kb/2129825`).

Cloning a VM

A VM deployed by cloning another VM creates an exact copy of the original VM. **Cloning** is the fastest method to deploy a new VM if an existing VM has the same features and applications you need for the new installation. When using the **Clone** option, the new VM will have exactly the same configuration as the source one (for instance, the same IP address will be configured within the guest OS or hostname). A new VM on the vSphere level will, of course, have a different UUID or MAC address.

 You can clone both running or powered-off virtual machines, but a new virtual machine will always be powered off, since the clone operation clones only the virtual machine files, not the state (content of the virtual memory).

This procedure allows you to save time during deployment because you simply need to clone and configure a few parameters.

To deploy a new VM by cloning an existing one, follow these steps:

1. From the vSphere Client, log in to the vCenter Server and access the inventory view. Right-click the VM to clone and select **Clone** | **Clone to Virtual Machine** to create a new VM.

2. Enter the name of the virtual machine and select the location in which to deploy the VM, then click **Next**.

3. Select a computer resource to allow the VM to access the resources of the selected object. If the compatibility checks succeed, click **Next** to continue.

4. Select the storage in which to store the configuration and disk files. Make sure you have sufficient space in the selected datastore. Specify the virtual disk format and click **Next**.

5. In **Select clone options**, you can customize the guest OS to prevent conflicts (a duplicate computer name or IP address already in use) and automatically power on the VM once it is deployed. Click **Next**.

6. In the Summary window, click **Finish** to begin the cloning process of the selected VM:

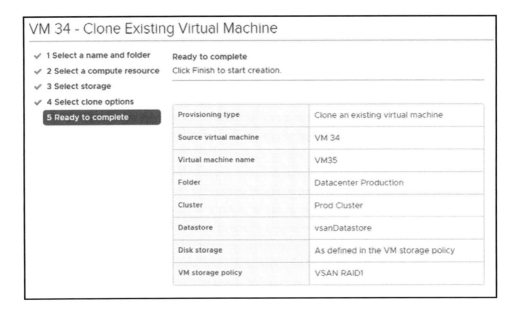

VM 34 - Clone Existing Virtual Machine

✓ 1 Select a name and folder
✓ 2 Select a compute resource
✓ 3 Select storage
✓ 4 Select clone options
5 Ready to complete

Ready to complete
Click Finish to start creation.

Provisioning type	Clone an existing virtual machine
Source virtual machine	VM 34
Virtual machine name	VM35
Folder	Datacenter Production
Cluster	Prod Cluster
Datastore	vsanDatastore
Disk storage	As defined in the VM storage policy
VM storage policy	VSAN RAID1

Clone to Template will clone an existing virtual machine to the new virtual machine template available in the Virtual Machines and Templates view. Clone as Template to Library will clone the source virtual machine and place the template in the content library.

Deploying a VM from a template

The deployment of a VM from a template is performed by creating a new VM from a copy of a template configured with specific virtual hardware and software. Template deployment is the recommended option if you need to deploy several machines with the same requirements. Proceed with these steps:

1. Go to the **VMs and Templates** inventory view and right-click on the template from which to deploy the new VM.

2. Select **New VM from This Template** to create a new VM based on the selected template.

3. Specify a name of the VM and specify the location in which to place the VM by selecting a datacenter or folders, depending on your organizational needs. Click **Next**.

4. Select a computer resource to allow the VM to access the resources of the selected object. If the chosen location causes compatibility issues, a warning message is displayed in the compatibility area. If the checks succeed, click **Next** to continue.

5. Select the datastore in which to store the VM files. You can specify the format of the virtual disk (we talked about the disk format in the *Virtual disks* section) you want to configure, then click **Next**.

6. In Select clone options, you can customize the guest OS to prevent conflicts due to a duplicate computer name or IP address and automatically power on the virtual machine once deployed. The guest OS customization allows you to modify the computer name, license, and network settings. When the desired option has been selected, click **Next**.

In the **Summary** window, click **Finish** to deploy the new VM based on the selected template.

There are multiple options for how to create a template:

- **Convert an existing (powered-off) virtual machine to a template**: In this situation, a source virtual machine will be removed from the inventory and a new template will be available. If you operate on the **Hosts and Clusters** view, the template will not be visible. You need to switch to **VMs and Templates** to access your templates. The source virtual machine will be kept on the original datastore with all its data, the only difference is that the .vmx configuration file will be renamed as .vmtx.

- **Clone an existing VM (powered off or powered on) to a template**: The source virtual machine will be kept intact and the new virtual machine will be transformed to the template.

 You cannot power on a template. If you need to upgrade your template, you need to convert the template back to the virtual machine, perform the necessary upgrade (for instance, patching the guest OS), and convert it back to the template.

VM customization Specifications

Usually, you do not need to run two copies of a virtual machine, instead you should perform additional customizations to the new virtual machine so that it has its own customized configuration.

By customization, we are referring to the following tasks (depending on the guest OS type):

- Changing the IP address
- Changing the hostname/computer name
- Changing the administrator/root password
- Setting the time zone
- Joining the computer to Active Directory Domain
- Running several initial scripts

To create a new VM customization specification, switch to **Policies and Profiles** and select VM customization specifications:

1. Configure the name of the customization specification and the target guest OS. Based on the selection, different options will be available for the customization. If you select Windows as the target guest OS, the following options will be available:

    - **Use custom SysPrep answer file**: The SysPrep answer file is used for the actual customization of the guest OS. If you do not select this option, you will manually configure the desired parameters in the **New VM Customization Specification** wizard. If you have an existing SysPrep file, you can use it instead of manual configuration. For more information about SysPrep, take a look at the official documentation: `https://docs.microsoft.com/en-us/windows-hardware/manufacture/desktop/use-answer-files-with-sysprep`.

    - **Generate a new security identifier (SID)**: With the change SID option, all of the deployed virtual machines can acquire a unique **security identifier (SID)**. A unique SID is required when joining a VM to the active directory.

2. The owner name and the organization name will change the `RegisteredOwner` and `RegisteredOrganization` registry keys in `HKEY_LOCAL_MACHINE\SOFTWARE\Microsoft\Windows NT\CurrentVersion`.

3. The computer name can either be provided during the clone/deploy wizard, it can be a fixed name in the VM customization specification, or a new name will be assigned based on the name of the virtual machine on the vSphere level.

4. You can directly assign a Windows license if you need to. If you do not assign the license, you will need to activate the guest OS once deployed.

5. You need to provide a new password for the local administrator account. You can choose whether the virtual machine should be logged in automatically once deployed.

6. You might need to change the time zone of the guest OS.

7. Invoke several commands inside the guest OS once deployed. You can either use native commands of the guest operation system, such as `netsh` for disabling the network interface, or you might use a more complicated script located inside the source template that will be invoked, for example, to extend the disk size.

8. In the network section, you can assign an IP address to the network interface. Note that based on the customization specification, the target virtual machine needs to have the exact number of virtual network adapters, as defined in the customization specification. If your customization specification includes settings for two NICs, the new virtual machine that will be deployed and customized by such a customization specification must also have two virtual NICs. The **Network** section of the customization profile is shown in the following screenshot:

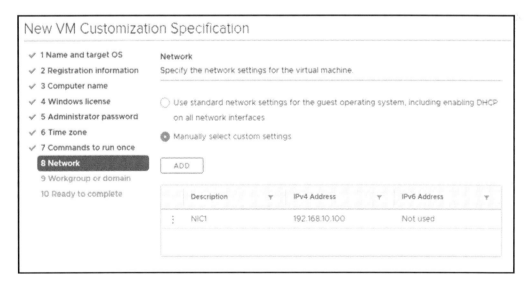

9. You have the option to automatically join this new virtual machine to the AD domain.

10. Once all inputs are filled in, you can review the settings and proceed with the creation of the VM.

Once the customization specification is created, you can choose the **Customize the operating system** clone option:

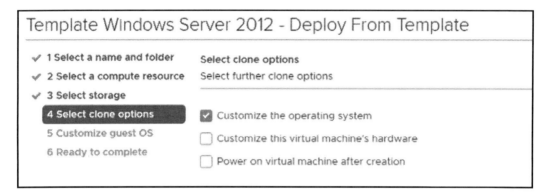

In the next step, all your available customization specifications will be displayed and, based on your selection, the new virtual machine will not only be cloned from a template but also customized with the configuration stored in the customization specification:

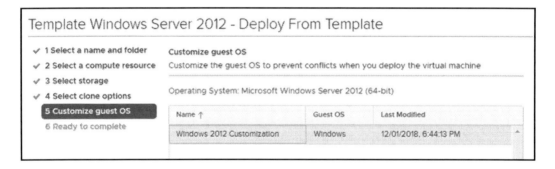

Content library

A content library is a container object to store templates, vApps, or other files that can be shared across multiple vCenter Server instances in the same or different locations to ensure consistency and compliance within the infrastructure.

vSphere 6.5 introduced new features and some enhancements that improve performance and recoverability. You can now mount an ISO directly from the content library, apply a guest OS customization during VM deployment, and update existing templates. The content library is included in the vSphere backup/restore service as well as the VCHA feature set (from VMware vSphere 6.5).

A VM template, a vApp template, or another type of file in a library is defined as a library item that can contain single or multiple files (ISO, OVF, and so on).

You can define multiple content libraries, and during the configuration, you specify on which datastore the content library will be stored. In this example, I have created two local content libraries. The first one is for ISO images and the second one holds all templates and external OVF files:

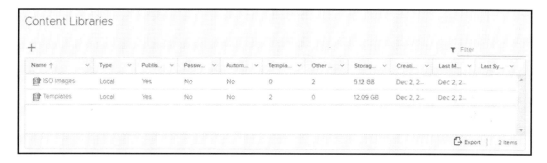

As you can see, each of the content libraries created its directory in the datastore, and the actual files are stored under folders with a UUID, not the name of the items.

Creating a content library

You can create two types of content library:

- **Local**: This is used to store items on a single vCenter Server instance that can be published to allow other users from other vCenter Servers to subscribe to it.
- **Subscribed library**: This is created when you subscribe to a published library and can be created in the same vCenter Server as the published library or a different vCenter Server instance.

If the subscribed library is created in a different vCenter Server, the option to download all contents or metadata can only be configured in the **Create Library** wizard. To keep the content of a subscribed library up to date, the subscribed library automatically synchronizes to the source published library on a regular basis. Synchronization of the subscribed library can also be done manually.

Local content library

Before you can subscribe to an existing library, you need to define the Local Content Library.

To create a Local Content Library, proceed as follows:

1. From the vSphere Client, access the vCenter Server and, from the menu, select **Content Libraries** and click on the create a new library icon with the + sign to open the create library wizard.
2. Enter a name and a description in the note field, then click **Next**.
3. Specify the type of content library you want to create (local or subscribed), then click **Next**. Select **Publish externally** to make the content of the library available to other vCenter Server instances. If you want the users to use a password when accessing the library, select **Enable authentication** and set a password. Check the **Optimize for syncing over HTTP** checkbox to create an optimized published library. This library is optimized to ensure lower CPU usage and faster streaming of the content over HTTP. This library is used as a central content depot for subscribed libraries:

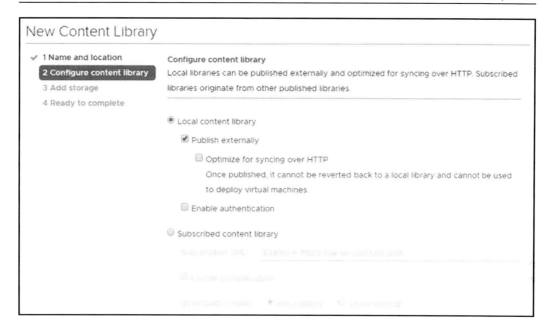

4. Select the datastore used to store the library's content and click **Next**.

5. Review the settings and click Finish to create the library.

Subscribed content library

A subscribed content library can synchronize its content with other content libraries. The idea is that you maintain only one content library (for example, in HQ) and all subscribed libraries will synchronize their content from the HQ without additional manual operations:

1. To subscribe to a content library, you need to have at least one content library defined on another vCenter server with the **Published Externally** flag set to **Yes**, as seen in the following screenshot:

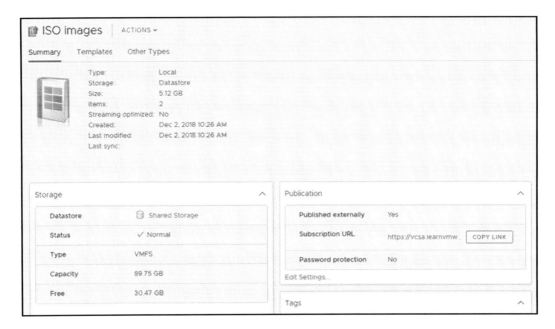

2. During the configuration of a subscribed library, you need the **Subscription URL**. You can quickly click the **COPY LINK** button to get the URL, or you can click on **Edit Settings** to access the information:

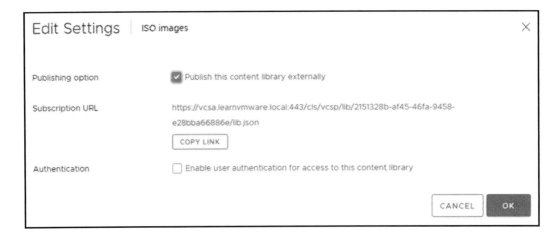

It is possible to have multiple Local and Subscribed Content Libraries in a single vCenter Server.

To create a new subscribed content library, perform the following tasks:

1. In a different vCenter server (vCenter does not need to be part of the Linked-Mode), switch to **Content Libraries** and create a new content library.
2. Provide a name for the new content library and click **Next**.
3. Select the subscribed content library option, provide a subscription URL, and provide authentication credentials if the authentication is configured. You have the option to either download all content automatically, or only download the metadata and download the item from the source content library once the item is accessed.
4. The files will be stored on a datastore, so select which datastore will back up the content library.
5. Confirm the configuration on the review screen:

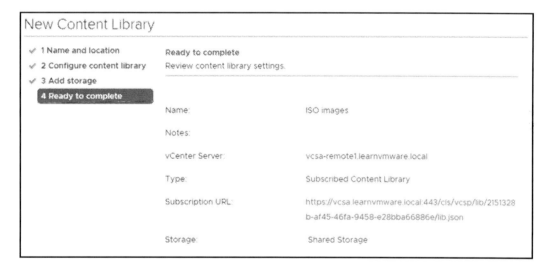

Once the content library is created, it will synchronize automatically from the source content library, and once the synchronization is complete, you will see the same content in the subscribed content library as in the original one:

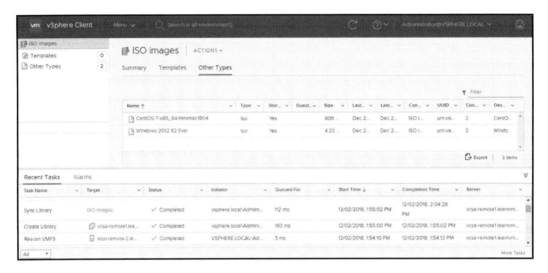

If you need to manually sync the content library (automatic synchronization is enabled by default) you can invoke manual synchronization from the **Actions** menu.

 You can find more details about synchronization intervals and timeouts at `https://docs.vmware.com/en/VMware-vSphere/6.7/ com.vmware.vsphere.vcenterhost.doc/GUID-1A5A5387-0E5C-4158- 9836-2544990EED00.html`.

Working with the content library

Content Libraries provide centralized access to all your ISO files, OVF templates, vApps, and any other files. Several tasks can be performed with content libraries. Let's walk through a few options.

Uploading ISO images

To upload ISO files, perform the following operations:

1. Right-click on the created content library and select the **Import item** option to import content to the library:

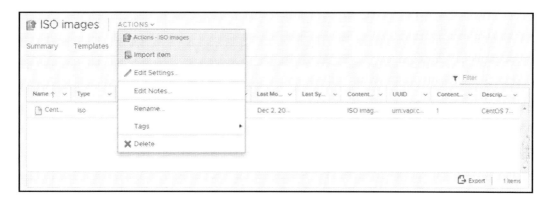

2. You can import content by specifying a URL or a local file. If you import the content from a local file, you locate the file using the **Browse** button. You can also edit the name of the item to identify the file better. Click **OK** to import the required item.

You can see what content is available in the library in the following screenshot. ISO images are stored under **Other Types**:

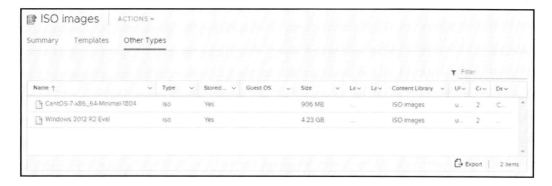

Uploading templates and OVF files

Existing templates can be cloned to the content library. You can also upload any OVF/OVA file, such as third-party appliances.

If you have an existing template in your inventory, you can clone it to the content library. The original template will not be removed from the inventory, and the clone will be available in the content library. Let's get started:

1. Right-click on the existing template and select **Clone to Library...**:

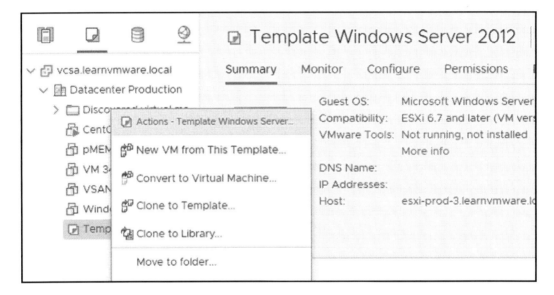

2. Specify in which content library the template should be cloned.
3. Once the wizard is closed, a new task will be launched. The existing template will be exported as an OVF file and uploaded to the content library.

Once the clone process is finished, you will see your new OVF template under the **Templates** tab in the content library. If the content is cloned from the template, you will also see the guest operating system version. For external OVF files uploaded to the content library, this information will not be available:

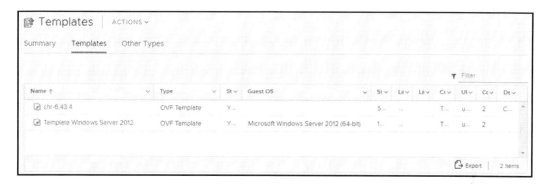

Deploying VMs from the content library

Once the OVF file is located in the content library, you can deploy a new VM from the content library. You cannot use guest OS customization scripts when the virtual machine is deployed from an OVF file in the content library:

1. Right-click on the datacenter or cluster and select **New Virtual Machine**. In the wizard, select **Deploy From Template**.
2. If the content library is configured, you will have the option to select the template from the content library.
3. Provide a name for the new VM and select in which datacenter it should be deployed.
4. As with any new virtual machine, select on which ESXi host or Cluster the VM will be deployed.

5. As items in the content library are OVF files, based on the selected item, you will see the details from an OVF manifest. If the template had been cloned from a template, no details would be provided, but if the template is a third-party OVF image, you might see different pieces of information here:

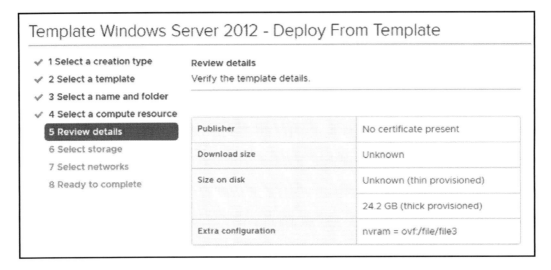

6. Choose on which datastore the new VM will be deployed
7. Change the mapping of the virtual network interface card. On the left, you have an original port group that was assigned to the template during creation. On the right, you can choose a target port group.
8. Review the settings and Confirm the deployment. Once the deployment starts, you will see deploy OVF template task running in the inventory.

ISO files from the content library

If you choose to use a content library to host your ISO installation images, you can easily access them when creating a new virtual machine:

1. Edit the settings of a virtual machine, select **CD/DVD drive 1,** and then select **Content Library ISO File**:

2. Select which ISO file you want to mount
3. Confirm the selection and close the edit settings to mount the ISO file to the virtual machine

Managing VMs

When VMs have been deployed in your infrastructure, you can start the administration using the available tools and features offered by vSphere Client. Several actions can be performed on VMs to keep a clean inventory and a healthy infrastructure. Let's take a look at some common procedures an administrator performs on a regular basis.

Adding or registering an existing VM

VMs can be created or deployed using the different methods shown previously. In some circumstances, you might need to put in your production environment a pre-created VM from another source. You may be wondering how to deploy this virtual machine.

First, using vSphere Client, you need to upload the VM files (generally the .vmx and .vmdk files) to an attached datastore that is reachable by the hosts. When the files are in the datastore, you have to register the VM to add it to the vCenter Server or the ESXi host inventory. Once the VM has been added to the inventory, you can start using and managing the VM.

To register a VM to the inventory, follow this procedure:

1. From the vSphere Client, log in to the vCenter Server and select the **Storage** view.
2. Select the storage and the folder in which the VM has been stored.
3. From the available files in the selected folder, select the file with the .vmx extension and click **Register VM...** to register the VM to the inventory:

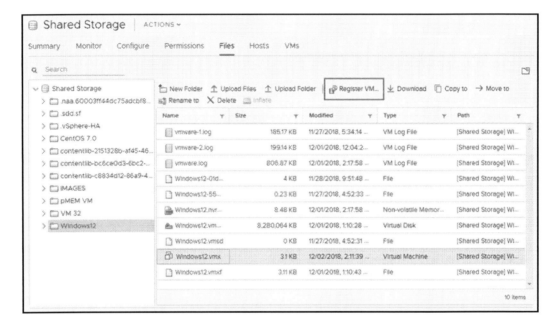

4. By default, the system populates the virtual machine name field, reading the info from the .vmx file. Enter a different name if you want to change the default value. Specify a location in which to run the VM and click **Next**.
5. Select the compute resource the VM will access to get the resources. If the compatibility checks succeed, click **Next** to continue.
6. When you are ready to complete, click **Finish** to register and add the VM to the inventory.

When the VM has been added to the inventory, you can power it on and manage it as you would do with other VMs.

Removing or deleting a VM

Removing and deleting a VM are two different but straightforward procedures that lead to different results. Removing a VM from the inventory doesn't delete the VM (the files remain in the same location in storage), but removes its view from the inventory, and it won't be listed anymore. Removing a VM from the inventory can be useful if you want to remove a no-longer-used VM, but you want to keep the data.

To remove a VM, the VM must be powered off. The procedure is quite simple:

1. Right-click on the VM to remove and select the **Remove from Inventory** option.
2. Click **YES** to confirm the removal:

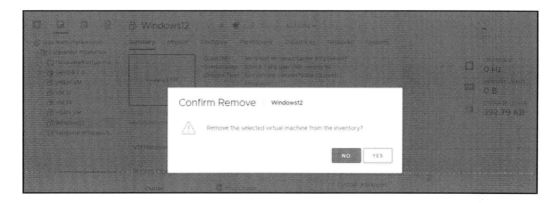

When you delete a VM instead, all VM files are removed from the datastore with no way to recover them if the deletion is done by mistake. *How do we recover a VM that has been deleted accidentally?* From the backup.

The deletion procedure is similar to what we just saw:

1. Right-click the powered-off VM (this option will be grayed out if the VM is still running) to delete and select the **Delete from Disk** option.
2. Click **YES** to confirm the deletion:

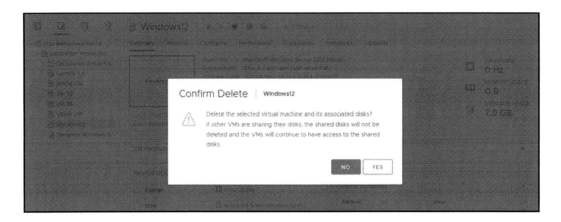

Managing the power state of a VM

In vSphere 6.7, you can change the VM power state in different ways. To change the power state, right-click the VM and select **Power** followed by the type of the state. You have the following states available:

- **Power On** and **Power Off**: This function powers the VM on or off immediately without any interaction with the guest OS. Be careful when powering off the VM, because the process doesn't perform a clean shutdown of open files and there is the risk of corrupting files that are not closed properly.
- **Suspend**: This feature suspends the VM, freezing its current state. When the VM is resumed, it starts from the state that was suspended.
- **Reset**: This command emulates the reset button of a physical computer.
- **Shut down guest OS**: This is the correct command to use to shut down the guest OS since it avoids data corruption. This function is available if Virtual Machine Tools is installed on the VM.
- **Restart guest OS**: This command is available only if Virtual Machine Tools is installed on the VM and it allows a graceful restart of the guest OS.

Managing VM snapshots

A snapshot takes the state of a VM at a specific point in time and allows you to revert to that state whenever you like. You can have several snapshots in a VM and, depending on the changes that have occurred, you may decide to keep the changes by deleting the snapshots, or to discard the changes by reverting to a previous snapshot.

A snapshot is taken on a per-VM basis and can be used for different situations. When a new patch is released from a vendor for the guest OS running on a VM, if something goes wrong during the upgrade process, the VM can become unresponsive and sometimes the blue screen of death may be displayed, in the case of a Windows guest OS. If the guest OS can't be recovered, the backup is the only lifeline you have that allows a quick recovery of the VM. If the failure occurs on a core VM and the process of restoration from a backup takes a long time, the users will not be happy because the services won't be available for a while.

Taking a snapshot before applying a patch is a trick that allows you to immediately revert to a working state of the VM before the patch was applied, with limited service disruption.

However, the use of snapshots has some limitations:

- Raw disks and **Raw device mapping** (**RDM**) physical mode disks are not supported, RDM with virtual compatibility mode is supported
- Independent disks are supported only if the VM is powered off
- VMs configured for bus sharing are not supported
- You can have a maximum of 32 snapshots in a chain, and a single snapshot should not be kept for more than 72 hours to avoid the snapshot storage location running out of space
- Keeping snapshots for a long time may negatively impact the performance of the VM
- For disks larger than 2 TB, snapshot creation can take a long time

Snapshots should not be used as a backup because if the files of the VM are lost, or the storage itself fails, the snapshot files are lost as well.

Creating a snapshot

To create a snapshot, follow these steps:

1. From the vSphere Client, right-click on the VM you want to process and select **Snapshots** | **Take Snapshot**.
2. Enter a name and provide a description. If the VM is powered on during snapshot creation, you have the option to snapshot the virtual machine's memory (grayed out if the VM is off). If this option is enabled, the RAM of the VM is also included in the snapshot. The quiesce guest file system option, which is only available if Virtual Machine Tools is installed, brings the on-disk data into a state that is suitable for backups, ensuring that backups are consistent and work as appropriate.
3. Click **OK** to take a snapshot of the selected VM.

When a snapshot is taken, multiple new files are created in the VM folder. These include .vmdk, -sparse.vmdk, .vmsd, and .vmsn, as shown at the following screenshot:

```
                                                      esxi-prod-1.learnvmware.local - PuTTY
[root@esxi-prod-1:/vmfs/volumes/5bfd67c0-72feebdf-aa85-000c299f4b65/Windows12] ls -lah
total 12662272
drwxr-xr-x    1 root     root        76.0K Dec  2 13:25 .
drwxr-xr-t    1 root     root        76.0K Dec  2 12:55 ..
-rw-------    1 root     root         4.0K Dec  2 13:24 Windows12-000001-d33fae10da35b0e9.vmfd
-rw-------    1 root     root        181.0M Dec  2 13:24 Windows12-000001-sesparse.vmdk
-rw-------    1 root     root          398 Dec  2 13:24 Windows12-000001.vmdk
-rw-------    1 root     root         4.0K Dec  2 13:24 Windows12-000003-4b07ec6d4eea6513.vmfd
-rw-------    1 root     root        198.0M Dec  2 13:26 Windows12-000003-sesparse.vmdk
-rw-------    1 root     root          398 Dec  2 13:25 Windows12-000003.vmdk
-rw-------    1 root     root         4.0K Nov 28 08:51 Windows12-01d62f107daab0ae.vmfd
-rw-r--r--    1 root     root          236 Nov 27 15:52 Windows12-5587bfce.hlog
-rw-------    1 root     root         4.0G Dec  2 13:25 Windows12-75718b10.vswp
-rw-------    1 root     root        30.9K Dec  2 13:24 Windows12-Snapshot1.vmsn
-rw-------    1 root     root        30.9K Dec  2 13:24 Windows12-Snapshot2.vmsn
-rw-------    1 root     root        40.0G Dec  2 13:24 Windows12-flat.vmdk
-rw-------    1 root     root         8.5K Dec  2 13:24 Windows12.nvram
-rw-------    1 root     root          606 Dec  2 13:21 Windows12.vmdk
-rw-r--r--    1 root     root          715 Dec  2 13:24 Windows12.vmsd
-rwx------    1 root     root         3.1K Dec  2 13:25 Windows12.vmx
-rw-------    1 root     root            0 Dec  2 13:25 Windows12.vmx.lck
-rw-------    1 root     root         3.1K Dec  2 13:24 Windows12.vmxf
-rwx------    1 root     root         3.1K Dec  2 13:25 Windows12.vmx~
-rw-r--r--    1 root     root        185.2K Nov 27 16:34 vmware-1.log
-rw-r--r--    1 root     root        199.1K Dec  1 11:04 vmware-2.log
-rw-r--r--    1 root     root        806.9K Dec  1 13:17 vmware-3.log
-rw-r--r--    1 root     root        323.0K Dec  2 13:24 vmware-4.log
-rw-------    1 root     root        245.2K Dec  2 13:25 vmware.log
-rw-------    1 root     root        110.0M Dec  2 13:25 vmx-Windows12-1970375440-1.vswp
[root@esxi-prod-1:/vmfs/volumes/5bfd67c0-72feebdf-aa85-000c299f4b65/Windows12]
```

Let's have a look at the files created when a snapshot is taken and their roles:

- `vmname-00000#.vmdk`: This is a text file that contains info about the snapshot and snapshot disks. For every snapshot taken, this file is created for each of the `.vmdk` files.
- `vmname-00000#-sparse.vmdk`: This is the delta disk file that represents the difference between the current state of the VM and the state at the time of snapshot creation.
- `vmname.vmsd`: This file holds snapshot information such as names, descriptions, and relationships between snapshots.
- `vmname.snasphot#.vmsn`: This stores the memory state of the VM when the snapshot is taken, and it is created each time you take a snapshot.

You can have a complex snapshot tree based on your requirements, and a snapshot chain does not need to be linear, as shown at the following screenshot:

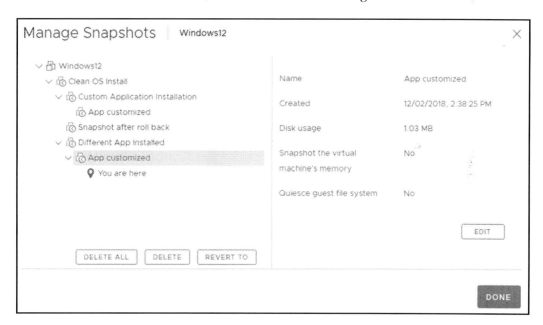

Reverting to a snapshot

If you need to, you can quickly revert to a previous snapshot using **REVERT TO** from the Snapshot Manager. If you revert to a snapshot, every change performed between the last snapshot and the current state will be discarded.

Committing changes

To commit changes and the current state of the VM, delta disks are merged with the base disks. This operation is done using the DELETE option in the Snapshot Manager:

- **DELETE**: Deletes the selected snapshot from a chain, consolidating the changes that occurred between the state of the snapshot and the previous disk state to the parent snapshot.
- **DELETE ALL**: All snapshots are deleted from the VM, consolidating, and writing the changes occurred between snapshots and previous delta disks to the base disks, merging them with the base VM disks. DELETE ALL is an alias for committing all changes, and your virtual machine will merge everything to the base disk. The result is that the VM will have only the base disk with the current running state.

Snapshot consolidation

Snapshot consolidation is a procedure that can be used when the delete or delete all operations fail. For example, consolidation may be required if the backup software that utilizes the snapshot technology is not able to remove redundant delta disks. If the snapshots are not removed, the VM performance may suffer, and the storage could run out of space. By performing a consolidation, these redundant delta disks are removed, keeping the VM in a healthy state.

To determine whether a VM requires consolidation, from the vSphere Client, select the vCenter Server, cluster, or host, and then click the **VMs** tab. If the **Needs Consolidation** column is not visible, click the arrow on the right side of the column head, select **Show/Hide** columns, and check the **Needs Consolidation** option:

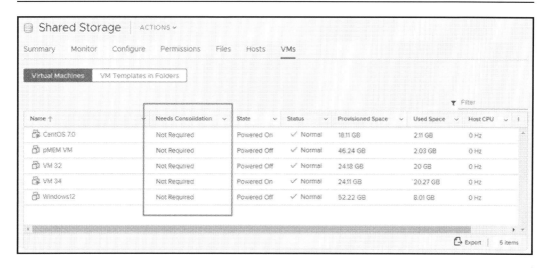

Importing and exporting VMs

The vSphere infrastructure allows you to import and export virtual machines. VMs that are deployed or exported from the inventory are usually referred as OVFs or OVAs.

Deploying Open Virtual Format (OVF) and Open Virtual Appliance (OVA) templates

Virtual machines can be exported in OVF and OVA formats and deployed in the same or different environments. OVA and OVF are compressed file packages that enable faster deployment and may contain more than one VM. From vSphere 6.5, the installation of the CIP is no longer required to import and export OVF or OVA templates.

The procedure to deploy a VM from an OVF or OVA file is similar to deployment from a template:

1. From the vSphere Web Client, right-click a valid inventory object (host, datacenter, cluster, or resource pool) and select the **Actions** | **Deploy OVF Template** option.
2. Click the **Choose Files** button to specify the .ovf file to use, or you can deploy the OVF directly from the URL.
3. Enter a name and select a location to deploy the VM to. Click **Next**.
4. Select the resource to run the deployed appliance and click **Next**. A validation check is performed.
5. Review the details to verify the configuration is correct. Click **Next** to define the storage to use.
6. Depending on the OVF, additional steps might be displayed, including the License Agreement and Configuration:

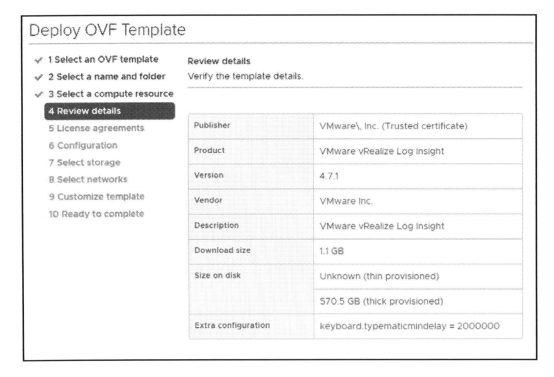

7. Under **Configuration**, you can perform additional configuration of the new VM. Those configuration options are based on the source OVF file and the author of the OVF.

8. Specify the virtual disk format and select the location in which to store the files. Click **Next** to continue.

9. Select the network to use from the **Destination Network** drop-down menu, then click **Next**.

10. In the **Customize template** section, you might be able to assign variables that will be slipstreamed to the new virtual machine for its initial configuration. Again, these variables are defined by the author of the OVF/OVA file:

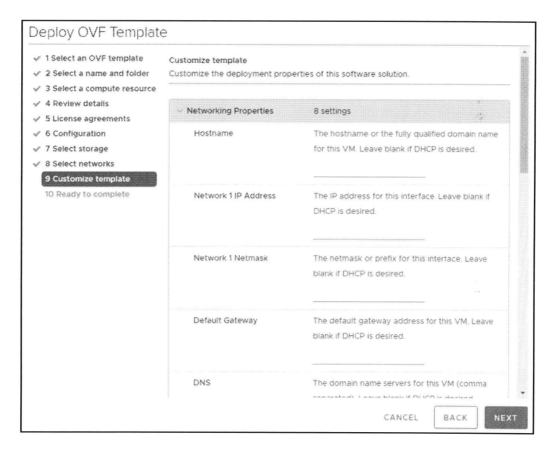

11. Click Finish to begin the deployment of the VM.

OVA and OVF files are commonly used to deploy third-party virtual appliances without a complete installation of some specific applications. Usually, specific deployment scripts are built into the virtual appliance, so all you need is to provide the initial configuration details in the OVF import wizard.

Exporting a virtual machine and an Open Virtual Format (OVF)

The OVF template can also be used to export a captured state of the VM in a compressed and sparse format. The procedure to export an OVF template requires that the VM is powered off before proceeding:

1. From the vSphere Client, right-click on the VM to export and select the **Template | Export OVF Template** option.
2. Specify the virtual machine name and, optionally, an annotation that can be useful to identify the VM configuration better. If you need to include additional information or configurations, such as BIOS UUID or MAC addresses, check Enable Advanced Options. Be careful if you enable these options because the portability will be limited. Click **OK** to proceed with the export.
3. Specify where to save each file associated with the template.

You can use OVF Export to transport your virtual machines between different environments or for cloud migrations. The OVF file has a generic structure so different service providers can deploy virtual machines exported as OVF appliances.

Converting VMs

There are some situations in which you might need to convert a physical machine into a VM or import a VM from a third party to take advantage of the scalability, reliability, security, and features provided by the vSphere platform. If you have old physical machines or physical machines running specific applications, OSes, and configurations that require time for a fresh reinstallation, and service downtime for an extended period is not tolerated, conversion to a VM might solve the problem.

You may also be requested to import VMs created for different virtual platforms in vSphere, and to run those VMs in a VMware environment, but they must be converted into a supported format.

To migrate the OS, applications, and data to the virtualization platform, the **VMware vCenter Converter** tool (available to download from the VMware website at `https://www.vmware.com/products/converter.html`) is the solution you should use to import a physical machine or VM into the vSphere environment.

You can perform two types of conversion:

- **Physical to virtual (P2V)**
- **Virtual to virtual (V2V)**

P2V conversion

P2V conversion is a procedure used to convert a physical computer into a VM. VMware vCenter Converter allows conversion from physical machines running Windows and Linux and supports both desktop and server editions. With the supported hot cloning feature, admins can convert a running machine in a non-disruptive way, with no downtime or reboot requirements.

To convert a physical server into a VMware vSphere machine, you can use VMware Converter:

1. Download and install VMware Converter on the source physical server

2. Click the **Convert machine** button and select **This local machine** as a source:

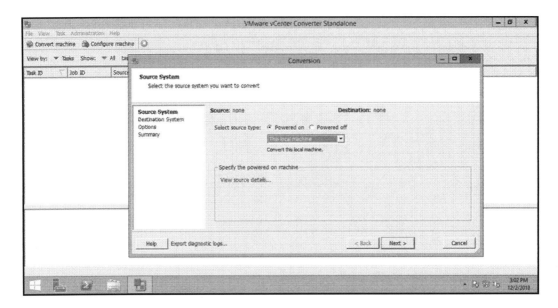

3. In **Destination System**, select vSphere infrastructure and provide an IP address or FQDN of the vCenter Server as well as the credentials.

4. Specify the name of the virtual machine and its location.

5. In the **Destination Location**, select on which cluster or ESXi server you want to deploy the virtual machine.

6. Options allow you to customize the P2V migration. You can, for example, define to which port group the NICs will be connected or how the virtual hardware will be defined for the new VM.

7. In the **Summary** tab, check the properties of the migration and, once you hit **Finish**, the migration will start.

Once the task is completed, you can access your converted server from the vSphere infrastructure.

Note that any changes to the source system during the migration will not be captured and migrated.

V2V conversion

V2V conversion refers to the migration of an OS, application programs, and data from a VM or disk partition to another VM or disk partition. VMware vCenter Converter supports the conversion from third-party VMs, such as Hyper-V and KVM to vSphere.

Other products can be used for V2V migrations:

- **StarWind V2V Converter**: `https://www.starwindsoftware.com/starwind-v2v-converter`
- **Acronis Backup and Recovery Solutions**: `https://www.acronis.com/en-au/virtualization/`
- **5nine V2V Easy Converter**: `https://www.5nine.com/5nine-v2v-easy-converter/`

Summary

In this chapter, we discussed VMs, a software computer composed by a file structure that specifies the configuration (`.vmx`) and the virtual disk used to store data (`.vmdk`) and core components, such as virtual and hardware resources, an OS, and Virtual Machine Tools. A VM can be deployed using different methods depending on the features requested. The use of a content library can simplify the deployment process, and it allows you to easily subscribe to a central content library from your remote sites to have unified access to the installation ISO files and OVF templates.

We have seen that, once installed, a VM can be added or removed from the inventory that keeps the VM data. Snapshots can be used to capture the state of a VM at a specific point in time so that we can quickly revert to a working version if necessary. A typical use case of snapshots is the patching process; before applying a new patch, taking a VM snapshot allows you to go back quickly in case of problems. Snapshots can be created and deleted, but sometimes consolidation is required when snapshot deletion fails.

We have also looked at the P2V and V2V migrations, which allow you to either virtualize your physical servers or migrate virtual machines between different virtualization technologies.

In the next chapter, we will explain how to allocate resources to VMs in an efficient way to avoid over-commitment, which can compromise performance and the functionality of the infrastructure.

Questions

1. What is the most recent Virtual Machine hardware version?

   a) 17
   b) 13
   c) 14
   d) 11
   e) 9

2. What is the most significant difference between using Open-VMtools compared to VMtools that are installed using an ISO image from VMware vSphere?

3. Name at least three different virtual network card types.

4. A thick provision lazy zeroed disk is zeroed during the creation of the disk:

   a) True
   b) False

5. A VMX file contains the data of the virtual disk, and a VMDK file contains the virtual machine configuration:

   a) True
   b) False

6. Describe the benefits of using templates compared to creating a virtual machine from scratch.

7. Which parts of the Windows operating system can be customized using VM Customization Specifications?

   a) Changing the IP address
   b) Setting the time zone
   c) The configuration of Windows Remote Management
   d) Slipstreaming MSI packages to the VM
   e) Changing the administrator/root password
   f) Automatically resizing the partition table
   g) Joining the computer to Active Directory Domain
   h) Running several initial scripts

8. What is the difference between a Local and a Subscribed Content Library?

9. True or false: In a single content library, you can store both ISO installation images and OVF templates.

10. How can you add a virtual machine to the inventory when the virtual machine is removed from the inventory?

11. What is the disadvantage of using snapshots? Which functions will not be available?

12. The Delete All option when working with snapshots will delete all snapshots and the virtual machine will be at the state it was at before taking the snapshots:

   a) True
   b) False

13. OVA and OVF templates can be further customized based on the developer of the appliance:

   a) True
   b) False

14. Explain the terms P2V and V2V.

Further reading

Check out the following links for more information on the topics covered in this chapter:

- **vSphere Virtual Machine Administration:** vSphere Virtual Machine Administration describes how to create, configure, and manage virtual machines in the VMware vSphere environment: `https://docs.vmware.com/en/VMware-vSphere/6.7/vsphere-esxi-vcenter-server-67-virtual-machine-admin-guide.pdf`.

- **Managing Virtual Machines:** Check out the official documentation available at the VMware site that describes every single aspect of virtual-machine management: `https://docs.vmware.com/en/VMware-vSphere/6.7/com.vmware.vsphere.vm_admin.doc/GUID-B7023DD7-F790-4DF8-89B4-FF09DA3DBFB1.html`.

- **VMware vCenter Converter Standalone User's Guide**: TheVMware vCenter Converter Standalone User's Guide provides information about installing and using VMware vCenter Converter Standalone: `https://www.vmware.com/pdf/convsa_61_guide.pdf`.

10
VM Resource Management

Maintaining a resource-optimal vSphere infrastructure is a critical day-to-day operation and should be performed with a strict focus on delivering adequate resources to the **virtual machines** (**VMs**) at any given time.

The resources of your vSphere infrastructure are limited, even though vSphere provides many overcommitment techniques so that you can assign more resources than you physically have, but you should try to avoid contention scenarios at all costs because such contention can significantly affect your applications' and workloads' performance.

One of the fundamental techniques that you can use to provide the best possible performance to your VMs is resources, limits, and shares, which you can use to fine-tune resource allocation to different vSphere objects, such as VMs, vApps, and resource pools.

Using vMotion, you can freely move your workloads within a vSphere cluster, allowing you to utilize the ESXi hosts evenly.

For more complex environment, you can also utilize **Distributed Resource Scheduler** (**DRS**), a cluster feature that is not only responsible for maintaining your cluster balance automatically but also provides advanced functions that allow you to specify how the VMs should be run concerning different affinity and anti-affinity rules.

Resource pools, on the other hand, can provide you with a pool of computing and memory resources that VMs inside the resource pool can consume without taking more than you have defined, and by using vApps you can even extend this functionality to complex application management, where you treat multiple VMs as a single logical application.

This chapter covers the following topics:

- Virtual machine resource management
- Virtual machine migration
- DRS
- Resource pools and vApps
- Network and storage resources

Virtual machine resource management

The number of VMs that can run on ESXi is not infinite, and optimization of resources ensures the best performance. In contrast to the physical world, where each server is often equipped with more resources than it needs, in a virtualized environment, you can allocate suitable resources to a VM based on its role and function.

An FTP server, for example, doesn't need to be equipped with a dual processor and 6 GB of RAM because the resources will be underutilized. By allocating a suitable amount of RAM and a suitable number of CPUs, you can obtain the best performance, saving resources for other VMs. Understanding how to manage and reallocate resources is then a key way to avoid overcommitment of resources (that is, when you have more demand than the available capacity), which can compromise the entire infrastructure's functionality.

Hosts and clusters (a group of hosts where the cluster owns the overall CPUs and RAM), as well as datastore clusters (a group of datastores), provide physical resources to the infrastructure. Default settings configured on a VM during creation are generally suitable, but sometimes may not ensure the correct allocation of resources. You can always edit the VM settings later on to adjust assigned resources in order to avoid issues due to lack of resources.

Reservations, limits, and shares

Not all VMs are the same. Some of them are used for business-critical workloads, some of them might be used for internal workloads, and some of the might be only some development and test VMs, and because of that, you want to treat them differently.

You should guarantee that your critical line-of-business application has some resources that are always available, but on the other hand, that your development and test VMs will never consume more than a certain amount of resources.

The most straightforward way to manage the resources of VMs is reservations, limits, and shares. We have already touched on these topics in previous chapters when we talked about network I/O control, but let's have a look at them in more detail.

Shares

Shares specify the priority of a VM to get resources during a period of contention. When resources in an ESXi host are limited, and the VMs compete to access resources, the VMs configured with higher shares will have higher priority to access more of the host's resources. Shares can be specified as high, normal, or low, with a ratio of 4:2:1, and are applied between siblings in the vSphere hierarchy.

If you do not use a resource pool or vApps, all your VMs will be on the same level in the hierarchy, and thus the shares will be split between all of them, as you can see in the following diagram:

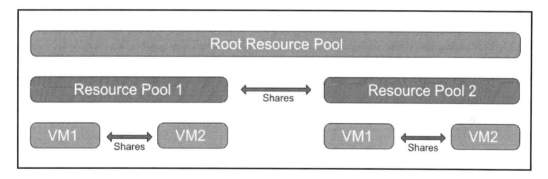

Keep in mind that the shares are only applied during contention. When there is no contention, they are not applied.

Reservations

Reservations specify the minimum allocation guaranteed to a VM. When the VM is powered on, the ESXi hypervisor assigns resources based on the specified minimum reservation regardless of whether the physical server is heavily loaded. Resources are allocated only when requested by the VM, and if the host's unallocated resources don't meet the reservation requirements, the VM cannot be powered on. The default reservation is set to 0.

To make it simple, if you make a reservation, the VM will always have a reserved amount of resources available, even during contention. When there is contention, VMs without a reservation must free up resources to the VMs with a reservation. For the remaining resources, the VMs will compete between each other based on the shares that they have.

Reservation, on the other hand, does not mean that the VM will lock such resources, and they will not be available for anybody else. If the VM does not use resources that are reserved, other VMs can freely use them.

Limits

Using limits, you can specify the maximum amount of resources a VM can use. If the limit is not set, a VM will consume up to the maximum amount of resources based on its configuration and the virtual hardware used. If a VM is configured with a limit, although it has some resources configured, it will never use more than specified by the limit. The default limit value is set to unlimited.

For example, you have a VM with 16 vCPUs, each running at 2.4 GHz, giving you a total of 38.4 GHz of computing resources, but you might want to configure the VM in a way that it will never consume more than 4.8 GHz of computing resources. From the guest OS perspective, it will have 16 CPUs, each running at 2.4 GHz.

CPU resources

For a vCPU, shares, reservation, and limit parameters can be configured:

- **Shares**: This parameter allows you to prioritize access to resources during resource contention. Shares determine how much CPU power in GHz will be provided to a VM.

- **Reservation**: This is used to specify the minimum CPU power in GHz guaranteed for a VM, and you can't reserve more CPU cycles than ESXi is capable of delivering. The host must have enough physical CPU capacity to satisfy the reservation; otherwise, the VM won't be able to power on.
- **Limit**: This is used to prevent a VM from accessing additional CPU power in GHz, even if they are available. The VM won't use more CPU cycles than specified in the limit.

To configure shares, reservation, and limit CPU parameters, follow these steps:

1. Right-click the VM to configure and select **Edit Settings**
2. Access the **Virtual Hardware** tab and expand the **CPU** item
3. Configure the parameters you need, and then click **OK** to confirm:

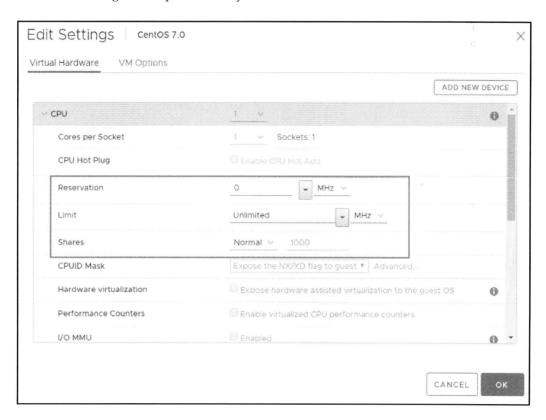

To improve resource management, CPU configuration can be enhanced by enabling additional components and parameters:

- **Hyperthreading**: This is a technology that allows a single physical processor core to behave like two logical processors. With this technology, a single processor core can execute two independent threads simultaneously, improving performance.
- **CPU affinity**: This is a configuration that assigns a specific VM to a specific physical CPU core and can be used for compliance to license requirements. CPU affinity should be used carefully because it can introduce potential issues, such as interfering with the ESXi host's ability to meet the reservation and shares that have been specified for a VM.

Memory resources

As with the CPU, shares, reservation, and limit are settings that are used to allocate and manage memory resources for a VM.

To configure shares, reservation, and limit parameters, proceed as follows:

1. Right-click the VM to configure and select **Edit Settings**
2. Access the **Virtual Hardware** tab and expand the **Memory** item
3. Set the appropriate values and then click **OK** to confirm:

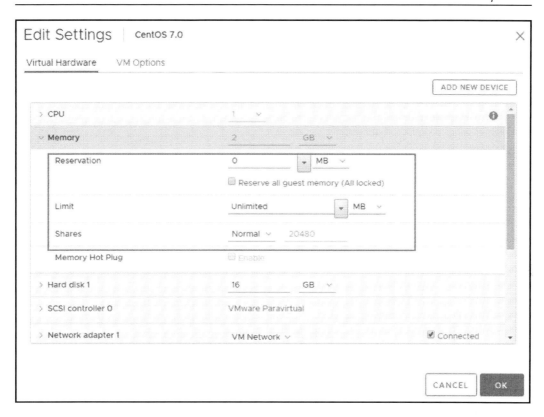

Although it is possible to configure the limit for memory resources, you should avoid doing that all costs because it will significantly affect the performance of the VM.

If you use a limit, from the perspective of the guest OS, the configured amount of memory will be presented, but only the subset of the memory will be physically available. *What about the rest of the resource?* You are right. It will be swapped at the ESXi level.

Although ESXi memory swapping is one memory reclamation technique, you should avoid it at all costs, because the guest OS is not aware of such swapping. This means it cannot effectively distribute the memory from within the guest OS.

Let's have a look at the following example:

- You have configured a VM with 8 GB of memory
- A limit is configured at 6 GB of memory

What is the result? The guest OS thinks it has 8 GB memory available, thus it is acting accordingly, but in reality, only 6 GB of memory is backed up with the physical memory of the ESXi host, and the swap file is backing the remaining amount of the memory (2 GB).

Since this is transparent to the guest OS, it is not able to manage the memory effectively and decide what parts of the programs should be placed in the swap file and what parts are actively used.

 It is always preferred to use swap on the guest OS level because in this case, the guest OS can effectively distribute the memory to the active applications.

VM swapping

By default, the swap file for each VM is created when you power it on, and it will be stored within the folder of the VM in a specific datastore.

The size of the VM's swap file equals the size of the VM's configured memory, unless you use reservations for the memory.

When no reservation is configured, the ESXi host cannot guarantee the amount of memory that will be served from physical memory and the size of memory that might be swapped due to contention.

When you reserve all memory for the VM, no swap file will be created because the ESXi hypervisor will ensure that the VM will always get the physical resources it needs.

If you set a partial reservation for the VM, the size of the swap file equals the configured memory size, minus the reservation.

ESXi host memory states

In times of contention, the ESXi host will use different techniques that allow you to overprovision the memory assignment for the VMs. As we already explained, overcommitment means that you assign more virtual resources than your physical hypervisor has. This is quite a common approach, but you need to be aware of what happens once all the VMs start to utilize such resources. This situation is called **contention**.

We have two different contentions when talking about resources: CPU and memory contention. There is nothing specific regarding CPU contention—the shares will simply kick in and the VMs will get the only subset of configured resources based on the shares. But for memory, it is more complicated.

vSphere 6.7 uses different reclamation techniques that you may already know from previous versions:

- **Transparent page sharing** (TPS)
    - Memory ballooning
    - Memory compression
    - Memory swapping

The memory reclamation technique you choose depends on the ESXi host's memory state. This is determined by the amount of memory available at a given time in the ESXi host.

If the amount of free memory is lower than a certain amount, different reclamation techniques will be used to free pages from physical memory.

There are five memory states of the ESXi hypervisor:

- **High state**: Enough free memory available
- **Clear state**: <100% of minFree
- **Soft state**: <64% of minFree
- **Hard state**: <32% of minFree
- **Low state**: <16% of minFree

You can quickly discover which memory state your ESXi hypervisor is in by using the `esxtop` command:

1. Connect to your ESXi hypervisor using `SSH`
2. Issue the `esxtop` command

3. Press *m* to switch to the memory view:

minFree is a dynamic value that depends on ESXi's physical memory configuration. For the first 28 GB of physical memory, minFree is set to 899 MB. For every 1 GB above 28 GB, you need to add 1% to memFree.

You can determine a minFree memory size based on the following table:

Physical memory	High state/clear state	Soft state	Hard state	Low state
28 GB	899 MB	575 MB	288 MB	143 MB
32 GB	939 MB	601 MB	300 MB	150 MB
48 GB	1,099 MB	703 MB	352 MB	176 MB
64 GB	1,259 MB	805 MB	403 MB	201 MB
128 GB	1,899 MB	1,215 MB	608 MB	304 MB
256 GB	3,179 MB	2,034 MB	1,017 MB	508 MB
384 GB	4,459 MB	2,854 MB	1,427 MB	713 MB
512 GB	5,739 MB	3,672 MB	1,836 MB	918 MB
768 GB	8,299 MB	5,311 MB	2,656 MB	1,328 MB
1,024 GB	10,859 MB	6,950 MB	3,475 MB	1,737 MB

Depending on the memory state, different memory reclamation techniques are invoked:

Memory state	Transparent Page Sharing	Ballooning	Compression	Swapping	Blocking
High	Standard TPS cycles				
Clear	ESXi actively calls TPS to collapse pages				
Soft	X	X			
Hard	X		X	X	

Memory state	Transparent Page Sharing	Ballooning	Compression	Swapping	Blocking
Low	X		X	X	X

Again, using `esxtop`, you can see what memory techniques are currently invoked and the amount of reclaimed memory:

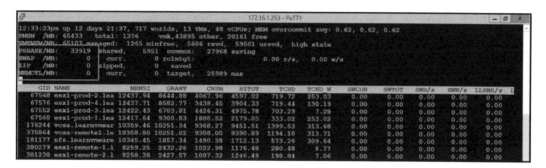

The following metrics are related to the ESXi reclamation techniques:

- `PSHARE`: Memory reclaimed using TPS
- `SWAP` : Memory reclaimed using ESXi host swapping
- `ZIP`: Memory reclaimed using compression
- `MEMCTL`: Memory reclaimed using ballooning

You can quickly identify your overall memory reclamation techniques that are in use from the vSphere client for each cluster:

1. Select the cluster you are interested in
2. Switch to the **Monitor** tab
3. Navigate to **Utilization**

Guest Memory is the graph you are interested in:

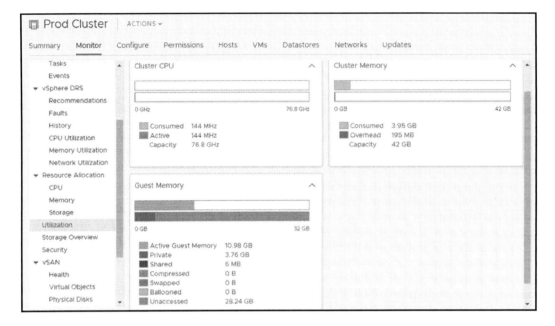

You can identify different memory reclamation techniques that are currently invoked by the ESXi hypervisor following this procedure:

1. Select your ESXi hypervisor
2. Switch to the **Monitor** tab
3. Click **Advanced** under **Performance**
4. Select the **Memory** view
5. Click **Chart Options**
6. Select the **Ballooned memory**, **Compressed**, **Shared**, and **Swap consumed** metrics:

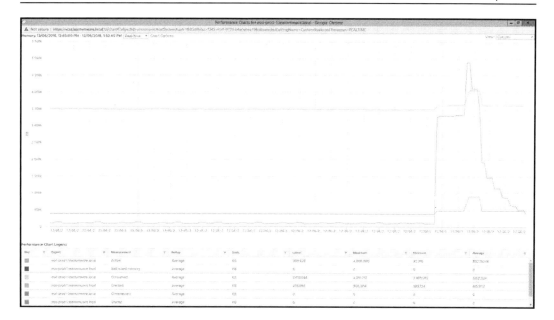

TPS

TPS has been around for a long time, and its purpose is to save memory at the host level. It is similar to storage deduplication, but this time focusing on the memory.

When multiple instances of VMs are run on the same ESXi hypervisor and access the same memory pages, they are stored only once. With TPS, the hypervisor will eliminate the redundant memory pages by mapping the identical content in only one memory page in the physical memory.

The TPS mechanism runs in the background and calculates a hash of the memory page. Those hashes are stored in a hash table and they are compared to each other by the ESXi server. If the ESXi kernel discovers two corresponding hashes, it will compare the content of the memory page. If the content is exactly the same, then only one memory page will be stored in the physical memory and the other one will be pointed to the same location.

Two types of memory sharing techniques are available:

- **Intra-VM:** Memory pages within the same VM will be deduplicated by TPS, but TPS will not share the memory pages between different VMs.
- **Inter-VM**: Memory pages within the same VM will be deduplicated by TPS and TPS will share the memory pages between different VMs.

There was a major change with vSphere 6.0 and Inter-VM TPS is now disabled by default.

There is no real-world example of exploiting Inter-VM memory sharing to inject malicious code as far we know, but as a security hardening best-practice, the behavior was rather changed.

If you are running a Service Provider environment, you should probably keep the settings at the default to prevent any malicious misuse of the feature. However, if you need, you can change the default behavior.

There are three possible values of `Mem.ShareForceSalting`:

- 2: Default value. No Intra-VM TPS
- 1: Intra-VM TPS will be used for VMs with the same `sched.mem.pshare.salt` advanced configuration option.
- 0: Inter-VM TPS works as expected.

For more informations about Intra-VM TPS, feel free to visit the following KB: `https://kb.vmware.com/s/article/2097593`.

 For Enterprise companies, I would suggest to switch to the old behavior and enabling Inter-VM TPS since the benefits of the TPS will—from my perspective—outweigh the possible security concerns. For service providers—from my perspective—I would use the same salt for all VMs belonging to the same customer, so the result will be that VMs from a single tenant can share memory pages between each other, but they can't share memory pages between different tenants.

Please note that `Mem.ShareForceSalting` is a per-host setting and `sched.mem.pshare.salt` is a per-VM setting.

You can change the `Mem.ShareForceSalting` settings from the vSphere client by following these steps:

1. Select your ESXi hypervisor
2. Switch to the **Configure** tab
3. Locate **Advanced System Settings** under **System**
4. Click **Edit**
5. Locate the `Mem.ShareForceSalting` configuration parameter and change it to the desired value, as shown in the following screenshot:

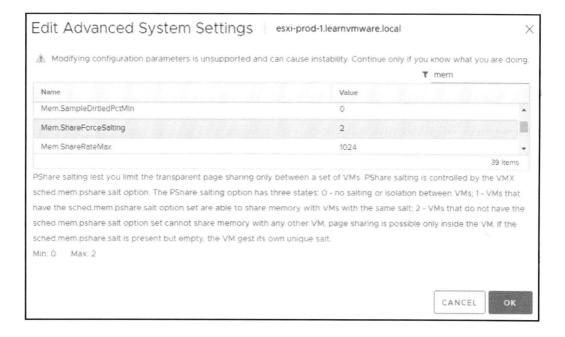

Ballooning

The hypervisor uses a memory reclamation technique called **memory ballooning** to reclaim the memory from a VM.

The ESXi server is not aware of the content of the memory page of the VM. Only the guest operating system knows what is inside and which memory pages are more important than the others.

That is why the balloon driver is an essential memory reclamation technique. Memory ballooning is not happening at the ESXi level but inside of each VM. As a part of VM tools, a specific balloon driver is installed into the guest operating system—vmmemctl.sys. As you already know, any driver running inside of the guest operating system, no matter whether the VM is Windows- or Linux-based, is run on the kernel level, thus having more significant priority over the user-space where the applications are being run.

As the balloon driver is invoked from within the guest operating system, the underlying operating system knows what is running inside and can decide what will be swapped to the virtual disk where the operating system is installed.

Let's have a look at the following example.

When there is no contention (the host is not in soft memory state), the balloon driver is deflated, consuming almost no memory resources, but when the contention occurs, the balloon driver starts to inflate. As we mentioned earlier, because it is from within the guest operating system, the OS will determine by itself what memory pages are not used (but still active) or are not accessed frequently. Those memory pages (in the virtual memory of the guest OS) will be swapped to the virtual disk. Once the contention is over, the memory balloon will deflate and the guest operating system will swap the memory pages from the system back to the virtual memory.

By default, the balloon driver (vmmemctl.sys) can reclaim up to a maximum of 65% of the physical guest memory. For example, your VM is allocated with 4,096 MB of memory. It can reclaim up to 2,662 MB using this technique.

Compression

ESXi provides a memory compression cache to improve VM performance whenever you use memory overcommitment. Memory compression is enabled by default. ESXi compresses virtual pages and stores them in memory when a host's memory becomes overcommitted.

 For more information, take a look at the following PDF: https://pubs.vmware.com/vsphere-51/topic/com.vmware.ICbase/PDF/vsphere-esxi-vcenter-server-51-resource-management-guide.pdf.

By default, up to 10% of VM memory can be compressed—the advanced system parameter Mem.MemZipMaxPct determines this value. The value is a percentage of the size of the VM and must be between 5 and 100 percent.

Compression is enabled by default, but if you want, you can disable the memory compression mechanism by using the `Mem.MemZipEnable` advanced system parameter.

Host swapping

This is the last resort technique that you do not want to be in. Since host swapping use the underlying storage infrastructure to swap page files from the memory to the disk and it is not aware of the content of the memory pages, it will significantly impact the performance of the VMs.

System swap is determinated automatically by the kernel of the ESXi server. You can alter the behavior by changing the **preferred swap location**. If no feasible option is available, then the system swap is not activated at all.

On the ESXi level, you can define the default location of the ESXi swap location:

1. Select your ESXi server
2. Switch to **Configure** tab
3. Select **System swap** under the **System**
4. Click **Edit** settings

Virtual machine migration

In vSphere 6.7, VMs can be moved from one host or storage to another using hot or cold migration. Wherever possible, hot migration is the preferred option to use to avoid service disruption because it performs a live migration of the VMs:

- **Hot migration**: A powered-on VM can be moved to a different host or datastore without service disruption using the vMotion or Storage vMotion features.
- **Cold migration**: This is the migration of a powered-off or suspended VM. You can move associated disks from one datastore to another and VMs are not required to be on shared storage. A cold migration can be performed manually or by scheduling a task.

There are two types of vMotion:

- Compute vMotion (otherwise known as standard vMotion) is responsible for migrating active state (the content of VM memory) between two ESXi hosts
- Storage vMotion (SvMotion) is responsible for the migration of the storage resources between two different datastores

Compute vMotion

vMotion has been around for more than fifteen years. The first version was introduced in 2003, which means it is a mature technology.

vMotion utilizes a similar technology (similar based on its behavior, but completely different from a technical perspective) as a snapshot. When you invoke vMotion, a snapshot of the memory is created, allowing new write operations to memory to be stored in a dedicated, known, section. Then, the content of the memory is migrated, and in the end, the data that has changed during the vMotion invocation are synced.

You might be wondering why you should use vMotion, so there is a list of several tasks that involves the use of vMotion:

- **ESXi maintenance mode**: If you have a DRS-enabled cluster, DRS will automatically migrate VMs from the ESXi host that is going into maintenance mode.
- **Troubleshooting**: You are experiencing one of the VMs behaving strangely. You can try to migrate it to a different ESXi hypervisor to determine if the problem is widespread or is only occurring on a single ESXi server.
- **Cluster balancing**: DRS might invoke vMotion to move VMs around the cluster for better resource balance.
- **Host standby:** DPM might invoke vMotion to move VMs from the ESXi host that is going into standby mode.
- **Affinity rules:** Some VMs should not be run together or should be run on the same ESXi hypervisor. If not, vMotion will be used to correct the situation.

Although it might sound like an easy task, many things are going on under the hood:

1. As a first step, vCenter server will validate whether the source VM can be run on the destination server.
2. Then, a new VM process is started on the second ESXi server and resources for the VM are reserved.
3. A memory checkpoint is initialized on the source VM so that all changes in the memory are written to the dedicated memory section.
4. The content of the memory is transferred over the network to the destination ESXi hypervisor.
5. Changes in memory during the transfer are again checkpointed and synced with the destination ESXi hypervisor. The checkpoint/checkpoint-restore operation might repeat several times.
6. The source VM is stopped and the remaining memory fragments are synced to the destination.
7. Once the vMotion process is finished, a reverse ARP packet is sent to the physical switches.

The **Notify Switches** option must be enabled on the virtual switch). Hard disk access is switched to the destination ESXi server.

8. The VM process running on the the source ESX hypervisor is terminated and deleted.

As stated, there will be multiple iterations of the memory checkpoints. The reason behind this is that if the VM is configured with a lot of memory and the memory is actively used, the delta between the creation of the checkpoint and the resulting changes will be quite large, meaning that the VM will be suspended for a quite long period. Therefore, multiple checkpoints are created when using vMotion.

Let's have a look at the following example:

Iteration number	Memory to transfer	Time for the transfer	Changes during the memory transfer
1	16,384 MB	30 seconds	3,072 MB
2	3,072 MB	8 seconds	512 MB
3	512 MB	2 seconds	64 MB
4	64 MB	0.25 seconds	4 MB

Iteration number	Memory to transfer	Time for the transfer	Changes during the memory transfer
5	4 MB	VM freeze for takeover	No new delta checkpoint created

vCenter server is responsible for validation, and it invokes the vMotion process on the ESXi hypervisors, but it is not involved in the actual data transfer. Therefore, an active vMotion process must always be allowed to run to completion, even if the vCenter server crashes.

As with any technology, specific prerequisites need to be met:

- The ESXi hypervisor must be licensed for vMotion
- The ESXi hypervisor must be configured with a VMkernel adapter with the vMotion service enabled on the adapter
- The ESXi hypervisor must have the same physical CPU or EVC must be configured
- The ESXi hypervisor must have shared storage accessible by the source and destination ESXi hypervisor

Moreover, there are of course certain limitations as well, which can be found at http://www.vmwarearena.com/vmware-interview-questions-vmotion/.

The migration of a VM is performed by following this procedure:

1. From vSphere Client, log in to vCenter Server, right-click the VM to move, and click the **Migrate** option.
2. In the migrate window, select the migration type to perform, choosing from the following options:
    - **Change computer resource only**: The VM is moved to a different compute resources, such as host, cluster, resource pool, or vApp. A powered-on VM is moved using vMotion.
    - **Change storage only**: The VM disks are moved to a different datastore on the same host. The storage vMotion feature is used to move a powered-on VM to a new datastore.
    - **Change both compute resource and storage**: Virtual disks are moved to a new datastore and computer resources are moved to another host. Cold or hot migration can be used to change the host and datastore. If the network of the VM is moved between distributed switches, network configuration and policies are transferred to the target switch.

3. Based on the migration type selected, you must then specify the compute resource, storage location, and vMotion priority (high or normal) to finalize the migration.

4. You also have the option to change the vNIC assignment during the vMotion invocation (such as changing the Port Group to which the VM belongs); this is handy if you do not use a distributed vSwitch, and the naming convention is not the same on the source and destination ESXi hypervisor.

Starting from vSphere 6.0, vMotion has been enhanced, introducing new functionalities such as Cross vSwitch vMotion, **Cross vCenter vMotion (xVC-vMotion)**, and **Long Distance vMotion (LD-vMotion)**:

- **Migrate to another virtual switch**: A VM can be migrated to a different type of virtual switch (standard or distributed) without reconfiguring the physical and virtual network. You can move the VM from a standard to a standard or distributed switch and from a distributed to another distributed switch.
- **Migrate to another datacenter:** During the migration, you can specify the target data center to move the VM between data centers. In the target data center, you can specify a dedicated port group on a distributed switch for network settings.
- **Migrate to another vCenter Server system:** VMs can be moved between vCenter Servers if they are connected in Enhanced Linked Mode, and also between vCenter servers that are located a long distance from each other.

Please note that it is even possible to migrate to a different vCenter server that is not connected using Linked Mode. Although this functionality is presented in the APIs, it is not possible to use the UI to invoke such a migration.

If you are interested in Shared-Nothing Cross vCenter Server migrations, you can use the Cross vCenter Workload Migration Utility, which is available at `https://labs.vmware.com/flings/cross-vcenter-workload-migration-utility`.

You can see **Cross vCenter Workload Migration Utility** GUI in the following screenshot:

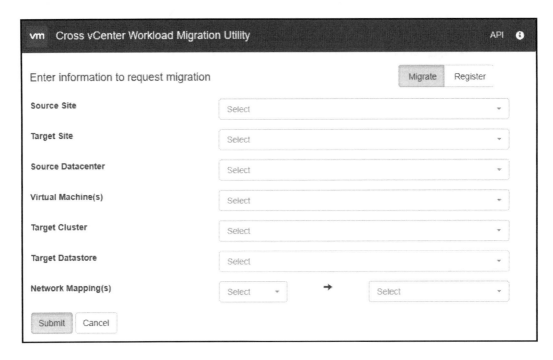

Storage vMotion

Storage vMotion works the same way as compute vMotion. The only difference is that the virtual disks and VM configuration files are moved between different datastores, not the memory between ESXi hypervisors.

Under the hood, again, a type of snapshot technology is used. When you invoke the storage vMotion, a new snapshot file is created on the datastore, and all write operations are performed on the snapshot. A base disk is switched to the read-only state so that the **Storage vMotion (SvM)** process can access it and the copy between datastores starts. Once the main VMDK file is transferred, the snapshot on the first snapshot is created, and the first snapshot is copied and merged to the base disk on the destination datastore. This process will be performed several times until only a small amount of data will be on the source datastore. At this time, again, the same as with compute vMotion, the VM is frozen, and the remaining bytes are copied and synced, and the VM is resumed from the new datastore.

The process of how to invoke storage vMotion is the same as with compute vMotion:

1. Select a VM and open the **Migrate** wizard.
2. Select the **Change storage only** option.
3. Select the destination datastore to which you would like to move the VM. You can also change the disk format from thin to thick or attach a different storage policy:

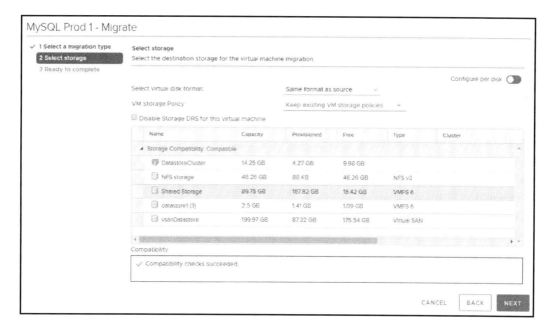

vMotion without shared storage

To perform vMotion, environments with shared storage are not required. For example, you can migrate a running VM between ESXi hosts with only local storage. When migrating a VM cross-cluster, the target cluster VM might not have access to the source cluster's storage.

Let's have a look at the VM that runs on a local datastore on the **esxi-prod-1** hypervisor. If we choose to migrate the compute resource only, the wizard will not allow us to migrate the VM to any other ESXi hypervisor, since the VM is backed up with local storage:

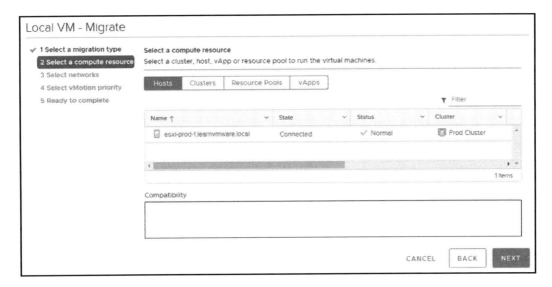

However, if we select **Change both compute resource and storage**, we will be able to migrate the VM to a different ESXi hypervisor and shared storage:

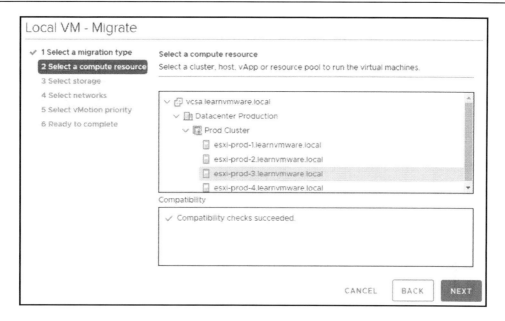

DRS

As discussed in `Chapter 5`, *Configuring and Managing vSphere 6.7*, a vSphere cluster is a collection of ESXi hosts that share resources and a management interface. Some of the vSphere's features are available only on the cluster level and DRS is one of them. Once the DRS is enabled on the cluster, the capability to automatically balance loads across the ESXi hosts will be available. vSphere DRS provides two main functions:

- Executing the placement of the just-powered-on VM on a specific host in the cluster
- Periodically (every 5 minutes by default), DRS checks the load on the cluster, providing recommendations for migration or automatically migrate the VM (using vMotion) to get a balanced cluster

If you have a DRS-enabled cluster and one of the hosts is heavily loaded compared to other host members, you might notice DRS doesn't vMotion any running VM off the host, leaving the workload unchanged. Until the ESXi host can satisfy resource demand from the VM, DRS doesn't perform any action. DRS ensures that the cluster is balanced, regardless of the workloads distributed on individual host members. To get balanced clusters and host members, there are third-party applications that provide real-time automation to allocate resources efficiently.

You can find a basic overview of your cluster's balance in the **Summary** tab of your vSphere cluster, as shown in the following screenshot:

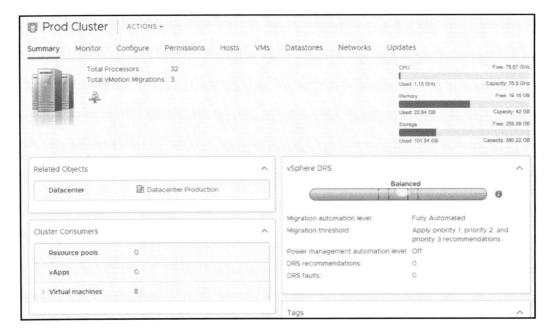

When a VM in a DRS-enabled cluster is powered on, the vCenter Server checks whether the cluster has enough resources to support the VM, that is, it performs admission control. If the available resources in the cluster are not sufficient to power on the VM, a warning message appears. If the resources are sufficient to support the VM, a recommendation on which host the VM should run is generated by the DRS and, based on the automation level configured in the cluster, one of the following actions is taken:

- The placement recommendation is executed automatically

- The placement recommendation is displayed, leaving the user with the option to accept or override

When DRS is disabled, no recommendations are provided, and VMs are not moved among the cluster's hosts.
To enable DRS in a cluster, proceed as follows:

1. From the vSphere client, log into vCenter Server and right-click the cluster in which you want to enable DRS and select **Settings**.
2. Under **Services**, select **vSphere DRS** and click the **Edit** button.

3. Enable the vSphere DRS option, and from the Automation drop-down menu, select the level of automation you want to apply to the cluster:
   - **Manual**: Placement and migration recommendations are displayed, but must be applied manually
   - **Partially Automated**: The initial placement is performed automatically, but migration recommendations are only displayed without running
   - **Fully Automated**: Placement and migration recommendations run automatically:

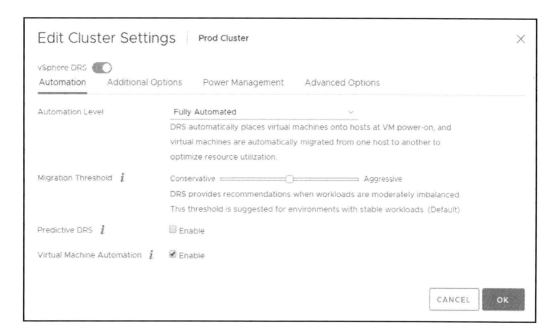

4. Select your **Migration Threshold:**
   - **Priority 1**: Those recommendations are not based on cluster imbalance but rather on system requirements such as anti-affinity and affinity rules, maintenance mode, or DPM.
   - **Priority 2 to 5**: Based on the cost/benefit of the VM migration, DRS rules are generated for priority 2 to 5. This configuration option basically adjusts the sensitivity of the DRS.

   For more information about DRS migration thresholds, feel free to visit the following website: `https://blogs.vmware.com/vsphere/2016/10/drs-migration-thresholds.html`.

5. If you have vRealize Operations in place, you can also enable **Predictive DRS**. With Predictive DRS, migration can occur even before your cluster is unbalanced based on historical data.
6. **Virtual Machine Automation** is enabled by default, and it gives you the option to override the automation level on a per-VM basis.

If you need to, you can also check the advanced parameters of DRS:

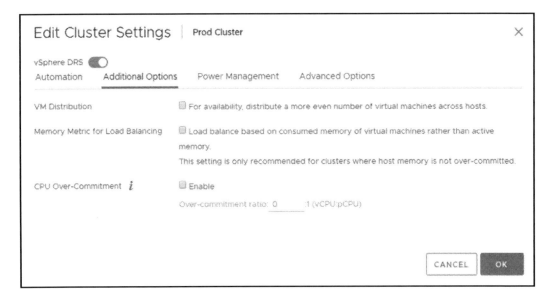

- **VM Distribution**: This setting overrules this logic and incurs the cost of migration to achieve a more even distribution of VMs. Please note that this setting will still keep VM happiness in mind, so even the distribution of VMs is done on a best-effort basis.

- **Memory Metric for Load Balancing:** This setting can be helpful for environments that attempt to minimize the impact of host failures or attempt to balance the load on network IP connections across the ESXi hosts in the cluster. Please note that this setting can increase the number of VM migrations without specifically benefitting the application's performance.

- **CPU Over-Commitment:** By default, DRS uses a default CPU over-commit (vCPU to pCPU) ratio that is approximately 80 to 1. A latency-sensitive workload can benefit from a lower CPU over-commit ratio by reducing the number of vCPUs waiting to be scheduled. This setting limits the number of vCPUs that can be powered on in the vSphere cluster.

 If DRS is disabled, resource pools configured in the cluster are removed.

Virtual network-aware DRS

Virtual network-aware DRS is a new feature that was introduced in vSphere 6.5, where DRS now also considers the network utilization when it generates the migration recommendations. If a host has **Transmit (Tx)** and **Receive (Rx)** rates of utilization of the connected physical uplinks that's greater than 80%, the VM won't be placed on that host. Network utilization is an additional check to evaluate whether a specific host is suitable for the VM.

Managing DRS rules

VM placement can be controlled using affinity rules. Affinity rules are useful for administrators to control how specific VMs should be placed in the host members of the cluster for performance and security reasons.

Let's have a look at the DRS-supported affinity rules.

VM-VM affinity rule

The VM-VM affinity rule is used to specify that selected VMs should run on the same host. You can configure this rule to improve performance. The anti-affinity rule behaves in precisely the opposite way, and it's used to ensure that some VMs are kept on different hosts.

Anti-affinity can be applied to AD domain controllers, for example, to keep them on different hosts to avoid AD issues in case one host fails. Only the DC running on the failed host is not available, while the others won't be affected, continuing to provide the authentication service with no interruption.

You can't enable two affinity rules if they clash. For example, if one rule is configured to keep VMs together and another rule keeps the same VMs separated, you can't enable both. In the event of a conflict between two affinity rules, the first rule takes precedence and the newer rule is disabled, as you can see in the following screenshot:

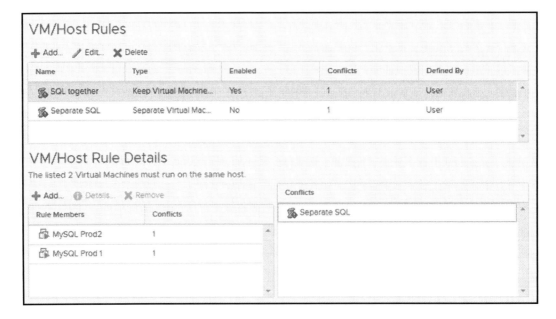

To create a VM-VM affinity rule, perform these steps:

1. From vSphere Client, right-click the cluster that you want to configure and select **Settings**.
2. Under **Configuration**, select **VM/Host Rules** and click the **Add** button.
3. Enter a name and select from the **Type** drop-down menu one of the available options:
   - **Keep Virtual Machines Together**: The specified VMs are kept together on the same host
   - **Separate Virtual Machines**: The specified VMs are separated on different hosts
4. Click the **Add** button to specify the VMs that must run with the specified rule. Click **OK** to save the configuration.

VM-Host affinity rule

The VM-Host affinity rule allows you to control which hosts in the cluster can run which VMs and requires that at least one VM DRS group and at least one host DRS group are created before managing host affinity rules.

The typical use case is about licensing, where only a subset of ESXi hosts are licensed for a particular software that the VM consumes; Oracle, for example. Without DRS, you would need either a dedicated cluster for Oracle VMs (because you need to assign an Oracle license to each physical server where the VM might run), or, by using DRS affinity rules, you can specify the subset of hosts that will be used by such VMs.

To create a VM-Host affinity rule, proceed as follows:

1. From vSphere Client, right-click the cluster to configure and select the **Settings** option.
2. Under **Configuration**, select **VM/Host group** and click on the **Add** button to create a VM group and a host group.
3. Specify a name and select from the **Type** drop-down menu the VM group. Click the **Add** button to add members to this group, and then click **OK** to save the configuration.
4. Repeat steps 2 and 3 to create a host group.
5. Now, under **Configuration**, select **VM/Host Rules** and click the **Add** button.

6. Enter a name and select from the **Type** drop-down menu the **Virtual Machines to Hosts**. Specify **VM Group** and the rule (for example, **Must run on hosts in a group**), select the **Host Group** to associate, and click **OK** to save the rule:

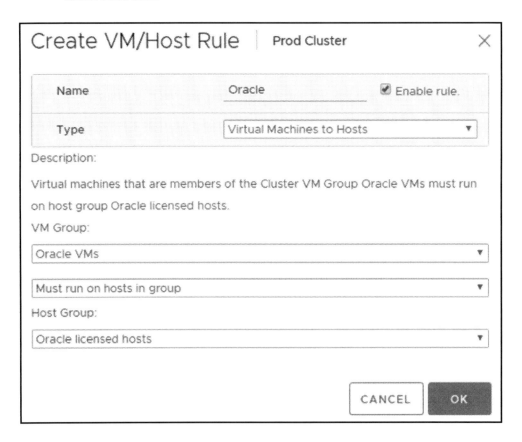

The options available for the rule can be one of the following:

- **Must run on hosts in group**: VMs in the selected VM group must run on host members of the specified host group. DRS will never break the rule, nor will vSphere HA. If there is only one ESXi host in the group, HA will not restart the server on the other nodes.
- **Should run on hosts in group**: VMs in the VM group should run on hosts of the specified host group, but it is not required. DRS will try its best to satisfy the rule, but in some cases, the rule might be broken.
- **Must not run on hosts in group**: VMs in the VM group must never run on host members of the specified host group. DRS will never break the rule.

- **Should not run on hosts in group**: VMs in the VM Group should not, but might, run on hosts of the specified host group. DRS will try its best to satisfy the rule, but in some cases, the rule might be broken.

DRS recommendations

If your DRS cluster is set to partially automated or manual mode, no migrations will be performed automatically by the DRS algorithm. You have to approve the recommendations manually.

You can check what recommendations are available in the Monitor tab of the DRS enabled cluster under vSphere DRS and Recommendations:

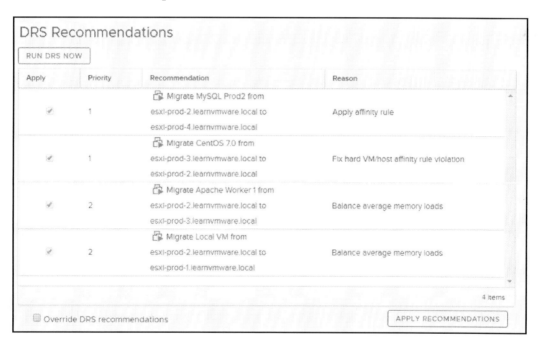

You can either apply all recommendations using the **APPLY RECOMMENDATIONS** button, or you can override them by selecting **Override DRS recommendations** and then select what recommendations you would like to apply.

Once you apply the DRS recommendation, vMotion will be issued to move the VMs between ESXi hypervisors.

In DRS history section, you can find what migrations were performed by DRS and when were they performed.

DRS utilization

DRS decisions are based on the overall utilization of your DRS-enabled cluster, and you can find the current utilization of three key components that are part of DRS decisions under the **Monitor** tab of the cluster, access the vSphere DRS subsection and select either CPU, memory, or network utilization:

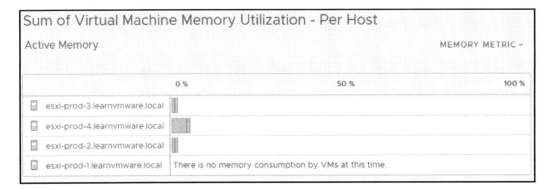

For memory utilization, you can switch between consumed and active memory consumption.

Managing power resources

Based on cluster resource utilization, a DRS-enabled cluster can reduce its power consumption by powering on or off ESXi hosts through the vSphere **Distributed Power Management (DPM)** feature.

Memory and CPU resources demanded by VMs in the cluster are compared with the total resource capacity that's available from the hosts in the cluster. If the cluster is providing excessive resources, one or more hosts are placed in standby mode by DPM and powered off after migrating the VM to other hosts. When the capacity that's provided is deemed not sufficient, DRS powers the host on, bringing them out of standby mode and vMotions the VMs to them.

vSphere DPM can use three protocols to bring a host out of standby mode:

- **Intelligent Platform Management Interface (IPMI)**
- Hewlett Packard **Integrated Lights-Out (iLO)**
- **Wake-On-LAN (WOL)**

vSphere DPM can put a host in standby mode only if at least one protocol is supported. If a host supports multiple protocols, the following order is used: IPMI, iLO, WOL.
Before you can start using DPM, you must configure the IPMI/iLO/WOL configuration for each ESXi host. To do that, perform the following operation for each ESXi hypervisor:

1. Switch to the **Configure** tab of the ESXi hypervisor
2. Navigate to **System** and select **Power management**
3. Click **Edit** to configure the IPMI/iLO settings for power management:

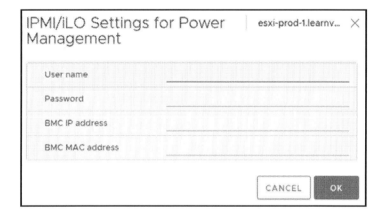

User name and **Password** are the credentials for the out-of-band management module. **BMC IP address** is the IP address of the module. You must also configure the MAC address of the BMC because it will be used for the Wake-On-Lan feature if IPMI / iLO communication fails.

After you configure the IPMI/iLO settings, do not forget to test the communication with the BMC module; otherwise, DPM might shut down the server, but powering on won't work. To do that, right-click on the ESXi hypervisor, and select **Power** and **Enter Standby Mode** to shut down the server. Once the server is offline, you can select the **Power On** operation to bring the server up.

You can invoke power management features of the ESXi server from the vSphere client as shown in the following screenshot:

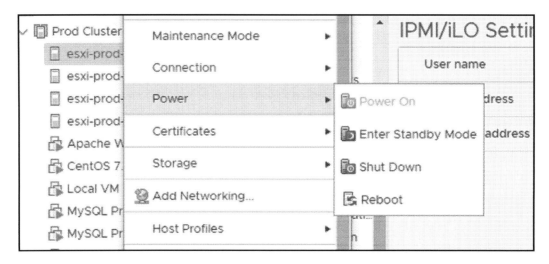

Resource pools and vApps

Resource pools are logical containers that can be used to allocate compute resources to a group of VMs (or child resource pools). The configuration options are exactly the same as with single VM—you can assign different reservations, shares, or limits for both CPU and memory resources on the resource pool, but compared to individual assignment to the VMs, resource pools provide a better and smoother management process and added scalability for the control of resources for groups of VMs.

Please note that resource pools can be used only in DRS-enabled clusters.

Resource pool configuration

To create a resource pool in a cluster (this procedure is similar for the single ESXi host), proceed as follows:

1. Right-click the cluster and select the **New Resource Pool** option.
2. Specify a name for the resource pool, giving a meaningful name that's useful to identify the resource scope better.

3. Specify how CPU and RAM resources should be allocated, and then click **OK**. When the resource pool has been created, you can start adding VMs to it. Share values set as **High**, **Normal**, or **Low** specify share values in a 4:2:1 ratio, as shown in the following screenshot:

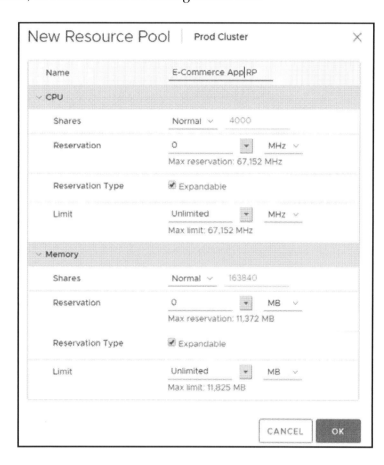

Reservations, **Limits**, and **Shares** work the same as with VMs. **Reservation Type** can be set to **Expandable** (we will discuss this specific type later).

Once you create a resource pool, you can quickly move VMs to the resource pool simply using the Drag and Drop function in the inventory.

You can also create a more complex structure of resource pools. Inside of the resource pool, you can create child resource pool(s) as well:

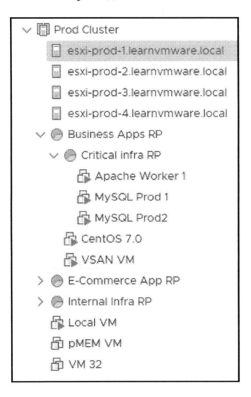

You may be wondering how resource pools work. To explain how they work, let's take a look at the following example. Three resource pools have been created that correspond to three different departments—**RP-PROD**, **RP-Internal**, and **RP-DEV**:

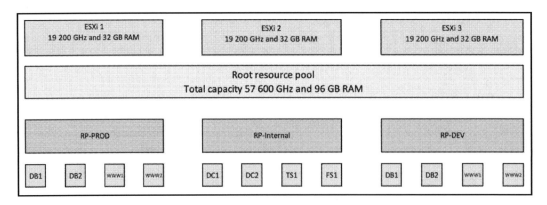

A configuration of the resource pools is shown in the following table:

Cluster	CPU shares	CPU limit	CPU reservation	Memory shares	Memory limit	Memory reservation
RP-PROD	Normal	Unlimited	20 GHz	Normal	Unlimited	32 GB
RP-Internal	Normal	Unlimited	10 GHz	Normal	Unlimited	16 GB
RP-DEV	Normal	10 GHz	0	Normal	16 GB	0

And following VMs are created:

VM	CPU	RAM	RP
DB1	8 vCPU / 19.2 GHz	16 GB	RP-PROD
DB2	8 vCPU / 19.2 GHz	16 GB	RP-PROD
WWW1	4 vCPU / 9.6 GHz	8 GB	RP-PROD
WWW2	4 vCPU / 9.6 GHz	8 GB	RP-PROD
DC1	1 vCPU / 2.4 GHz	4 GB	RP-Internal
DC2	1vCPU / 2.4 GHz	4 GB	RP-Internal
TS1	4v CPU / 9.6 GHz	12 GB	RP-Internal
FS1	2 vCPU / 9.6 GHz	8 GB	RP-Internal
WWW1	2 vCPU / 4.8 GHz	8 GB	RP-DEV
WWW2	2 vCPU / 4.8 GHz	8 GB	RP-DEV
DB1	4 vCPU / 9.6 GHz	16 GB	RP-DEV
DB2	4 vCPU / 9.6 GHz	16 GB	RP-DEV

Our clusters consist of three ESXi hosts, each containing eight physical CPU cores at 2.4 GHz and 32 GB RAM.

The overall cluster capacity is 57.6 GHz of CPU power and 96 GB RAM. If every VM consumes 100% of the configured resources, the total amount of required resources is 110.4 GHz and 124 GB of memory, which does not fit the cluster. Now, the resource pools come into play. Let's assume that all VMs are 100% utilized; *what will the resource allocation for the VMs be?*

First, the reservation must be satisfied. Based on that, we have 27.6 GHz of CPU power to be distributed and 48 GB of memory.

Resource pools are configured on the same level. Thus, the remaining resources are divided between resource pools using shares:

Resource pool	Reservation for CPU	Remaining resources based on shares for CPU	Total available resources for CPU	Reservation for memory	Remaining resources based on shares for memory	Total available resources for memory
RP-PROD	20 GHz	9.2 GHz	29.2 GHz	32 GB	16 GB	48 GB
RP-Internal	10 GHz	9.2 GHz	19.2 GHz	16 GB	16 GB	32 GB
RP-DEV	0	9.2 GHz	9.2 GHz	0	16 GB	16 GB

So now the shares, reservations, and limits will be applied if they are configured on the individual VMs within the resource pool. If no RLS on the VMs are configured, each VM will get an equal amount of resources, so in the case of RP-PROD VMs the allocation will be as follows (no RLS is configured on any VM):

VM	CPU	RAM	RP
DB1	7.3 GHz	16 GB	RP-PROD
DB2	7.3 GHz	16 GB	RP-PROD
WWW1	7.3 GHz	8 GB	RP-PROD
WWW1	7.3 GHz	8 GB	RP-PROD

Memory allocation is not affected because the total size of configured memory does not exceed the Total Available Resource for Memory, but the CPU will be throttled for the VMs since the required power is 57.6 GHz, but the Total Available Resource for CPU is 29.2 GHz.

Using resource pools, resources assigned to a group of VMs can be adjusted from a single point with no need to edit every single VM.

Keep in mind that you can configure RLS settings on multiple levels, so the resource hierarchy might be quite complicated to calculate.

Expandable resource pool

An expandable option is related to the reservation that's configured on the resource pool. If you use reservation on the VM, DRS makes sure that the resources are available and if not, the VM will not be started.

Imagine a situation where you have created a resource pool with 15 GHz of CPU resources and then four VMs, each with 5 GHz of CPU resources reserved.

If you try to power-on all of the VMs and expandable reservation is not checked, only the first three VMs will be powered on, not the last one.

Why? The first VM will claim 5 GHz of CPU resources from the RP (which has a reservation of 15 GHz), the second one and the third will do the same, but when the fourth VM tries to claim resources, there won't be enough resources since the remaining capacity of the resource pool is 0 GHz, and the VM wants to claim 5 GHz, as shown in the following diagram:

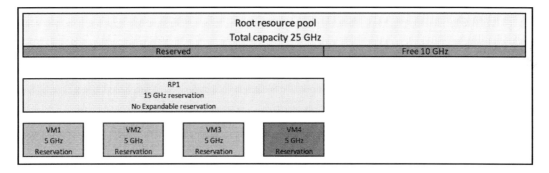

If you enable expandable reservation, the remaining capacity will be reserved on the parent resource pool (if multiple parent-child resource pools are configured) or from the root resource pool (total cluster capacity):

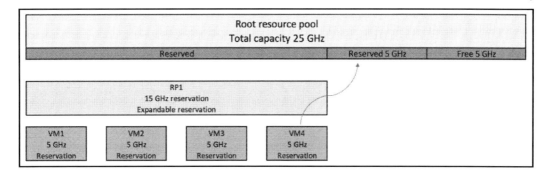

So, again, multiple resource pools (parent-child) can be configured, so if the expandable resource pool cannot satisfy the resource reservation, it will try to reserve the resources on the parent object. If the parent resource pool has the expandable option configured, it will try to reserve the resources on its parent object. If the expandable option is not enabled, the resource reservation fails, and the VM is not powered on.

Resource allocation monitoring and calculations

As you have already seen, working with the reservations, shares, and limits on multiple levels might be a tricky job, and unfortunately, there is no mechanism directly built into vSphere to help you with the calculations.

You can either use Excel or any other tool to calculate the resources and model what-if scenarios based on the resource consumption. You can use DRS Entitlement Viewer, a free tool available at VMware Labs (`https://labs.vmware.com/flings/drs-entitlement-viewer`).

DRS Entitlement Viewer is a small application that can integrate with the vSphere web client (HTML5 only), and it can do all the calculations for you:

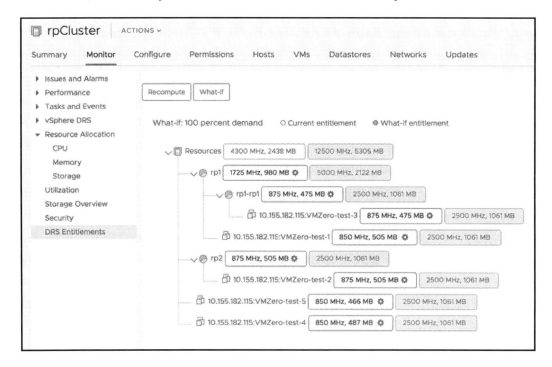

I would strongly suggest installing this Fling to your vSphere environment, especially if you are working with multiple resource pools and you have configured RLS settings on multiple items.

The installation is simple—all you need to do is download the Fling itself and follow these instructions:

1. Unzip the plugin package to the `/usr/lib/vmware-vsphere-ui/plugin-packages/` folder.
2. Add the advanced options to the cluster:
   - `CompressDrmdumpFiles`– 0
   - `DrmdumpResActions`– 1

3. Restart the vsphere-ui service:
   - `service-control --stop vsphere-ui`
   - `service-control --start vsphere-ui`

Once installed, you can see the new DRS entitlements section under the **Monitor** tab for each cluster.

Managing resource pools

Once created, you can edit, delete, add, or remove VMs from the resource pools:

- **Edit a resource pool**: From the vSphere client, right-click on the object and select **Edit Resource Settings**. Change the CPU and RAM settings and then click **OK** to confirm.
- **Delete a resource pool**: From the vSphere client, right-click the resource pool and select **Delete**. Click **OK** to confirm the deletion. Deleting a resource pool doesn't delete the VM it contains.
- **Adding a VM**: A VM can be added to a resource pool during the creation process using the migrate functionality or using the drag and drop feature.
- **Removing a VM**: From a resource pool, right-click on the VM to remove, and select the option **Migrate to move it to another resource pool**. Use the drag and drop feature to move a VM off the resource pool instead.

vApps

VMware vApps is perhaps one of the most underutilized features of vCenter Server. A vApp is an application container, such as a resource pool.

You can assign multiple VMs to a vApp and then treat this set of VMs as a single application. You can configure the startup and shutdown order of the VMs or monitor the utilization and health of the vApp itself, instead of individual VMs.

Let's imagine a situation—you have a two-tier application, consisting of two database servers and one web frontend server. Those VMs are used only for this e-commerce application, so you can create a vApp and move VMs inside the vApp. On the vApp level, you can configure the resource parameter in terms of reservations, limits, and shares for the whole vApp, not the individual VMs, and you can treat the vApp like a VM. Let's say you need to deploy another instance of the application. All you need to do is to clone the whole vApp instead of cloning all of the VMs. Lastly, you can configure the boot and shutdown order of the VMs within a vApp. First, you need to start the databases, and only after that do you start the web frontend.

Creating a vApp is a straightforward process:

1. In the **Hosts and Clusters** view, click in the inventory and select **New vApp**
2. A vApp can be created on the ESXi hypervisor, in a cluster, or even inside the parent resource pool
3. Provide a name and location for the vApp
4. You have an option to configure the resource allocation of the vApp, the same as with a resource pool
5. Review the settings and create a vApp

Once the vApp is created, you can drag and drop VMs to the vApp:

In the Hosts and Cluster view, you can see individual VMs in the vApp. In the **Virtual Machines and Templates** view, all you can see is the vApp itself.

You can configure the vApp to change the resource allocation settings or to configure the **Startup** and **Shutdown** order:

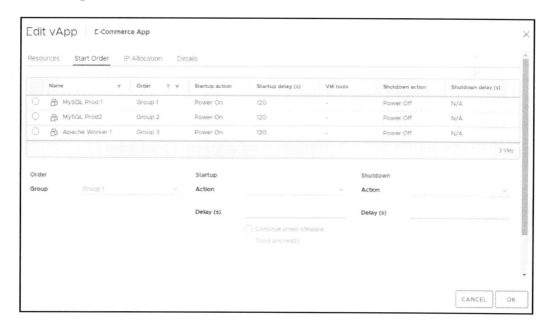

A VM within the vApp can be part of a single group, but multiple VMs can also be part of a single group. For instance, you have three web frontend servers. You do not care in which order the individual frontend servers start, but you need to start them only after the HTTP load balancer successfully starts. In such a case, you create two groups. Load balancers will be placed in **Group 1**, and all web frontend servers will be placed in **Group 2**.

Now, if you decide to shut down the whole vApp, you can click on the vApp and select shutdown or power off, and all VMs within the vApp will be turned off based on the start order.

Using the resource allocation on the vApp level, you can easily configure reserved resources for the vApp (the same as with resource pool) or the limits. Then, on the individual VMs inside the vApp, you can configure shares that will be applied during the resource contention of the vApp.

You can check the current vApp resource utilization in the **Monitor** tab of the **Utilization** section:

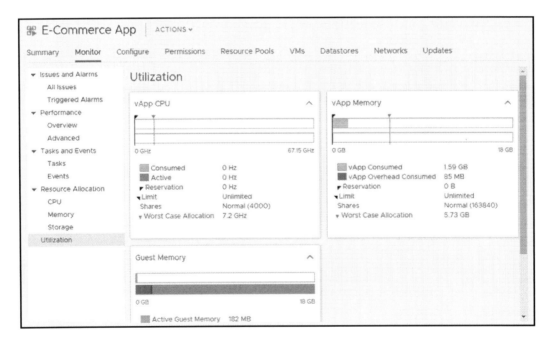

Network and storage resources

vSphere 6.7 includes additional resource management features that are useful for optimizing the virtual infrastructure performance and the efficiency of hardware components, such as storage devices and network resources.

Network resources can be allocated and controlled through the vSphere Network I/O Control feature to solve situations of resource contention. Network resources were discussed in `Chapter 7`, *Managing Networking Resources*.

Storage I/O Control (SIOC), **Storage DRS (SDRS)**, **Storage-Based Policy Management (SBPF)**, and other storage-related features (they were covered in `Chapter 8`, *Managing Storage Resources*), are used to control and optimize storage performance and resource availability.

From the single VM perspective, the configuration is the same as with computing resources. You can configure reservations, limits, and shares for both network and storage resources.

Summary

This chapter explained how to allocate resources to VMs in an efficient way to avoid overcommitment of resources, which can compromise performance and infrastructure functionality. We have explained how reservations, limits, and shares can be configured and how they affect the overall performance of the VMs using the **Distributed Resource Scheduler (DRS)** and resource pools.

VMs can be hot or cold migrated to different hosts or different storage devices using the vMotion and Storage vMotion features. Keep in mind that shared storage is not a requirement for vMotion.

vApps can be also used to manage the entire application as a single logical container that consists of multiple VMs, and it allows you to fine-tune the resource allocation in the same way as the resource pools.

The next chapter will cover different high availability features of VMware vSphere, such as vSphere HA and Fault Tolerance. We will also cover different disaster recovery techniques, such as vSphere Replication and Site Recovery Manager, as well as business continuity approaches, such as VM clustering and stretched cluster configurations.

Questions

1. Reservations and limits are configured on the VM level, but shares can be configured on the Resource Pool.

   a) True
   b) False

2. Please describe the difference between reservations, limits, and shares.

3. Transparent Memory Sharing is disabled by default for Inter-VM page sharing.

   a) True
   b) False

4. There are five memory states of the ESXi hypervisor—what are they?

5. Based on the memory state of the ESXi server, different memory-saving techniques are used. What is the correct order of those techniques based on the negative impact to the VM?

   a) TPS, compression, ballooning, swapping
   b) Ballooning, compression, TPS, swapping
   c) Swapping, compression, ballooning, TPS
   d) TPS, ballooning, compression, swapping

6. Describe the ballooning functionality.

7. In vSphere 6.7, you can perform migration of the VM, even if there is no shared storage in place.

   a) True
   b) False

8. Please describe the function of the vSphere Distributed Resource Scheduler.

9. DRS affinity and anti-affinity rules can be used only when DPM is enabled.

   a) True
   b) False

10. Describe the function of resource pools.

11. Expandable resource pools mean that the limit of the resource pool can be automatically adjusted if free resources are available on the parent object.

    a) True
    b) False

12. Using vApps, you can configure the following settings:

    a) Reservations, shares, limits, startup and shutdown order of the VMs, guest OS installation and affinity, and anti-affinity rules
    b) Reservations, shares, limits, startup and shutdown order of the VMs
    c) Startup and shutdown order of the VMs and CPU resource allocation
    d) Reservations, shares, limits, startup and shutdown order of the VMs, and port group assignment of the VMs

Further reading

- **vSphere Resource Management**: `https://docs.vmware.com/en/VMware-vSphere/6.7/vsphere-esxi-vcenter-server-67-resource-management-guide.pdf`
- **Performance Best Practices for VMware vSphere 6.7**: This book provides performance tips that cover the most performance-critical areas of VMware vSphere
  6.7. `https://www.vmware.com/content/dam/digitalmarketing/vmware/en/pdf/techpaper/performance/vsphere-esxi-vcenter-server-67-performance-best-practices.pdf`.

Section 3: Advanced Topics 3

In this section, we are going to cover several advanced topics, such as security, availability, disaster recovery, troubleshooting, and monitoring. Availability and disaster recovery will be broadly covered, because these are two of the critical aspects of every vSphere infrastructure, but you will learn a lot about different topics that you can use to improve your virtual environment as well.

The following chapters are included in this section:

- Chapter 11, *Availability and Disaster Recovery*
- Chapter 12, *Securing and Protecting Your Environment*
- Chapter 13, *Analyzing and Optimizing Your Environment*
- Chapter 14, *Troubleshooting Your Environment*

11
Availability and Disaster Recovery

This chapter will focus on specific availability (and resiliency) solutions in vSphere, whereas , with the VMware technology, it is possible to create an entire HA infrastructure on every level.

When we think about how we can work with all the benefits of VMware solutions, we see a lot of positions and levels where it is possible to protect the infrastructure. Still, the physical and infrastructural parts of your environment are really important and crucial, so the right design and configuration are needed for your hardware, such as servers, switches, storage, and **host bus adapter (HBA)**, in order to design and configure all of them without a potential single point of failure.

However, only the infrastructure level is essential and must be resilient. Also, workloads need a good HA level according to business requirements and needs. There are not only several native solutions that can be used, such as NIC teaming, multipathing for storage, vSphere **High Availability (HA)**, and vSphere **Fault Tolerance (FT)**, but also other solutions, typically from the physical world, such as guest clustering.

In this chapter, we will cover the following topics:

- vSphere HA
- vSphere FT
- Virtual machine clustering
- Virtual machine backup
- VMware vSphere Replication
- Disaster recovery and disaster avoidance
- VMware solutions

VMware vSphere HA

vSphere HA is the most commonly used technology in the vSphere Suite in terms of HA. vSphere HA is responsible for restarting VMs in cases of ESXi downtime. Highlighting the word **restart** is crucial. There is a hard restart of the VM on the other ESXi hypervisor within the same vSphere cluster.

 Keep that in mind that your OS will boot from scratch after the HA event because, in such an event, it is not possible to synchronize the memory of the VM between hosts.

We will have a look at the different aspects of the vSphere HA in the next few sections, but now let's have a look at how to enable HA.

vSphere HA configuration

Configuring vSphere HA is a part of the cluster configuration in vSphere Web Client; click on the **EDIT...** button in the **vSphere Availability** area, as shown in the following screenshot:

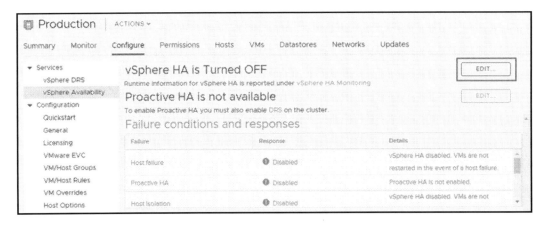

Configuration in the basic state is straightforward; click on the **Turn ON vSphere HA** checkbox and then **OK**:

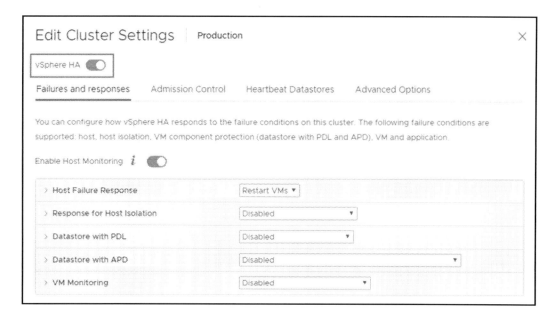

Under the **Recent Tasks** area, you can see **Configuring vSphere HA** on each host, so wait for success on all hosts of the cluster:

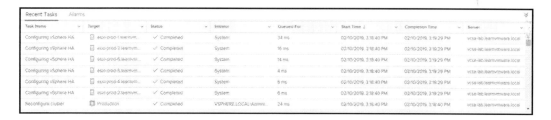

When you click on **Turn ON** on every ESXi host in the cluster, a special agent called **Fault Domain Manager** (**FDM**) is installed. A log specific to the FDM agent is available on each host in the `/var/log/fdm.log` file.

Now we have to enable HA and protect VMs. When a host fails, vSphere HA restarts the VMs on other hosts in the cluster. In each cluster, there is a master host that is responsible for managing all other slave hosts, and the master node reports the current state of the cluster to the vCenter server. The vCenter server is used to configure the vSphere HA, but the master node is responsible for HA events, so even if your vCenter server is not available, the vSphere HA will work as expected.

To configure vSphere HA, we have the following requirements:

- **Right license**: Minimal Essential Plus
- **Two hosts minimal**: 64 hosts, which is the maximum per cluster in vSphere 6.0 and 6.5
- **At least two share datastores**: These are required for datastore heartbeats, but you can also have a single shared datastore (in this case, you need an advanced option to remove the warning on the datastore numbers)
- **vCenter Server**: Needed to configure vSphere HA, but is not involved in actual HA failovers

vSphere HA heartbeats

Heartbeats are used to ensure that the host is up and running. If no heartbeats are received within a configured timeframe, the host is considered down, and the HA event will occur, restarting the VMs running on the unresponsive host.

There are two kind of heartbeat:

- **Network heartbeat**: The master node will periodically check if the slave node is available over the network using ICMP pings.
- **Storage heartbeat**: Each ESXi hypervisor stores an empty file on the shared datastore, which is exclusively locked by the ESXi hypervisor. If the file is not locked, it means that the hosts have lost access to the storage.

vSphere HA network heartbeats

The master ESXi server sends ICMP pings to the slave hosts over the management network. The management network is a port group that is configured for management traffic.

Also, by default, the default gateway is used as an **isolation address**. When the slave doesn't receive any network heartbeats from the master, it will try to reach its isolation address. If the isolation address is not reachable, the slave host will be considered isolated—meaning that access to the network is limited; based on your preferences, you can choose what to do with the VMs by configuring **Response for Host Isolation**:

You can change the isolation address from the default gateway to any other IP address based on your network design by using the advanced `das.isolationaddress[0-9]` cluster parameter. There can be up to 10 different isolation address.

It is also recommended to have a physical network that's highly available, so always use dual physical NICs to carry your management traffic as well as two physical switches to provide maximum network availability:

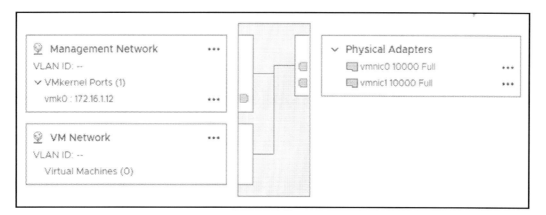

vSphere HA storage heartbeats

In addition to network heartbeats, storage heartbeats were introduced to increase the resilience of the infrastructure.

By default, two different shared datastores will be used for storage heartbeats, again to increase the resilience of the infrastructure. It is possible, however, to configure an advanced setting, das.heartbeatDsPerHost, to change the value to a different number of datastores, or das.ignoreInsufficientHbDatastore, set to true to ignore the warning.

The following screenshot is the configuration page for **Heartbeat Datastores**:

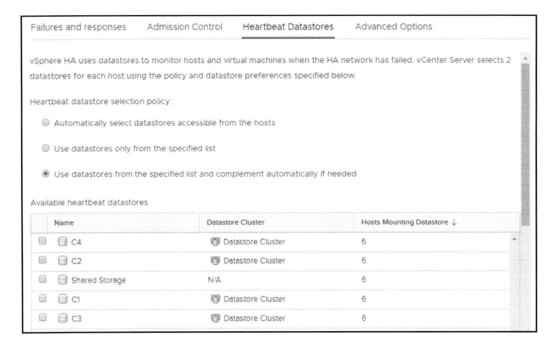

Storage heartbeats are used only when network heartbeats have failed. Each host will create a specific file on the shared datastore that can be accessed by all other ESXi hosts. This file, host-XXXX-hb, is an empty file. The corresponding ESXi hypervisor exclusively opens that. If the ESXi hypervisor loses access to the storage, the master ESXi node will discover that the lock from the file disappears, meaning that the host has lost access to the storage and an HA event will occur.

vSphere HA protection mechanism

How does HA work? Each ESXi server that is a part of the cluster will maintain its `poweron` file, which contains the list of VMs running on the host. This file is located on your `vmfs` volumes in the hidden. `vSphere-HA/<FDM cluster ID>` directory, as shown in the following screenshot:

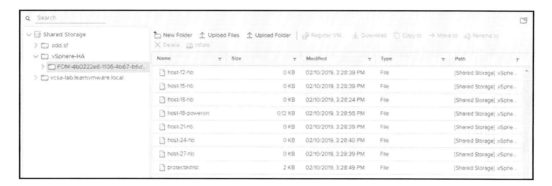

The `poweron` file is not just used only to track which VMs are running but also for identification if the host is isolated . The first line of the `poweron` file contains the isolation identification, and it contain either a 0 (zero) or a 1. A 0 means that the host is not isolated, and a 1 means that it is isolated. The master is responsible for informing vCenter about the isolation status of the host.

When the lock from the heartbeat file is lost, the master ESXi node will check the corresponding `poweron` list and initiate a restart of the VMs on the other ESXi nodes.

Virtual Machine Component Protection (VMCP)

VMCP is a new technology from vSphere 6.0. VMCP protects storage failures, used typically for block-based storage. Before vSphere 6.0, vSphere HA only protected hosts by monitoring network failures; if the FDM agent is not able to talk with other agents, it can be considered in a fault state by the other agents, and it will be considered in an isolated state itself.

The following two types of storage failure can now be handled:

- **PDL**: When the storage array has lost access to the device (the device is offline or unavailable) then a specific SCSI sense code is sent to the ESXi server. When PDL situation occurs, the ESXi server will stop sending I/O commands to the device.
- **APD**: If the ESXi host is not able to reach the storage array at all (no SCSI sense codes are received) then the storage device is marked as unavailable, but since the ESXi server validates the status of the storage array, it will still try to resend I/O commands to the device until APD Timeout is reached.

When you want to use VMCP, you must configure the **Failures and responses** tab of the configuration:

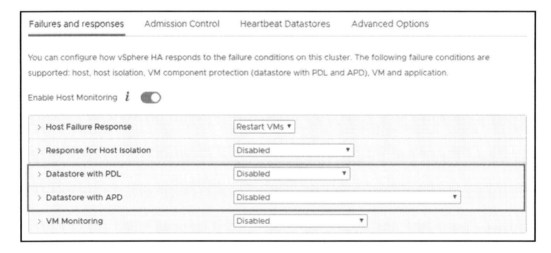

The VMCP recovery workflow is shown in the following diagram:

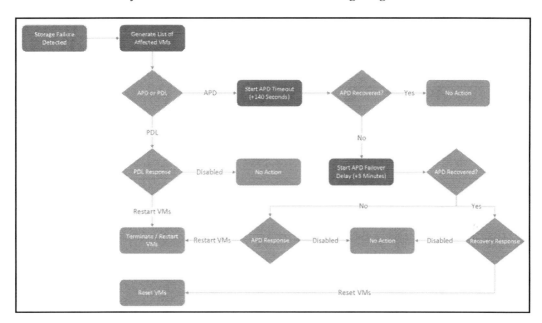

Proactive HA

Proactive HA is a new feature integrated with server vendor monitoring systems. The idea is to provide HA to VMs even before an actual failure occurs. For example, the server has two redundant power supplies, and one of them fails. There is no direct impact on the ESXi server itself, but this condition might lead to downtime when the second power supplies fail. With proactive HA, you can evacuate the VMs from the affected ESXi hypervisor event before it becomes unresponsive.

When any of the hardware fails, it is marked by the hardware monitoring agent as unhealthy. Based on the configuration, vCenter Server will classify the hardware failure as **degraded** or **severely degraded** and the host is placed in a specific state called **quarantine mode**.

In quarantine mode, DRS won't use the affected ESXi server for the placement of any new VMs, and it might even proactively evacuate the VMs of the ESXi host. Evacuation will only take place in situations when the migration will not affect the performance of the VMs. There is an option to place the host into **maintenance mode** as the result of degraded state.

Remediation actions available with proactive HA include:

- **Quarantine mode for all failures**: Quarantined hosts are not used to run new VMs, but currently running VMs will still be run on the top of the quarantined host.
- **Mixed mode (quarantine mode for moderate and maintenance mode for severe failure)**: If the host suffers from moderate degradation, the VMs will be kept running on the host, but new VMs will not be run on the host. However, all VMs will be migrated off the host in severe failures.
- **Maintenance mode for all failures**: All VMs will be migrated off the host no matter whether moderate or severe degradation occurred.

Admission control

Admission control guarantees vSphere HA failover by ensuring enough spare failover capacity within the cluster. If you have four ESXi hosts and all of them are utilizing almost 100% of the total compute capacity, and one of the ESXi hypervisors fails, the VMs will be restarted, but the remaining hosts won't be able to provide the required number of the resources other VMs thus performance will be degraded. Admission control takes care of that by reserving resources for the failover.

Configuration is at the cluster level under the **vSphere Availability** section, as follows:

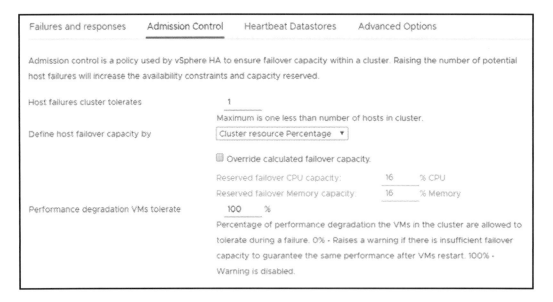

You can define the host's failover capacity using one of the following options:

- **Disabled**: No admission control is configured, and no resources are reserved for failover.
- **Slot Policy (powered-on VMs)**: A slot is a logical representation of memory and CPU resources. A slot is the memory and CPU reservation required for any powered-on VMs in the cluster. Slot Policy can do good work in the environment where there is a very similar VM with the same CPU memory configuration. When you have a lot of small VMs and two monster VMs, it is not a very good situation because the reservation selects the most significant value. You can change this value for the CPU slot size and memory slot size through **Advanced Options.**
- **Cluster resource Percentage**: You can design vSphere HA to perform affirmation control by holding a particular level of group CPU and memory assets for recuperation from host failure. vSphere HA calculates CPU and memory. CPU calculation uses CPU reservation for powered-on VMs. If you don't use reservation HA, use the default value of 32 MHz. The memory calculates the memory reservation and memory overhead of each powered-on VM; the default value is **0** MB. You can override the calculated failover capacity.
- **Dedicated failover hosts**: This is the last option for defined failover hosts. You can specify and dedicate failover hosts. vSphere HA uses such hosts when it needs failover actions or has insufficient resources.

You can find more information about different **Admission Control** policies at `https://docs.vmware.com/en/VMware-vSphere/6.7/com.vmware.vsphere.avail.doc/GUID-85D9737E-769C-40B6-AB73-F58DA1A451F0.html`.

Then, there is a new option called **Performance degradation VMs tolerate**. This new setting in vSphere 6.5, if set, will issue a notice when a host disappointment would cause a decrease in VM execution depending on the genuine asset, not simply arranged reservations.

VM restart and monitoring

You can override specific vSphere HA (but also **vSphere DRS**) configurations for specific VMs directly from the cluster level. In the **Configure** tab, under the **Configuration** menu, select **VM Overrides**:

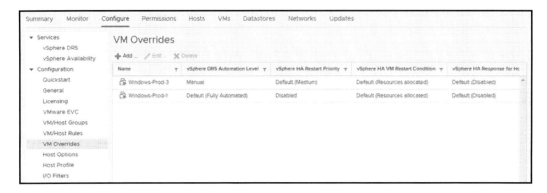

The first option is the automation level, but it's related to vSphere DRS. For vSphere HA, you can specify different restart priorities or disable vSphere HA completely, as follows:

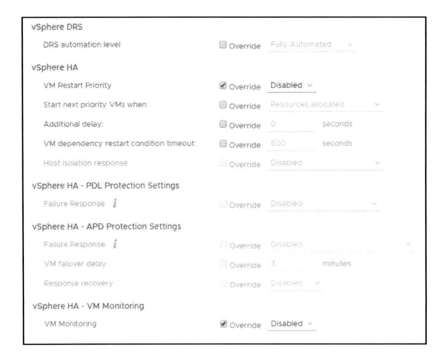

Note that starting with vSphere 6.5 there are two new levels (lowest and highest) to provide more control. If a VM does not need to be restarted (for example, for test purposes), you can also disable vSphere HA.

The next option is called **Start next priority VMs when,** which define a condition on when the next VM should be restarted. For example, you can choose the **Guest Heartbeats detected** option:

To monitor vSphere HA, it is possible to use the **Monitor** tab, and the **vSphere HA** section on it containing various information about the overall vSphere HA configuration, configuration issues, datastores under APD conditions, or advanced runtime information.

VMware vSphere FT

VMware vSphere FT is a way to improve the availability level for critical VMs, with a *zero-downtime technology*.

vSphere FT works by continuously replicating the state of the VM between two different ESXi hosts. As a result there are two identical copies of a VM—the primary VM and the secondary VM (sometimes called shadow VM). Each VM has its own set of configuration files, VMX and VMDK files, which vSphere FT automatically keeps synchronized.

When the physical ESXi server where the primary VM is running fails, the secondary VM (shadow VM) automatically takes over and resumes normal operations.

VMware vSphere FT also has some limits—for each VM, it supports a maximum of 4 vCPUs and 64 GB RAM. For each host, it supports a maximum of 4 fault-tolerant VMs. VMware vMotion migration is supported for both VMs, as are the different virtual disk formats and the native backup capability (using VM snapshots).

The requirements for vSphere FT are as follows:

- The physical CPU used in hosts for FT must be the same family or **Enhanced vMotion Compatibility** (**EVC**) must be configured on the cluster.
- The network for FT logging must use a 10 Gbps speed. A dedicated FT network is highly recommended.
- For licensing, only Enterprise Plus allows up to 4 vCPUs; with the Standard Editions, the maximum is 2.

FT provides the following HA benefits:

- Continuous availability with zero downtime and zero data loss:
    - Transparent to guest OS
    - Independent on guest OS and application; any VM or application can be protected using FT technology
    - Zero-downtime failover from primary to secondary VM
- Fault tolerance improvements in vSphere 6.x:
    - Now you can protect VMs with up to 4 vCPUs and 64 GB RAM
    - vMotion is supported for both the primary and secondary VM
    - Supports backing up FT VMs
    - All disk types are supported (thin, thick eager-zeroed and thick lazy zeroed)
    - Each VM has its own set of VM files, such as `.vmx` and `.vmdk`, and both can be on different datastores:

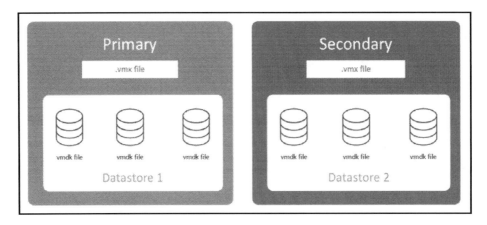

Features not supported for FT-enabled VMs are as follows:

- **Storage vMotion**: Storage vMotion cannot be used in conjunction with FT-enabled VMs.
- **Linked clones**: With FT, you can use the Linked Clones functionality.
- **VMCP**: If you use VMCP, VM overrides are automatically created for each FT-enabled VM and the VMCP is disabled for the VMs.
- **Virtual volume datastores:** VVoLs are not supported with FT. FT-enabled VMs cannot use the VVoL datastore.
- **Storage-based policy management:** SPBM policies cannot be used together with FT-enabled VMs.
- **Snapshots**: VM must not have any snapshots once FT is enabled. Besides, it is not possible to take snapshots of VMs on which FT is enabled. Otherwise, the following error will be displayed:

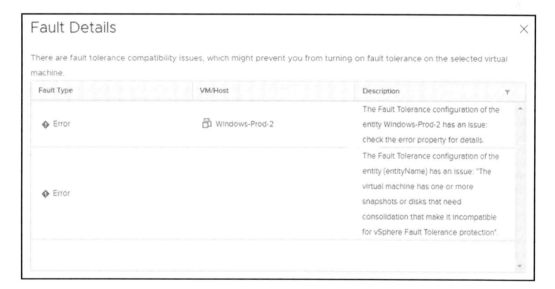

 For more information about Fault Tolerance, please visit the official paper, **VMware vSphere 6 Fault Tolerance Architecture and Performance**, at `https://www.vmware.com/files/pdf/techpaper/VMware-vSphere6-FT-arch-perf.pdf`.

FT configuration

The configuration of the FT is a simple process. It is performed on the individual VM level.

As FT traffic might generate a significant amount of bandwidth, it is highly recommended you use a dedicated physical network interface card for such reasons. If you are not able to dedicate a NIC for FT traffic, you should consider using other **Quality of Service (QoS)** features such as **Network IO Control** to guarantee specific bandwidth to different traffic types on the shared physical media.

In both cases, prior to configuring the FT on the VM, you need to configure a VMkernel port that will be used for FT traffic and enable the **Fault Tolerance logging** service on the adapter. Again, it is highly recommended you use a dedicated VMkernel adapter for FT traffic, although you can, of course, enable the **Fault Tolerance logging** service on the existing adapter:

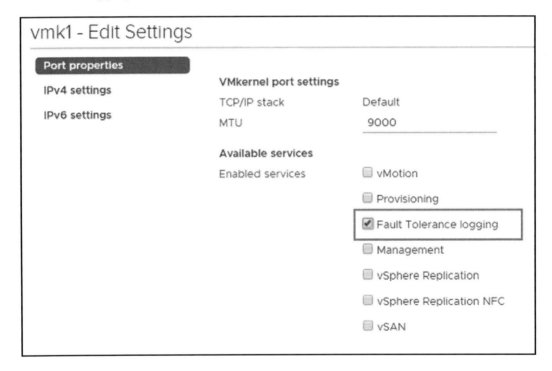

Once the network configuration is done, VMware vSphere FT can be easily activated or deactivated. To turn on this feature, right-click on the VM, select **Fault Tolerance**, and **Turn On Fault Tolerance**:

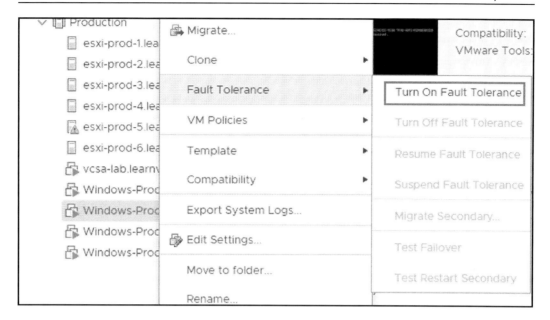

You need to select which datastore the secondary VM will be stored on as well as which ESXi hypervisor it should run on.

You cannot select the same ESXi or datastore as the one the source VM is located in.

Once the FT is configured, you might notice that the icon of the VM has changed so you can quickly identify those VMs protected by FT:

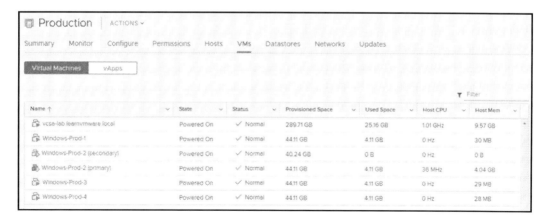

Working with FT-enabled VM

When the FT is enabled, you can perform several FT-related operations on the VM:

- **Turn Off Fault Tolerance**: The secondary VM is deleted, and FT is unconfigured on the primary VM.
- **Suspend Fault Tolerance**: FT logging is suspended, so the VMs are not in synchronization anymore, but the secondary VM is not removed from the infrastructure.
- **Resume Fault Tolerance**: Resumes the FT logging after the suspend operation; any changes made to the primary VM will be synced to the secondary VM and standard operations will resume, resulting in continuous synchronization of the primary and secondary VM.
- **Migrate Secondary**: You can migrate the secondary VM to the different ESXi hosts, for example, in case you need to perform maintenance on the ESXi hypervisor that hosts the secondary VM.
- **Test Failover**: In this situation, the primary VM is switched between two different hosts and the secondary VM begins the synchronization process from the beginning. This is a non-intrusive test for the primary VM.
- **Test Restart Secondary**: The secondary VM is stopped and destroyed and the new secondary VM is started and synced with the primary VM.

FT performance implications

VMs protected by FT will have lower performance due to the fact that every single CPU instruction, memory change, or storage I/O needs to be replicated to the secondary VM. Depending on the workload, FT might also generate extensive network traffic.

As with almost any technology, there is always some trade-off. In case of FTs, you get zero-downtime for your VMs and applications, but with a performance hit on the VM.

DVD Store is a benchmarking utility that can measure the maximum throughput of the SQL server:

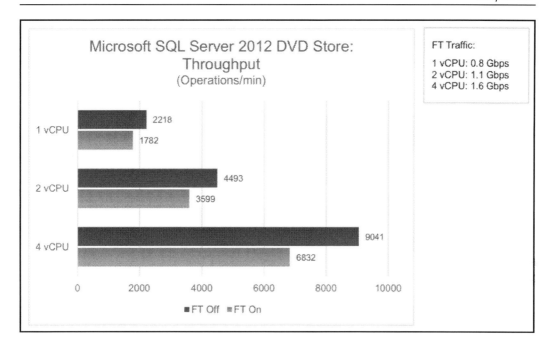

As you can see, in the case of the DVD Store, the difference between FT-protected and unprotected VMs is between 20-30%, depending on the number of vCPUs.

Another benchmark you can use to measure your CPU performance is to compile a Linux kernel. This is a CPU-intensive operation, and as you can see, the difference between FT-protected and unprotected VMs is 10-20%:

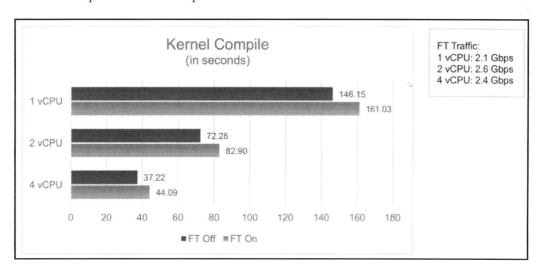

Also keep in mind that your physical network carried out the synchronization between VMs, and depending on the application you run inside the VM, it can generate a significant amount of data.

 For more information about FT architecture and performance, feel free to check the official technical paper at `https://www.vmware.com/files/pdf/techpaper/VMware-vSphere6-FT-arch-perf.pdf`.

Virtual machine clustering

Virtual machine clustering is an infrastructure configuration, where two systems and applications act as a *single, logical unit*. There is no direct connection to VMware vSphere. Clustering must be supported by the underlying operating system or the application itself.

In general, both systems must have simultaneous write access to the storage device so both can act as a primary or standby instance.

Mission-critical systems such as production databases are usually clustered, so in any situation, you have at least one instance available. For this reason, you can't use VMware HA technology because, as we have already explained, the VM restarts during the HA failover, resulting in application downtime. You can, in theory, use FT, but there will be limitations as well. In the case of FT, there are two significant disadvantages—performance degradation and support for a maximum of 4 vCPUs.

Clustering does not have such negatives, but configuration dramatically depends on the application.

VMware vSphere supports the following clustering options:

- **Cluster-in-a-Box**: This is when VMs are clustered on the same ESXi host. The shared disks or quorum (either local or remote) are shared between the VMs. CiB can be used in test or development scenarios. However, this solution does not protect in the event of hardware failure.
- **Cluster-out-of-the-Box**: The cluster is deployed to two VMs and the two VMs are running across two different ESXi hosts. This protects against both software and hardware failures. Physical RDMs are the recommended disk choice. Shared storage/quorum should be located on a fiber channel SAN or via an in-guest iSCSI initiator.

- **VM and physical server clustering**: This involves one cluster node running natively on a physical server, while the other runs as a VM. This mode can be used to migrate from a physical two-node deployment to a virtualized environment. Physical RDMs are the recommended disk option here. Shared storage/quorum should be located on a fiber channel SAN or through an in-guest iSCSI initiator.

Different cluster solutions are shown in the following diagram:

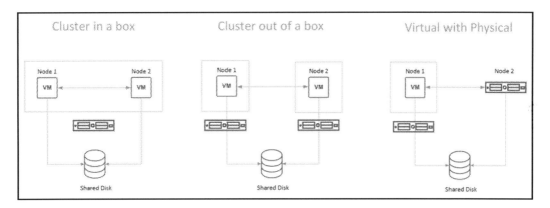

Clustering features available in VMware vSphere

Many features can be used for guest OS or application clustering within VMware vSphere. There are always pros and cons for each type depending on your use case:

- **SCSI bus sharing for virtual disks on VMFS volume**: You can enable simultaneous access to the single disk for multiple VMs
- **SCSI bus sharing for RDM devices**: In this case, there is no virtual disk located on the VMFS datastore, but the device is mapped using **Raw Device Mapping** (**RDM**) as a disk to the VMs
- **Multi-writer flag on the virtual disk**: No bus sharing is involved, but the disk is unlocked for simultaneous operations from the VMs
- **In-guest iSCSI**: There is no shared disk on the vSphere level, the disk is mapped from the guest OS.

Although VMware vSphere supports different storage configurations that can be used for clustering, always check the vendor or VMware knowledge base to check if your application supports such configuration. If something can be configured and works as expected, it does not mean that such a configuration is fully supported. For example, with **Microsoft Windows Server Failover Clustering (WSFC)**, you can configure bus sharing for the disks located on the VMFS volume (no RDM), but it is supported only for CiB deployment, not CAB, although it works.

The following are the supported shared storage configurations:

Storage type	CiB	CAB	VM and physical
Virtual disks	Yes	No	No
Pass-through RDM (physical compatibility mode)	No	Yes	Yes
Non-pass-through RDM (virtual compatibility mode)	yes	No	No

Cluster-related configuration parameters are as follows:

- **SCSI Controller settings**:
    - **Disk types**: You have the choice of VMDK, virtual RDM (virtual compatibility mode), or physical RDM (physical compatibility mode).
    - **SCSI bus-sharing setting**: Virtual sharing policy, or physical sharing policy, or none.
- **SCSI bus sharing values**:
    - **None**: Used for disks that aren't shared in the cluster (between VMs) or when a multi-writer flag is used.
    - **Virtual**: Use this value for CiB deployments.
    - **Physical**: Recommended for CAB or physical and virtual deployments.
- **Raw Device Mapping (RDM) options**:
    - **Virtual compatibility mode**: In this situation, RDM acts identically to the virtual disk file, and you can use standard virtual disk benefits such as cloning or snapshots.
    - **Physical compatibility mode**: In this situation, RDM has direct access to the SCSI device. This mode is especially usefully for applications that need low-level control over the device.

Please note that your operating system and application must be cluster-aware. You can only map the same disk to multiple VMs assuming both of them will have read/write access to the device.

When working with cluster configuration, always follow the official configuration guide of the vendor of the application or the operating system. Any misconfiguration can lead to serious cluster issues or event data corruption.

RDM device and multi-writer flag

This is probably one of the most common clustered deployments, but always follows the official documentation from VMware or your application vendor for specific configurations. In this example, I assume that a VM is already configured and the operating system is installed. An initial VM has a single virtual disk on the VMFS datastore connected to SCSI controller 0:

1. Power off the VM and edit the settings of the virtual hardware.
2. Assign a new SCSI controller 1:
    1. **Type**: **VMware Paravirtual**
    2. **SCSI Bus Sharing**: **None**
3. Create a new RDM disk and attach it to SCSI controller 1:
    - **Compatibility Mode**: **Physical**
    - **Sharing**: **Multi-writer**:

4. Start the first VM.

5. From the guest OS (assuming it is Windows Server), rescan the storage devices.

6. Bring the disk online and create a new simple volume.

7. Power off the second VM that should be part of the cluster.

8. Assign a new SCSI controller 1:
   - **Type: VMware Paravirtual**
   - **SCSI Sharing: None**

9. Assign the disk created in step number 3 using **Add existing disk.**

10. Set the sharing policy to **Multi-writer.**

11. Start the second VM.

12. Rescan the storage devices, and you should see the shared disk.

13. Proceed with Oracle RAC/Microsoft Cluster Services deployment.

If you forget to enable the multi-writer flag, the following error will be displayed:

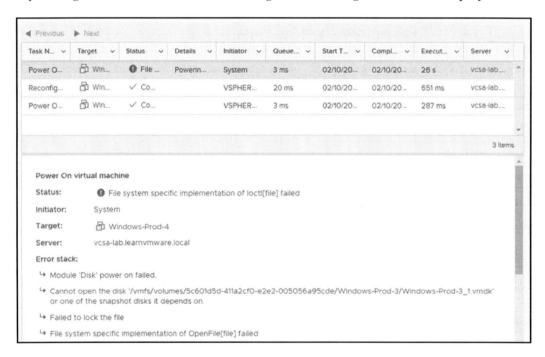

Before the Oracle or Microsoft cluster is configured, do not copy anything to the new disk from within the guest operating system.

You should also configure **DRS anti-affinity VM rules** to keep the VMs on the different ESXi hypervisor.

Working with clusters is not an easy task, and as already stated, any minor misconfiguration can lead to severe problems. From my perspective, I would recommend switching to scaled-out solutions instead of clustered ones because such deployments provide the same availability as clusters, but they do not involve any advanced configuration on the vSphere level. In-guest bunching arrangements that don't utilize a common plate design, for example, **SQL Mirroring, SQL Server AlwaysOn Availability Group,** and **Exchange Database Availability Group**, don't require unequivocal help explanations from VMware. These setups don't require extra VMware consideration with respect to a particular stockpiling convention or various hubs and can be conveyed on VMs in much the same way as on physical devices.

For more information, feel free to visit the following articles at `https://kb.vmware.com/s/article/1034165` for multi-writer information and `https://kb.vmware.com/s/article/2147661` for failover clustering guidelines.

Virtual machine backup

The choice of the suitable backup solution for an infrastructure depends on what you need to protect—configurations, data, VM, applications, or a complete system state.

Depending on that, backup solutions can be categorized as follows:

- **Backup with an agent**: This solution is intended for the protection of a physical environment or specific configurations such as a VM cluster. Vendors such as Arcserve and Veritas Backup Exec provide this solution type.
- **Native backup for VMware**: This was developed explicitly for virtualized environments, and is the recommended solution for a virtualized environment because it takes the benefits of vSphere features (for example, snapshots technology). Veeam, Nakivo, Altaro, Vembu, and HPE are some vendors that provide backup solutions for virtual infrastructure.
- **Hyper-scale backup**: Vendors such as Rubrik and Cohesity provide ready-to-use backup solutions based on appliances installed in the infrastructure.

Let's discuss the protection of infrastructure components and the tools used to guarantee maximum availability.

Transport modes

Software backup solutions use different protocols called transport modes to retrieve VM data from storage. The transport mode to use for backups depends on the design of the network and the storage architecture.

Four main transport modes are supported for handling data:

- **Network Block Device (NBD)**: The ESXi host reads data from the storage and sends it to the application, across the network, using the NBD protocol. This mode can be used in any infrastructure configuration and is the simplest method to implement.
- **Network Block Device Secure Sockets Layer (NBDSSL)**: This is the same as NBD but uses SSL to encrypt the data passed over the TCP/IP connection.
- **SCSI HotAdd**: This is a LAN-free data transfer mode where the .vmdk files of a VM are attached to the backup application. Data won't go through the network but is read and written directly from/to the datastore. In many environments, this is the preferred mode.
- **Direct SAN**: In this, data is read directly from the SAN or iSCSI LUN; this provides the fastest data transfer speed. Direct SAN transport mode is recommended if the VM's disks are stored on shared SAN LUNs connected to the ESXi host over FC, FCoE, and iSCSI.

Not all transport modes can be used in all cases: for example, with virtual volumes direct SAN mode is not supported.

Also, some specific backup products can implement other specific transport modes (for example, direct NFS with Veeam Backup and Replication).

Backup solutions for VMware vSphere

The market offers several valid solutions you can choose from, and backup product selection must consider different elements, such as infrastructure complexity, supported platforms, backup types, licensing, and budget.

Depending on what you need to back up, the software solution you choose must provide specific features to meet the requirements. For example, to back up Microsoft SQL Servers, application-aware backups with log truncate features must be supported to ensure database consistency. If you are still performing backups on tape, make sure the product supports tapes.

Since the available backup solutions provide different options, capabilities, and pricing, some popular backup products specific to virtual environments will now be briefly illustrated to show what the market is offering. The listed vendors and product order don't follow any classification or preference.

Veeam Backup and Replication

Veeam offers robust and powerful backup and replication features to protect entire virtual infrastructures. It's a backup solution for enterprises but also for SMBs.

It's installation supports Windows OSes only. The management of the application can be done through a console deployed on the administrator's computers or with a web-based console. Despite its simplicity, Veeam protects the infrastructure in a very robust and reliable way.

The main features of Veeam are as follows:

- **Backup**: Full VM backup, incremental backup, copy backup, cloud backup (AWS, Azure, Veeam Cloud Connect), tape backup, replication, cloud replication.
- **Restore**: Restore full VM, Instant File Recovery, Instant VM Recovery, Instant Object Recovery (AD, Exchange, Microsoft SQL, SharePoint, Oracle).
- **Licensing**: This is per physical CPU socket.
- **Available in three editions**: It is available in Standard, Enterprise, and Enterprise Plus. Veeam also provides an Essential version with an affordable price that is designed for small organizations with fewer than 250 employees and is limited to 6 CPU sockets. A Free Edition is available but is limited to full backups only, and vPower, VMs replication, and scripting features are not available.

NAKIVO Backup and Replication

NAKIVO Backup and Replication is a backup solution for SMBs and enterprises and can be deployed on both Windows and Linux OS or as a virtual appliance, allowing you to save some Windows licenses. Management is done through a simple, comfortable, and intuitive HTML5-based console that guides the user through the configuration steps required by the backup or restores procedures.

The installation and usage are, and this product offers all the features required by modern data centers. You need a few minutes to get the software up and running.

The main features of NAKIVO Backup and Replication are as follows:

- **Backup**: Full VM backup, incremental backup, copy backup, replication, cloud backup (AWS), cloud replication.
- **Restore**: Restore full VMs, Instant File Recovery, Instant Object Recovery (AD, Exchange), Instant VM Recovery.
- **Licensing**: This is per physical CPU socket.
- **Available in three editions**: This is available in Basic, Pro, and Enterprise editions. An Essential version is also available with an affordable price for the Pro and Enterprise Editions, designed for SMBs, and limited to a maximum of 6 socket licenses per organization. A Free Edition is available and supports up to two VMs.

Altaro VM Backup

Altaro VM Backup is a backup solution for SMBs deployed to the Windows platform. It offers all the features required by the Disaster Recovery(DR) to protect VMware virtual infrastructures. A dedicated Windows machine is not required, and there is no need for third-party software dependencies such as Microsoft SQL. The product is easy to use, with an intuitive design, and provides full control over backup jobs across all hosts.

You can manage the application from a console that is deployed on the administrator's computers and can be used as a central monitoring station for several Altaro VM instances.

The main features of Altaro VM Backup are as follows:

- **Backup**: Full VM backup, incremental backup, copy backup, cloud backup (Azure), replication.
- **Restore**: Restore full VMs, Instant File Recovery, Instant Object Recovery (Exchange), Instant VM Recovery.
- **Licensing**: This is per physical host with unlimited sockets/CPUs.
- **Available in three editions**: It is available in Standard, Pro, and Enterprise editions. A Free Edition is also available and supports protection for two VMs.

Vembu VMBackup

Vembu is a backup and DR software solution that can be deployed on the Windows and Linux platforms or as a virtual appliance. It is suitable for data centers and small and medium businesses with enterprise-level features. Backup copies of your backups can be sent to offsite storage or to Vembu Cloud, which provides data redundancy and DR.

The main features of Vembu VMBackup are as follows:

- **Backup**: Full VM backup, incremental backup, copy backup, cloud backup (Vembu Cloud), replication.
- **Restore**: Restore full VMs, Instant File Recovery, Instant VM Recovery, Instant Object Recovery (Microsoft Exchange, SharePoint, SQL, and AD).
- **Licensing**: This is per physical CPU socket.
- **Two editions available**: It is available in two editions—BDR Suite and Free. The Free Edition supports a maximum of three VMs.

Deduplication appliances

Data that needs protecting is continuously growing, and the available space on storage devices is never enough. To reduce the space occupied by backup files on storage devices, deduplication technology allows a reduction in storage space consumption.

Deduplicated storage should be used mainly as secondary targets due to their design. These storage systems are often developed to optimize write operations, but random read I/O performance may suffer.

Hyper-scale solutions

Hyper-scale is an architecture capable of scaling appropriately as increased demand is added to the system. This architecture is composed of individual servers, referred to as nodes, that provide resources in terms of compute, storage, and networking, and are put together in a cluster and managed as a single entity.

The advantage of hyper-scale is its architecture, which can be expanded as demand grows by merely adding new nodes to the cluster.

Cohesity

Cohesity DataPlatform is a hyper-converged platform solution that consolidates and manages secondary data with scale. Cohesity offers secondary storage devices with global deduplication, compression, and encryption.
The Cohesity appliance is installed with a proprietary OS and distributed filesystem. The design allows for scaling to any capacity.

When using a Cohesity solution, you have two main benefits:

- You can eliminate secondary storage silos and consolidate backups.
- You can control all your secondary data operations with converged data protection.

Rubrik

Rubrik is a cloud data management solution for protecting workloads that deliver a data management platform for enterprises in private, public, and hybrid cloud environments.

The Rubrik solution is deployed as an appliance to insert in the rack and power on. The scale-out hardware combined with robust backup software manages, with a single platform, all data in the cloud or on-premise for automated backup, DR, archival, and search, in a simple, scale-out platform built for the hybrid cloud.

VMware vSphere Replication

vSphere Replication is extension to vCenter Server, and it provides hypervisor VM replication and recovery. vSphere Replication is an alternative to storage-based replication and can be used together with the **Site Recovery Manager** (**SRM**) for more advanced scenarios.

vSphere Replication can provide very cost-efficient, simple, and powerful replication at the VM level, using scheduled asynchronous file-based replication. It is more cost-efficient because it reduces both storage costs and replication costs, and also because it's included in all editions, starting from the Essential Plus edition.

It is important to emphasize that vSphere Replication is based on asynchronous replication with a minimal recovery point objective of 5 minutes. Based on this technical limitation, you can't protect your site in real time, and you might even lose data from the past 5 minutes if any problems occur on the primary site.

One interesting aspect is that vSphere Replication does not use VM snapshots at. On the other hand, it is strictly dependent on the vCenter Server for its configuration and management.

vSphere Replication installation

Technology that is used by vSphere Replication is already included in VMware vSphere, but to leverage it, you need to download the vSphere Replication appliance, which will hook to the vSphere APIs and provide the UI.

Once the appliance is deployed and configured, it provides a native vSphere plugin that will be available through your vCenter Server, leading to full integration with the vSphere Suite.

The initial installation and configuration are a straightforward process:

1. Download the ISO for the vSphere Replication appliance from the `my.vmware.com` portal.

2. Deploy the OVF template from the ISO file, as you already know how to do this (that is, select OVF and VMDK files, select the destination cluster and storage, map the VM to the correct port group, and customize the appliance).

3. Once the vSphere Replication appliance is deployed, you need to link it to the vCenter Server. To do that, connect to the management interface of **vRealize Automation (vRA)** at `https://<replication appliance IP/FQDN>:5480`:

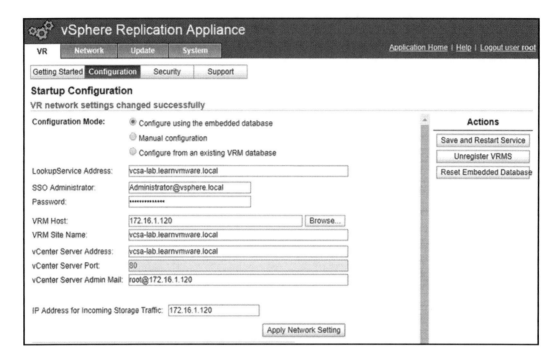

Once the binding is configured, you will be able to access vRA directly from the vSphere client.

Working with vSphere Replication

In past adaptations of VMware vSphere Replication, there was a different route called vSphere Replications. VMware has solidified this under **Site Recovery**:

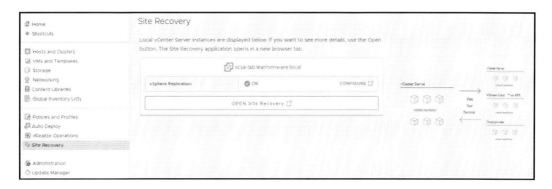

Configuring vSphere Replication

To configure vSphere Replication, follow these steps:

1. From the vSphere client, select the VM you need to replicate and select **All Site Recovery Actions** and **Configure Replication**.
2. The new UI will be launched.
3. First, the wizard will validate whether the VM can be configured for replication.
4. In the next step, you can select the replication target. As a replication target, you can use either the same vCenter server (the VM will be replicated to another local VM) or a remote vCenter server (the VM will be replicated to another site).
5. In the target datastore, you have to select on which datastore the data will be replicated.

6. The last step is to configure your replication option, especially **Recovery Point Objective (RPO)** and point in time snapshots, should you wish to use them:

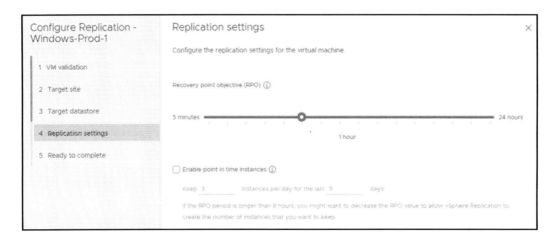

Once the replication is configured, you can access the vSphere Replication UI to see the status of all replicated VMs and their last synchronization, and you have an option to recover from the replica:

Disaster recovery and disaster avoidance

A **disaster** is any event that halts business activity on a large scale. In most cases, we are talking about natural disasters, but there are also human-made disasters, and all of them can happen at any time without warning.

These disasters could impact technologies and IT services. Of course, there are other and more critical aspects, such as risk to human life, but for **Business Continuity(BC)**, we put the main focus on business-critical services and applications.

DR provides BC in the event of a disaster, and may be just localized on equipment (such as a single server) or globally on an entire site. Business will be recovered by following a specific DR plan; it is just a subset of the **Business Continuity Plan** (**BCP**). In the case of a disaster that impacts an entire site or region, usually, the recovery process uses a remote location called a disaster recovery site.

DR is essential to ensure the continuation of business after a disaster. DR can also be required in several regulatory compliances. Effective DR is a critical part of a BCP must address the following three organizational requirements:

- **Minimize risks**: Having a BC plan does not eliminate all risks if you cannot be sure that the plan is reliable or practicable. The DR plan could be difficult to implement, and for several organizations, it may have some business impacts and possible risks.
- **Minimize downtime:** The consequences of extended downtime can be critical for business, recognition, and productivity. For most companies, a service disruption of ten or more days could be a total disaster and lead to the company closing.
- **Control costs:** Traditional disaster recovery plans are often limited in scope because of the cost, but you must find a trade off between costs and risk mitigation.

Although everyone realizes the importance of a DR plan, some organizations do not have the proper level of DR protection that they need. Only after a real disaster do they fully understand the importance of DR and the real impact that a disaster can have on their business.

Legacy solutions and processes to activate applications in the DR site usually require complex runbooks and manual procedures to execute the failover process. They may require highly specialized staff with vertical skills, large time investments, and high levels of coordination from several teams that are responsible for different layers of the infrastructure.

The main challenges that must be handled by DR in order to have a successful and effective plan are as follows:

- **Complexity**: Usually data center recovery plans are complex processes because, to guarantee the correct recovery of entire business services, they must deal with all the inter-dependencies between applications, hosts, networks, storage, and other infrastructural and organizational aspects.

- **Lack of predictable and reliable recovery**: Recovery plans documented in run books can be incomplete and may quickly fall out of sync with rapidly evolving deployments. Most enterprises test their recovery plan only twice a year or less.
- **High cost**: Legacy DR solutions require significant capital and operating expenditures. The DR site typically requires a dedicated duplicate server infrastructure. As defined by Gartner in *Survey Analysis: IT Disaster Recovery Management Spending and Testing Activities Expand in 2012, July 2012*:

  > *"The net result is that legacy disaster recovery solutions are regarded as non-strategic and costly insurance policies with very questionable returns. At best, only a few mission-critical applications get the privilege of site-level protection."*

Two of the fundamental parameters that characterize a BC/DR plan are the **Recovery Point Objective (RPO)** and **Recovery Time Objective (RTO)**:

- RPO refers to how much data you can lose. RPO usually refers to the time that has elapsed between last backup and the failure.
- RTO refers to how long it will take to recover from the failure. Usually, the duration of the restore procedure is referred as Recovery Time Objective.

In a perfect world, you would want to have those numbers near zero, but the cost of such a solution would be extremely high. In the real world, you need to find a balance between the cost of a BC/DR solution versus the potential risks of failure.

DR of a virtual data center

Protecting a virtual workload is much easier compared to protecting a physical data center, in a legacy way, for several reasons:

- **Virtualization provides encapsulation**: A VM is usually a set of files that can be easily managed.
- **Virtualization provides hardware independence**: Where a VM can run as it is (without any changes) on different hardware, maybe also with different sizing, but using the same hypervisor (or a compatible one).
- **Different types of data replication can be used**: From traditional storage array replication to VM replication.

- **On the DR site, you can, potentially, and for a limited number of workloads**: Use a single server that has enough computing and storage capacity.
- **Cloud Disaster Recovery as a Service (DRaaS)**: This solution is possible and practical.

All of the preceding benefits make it possible and convenient to provide a low RPO and a low RTO for the entire data center (or a large set of it), not just for the first tier of business-critical applications and services. Also, we have to consider that most companies are already leveraging virtualization, with a virtualization-first approach, also dictated for BC and DR requirements.

DR versus disaster avoidance

Disaster avoidance, as the name suggests, is a way to avoid or lessen the likelihood that a catastrophe will happen (through human blunders), or guarantee that, on the off-chance that, such a disaster occurs, the impact upon the association's innovation frameworks will be limited as far as possible.

The idea of disaster avoidance provides better resilience rather than good recovery, but to use it, you cannot rely only on infrastructure availability solutions, which are mostly geographically limited to a specific site; you also need to look at how to provide better application availability and redundancy in the wake of foreseeable disruptions.

Multi-datacenter (or multi-region cloud) replication is one part of the solution. The second part is having active-active data centers or having applications spread between multiple sites that provide service availability.

Most new cloud-native applications are designed for this scenario. However, there are also some examples of traditional applications with HA concepts at the application level that can also work geographically, such as **DNS services**, **Active Directory Domain Controller (AD DC)**, Exchange **database availability group (DAG)**, and **SQL AlwaysOn** clusters. In all these cases, one system can fail, but the service will not be affected because another node will provide it. Although solutions such as Exchange DAG or SQL AlwaysOn rely on internal cluster services, applications designed with HA solutions usually use loosely coupled systems without shared components (except, of course, the network, but it can be a routed or geographical network).

An interesting examples of the infrastructure layer is a stretched cluster, or metro cluster.

DR versus stretched clusters

A stretched cluster, sometimes called a **metro cluster** or **metro storage cluster**, is a deployment model in which two or more host servers are part of the same logical cluster but are located in separate geographical locations, usually two sites. In a stretched cluster, the two groups of servers (in each site) are usually used to provide HA and load balancing features and capabilities:

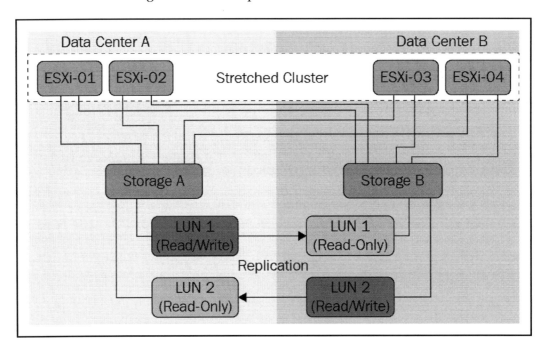

This allows proactive behavior in order to avoid or minimize service outages, using disaster avoidance; if a disaster affects an entire site, the second one will manage all the resources and services. Although a stretched cluster can be used for disaster recovery and not only for disaster avoidance, there are some possible limitations on using a stretched cluster as DR as well:

- A stretched cluster can't protect you from site link failures and can be affected by the split-brain scenario.
- A stretched cluster usually works with synchronous replication; that means a limited distance, but also makes it difficult to provide multiple restore points with different timings.
- Bandwidth requirements are high, to minimize storage latency. So you not only need reliable lines, but also enough capacity.
- A stretched cluster can be more costly than a DR solution, but of course, can also provide disaster avoidance in some cases.

In most cases where a stretched cluster is used, there might be a third site acting as a traditional DR; in this way, a multi-level protection approach is used.

VMware solutions

In the past, business continuity was the first driver of virtualization; virtualization not only helps with server consolidation and driving down costs across IT organizations, but can also improve availability, resilience, and recoverability for business-critical applications and services.

VMware provides a holistic approach to protecting your IT environment and all applications running on the vSphere platform from a variety of factors that can cause application downtime, including unplanned events such as server failures and even planned events such as server maintenance. These solutions provide simple, cost-effective protection with a standard solution for all your applications and services.

VMware BC-related solutions cover the following:

- **Local availability**: Some products and technologies protect applications against the downtime of individual hosts. This includes vSphere HA and FT for unplanned downtime, as well as vMotion and storage vMotion for planned downtime.

- **Data protection**: There are solutions to back up entire VMs, including OSes, application binaries, and application data, in a simple non-disruptive manner. A third-party solution can use VMware storage APIs for data protection to enable native VM backup.
- **Disaster recovery**: vSphere Replication is an exciting addition to the vSphere platform, providing a cost-efficient and straightforward way to implement VM-based replication. For DR orchestration, vCenter SRM leverages vSphere and vSphere Replication (or storage-based replication) to protect applications against site failures and to streamline planned migrations.
- **Disaster avoidance**: **vSphere Metro Storage Cluster** (**vMSC**) is a configuration option, introduced in vSphere 5, that allows the use of stretched clusters.

You can find more details in **Mastering Disaster Recovery: Business Continuity and Virtualization Best Practices** at `http://download3.vmware.com/elq/img/EMEA/EMEA11122/pdf/VirtMngt_MasteringDisasterRecovery_WhitePaper_Q410_EN.pdf?cid=70180000000wCtz`.

VM Replication

VMware vSphere Replication is a BC/DR solution that enables you to replicate VMs to the same vCenter Server or even to a different vCenter Server running on another site. You can also utilize third-party service providers who offer disaster recovery to cloud solutions where the primary VM is replicated to the service provider environment.

vSphere Replication is a available for both vCenter Server for Windows and for vCenter Server Appliance, and it is included in every license starting from Essentials Plus.

Once you enable the replication, any VM can be replicated to the other site. If it is required (for example, because of low bandwidth between sites), the initial replica can be transported using offline media, and once it is at the targeted site, the delta data is transferred over the network. Only the changed blocks are transferred between sites using the **Change Block Tracking** (**CBT**) feature of vSphere.

You have the option defining your own RPO ranging from 5 minute to 24 hours depending on your needs, and you are able to use **multiple points in time** (**MPIT**), in which case you will be able to store up to 24 snapshots of each replicated VM.

Of course, this is not the only VM-based replication solution; several third-party products provide more features and capabilities. Most native backup products also have VM Replication features, and so, in this case, they could be cost-effective solutions, especially if you already have that specific backup product.

There are also some replication products that can replicate VMs not only across the same virtualization platform but also across different types of hypervisor such as **Zerto**. You can find more information about the technology at `https://www.zerto.com/solutions/use-cases/cross-hypervisor-replication-vmware-hyper-v-aws/`

Stretched cluster

A VMware vMSC configuration is a certified solution that combines vSphere clustering with array-based replication. Such solutions are commonly deployed in environments where the distance between data centers is limited since array-based replication requires low latency between sites.

vMSC infrastructures are implemented with the goal of reaping the same benefits that HA clusters provide to a local site, in a geographically dispersed model with two data centers in different locations.

A vMSC infrastructure is necessarily a **stretched cluster**. The architecture is built on the premise of extending what is defined as *local* in terms of network and storage to enable these subsystems to span regions, resulting in a single logical infrastructure consisting of the resources from both of the sites.

VMware vMSC is just a configuration option for a vSphere cluster, where half of the virtualization hosts are on one site and the other half is on a second site. Both sites work in an active-active way, and common vSphere features such as vMotion and vSphere HA can be used.

The only restrictions are that vMotion must support higher latency (this is possible in the Enterprise Plus Edition), that all VMs must reside on the same layer 2 networks (that means a stretched network is needed, or some other network virtualization technique), and that the storage part can provide active-active access from both sites (there are several types of storage certified for vMSC).

On account of a site catastrophe, vSphere HA will give start the VMs on the other site.

VMware vSAN in the Enterprise Edition can also provide the stretched shared storage part; in this way, it's possible to build a complete stretched cluster using vSphere as a core infrastructure component for both compute and storage components:

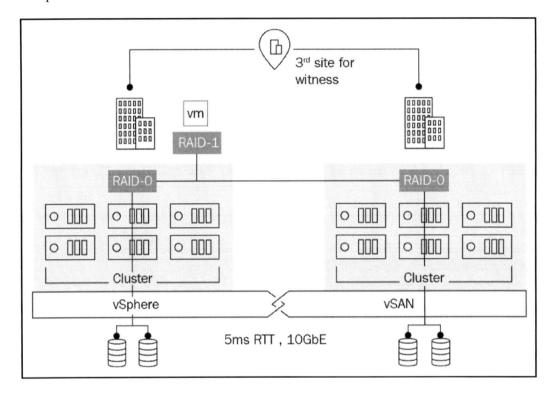

SRM

VMware's disaster recovery solution is called SRM. SRM is mechanization programming that incorporates a hidden replication innovation to give strategy-based administration, non-problematic testing, and computerized coordination of recuperation designs. It gives accessibility to the VMs when disasters occur:

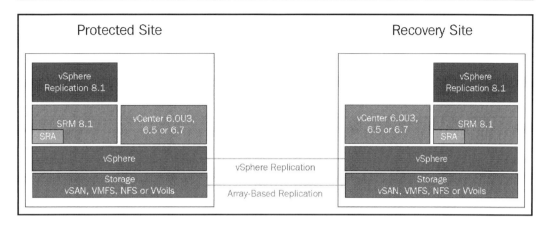

SRM uses vSphere Replication and supports a broad range of array-based replication solutions available from various VMware storage partners. SRM integrates tightly with VMware vSphere Web Client and vCenter Server, and it also takes advantage of **software-defined datacenter** (**SDDC**) by integrating NSX and vSAN.

As written, cross-site replication at the VM or storage level is just the first step for DR. You will then need an entire set of rules to define how to recover your VMs in the case of the primary site failure. SRM delivers several features and functions, including centralized recovery plans, non-disruptive testing, and automated orchestration, both for fail-over (in the case of DR) and fail-back (in case the original site has been recovered).

Adding extended stockpiling to a SRM sending on a very basic level diminishes recuperation times; on account of a catastrophe, recuperation is a lot quicker because the extended stockpiling design that empowers synchronous information composes and peruses on the two destinations.

Please note that the SRM model for active-active data centers is fundamentally different from the model used in the VMware vMSC. SRM uses two vCenter Server instances, one on each site, instead of stretching the vSphere cluster across sites.

Adding SRM to a stretched storage deployment allows users to benefit from key features of SRM that are not present in vMSC, such as centralized recovery plans, orchestrated recovery, and non-disruptive automated testing.

Summary

Protection of the virtual infrastructure is an essential topic for every administrator, to limit potential service disruption.

Virtual servers are the most critical infrastructure components since they provide services to the business. Suitable protection of VMs is therefore required to ensure data protection and business continuity.

In this chapter, we described specific availability (and resilience) solutions in vSphere, including the new vSphere HA features, Proactive HA, and Admission Control.

vSphere HA is the essential high-availability mechanism built into the vSphere suite that is responsible for VM restarts when the underlying ESXi hypervisor is unavailable.

Although vSphere HA can provide an essential and convenient availability level for all workloads, with minimum effort and cost, it's not suitable for business-critical workloads. In this case, other solutions can be used, such as vSphere FT or traditional (from the physical world) solutions, such as guest clustering.

This chapter also provided a general overview of some backup solutions available on the market that protect virtual environments. Hyper-scale technology is quite a new solution that reduces the management of workload protection, providing appliances that are ready to go.

We have also described different business continuity and disaster recovery approaches, the overall benefits of BC/DR solutions, and specific VMware products and features that lead to the maximum uptime for your virtual datacenter.

vSphere Replication can be used for business continuity and disaster recovery situations without additional investment compared to traditional storage replication solutions, and can be further extended by the SRM to fully automated disaster recovery.

Questions

1. vSphere HA will always restart the VM in case of failover.

    a) True
    b) False

2. Two kinds of heartbeats are used in conjunction with vSphere HA. What are their exact names?

        a) Network heartbeat
        b) IP heartbeat
        c) File heartbeat
        d) Storage heartbeat
        e) TCP/IP heartbeat

3. A specific file, `host-XX-hb`, is created on the shared datastore once the vSphere HA is configured. Please describe the use of this file.

4. An **All-Path-Down (APD)** situation is announced by SCSI sense code from the storage array.

        a) True
        b) False

5. What three types of admission control can be configured (except disabling the option)?

        a) Slot Policy
        b) ESXi resource policy
        c) Cluster resource percentage
        d) Dedicated failover host
        e) Datastore clusters

6. Name at least three technologies or functions that you cannot use in conjunction with Fault Tolerance.

7. You can use any VMkernel adapter for FT logging traffic. When multiple VMkernel adapters are configured, based on the election mechanism, the correct one will be used.

        a) True
        b) False

8. Please describe some disadvantages of Fault Tolerance.

9. VM clustering can be used to improve the performance of the individual VM.

        a) True
        b) False

10. vSphere Replication provides continuous synchronous replication for VMs.

   a) True
   b) False

11. Describe two essential parameters for every disaster recovery plan—RTO and RPO.

12. What is the most significant difference between the Site Recovery Manager and vMSC in terms of the number of vCenter Servers?

Further reading

Read the following articles for more information:

- **vSphere Availability**: vSphere Availability describes solutions that provide business continuity, including how to establish vSphere HA and vSphere FT. `https://docs.vmware.com/en/VMware-vSphere/6.7/vsphere-esxi-vcenter-server-67-availability-guide.pdf`

- **Setup for failover clustering and Microsoft cluster service**: `https://docs.vmware.com/en/VMware-vSphere/6.5/vsphere-esxi-vcenter-server-651-setup-mscs.pdf`

- **VMware vSphere Metro Storage Cluster recommended practices**: `https://www.vmware.com/content/dam/digitalmarketing/vmware/en/pdf/techpaper/vmware-vsphere-metro-storage-cluster-recommended-practices-white-paper.pdf`

- **Disaster Recovery Using VMware vSphere Replication and vCenter Site Recovery Manager - Second Edition**: `https://www.packtpub.com/virtualization-and-cloud/disaster-recovery-using-vmware-vsphere-replication-second-edition`.

Securing and Protecting Your Environment

12

One of the pillars of virtualization is the VM isolation property, which can protect the host layer from the VM effectively. Although some possible attacks have been found, virtualization remains an exciting approach to improve the security of your infrastructure. Securing and hardening your vSphere infrastructure should be considered one of the most important steps toward making your infrastructure as reliable as possible.

A new trend is now also to protect VMs from the underlying infrastructure; for example, in the case of a public cloud service, consumers may have some concerns about the security and privacy of their data. VMware offers different encryption mechanisms that make your data private no matter where they are being run.

This chapter will cover the following topics:

- Tuning and hardening guidelines
- vCenter and ESXi security
- Working with encryption and securing VMs

Security and hardening concepts in vSphere

Security is a complete process flow with an entire life cycle; depending on the model that will be used, the first part of the process is usually product-agnostic, but there is a part that's dependent on the different products and their features and capabilities.

Following VMware's vision, the five pillars of cyber hygiene are as follows:

- **Least privilege**: This is the standard and most reasonable approach, which applies to user accounts, service accounts, and services in general (for example, used ports).
- **Micro-segmentation**: Using NSX, it's finally possible to bring network control at the VM level with granular security rules. Considering also the new product, VMware AppDefense, VM security can be enforced at both network and application levels.
- **Encryption**: Data must be protected at each level, and for the physical level, encryption is the only way to ensure proper protection. We will discuss this later in the chapter.
- **Multi-factor authentication (MFA)**: Authentication is usually the weakest part, mostly due to passwords that are too simple (or passwords that are not changed periodically). We will discuss this later in the chapter.
- **Patching**: Keeping your software components up to date is crucial for the security aspect, but it's also essential for implementing new features. We will discuss this more in `Chapter 6`, *Life Cycle Management, Patching, and Upgrading*.

Hardening vSphere

Hardening is the process of securing a system, a service, or an entire infrastructure, by reducing the attack surface and minimizing the possible vulnerabilities. VMware has built **Security Hardening Guides**, which can found at `https://www.vmware.com/security/hardening-guides.html`, to provide prescriptive guidance for customers on how to deploy and operate VMware products in a secure manner.

The vSphere 6.7 Security Configuration Guide is a spreadsheet file with several guidelines classified with a risk profile, useful as a checklist for tuning, with rich metadata for guideline classification and risk assessment. There are also some example scripts for enabling security automation. For more information on how to read them and how the guidelines have changed since the previous release, see `https://blogs.vmware.com/vsphere/2018/11/announcing-the-vsphere-6-7-update-1-security-configuration-guide.html`.

The vSphere 6.7 Security Configuration Guide isn't a compliance tool; it can be used for compliance, but it's not automatically enforced. It's mostly a set of guidelines that attempt to explain security risks. Also, the guidelines may or may not apply to specific customer cases.

Authentication and identity

The vCenter **Single Sign-On** (**SSO**) authenticates a user against the identity source (configured in the vCenter SSO). Identity sources define how and where to verify user credentials. vSphere supports several identity source types:

- **Local SSO domain**: Default SSO domain created during the installation of the PSC. This is a default identity source.
- **Active directory (native)**: When the PSC is joined to an AD domain, it is possible to use the domain or the forest as an authentication source using Kerberos authentication.
- **LDAP (active directory)**: Use this if you don't want to join the PSC to the AD domain, or if you are using a lightweight active directory.
- **LDAP (OpenLDAP)**: Use this if you have an open source LDAP server (such as OpenLDAP).
- **Local OS**: The user defined in the SAM (for a Windows-based PSC) or the /etc/passwd and /etc/shadow file (for a Linux-based PSC).

You can define as many identity sources as you need, but only one of them can be a default identity source. When an identity source is set as the default, you do not need to include the domain name as a part of the username (user@mydomain.com) as the domain name will be appended automatically, so all you need to do is to provide a username without a domain suffix.

SSO configuration

By default, only the administrator of the local SSO domain has permission to access a vSphere SSO configuration:

1. From the web client, select **Administration**
2. Under SSO, select **Configuration**

3. Switch to the **Identity Sources** tab, as shown in the following screenshot:

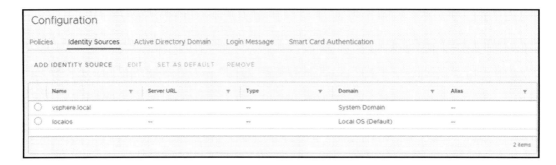

Password management

As vSphere is one of the most critical infrastructure components, it is critical to use strong passwords that are not easily guessed, and that is difficult for password generators. Password strength and complexity rules apply to all passwords, including hosts users (such as root).

ESXi uses the `pam_passwdqc.so` plugin to set the strength and the complexity of the host's passwords. You can define the password quality using the host's advanced system settings, called `Security.PasswordQualityControl`.

ESXi 6.0 has presented another lockout feature; a limit of 10 failed logins is permitted before the account is locked. The account is unlocked after two minutes by default. In the host's events, you will see the following row:

```
Remote access to ESXi local user account 'LOGINNAME' has been locked
for 120 seconds after ### failed login attempts.
```

Account locking works for access through SSH and the vSphere web services SDK. It does not apply to the DCUI and ESXi Shell.

If you are using a local SSO domain, you can enforce password and lockout policies to force the users to use complex passwords with specific requirements:

TIP If you are using AD users, both for hosts and vCenter, then the password policies are enforced by the AD GPO.

There are also password expiration rules for the virtual appliance local users, in case you are using vCSA for vCenter and/or the PSC components. Be sure also to check those settings:

1. Log in to the VAMI interface of the vCSA

2. Select the **Administration** tab from the navigator

3. Configure the desired options related to the password policy, as shown in the following screenshot:

Password	CHANGE
Password requirements	1. Must have at least six characters. 2. Should not be any of your previous five passwords.

Password expiration settings	EDIT
Password expires	Yes
Password validity (days)	90
Email for expiration warning ⓘ	Unset
Password expires on	May 11, 2019, 2:00:00 AM

Role-Based Access Control (RBAC)

The RBAC approach aims to limit individual users permissions based on their assignment within the organization by mapping the user accounts to the groups that are defined by the organization.

In VMware vSphere, you can find three core components of RBAC:

- **Roles**: A role is a specific subset of privileges based on the user's assignment.
- **Permissions**: Each task that can be performed is connected to a specific permission. To power off a VM, you need to have permission. Several permissions form a role.
- **Users and groups**: A role is mapped to a user and a particular vSphere object (such as a data center, cluster, or single VM).

Permissions are assigned according to the RBAC model, where you are matching the object (if the permission is not global), the user, or the group with the right role. A role is just a set of permissions, and you can use predefined roles or build (or copy) new ones.

Try to avoid certain mapping roles to specific users. Always map a role to the group instead and add a user to the group.

Users and groups could be used to define vSphere permissions at two different levels:

- **Inventory object level**: This is the traditional way to add permissions, by matching a user or group with a specific vSphere role on a specific object. It is useful if you need to delegate some management tasks:

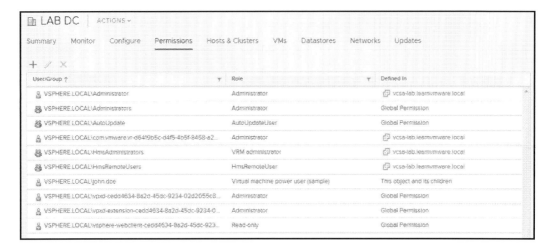

- **Global level:** This is an option where you can define global permissions (with a specific role) on the entire infrastructure (at the PSC level, thus this global permission will be applied to all vCenter Servers linked to the PSC):

Starting with vSphere 6.0 Update 2, you can include a login banner with your environment. You can enable and disable the login banner from the SSO configuration, and you can require that users click an explicit **Consent checkbox**:

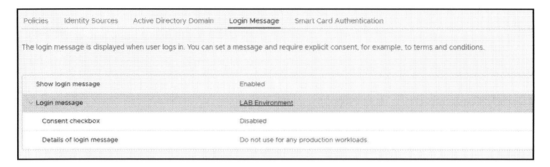

Active directory integration

The vCenter Server has an internal user database that allows you to add and manage users with the vSphere Web Client. User management and SSO is provided by the PSC, which has been available since vSphere 6.0. In a large environment, you might want to connect your virtualization infrastructure to a centrally managed AD.

We have already covered basic active directory integration in Chapter 5, *Configuring and Managing vSphere 6.7*, so let's focus on advanced topics.

MFA

MFA grants user access only after successfully presenting several separate pieces of evidence to an authentication mechanism, usually at least two of the following categories—knowledge (something they know), possession (something they have), and inherence (something they are).

Two-factor authentication (**2FA**) is a type of MFA where just two components are used. Starting with vSphere 6.0 Update 2, it is possible to have 2FA using the following:

- **Smart cards** (UPN-based **Common Access Card** (**CAC**))
- **RSA SecurID** token

vCenter SSO supports only native SecurID and does not support **Remote Authentication Dial-In User Service (RADIUS)**.

Smart cards

A smart card is a small plastic card with an embedded integrated circuit chip that can be read by a smart card reader (many laptops may have one integrated). To enable smart card authentication for vCenter authentication, you must first set up your clients before users can log in using a smart card:

- **With vSphere 6.0**: Verify that the Client Integration Plugin is installed.
- **With vSphere 6.5 and 6.7**: Verify that the Enhanced Authentication Plugin is installed.

Then the configuration of the PSC is a little different in versions 6.0 and 6.5. For the latest version, before you can enable smart card authentication, you must correctly configure the reverse proxy from the command line on the PSC (or the vCenter if you have an embedded deployment). You have to create a trusted client **Certificate Authority (CA)** store that contains the trusted issuing CA's certificates for the client certificate.

For a Linux-based PSC, these are the possible commands:

```
cd /usr/lib/vmware-sso/
openssl x509 -inform PEM -in xyzCompanySmartCardSigningCA.cer >>
/usr/lib/vmware-sso/vmware-sts/conf/clienttrustCA.pem
```

Then you have to modify the `config.xml` file with the following changes:

```
<http>
 <maxConnections> 2048 </maxConnections>
 <requestClientCertificate>true</requestClientCertificate>
 <clientCertificateMaxSize>4096</clientCertificateMaxSize>
 <clientCAListFile>/usr/lib/vmware-sso/vmware-
sts/conf/clienttrustCA.pem</clientCAListFile>
 </http>
```

And finally, restart the service:

```
/usr/lib/vmware-vmon/vmon-cli --restart rhttpproxy
```

Then verify that an enterprise **Public Key Infrastructure** (**PKI**) is set up in your environment and that certificates meet the following requirements:

- A **User Principal Name** (**UPN**) must correspond to an AD account in the **Subject Alternative Name** (**SAN**) extension
- The certificate must specify client authentication in the **Application Policies** or **Enhanced Key Usage** fields, or the browser does not show the certificate

At this point, you can enable smart card authentication from the SSO configuration menu.

Starting with ESXi 6.0, it's also possible to use smart card authentication to log in to the ESXi DCUI by using a **Personal Identity Verification** (**PIV**), CAC, or SC650 smart card instead of specifying a username and password.

Under **Configure** | **System**, select the authentication services (described before for AD authentication) and you will see the current **Smart Card Authentication** status and a list of imported certificates:

In the **Smart Card Authentication** panel, you can click the **EDIT...** button and select the **Certificates** page to add trusted CA certificates, for example, root and intermediary CA certificates.

RSA SecurID

SecurID setup is supported only from the command line on vCenter Server version 6.0 or later. The configuration is well explained in the following blog post: `https://blogs.vmware.com/vsphere/2017/07/using-vcenter-login-banner-rsa-securid-support.html`.

Then the integration is quite simple on the web client authentication page:

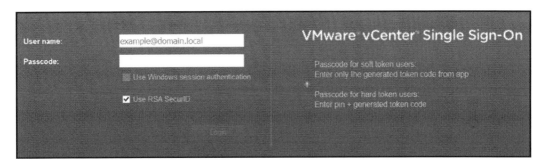

RSA authentication manager requires that the user ID is a unique identifier that uses 1 to 255 ASCII characters. The characters ampersand (&), percent (%), higher than (>), less than (<), and single quote (`) are not allowed. Also, the RSA SecurID agent that is integrated into the PSC component of vCenter does not support PIN resets.

vCenter Server, ESXi, and VM hardening

VMware vSphere environments are sometimes deployed using the default configuration of many features and services and they are not regularly checked for potential improvements in terms of VMware security standards and best practices.

VMware regularly updates its hardening guides available at `https://www.vmware.com/security/hardening-guides.html` which provides essential information and recommendations on how to make the vSphere infrastructure more secure.

We have tried to pinpoint several of the most essential aspects of the vSphere infrastructure hardening in the following sections.

ESXi hardening

To protect the ESXi hosts against unauthorized intrusion and misuse, consider the following options for improving infrastructure security:

- **Limit user access:** This is done by restricting user access to the management interface and enforcing access security policies such as setting up password restrictions. Lockdown mode could be used to limit access to the hosts to all users. Otherwise, a centralized authentication could be useful to manage security groups and related roles (for example, with AD).

- **Limit shell access:** ESXi Shell (locally, but also through ESXi SSH access) has several privileged accesses to certain parts of the host. Therefore, they provide only trusted users with ESXi Shell login access. Usually, it is safe to keep both ESXi Shell and SSH access disabled to prevent direct access to the ESXi CLI. In this case, you can still use `esxcli` remotely or another remote CLI.

- **Limit services**: You can run ESXi essential services only. Some hardware vendors have specific agents that can run on ESXi hosts, but check their support and security level before running any third-party agents or services on ESXi hosts.

- **Limit network connections:** ESXi has a personal firewall (starting from ESXi 5.0) and, by default, is closed on most ports. When you enable a service, it also opens the right ports. Although you can manually open ports with the predefined firewall rules, and you can also build new custom ESXi firewall rules, it would be better to try to keep the ESXi firewall rules management entirely automatic. The personal firewall does not protect you from **Denial-of-Service (DoS)** attacks, so still keep your ESXi VMkernel interfaces on protected networks and still use perimeter firewalls.

- **Use secure connections:** By default, weak ciphers are disabled, and SSL secures all communication from clients. The exact algorithms used for securing the channel depend on the SSL handshake. VMware vSphere 6.0 introduces a certification authority to help in certification management. Starting with vSphere 6.5, the **Transport Layer Security (TLS)** protocol versions 1.0, 1.1, and 1.2 are enabled by default.

- **Patch your hosts:** Use only VMware sources to upgrade or patch ESXi hosts. VMware does not support upgrading these packages from any source other than a VMware source.

- **Check VMware Security Center**: VMware monitors all security alerts that could affect ESXi security and, if necessary, issues a security patch. If you regularly check the VMware Security Center site, you can find any alerts that might impact the environment.

You can check the official guide, **General ESXi Security Recommendations**, at `https://docs.vmware.com/en/VMware-vSphere/6.7/com.vmware.vsphere.security.doc/GUID-B39474AF-6778-499A-B8AB-E973BE6D4899.html`.

Lockdown mode

When you connect ESXi to vCenter, to increase the host's security, you can put the ESXi host in lockdown mode. Lockdown mode restricts remote users from directly logging in to this host. It can be accessed only through local console or an authorized centralized management application. It is possible to modify lockdown mode configuration in the host settings, or from the **Direct Console User Interface** (DCUI).

In vSphere 6.7, lockdown mode has multiple settings and a user exception list. This allows users and solutions to be excluded from the lockdown mode settings. The following are the different configuration options:

- **Disabled**: Lockdown mode is disabled.
- **Normal**: DCUI is not blocked. Privileged user accounts can still log in to the ESXi host console and exit lockdown mode.
- **Strict**: DCUI is stopped and is only accessible through vCenter:

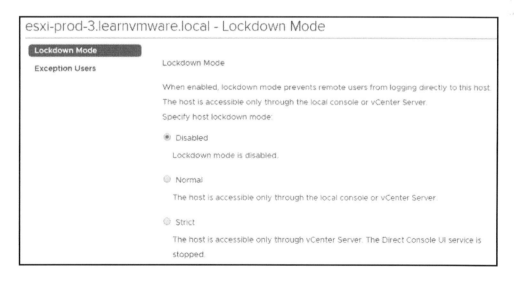

Strict mode dramatically reduces the manageability of the hosts, because CLI commands cannot be executed from an administration server or script. There is an option to access the ESXi server even under strict lockdown mode but only for users defined in **exception users.** Users in this list retain their original permissions allowing them to interact with the ESXi. Typically, user accounts used for integration purposes, third-party solutions, or external applications are included in the exception users.

Networking

If you are using distributed virtual switches, some specific network security configurations can be managed only from the most advanced settings. For example, to enable the **Bridge Protocol Data Unit (BPDU)** filter, you must use a host advanced setting, `Net.BlockGuestBPDU`, as described in **KB 2047822: Understanding the BPDU Filter feature in vSphere,** at `https://kb.vmware.com/kb/2047822`.

Of course, the security policies (promiscuous mode, MAC address change, and forge packets) for the virtual switches are still relevant, but for distributed virtual switches, they are all rejected by default (starting with vSphere 5.1).

Virtual switches do not provide firewall functions (ESXi personal firewall works only on VMkernel ports); to implement micro-segmentation, you need solutions such as NSX, although you can achieve some necessary protection using filtering rules on the distributed vSwitch.

Transparent Page Sharing (TPS)

Recent academic research has demonstrated that it is theoretically possible to leverage TPS to gain unauthorized access to data under certain highly controlled conditions. For more information, see `https://blogs.vmware.com/security/2014/10/transparent-page-sharing-additional-management-capabilities-new-default-settings.html`.

For this reason, in vSphere 6.x, TPS is disabled across different VMs but is still working inside individual VMs. It is still possible to enable it on the entire ESXi, by following **KB 2097593: Additional Transparent Page Sharing management capabilities and new default settings** at `https://kb.vmware.com/kb/2097593`.

VIB acceptance level

By default, ESXi only allows signed **vSphere Installation Bundles** (**VIBs**), because an unsigned VIB represents untested code installed on an ESXi host. You can change the acceptance level for each host, in the **Configure** | **System** | **Security Profile** menu, under the **Host Image Profile Acceptance Level** option:

The host image profile supports the four acceptance levels:

- **VMware Certified**: VIBs created, tested, and signed by VMware.
- **VMware Accepted**: VIBs created by a VMware partner but tested and signed by VMware.
- **Partner Supported**: VIBs created, tested, and signed by a certified VMware partner.
- **Community Supported**: VIBs that have not been tried by VMware or a VMware partner. Community Supported VIBs are not upheld and don't have a computerized mark. To ensure the security and respectability of your ESXi, don't permit unsigned Community Supported VIBs to be introduced on your hosts.

Host encryption mode

Encryption mode determines whether the host is ready to accept key material. When enabled, core dumps are always encrypted. Enable encryption mode only if the host is secured from unauthorized access to avoid leaking sensitive cryptographic data.

This setting can be configured from the **Configure** | **System** | **Security Profile** menu, under the **Host Encryption Mode** option:

ESXi Secure Boot

For ESXi, Secure Boot is possible using the digital signature of all VIB components, like a cryptographic assurance. By utilizing that computerized endorsement in the host UEFI firmware, at boot time, the approved ESXi VMkernel will in this way approve each VIB against the same certificate:

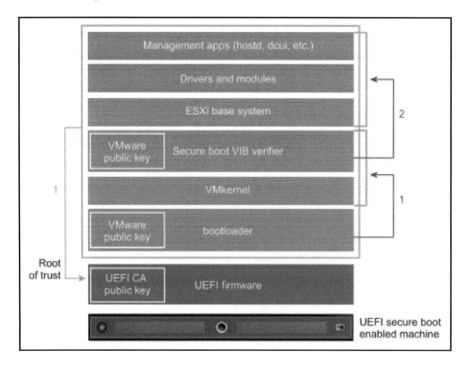

When ESXi Secure Boot is enabled, you will not be able to install unsigned code on ESXi forcibly.

For more information on how to enable this feature and some possible issues, for example, during the upgrade process, see the following post: `https://blogs.vmware.com/vsphere/2017/05/secure-boot-esxi-6-5-hypervisor-assurance.html`.

vCenter hardening

By using the vCSA, as also suggested by VMware, you can use the same VM hardening suggestions and also benefit from a hardened OS. By default, shell access is disabled. SSH can be enabled during deployment, but you still access the vCSA with a limited set of commands (anyway, enabling the full shell is quite easy).

Similar best practices to the ESXi hypervisor apply to the vCenter Server as well, with a few additional recommendations related to PSC:

- **Check password expiration**: The default vCenter SSO password lifetime is 90 days.
- **Configure NTP**: This ensures that all systems use the same relative time source (including the relevant localization offset). Synchronized systems are essential for vCenter SSO certificate validity, and the validity of other vSphere certificates.

VM hardening

The hardening guide describes a lot of specific VM options but, starting with ESXi 6.0 Patch 5, many of the VM advanced settings are now set to be *secure* by default. This means that the desired values in the Security Configuration Guide are the default values for all new VMs and you don't have to set them manually anymore.

For more information, see the blog post at `https://blogs.vmware.com/vsphere/2017/06/secure-default-vm-disable-unexposed-features.html`.

For VMs, several specific hardening operations should be considered:

- Use templates to deploy VMs
- Minimize use of the VM console
- Prevent VMs from taking over resources
- Disable unnecessary functions inside VMs

For more information, check the official documentation at `https://docs.vmware.com/en/VMware-vSphere/6.7/com.vmware.vsphere.security.doc/GUID-14CCC8CD-D90D-4227-B2C3-0A93D3C023BA.html`.

It is recommended to disable or remove any virtual hardware that is not vital for the VM (such as the floppy drive). The same security principles as physical servers apply to the VMs:

- Protect the BIOS of the server with the password
- Patch the OS and application
- Enable **Secure Boot**
- Protect the server with the firewall (if connected to an unsecured network)

For virtual networking, NSX can provide the micro-segmentation capability to enforce network security directly at the VM virtual NIC level. Also, at VMworld 2017, a new product was announced—**VMware AppDefense**, a data center endpoint security product that protects applications running in virtualized environments. AppDefense works inside the VMs (as compared to NSX, which only works at the network level) and understands how applications are supposed to work regularly and monitors all changes to that behavior state that indicate a threat.

VM Secure Boot

In an OS that supports UEFI Secure Boot, each piece of boot software is signed, including the bootloader, the OS kernel, and OS drivers.
VM Secure Boot has some essential requirements:

- Virtual hardware version 13 or later
- EFI firmware in the VM boot options
- Guest OS that supports UEFI Secure Boot

Some examples of a supported OS are Windows 8 and Windows Server 2012 or newer, VMware ESXi 6.5 and Photon OS, RHEL/Centos 7.0, and Ubuntu 14.04.

You can enable Secure Boot using the vSphere Web Client in the **VM Options** section of the selected VM:

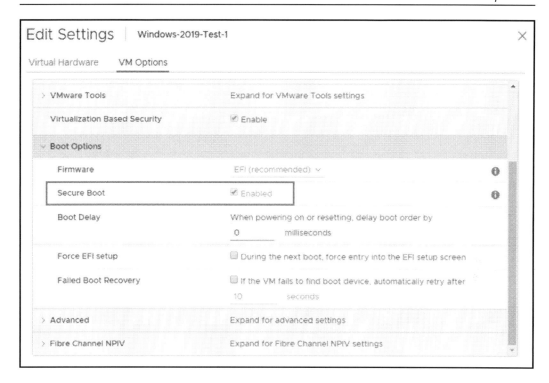

 You cannot upgrade a VM that uses BIOS boot to a VM that uses UEFI boot. Only if a VM already uses UEFI boot and the OS supports UEFI Secure Boot can you enable Secure Boot.

Other security aspects

Several other aspects should be considered for security, such as **log management** and **system monitoring**; both of these are useful not only for the security of your environment but also for its manageability.

Another common aspect that will be discussed is certification management, which has been widely improved starting with vSphere version 6.0.

Log management

ESXi has run a syslog administration (`vmsyslogd`) that logs messages from the VMkernel and other framework parts to log records. The log destination can be configured from the vSphere Client; select the host and click **Configure** | **Settings** | **Advanced System Settings**. By default, the `Syslog.global.logDir` parameter is set to `/scratch/log`.

ESXi can be designed to store log documents on an in-memory filesystem. This happens when the host's `/scratch` registry is connected to `tmp/scratch`. When this is done, just a solitary day of logs is put away at once. For more information on ESXi partitions, see `Chapter 5`, *Configuring and Managing vSphere 6.7*.

You can also set a Syslog Server, both with the GUI (under the advanced settings) or with the CLI, for example, from ESXi Shell:

```
esxcli system syslog config set —loghost tcp://SYSLOG_IP:514
esxcli system syslog reload
```

You can use more Syslog Servers using a comma, or also use SSL connections instead of plain TCP (or UDP); in this case, you must use the syntax `ssl://SYSLOG_SERVER:1514`.
For more information, see **KB 2003322**: **Configuring syslog on ESXi** at `https://kb.vmware.com/kb/2003322`.

You can use an external third-party Syslog Server or the following VMware solutions:

- **VMware Syslog Collector**: Included in vCenter Server. It supports TLS protocol versions 1.0, 1.1, and 1.2. However, it does not have a simple way to analyze logs.
- **VMware vRealize Log Insight server**: A dedicated product also used to correlate different logs and get to the root cause of issues more quickly and efficiently.

Monitoring protocols

By default, SNMP is not enabled on hosts, either as a service or as a configured node. If you want to enable the SNMP service, to use this protocol, then, for each host, the proper trap destination should be configured as the correct community.

Also on vCenter Server, you can enable sending traps on different alarms, but the SNMP receivers must be set in the general configuration. If SNMP is not being used, it might be better to keep it disabled; if it is not configured correctly, monitoring information can be collected from a malicious host that can then use this information to plan an attack.

To configure SNMP receivers, perform the following configuration:

1. Select your vCenter server in the navigator and switch to the **Configure** tab.
2. Under **Settings**, switch to **General** and click the **Edit...** button.
3. Select the **SNMP receivers** section in the menu and configure the receiver URL (IP address), port, and SNMP community name:

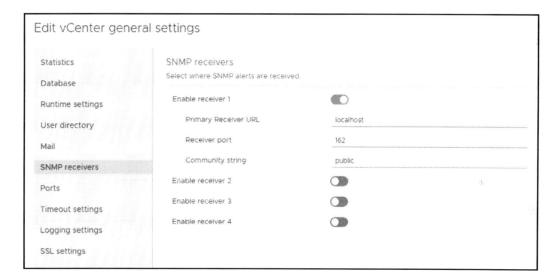

Certification management

Starting with vSphere 6.0, the new PSC component includes not only the SSO part but also a certification authority, **VMware Certificate Authority (VMCA)**, for certification management of all vSphere infrastructure components. This simplifies not only the certification management (with auto-enrollment for expired certificates) but also the trust between the different connections.

In this environment, the vSphere certificates are generated and issued by the VMCA and stored by the **VMware Endpoint Certificate Store** (**VECS**). However, to avoid browser warnings, you need to trust the VMware's CA by adding it in your certification chain. First of all, you need to get the CA root certificate. You can directly download it from the vCenter home page, under **Download trusted root CA certificates**:

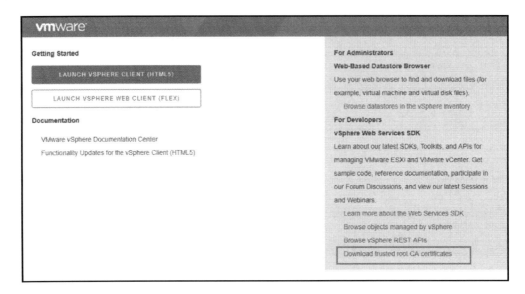

You will download a simple download `.zip` file that contains both the CA certificate and the revocation list.

To import the certificate, you can use different approaches for a Windows system:

- **Import manually**: For Internet Explorer, Edge, and Chrome, you can double-click on the certificate and import it into the trusted CA. Firefox has a different certificates repository.
- **Import by using GPO**: Under **Computer Configuration** | **Windows Settings** | **Security Settings** | **Public Key Policies** | **Trusted Publishers**, you can import existing certificates. Be sure to import it into the **Trusted Root Certification Authorities** store.
- **Add as an intermediate CA**: In your existing CA authority.

Otherwise, you can replace the CA certificate of VMCA, or don't use it at all and manage all the certificates as in the past. For more information, see **VMware KB 2097936: How to use vSphere 6.x Certificate Manager** at `https://kb.vmware.com/kb/2097936`.

If you have an existing PKI within your infrastructure, you can easily replace the VMCA root certificate (self-signed) by a new (signed) certificate from your enterprise authority. In this scenario, the VMCA certificate is an intermediate certificate. VMCA provisions vCenter Server components and ESXi hosts with certificates that include the full certificate chain.

VMCA can only be managed using the CLI. There is no UI available yet. If you need to access VMCA configuration utility, simply log in to the vCSA (or dedicated PSC) and issue the following command:

`/usr/lib/vmware-vmca/bin/certificate-manager`

The certificate manager will be displayed as follows:

Please be sure that you have enabled SSH access to the vCSA. You can check the configuration through the VAMI interface of the vCSA under the **Access** menu option.

Encryption options of the vSphere

Some vSphere infrastructures are located strictly on-premise, where the local IT department has full control over the entire infrastructure, but maintaining a hybrid infrastructure can become a security challenge.

Every time your data leaves your organization, for example, if part of the infrastructure is located in an external data center, you should always encrypt such data since it is the most valuable asset of every company.

VMware vSphere can be leveraged to encrypt data in different levels:

- **Encryption at rest**: Data is encrypted on the storage infrastructure, in the other words, where it resides
- **Encryption during transit**: Data is encrypted when transmitted over an unsecured channel

Protecting the data at rest

There are different possible options to store your data securely, which are as follows:

- **Encryption at storage physical level**: This is done by using **self-encrypting drives (SEDs)** using full disk encryption, also known as hardware-based **full-disk encryption (FDE)**. **Opal Storage Specification** is a set of specifications for SEDs developed by the Trusted Computing Group. However, these types of disks are quite costly and also require controllers or storage that support this feature.
- **Encryption at storage logic level**: This is done by using vSAN encryption that uses an AES 256 cipher and eliminates the extra cost, limitations, and complexity associated with purchasing and maintaining SEDs. vSAN datastore encryption is enabled and configured at the datastore level. In other words, every object on the vSAN datastore is encrypted when this feature is enabled.
- **Encryption at VM level**: This is a new feature of the vSphere 6.5 Enterprise Plus edition. Previously, it was only possible with third-party products.
- **Encryption inside the VM**: Consider, for example, using Microsoft BitLocker, or using a Linux-encrypted filesystem (with `losetup`, `luks`, or other tools).

For more information, check the following guide, **How vSphere Virtual Machine Encryption Protects Your Environment**, available at `https://docs.vmware.com/en/VMware-vSphere/6.7/com.vmware.vsphere.security.doc/GUID-8D7D09AC-8579-4A33-9449-8E8BA49A3003.html`.

VM encryption

A new feature introduced in vSphere 6.5 is the encryption of VMs, which secures the VMDK virtual disks (also `.vmx` and `swap` files are encrypted), making the stored data unreadable.

To get the benefits of encryption, you need to connect vCenter Server to a **Key Management Server** (**KMS**) that provides the necessary keys to encrypt and decrypt VMs using the **Key Management Interoperability Protocol** (**KMIP**) protocol. To establish the connection between KMS and vCenter Server, the KMS performs a certificate exchange.

The components required to allow VM encryption features are the following:

- **KMS**: Generates and stores the keys passed to the vCenter Server to encrypt and decrypt the VMs.
- **vCenter Server**: This is the only component that can log in to the KMS to obtain the keys and push them to ESXi hosts. KMS keys are not stored in vCenter Server, which keeps a list of key IDs only.

A KMS cluster configured in vCenter Server requires that all KMS instances added to the cluster are from the same vendor and must replicate keys. If you use different vendors in different environments, you can create a KMS cluster for each KMS specifying the default cluster. The first cluster added becomes the default cluster.

Be sure to use only a certified KMS provider. Some KMS providers are as follows:

- **HyTrust KeyControl**: `https://www.hytrust.com/`
- **IBM Security Key Lifecycle Manager**: `http://www-03.ibm.com/software/products/en/key-lifecycle-manager`
- **Thales Vormetric Data Security Manager**: `https://www.thalesesecurity.it/products/data-encryption/vormetric-data-security-manager`
- **Gemalto SafeNet KeySecure**: `https://safenet.gemalto.com/data-encryption/enterprise-key-management/key-secure/`

You can have a look at HCL for certified KMS providers at `https://www.vmware.com/resources/compatibility/search.php?deviceCategory=kms`.

 A KMS is required to enable and use vSAN encryption as well. Multiple KMS vendors are compatible, including HyTrust, Gemalto (SafeNet), Thales e-Security, CloudLink, and Vormetric.

Access to the encrypted virtual disk requires the correct key owned only by the VM that manages the virtual disk. An unauthorized VM that tries to access the encrypted VMDK without the correct key will receive only meaningless data. No additional hardware is required for the encryption/decryption operation, and performance is improved if the processor used supports the AES-NI instruction set, because encryption is CPU-intensive. AES-NI should be enabled in your BIOS, and the VM needs to be powered off before proceeding.

To encrypt VMs, you first need to configure a KMS in vCenter Server:

1. From the vSphere Web Client, select **vCenter Server** in the inventory and select the **Configure** tab. Expand More and select **Key Management Servers** to access the KMS management section.

2. Click the Add KMS icon to add the KMS server (you must have one in your network). Specify the required parameters and click **OK** to save the configuration:

Add KMS	×
KMS cluster	Create new cluster ∨
New cluster name	
	☑ Make this the default cluster
Server name	
Server address	
Server port	
Proxy address	Optional
Proxy port	Optional
User name	Optional
Password	Optional

3. Once the KMS server is successfully added to vCenter Server, the **Connection Status** column is displayed as **Normal**. Once you have configured the KMS server, you can start encrypting VMs:

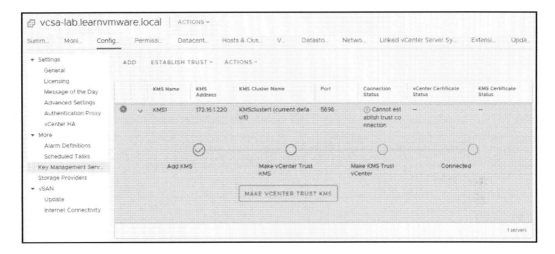

Change the storage policy of a VM by following this procedure:

1. From the vSphere Client, access **vCenter Server**, and right-click the VM to encrypt. Select **VM Policies | Edit VM Storage Policies**.

2. From the **VM storage policy** drop-down menu, select the **VM Encryption Policy** option to encrypt the VM and click **OK**:

3. When the encryption process has completed, the VM hardware area in the VMs **Summary** tab displays the **Encryption** field which indicates which components are encrypted.

Here are some recommendations for using encrypted VMs:

- PSC and vCenter Server VMs should not be encrypted.
- The support bundle used to decrypt a core dump is generated using the ESXi host key. If the host is rebooted, the host key may change, and the support bundle can no longer be generated with a password and you might not be able to decrypt core dumps located in the support bundle as well. For this reason, if the host crashes, you should retrieve the support bundle as soon as possible.
- Since .vmx files and .vmdk descriptor files contain the support bundle, you should not edit these files; otherwise, the VM becomes unrecoverable.

Encryption and decryption of a VM can also be performed using PowerCLI:

- To encrypt a VM, run the following command:

```
Get-VM -Name <vmname> | Enable VM encryption
```

- To decrypt a VM, use the following command:

```
Get-VM -Name <vmname> | Disable VM encryption
```

Encrypted VMs can be a potential challenge for native backup programs, but there is a way to permit backup of those encrypted files in a clear format, to permit indexing and granular restore. Several backup products already support this feature.

Also, you have to consider the following caveats:

- vSphere FT, vSphere Replication, and content library do not work with VM encryption.
- Snapshot operations have some limitations; for example, you cannot select a snapshot of the VM's memory checkbox.
- Cloning an encrypted VM or performing a storage vMotion operation and changing the disk format may not work.
- You cannot encrypt a VM and its disks by using the **Edit Settings...** menu. You have to use the storage policy.
- When you detach a disk from a VM, the storage policy information for the virtual disk is not retained.
- OVF export is not supported on an encrypted VM.
- You can use vSphere VM encryption with IPv6 in mixed mode, but not in a pure IPv6 environment.

- The vCenter Server becomes more critical; only vCenter Server has credentials for logging in to the KMS. Your ESXi hosts do not have those credentials. vCenter Server obtains keys from the KMS and pushes them to the ESXi hosts.

> If you want to try VM Encryption, for PoC or Dev and Test environments, you can follow William Lam's post, **KMIP Server Docker Container for evaluating VM Encryption in vSphere 6.5**, available at `https://www.virtuallyghetto.com/2016/12/kmip-server-docker-container-for-evaluating-vm-encryption-in-vsphere-6-5.html`.

Protecting data in motion

Protecting the stored data is only a part of the data security; you also need to encrypt or make secure the network connections and how data is moved. Data in motion is trickier to protect. The best way is always to use secure channels and communication.

At the VM level, it is a problem that is addressed and managed as in any physical environment. Do not only use VLAN (or VXLAN) to segregate traffic, but use the right network traffic rules (in this case, NSX can help with micro-segmentation) and try to avoid clear text network communication.

However, you have also the infrastructure to consider. VMware vSphere management traffic is already on SSL connections since version 3.5, but other types of traffic are usually not encrypted, such as vMotion (until vSphere 6.5), or FT logging or storage traffic based on IP, such as **iSCSI** or **NFS traffic**.

If you need to transfer data over an unsecured channel, always use network encryption such as **MACsec** or **IPsec**.

Encrypted vMotion

The vMotion encryption feature isn't merely an encryption of the entire network channel for the vMotion traffic. There aren't certificates to manage.

The encryption happens on a per-VM level; when the VM is migrated, a randomly generated, one-time-use 256-bit key is generated by vCenter (it does not use the KMS). In addition, a 64-bit nonce (an arbitrary number used only once in a crypto operation) is also generated. The encryption key and nonce are packaged into the migration specification sent to both hosts. At that point, all the VM vMotion data is encrypted with both the key and the nonce, ensuring that communications can't be used to replay the data:

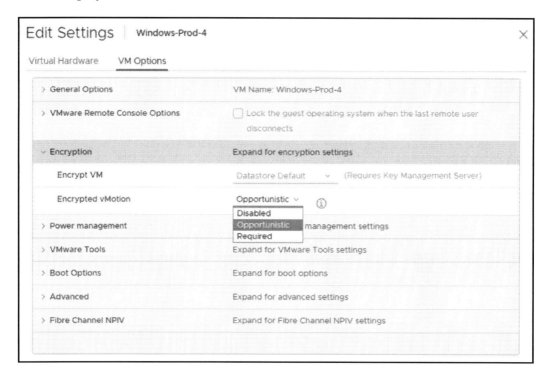

Three options regarding encrypted vMotion are available:

- **Opportunistic**: If the source and destination ESXi host supports **Encrypted vMotion**, Encrypted vMotion will be used. If one of the hosts does not support encrypted vMotion, regular (unencrypted) vMotion will be used.
- **Required**: Both source and destination ESXi host must be capable of encrypted vMotion. If the host is non-compliant, the vMotion will fail. In other words, encrypted vMotion will always be used.
- **Disabled**: No encrypted vMotion will be used at all, only regular (unencrypted) vMotion will be used.

Summary

Security has become a critical part of any implementation, also for virtual environments. In addition to the security and hardening aspects of vSphere, the new version 6.7 introduces some essential new features related to this aspect, such as audit-quality logging of vSphere events, VM encryption, encrypted vMotion, Secure Boot support for VMs, and Secure Boot plus cryptographic hypervisor assurance for ESXi.

We have explained some security topics, such as security and hardening concepts in vSphere, new security options in vSphere 6.7, and how to design for security covering all three critical aspects of the vSphere suit to harden: vCenter Server, ESXi hypervisor, and the VM.

Encryption is one of the crucial tasks, especially when the data is not stored within the company, and the vSphere suite allows us to quickly implement encryption for data at rest as well as for data in transit.

In the next chapter, we focus on the optimization and analysis of your vSphere 6.7 environment using all the advanced functions that are available within VMware vSphere suite and related products such as vRealize Operations and vRealize Log Insight as well.

Questions

1. Name at least three security and hardening principles in VMware vSphere.
2. What is not a valid identity source?

    a) Local Single Sign-On Domain
    b) OpenLDAP
    c) Local OS
    d) LDAP (Active Directory)
    e) Network Identity Server
    f) LDAP (Native)

3. The password management feature of SSO configuration can be used to effect password policy for active directory users.

> a) True
> b) False

4. What is the correct workflow for assigning permissions in VMware vSphere?

> a) Assign several permissions and form a role, and assign the role to the vSphere object together with the user or group.
> b) Assign several permissions to a user or group on the vSphere object.

5. Describe the benefits of using **two-factor authentication (2FA)**.
6. Lockdown mode can be used to disable SSH access to the ESXi hypervisor once managed by the vCenter server:

> a) True
> b) False

7. In vSphere 6.x, several adjustments were made regarding transparent memory sharing. Please describe those significant changes.
8. For VM Secure Boot, several prerequisites must be met. What are they?

> a) Virtual hardware version 13 or later
> b) Snapshots cannot be used
> c) Virtual hardware version 14 or later
> d) GuestOS that supports UEFI secure boot
> e) FT can be only configured once the guestOS is installed
> f) EFI firmware in the VM boot options

9. Please describe the function of **VMware Certificate Authority (VMCA)**.
10. For VM encryption, KMS must be configured. Do you need a third-party application to do that, or do you just need vCenter server?
11. Encrypted vMotion can be configured. What is the difference between opportunistic and required settings?

Further reading

Read the following articles for more information:

- **vSphere security**: vSphere security provides information about securing your vSphere environment for VMware vCenter Server and VMware ESXi and it focuses on the following subjects:
    - Permissions and user management
    - Host security features
    - Virtual machine encryption
    - GuestOS security
    - Managing TLS protocol configuration
    - Security best practices and hardening
    - vSphere privileges

  For more information refer to `https://docs.vmware.com/en/VMware-vSphere/6.7/vsphere-esxi-vcenter-server-67-security-guide.pdf`.

- **VMware security advisories**: VMware's security advisories document remediation for security vulnerabilities that are reported in VMware products. For more information, refer to `https://www.vmware.com/security/advisories.html`.

- **Cybersecurity – attack and defense strategies**: The book will start talking about the security posture before moving to Red Team tactics, where you will learn the basic syntax for the Windows and Linux tools that are commonly used to perform the necessary operations. You will also gain hands-on experience of using new Red Team techniques with powerful tools such as Python and PowerShell, which will enable you to discover vulnerabilities in your system and how to exploit them. Moving on, you will learn how a system is usually compromised by adversaries, and how they hack a user's identity, and the various tools used by the Red Team to find vulnerabilities in a system. For more information, refer to `https://www.packtpub.com/networking-and-servers/cybersecurity-attack-and-defense-strategies`.

13
Analyzing and Optimizing Your Environment

In this chapter, we will show how it is possible to monitor and optimize your vSphere environment. Here, we will look at **virtual machine** (**VM**) optimization through the vSphere approach, as well as through the guest OS approach.

This chapter focuses on monitoring different critical resources, such as computing, storage, and networking, across the ESXi hosts, resource pools, and clusters. Other tools, such as vRealize Operations and third-party tools, will also be described briefly.

In this chapter, we will cover the following topics:

- How to monitor and optimize your vSphere environment
- VM optimization
- The importance of log management
- vRealize Operations
- Third-party monitoring tools

Monitoring a virtual environment

So, *how can we monitor the environment?* You can use two ways—first, through an OS VM approach and second, through a third-party tools approach. We can use two views to monitor the environment:

- **Inside the guest OS tools**: Task Manager, top or monitoring agents installed inside of the guest OS
- **Outside the guest OS tools**: vCenter Server performance charts or ESXTOP

For specific tasks, such as long-term monitoring, GUI tools are usually more powerful, but for quick identification of bottlenecks or troubleshooting, I usually prefer **command-line interface** (**CLI**). As we are covering mainly the VMware world, we will not cover how to monitor your VMs from the guest OS perspective, but we will instead focus on vSphere monitoring itself.

vSphere monitoring

There are many options related to monitoring your vSphere environment, but most commonly you will use the performance monitoring capabilities of vCenter Server. There is an option to monitor your VMs directly from the ESXi web client, but as you have already learned, ESXi hypervisor does not contain a database, thus performance data is only available for the past 60 minutes. Anything older is automatically discarded. On the other hand, with vCenter Server, you can store performance data for years.

vCenter Server statistics levels

Statistics levels determine the overall size of the performance data within vCenter Server. Based on your preferences, you can alter how long the data will be stored for as well as the individual metrics for different interval durations.

There are five interval durations when working with performance graphs:

- **Real-time**: This data is not stored in the database, but the individual ESXi host is queried when such data is requested. Every 20 seconds, the sample of data is retrieved.
- **Last day**: Real-time statistics are aggregated to 5-minute intervals and stored in the database.
- **Last week:** The last day's statistics are aggregated to 30-minute intervals and stored in the database.
- **Last month**: The last day's statistics are aggregated to 2-hour intervals and stored in the database.
- **Last year**: The last month's statistics are aggregated to 24-hour intervals and stored in the database.

For each duration, you can configure the *statistic level from 1 to 4*. Each statistic level contains a different set of performance counters. With **Level 1**, you get the most useful set of performance counters, and with **Level 4** you get a complete set of all performance counters available in vCenter Server. Of course, the statistic level will affect the overall size of the performance data that will be stored, as shown in the following screenshot:

For more information about statistic levels, feel free to check the official documentation at `https://docs.vmware.com/en/VMware-vSphere/6.7/com.vmware.vsphere.vcenterhost.doc/GUID-25800DE4-68E5-41CC-82D9-8811E27924BC.html`.

Performance monitoring with vCenter Server

Each object can be monitored from vCenter Server no matter the type. You can monitor your ESXi hypervisor, single VM, specific resource pool, cluster, or even data center object here.

Based on what object you select, different metrics are available based on such item, but for all objects, you can access performance monitoring using the **Monitor** tab and the **Performance** option, as shown in the following screenshot:

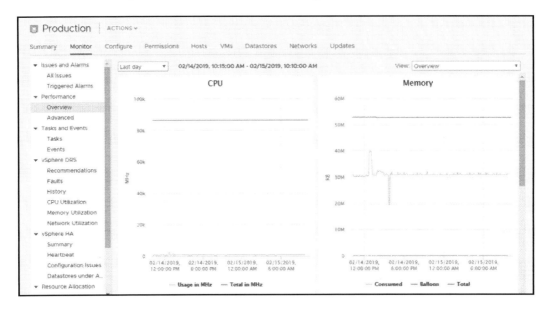

For all objects, the following options are available:

- **Overview**: Based on the selected object, the most useful graphs are displayed. There will be different overview content for the data center object and the VM object.
- **Advanced**: Using this option, you can drill down to the individual components of the selected object.

Using the **Advanced** option, you can gain access to different component monitoring options. When you switch to the **Advanced** mode, you can select what view you are interested in. Based on the view, different performance counters related to such a view will be displayed. In the following screenshot, you can see the available views for the ESXi hypervisor object:

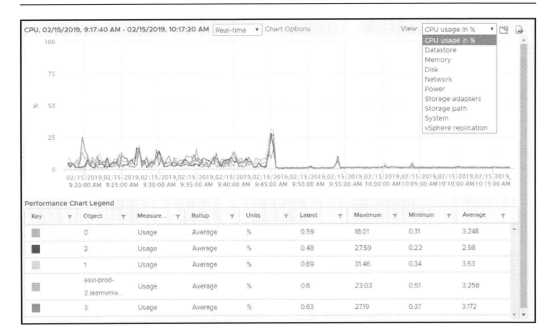

Are you looking for a specific performance counter that is not displayed? Don't worry, only preselected performance counters are displayed by default, but you have an option to select individual performance counters in each view by clicking on the **Chart Options** link.

Here, you can see all of the available performance counters, and you can adjust the graph based on your needs.

The following options are available:

- **Chart Metrics**: You can switch to the different components you are interested in.
- **Select counters for this chart**: Individual performance metrics are available.
- **Timespan**: You can either select existing a preset (**Real-time**, **Last day/week/month/year**), or you can specify a custom range.
- **Chart Type**: Sometimes different chart types are more useful than the default line graph.
- **Select the object for this chart**: You can specify individual objects here. For example, you can monitor only a single physical CPU or even a core for the ESXi hypervisor. Another example might be an individual **virtual NIC** (**vNIC**) of the VM.

An example of **Chart Options** for ESXi hypervisors is shown in the following screenshot:

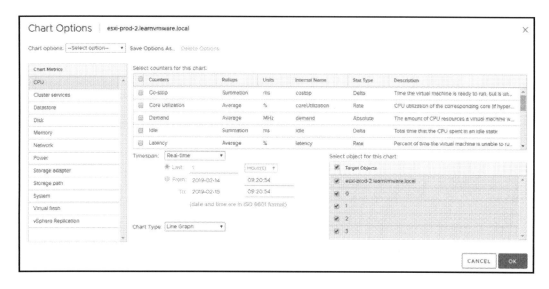

Once you define your custom chart, you have an option to either export the graph, or open the graph in a new window (indicated by two small icons in the top right-hand side of the chart), as shown in the following screenshot:

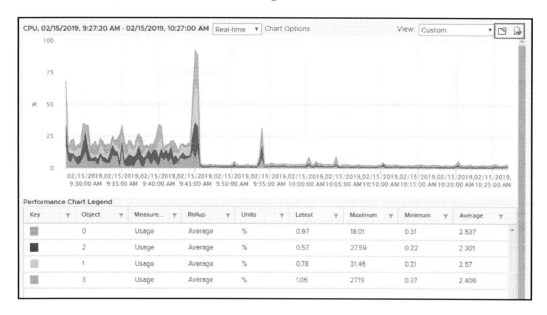

Using export, you can export the chart directly from the vCenter Server in the following formats:

- PNG
- JPG
- SVG
- CSV

Sometimes, it's also handy to open the graph in a new window for a more detailed view without being limited by the window size of the vCenter Server UI.

ESXi health

There is a new option integrated into vCenter Server 6.7, and that is the online health check of your ESXi hypervisor.

Using this option, you can automatically check against VMware recommendations regarding the physical hardware and driver versions and several vSphere configuration options.

Not only can you see what is not correct in your infrastructure, but you can also display the details of such a warning, as well as having an option to open the related KB using the **Ask VMware** option, as shown in the following screenshot:

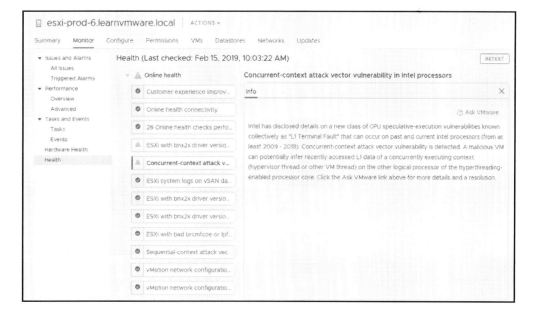

Working with alarms

vCenter Server contains several predefined alarms, but there is an option to define your custom alarms as well. This feature is sometimes overlooked, although it provides a comprehensive option to better monitor your vSphere environment.

Default alarms are enabled by default, but you have an option to disable a particular alarm if needed. You can check the exact configuration of the alarm. Alarms are defined at the vCenter level. To access the configuration, select your vCenter Server and, from the **Monitor** tab, switch to the **Alarm Definitions** option, as shown in the following screenshot:

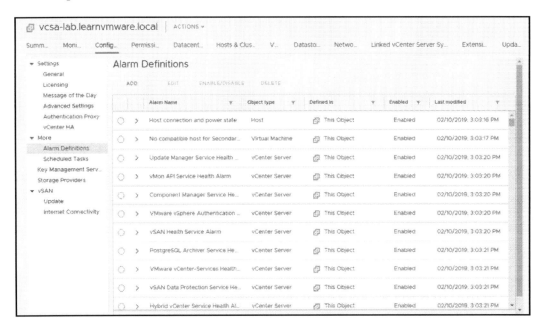

To create a custom alarm, perform the following steps:

1. Click on the **ADD** button in **Alarm Definitions.**
2. Provide the name of the alarm, description, and target type. Based on the target type, different rules that could trigger the alarm will be available.
3. Define the rule that will trigger the alarm. For example, you can raise the alarm when the CPU usage of the VM is above 90% for more than 15 minutes, as shown in the following screenshot:

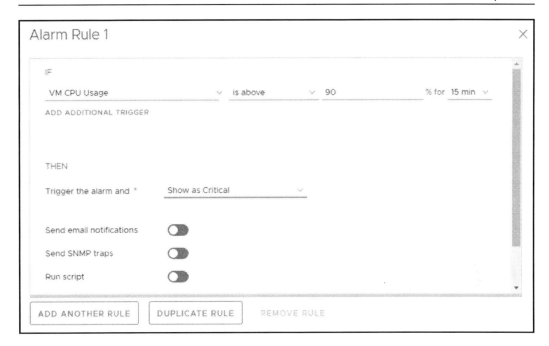

4. Using the **THEN** clause, you can select whether the object will be in a warning state or critical, and you can also specify to send an email notification, SNMP trap, or even run a custom command.

5. In **Reset Rules**, you can configure what condition will bring the object back to normal state and again, an email, SNMP trap, or script can be run once the condition has changed to **Normal**.

6. Review the alarm definition and save the configuration, as demonstrated in the following screenshot:

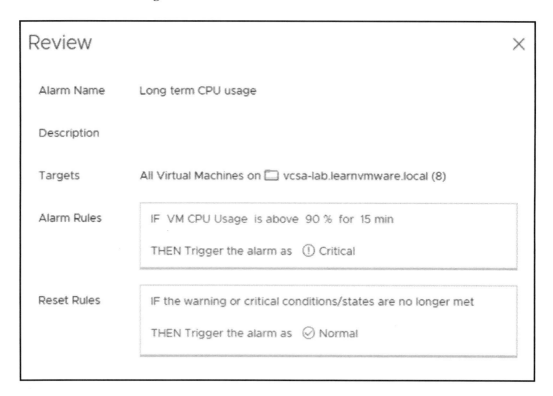

CLI monitoring

CLI monitoring is usually used for troubleshooting, or when you need to see specific performance counters in real-time. There are two options that you can use for CLI-based monitoring:

- ESXTOP
- PowerCLI

ESXTOP

The `esxtop` command is available at the hypervisor level, so you need to connect to your ESXi hypervisor over **Secure Shell** (**SSH**) first, before you can issue the command.

Once you are logged-in, all you need to do is issue the `esxtop` command from the command line, as shown in the following screenshot:

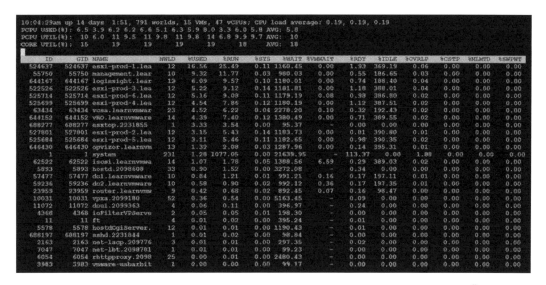

The windows are automatically refreshed every 5 seconds so you can see what exactly is going on.

ESXTOP has a number of different views you can switch to:

- CPU view
- Interrupt view
- Memory view
- Network view
- Disk adapter view
- Disk device view
- VM disk view
- Power management
- vSAN

To switch to the different view, hit *h* to see what views are available and their corresponding shortcuts, as demonstrated in the following screenshot:

```
Interactive commands are:

fF          Add or remove fields
oO          Change the order of displayed fields
s           Set the delay in seconds between updates
#           Set the number of instances to display
W           Write configuration file ~/.esxtop60rc
k           Kill a world
e           Expand/Rollup Cpu Statistics
v           View only VM instances
L           Change the length of the NAME field
l           Limit display to a single group

Sort by:
        U:%USED          R:%RDY              N:GID
Switch display:
        c:cpu            i:interrupt      m:memory       n:network
        d:disk adapter   u:disk device    v:disk VM      p:power mgmt
        x:vsan
```

You also have an option to sort the items based on different metrics. Again, all the available commands are available from the help view, which you can switch to using the *h* key.

There are a lot of metrics available through ESXTOP, and Duncan Epping wrote a great series of blog posts about ESXTOP available at http://www.yellow-bricks.com/esxtop/.

You can also check the following article about interpreting ESXTOP counters at https://communities.vmware.com/docs/DOC-9279.

PowerCLI

If you prefer PowerCLI, you can use it for CLI-based monitoring as well. From my perspective, it is an excellent tool because it allows you to monitor not only an individual ESXi hypervisor, but you can connect directly to vCenter Server to monitor multiple objects in your inventory.

We already discussed how to install and work with PowerCLI in Chapter 5, *Configuring and Managing vSphere 6.7*. So, let's start with the monitoring itself.

As a first step, you need to connect to your ESXi hypervisor or vCenter Server, as follows:

```
Connect-VIServer
```

If you are not sure what parameters are available with a particular command, you can always check the help of a command using the Get-Help command.

As a next step, you will probably want to know what statistics are available for a particular object through the following command:

```
Get-StatType -Entity VMname
```

Based on your statistics-level configuration, different metrics will be available, as follows:

```
cpu.usage.average
cpu.usagemhz.average
cpu.ready.summation
mem.usage.average
disk.usage.average
net.usage.average
sys.uptime.latest
disk.used.latest
disk.provisioned.latest
disk.unshared.latest
```

Lastly, you can retrieve particular metric using the Get-Stat command, as follows:

```
Get-Stat -Entity VMname -Disk -IntervalSecs 30
```

A similar output will be retrieved:

```
MetricId Timestamp Value Unit Instance
-------- --------- ----- ---- --------
disk.usage.average 2/15/2019 11:16:20 AM 51 KBps
disk.usage.average 2/15/2019 11:16:00 AM 46 KBps
disk.usage.average 2/15/2019 11:15:40 AM 165 KBps
disk.usage.average 2/15/2019 11:15:20 AM 81 KBps
disk.usage.average 2/15/2019 11:15:00 AM 67 KBps
disk.usage.average 2/15/2019 11:14:40 AM 60 KBps
disk.usage.average 2/15/2019 11:14:20 AM 52 KBps
```

For more information, feel free to visit the official PowerCLI reference guide available at https://www.vmware.com/support/developer/PowerCLI/PowerCLI651/html/.

VM optimization

VM configuration is one of the most crucial decisions you can make in your environment. There are several recommendations and best practices that you should follow to optimize your VM hardware and improve the performance of the infrastructure.

These recommendations are generic, and at your environment, you might not apply all of them. There is nothing like a golden rule here, but the first recommendation is to know your workloads.

Using the default VM templates

Based on the guest OS you want to run inside the VM, make sure you have selected the best possible virtual hardware. VMware optimizes the default VM templates, so you should stick with them.

Based on the OS family and the guest OS version, the wizard will automatically choose the best set of components for the VM.

With every new vSphere version, several improvements and features are available. vSphere 6.7 uses virtual hardware 14, and for example, a persistent memory device is available for the VMs.

Using only the necessary virtual hardware

You should check that you are using only the necessary virtual hardware that your VM requires. Do you need a virtual floppy drive more than one SCSI controller? If not, remove those devices. This will optimize the VM, so that it uses less memory and fewer CPU cycles from the underlying ESXi host, which, in turn, will help you to achieve higher consolidation ratios.

Choosing the correct virtual network adapter

Some older legacy adapters have been replaced over time, and it is essential to upgrade them in your VM. Also, for high-performing VMs, it is strongly recommended to use **paravirtualized devices** instead of emulated devices. For example, **VMXNET Generation 3** (**VMXNET3**) is the latest paravirtualized adapter with multi-queue support, IPv6 offloads, and MSI/MSI-X delivery interruption providing the best possible network performance for your VMs.

VMware tools

Always use the latest version of VMware tools. VM tools are a suite of **device drivers** and **management components** that are installed in the guest OS after OS installation. Although your VMs can run without VM tools, it is strongly suggested to install VM Tools as well as checking for the new versions that might improve some functions of the VM. Every time you upgrade your underlying ESXi hypervisors, you should also upgrade VM tools inside each VM.

Paravirtual SCSI (PVSCSI) storage controller

The PVSCSI storage controller that is used to attach virtual disks in your VM is the most advanced performing storage adapter available today. Compared to traditional emulated LSI storage controllers, it provides **higher I/O** and **lower CPU utilization** for the VM.

Please note that some guest OSes do not include the driver by default, so when you start the installation without the driver, the installer might directly complain that there is no disk to install the system.

Don't use snapshots in production

Snapshots are great for short-term tasks, such as performing some change or upgrade, but they could have a significant impact on the performance. Keep in mind that if the VM has a snapshot, you can't resize the virtual disk, and based on the amount of data written to the snapshot file, the merge of such a snapshot can take a lot of time.

Don't oversize your VMs

Of course, if your VM has fewer resources that it needs, it might affect the performance, but there is a problem with oversized VMs as well.

The VMware ESXi CPU scheduler allocates physical CPU time slots to vCPUs in VMs. If your VMs are configured with multiple vCPUs, the CPU scheduler must wait for physical CPUs to become available. Unused vCPUs will continue to consume system resources even when the system isn't using them. If other single-vCPU VMs use the system, your multi-vCPU VM will have to wait for CPU time.

VMware OS Optimization Tool (OSOT)

Some of the optimizations can be easily performed by yourself, but some of them – especially optimizing the guest OS—might be tricky.

The optimization tool includes customizable templates to enable or disable Windows system services and features, per VMware recommendations and best practices and across multiple systems. Since most Windows system services are enabled by default, the optimization tool can be used to disable unnecessary services and features to improve performance quickly.

You can perform the following actions using the VMware OSOT:

- Local analyze/optimize
- Remote analyze
- Optimization history and rollback
- Managing templates

Based on the selected template, different services or registry keys will be changed during the optimization, as shown in the following screenshot:

You can download the VMware OSOT for free at `https://labs.vmware.com/flings/vmware-os-optimization-tool`.

Log management

We will cover different log files available for troubleshooting in `Chapter 14`, *Troubleshooting Your Environment*. However, for now, I would like to focus on the importance of long-term log and event collection of your environment. You should not only monitor your vSphere infrastructure, but other components of the physical infrastructure or even VMs to get a better understanding of what is going on within your environment.

Manual log and event checking might be useful for troubleshooting, but you should consider deploying some centralized tools that can be used for long-term analysis of the environment.

vRealize Log Insight

VMware itself develops this tool, which can be used as a single location to collect and analyze all logs (not only VMware-related ones). You can find additional information about vRealize Log Insight at `https://www.vmware.com/products/vrealize-log-insight.html`.

vRealize Log Insight is available as an **OVA appliance**, so the installation to the environment is a pretty easy task.

Once Log Insight is installed, you can easily integrate different solutions to Log Insight to start digesting all the logs and events. Based on your integrations, different views and dashboards will be available, as demonstrated in the following screenshot:

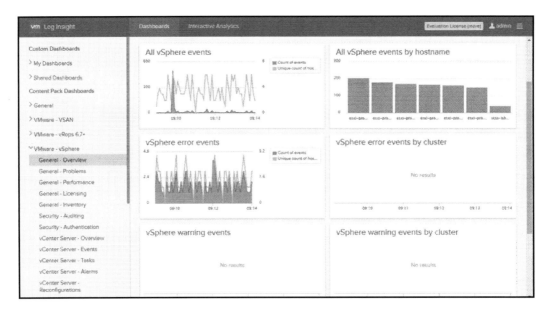

The great power of vRealize Log Insight is the **Interactive Analytics** view, where you can quickly drill down through your infrastructure and discover anything you wish, as shown in the following screenshot:

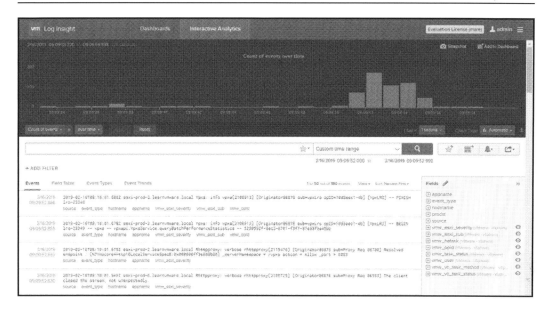

You can also use this tool for Microsoft, Veeam, Cisco, or other solutions only if the content pack is installed from the marketplace:

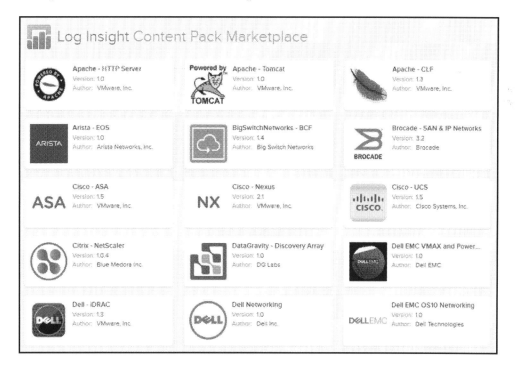

vRealize Operations

vRealize Operations Manager helps you to monitor and report your environment. vRealize Operations is a powerful tool which collects complex information about all objects in your VMware environment. Although long-term monitoring is available in vCenter Server itself, with vRealize Operations, you can get a more in-depth understanding of your environment, as well as different predictions based on your workloads.

For more information, refer to the following link: `https://www.vmware.com/ products/vrealize-operations.html`.

vRealize Operations installation

vRealize Operations is fully integrated into the vSphere 6.7, and you can start the installation directly from the vSphere Web Client by selecting **vRealize Operations** from the menu. If no vRealize Operations are deployed yet, you will have an option to start the installation from there:

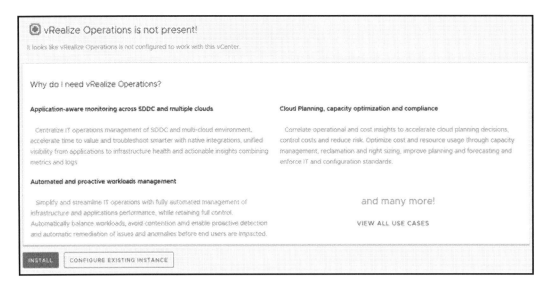

The installation procedure of vRealize Operations is as follows:

1. Navigate to the **vRealize Operations** menu and select **Install.**
2. You have the option to select either an online or an offline install type. With online installation, you do not need to download anything from the internet; the installer will do that for you.
3. In the next step, you need to connect to the vCenter Server providing the FQDN, username, and password.
4. In **Environment Details**, you need to select on which data center or cluster the new vRealize Operations appliance will be deployed, on which datastore the VM will be stored, and to which port group you should connect vRealize Operations.
5. In the last step, all that remains is the network configuration, such as IP address, gateway, or subnet mask.
6. In the **Summary** view, you have an option to verify everything and start the installation, as shown in the following screenshot:

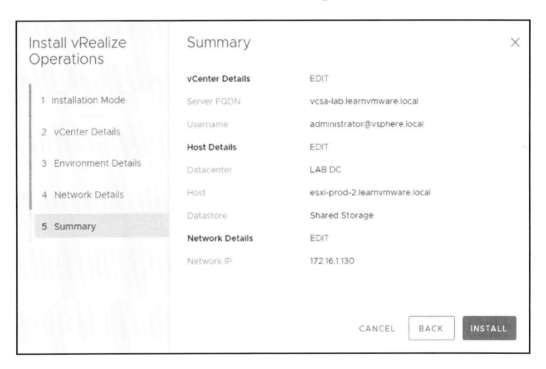

Once you hit **INSTALL**, you might notice that several tasks will be executed in the environment, as shown in the following screenshot:

Once the installation is finished, you will have an option to open vRealize Operations directly from the vSphere client, as shown in the following screenshot:

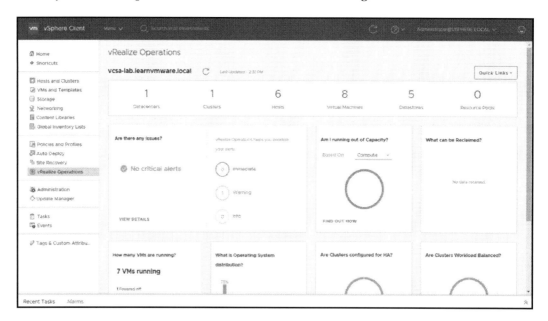

vRealize Operations analytics

There are many different views that you can have a look at using vRealize Operations, so let's show you several interesting views and dashboards that will be available to you:

- **VM Configuration dashboard**: You can find exciting information about your VM configuration in the following screenshot:

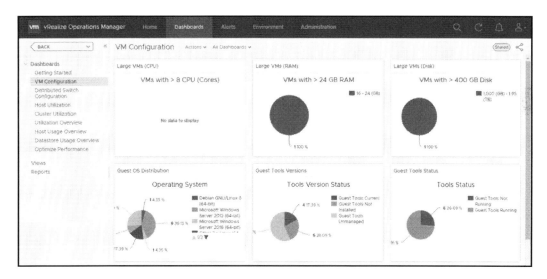

- **Capacity Allocation**: Certain resource over-subscriptions can affect your vSphere environment. You can find your **current over subscriptions** and **physical-to-virtual resource mapping** in this report, as shown in the following screenshot:

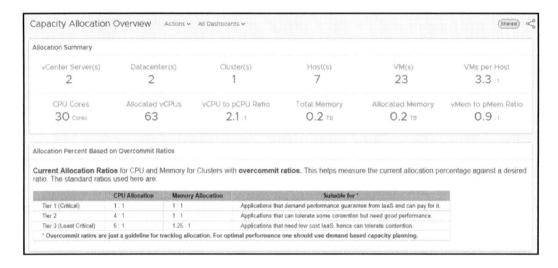

- **Rightsizing**: *Are your VMs oversized or undersized? Should you increase CPU or memory allocation to specific VMs, or, on the other hand, have you configured more resources than the VMs require?*

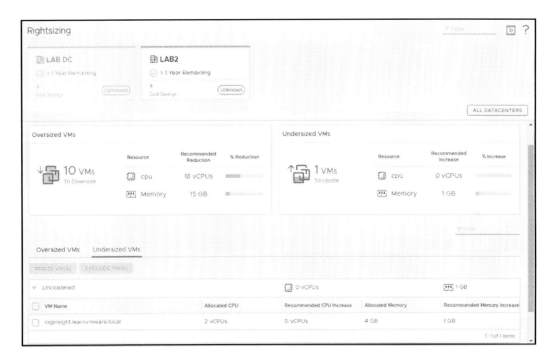

vRealize Operations integrations

vRealize Operations can be integrated with different products as well as allowing you to monitor the infrastructure end-to-end.

For such integration, management packs are used. For VMware solutions, management packs are already included in vRealize Operations, and all you need to do is configure the integration. vRealize Operations also supports the installation of third-party management packs, as you can see in the following screenshot:

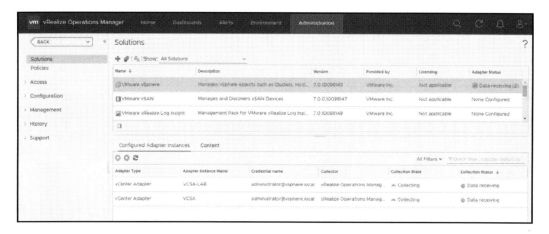

These management packs are distributed as `.pak` files, which you can obtain from your vendor, or you can have a look at the VMware marketplace located at `https://marketplace.vmware.com/vsx/?contentType=1` to see whether there is a management pack for your solution.

We could write a book just about vRealize Operations, but the best way to learn the product is to download the trial and play with it.

Other monitoring tools

If you wish, you can use only VMware products to monitor and manage your environment. However, there are other options available as well. It is beyond the scope of this chapter to describe all of them, so let's stick with a few tools I have worked with and would recommend.

Veeam ONE

Veeam is a well-known player in the backup and availability world that also provides monitoring tools. The core product is called **Veeam ONE**, and it is distributed as an executable file that you directly install on the top of any Windows-based VM.

Veeam ONE integrates seamlessly into your entire IT environment, providing complete visibility into virtual and Veeam-protected cloud and physical workloads. It provides monitoring, reporting, and intelligent tools to help your business with the automation and control you need to maintain availability, by protecting against potential problems before operational impact.

The following functionality is available with Veeam ONE:

- Real-time dashboards with drill-down views in one click
- More than 200 pre-set alarms based on best practices
- Detailed heat maps with deep visibility into backup repositories and proxies
- Enhanced business view to easily group and monitor the health states of VMs and agents
- Extensive KB connected to each alarm
- Detailed information to help you isolate root cause and quickly resolve issues
- Specific alarm dashboards designed to reduce discovery and troubleshooting times
- Dashboards for backup infrastructure performance and trends
- Dashboards for top consumers by any resource

Veeam ONE comes in two different editions: the Community edition with a limited set of functionality, and the full-featured product for large environments. You can have a look at the comparison at `https://www.veeam.com/products-edition-comparison.html`.

Different dashboards and views are available in Veeam ONE. The overall health of the environment is shown in the following screenshot:

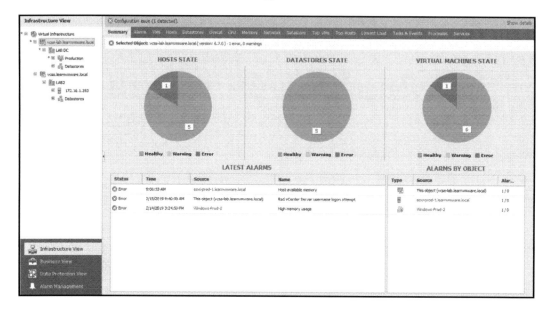

The top VMs in the inventory are shown in the following screenshot:

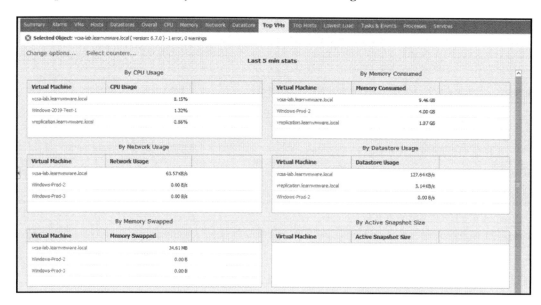

Opvizor

Opvizor's Performance Analyzer is a performance monitoring and optimization product for virtual environments, specializing in VMware vSphere. Performance Analyzer presents a dashboard that is simultaneously comprehensive and easy to understand and use, but it is also extremely customizable.

Opvizor Performance Analyzer is distributed as an OVA appliance, which you can download from the Opvizor website at `https://www.opvizor.com/how-it-work`.

Again, different views and dashboards are available once the Performance Analyzer digests enough data.

The ESXi host troubleshooting view is shown in the following screenshot:

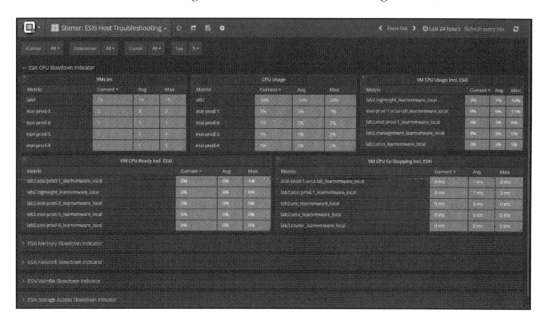

The VM cluster performance is shown in the following screenshot:

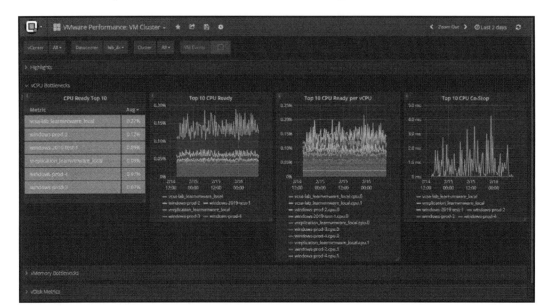

Summary

This chapter covered the vSphere native tools that can be used to monitor performance and other optimization techniques in a virtual environment.

Monitoring is a critical task to the improvement of the virtual environment and the workloads for performance and efficiency. This chapter focused on monitoring different critical resources, such as computing, storage, and networking, across ESXi hosts, resource pools, and clusters.

To better understand your environment, you should consider deploying a centralized log and event solution or performance monitoring solutions, such as vRealize Log Insight or vRealize Operations. We have also covered other monitoring solutions that you should check as well.

In the next chapter, we will focus on troubleshooting your virtual data center using different tools and techniques.

Questions

1. What are the default performance monitoring time ranges available in vCenter Server?

   a) Real-time
   b) Last hour
   c) Last day
   d) Last week
   e) Last month
   f) Last year

2. Only VMs and ESXi hypervisors can be monitored using the performance monitoring option:

   a) True
   b) False

3. What tools can be used for CLI-based monitoring?

   a) Esxcli
   b) Esxtop
   c) PowerCLI
   d) Esxmonitor

4. E100e vNIC provides better performance than VMXNET3:

   a) True
   b) False

5. Name at least three optimization techniques related to VMs.
6. What is the name of the event and log management solution from VMware?
7. A vRealize Operation is a tool that can be used for automation and orchestration of your virtual data center:

   a) True
   b) False

Further reading

Read the following articles for more information:

- **vSphere monitoring and performance**: VMware provides several tools to help you monitor your virtual environment and locate the source of potential issues and current problems.`https://docs.vmware.com/en/ VMware-vSphere/6.7/vsphere-esxi-vcenter-server-67-monitoring- performance-guide.pdf`.

- **Performance best practices for VMware vSphere 6.7**: This book provides performance tips that cover the most performance-critical areas of VMware vSphere 6.7. `https://www.vmware.com/content/dam/digitalmarketing/vmware/en /pdf/techpaper/performance/vsphere-esxi-vcenter-server-67- performance-best-practices.pdf`.

14
Troubleshooting Your Environment

Although VMware vSphere is a reliable platform, sometimes unexpected events occur. In this chapter, we will show you how it is possible to troubleshoot and repair your VMware infrastructure. You might not become a troubleshooting master, but you will learn enough to be ready for any situation that might arise. This chapter will cover the native tools used to troubleshoot performance issues and other issues to improve the virtual environment and workloads.

In this chapter, we will cover the following topics:

- What is troubleshooting?
- Troubleshooting a virtual environment
- Logs
- Troubleshooting vSphere components

What is troubleshooting?

Troubleshooting (TRBL) is a complete process where you (in the role of VMware administrator) identify an issue, try to find the origin of the problem, and define the way to resolve it.

The main steps involved during the troubleshooting process are therefore the following:

1. Defining the problem
2. Identifying the cause of the problem
3. Resolving the problem

The complexity of VMware environments is that different layers are involved, and the problem could impact any of the component for different reasons:

- Hardware failures
- Software problems
- Network problems
- Resources contention
- Mistakes in configuration

A big mistake that occurs quite often is considering TRBL only when your environment has failed, for example, with a **Purple Screen of Death** (**PSOD**) error. NO! TRBL is about all problems, and you should start TRBL when there is a problem or when users report problems in terms of performance, reliability, or usability.

The first step of every TRBL process is collecting all the symptoms. Here, you must be careful because the symptoms and the origin of the problem can be entirely different. This stage is crucial for gathering additional information to define the problem.

The typical questions may be—*Can the problem be reproduced? What is the scope? Did the system change before we got notification of the problem? Is the problem documented in the VMware Knowledge Base (KB)?*

When you have all of this information, you can start TRBL from the following three components:

- You start on the VM OS level and continue down to the hardware
- You start at the hardware level and continue up to the VM OS level
- You can start in the middle, at the VMkernel level, and continue up or down

After identifying the cause, you must specify the level of the problem to be fixed for your production environment, assigning a priority:

- **High**: Resolve as fast as a possible
- **Medium**: Resolve during the first possible window
- **Low**: You can wait for the next maintenance window

Solutions levels can be classified as follows:

- **Short**: Typical workaround
- **Long**: Reconfigure or change the advanced configuration

A problem's solution may require the use of different solutions together. But I think the theory is done with, and we can start with some real examples of how to troubleshoot your production environment.

Troubleshooting a virtual environment

From my perspective, GUI tools are not the ideal tools to use for TRBL. You will mostly stick with the logs and CLI commands to dig down into your environment if something goes wrong.

Although some GUI tools might be handy, such as **vRealize Operations** or **vRealize Log Insight** (discussed in the previous chapter), we will focus on the CLI tools for troubleshooting.

CLI tools

The CLI is the most useful option for TRBL. There are a lot of CLIs available that are used for TRBL in a VMware environment:

- **vSphere ESXi shell**: esxcli, which is the new CLI
- **vSphere command-line interface vCLI**: esxcfg-*, which is the old CLI

Both CLIs can be used directly from an ESXi host, and the ESXi shell must be enabled in the **Direct Console User Interface** (**DCUI**). You can access the DCUI from the physical console of the host, and also remotely by using a specific hardware vendor card, such as iDRAC for Dell or iLO for HP. When you want to use the CLI using a **remote SSH** session (**PuTTY** is a popular SSH client you can use), SSH protocol must be enabled. The second place where the configuration can be set is through vCenter Server in the Security Profile tab.

esxcli commands

How do we use esxcli? Follow these steps:

1. When you write the basic esxcli command and press *Enter*, you will see all the possible commands:

    ```
    [root@esxi-prod-1:~] esxcli
     Usage: esxcli [options] {namespace}+ {cmd} [cmd options]
    ```

```
Available Namespaces:
device Device manager commands
esxcli      Commands that operate on the esxcli system
itself
            allowing users to get additional information.
fcoe        VMware FCOE commands.
graphics    VMware graphics commands.
hardware    VMKernel hardware properties and commands for
            configuring hardware.
iscsi       VMware iSCSI commands.
network     Operations that pertain to the maintenance of
            networking on an ESX host. This includes a wide
            variety of commands to manipulate virtual
networking
            components (vswitch, portgroup, etc) as well as
local
            host IP, DNS and general host networking
settings.
...
```

We can continue by adding the other namespaces to the ESXi command. Another namespace is `network`, for example. `esxcli` is just a kit composed of a sequence of commands and namespaces.

2. Type `esxcli network` and press *Enter*:

```
[root@esxi-prod-1:~] esxcli network
Usage: esxcli network {cmd} [cmd options]

Available Namespaces:
ens         Commands to list and manipulate Enhanced
Networking
            Stack (ENS) feature on virtual switch.
firewall    A set of commands for firewall related
operations
ip          Operations that can be performed on vmknics
multicast   Operations having to do with multicast
nic         Operations having to do with the configuration
of
            Network Interface Card and getting and updating
the
            NIC settings.
port        Commands to get information about a port
sriovnic    Operations having to do with the configuration
of
            SRIOV enabled Network Interface Card and
getting and
            updating the NIC settings.
```

```
vm          A set of commands for VM related operations
diag        Operations pertaining to network diagnostics
....
```

3. To find out the IP addresses of all of the VMkernel ports, use the following `esxcli` command:

```
[root@esxi-prod-1:~] esxcli network ip interface ipv4
address list
Name IPv4 Address IPv4 Netmask IPv4 Broadcast Address Type
Gateway DHCP DNS
---- -------------- ------------- ---------------- --------
---- ------------ --------
vmk0 172.16.1.11 255.255.255.0 172.16.1.255 STATIC
172.16.1.254 false
vmk1 172.16.2.1 255.255.255.0 172.16.2.255 STATIC 0.0.0.0
false
vmk2 192.168.101.11 255.255.0.0 192.168.255.255 STATIC
0.0.0.0 false
vmk3 192.168.101.12 255.255.0.0 192.168.255.255 STATIC
0.0.0.0 false
```

4. Once you have found the VMkernel port IP address, you need to know where the TCP/IP stack is. To achieve this, type the following command:

```
[root@esxi-prod-1:~] esxcli network ip interface list
vmk0
 Name: vmk0
 MAC Address: 00:50:56:a9:8a:3f
 Enabled: true
 Portset: vSwitch0
 Portgroup: Management Network
 Netstack Instance: defaultTcpipStack
 VDS Name: N/A
 VDS UUID: N/A
 VDS Port: N/A
 VDS Connection: -1
 Opaque Network ID: N/A
 Opaque Network Type: N/A
 External ID: N/A
 MTU: 1500
 TSO MSS: 65535
 RXDispQueue Size: 1
 Port ID: 33554438
```

To avoid problems in the production environment, I recommend trying all available CLI commands for storage, devices, and so on in a lab environment or using the VMware **Hands-On Lab (HoL)**. VMware HoL is free and available online at `http://labs.hol.vmware.com`.

esxcfg-*

There is also another set of CLI commands that start with `esxcfg-*`. These commands are a little bit older, but still very useful. They can be used from the ESXi host's shell.

In the following example, you can see a duplicated CLI for the same output as `esxcli`. Yes, any CLI duplicates `esxcli`.

To see all the available commands, you can type `esxcfg-`, followed by a double hit of the *Tab* button. You will be able to see all possible `esxcfg-` CLI commands:

```
[root@esxi-prod-1:~] esxcfg-
esxcfg-advcfg esxcfg-hwiscsi esxcfg-ipsec esxcfg-nas esxcfg-resgrp
esxcfg-swiscsi esxcfg-vswitch esxcfg-dumppart esxcfg-info esxcfg-
module esxcfg-nics esxcfg-route esxcfg-vmknic
esxcfg-fcoe esxcfg-init esxcfg-mpath esxcfg-rescan esxcfg-scsidevs
esxcfg-volume
```

Using the `esxcfg-vmknic -l` command, you can find all `vmk` IP address, and the net stack in a more natural way than with `esxcli`:

Next, an excellent CLI to use is `esxcfg-vswitch -l`, which lists all vSwitches and vDSes:

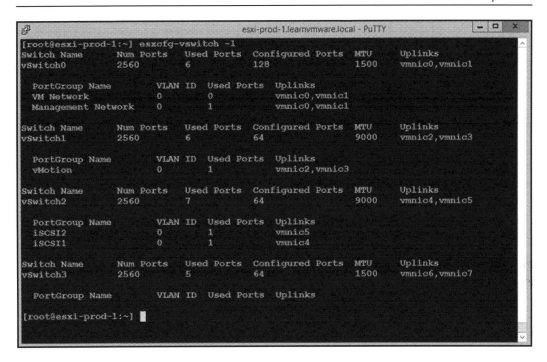

Ruby vSphere console

The next CLI that is very useful in real life is the Ruby vSphere console. The Ruby vSphere console is a part of the vCenter Appliance 6.7, and is accessible by typing `rvc`.

You can install `rvc` in your notebook or use a Docker container. The `rvc` command is often used for TRBL vSAN. You can find a great post about it here: `https://blogs.vmware.com/kb/2016/10/tips-tricks-ruby-vsphere-console-rvc-managing-virtual-san-environment.html`:

```
Command> rvc
Install the "ffi" gem for better tab completion.
WARNING: Nokogiri was built against LibXML version 2.9.4, but has
dynamically loaded 2.9.8
Host to connect to (user@host): localhost
Using default username "administrator@vsphere.local".
password:
Welcome to RVC. Try the 'help' command.
0 /
1 localhost/
>
```

Once you are connected, you can browse the available commands using `help`:

```
> help
Namespaces:
alarm
basic
cluster
connection
core
datacenter
datastore
device
diagnostics
...
```

To see commands in a namespace, use `help namespace_name`. To see detailed help for a command, use `help namespace_name.command_name`.

Here's a list of the available commands for VMs:

```
help vm
Commands:
annotate: Change a VM's annotation
answer: Answer a VM question
bootconfig: Alter the boot config settings
clone: Clone a VM
create: Create a new VM
extra_config: Display extraConfig options
find: Display a menu of VMX files to register
ip: Wait for and display VM IP addresses
kill (kill, k): Power off and destroy VMs
...
```

vim-cmd

The `vim-cmd` command could be a very good CLI when you need to start a VM, for example, the vCSA:

```
[root@esxi-prod-1:~] vim-cmd
Commands available under /:
hbrsvc/ internalsvc/ solo/ vmsvc/
hostsvc/ proxysvc/ vimsvc/ help
```

For example, with the `vmsvc` namespace, you can manage the power status of a VM:

```
[root@esxi-prod-1:~] vim-cmd vmsvc/
Commands available under vmsvc/:
acquiremksticket get.snapshotinfo
acquireticket get.spaceNeededForConsolidation
createdummyvm get.summary
destroy get.tasklist
device.connection getallvms
device.connusbdev gethostconstraints
device.ctlradd message
device.ctlrremove power.getstate
device.disconnusbdev power.hibernate
device.diskadd power.off
device.diskaddexisting power.on
...
```

The first step is to list all VMs because we need the **VM identificator** (**VMID**) to power it on:

```
[root@esxi-prod-1:~] vim-cmd vmsvc/getallvms
Vmid Name File Guest OS Version Annotation
19 Windows-Prod-1 [C2] Windows-Prod-1/Windows-Prod-1.vmx
windows8Server64Guest vmx-14
20 Windows-Prod-4 [C1] Windows-Prod-4/Windows-Prod-4.vmx
windows8Server64Guest vmx-14
21 Windows-2019-Test-1 [Shared Storage] Windows-2019-
Test-1/Windows-2019-Test-1.vmx windows9Server64Guest vmx-14
```

When we know the correct VMID, we can power on the VM:

```
[root@esxi1:~] vim-cmd vmsvc/power.on 19
```

With `vim-cmd`, you can try a lot of further commands. In the following example, the following command is used to get network information for VM `19`:

```
[root@esxi-prod-1:~] vim-cmd vmsvc/get.network 19
Networks:

(vim.Network.Summary) {
 network = 'vim.Network:HaNetwork-VM Network',
 name = "VM Network",
 accessible = true,
 ipPoolName = "",
 ipPoolId = <unset>
}
```

vcsa-cli

The next CLI is part of the vCSA, and you can use the `api` command. To see all available commands, you can use `help api list`:

```
Command> help api list
Supported API calls by this server:
com.vmware.appliance.version1.access.consolecli.get
com.vmware.appliance.version1.networking.ipv6.list
com.vmware.appliance.version1.access.consolecli.set
com.vmware.appliance.version1.networking.ipv6.set
com.vmware.appliance.version1.access.dcui.get
com.vmware.appliance.version1.networking.proxy.delete
com.vmware.appliance.version1.access.dcui.set
com.vmware.appliance.version1.networking.proxy.get
com.vmware.appliance.version1.access.shell.get
com.vmware.appliance.version1.networking.proxy.set
com.vmware.appliance.version1.access.shell.set
com.vmware.appliance.version1.networking.proxy.test
...
```

See the following example:

```
Command> api com.vmware.appliance.health.mem.get
Health: green
```

In real life, a VMware administrator needs other commands on the vCSA to restart components, such as the vSphere Web Client:

```
Command> service-control --list
vmware-updatemgr (VMware Update Manager)
vmafdd (VMware Authentication Framework)
vmware-eam (VMware ESX Agent Manager)
vmcam (VMware vSphere Authentication Proxy)
...
```

Restarting the vSphere Web Client service is quite easy from the command line:

```
Command> service-control --stop vsphere-client
Command> service-control --start vsphere-client
```

You should also know basic Linux commands such as `tail`, `vi`, `more`, `less`, `grep`, and `ls` for the TRBL process.

PowerCLI

We can't forget **PowerCLI**, of course. PowerShell lovers will love PowerCLI or PowerNSX. As you already know, you must first log in to the ESXi or vCenter server:

```
Connect-VIServer IP/FQDN
```

You can easily get information about hosts with the `Get-VMHost` command:

```
PS C:\> Get-VMHost

Name ConnectionState PowerState NumCpu CpuUsageMhz CpuTotalMhz
MemoryUsageGB MemoryTotalGB Version

---- --------------- ---------- ------ ----------- ----------- -------
------ ------------- -------
esxi-prod-5.learn... Connected PoweredOn 4 98 14396 5.997 11.999 6.7.0
esxi-prod-4.learn... Connected PoweredOn 4 142 14396 3.440 11.999
6.7.0
esxi-prod-6.learn... Connected PoweredOn 4 75 14396 1.437 11.999 6.7.0
esxi-prod-2.learn... Connected PoweredOn 4 870 14396 10.978 11.999
6.7.0
esxi-prod-1.learn... Connected PoweredOn 4 309 14396 1.565 11.999
6.7.0
esxi-prod-3.learn... Connected PoweredOn 4 156 14396 6.032 11.999
6.7.0
```

We already discussed in Chapter 5, *Configuring and Managing vSphere 6.7*, how to install and work with PowerCLI. Additional information can be found at `https://learnvmware.online/2018/03/05/vmware-powercli-10-released/`.

I think that your brain is now full of CLI and commands. However, at this moment, it is not essential to remember every CLI. We need to know and remember what is possible and which CLI can be used for the different parts of the TRBL process.

Logs

For TRBL, it is vital to know where the logs are located. In vCSA, log files are stored in `/var/log/`.

If you login to the vCSA, bash shell is not accessible directly after the login. To access the bash shell, you need to issue the `shell` command first:

```
Command> shell
Shell access is granted to root
```

```
root@VCSA-lab [ ~ ]#
root@VCSA-lab [ ~ ]# cd /var/log/vmware
root@VCSA-lab [ /var/log/vmware ]# ls
```

Detailed log locations and descriptions can be found in the VMware KB at `https://kb.vmware.com/s/article/2110014?language=en_USr=2Quarterback.validateRoute=1KM_Utility.getArticleData=1KM_Utility.getArticleLanguage=2KM_Utility.getArticle=1`.

ESXi host logs

The ESXi host log files are very similar to vCSA logs and can be found in the `/var/log/` directory of the host:

```
[root@esxi-prod-1:/var/log] ls -lah
total 444
drwxr-xr-x 1 root root 512 Feb 16 15:48 .
drwxr-xr-x 1 root root 512 Feb 11 20:14 ..
-rw-rw-rw- 1 root root 82 Feb 16 15:48 .vmsyslogd.err
-rw-r--r-- 1 root root 10.0K Feb 16 15:48 .vmsyslogd.err.1
drwxr-xr-x 1 root root 512 Feb 11 20:12 EMU
lrwxrwxrwx 1 root root 21 Feb 16 15:48 Xorg.log ->
/scratch/log/Xorg.log
lrwxrwxrwx 1 root root 21 Feb 16 15:48 auth.log ->
/scratch/log/auth.log
-rw-rw-rw- 1 root root 56.7K Feb 11 20:14 boot.gz
lrwxrwxrwx 1 root root 22 Feb 16 15:48 clomd.log ->
/scratch/log/clomd.log
lrwxrwxrwx 1 root root 29 Feb 16 15:48 clusterAgent.log ->
/scratch/log/clusterAgent.log
lrwxrwxrwx 1 root root 33 Feb 16 15:48 cmmdsTimeMachine.log ->
/scratch/log/cmmdsTimeMachine.log
lrwxrwxrwx 1 root root 37 Feb 16 15:48 cmmdsTimeMachineDump.log ->
/scratch/log/cmmdsTimeMachineDump.log
-rw-r--r-- 1 root root 36.1K Feb 12 09:17 configRP.log
-rw-r--r-- 1 root root 0 Feb 11 20:12 cryptoloader.log
lrwxrwxrwx 1 root root 24 Feb 16 15:48 ddecomd.log ->
/scratch/log/ddecomd.log
lrwxrwxrwx 1 root root 25 Feb 16 15:48 dhclient.log ->
/scratch/log/dhclient.log
lrwxrwxrwx 1 root root 20 Feb 16 15:48 epd.log -> /scratch/log/epd.log
...
```

When you use the `ls -lah` command, you may notice an important key point about ESXi logs; all logs on the host are symbolic links to `/scratch/log/`. When you install the ESXi host on an SD card, a warning message related to non-persistent storage may appear when the installation has completed. To fix this, you must create a datastore and redirect the logs to that datastore (we covered scratch partition in `Chapter 5, Configuring and Managing vSphere 6.7`).

Also, check out **VMware KB 2032823: System logs are stored on non-persistent storage at the address** at `https://kb.vmware.com/s/article/2032823?language=en_US`.

As a first step, I recommend checking the `vmkernel.log` log file:

```
[root@esxi-prod-1:/var/log] tail -f vmkernel.log
2019-02-16T15:55:37.094Z cpu3:2317032)Swap: vm 2317014: 5104: Finish
swapping in migration swap file. (faulted 0 pages). Success.
2019-02-16T15:55:37.144Z cpu2:2099363)Config: 703: "SIOControlFlag2" =
0, Old Value: 1, (Status: 0x0)
2019-02-16T15:55:38.486Z cpu0:2317158)DLX: 4319: vol 'Shared Storage',
lock at 10395648: [Req mode 1] Checking liveness:
2019-02-16T15:55:38.486Z cpu0:2317158)[type 10c00002 offset 10395648 v
1968, hb offset 3571712
gen 25, mode 1, owner 5c61c947-9f3a90a4-5da3-005056a97911 mtime 47191
num 0 gblnum 0 gblgen 0 gblbrk 0]
2019-02-16T15:57:17.473Z cpu2:2097177)ScsiDeviceIO: 3068:
Cmd(0x459a40b33c40) 0x1a, CmdSN 0x8fdf from world 0 to dev
"mpx.vmhba1:C0:T0:L0" failed H:0x0 D:0x2 P:0x0 Valid sense data: 0x5
0x20 0x0.
2019-02-16T15:58:28.574Z cpu2:2315918)WARNING: UserSocketInet: 2266:
python: waiters list not empty!
2019-02-16T15:58:28.575Z cpu2:2315918)WARNING: UserSocketInet: 2266:
python: waiters list not empty!
2019-02-16T15:58:28.968Z cpu0:2317573)WARNING: MemSchedAdmit: 1226:
Group vsanperfsvc: Requested memory limit 0 KB insufficient to support
effective reservation 10596 KB
```

There are also other ways to check ESXi logs. One way is using the DCUI from the ESXi console.

Another way is using a web browser and pointing it at your ESXi host using
`https://ESXi_IP/host`. After providing the correct ESXi credentials, you will see
something like the following screenshot:

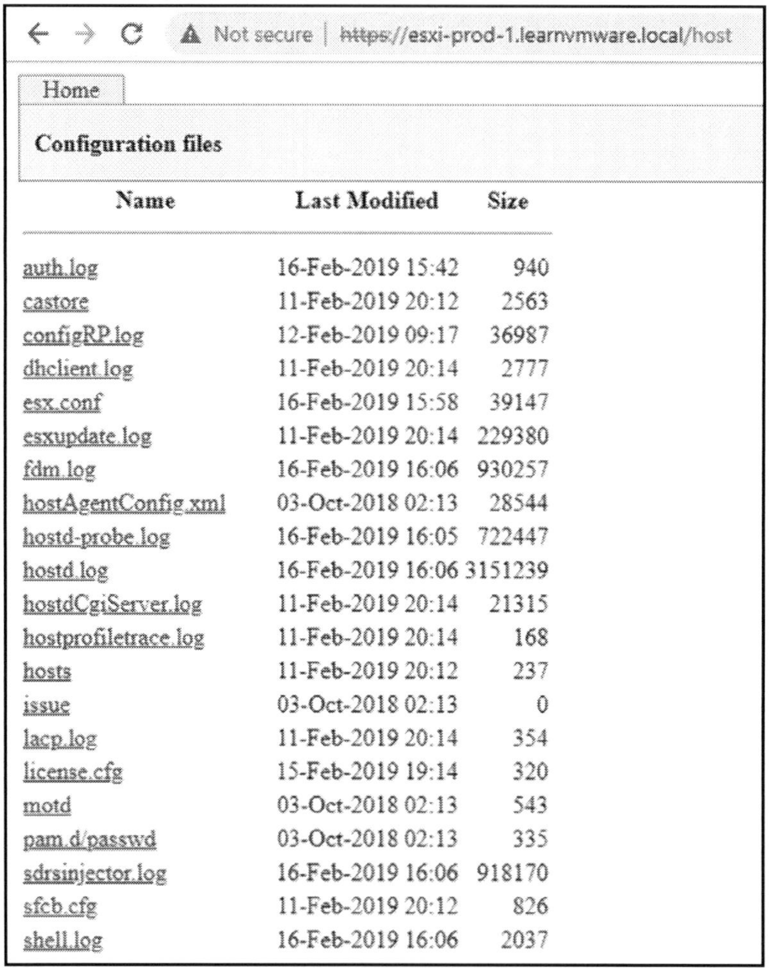

Troubleshooting vSphere components

Now that we have learned a lot about CLI or GUI commands and tools, we can start with specific TRBL aspects.

TRBL can be focused on different infrastructural parts, such as the ESXi hosts or the vCenter Server, the network, storage, or can be directly performed at the VM level. Depending on the different issues, it could be better to adopt a bottom-up or top-down approach.

Troubleshooting the vCenter Server

TRBL problems and errors with vCenter Server and ESXi or clusters can be straightforward. One possible issue could be only that some services are no longer working.

The first action to perform during the troubleshooting of a problem that has occurred in the vCenter Server is to restart the service using the `service-control` command:

```
Command> service-control --list
vmware-vpostgres(VMware Postgres)
vmware-imagebuilder(VMware Image Builder Manager)
vmware-cm (VMware Component Manager)
vmware-vpxd (VMware vCenter Server)
...

Command> service-control --stop vmware-vpxd and service-control --
start vmware-vpx
```

When you see a problem in `vmkernel.log`, you can check the next important component, that is, the vCenter Server database. Typical problems are disk capacity, CPU, and RAM. With vCSA, the only database that can be used is PostgreSQL, but with the Windows version of vCenter Server, both Microsoft SQL Server and Oracle can be used.

For the Windows-based vCenter Server, you may use the available monitoring tools as a part of the database that's used, such as the Management Studio for MS SQL or SQL Developer for Oracle. When you are using the vCSA, life is more much more comfortable, and you can use the new management console, **vCenter Server Appliance Management Interface (VAMI)**, which is accessible through the browser at `https://VCFQDN or IP:5480`:

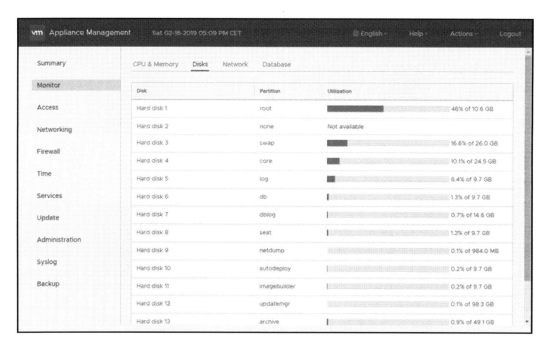

To verify the disk usage, you can go to the **Monitor** and **Disks** tab of the VAMI and check the reported value.

The next step to solve problems related to the database is to try and restart PostgreSQL using the `service-control` command. Next, it is usually useful to restart the problematic vSphere Web Client.

You can use any backup feature that's available so that the vCSA can restore the database.

Troubleshooting the ESXi host

A typical problem you may face with the ESXi host is the fatal PSOD error, as shown in the following screenshot:

```
VMware ESXi 6.7.0 (Releasebuild-10302608 x86_64)
CrashMe
ESXinVM cr0=0x80010031 cr2=0x61d04bdfe0 cr3=0x131cc4000 cr4=0x142768
*PCPU2:2335756/vsish
PCPU  0: SSUU
Code start: 0x41802c400000 VMK uptime: 4:20:58:45.272
0x451a0401b360:[0x41802c50ac15]PanicvPanicInt@vmkernel#nover+0x439 stack: 0x430459d24010
0x451a0401b400:[0x41802c50ae48]Panic_NoSave@vmkernel#nover+0x4d stack: 0x451a0401b460
0x451a0401b460:[0x41802c6f32ee]CrashMeCurrentCore@vmkernel#nover+0x03b stack: 0x61d04bd
0x451a0401b560:[0x41802c6f3b7e]CrashMe_VsiCommandSet@vmkernel#nover+0xd7 stack: 0x0
0x451a0401b5a0:[0x41802c402444]VSI_SetInfo@vmkernel#nover+0x369 stack: 0x451a0401b690
0x451a0401b620:[0x41802cbabd53]UW64VMKSyscallUnpackVSI_Set0(user)#<None>+0x2d0 stack: 0x0
0x451a0401bed0:[0x41802cb3b660]User_UWVMK64SyscallHandler@(user)#<None>+0x249 stack: 0x5f278753f88d24ac
0x451a0401bf30:[0x41802c55f648]SyscallUWVMK64@vmkernel#nover+0x90 stack: 0x0
base fs=0x0 gs=0x418040800000 Kgs=0x0
2019-02-11T19:13:22.832Z cpu1:2030311)Warning: /vmfs/devices/char/vmkdriver/usbpassthrough not found
Coredump to disk. Slot 1 of 1 on device mpx.vmhba0:C0:T0:L0:9.
Finalized dump header (14/14) DiskDump: Successful.
No file configured to dump data.
No port for remote debugger. "Escape" for local debugger.
```

This crash is a problem that can be related to CPU, RAM, modules, hardware, or a software bug. When you see this error through iDRAC or iLO, you should take a photo or screenshot to support VMware. You can also try checking the VMware KB to find a resolution. *Did you experience PSOD after an ESXi upgrade?* A possible quick solution to fix this error is to perform an ESXi downgrade. This problem may also occur when you change RAM or firmware in HBA. All of these situations can be potentially problematic for ESXi.

Another way to troubleshoot the problem is to gather maximum information from PSOD, such as the most recent changes in the environment, and restart the ESXi host to create the log bundle requested by the VMware support. The log bundle can be created with a GUI or a CLI with the `vm-support` command.

Does the PSOD occur only on one ESXi host or all ESXi hosts with Qlogic FC HBA? Is it a specific ESXi build that's affected by the problem? You must know this information because it can help you resolve the root problem.

The worst situation you can face is when the VMkernel is in the stopped status, and the ESXi host is not responding. When the VMkernel is busy and doesn't work correctly, as a possible solution, you can try to reboot the host. After rebooting the ESXi, it is very important to gather logs and performance statistics for the support.

You can initiate PSOD using the following command:
```
vsish -e set /reliability/crashMe/Panic 1
```

Troubleshooting cluster HA or DRS

Problems with cluster HA or DRS may occur at any time. If you have a problem with vSphere HA, you must first check the HA logs stored in `/var/log/fdm.log`. A typical problem can occur during the installation of the FDM agent (HA agent) to the ESXi host. The relevant logs are located in `/var/log/esxupdate.log`.

If you have a problem with the `/root` partition space, it is possible to control the partition through the CLI with the `vdf` command.

Other possible problems in the cluster can be related to VMkernel ports, VMs reservation on the target host, and incorrect network time. If the time is not synced in the VMware environment, you can have issues. Another typical vMotion issue is often due to misconfiguration of the IP address or VLANs.

To check the VMkernel, you can use the `ping` command, but when using the vMotion stack, you should use the `++netstack=vmotion` parameter.

DRS can also cause a problem with vMotion. Keep in mind that DRS uses vMotion to balance resources. Sometimes, a problem is simply due to DRS misconfiguration (manual or fully automated setup) or related to DRS rules.

Troubleshooting a virtual network

Every administrator around the world may have problems with the network connection, and the first action to begin the TRBL process is the use of the `ping` command. Yes, an easy ping can help you, but you have to ping from all directions: ESXi to vCSA and vCSA to ESXi. A typical possible TRBL scenario is when the network is misconfigured, the VLAN is not set up correctly, NIC teaming is not configured correctly, a port on a switch may be down, or there is a hardware problem with a VMNIC or with a physical switch.

The following CLIs can help you identify the problem:

- `esxcfg-vswitch`
- `esxcfg-vmknic`
- `esxcli network`
- `esxcfg-nics`

In TRBL you must, of course, understand what **vSphere Standard Switch** (**vSS**) and **vSphere Distributed Switch** (**vDS**) are. The problem can be anywhere, from the virtual machines to the physical network, software, or hardware.

A very good CLI command for TRBL network is `esxcli network`. For example, a command that can be used to enable or disable a VMNIC is `vmnic`, followed by the `up` or `down` parameters:

```
esxcli network nic down -n vmnic2
esxcli network nic up -n vmnic2
```

Network cards can be checked and listed using the `esxcli network nic list` command:

```
[root@esxi-prod-1:/] esxcli network nic list
Name PCI Device Driver Admin Status Link Status Speed Duplex MAC
Address MTU
Description
------ ------------ -------- ------------ ----------- ----- ------ ---
-------------- ---- ------------------------------------------------
vmnic0 0000:0b:00.0 nvmxnet3 Up Up 10000 Full 00:50:56:a9:8a:3f 1500
VMware Inc. vmxnet3 Virtual Ethernet Controller
vmnic1 0000:13:00.0 nvmxnet3 Up Up 10000 Full 00:50:56:a9:ac:78 1500
VMware Inc. vmxnet3 Virtual Ethernet Controller
vmnic2 0000:1b:00.0 nvmxnet3 Up Up 10000 Full 00:50:56:a9:2a:5c 9000
VMware Inc. vmxnet3 Virtual Ethernet Controller
vmnic3 0000:04:00.0 nvmxnet3 Up Up 10000 Full 00:50:56:a9:5c:de 9000
VMware Inc. vmxnet3 Virtual Ethernet Controller
vmnic4 0000:0c:00.0 nvmxnet3 Up Up 10000 Full 00:50:56:a9:47:f1 9000
VMware Inc. vmxnet3 Virtual Ethernet Controller
vmnic5 0000:14:00.0 nvmxnet3 Up Up 10000 Full 00:50:56:a9:07:f3 9000
VMware Inc. vmxnet3 Virtual Ethernet Controller
vmnic6 0000:1c:00.0 nvmxnet3 Up Up 10000 Full 00:50:56:a9:93:db 1500
VMware Inc. vmxnet3 Virtual Ethernet Controller
vmnic7 0000:05:00.0 nvmxnet3 Up Up 10000 Full 00:50:56:a9:7c:20 1500
VMware Inc. vmxnet3 Virtual Ethernet Controller
```

A typical problem that's due to misconfiguration is the selection of a bad virtual machine's port group. Changing to the correct VLAN fixes this problem.

If the management network is misconfigured (the change results in losing the host connection to the vCenter Server), the change is rolled back automatically to the previous configuration.

For additional information, check out **VMware KB 2032823**: **Understanding network rollback and recovery in vSphere 5.1 and later** at `https://kb.vmware.com/s/article/2032908`.

Troubleshooting storage

When you want to resolve problems with storage quickly, you must understand the architecture. There is a big difference between NFS and VMFS filesystems, or if DAS, FC, FCoE, iSCSI, or the new vSAN or VVOL are used. Two great friends will be `esxcli storage` and `esxcli iscsi` for particular use with iSCSI storage.

A problem you may need to analyze is the space occupied on the datastore. Use the `df -h` command to do so:

```
[root@esxi-prod-1:/var/log] cd /vmfs/volumes/
[root@esxi-prod-1:/vmfs/volumes] df -h
Filesystem Size    Used    Available Use%    Mounted on
VMFS-6     499.8G  135.0G  364.8G    27%     /vmfs/volumes/Shared
Storage
VMFS-6     49.8G   5.5G    44.2G     11%     /vmfs/volumes/C1
VMFS-6     49.8G   9.4G    40.4G     19%     /vmfs/volumes/C2
VMFS-6     49.8G   5.6G    44.1G     11%     /vmfs/volumes/C3
VMFS-6     49.8G   1.6G    48.1G     3%      /vmfs/volumes/C4
vfat       249.7M  155.3M  94.4M     62%     /vmfs/volumes/c931af73-
                                             7283cfde-5f11-b0b5ca4e48fc
vfat       285.8M  174.2M  111.6M    61%     /vmfs/volumes/5c60274d-
                                             50968070-edd0-005056a95cde
vfat       4.0G    19.8M   4.0G      0%      /vmfs/volumes/5c602753-
                                             c9175297-8143-005056a95cde
vfat       249.7M  155.3M 94.4M      62%     /vmfs/volumes/4a41ca7c-
                                             4c35da2c-e33e-88f6e0f74792
```

Troubleshooting VMs

The last component you may need to troubleshoot is the VMs. Typical issues are related to power-on, delete, misconfiguration, and resources.

To list the files belonging to a specific VM, use the `ls -lah` command:

```
[root@esxi-prod-1:/vmfs/volumes/5c601d26-2c3ab9f8-
e0ab-005056a95cde/VCSA-lab.learnvmware.local] ls -lah
total 36349248
drwxr-xr-x 1 root root 88.0K Feb 16 15:50 .
drwxr-xr-t 1 root root 76.0K Feb 14 12:07 ..
-rw-r--r-- 1 root root 92 Feb 16 15:20 VCSA-
lab.learnvmware.local-1af96f43.hlog
-rw------- 1 root root 10.0G Feb 11 20:35 VCSA-
lab.learnvmware.local-1af96f43.vswp
-rw------- 1 root root 12.0G Feb 16 16:16 VCSA-lab.learnvmware.local-
flat.vmdk
-rw------- 1 root root 8.5K Feb 14 15:22 VCSA-
lab.learnvmware.local.nvram
-rw------- 1 root root 546 Feb 16 15:20 VCSA-
lab.learnvmware.local.vmdk
-rw-r--r-- 1 root root 0 Feb 10 13:48 VCSA-lab.learnvmware.local.vmsd
-rwxr-xr-x 1 root root 4.1K Feb 16 15:20 VCSA-
lab.learnvmware.local.vmx
-rw------- 1 root root 0 Feb 16 15:20 VCSA-
lab.learnvmware.local.vmx.lck
-rwxr-xr-x 1 root root 4.1K Feb 16 15:20 VCSA-
lab.learnvmware.local.vmx~
lab.learnvmware.local_8-flat.vmdk
-rw------- 1 root root 546 Feb 11 20:13 VCSA-
lab.learnvmware.local_8.vmdk
-rw------- 1 root root 10.0G Feb 11 20:14 VCSA-
lab.learnvmware.local_9-flat.vmdk
-rw------- 1 root root 548 Feb 11 20:13 VCSA-
lab.learnvmware.local_9.vmdk
-rw-r--r-- 1 root root 222.3K Feb 16 07:20 vmware-185.log
-rw-r--r-- 1 root root 223.8K Feb 16 08:00 vmware-186.log
-rw-r--r-- 1 root root 222.3K Feb 16 08:50 vmware-187.log
-rw-r--r-- 1 root root 228.4K Feb 16 11:15 vmware-188.log
-rw-r--r-- 1 root root 228.2K Feb 16 13:50 vmware-189.log
-rw-r--r-- 1 root root 226.0K Feb 16 15:20 vmware-190.log
-rw-r--r-- 1 root root 183.7K Feb 16 16:09 vmware.log
-rw------- 1 root root 110.0M Feb 16 15:19 vmx-VCSA-
lab.learnvmware.local-452554563-1.vswp
```

During the TRBL process, `vmware.log` is the virtual machine's log file, which helps you to understand the problem better. In this log, you will see all the details about the problem. The name of the log file, `vmware.log`, is the same for each VM.

Many problems are due to resources, resource pools, and vApp, thus you should be very careful. If it is not a requirement, don't use reservations or limits for VMs.

Although TRBL can fix most problems, there are situations where restoring a VM from the backup is the only possible solution. Backup is an essential part of vSphere management.

Summary

In this chapter, you have learned how to perform different TRBL operations based on the component affected.

We have covered overall TRBL techniques, and we have looked at different vSphere commands we can use for TRBL. Although you may use some GUI tools for TRBL, you will usually stick with the CLI-based commands for their ease of use.

We have covered different CLI commands that you can use to troubleshoot your vCenter Server or ESXi host, and we have gone through different vSphere components that might be necessary to troubleshoot.

Finally, we covered several everyday situations that might require TRBL.

This concludes the second part of this book, and in the last part, we will have a look at how you can extend your vSphere knowledge and experience with vSphere Lab.

Questions

1. What are the valid commands on the ESXi level that can be used for TRBL?

   a) `esxcli`
   b) `esxcfg-*`
   c) `cfgtool-*`
   d) `vim-cmd`
   e) `esxconfig`

2. What is the valid command at the vCenter Server level that can be used for TRBL?

> a) `pyvc` (Python vSphere Console)
> b) `rvc` (Ruby vSphere Console)
> c) `pvc` (Perl vSphere Console)

3. In which folder (on the ESXi server) can you find logs?

> a) `/logs/`
> b) `/var/vsphere/log/`
> c) `/var/log/`
> d) `/esxi/log/`

4. You can restart individual vCenter Server services both from the CLI and the GUI:

> a) True
> b) False

5. What does PSOD refer to?

Further reading

Read the following article for more information:

vSphere troubleshooting: vSphere Troubleshooting describes troubleshooting issues and procedures for VMware vCenter Server implementations and related components.

For more information, refer to `https://docs.vmware.com/en/VMware-vSphere/6.5/vsphere-esxi-vcenter-server-651-troubleshooting-guide.pdf`.

Section 4: Building Your Lab Environment

This section focuses on how to build your lab environment, and different approaches and considerations regarding how the lab can be implemented (including physical servers, desktop virtualization, and utilizing a dedicated server from the service provider). At the end of the section, there will be detailed example of how the lab environment could look, with step-by-step instructions and a how-to cookbook.

This section includes the following chapter:

- Chapter 15, *Building Your Own VMware vSphere Lab*

15
Building Your Own VMware vSphere Lab

In this chapter, we will focus on different techniques that can be used to enhance your VMware vSphere skills. The majority of the chapter will look at various aspects of building your lab, including different approaches you can take and the pros and cons of each.

After that, we will cover one particular solution in more detail, which is having a vSphere lab environment running on the dedicated physical server in the data center. We will learn how to install and configure different components of the lab.

Running your vSphere lab should be one of your primary concerns, since, with your lab, you can test any component of VMware vSphere and gain the required experience and knowledge.

In this chapter, we will cover the following topics:

- The importance of lifelong learning
- Choosing the right platform
- Software components and licensing
- Architecture and logical design
- A detailed implementation guide

The importance of lifelong learning

It is always advantageous for professionals in the IT field to have a home lab environment, because it enables you to experiment with different technologies. It is always a great learning experience to build a lab from scratch by yourself. Building your own VMware vSphere lab is much easier than you might think and it will enable you to extend your VMware skills and further your career.

Why build a lab?

There are many reasons why someone would want to build a virtualization lab. Two of the most common reasons are the following:

- **Exam study**: Before you apply for an exam, you need to test everything and be entirely sure about how different components interact. You also need to be confident with the different configuration options and have an awareness of how to perform different tasks.
- **Hands-on learning**: One of the most common reasons for running a lab is to be able to gain real hands-on experience. You can, of course, read books or watch videos about different components of VMware vSphere, but being able to configure and maintain the environment by yourself is an essential skill.

If you don't wish to run your own lab, there are other options. We'll take a look at a few of these in the following sections.

VMware Hands-On Lab (HOL)

If you need to test specific products without running an environment, you can check out **VMware Hands-On Labs (HOLs)**, which can be found at the following link: `https://labs.hol.vmware.com/HOL/catalogs/catalog/1212`.

Here, you can find numerous instant-access labs that you can use to evaluate certain products. The nice thing about HOLs is that the infrastructure is ready within a few minutes and you get a comprehensive lab guide that will guide you through different scenarios. Moreover, it's free!

The VMware HOLs catalog looks as follows:

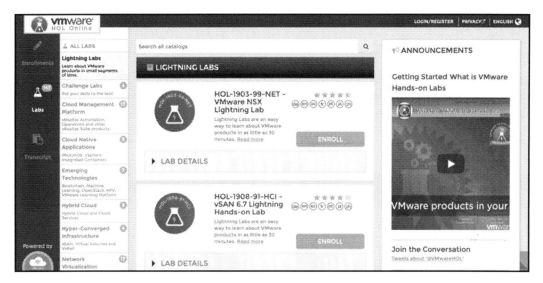

VMware forums

If you are looking for unofficial support, or you would like to discuss a particular situation within your VMware environment, you can also check out VMware Communities at the following link: `https://communities.vmware.com/welcome`. You can find numerous forums here based on the products with which you are facing some issues or difficulties.

The most useful forums include the following:

- **VMware vSphere**: `https://communities.vmware.com/community/vmtn/vsphere/content?filterID=contentstatus[published]~objecttype~objecttype[thread]`

- **vCenter Server**: `https://communities.vmware.com/community/vmtn/vcenter/content?filterID=contentstatus[published]~objecttype~objecttype[thread]`

- **VMware NSX**: `https://communities.vmware.com/community/vmtn/nsx`

- **VMware vSAN**: `https://communities.vmware.com/community/vmtn/vsan/content?filterID=contentstatus[published]~objecttype~objecttype[thread]`

Blogs

A lot of useful information can be found on different blogs. I would strongly recommend the following blogs so that you don't miss any new features or configuration walk-throughs.

There are two kinds of blogs:

- **Official**: Run by different VMware departments
- **Unofficial**: Run by freelancing VMware consultants or sometimes even by VMware employees

The following are official blogs:

- **VMware vSphere Blog**: https://blogs.vmware.com/vsphere/
- **VMware VROOM! Blog**: https://blogs.vmware.com/performance/
- **VMware PowerCLI Blog**: https://blogs.vmware.com/powercli/
- **Network Virtualization**: https://blogs.vmware.com/networkvirtualization/

A number of personal blogs you should check out are listed here:

- **Yellow Bricks**: http://www.yellow-bricks.com
- **virtuallyGhetto**: https://www.virtuallyghetto.com
- **CormacHogan**: https://cormachogan.com
- **ESXvirtualization**: https://www.vladan.fr
- **LearnVMware**: https://learnvmware.online
- **VirtualGeek**: https://virtualgeek.typepad.com
- **vNinja**: https://vninja.net
- **VMGuru**: https://vmguru.com

Choosing the right platform

A VMware lab can come in many forms. You can use standard rack servers installed in your basement, you can use your desktop PC, you can run several small PCs as an Intel **Next Unit of Computing** (**NUC**) to host your ESXi servers, you can rent a physical server from a number of service providers, or you can use a cloud environment to host your virtual ESXi hypervisors.

The aim is to find the sweet spot between cost and functionality. Of course, it would be nice to run your blade chassis with multiple physical servers and fiber-channel storage, but the cost of such a solution would probably be too high.

It is important to note that whatever your decision, in most cases, it won't be supported by VMware at all. You can't expect any support from the VMware support team and you will be responsible for any problems you have with your lab. In order to get official support, you need to have all hardware components listed in the **Hardware Compatibility List** (**HCL**). However, community support is still available. If you run into any problems, you can try asking a question on the public VMware forums at the following link: `https://communities.vmware.com/index.jspa`.

No matter what platform you choose, you should carefully plan the resources the platform will require and any additional hardware you might need. Think about the following questions:

- Which CPU and memory resources do you need?
- What is the size of the storage and what is its performance like?
- Do you need additional physical components, such as switches or storage arrays?
- Where will the lab be located?
- What will the energy consumption of your lab be like?

Another factor might be the time span of the lab or **proof of concept** (**PoC**):

- **Short-term**: You only need to run the lab for a few weeks or months to test the individual components or for exam preparation
- **Long-term**: You would like to run the lab for months or even years so that you have an environment that you can come back to whenever you need it

The duration of the lab project or PoC will, of course, affect the overall cost of the solution. Let's take a look at the different options for your lab and their pros and cons.

Standard rack servers

This kind of server is commonly used by enterprise companies in their data center. You might get lucky and find refurbished servers at a fraction of the original cost. Usually, when companies are refreshing their hardware infrastructure, they sell older servers.

The advantages of using a standard rack server are as follows:

- They are similar to production servers
- They have adequate compute resources
- They are easy to scale by adding more servers

The disadvantages of using a standard rack server are as follows:

- They are expensive
- They consume a lot of power (this is especially the case for older hardware)
- They require additional physical network infrastructure
- They are large in size
- They are noisy

You can find many refurbished servers on eBay at `https://www.ebay.com/b/Computer-Servers/11211/bn_886971` or on some specialized sites including `https://www.bargainhardware.co.uk/refurbished-servers`.

Desktop PC

For a small lab, even your home PC could be enough, but it depends on what you want to test. Do you need to run a single ESXi server? If so, a VMware Workstation will do the trick. Once you get serious, however, you might encounter problems with the resources of your home PC.

Today, traditional home PCs might have 16 GB of memory, with some more expensive configurations having up to 32 GB. To run a single vCenter Server appliance, you will need 10 GB of memory. If you require additional ESXi servers, nested virtual machines, vRealize Operations, or even NSX, you will reach the resource limits quite quickly.

The advantages of using a Desktop PC are as follows:

- They are cheap
- They are often already available
- There is no need for additional infrastructure

The disadvantage of using a Desktop PC is that you will often not have enough resources available for more complex setups.

Small, dedicated PCs

A lot of people use NUCs or similar platforms for their labs. In this case, you have several dedicated small servers, each usually equipped with 32 GB of memory and local SSD storage.

The advantages of using small, dedicated PCs are as follows:

- They are small
- They are easy to scale by adding more servers

The disadvantages of using small, dedicated PCs are as follows:

- They are expensive
- They require additional physical network infrastructure
- You will have limited upgrade options for CPU and memory

Cloud-based solutions

If you do not want to invest in any physical hardware, you might be interested in a cloud-based option. In this case, you are renting virtual resources like any other customer on the public cloud, but inside the virtual machine, a virtualized ESXi server is running.

This approach might be ideal for short-term projects, where you pay only for resources that you have used over a period of time. For a long-term project, however, the price might not be that attractive when compared to physical servers.

The advantages of using cloud-based solutions are as follows:

- They can be deployed within minutes
- They can be cheap for short-term projects
- They are software defined, so there is no need for any additional infrastructure

The disadvantages of using cloud-based solutions are as follows:

- They can be expensive for long-term projects
- The solution is delivered as is, and you can't customize some of the components

Note that you can't run ESXi inside a virtual machine. The service provider must explicitly support this function (nested virtualization). If you try to install an ESXi hypervisor on an Amazon AWS EC2 instance, for example, it won't work correctly. Several companies specialize in nested environments. These include Ravello (`https:/ /cloud.oracle.com/en_US/ravello`) and VMlabs (`https://www.vmlabs.io`).

A dedicated server in a data center

In my opinion, this is the optimal solution. You can either host your server in the data center, or you can rent a server, depending on your requirements. When you are running your own dedicated server, you have complete control of the environment, and you can tweak the server as you need to.

In this situation, nested virtualization is used. First, the ESXi hypervisor is installed on the physical server and then you create several other virtual machines that will be used to host your virtual ESXi servers.

The advantages of using a dedicated server in a data center are as follows:

- You have complete control of the servers
- There is no need for any additional physical network infrastructure because everything is virtualized
- It can be cheap for short-term projects
- You will have sufficient compute resources

The disadvantage of using a dedicated server in a datacenter is that it can be cheap for long-term projects.

There are many service providers that you can use to rent a physical server. I tend to use servers from OVH (`https://www.ovh.com`).

Software components and licensing

Now, when you have chosen your ideal hardware platform, you need to think about which software licenses you need in order to install and run the environment successfully.

There are many components that you need to license, especially if you want to build everything from scratch. In some cases, cloud-based solutions do not need to be licensed, because the licenses are already included in the service price.

Let's cover the most common software components that you might need to use in your lab.

VMware licensing

Let's start with VMware itself. Most products can be tested for free with the evaluation version through the Eval center at the following link: `https://www.vmware.com/try-vmware.html`.

The following products can be downloaded as 60-day eval versions:

- **VMware vSphere**: `https://www.vmware.com/go/evaluate-vsphere-en`
- **VMware vSAN**: `https://www.vmware.com/go/try-vsan-dl-en`
- **VMware Horizon**: `https://www.vmware.com/go/try-horizon-view-dl-en`
- **vRealize Operations**: `https://www.vmware.com/go/try-vrealize-ops-dl-en`
- **vRealize Log Insight**: `https://www.vmware.com/go/try-log-insight`
- **Site Recovery Manager**: `https://www.vmware.com/go/try-srm`

However, some products can't be downloaded. VMware NSX and vRealize Automation, for example, are no longer available for download.

For some VMware products, you can test solutions already deployed for you using the cloud offerings located at the following link: `https://cloud.vmware.com`.

VMware EVALExperience

This is an excellent program that you can join through **VMware User Group** (**VMUG**) membership. Standard VMUG membership is free, and it gives you several benefits, which you can check at the following link: `https://www.vmug.com`.

There is a paid membership as well, called VMUG Advantage, which allows you to access the following additional benefits:

- EVALExperience
- 20% discount on VMware training classes
- 20% discount on VMware certification exams
- 35% discount on VMware certification exam preparation workshops (VCP-NV)

- 35% discount on VMware lab connect
- $100 discount on VMworld attendance
- Extended trials of VMware cloud services

Membership of the advantage program costs $200 per year, but it is worth it. The most exciting offering is the EVALExperience program. VMware's EVALExperience gives you exclusive access to 365-day evaluation licenses for a selection of VMware solutions, for personal use in a non-production environment. It includes the following products:

- VMware vCenter Server v6.x Standard
- VMware vSphere ESXi Enterprise Plus with Operations Management (six CPU licenses)
- VMware NSX Enterprise Edition (six CPU licenses)
- VMware vRealize Network Insight
- VMware vSAN
- VMware Site Recovery Manager
- VMware vRealize Log Insight
- VMware vRealize Operations
- VMware vRealize Automation 7.3 Enterprise
- VMware vRealize Orchestrator
- VMware vCloud Suite Standard
- VMware Horizon Advanced Edition
- VMware vRealize Operations for Horizon
- VMware Fusion Pro 11
- VMware Workstation Pro 15

For the price of $200, you get the licenses for all vSphere products you might ever need, which is an impressive offering. Plus, it saves you having to reinstall the environment every 60 days!

If you would like to join the program, visit the following link: `https://www.vmug.com/Join/EVALExperience`.

Windows licensing

You will probably use Windows Servers within your inventory as well as some Microsoft applications such as the SQL database. Fortunately, Microsoft has an eval program as well. This allows you to run any software component for 180 days to test it. You can download different software at the following link: `https://www.microsoft.com/en-us/evalcenter/`.

The following two components are likely to be the most interesting:

- **Windows Server:** `https://www.microsoft.com/en-us/evalcenter/evaluate-windows-server-2019`
- **SQL Server:** `https://www.microsoft.com/en-us/evalcenter/evaluate-sql-server-2017-rtm`

Note that you can download the older versions as well, so if you prefer to stick with Windows Server 2012 R2, you can still download it from the Evaluation Center.

Other software components

Once you have obtained the core licenses, it is time to start thinking about the whole environment, including how you will interconnect the core components and which additional licenses or software you might need.

Storage

Which storage solutions will you use? There are many options for how to provide storage to your ESXi infrastructure:

- Windows Server with file services (iSCSI target)
- Open source Linux-based storage solutions such as **FreeNAS** (`https://www.freenas.org`)
- Software-defined storage solutions such as HPE VSA or EMC ScaleIO

Networking

Depending on how your infrastructure will be interconnected with the outside network, you might need to run some firewall appliances that provide access to the lab, **Network Address Translation** (**NAT**) and routing features, or even to the VPN connection.

Many vendors offer either free products or at least evaluation versions of virtual appliances:

- **Cisco Cloud Services Router 1000V Series**: `https://www.cisco.com/c/en/us/products/routers/cloud-services-router-1000v-series/index.html`
- **Juniper vSRX Virtual Firewall**: `https://www.juniper.net/us/en/products-services/security/srx-series/vsrx/`
- **VyOS**: `https://vyos.io`
- **MikroTik RouterOS**: `https://mikrotik.com/software`

You might even try to simulate complex physical networks to test some advanced networking features such as leaf-spine design or VXLANs. To do this, you will need to deploy a specific virtual machine that will act as a switch for your environment.

Cumulus Linux is one of the most frequently deployed network operating systems that can be installed within the virtual machine as well. This can be found at the following link: `https://cumulusnetworks.com/products/cumulus-linux/`.

Architecture and logical design

You might have realized by now that building a lab isn't as simple as you might think. For those who are interested in how I built the lab that I used during the writing of this book, you can follow this detailed guide.

I chose to rent a dedicated server from OVH. This was for the following reasons:

- For my on-site training, I needed a lot of resources (256 GB of RAM or more)
- I did not need to run the server all the time
- I did not want to pay any setup fees
- I needed to be able to order as many public IP addresses as necessary for the project
- There were months when I didn't need to run the lab at all
- There were other months in which I needed a different hardware platform with different resources
- I needed to access the lab from anywhere

Based on these requirements, I decided that it did not make sense to use my hardware because the costs would have been too high. The cloud solution did not work for me either, because I needed to have complete access to the environment and I needed to be able to tweak it as much as necessary.

Let's take a look at the architecture of my lab and its logical design.

The architecture of the lab

I used a single physical server. The first ESXi server is installed on the top of the server. I call the ESXi hypervisor **MasterESXi**. This MasterESXi then hosts multiple VMs, some of which are used to provide infrastructure services, such as DNS, **Active Directory (AD)** services, or iSCSI storage, to the lab. Other VMs are used as nested ESXi hypervisors. Let's take a look at the overall architecture:

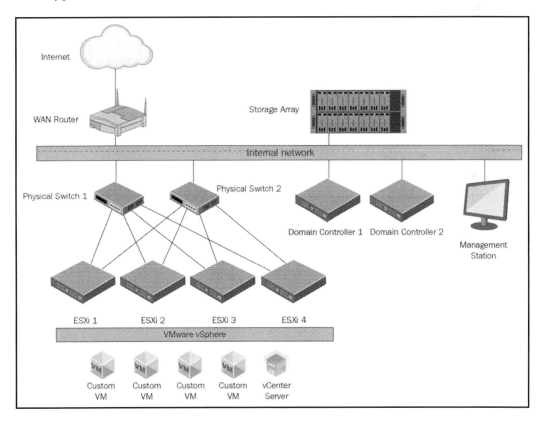

Let's now take a look at the different components of the lab.

The Master ESXi hypervisor

This is an ESXi hypervisor running on the bare metal server in the data center. There is no shared storage at all, only local storage that is used for virtual machines. This ESXi hypervisor is used to host all virtual infrastructure machines, such as the **Active Directory Domain Controller** (**AD DC**), the management station, the iSCSI server, and the virtual router. All virtual ESXi servers are running on top of the Master ESXi server.

iSCSI storage

As you already know, we need to provide shared storage to our ESXi servers if we want to use different cluster features such as **HA** or **DRS**. As a result, I have a virtual machine that hosts the iSCSI target service. All virtual ESXi servers are connected to that storage over iSCSI.

Virtual router

You need to provide management access to the environment. You also need to configure the routing between different subnets within your lab. My virtual router supports VLANs, so I can quickly test multiple port groups with different VLAN tags. You can also use a virtual router to provide services such as a DHCP server or NAT.

Management station

I prefer to install all necessary software on a management station (or a jump-host server if you prefer) so that I do not need to install any software directly to my laptop or home PC. Another reason for using a management station is that it is run within the environment and you are accessing the station over RDP remotely. This means that the interconnection within the lab is much faster than over the internet.

AD

In many enterprise environments, there is an AD in place. It would be good to test all the integrations between your vSphere environment and AD. Also, if you need to test different roles and permissions, it is useful to test these against AD (or any other LDAP server) instead of the local SSO domain.

IP address plan

In the lab, there will be multiple IP subnets and port groups. Let's take a look at the different sections of the IP address plan. As a DNS server, use the IP addresses of the primary and secondary domain controllers. In my case, these are `172.16.1.1` and `172.16.1.2`.

Management network

The management network is used for management communication between different components:

Management network 172.16.1.0/24		IP address	DNS name
vSphere infrastructure			
	ESXi-prod-1	172.16.1.11	esxi-prod-1.learnvmware.local
	ESXi-prod-2	172.16.1.12	esxi-prod-2.learnvmware.local
	ESXi-prod-3	172.16.1.13	esxi-prod-3.learnvmware.local
	ESXi-prod-4	172.16.1.14	esxi-prod-4.learnvmware.local
	vCenter Server	172.16.1.100	vcsa.learnvmware.local
Internal Infrastructure			
	Domain Controller 1	172.16.1.1	dc1.learnvmware.local
	Domain Controller 2	172.16.1.2	dc2.learnvmware.local
	Management workstation	172.16.1.250	mgmt.learnvmware.local
Network infrastructure			
	Default gateway	172.16.1.254	

vMotion network

This is the dedicated network for vMotion:

vMotion network 172.16.2.0/24		IP address
VMware vSphere		
	ESXi-prod-1	172.16.2.1
	ESXi-prod-2	172.16.2.2
	ESXi-prod-3	172.16.2.3
	ESXi-prod-4	172.16.2.4

iSCSI network

This is the dedicated network for iSCSI traffic between ESXi hypervisors and the shared storage array:

iSCSI network 192.168.0.0/16		IP address
VMware vSphere	ESXi1 iSCSI1	192.168.100.11
	ESXi1 iSCSI2	192.168.100.12
	ESXi2 iSCSI1	192.168.100.21
	ESXi2 iSCSI2	192.168.100.22
	ESXi3 iSCSI1	192.168.100.31
	ESXi3 iSCSI2	192.168.100.32
	ESXi4 iSCSI1	192.168.100.41
	ESXi4 iSCSI2	192.168.100.42
	Storage SP1	192.168.10.1
	Storage SP2	192.168.10.2

Production network

This is the simulation of the production network. Different VLANs are used in the production network to test network connectivity:

Production network 1 - VLAN 10	
VMs	10.0.10.1-253
GW	10.0.10.254
Production network 2 - VLAN 20	
VMs	10.0.20.1-253
GW	10.0.20.254
Production network 3 - VLAN 30	
VMs	10.0.30.1-253
GW	10.0.30.254

A detailed implementation guide

In this example, I am using a dedicated server provided by OVH.com. As mentioned previously, however, you can use any server you like. At this stage, I have a bare metal server and a fresh copy of ESXi 6.7 U1 installed on the top of the server:

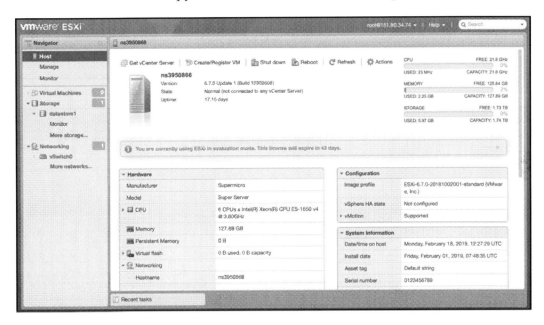

Master ESXi server configuration

First, we need to configure our Master ESXi server so that it will be possible to host our virtual machines. Before we do that, we need to start with the network configuration of the Master ESXi server.

Network configuration

Let's have a look at the network topology of the Master ESXi hypervisor first:

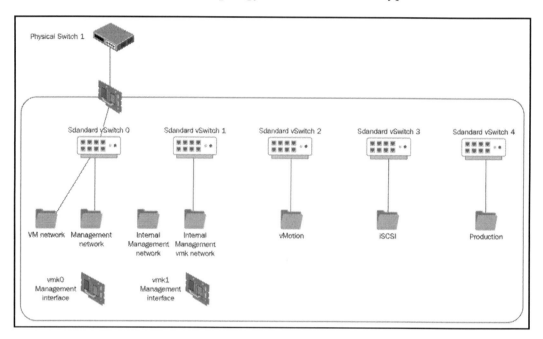

Virtual switches

As a first step, we need to define our virtual switches. The following vSwitches will be created:

vSwitch name	Uplinks	MTU	Description
vSwitch1	No	1500	Used for management of the network
vSwitch2	No	1500	Used for vMotion
vSwitch3	No	9000	Used for iSCSI
vSwitch4	No	1500	Used for the production network

Because we will be running nested virtualization, all security policies must be set to
Accept:

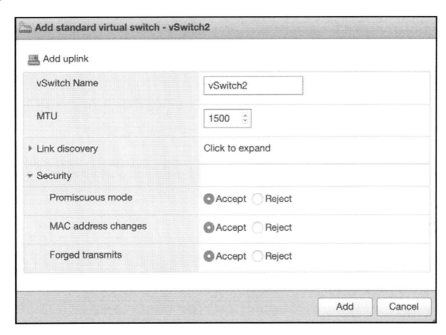

You can check the following article, which explains why the security policy must be
changed: `https://www.virtuallyghetto.com/2013/11/why-is-promiscuous-mode-forged.html`.

Port groups

Next, we need to define port groups that will be used to connect our virtual
machines:

Name	vSwitch	VLAN ID	Notes
Internal management	vSwitch1	0	
Internal management—vmk	vSwitch1	0	For vmk1
vMotion	vSwitch2	0	
iSCSI	vSwitch3	0	
Production	vSwitch4	4095	ESG trunking must be enabled with VLAN 4095

On the Master ESXi level, we need one additional VMkernel port that will be used for management from our management station:

Name	Port group	IP address	Services
vmk1	Internal management—vmk	172.16.1.253	Management

Virtual machines

Now, when we have configured the networking of the Master ESXi server, let's create several virtual machines that will be used for our lab. In my case, I am running all VMs with a thin disc. Of course, your resource configuration might be different, so take this as an example only:

VM name	CPU	RAM	HDD	OS	Notes
DC01.learnvmware.local	1	2	20	Windows	Domain controller 1
DC02.learnvmware.local	1	2	20	Windows	Domain controller 1
Mgmt.learnvmware.local	2	4	40	Windows	Management station
iSCSI	4	4	20	Windows	iSCSI storage array
Esxi-prod-1.learnvmware.local	2	12	10	ESXi	vESXi1
Esxi-prod-2.learnvmware.local	2	12	10	ESXi	vESXi2
Esxi-prod-3.learnvmware.local	2	12	10	ESXi	vESXi3
Esxi-prod-4.learnvmware.local	2	12	10	ESXi	vESXi4

Let's take a look at the network configuration of the virtual machines:

Virtual machine	Interface type	Port group
DC01	E1001	Internal management
DC02	E1001	Internal management
Mgmt	E1001	Internal management
iSCSI	E1001	Internal management
iSCSI	VMXNET3	iSCSI
iSCSI	VMXNET3	iSCSI
ESXi	VMXNET3	Internal management
ESXi	VMXNET3	Internal management
ESXi	VMXNET3	vMotion
ESXi	VMXNET3	vMotion
ESXi	VMXNET3	iSCSI
ESXi	VMXNET3	iSCSI
ESXi	VMXNET3	Production
ESXi	VMXNET3	Production

For all Windows-based virtual machines, install Windows Server 2012 R2 as a base OS, configure the computer name and the IP address, enable remote desktop services, and change the firewall settings if necessary. Also, install VMtools to the guestOS.

For ESXi-based virtual machines, install vSphere 6.7U1.

 Note that at this stage, the network connectivity is still unavailable to the external network. Only connections inside the internal management network will work.

Virtual router

As a virtual router, I am using **RouterOS** from MikroTik, but feel free to install any vRouter with which you have hands-on experience.

RouterOS can be downloaded from `https://mikrotik.com/download`. Once you register your account on `Mikrotik.com`, you can obtain a free 60-day evaluation license.

Let's deploy the OVA package from MikroTik. There is a specialized appliance type called **Cloud Hosted Router** that is built to be run in virtualized environments:

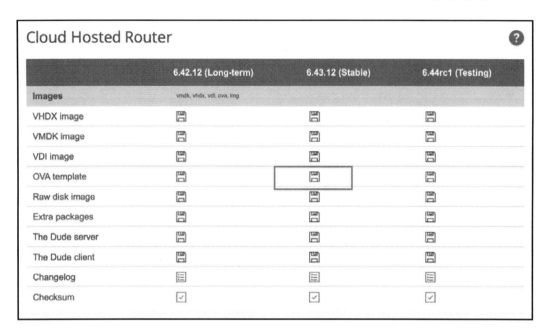

Once you have deployed the virtual router, all you need to do is to assign more virtual network adapters:

vNIC ID	Port group
Network adapter 1	VM network
Network adapter 2	Internal management
Network adapter 3	Production

Virtual router configuration

Before we can communicate between multiple IP subnets, we need to configure our virtual router correctly:

Interface name	IP address	Port group
Eth1	x.x.x.x	VM network (public IP address from the service provider)
Eth2	172.16.1.254/24	Internal management

At this stage, we can use any GUI to configure our router. We do this using CLI. In my example, you can see the configuration of the RouterOS as follows:

```
ip address add address=X.X.X.X/X interface=ether1
ip address add address=172.16.1.254/24 interface=ether2
```

For the default gateway, you can use the following command:

```
ip route add address=0.0.0.0/0 dst-address=Y.Y.Y.Y
```

In these commands, X.X.X.X is the public IP address from the service provider, and Y.Y.Y.Y is the gateway that you have been assigned.

If you have configured everything correctly, you should now be able to connect to the GUI configuration interface of the RouterOS using the public IP address:

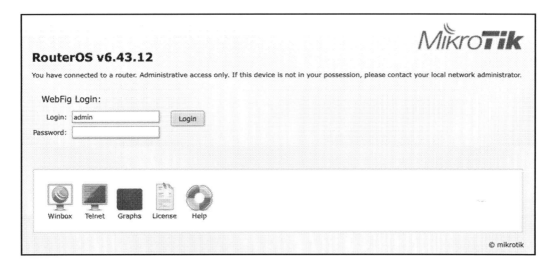

Firewalls and access to the virtual router

RouterOS, by default, does not use a password for the admin user. The first thing you should do is to change the blank password to something else. From the GUI menu, select **System | Users** and select the default admin user and change its password.

Then, it is recommended to limit the connection to the management interface of the RouterOS using firewall rules. Switch to **IP | Firewall** from the menu and define the following firewall rules:

ID	Chain	Source address	Action	Notes
0	Input	z.z.z.z	Permit	Your home IP address, so you can connect to the virtual router
1	Input	172.16.1.0/24	Permit	Allows connectivity from the management network
2	Input	10.0.0.0/8	Permit	Allows connectivity from the production network
3	Input		Permit	Check only the **related** and **established** options in the **connection state**
4	Input		Drop	Drop anything that is not permitted

These rules are shown in the following screenshot:

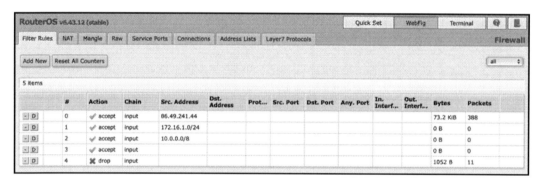

Next, we need to configure NAT so that our virtual machines will be able to connect to the internet and so that we can connect to our management station. Two rules should be defined in the **NAT** tab:

ID	Chain	Action type	Notes
0	srcnat	masquerade	
1	dstnat	dst-nat	Fill in the destination address (the public IP of the virtual router) and port 3389. In **Action**, select dst-nat. The **To Address** value will be 172.16.1.250 and the **To Port** value should be 3389.

The following screenshot contains the NAT rules:

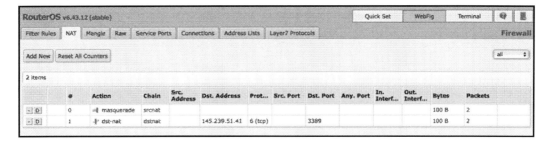

DNS configuration

Our virtual router must be able to translate DNS records, so we need to configure the DNS servers. To do that, select **IP | DNS** and fill in your favorite DNS servers in the **Servers** field:

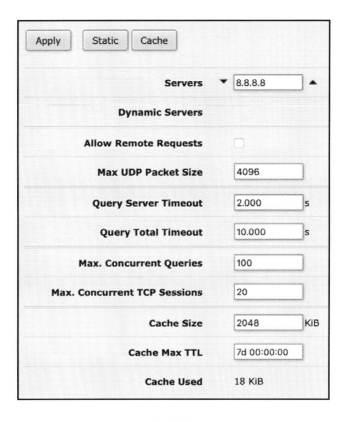

License configuration

By default, RouterOS runs with an evaluation version that is capped at 1 Mbps. You can obtain a 1 Gbps license for free; all you need to do is specify the username and password that you created during registration at `Mikrotik.com`.

Switch to **System | License** and click **Renew License**. You need to fill in your username and password and the desired license type. **P1** is a 1 Gbps license, **P10** is a 10 Gbps license, and **P unlimited** has no cap at all.

Once you have configured the username and password, you should see that you have successfully obtained a trial license:

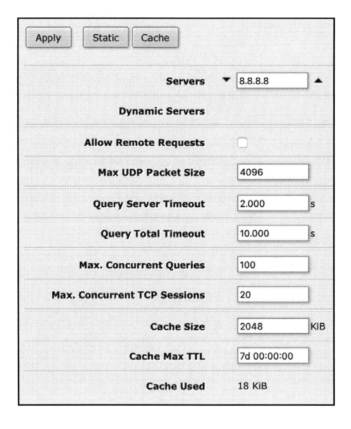

VLAN configuration

We then need to configure our virtual router to support VLANs. Switch to **Interface** from the main menu and select **New VLAN interface.** Three VLANs need to be created with the following properties:

- The VLAN IDs are 10 20, and 30
- The interface is ether2
- The names are vlan10, vlan20, and vlan30

You can also use the following CLI command:

```
interface vlan add interface=ether3 vlan-id=10 name=VLAN10
```

The interface configuration should appear as follows:

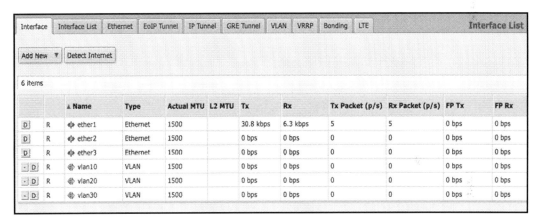

We now need to configure an L3 interface for the new VLANs so that the virtual machines that are connected to them will be able to reach the IP interface of the virtual router.

To do this, switch to **IP | Addresses** from the main menu and add the following three IP addresses:

IP address	Interface
10.0.10.254/24	vlan10
10.0.20.254/24	vlan20
10.0.30.254/24	vlan30

The IP configuration should appear as follows:

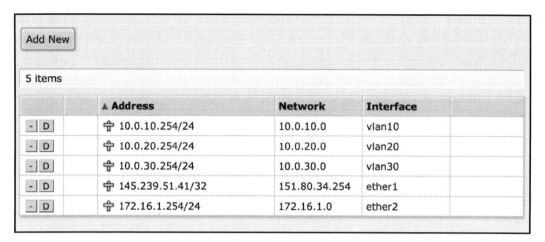

Windows infrastructure

We have two new virtual machines that will be used as domain controllers, so let's have a look at the configuration of the Windows environment.

Once you have installed the guestOS and VMtools, configured the IP address, and changed the computer name, proceed with the AD installation.

DC01.learnvmware.local

This will be our first AD DC. The installation of AD is quite a straightforward process. All you need to do is install the AD server role on the server.

From **Server Manager**, click **Manage,** and then select **Add Roles and Features**:

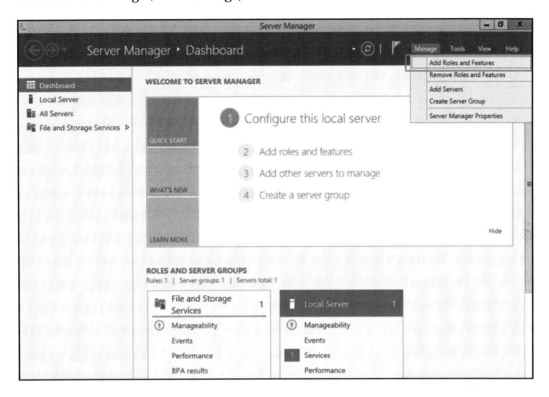

In the installation type, select role-based installation:

1. Select your server (dc01).
2. Select **Active Directory Domain Services Role** and add the required features:

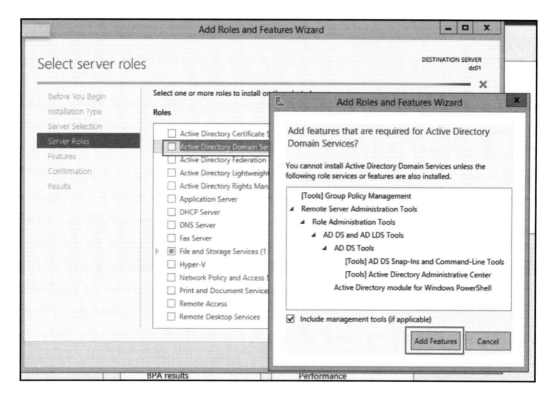

There is no need to select any additional features, so let's finish the wizard. It will take some time to install the required files, and once everything is installed, you can proceed with the AD configuration.

To do that, all you need to do is to click on **Promote this server to a domain controller**:

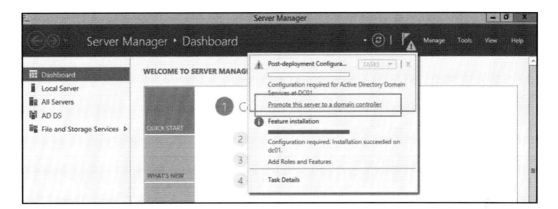

In **Deployment Configuration**, select **Add a new forest** and specify your local active directory domain. In this example, this is `learnvmware.local`:

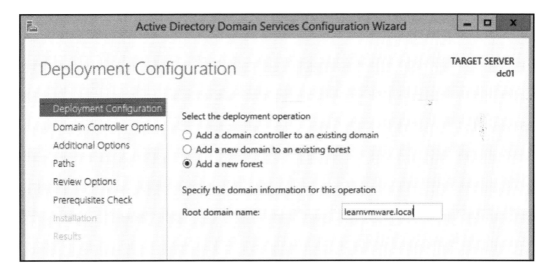

In the next step, do not change anything except the **Directory Services Recovery Mode** (**DSRM**) password, which is a required field.

It is beyond the scope of this guide to cover AD itself, so let's proceed with the installation and keep all the defaults as the wizard suggests.

Once the installation is over, the server will automatically reboot to finish the **Active Directory Federation Services** (**ADFS**) installation.

DC02.learnvmware.local

With our secondary domain controller, the process will be slightly different. As a first step, we will join this computer to our new AD domain. To do this, click on Configure this local server and then click on the **Workgroup** link. Then, follow the instructions as follows:

1. Click the **Change** button.
2. Select the domain and fill in your domain name as configured. You will need to provide an AD username and password. This would be the password you configured when you were installing Windows Server on dc01 in the first place:

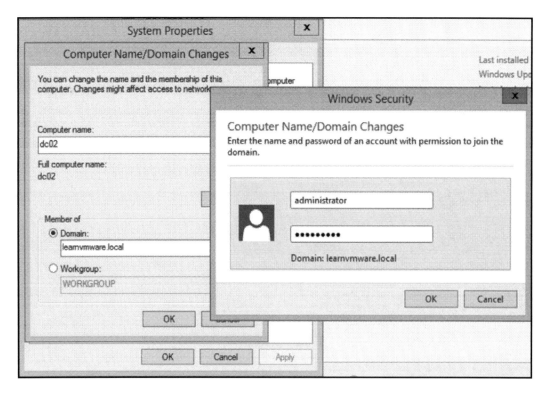

3. Reboot the server. After the server is rebooted, do not forget to log in as a domain administrator: DOMAINNAME\administrator.

4. Now, you need to install the ADFS role as described in the *DC01.learnvmware.local* section. The only difference would be that during the ADFS configuration, you will select **Add a domain controller to an existing domain**:

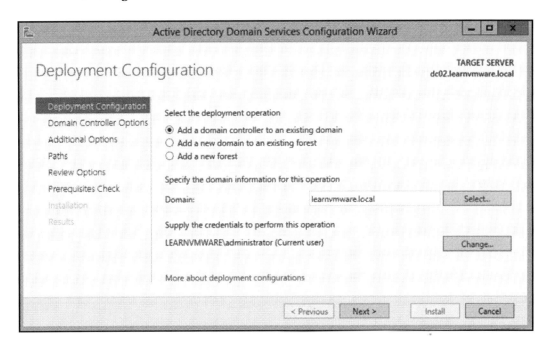

Finish the installation wizard and reboot the server.

Congratulations ! You have successfully deployed your AD infrastructure! It's now time to move on to other servers.

Mgmt.learnvmware.local

On this server, all we need to do is to join this computer to the AD domain as described in the *DC02.learnvmware.local* section.

This server will be used as a jump-host to the lab. Because we have already configured the NAT, you should be able to connect to the server using the remote desktop protocol.

We would now like to install several remote management tools on the server so that we can connect to the AD directly from our management server:

1. Again, click on **Manage** and select Add or Remove features.
2. Do not select any role to install.

As the feature to install, select the **AD DS and AD LDS Tools** and **DNS Server Tools** under **Remote Server Administration Tools**:

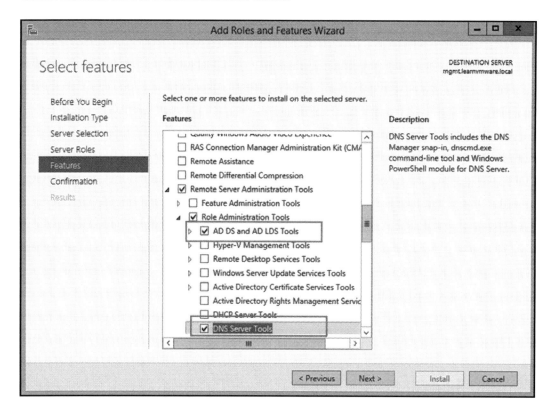

Once installed, you should see the new management snap-ins in the **Tools** menu:

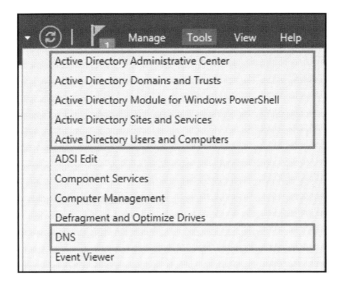

iscsi.learnvmware.local

Again, this server needs to be joined to the AD first. Once the server is part of the AD domain, we will install the iSCSI target service that will be used for our shared storage. Before we do that, we need to perform several reconfigurations on the Master ESXi level.

Storage design

Right now, our iSCSI virtual machine has only a single small disk, but we need to provide a much larger space for our vSphere infrastructure. We need to assign a new virtual disk to the iSCSI virtual machine.

Bear in mind that for optimal performance, you should attach this new virtual disk to the PVSCSI controller and the disk type should be **Thick provisioned, eagerly zeroed**:

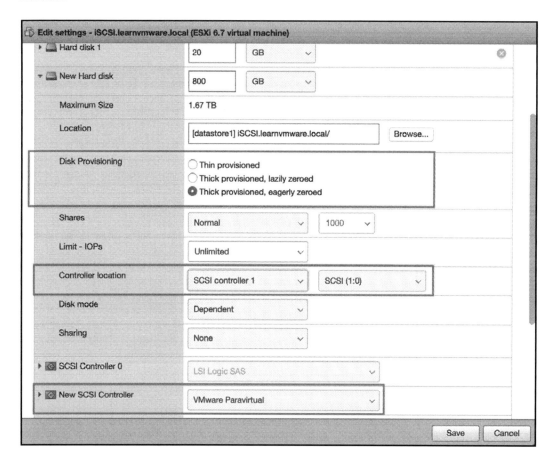

iSCSI target configuration

Now that we have attached our new virtual disk to the VM, we need to bring it online and format it. Follow these steps:

1. From **Tools**, select **Computer Management** and **Disk Management** under the **Storage** menu. As you can see, our guest OS can correctly see the new device:

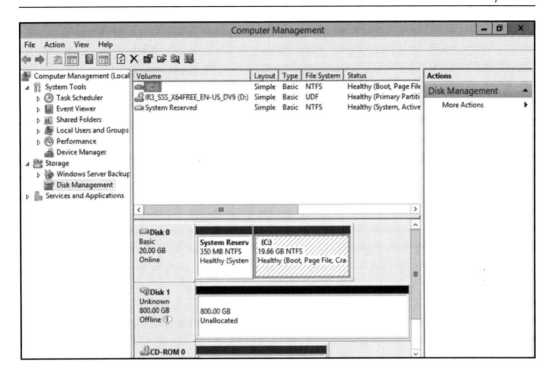

2. Right click on **Disk 1** and select **Online**.
3. Once the disk is online, right-click it again and select **Initialize**.

All that is left to do now is to create a new partition that will be used to store our iSCSI disks:

1. Right-click on the **Unallocated** space.
2. Select **New Simple Volume...**.
3. Assign a new drive letter, format the volume with NTFS, and provide a name for the volume if required. You should then be able to see that the disk is online and the new partition is created:

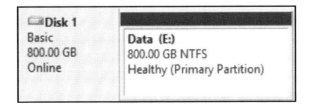

Once the disk is online, you can install the iSCSI target role. To do that, merely launch the add or remove roles and features wizard and select the **iSCSI Target Server** role:

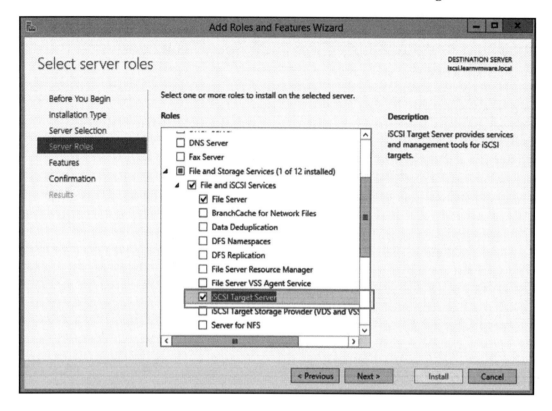

DNS configuration

For our vSphere infrastructure, we will need valid A DNS records. Let's add these to the DNS:

1. From the management server, click on **Tools** and select **DNS**.
2. Since the DNS service is not installed on our management station, we need to select one of our domain controllers. For example, let's choose dc01:

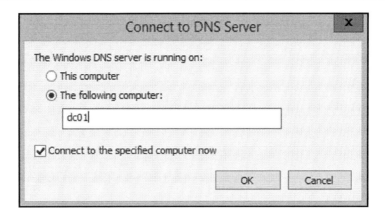

3. Once you are connected, navigate to your AD domain from the menu on the left:

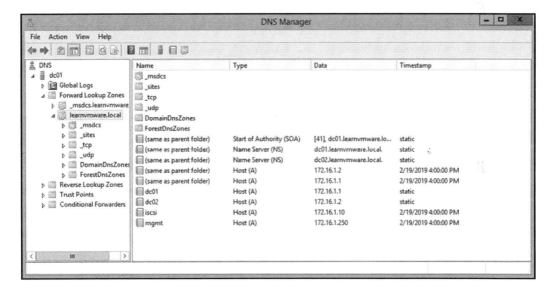

4. Now, we need to add several **A** records. Right-click on the right-hand side and select **New Host (A or AAA)...** and fill in the IP address and name.

The following DNS records will be required:

IP address	DNS name
172.16.1.100	vcsa.learnvmware.local
172.16.1.11	esxi-prod-1.learnvmware.local
172.16.1.12	esxi-prod-2.learnvmware.local
172.16.1.13	esxi-prod-3.learnvmware.local
172.16.1.14	esxi-prod-4.learnvmware.local

Centralized management

Once we have deployed our AD, we can benefit from centralized management. We will use our management server for all tasks within our AD Domain. Before we can do that, however, we need to add the other computers that will be managed from the management server:

1. From **Server Manager**, select **Add other servers to manage**, as shown in the following screenshot:

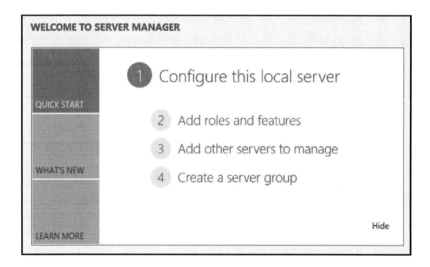

2. In the wizard, you can click the **Find Now** button to display all computer accounts from the AD. Select them and move them to the right:

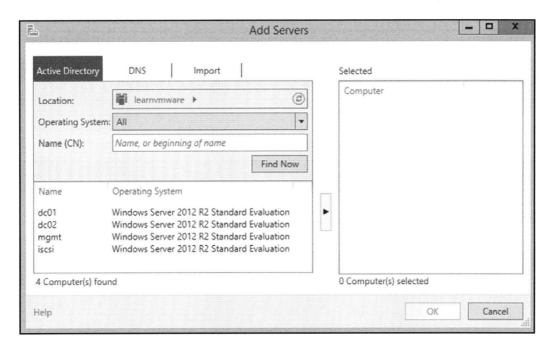

3. Once the servers are added, we can, for example, configure our iSCSI target service directly from our management station.

iSCSI target configuration

If you are logged in to either the management server or the iSCSI server, you can quickly provision a new disk that will be exported as an iSCSI volume:

1. Open **Server Manager** and, under **File and Storage Services**, select **iSCSI**:

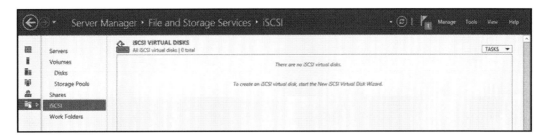

2. First, we need to configure our iSCSI device. Click on **Tools** and select a new iSCSI device.

3. Select the server on which the iSCSI device will be configured and the volume to store the content of the device:

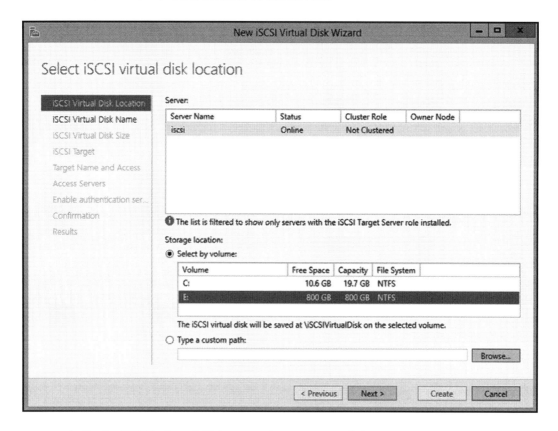

4. In the iSCSI virtual disk, provide a name and description for the new iSCSI disk.

Now, you have the option to configure the size of the disk and its type. I have decided to create a 500 GB volume, as shown in the following screenshot:

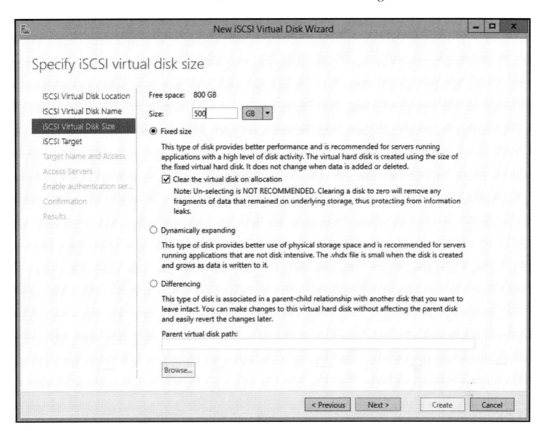

Since we have not defined any iSCSI target, we need to define it now. The first step is to provide the name of the iSCSI target.

In **Access Servers**, you can define which iSCSI initiators will be able to connect to our storage. There are multiple options for how to identify the iSCSI initiator, but the most commonly used methods are using the IQN or the IP address.

Let's stick with a good old-fashioned IP addresses and provide the IP addresses of the VMkernel interfaces that will be used to connect to our iSCSI target (you can find the IP addresses in the IP address plan):

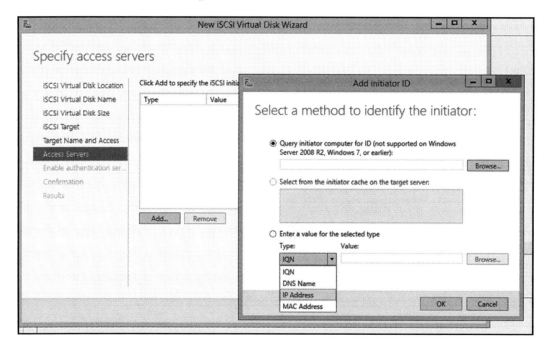

If you need to, you can also enable **CHAP authentication** for your iSCSI target. Then, confirm the creation of the new iSCSI device and the iSCSI target. You should be able to connect to the iSCSI server through iSCSI. You'll then be able to access the 500 GB volume.

ESXi servers

Your virtual ESXi servers should be installed at this stage, so let's start with the configuration.

The first task will be to configure the management network of our virtual ESXi hypervisors. To do that, you need to access the **DCUI** console from the Master ESXi servers:

```
VMware ESXi 6.7.0 (VMKernel Release Build 10302608)

VMware, Inc. VMware7,1

2 x Intel(R) Xeon(R) CPU E5-1650 v4 @ 3.60GHz
12 GiB Memory



To manage this host go to:
http://169.254.100.28/ (Waiting for DHCP...)
http://[fe80::20c:29ff:fe21:8068]/ (STATIC)

        Warning: DHCP lookup failed. You may be unable to access this system until you customize its
        network configuration.
```

As you already know, to configure the IP address, you need to access the **Configure Management Network** option in the DCUI. In the interfaces, you have to select the physical NICs that are connected to the management network. In my case, these are `vmnic0` and `vmnic1`. No VLANs are used in the environment, so there is no need to configure them. All that remains is the IP configuration and the DNS settings.

Once you have successfully configured the IP and DNS settings, do not forget to test the configuration using the **Testing Management Network** option:

```
Testing Management Network

You may interrupt the test at any time.


Pinging address #1 (172.16.1.254).                        OK.
Pinging address #2 (172.16.1.1).                          OK.
Pinging address #3 (172.16.1.2).                          OK.
Resolving hostname (esxi-prod-1.learnvmware.local).       OK.

                                                  <Enter> OK
```

Now, when the management connectivity is configured, we can switch to the web client of the ESXi servers and continue from there.

Network configuration

Let's take a look at the network configuration of our virtual ESXi servers:

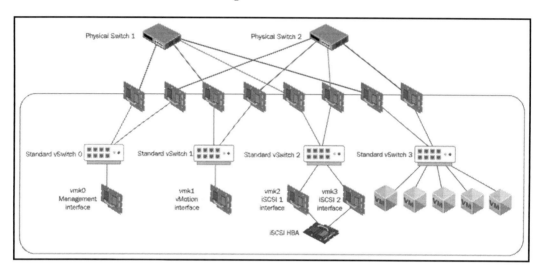

It looks a bit complicated, but you will soon get familiar with the design. I won't cover all the ESXi servers; I'll only cover the first one, since the configuration is the same for each apart from the IP addresses.

vSwitches

The following vSwitches need to be created:

vSwitch name	MTU	Physical adapters	Notes
vSwitch1	1500	vmnic2, vmnic3	vMotion
vSwitch2	9000	vmnic4, vmnic5	iSCSI
vSwitch3	1500	vmnic6, vmnic7	Production traffic

The configuration should end up looking as follows:

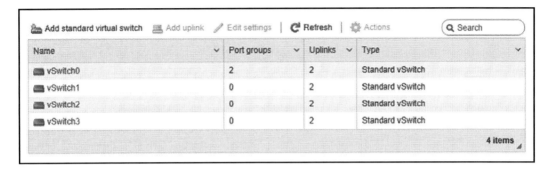

Port groups

The following port groups need to be created:

Port group name	vSwitch	VLAN tag	Notes
vMotion	vSwitch1	0	vMotion
iSCSI1	vSwitch2	0	iSCSI PG 1
iSCSI2	vSwitch2	0	iSCSI PG2
VM10	vSwitch3	10	VM test PG 1
VM20	vSwitch3	20	VM test PG 2
VM30	vSwitch3	30	VM test PG 3

In the following screenshot, you can see the port groups that need to be configured:

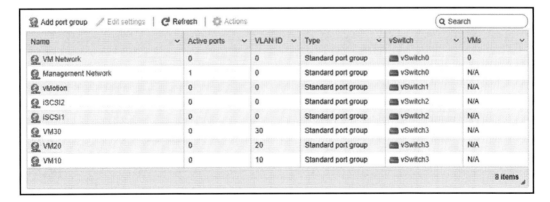

There is one more task we need to do related to our iSCSI port groups. As you already know, if you need to work with storage multipathing, you must ensure that the VMkernel ports that are used to bind to the iSCSI initiator are not balanced over multiple **vmnics**. To do this, open the configuration of the first iSCSI port group and override the failover order. For the iSCSI1 port group, we will only use **vmnic4**. For the iSCSI2 port group, only **vmnic5** will be used. This is shown in the following screenshot:

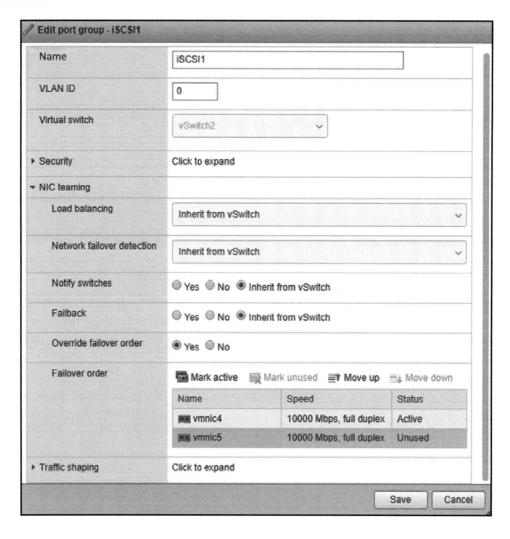

VMkernel ports

To enable our ESXi server to communicate over the network, we have to configure the following VMkernel ports:

VMkernel port name	IP address	Port group
Vmk1	172.16.2.1	vMotion
Vmk2	192.168.100.11	iSCSI 1
Vmk3	192.168.100.12	iSCSI 2

These can be seen in the following screenshot:

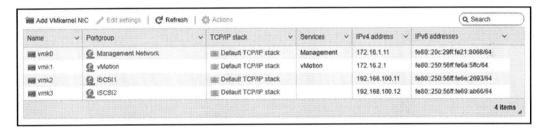

Network verification

Once you have configured your network, you can verify the connectivity from the CLI of the ESXi server. To do that, connect to your ESXi server using **SSH** (don't forget to start the SSH service if you have not done so already) and issue the `vmkping` command.

The following IP addresses should be accessible:

```
[root@esxi-prod-1:~] vmkping 192.168.10.1
PING 192.168.10.1 (192.168.10.1): 56 data bytes
64 bytes from 192.168.10.1: icmp_seq=0 ttl=128 time=0.285 ms
64 bytes from 192.168.10.1: icmp_seq=1 ttl=128 time=0.281 ms

[root@esxi-prod-1:~] vmkping 192.168.10.2
PING 192.168.10.2 (192.168.10.2): 56 data bytes
64 bytes from 192.168.10.2: icmp_seq=0 ttl=128 time=0.302 ms
64 bytes from 192.168.10.2: icmp_seq=1 ttl=128 time=0.200 ms
```

If any of the servers are not responding, make sure that the Windows Firewall is not blocking the communication.

You can also check the ARP table of the ESXi server by using the following command:

```
[root@esxi-prod-1:~] esxcli network ip neighbor list
 Neighbor Mac Address Vmknic Expiry State Type
 ------------ ------------------ ------ -------- ----- -------
 172.16.1.250 00:0c:29:ec:1c:12 vmk0 858 sec Unknown
 172.16.1.1 00:0c:29:3f:6f:3d vmk0 1099 sec Unknown
 172.16.1.2 00:0c:29:ad:b5:d4 vmk0 1102 sec Unknown
 192.168.10.2 00:0c:29:95:16:36 vmk2 1096 sec Unknown
 192.168.10.1 00:0c:29:95:16:40 vmk2 1088 sec Unknown
```

At this stage, you should be able to access all the network resources of our lab. It's time to take a look at the storage configuration.

Storage configuration

As you know, we are working with the iSCSI-based storage array. We will be using a software-based iSCSI initiator on the ESXi server. To configure the software-based iSCSI initiator, switch to the **Storage** view and the **Adapters** tab and select **Configure iSCSI**:

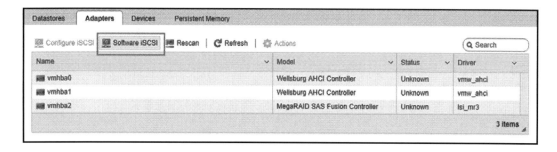

The new configuration wizard will be shown, as demonstrated in the following screenshot:

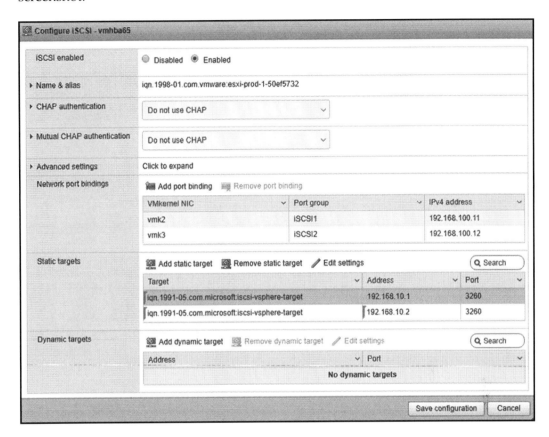

All you need to do is to enable the iSCSI initiator, bind your two new VMkernel adapters to the iSCSI initiator (**vmk2** and **vmk3**), and configure the static iSCSI target.

To obtain the name of your iSCSI target, open the **File and Storage Services** view from **Server Manager** and select the **iSCSI** option. In the following screenshot, you can see the iSCSI target name:

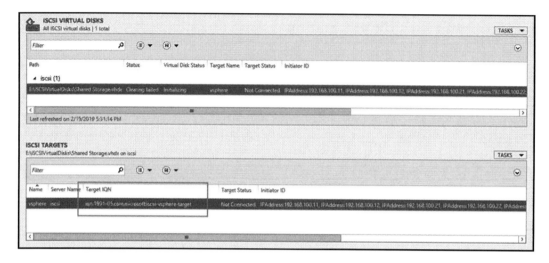

Once the iSCSI initiator is configured, the adapters are automatically rescanned by the ESXi server. If you have done the configuration correctly, you should be able to see your iSCSI device from the **Device** view, as shown in the following screenshot:

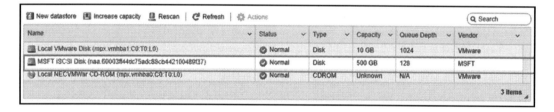

The final step that needs to be undertaken is to create a new datastore. To do this, switch to the **Datastore** view, click on **New datastore**, and select a new iSCSI disk, as shown in the following screenshot:

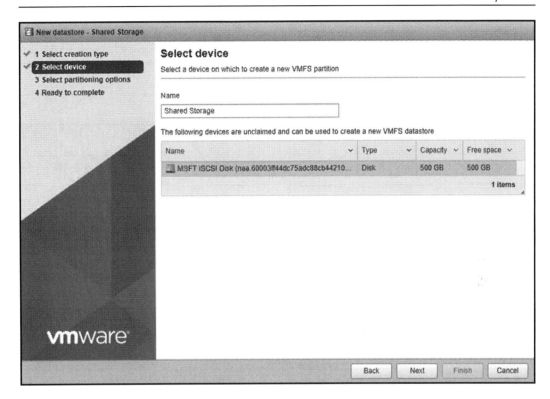

If you would like to test features such as Storage DRS, you will need multiple datastores and datastore clusters configured. You can provision more iSCSI disks on the iSCSI target server. After you rescan the iSCSI adapter within ESXi, you will see the additional devices.

You have successfully configured your first ESXi server. All you need to do now is to configure the remaining three ESXi servers so you end up with four fully configured ESXi hypervisors.

The vCenter Server

Now, when we have our ESXi servers installed, it is time to install the vCenter Server. To do that, just plug in the ISO image of the vCSA downloaded from the VMware website and follow the installation wizard:

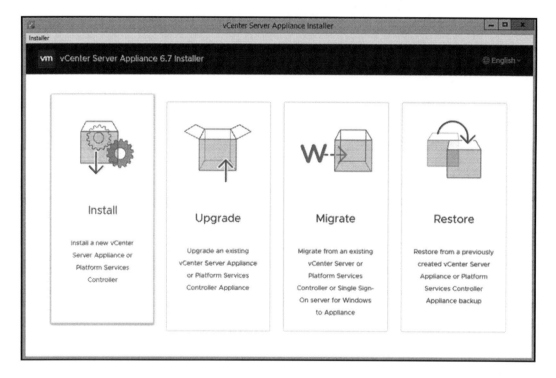

In our case, we will be working with the embedded deployment mode, in which both the vCenter Server and PSC are deployed on the same appliance.

As a destination location for the installation, use our first ESXi server, `esxi-prod-1.learnvmware.local`. You need to provide the root password before you can proceed:

1. In the **Deployment size** option, select your desired infrastructure size. For most lab environments, the **Tiny** deployment size is sufficient.
2. Now, we need to select which datastore we will deploy the vCenter Server Appliance on. Make sure you select your iSCSI shared storage. If you want to save some storage space, select **Enable Thin Disk Mode** for the virtual disks:

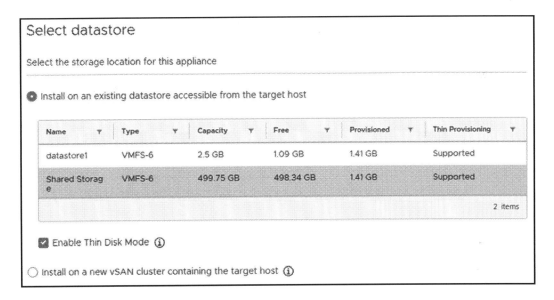

In the next stage, provide the network configuration for your vCSA. According to our IP address plan, you should fill in the following values:

- **Port group**: **VM Network**
- **FQDN**: `vcsa.learnvmware.local`
- **IP address**: `172.16.1.100`
- **Netmask**: `255.255.255.0`
- **Gateway**: `172.16.1.254`
- **DNS**: `172.16.1.1,172.16.1.2`

The following screenshot shows the network configuration:

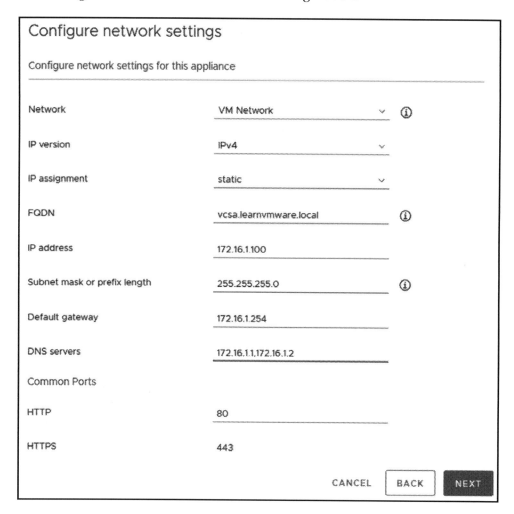

Review the network settings and proceed with the installation. If you check your first ESXi host, `esxi-prod-1.learnvmware local`, you should see that the installation wizard has initiated the deployment task:

Once this stage is completed, we can proceed with the configuration of the PSC. All we need to do is provide the default **Single-Sign-On domain name** and the **administrator** password, as shown in the following screenshot:

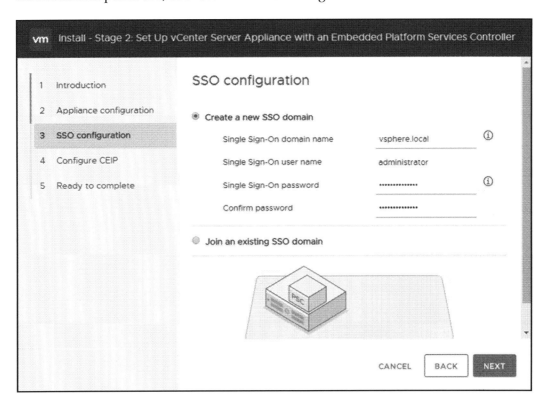

That's it. You have now successfully deployed your vCenter Server Appliance and you can try to log in to the system:

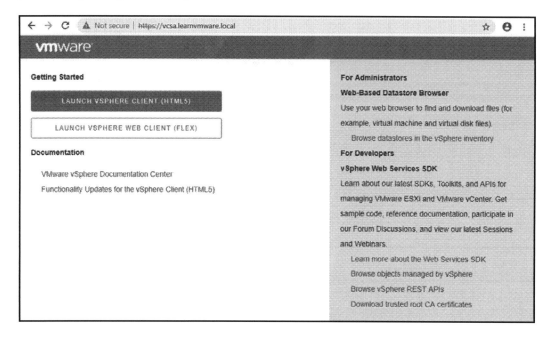

vSphere configuration

Now, when all your components are deployed and configured, you can start working on the vSphere configuration. I am not going to cover everything here; after all, it is your lab, so feel free to test anything we have covered or any other feature or technology you are interested in.

What we will do at this stage is configure our first data center object and vSphere cluster. As you already know, every vSphere object is related to the data center, so we need to create our first data center object. Now, when we have a data center, we can create our first vSphere cluster. If you would like to enable some cluster services at this stage, feel free to do so. In this example, however, I'm just going to create a default cluster without any additional services:

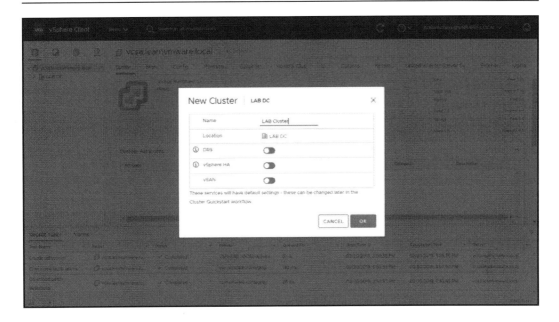

As a final step, let's add our four ESXi hypervisors to the cluster, as shown in the following screenshot:

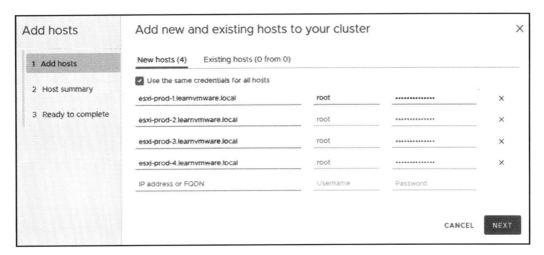

Finally, you should see your four ESXi hypervisors residing in your new vSphere cluster:

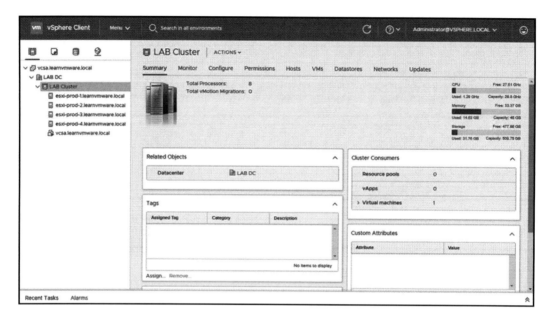

That's it! Congratulations ! You now have a lab environment in which you can test anything you need to.

Summary

In this chapter, we have covered the different resources you can use to extend your VMware vSphere skills and looked at how to build your own vSphere lab. We have covered some approaches you can take to build your lab, including running the lab on your laptop, cloud-based solutions, and physical servers in the data center. You have also learned the pros and cons of each solution.

After that, we covered the building blocks of the lab. We looked at the network, the storage design, and which software and licenses you need. Finally, we provided you with a blueprint of what the lab might look like, and you learned how to set up the entire lab infrastructure by yourself.

Assessment

Chapter 1: Evolution to vSphere 6.7

1. (a) VMware vSphere, (d) VMware vSAN, (f) VMware NSX
2. (c) VMware vSphere ROBO edition
3. (a) Full integration with on-premises infrastructure, (b) Deep integration of VMware vSphere, vSAN, and NSX, (c) Pay-as-you-go payment model based on the number of ESXi hypervisors, (d) Fully managed environment, (e) Zero investment costs, (f) Dedicated hardware
4. (a) Yes
5. (b) No
6. (b) VMware Distributed vSwitch, (c) VMware Distributed Resource Scheduler, (f) Network I/O Control
7. (a) Hardware support

Chapter 2: Designing and Planning a Virtualization Infrastructure

1. (a) Plan, (d) Do, (f) Check, (g) Act
2. (b) Better power utilization compared to standard servers, (c) Higher density, (e) Centralized management through blade chassis
3. (b) Leaf-spine architecture
4. (b) Conceptual design, (d) Logical design, (e) Physical design
5. (d)

Chapter 3: Analysis and Assessment of Existing Environments

1. (b) An application requires an HW USB key connected to the system, (c) Application vendor limitations, (d) High-performance system with a lot of compute resources, (e) Proprietary hardware used within the system
2. VMware Capacity Planner, vSAN sizing tools, Dell Live Optics, Microsoft Assessment and Planning toolkit, RVtools, VMware vRealize Operations, **vSphere Optimization Assessment** (**VOA**), VMware vSphere Health Check, Runecast, Opvizor, CloudPhysics
3. (b) False
   MAP Toolkit can be used for Linux environments as well.
4. The products, tools, or services offered by VMware are discussed as follows:
   - (a) **VMware vSphere Health Check**: VMware or professional partner services provide this and it's based on a virtual appliance (or also a standalone package) that can connect to your VMware infrastructure and analyze it, with a great report generator. At this point, it's only available for VMware employees or selected partners.
   - (b) **VMware vRealize Operations**: The primary purpose of this tool is monitoring, in a proactive way, a virtual (and in some parts also physical) infrastructure. However, it can also provide some useful insights for capacity and resource planning, and also for resource optimization and resource reclaiming.
   - (c) **vSAN Assessment**: Collect data about your existing vSphere storage environment in just one week and get the technical and business recommendations you need for a vSAN design.
   - (d) **vSphere Optimization Assessment**: Using this tool you can access the overall reports for your multi-cloud environments from the single console. Primary focus is on the optimization, right-sizing, capacity and costs.
5. (a) True
   DVDstore or HCIBench as an example

Chapter 4: Deployment Workflow and Component Installation

1. vCenter Server and ESXi hypervisor
2. (b) No.
   VMware vSphere 6.5 U2 cannot be upgraded directly to 6.7 but you might upgrade do 6.7U1.
3. (b) Hardware Compatibility List.
4. Manual installation using ISO media, Automatic installation using kickstart files and Automatic installation using vCenter Server and Auto Deploy feature.
5. Remote device is a block device connected to ESXi server from the external storage array.
6. (a) Yes
   You can upgrade ESXi server through ISO installation media.
7. (b) False
   You need to run your own TFTP server.
8. (d) Performance Service Center
9. License costs, Ease of deployment, vCSA HA feature, Automatic backups, Enhanced Link-Mode, Direct installation on the new VSA cluster.
10. (b) False
    vCenter Server HA is available only for vCSA not the Windows version.

Chapter 5: Configuring and Managing vSphere 6.7

1. (c) HTTPS, (e) SSH
2. It is important to have consistent time settings within the whole infrastructure. Some services strongly relies on the time synchronization and troubleshooting is much easier when the time is synchronized as well
3. (b) False
4. If the vCenter Server crash you would like to be able to restore the whole configuration from the backup. As a best-practice it is advised to perform the backups on the vCSA level through VAMI interface, not the infrastructure level backups using backup solutions like Veeam.

5. (b) False
6. vCenter Essentials can manage up to three hosts. vCenter Foundation can manage up to four hosts and vCenter Server Standard has no limitation in the number of managed hosts.
7. (a) Active Directory, Open LDAP, LocalOS, and Local Domain
8. (a) ESXi server and vCSA
9. Yes
10. (b) False
11. PowerCLI, vCLI, **vRealize Orchestrator (vRO)**, vSphere Web Services SDK, REST APIs, CLI

Chapter 6: Life Cycle Management, Patching, and Upgrading

1. (b) vCSA 6.5 with embedded PSC to vCSA 6.7 with embedded PSC, (d) vCenter Server for Windows with external PSC to vCSA with External PSC, (f) vCenter for Windows 6.5 with embedded PSC and embedded database to vCenter 6.7 for Windows with embedded PSC and embedded database
2. (b) False
3. (a) vSphere Update Manager, (c) The `esxcli` tool, (d) ISO installation media
4. (a) True
5. Critical Host Patches, Non-Critical Host Patches, VMware Tools Upgrade to Match Host, VM Hardware Upgrade to Match Host and VA Upgrade to Latest
6. (b) False
7. The Migration assistant serves two purposes. The first is running pre-checks on the source Windows vCenter Server. The Migration Assistant displays warnings of installed extensions and provides a resolution for each. It will also show the source and the destination deployment types. The second purpose of the MA is copying the source Windows vCenter Server data. By default, the configuration and inventory data of the Windows vCenter Server is migrated.
8. (a) True

Chapter 7: Managing Networking Resources

1. (b) False
2. VLAN is a broadcast domain so that you can be segmenting Ethernet broadcast domains with VLANs. Network ports might be configured with one (access or untagged mode) or multiple VLANs (trunk or tagged mode).802.1Q trunking modifies Ethernet frames to add a numeric tag. Using this tag can forward frames to different VLANs.
3. (b) False
4. Inbound traffic shaping, Centralized management, PVLAN support, Netflow export support, Port mirroring, Multicast support, Traffic filtering, Network IO control, Enhanced LACP Mode.
5. vSwitch, Port Group, VMkernel adapters, TCP/IP Stacks
6. (b) Promiscuous mode, (c) MAC address changes, (e) Forged transmits
7. (a) True
8. (a) Active adapters, (c) Standby adapters, (e) Unused adapters
9. (b) False
10. (b) False
11. CDP and LACP
12. (a) MTU configuration, (b) VLAN configuration
13. (a) True
14. SR-IOV is a specification that allows a single **Peripheral Component Interconnect Express** (**PCIe**) physical device under a single root port to appear as multiple separate physical devices to the hypervisor or the guest operating system.
SR-IOV uses **physical functions** (**PFs**) and **virtual functions** (**VFs**) to manage global functions for the SR-IOV devices. PFs are full PCIe functions that are capable of configuring and managing the SR-IOV functionality. It is possible to configure or control PCIe devices using PFs, and the PF has full ability to move data in and out of the device. VFs are lightweight PCIe functions that support data flowing but have a restricted set of configuration resources.

Chapter 8: Managing Storage Resources

1. All-Flash Arrays consists only from (different) SSD devices. Hybrid Arrays use the mix of SSD devices and magnetic disks.

2. SAS, FC, FCoE, iSCSI and NFS

3. (b) False

4. RAW capacity is the total capacity of all devices. USABLE capacity is the capacity that can be consumed by the ESXi hypervisor after the RAID overhead or other overheads are deducted from raw capacity.

5. (b) No

6. (a) Host Bus Adapters, (e) SAN Switches, (f) SAN WWN replicator

7. There is no essential difference. In both cases you can access the block device. In case of software adapter you can't boot from the block devices. Hardware adapter provides better performance.

8. (a) True

9. (b) BusLogic Logic SAS, (c) VMware Paravirtual (or PVSCSI), (d) NVMe Controller

10. Software iSCSI adapter is a software component run within ESXi kernel. A dependent hardware iSCSI adapter is a third-party adapter that depends on VMware networking, and iSCSI configuration and management interfaces provided by VMware. When installed on a host, it presents its two components, a standard network adapter and an iSCSI engine, to the same port. The iSCSI engine appears on the list of storage adapters as an iSCSI adapter (vmhba). Although the iSCSI adapter is enabled by default, to make it functional, you must first connect it, through a virtual VMkernel adapter (vmk), to a physical network adapter (vmnic) associated with it. An independent hardware iSCSI adapter is a specialized third-party adapter capable of accessing iSCSI storage over TCP/IP. This iSCSI adapter handles all iSCSI and network processing and management for your ESXi system.

11. (b) False

12. (c) Reservations, Limits, and Shares

13. **All Paths Down (APD)** and **Permanent Device Lost (PDL)**

14. (b) False

15. 5 disk groups, each consisting of 7 capacity devices and 1 caching device.

Chapter 9: VM Deployment and Management

1. (c) 14
2. Both solution provides the same functionality but Open-VMtools can't be upgraded and managed by Update Manager.
3. VMXNET2, VMXNET3, E1000, E1000e, SR-IOV passthrough, Flexible
4. (b) False
5. (b) False
6. Using template functionality you can create a master image of your VM that will be used for further deployment. This approach speeds up the deployment process compared to creating VMs from scratch.
7. (a) Changing the IP address, (b) Setting the time zone, (e) Changing the administrator/root password, (g) Joining the computer to Active Directory Domain, (h) Running several initial scripts
8. Subscribed Content Library connects to the Local Content Library and download all content from there.
9. True
10. By browsing the datastore where the VM is stored and adding the VM to the inventory using .vmx file.
11. Snapshots might affect the performance of the VM. If the snapshot is presented, you are not able to increase the disk size.
12. (b) False
13. (a) True
14. P2V refers to physical to virtual conversions and V2V refers to different virtual to virtual conversions (for example between different virtualization platforms).

Chapter 10: VM Resource Management

1. (b) False
2. The differences between reservations, limits, and shares are as follows:
   - **Reservations** specify the minimum allocation guaranteed to a VM. When the VM is powered on, the ESXi hypervisor assigns resources based on the specified minimum reservation regardless of whether the physical server is heavily loaded.

- **Using limits**, you can specify the maximum amount of resources a VM can use. If the limit is not set, a VM will consume up to the maximum amount of resources based on its configuration and the virtual hardware used.
- **Shares** specify the priority of a VM to get resources during a period of contention. When resources in an ESXi host are limited, and the VMs compete to access resources, the VMs configured with higher shares will have higher priority to access more of the host's resources. Shares can be specified as high, normal, or low, with a ratio of 4:2:1, and are applied between siblings in the vSphere hierarchy.

3. (b) False
4. High state, clear state, soft state, hard state and low state
5. (d) TPS, ballooning, compression, swapping
6. The hypervisor uses a memory reclamation technique called memory ballooning to reclaim the memory from a VM. The ESXi server is not aware of the content of the memory page of the VM. Only the guest operating system knows what is inside and what is more important compared to other memory pages. Ballooning is used to inflate and deflate the balloon driver within the guestOS and force the guestOS to swap content of the memory pages to the virtual disk.
7. (a) True
8. Primary focus of DRS is to distribute the load generated by VMs between ESXi hosts.
9. (b) False
10. Resource pools are logical containers that can be used to allocate compute resources to a group of VMs (or child resource pools).
11. (a) True
12. (b) Reservations, shares, limits, startup and shutdown order of the VMs

Chapter 11: Availability and Disaster Recovery

1. (a) True
2. (a) Network heartbeat, (d) Storage heartbeat

3. Storage heartbeats are used only when the network heartbeats have failed. Each host will create a specific file on the shared datastore that can be accessed by all other ESXi hosts. This file, host-XXXX-hb, is an empty file. The corresponding ESXi hypervisor exclusively opens that. If the ESXi hypervisor loses access to the storage, the master ESXi node will discover that the lock from the file disappears, meaning that the host has lost access to the storage and an HA event will occur.

4. (b) False

5. (a) Slot Policy, (c) Cluster resource percentage, (d) Dedicated failover host

6. Storage vMotion, Linked clones, VMCP, Virtual volume datastores, Storage-based policy management, Snapshots

7. (b) False

8. Maximum support of 2 vCPUs (Standard Edition) and 4 vCPUs (Enterprise Plus Edition). Performance hit to the FT-Enabled virtual machine. High network utilization for FT traffic.

9. (b) False

10. (b) False

11. RPO refers to how much data you can lose. It is the time that has elapsed between last backup and the failure. RTO refers to how long it will take to recover from the failure. Usually, the duration of the restore procedure is referred as Recovery Time Objective.

12. In vMSC environment, the infrastructure is stretched between two sites but those two sites are managed by single vCenter Server as one logical site. With SRM, two independent site are managed by two independent vCenter Servers installed in each site.

Chapter 12: Securing and Protecting Your Environment

1. Least privilege, Micro-segmentation, Encryption, **Multi-factor authentication (MFA)**, Patching.

2. (e) Network Identity Server

3. (b) False

4. (a) Assign several permissions and form a role, and assign the role to the vSphere object together with user or group.

5. 2FA grants user access only after successfully presenting several separate pieces of evidence to an authentication mechanism, usually at least two of the following categories—knowledge (something they know), possession (something they have), and inherence (something they are).

6. (a) True

7. In vSphere 6.x, TPS is disabled across different VMs (Inter-VM TPS) but is still working inside individual VMs (Intra-VM TPS).

8. (a) Virtual hardware version 13 or later, (d) GuestOS that supports UEFI secure boot, (f) EFI firmware in the VM boot options

9. **VMware Certificate Authority** (**VMCA**) is used for certification management of all vSphere infrastructure components.

10. You need external KMS server. vCenter Server does not include Key Management Services features.

11. With opportunistic setting, Encryption vMotion will be used if the source and destination ESXi server supports Encrypted vMotion. If one of the servers does not support EvM, unencrypted vMotion will be used. Using required setting Encrypted vMotion will be enforced. If source or destination ESXi servers does not supports EvM, migration fails.

Chapter 13: Analyzing and Optimizing Your Environment

1. (a) Real-time, (c) Last day, (d) Last week, (e) Last month, (f) Last year

2. (b) False

3. (b) Esxtop, (c) PowerCLI

4. (b) False

5. Use the default VM templates, Use only the necessary virtual hardware, Choose the correct virtual network adapter, VMware tools, Paravirtual SCSI (PVSCSI) storage controller, Don't use snapshots in the production, Don't oversize your VMs.

6. vRealize Log Insight

7. (b) False

Chapter 14: Troubleshooting Your Environment

1. (a) `esxcli`, b) `esxcfg-*`, d) `vim-cmd`
2. (b) `rvc` (Ruby vSphere Console)
3. (c) `/var/log/`
4. (a) True
5. Purple Screen of Death. Kernel Panic screen of the ESXi hypervisor

Other Books You May Enjoy

If you enjoyed this book, you may be interested in these other books by Packt:

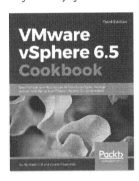

VMware vSphere 6.5 Cookbook - Third Edition
Abhilash G B, Cedric Rajendran

ISBN: 978-1-78712-741-8

- Upgrade your existing vSphere environment or perform a fresh deployment
- Automate the deployment and management of large sets of ESXi hosts in your vSphere Environment
- Configure and manage FC, iSCSI, and NAS storage, and get more control over how storage resources are allocated and managed
- Configure vSphere networking by deploying host-wide and data center-wide switches in your vSphere environment
- Configure high availability on a host cluster and learn how to enable the fair distribution and utilization of compute resources
- Patch and upgrade the vSphere environment
- Handle certificate request generation and renew component certificates
- Monitor performance of a vSphere environment

vSphere High Performance Cookbook - Second Edition
Kevin Elder, Christopher Kusek, Prasenjit Sarkar

ISBN: 978-1-78646-462-0

- Understand the VMM Scheduler, cache aware CPU Scheduler, NUMA Aware CPU Scheduler, and more during the CPU Performance Design phase
- Get to know the virtual memory reclamation technique, host ballooning monitoring, and swapping activity
- Choose the right platform while designing your vCenter Server, redundant vCenter design, and vCenter SSO and its deployment
- Know how to use various performance simulation tools
- Design VCSA Server Certificates to minimize security threats
- Use health check tools for storage and boost vSphere 6.5's performance with VAAI and VASA

Leave a review - let other readers know what you think

Please share your thoughts on this book with others by leaving a review on the site that you bought it from. If you purchased the book from Amazon, please leave us an honest review on this book's Amazon page. This is vital so that other potential readers can see and use your unbiased opinion to make purchasing decisions, we can understand what our customers think about our products, and our authors can see your feedback on the title that they have worked with Packt to create. It will only take a few minutes of your time, but is valuable to other potential customers, our authors, and Packt. Thank you!

Index

A

access control lists (ACLs) 285
Active Directory (AD) 177, 651
Active Directory Domain Controller (AD DC)
  537
active directory integration
  about 554
  MFA 554
active memory 107
Address Resolution Protocol (ARP) 280
admission control
  about 510, 511
  policies, reference 511
All-Flash Array (AFA) 341
All-Paths-Down (APD)
  about 375
  reference 377
Altaro VM Backup
  about 528
  features 528
alternate boot bank 187
AppDefense 40
approaches, CaaS solution
  PKS, using 21
  VIC, using 21
  vRealize Automation, using 21
architecture, virtualization lab
  AD 652
  iSCSI storage 652
  management station 652
  Master ESXi hypervisor 652
  virtual router 652
assess
  about 71
  assumptions 72
  constraints 72

design objective 72
requirements 72
risks 72
Asymmetric Logical Unit Access (ALUA) 380
Auto Deploy installations
  stateful installation 154
  stateless caching installation 152
  stateless installation 152
Auto Deploy, modes
  stateful 152
  stateless 152
  stateless caching 152
Auto Deploy
  DHCP, configuring 146
  TFTP, configuring 147, 148
  working 145

B

backup solutions, VMware vSphere
  Altaro VM Backup 528
  NAKIVO Backup and Replication 527
  Veeam Backup and Replication 527
  Vembu VMBackup 529
benchmarks, virtual environment
  DVD Store 118
  Hyper-Converged Infrastructure Benchmark
    (HCIBench) 118
blogs
  official 642
  unofficial 642
Bridge Protocol Data Unit (BPDU) 560
Business Continuity Plan (BCP) 535
Business Continuity(BC) 534

C

capacity utilization report
  reference 123

Certificate Authority (CA) 555
certification management 567, 568, 569
Change Block Tracking (CBT) 540
Cisco Discovery Protocol (CDP) 291, 320
CLI tools, used for troubleshooting virtual
   environment
  esxcfg-* 618
  esxcli commands 615
  PowerCLI 623
  Ruby vSphere console 619
  vcsa-cli 622
  vim-cmd 620
CLI-based monitoring
  about 590
  ESXTOP 591
  PowerCLI 592
Client Integration Plugin (CIP) 178
cloning 415
cloud-based solutions
  advantages 645
  disadvantages 645
cluster design
  types 79
cluster
  creating 216
  host, removing 217
  managing 211
clustering features, VMware vSphere
  multi-writer flag 523, 524, 525
  RDM device 523, 524, 525
clustering options, VMware vSphere
  Cluster-in-a-Box 520
  Cluster-out-of-the-Box 520
  VM and physical server clustering 521
Cohesity DataPlatform 530
command-line interface (CLI) 180
Common Access Card (CAC) 554
common rules 365
components, for configuring in VM
  network adapter 398
components, Role-Based Access Control
  (RBAC)
  groups 552
  permissions 552
  roles 552

users 552
components, virtual machine tools
  VMware device drivers 407
  VMware services 407
  VMware user process 407
components, virtual machine
  about 396
  file structure 403, 404
  virtual hardware 396
  virtual machine tools 405, 406
components, vSphere
  ESXi hypervisor 128
  vCenter Server 128
components, VVols
  about 383
  array 383
  object 383
  protocol Endpoint (PE) 383
  Storage Container (SC) 383
  VASA provider (2.0) 383
computing 64
configuration health report
  reference 123
configuration maximums
  about 37
  ESXi 6.7 hypervisors 38
  vCenter Server 6.7 39
configuration options, distributed vSwitch
  health check 325
  Link Aggregation Control Protocol (LACP)
   321, 322, 323
  NetFlow 324
  port mirroring 325
  private VLAN (PVLAN) 323, 324
  topology 320, 321
consumed memory 107
Containers-as-a-Service (CaaS) 21
content library
  about 421
  creating 422
  ISO files, creating from 430, 431
  ISO images, uploading 427
  local content library 422, 423
  OVF files, uploading 428
  subscribed content library 422, 423, 424,

425
  templates, uploading 428
  VMs, deploying from 429, 430
  working with 426
Continuous Integration/Continuous Deployment
  (CI/CD) 21
controllers, for VM physical level
  about 352
  BusLogic 352
  LSI logic parallel 352
  LSI logic SAS 352
  NVMe 352
  VMware paravirtual (or PVSCSI) 352
converged network adapters (CNA) 132
core services, PSC
  Certificate Management 157
  SSO 157
  VMware License Service 157
CPU Benchmarks
  reference 106
CPU resources
  limit 453
  reservation 453
  shares 452
Customer Experience Improvement Program
  (CEIP) 79, 165, 248
cyber hygiene
  pillars 548

D

data center
  creating 212
  managing 211
database availability group (DAG) 537
datacenter bridging (DCB) 358
datastore, VMware vSphere
  about 348
  Network FileSystem (NFS) datastores 348
  VMware FileSystem (VMFS) datastores 348
  vSAN datastore 348
  VVol 348
de-encapsulation 279
dedicated server
  advantages 646
deduplication appliances 529

deduplication
  types 344
Define-Measure-Analyze-Improve-Control
  (DMAIC) 55
Dell Live Optics
  about 113
  reference 113
Denial-of-Service (DoS) attacks 558
deployment rules
  creating 149, 151
design
  about 73
  best practice 86
  conceptual design 74
  conceptual design, categories 74
  documentation, representing 86
  logical design 75
  physical design 77
  reference architecture 87
Desktop PC
  advantages 644
direct access 375
Direct Console User Interface (DCUI) 179,
  559, 615
direct memory access (DMA) 333
Direct SAN transport mode 526
Directory Services Recovery Mode (DSRM)
  669
disaster avoidance 534, 535, 537
disaster recovery
  about 534, 535
  for virtual data center 536
  versus disaster avoidance 537
  versus stretched clusters 538, 539
disk metrics 108
disk mode, virtual disk
  dependent 400
  independent-nonpersistent 400
  independent-persistent 400
distributed port groups
  creating 316, 318
Distributed Power Management (DPM) 482
Distributed Resource Scheduler (DRS) 40,
  128, 240, 339, 449
distributed virtual networking

managing 310
distributed vSwitch
    configuration options 319, 320
    creating 310
    ESXi host, attaching 312, 313, 316
    overview 287, 289
    properties 319, 320
    versus standard virtual switch (vSwitch) 289
Domain Controllers (DCs) 183
Drive Writes Per Day (DWPD) 345
DRS rules
    VM-Host affinity rule 479
    VM-VM affinity rule 478
DRS
    about 473, 474, 476
    power resources, managing 482
    recommendations 481
    rules, managing 477
    utilization 482
    virtual network-aware DRS 477
DVD Store
    about 118
    reference 118
Dynamic Host Configuration Protocol (DHCP)
    179
    configuring 146

E

Eager Zeroed Thick (EZT) 371
eBay
    reference 644
Elastic Load Balancing (ELB) 24
Elastic Network Interface (ENI) 24
Embedded Platform Service Controller
    vCSA, installing with 168
encapsulation 279
encrypted vMotion
    about 575, 576
    options 576
encrypted VMs
    recommendations 574
encryption 548
encryption options, vSphere
    about 569
    encryption at rest 570

encryption during transit 575
End of Availability (EoA) 189
End User License Agreement (EULA) 138
Enhanced vMotion Compatibility (EVC) 217,
    514
Enterprise License Agreement (ELA) 92
Enterprise Multi-Level Cells (eMLCs) 345
enterprise, scenarios
    about 90
    design decisions 91
    main constraints 91
    main risk 91
    requirements 90
ESXi 6.7 partition layout
    about 184
    boot banks 187
    scratch partition 187
ESXi CLI
    port group, creating from 301
    vSwitch, creating from 296, 297
ESXi Compatibility Checker
    reference 46, 249
ESXi configuration
    about 178
    centralized log management 188
    ESXi 6.7 partition layout 184
    management network configuration 179
    vRealize Log Insight 189
ESXi deployment plan
    about 130
    hardware platform, selecting 130, 131, 132
    network configuration, defining 132, 133
    storage architecture, identifying 132
ESXi hardening
    about 558
    host encryption mode 561, 562
    lockdown mode 559
    networking 560
    Transparent Page Sharing (TPS) 560
    VIB acceptance level 561
ESXi host client
    port group, creating from 298, 299, 300
    VMkernel adapter, creating from 302, 303
    vSwitch, creating from 290, 292, 293, 295
ESXi host memory states

about 457, 459
balloning 463
compression 464
host swapping 465
TPS 461
ESXi host
about 78
attaching, to distributed vSwitch 312, 313, 316
compute 79, 80
management 85
network connectivity 83, 84
storage 81, 82
ESXi hypervisor
about 128
memory states 457
ESXi installation
about 134
Auto Deploy installation 143
interactive installation 137, 139
location 134, 135
unattended installation 139, 141, 143
ESXi logical level
storage types 348, 349
ESXi physical level
storage types 349
ESXi Secure Boot 562, 563
ESXi servers
about 682
network configuration 684
storage configuration 688, 691
ESXi
backing up 190
backing up, with CLI 191
backing up, with PowerCLI 192
backing up, within single vCenter server 192
configuring, with AD authentication 202
deployment, preparing 136
restoring 190
restoring, with CLI 191
restoring, with PowerCLI 192
existing tools, physical environment
Dell Live Optics 113
Microsoft Assessment and Planning (MAP)
Toolkit 113

Virtual Storage Area Network (vSAN) sizing
tools 112
VMware Capacity Planner (VCP) 112
existing tools, virtual environment
Hybrid Cloud Assessment 120
RVTools 120, 121
Virtual Desktop Infrastructure (VDI)
assessment 120
Virtual Network Assessment (VNA) 120
VisualESXtop 120
VMware vRealize Operations 119
VMware vSphere Health Check 119, 123
VMware {code} vCheck vSphere 120
vSAN Assessment 120
vSphere Optimization Assessment (VOA)
119, 122

F

Fault Domain Manager (FDM) 503
Fault Tolerance (FT) 108, 285, 501
FC storage
about 355, 356
FCoE 357
features, storage DRS
deduplication 374
storage replica (SR) 374
storage tier 374
thin provisioning 374
features, VMware vSphere 6.7
about 26
ESXi Quick Boot 30
ESXi single-reboot upgrades 29
hybrid linked mode 35
improved vCenter backup management 28
improved vCenter Server Appliance (vCSA)
monitoring 27
Instant Clone 36
Microsoft virtualization-based security (VBS)
33
per-VM Enhanced vMotion Compatibility
(EVC) 34
Remote Direct Memory Access (RDMA)
support 31
TPM 2.0 33
Virtual Trusted Platform Module (vTPM) 32

vSphere Client (HTML-5) 26
vSphere persistent memory 32
Fiber Channel over Ethernet (FCoE) 31
Fibre Channel (FC) 132, 339
file structure 403, 404
files, virtual machine
  .log 404
  .nvram 404
  .vmdk 403
  .vmx 403
  .vswp 404
  log files 405
  snapshot files 405
  swap file 405
  VMDK files 405
FreeNAS
  reference 649
FT-enabled VM
  working with 518
full-disk encryption (FDE) 570
fully qualified domain name (FQDN) 180
functional requirements (FRs) 73

G

General Data Protection Regulation (GDPR) 24
General ESXi Security Recommendations
  reference 559
Google Cloud Platform (GCP) 16
GUID Partition Table (GPT) 185

H

hardening 548
hardening guides, VMware
  reference 557
Hardware Compatibility List (HCL) 85, 117,
  248, 643
hardware considerations
  about 59
  network design considerations 68
  physical form factor considerations 59
  storage design considerations 67
health check, distributed vSwitch
  about 325
  MTU 325
  network adapter teaming 325

  VLAN 325
High Availability (HA) 339, 501
Horizon 7 20
host bus adapters (HBAs) 132
host image profile
  acceptance levels 561
hosts
  managing 211, 218
  managing, with tags 219
  managing, with tasks 220
  profiles, managing 221, 224
  tasks, scheduling 220
Hybrid Cloud Assessment
  reference 120
Hybrid Cloud Extension (HCX) 21
Hybrid Linked Mode (HLM) 24
Hyper-Converged Infrastructure (HCI)
  about 65, 112, 341, 384
  reference 66
Hyper-Converged Infrastructure Benchmark
  (HCIBench)
  about 118
  reference 119
hyper-converged servers
  about 64
  resource comparison 64
  systems 65
hyper-scale solutions
  about 529
  Cohesity DataPlatform 530
  Rubrik solution 530

I

identity source types, vSphere
  active directory (native) 549
  LDAP (active directory) 549
  LDAP (OpenLDAP) 549
  local OS 549
  local SSO domain 549
iDRAC 117
image profile
  creating 148, 149
implementation guide 655
improved waterfall model 57, 59
InfiniBand (IB) 63

Information Technology Infrastructure Library (ITIL) 56
input/output operations per second (IOPS) 75, 108
Instant Clone Architecture, in vSphere 6.7
  reference 374
Integrated Lights-Out (iLO) 117
Internet Small Computer System Interface (iSCSI) 339
IP address plan
  about 653
  iSCSI network 654
  management network 653
  production network 654
  vMotion network 653
IPsec 575
IPv6 283
iSCSI Extension for RDMA (iSER) 31
iSCSI storage
  about 358, 359, 360
  dependent hardware iSCSI adapter 358
  independent hardware iSCSI adapter or iSCSI HBA 358
  software iSCSI adapter 358
  types 358
iscsi.learnvmware.local server
  about 673
  iSCSI target configuration 674
  storage design 673
ISO files
  using, from content library 430, 431
IT Infrastructure Library (ITIL) 56

K

KB 1027206
  reference 117
Key Management Interoperability Protocol (KMIP) 571
Key Management Server (KMS)
  about 571
  configuring, in vCenter Server 572, 573
Kiwi syslog server
  reference 190

L

Large File Block (LFB)
  about 371
  reference 371
Lazy Zeroed Thick (LZT) 371
least privilege 548
lifelong learning
  importance 640
Link Aggregation Control Protocol (LACP) 321, 322, 323
Link Aggregation Group (LAG) 321
Link Layer Discovery Protocol (LLDP) 320
local content library
  creating 422, 423
local memory 80
log management
  about 566, 597
  vRealize Log Insight 598, 599
logs
  about 623
  ESXi host logs 624, 625, 626
LUN masking 356

M

MAC learning process 280, 281
MAC tables 280, 281
MACsec 575
Magic Quadrant (MQ) 17
maintenance mode 509
management network configuration
  about 179, 180
  ESXi firewall 182
  Network Time Protocol (NTP), configuring 183
  Secure Shell (SSH) access, enabling 180
  Sell (SSH) access, enabling 182
Master ESXi server configuration
  about 655
  network configuration 656
  vCenter Server 692
  virtual ESXi servers, installing 682
  virtual machines 658
  virtual router 659
  virtual router configuration 660

vSphere configuration 696
Windows infrastructure 666
MasterESXi 651
Maximum Transmission Unit (MTU) 281, 282
memory 397, 398
memory counters
  reference link 107
memory metrics 106
metrics
  disk metrics 108
  from physical environment 105
  memory metrics 106
  network metrics 108
  processor metrics 105
metro cluster 538
MFA
  about 554
  RSA SecurID 557
  smart cards 555
micro-segmentation 548
Microsoft Assessment and Planning (MAP)
  Toolkit
  about 113
  reference 114
Microsoft Windows Server Failover Clustering
  (WSFC) 522
minFree 458
monitoring tools
  about 606
  Opvizor 609, 610
  Veeam ONE 607
multi-datacenter 537
multi-factor authentication (MFA) 548
Multi-Level Cell (MLC) 345
multiple points in time (MPIT) 540

N

NAKIVO Backup and Replication
  about 527
  features 528
nel over Ethernet (FCoE) 339
NetFlow 324
netstacks 307
network 64
network adapter 398, 399

Network Address Translation (NAT) 649
network and storage resources 495
network bandwidth allocation
  configuring, on VM 330
Network Block Device (NBD) 526
Network Block Device Secure Sockets Layer
  (NBDSSL) 526
network configuration, master ESXi server
  configuration
  port groups 657
  virual switches 656
network configuration, virtual ESXi servers 687
  about 684
  port groups 685
  VMkernel ports 687
  vSwitches 684
network configuration
  hosts 326
  ports 326
  VM 326
network design considerations
  about 68
  leaf-spine architecture 70, 71
  three-tier architecture 69
Network I/O Control (NIOC)
  about 277, 317, 327, 328
  network bandwidth allocation, configuring on
    VM 330
  network resource pools, creating 328, 330
Network Interface Card (NIC) 108
network metrics 108
network partition (NPAR) 357
network resource pools
  creating 328, 330
network-attached storage (NAS) 361
Next Unit of Computing (NUC) 642
NFS storage 361, 362
NIC types
  E1000 398
  E1000E 398
  flexible 398
  VMXNET 399
  VMXNET 2 (Enhanced) 399
  VMXNET 3 399
non-functional requirements (NFRs) 73

non-uniform memory access (NUMA) 79
non-volatile dual in-line memory module
    (NVDIMM) module 32, 353
Non-Volatile Memory (NVM) devices 353
NSX
  AppDefense 19
  NSX Cloud 19
  NSX for vSphere (NSX-V) 19
  NSX Transformers (NSX-T) 19

O

Observe-Plan-Do-Check-Act (OPDCA) 55
Opal Storage Specification 570
Open Virtual Appliance (OVA)
  templates, deploying 439, 440, 441
Open Virtual Format (OVF)
  exporting 442
  templates, deploying 439, 440, 441
Opvizor
  about 609
  reference 609
OS
  installing, on virtual machine 413
OSI model
  about 278, 279
  chart, reference 279
OVH
  reference 646
OVT
  about 407
  installing, in VM 407, 408

P

paravirtualized device 595
password management 550, 551
patches
  remediating 263
  staging 262
patching 548
performance bottlenecks report
  reference 123
Performance degradation VMs tolerate 511
Peripheral Component Interconnect express
    (PCIe) 331
Permanent Device Loss (PDL) 375

reference 377
persistent memory (PMem) 353
Personal Identity Verification (PIV) 556
physical design 77
physical environment
  analyzing, before virtualizing 103
  existing tools. analyzing 111
  metrics 105
  workloads, virtualizing 109
physical form factor considerations
  about 59
  blade server 62, 64
  hyper-converged servers 64
  standard rack servers 59, 62
physical functions (PFs) 331
physical NICs
  working with 305, 306
physical-to-virtual (P2V) 103
Pivotal Container Service (PKS) 15
Pivotal Container Service (PKS), components
  BOSH 16
  Control Plane 16
  Kubernetes 16
  Project Harbor 16
  VMware NSX-T 16
Plan-Do-Check-Act (PDCA) 54
Plan-Do-Study-Act (PDSA) 55
Platform Services Controller (PSC) 183
Pluggable Storage Architecture (PSA)
  about 379
  multipathing 380
PMem technology
  datastore 353
  direct-access mode 353
  storage policy 354
PMem
  reference 355
port groups
  creating, from ESXi CLI 301
  creating, from ESXi host client 298, 299, 300
  creating, from vCenter Server 300, 301
  working with 297
port mirroring 325
power states, VM
  power off 434

power on 434
reset 434
restart guest OS 434
shut down guest OS 434
suspend 434
PowerCLI
  reference 593
  script examples 228
  used, for automating tasks 225, 226
Preboot Execution Environment (PXE) 136
primary boot bank 187
Primary Domain Controller (PDC) 183
private VLAN (PVLAN) 323, 324
proactive HA 509, 510
processor metrics 105
products, V2V migrations
  references 445
Professional Services Organization (PSO) 112
proof-of-concept (PoC) 119, 643
protocols, VMware ESXi
  about 350
  CNA adapters for FCoE or iSCSI 350
  fibre Channel Host Bus Adapter (FC HBA)
    350
  InfiniBand HCA 350
  iSCSI HBA 350
  monitoring 566, 567
  RDMA over Converged Ethernet (RoCE) 350
PRTG
  reference 190
PSC
  about 155
  embedded 156
  external 156
  Linked Mode 158
Public Key Infrastructure (PKI) 556
Pumpkin TFTP
  reference 148
Purple Screen of Death (PSOD) 614
PuTTY 615

Q

qualities, design
  about 75
  availability 75

manageability 75
performance 75
recoverability 75
security 75
Quality of Service (QoS) 333, 516
quarantine mode 509

R

RAID 1 135
Ravello
  reference 646
RAW capacity 82
Raw Device Mapping (RDM) 399, 435
  about 351
  compatibility 375
Read-Only Domain Controller (RODC) 200
Recovery Point Objective (RPO) 534, 536
Recovery Time Objective (RTO) 536
Redundant Array of Independent Disks (RAID)
  342
Remote Authentication Dial-In User Service
  (RADIUS) 555
remote direct memory access (RDMA) 350
Remote Office Branch Office (ROBO) editions
  44
replication
  types 344
resource management, improving
  CPU affinity 454
  hyperthreading 454
resource pools
  about 484
  configuration 484, 487
  expandable resource pool 488
  managing 491
  resource allocation monitoring 490
Reverse Address Resolution Protocol (RARP)
  294
ROBO, scenarios
  about 95
  design decisions, examples 97
  main constraint 96
  requirements 96
  requirements, example 96
  risks 97

Role-Based Access Control (RBAC)
  about 552
  components 552
RSA SecurID 557
Rubrik solution 530
Rufus 136
RVTools
  about 120, 121
  reference 120

S

scenarios
  enterprise 90
  ROBO 95
  small and medium-sized business (SMB) 92
  types 90
SCSI HotAdd 526
Secure Digital (SD) 135
Secure Shell (SSH) 591
security 547
Security Hardening Guides, VMware
  reference 548
Security Support Provider Interface (SSPI) 200
self-encrypting drives (SEDs) 570
Service Level Agreement (SLA) 382
scrvice level agreement (SLA) 54
Service Principal Name (SPN) 201
single point of failure (SPOF) 75
Single Root I/O Virtualization (SR-IOV)
  about 331
  enabling 332
  VM, configuring 333
Single Sign-On (SSO) 75, 239, 549
Single-Level Cell (SLC) 345
SIOC
  about 362
  limits 363
  reservations 363
  RLS calculations 364
  shares 363, 364
  versions 365, 367, 368
Site Recovery Manager (SRM) 530, 543
small and medium-sized business (SMB),
    scenarios
  about 92

design decisions 94, 95
main constraint 93
requirements 93
risks 94
small and medium-sized enterprise (SME) 92
Small File Block (SFB) 371
Small Office/Home Office (SOHO) 93
small, dedicated PCs
  advantages 645
  disadvantages 645
smart cards 555
snapshot consolidation 438
Snapshot Manager
  DELETE ALL option 438
  DELETE option 438
snapshots
  about 435
  changes, committing 438
  creating 436
  limitations 435
  reverting to 438
  roles 437
SNMP receivers
  configuring 567
software components
  about 649
  and licensing 646
  networking 650
  storage 649
  VMware licensing, download link 647
  Windows licensing 649
software-defined datacenter (SDDC) 12, 64,
    543
SolarWind TFTP Server
  reference 148
solid-state drives (SSDs) 82
Splunk Light
  reference 190
SQL Server
  reference 649
SSD
  types 345
standalone ESXi servers upgradation
  about 248
  boot banks, using 253

ESXi compatibility checker, using 249
ESXi hosts, updating/patching through
  command line 251
ESXi hosts, updating/patching through
  installation ISO 250
standard virtual networking
  managing 290
  physical NICs, working with 305, 306
  port groups, working with 297
  TCP/IP stacks 307, 308, 309
  VMkernel adapters, working with 302
  vSwtich, creating 290
standard virtual switch (vSwitch)
  overview 285, 286
  versus distributed vSwitches 289
Standardize-Do-Check-Act (SDCA) 55
StarWind 384
storage and availability products
  VMware Site Recovery Manager (SRM) 18
  VMware vSAN 18
storage architectures types, VMware
  about 380
  active-active storage system 380
  active-passive storage system 380
  asymmetrical storage system 380
  fixed 380
  most Recently Used (MRU) 381
  round Robin (RR) 381
  virtual port storage system 380
storage arrays
  about 341
  AFA 345, 346
  Asymmetric Logical Unit Access (ALUA) 346
  deduplication 343
  device types 344
  performance 342
  RAID level 343
  replication 344
  SSD 345, 346
  types 341
storage configuration, VMware vSphere
  about 355
  FC storage 355, 356
  iSCSI storage 358, 359, 360
  NFS storage 361, 362

storage controller
  about 401
  BusLogic 402
  LSI Logic Parallel 402
  LSI Logic SA 402
  SATA 402
  SCSI 402
  VMware Paravirtual 402
storage design considerations
  about 67
  software-defined 67
  standard arrays 67
Storage Distributed Resource Scheduler
  (SDRS)
  about 362, 368, 495
  anti-affinity rules 370
  datastore clusters 370
  features 374
  functions 369, 370
  versus storage tiering 368
storage features
  about 371
  All-Paths-Down (APD) 375
  automatic space reclaim 372, 373
  Flash Read Cache 377
  instant clones, versus linked clones 373
  Permanent Device Loss (PDL) 375
  RDM 375
  storage DRS, versus storage tiering 374, 375
  Virtual Machine File System (VMFS) 6 371
Storage I/O Control (SIOC) 495
storage integration
  about 378
  Pluggable Storage Architecture (PSA) 379
  VASA 382
  VMware vSphere APIs for I/O Filtering (VAIO)
  382
  VMware vSphere SPBM 378
  VMware vStorage API for Array Integration
  (VAAI) 381
  VVols 382, 384
Storage Policy-Based Management (SPBM)
  365, 378
storage types, ESXi physical level
  about 349

block-based storage 349
NFS storage 349
storage types, VM logical levels
  eager zeroed thick Virtual Machine Disk
    (VMDK) 350
  thick or lazy zeroed thick VMDK 350
  thin VMDK 350
Storage-Based Policy Management (SBPF)
  495
storage
  about 64, 340, 341
  enterprise-class storage, classification ways
    340
StorMagic 384
stretched clusters
  about 541, 542
  versus disaster recovery 538, 539
Subject Alternative Name (SAN) 556
subscribed content library
  about 423
  creating 424, 425, 426
switches
  used, for virtual networking 284, 285

T

tasks
  automating, with scripts 224
TCP/IP stacks 307, 308, 309
template
  virtual machine, deploying from 416, 417
TFTP
  configuring 147, 148
Tftpd32
  reference 148
three-tier architecture
  about 69
  Access Layer 69
  Core Layer 70
  Distribution Layer 70
tools, for vCSA 6.5 to 6.7 upgradation
  CLI interface 239
  graphical interface 239
topology 320, 321
traffic filtering and marking policy 334
Transmission Control Protocol (TCP)

versus User Datagram Protocol (UDP) 283
Transparent Page Sharing (TPS) 398, 457,
  560
Transport Layer Security (TLS) 558
transport modes
  about 526
  Direct SAN transport mode 526
  Network Block Device (NBD) 526
  Network Block Device Secure Sockets Layer
    (NBDSSL) 526
  SCSI HotAdd 526
Trivial File Transfer Protocol (TFTP) 143
troubleshooting (TRBL) 613, 614, 615
Turbonomic virtual monitor
  reference 121
two-factor authentication (2FA) 554
types, anti-affinity rule
  about 370
  VM anti-affinity rules 370
  VMDK anti-affinity rules 370
types, VMCP
  APD 376
  PDL 376

U

U-size 60
unattended ESXi installation
  boot options 140, 141
UNETbootin 136
Update Manager 128
Update Manager Download Service (UMDS)
  254
USABLE capacity 82
User Datagram Protocol (UDP)
  versus Transmission Control Protocol (TCP)
    283
User Principal Name (UPN) 556

V

VAAI UNMAP 372
vApps 484, 492, 494
VASA 382
VCDX
  reference 74
vCenter HA

configuring 169, 170, 171, 172, 173
vCenter hardening 563
vCenter High Availability (VCHA) 239
vCenter REST API
   used, for automating tasks 229
vCenter Server Appliance (vCSA)
   about 85, 128, 177
   deploying, features 163
   deployment 161
   pointing, with embedded PSC to an external
      PSC 205
   repointing, to another external PSC 204
   SSO password, resetting 206
   updating 268
   updating, through command line 269
   updating, with VAMI 270
vCenter Server Appliance Management
      Interface (VAMI) 193, 240
vCenter Server, components
   about 154
   PSC 155
vCenter Server, services
   Auto Deploy 160
   Inventory Service 160
   Network Dump Collector 160
   profile driven storage 160
   Syslog Collector 160
   Web Client 160
vCenter Server
   about 85, 128, 159
   host, adding 213
   host, disconnecting from 215
   host, removing 216
   installation, on server 161
   port group, creating from 300, 301
   VMkernel adapter, creating from 304, 305
   vSwitch, creating from 295, 296
vCenter, migrating from Windows 6.5 to vCSA
   6.7
   about 244
   procedure 245, 248
vCenter, upgrading from Windows 6.5 to 6.7
   242
   PSC upgrade 243
   vCenter Server 243

vCenter
   migrating, for Windows to vCSA 160
vCPUs 397
vCSA 6.5
   upgrading, to vCSA 6.7 240, 242
vCSA configuration
   about 193
   AD integration 200, 202
   and PSC 204
   backup procedure 208
   exporting 208
   importing 208
   licensing 195
   restoration procedure 209
   roles and permissions 197, 200
   setup, with VAMI 193
vCSA HA
   about 168
vCSA PSC
   installing 164, 165
vCSA setup, with VAMI
   about 193
   DNS, modifying 194
   IP address, modifying 194
   password, modifying 195
   support bundle, exporting 194
   time synchronization, configuring 195
vCSA vCenter
   installing 166, 167
vCSA, updating via command line
   about 269
   patches, remediating 269
   patches, staging 269
vCSA
   installing, with Embedded Platform Service
      Controller 168
Vdbench 118
Veeam Backup and Replication
   about 527
   features 527
Veeam ONE
   about 607
   reference 121, 607
Vembu VMBackup
   about 529

features 529
vFlash 377
virtual data center
  disaster recovery 536
Virtual Desktop Infrastructure (VDI) 76, 120
virtual disks
  about 399
  disk mode 400
  thick provision eager zeroed 399
  thick provision lazy zeroed 399
  thin provision 400
virtual environment, troubleshooting
  about 615
  CLI tools, using 615
virtual environment
  assessing 115
  benchmarks 118
  cloud-based monitoring tools 121
  discovery 115, 117
  existing tools, analyzing 119
  health check 118
  inventory, building 115, 117
virtual functions (VFs) 331
virtual hardware
  about 396
  memory 397, 398
  network adapter 398, 399
  storage controller 401
  vCPUs 397
  virtual disks 399
virtual infrastructure project
  improved waterfall model 57, 59
  ITIL v3 56
  methodologies 54
  Plan-Do-Check-Act (PDCA) 54
  planning 54
  waterfall 56
  waterfall model 55
Virtual LAN (VLAN) 282
virtual machine backup
  about 525
  with deduplication appliances 529
  with hyper-scale solutions 529
  with transport modes 526
virtual machine clustering 520, 521

Virtual Machine Component Protection (VMCP)
  508, 509
Virtual Machine Disk (VMDK) 116
virtual machine migration 465, 466, 470, 472
virtual machine resource management
  about 450
  CPU resources 452
  ESXi host memory states 457, 459, 460
  limits 450, 452
  memory resources 454, 456
  reservations 450, 452
  shares 450, 451
  VM swapping 456
virtual machine tools
  about 405, 406
  components 407
  features 406
  installing 414
  OVT 407, 408
  reference 407
virtual machine
  about 177
  adding 431
  CLI monitoring 590
  cloning 415, 416
  components 396
  configuring, for SR-IOV 333
  converting 443
  creating 409, 410, 411
  customization specifications 418, 419, 420
  default hardware version, setting 412
  deleting 434
  deploying 408
  deploying, from content library 429, 430
  deploying, from template 416, 417
  exporting 439, 442
  files 405
  hardware version 411, 412
  importing 439
  managing 431
  monitoring 581
  OS, installing on 413
  P2V conversion 443, 444
  power state, managing 434
  registering 432

removing 433
  V2V conversion 445
  vSphere monitoring 582
Virtual Network Assessment (VNA) 120
virtual networking
  with switches 284, 285
virtual NIC (vNIC) 585
virtual NUMA (vNUMA)
  reference 397
virtual router configuration
  about 660, 663
  firewalls 661
  license configuration 664
  VLAN configuration 665
Virtual Storage Area Network (vSAN) sizing
  tools 112
virtualization lab
  architecture 650, 651
  building, benefits 640
  IP address plan 653
  logical design 650
VisualESXtop
  about 120
  reference 120
VM encryption 571
VM hardening 563, 564
VM logical levels
  storage types 350, 351
VM networking
  migrating, to other network 326
VM optimization
  about 594
  default VM templates, using 594
  oversized VMs, avoiding 596
  paravirtual SCSI (PVSCSI) storage controller 595
  snapshots, avoiding 595
  virtual hardware, using 594
  virtual network adapter, selecting 595
  VMware OS Optimization Tool (OSOT) 596
  VMware tools 595
VM physical level
  storage types 352
VM Replication 540
VM Secure Boot 564

VM snapshots
  managing 435
VMFork 36
vmhba 357
VMkernel adapters
  creating, from ESXi host client 302, 303
  creating, from vCenter Server 304, 305
  working with 302
VMlabs
  reference 646
vMotion 128
VMware AppDefense 564
VMware BC-related solutions 539
VMware Capacity Planner (VCP)
  about 112
  reference 112
VMware Certificate Authority (VMCA) 567
VMware Cloud Foundation
  reference 13
VMware Cloud Provider Program 92
VMware Cloud, on AWS
  about 21
  certifications 24
  hardware specifications and sizing 22
  interconnection with on-premises
    SDDCnterconnection with on-premises
    SDDC 24
  native AWS services, connectivity 24
  physical location 23
  pricing 23
VMware Cloud
  reference 22
VMware Compatibility Guide
  reference 131
VMware Endpoint Certificate Store (VECS) 568
VMware Enhanced Authentication plugin
  installing 203
VMware flings 46
VMware forums 641
VMware Hands-On Labs (HOLs)
  about 640
  reference 640
VMware Infrastructure Software Development
  Kit (VI SDK) 121
VMware Knowledge Base (KB)

reference 204
VMware lab, options
  about 643
  cloud-based solutions 645
  dedicated PCs 645
  dedicated server, in data center 646
  desktop PC 644
  standard rack servers 643
VMware lab
  long-term 643
  selecting 642
  short-term 643
VMware online depot
  reference 148
VMware OS Optimization Tool (OSOT)
  reference 597
VMware solutions 539
VMware Syslog Collector 566
VMware User Group (VMUG)
  reference 647
VMware Validated Design (VVD) 87, 88, 89
  reference 89
VMware vCenter Converter tool
  reference 443
VMware vRealize Log Insight server 566
VMware vRealize Operations
  about 119
  reference 119
VMware vSAN
  about 384, 385
  all-flash mode 386
  configuration 386, 388
  designing 385
  device considerations 386
  health monitoring 389
  hybrid deployment 386
  planning 385
  policies 390
  VM, creating 390, 391
VMware vSphere 6.7
  configuration maximums 36
  editions 39, 196
  features 25
  upgrade paths 48
  upgrade, avoiding 47

upgrade, reasons 46
  upgrading, reasons 45
VMware vSphere APIs for I/O Filtering (VAIO) 382
VMware vSphere Design Workshop course
  reference 74
VMware vSphere ecosystem
  about 17
  cloud management 20
  cloud-native workloads 21
  computing 17
  data centers 17
  End user computing 20
  network and security 18
  storage and availability 17
VMware vSphere Editions 40
VMware vSphere Essentials Kits 44
VMware vSphere Health Check
  about 119, 123
  reference 119
VMware vSphere HTML5 client
  using 178
VMware vSphere SPBM 378
VMware vSphere storage types
  about 346, 348
  at ESXi logical level 348, 349
  at ESXi physical level 349
  at VM logical levels 350, 351
  at VM physical level 352
VMware vSphere
  about 9
  backup solutions 526
  clustering features 521
  IT priorities 10
  strategy 11
  virtualization, versus containers 13
VMware vStorage API for Array Integration
  (VAAI) 381
VMware {code} vCheck vSphere
  about 120
  reference 120
VMware
  reference 87, 251
VMXNET Generation 3 (VMXNET3) 595
vNetwork Distributed Switch (vDS) 284

vNetwork Standard Switch (vSS) 284
vRealize Log Insight
  about 189
  free syslog servers 190
  reference 598
  syslog configuration 190
vRealize Network Insight (vRNI) 20, 120, 324
vRealize Operations
  about 600
  analytics 603
  installation 600, 602
  integrations 605
vRealize Orchestrator (vRO) 224
vSAN Assessment 120
vSAN licensing, versus vSAN features
  reference 385
vSAN ReadyNode
  reference 65
vSAN ReadyNode™ Sizer
  reference 112
vSphere 6.7 environment
  major updates 236
  minor updates 236
  patching 236
vSphere 6.7 Security Configuration Guide
  reference 548
vSphere 6.7 workflow
  about 237
  migration 239
  pre-migration 238
  validation 239
vSphere 6.7
  deployment procedure 129
  features 162
  flow, upgrading to 237
  procedure plan 237
vSphere components
  cluster HA or DRS, troubleshooting 630
  ESXi host, troubleshooting 629
  storage, troubleshooting 632
  troubleshooting 627
  vCenter Server, troubleshooting 627
  virtual network, troubleshooting 630
  VMs, troubleshooting 633
vSphere distributed switch (vDS) 212

vSphere FT
  about 513, 514, 515
  configuring 516, 517
  performance implications 518, 520
vSphere HA heartbeats
  about 504
  network heartbeat 504, 505
  storage heartbeat 504, 505, 506
vSphere HA
  about 502
  admission control 510, 511
  configuring 502, 503
  overriding, for VM from cluster level 512, 513
  protection mechanism 507
vSphere Installation Bundles (VIBs) 148, 561
vSphere Integrated Containers (VIC)
  about 14
  Container management portal 15
  Container Registry 15
  engine 14
vSphere Management Assistant (vMA) 224
vSphere Metro Storage Cluster (vMSC) 540
vSphere monitoring
  alarms, working with 588, 590
  ESXi health 587
  performance monitoring 583, 587
  vCenter Server statistics levels 582, 583
vSphere On-disk Metadata Analyzer (VOMA)
  372
vSphere Optimization Assessment (VOA)
  about 119, 122
  capacity assessment 123
  configuration health 123
  performance assessment 123
  pre-migration 238
  reference 119
vSphere permissions, users and groups
  global level 553
  inventory object level 553
vSphere Replication
  about 530, 531
  configuring 533, 534
  installing 531, 532
  working with 532
vSphere SSO configuration

about 549, 550
password management 550, 551
vSphere Update Manager (VUM) 128, 235
vSphere
  components 128
  encryption options 569, 570
  hardening 548
  identity source types 549
  security 547
  workflow 128
vStorage APIs for Storage Awareness (VASA) 378
vSwtich
  creating 290
  creating, from ESXi CLI 296, 297
  creating, from ESXi host client 290, 292, 293, 295
  creating, from vCenter Server 295, 296
VUM
  about 254
  baseline groups 259
  baselines, attaching 260
  baselines, detaching 260
  baselines, working with 257
  configuring 254, 256
  hosts, scanning 261
  used, for upgrading hosts 264
  VM hardware, upgrading 266

VM tools, upgrading 267
VMs, scanning 261
VVols
  about 382, 384
  reference 383
VXLAN
  reference 279

W

waterfall model 55, 56
Windows infrastructure
  about 666
  centralized management 678
  DC01.learnvmware.local 666, 669
  DC02.learnvmware.local 670, 671
  DNS configuration 676
  iSCSI target configuration 679, 681
  iscsi.learnvmware.local 673
  Mgmt.learnvmware.local 671
Windows Management Instrumentation (WMI) 112
Windows Server
  reference 649
Wireshark
  reference 325
Workspace ONE 20
World Wide Name (WWN) 356

Made in the USA
San Bernardino, CA
28 August 2019